Mauritius, Réunion & Seychelles

Joseph Bindloss
Sarina Singh
Deanna Swaney
Robert Strauss

LONELY PLANET PUBLICATIONS
Melbourne • Oakland • London • Paris

Mauritius, Réunion & Seychelles
4th edition – January 2001
First published – December 1989

Published by
Lonely Planet Publications Pty Ltd ABN 36 005 607 983
90 Maribyrnong St, Footscray, Victoria 3011, Australia

Lonely Planet Offices
Australia Locked Bag 1, Footscray, Victoria 3011
USA 150 Linden St, Oakland, CA 94607
UK 10a Spring Place, London NW5 3BH
France 1 rue du Dahomey, 75011 Paris

Photographs
    of the images in this guide are available for licensing from
Lonely Planet Images.
email: lpi@lonelyplanet.com.au

Front cover photograph
Creole architecture detail (Olivier Cirendini)

ISBN 0 86442 748 4

**Although the authors
and Lonely Planet try
to make the informa-
tion as accurate as
possible, we accept
no responsibility for
any loss, injury or
inconvenience
sustained by anyone
using this book.**

Contents – Text

RÉUNION

SEYCHELLES

Contents – Maps

The Authors

Joseph Bindloss

Joseph (Joe) was born in Cyprus, grew up in England and has since lived and worked in several other countries, though he currently calls London home. Joe gravitated towards journalism after a degree in biology eliminated science from his future career choices, but he has also worked as a mural painter, surveyor and sculptor. He first developed wanderlust on family trips through the Mediterranean in an old VW Kombi. Joe has also worked on Lonely Planet guides to Australia and the Philippines.

Sarina Singh

A passionate traveller for as long as she can remember, Sarina took the plunge and bought a one-way ticket to India after completing a business degree in Melbourne, Australia. She did a corporate traineeship with the Sheraton Hotel in New Delhi, then worked as a foreign correspondent and freelance journalist. Other Lonely Planet books Sarina has worked on include *Africa on a shoestring*, *India*, *Rajasthan*, *Sacred India*, *Out to Eat – Melbourne*, *Out to Eat – Sydney* and *Aboriginal Australia & the Torres Strait Islands*.

Deanna Swaney

After her university studies, Deanna made a shoestring tour of Europe and she has been addicted to travel ever since. Despite an erstwhile career in computer programming, she avoided encroaching yuppiedom in the arctic wastes of midtown Anchorage by making a break for South America, where she wrote Lonely Planet's *Bolivia* guide. Subsequent travels resulted in six more guides: *Iceland, Greenland & the Faroe Islands*, *Tonga*, *Norway*, *Samoa*, *The Arctic* and *Zimbabwe, Botswana & Namibia*. In between, Deanna contributed to Lonely Planet's *Madagascar & Comoros*, *Southern Africa*, *Brazil* and *Russia, Ukraine & Belarus*, as well as shoestring guides to Africa, South America and Scandinavia.

Robert Strauss

In the early 1970s Robert Strauss took the overland route to Nepal and then studied, taught and edited in England, Germany, Portugal and Hong Kong. He has contributed to Lonely Planet's *China*, *Tibet*, *Brazil* and *Bolivia* guidebooks and has contributed photos and articles to magazines, newspapers and other books in the USA, Australia and Asia.

FROM JOSEPH

Thanks firstly to all the readers who wrote in with information and advice. In Mauritius, thanks to the staff at Aquarelle and the Nice Place Guest House for providing a home away from home to work from. In the Seychelles, thanks to the attentive staff at the tourist office in Victoria. In Réunion, credit is due to the French and English students of St-Denis for giving me the inside track on nightspots, cheap eats and budget car hire.

This Book

The 1st edition of *Mauritius, Réunion & Seychelles* was written by Robert Willox in 1989. The 2nd edition was updated by Robert Strauss and Deanna Swaney, and the 3rd edition was updated by Sarina Singh. This 4th edition was updated by Joe Bindloss. Michael Aw and Lawson Wood contributed to the special section 'Underwater Worlds'.

FROM THE PUBLISHER

This edition of *Mauritius, Réunion & Seychelles* was coordinated in Lonely Planet's Melbourne office by Kerryn Burgess (editor) and Rod Zandbergs (cartographer and designer). Hilary Rogers, Adam Ford, Bruce Evans, Justin Flynn and Joanne Newell assisted on the editorial sides of things, while Hunor Csutoros drew the climate charts, Quentin Frayne updated the Language chapter, Kelli Hamblet and Martin Harris drew the illustrations, and Maria Vallianos designed the cover.

Acknowledgments

Many thanks to the travellers who used the last edition and wrote to us with information, advice and anecdotes:

Robert Adams, Alan Aitchison, Graeme Aitkin, Dr Bernhard Assmus, Janet Astle, Michael Badman, Paul Bahher, Chris & Eveline Bakaloudi, Vicky & Liam Barrett, Stuart Barrow, Joshua Berry, Rom L Billiet, Tom Blakeley, Cathy & Dick Blenko, Piet Bommer, Helen Bottrill, Helen & Richard Brain, Monica Chang, Ada Cheung, Dawn Clairmonte, John Collins, Katie Cooke, Huw Cordey, Sharon Croome, Hannah de Angelis, Francois de Maroussem, Julia W Deather, L Donaldson, Dr R A Duncan, Brian Ellis, Carrie Garavan, Robert Garnett, Paolo Gemma, Mark Grice, Bram Gruwez, Hitbans Gujadhur, Amber & Ken Gunther, Chris Hall, Maureen Hammond, Sandra Hanks Benoiton, Ed Harland, Stephan Hasselberg, Alice Henders, Jean Hendry, Michael Jaksch, Richard Jenner, Todd Johnson, Wally Jones, Malgorzata Kragora, Falk Krause, Robert R Krueger, Wendy Lindeman, Guido Marchionni, Alicia & Steve Merrett, Roland Muller, Pavel Novak, Judy Papineau, Vinod Persand, Stefaan Persoons, Angela Pistoia, Diane Porter, Arnout J Punt, Philippe Quix, Helen Ranger, Alexandra Richards, Kim Rothbart, John Sahar, Pieter Santen, Alison & George Sassoon, Willem Schipper, G & P Scott, Vishnee Seenundun, Dr M S Smith, Susanne Speidel, Mr & Mrs J Stamp, Mia Steenholt, David Swabey, Tony Talarico, Louise Theophanous, Albert G Valks, Erwin van Engelen, M Verheyen, Arlinde Vletter, Fredy Wehrili, Erik Wilbers, Kathryn Young.

Foreword

ABOUT LONELY PLANET GUIDEBOOKS

The story begins with a classic travel adventure: Tony and Maureen Wheeler's 1972 journey across Europe and Asia to Australia. Useful information about the overland trail did not exist at that time, so Tony and Maureen published the first Lonely Planet guidebook to meet a growing need.

From a kitchen table, then from a tiny office in Melbourne (Australia), Lonely Planet has become the largest independent travel publisher in the world, an international company with offices in Melbourne, Oakland (USA), London (UK) and Paris (France).

Today Lonely Planet guidebooks cover the globe. There is an ever-growing list of books and there's information in a variety of forms and media. Some things haven't changed. The main aim is still to help make it possible for adventurous travellers to get out there – to explore and better understand the world.

At Lonely Planet we believe travellers can make a positive contribution to the countries they visit – if they respect their host communities and spend their money wisely. Since 1986 a percentage of the income from each book has been donated to aid projects and human rights campaigns.

Updates Lonely Planet thoroughly updates each guidebook as often as possible. This usually means there are around two years between editions, although for more unusual or more stable destinations the gap can be longer. Check the imprint page for publication dates.

Between editions up-to-date information is available in two free newsletters – the paper *Planet Talk* and email *Comet* (to subscribe, contact any Lonely Planet office) – and on our Web site at www.lonelyplanet.com. The *Upgrades* section of the Web site covers a number of important and volatile destinations and is regularly updated by Lonely Planet authors. *Scoop* covers news and current affairs relevant to travellers. And, lastly, the *Thorn Tree* bulletin board and *Postcards* section of the site carry unverified, but fascinating, reports from travellers.

Correspondence The process of creating new editions begins with the letters, postcards and emails received from travellers. This correspondence often includes suggestions, criticisms and comments about the current editions. Interesting excerpts are immediately passed on via newsletters and the Web site, and everything goes to our authors to be verified when they're researching on the road. We're keen to get more feedback from organisations or individuals who represent communities visited by travellers.

Lonely Planet gathers information for everyone who's curious about the planet – and especially for those who explore it first-hand. Through guidebooks, phrasebooks, activity guides, maps, literature, newsletters, image library, TV series and Web site we act as an information exchange for a worldwide community of travellers.

Research Authors aim to gather sufficient practical information to enable travellers to make informed choices and to make the mechanics of a journey run smoothly. They also research historical and cultural background to help enrich the travel experience and allow travellers to understand and respond appropriately to cultural and environmental issues.

Authors don't stay in every hotel because that would mean spending a couple of months in each medium-sized city and, no, they don't eat at every restaurant because that would mean stretching belts beyond capacity. They do visit hotels and restaurants to check standards and prices, but feedback based on readers' direct experiences can be very helpful.

Many of our authors work undercover, others aren't so secretive. None of them accept freebies in exchange for positive write-ups. And none of our guidebooks contain any advertising.

Production Authors submit their raw manuscripts and maps to offices in Australia, USA, UK or France. Editors and cartographers – all experienced travellers themselves – then begin the process of assembling the pieces. When the book finally hits the shops, some things are already out of date, we start getting feedback from readers and the process begins again...

WARNING & REQUEST

Things change – prices go up, schedules change, good places go bad and bad places go bankrupt – nothing stays the same. So, if you find things better or worse, recently opened or long since closed, please tell us and help make the next edition even more accurate and useful. We genuinely value all the feedback we receive. Cathy Viero coordinates a well travelled team that reads and acknowledges every letter, postcard and email and ensures that every morsel of information finds its way to the appropriate authors, editors and cartographers for verification.

Everyone who writes to us will find their name in the next edition of the appropriate guidebook. They will also receive the latest issue of *Planet Talk*, our quarterly printed newsletter, or *Comet*, our monthly email newsletter. Subscriptions to both newsletters are free. The very best contributions will be rewarded with a free guidebook.

Excerpts from your correspondence may appear in new editions of Lonely Planet guidebooks, the Lonely Planet Web site, *Planet Talk* or *Comet*, so please let us know if you *don't* want your letter published or your name acknowledged.

Send all correspondence to the Lonely Planet office closest to you:

Australia: Locked Bag 1, Footscray, Victoria 3011
USA: 150 Linden St, Oakland, CA 94607
UK: 10A Spring Place, London NW5 3BH
France: 1 rue du Dahomey, 75011 Paris

Or email us at: talk2us@lonelyplanet.com.au

For news, views and updates see our Web site: www.lonelyplanet.com

HOW TO USE A LONELY PLANET GUIDEBOOK

The best way to use a Lonely Planet guidebook is any way you choose. At Lonely Planet we believe the most memorable travel experiences are often those that are unexpected, and the finest discoveries are those you make yourself. Guidebooks are not intended to be used as if they provide a detailed set of infallible instructions!

Contents All Lonely Planet guidebooks follow roughly the same format. The Facts about the Destination chapters or sections give background information ranging from history to weather. Facts for the Visitor gives practical information on issues like visas and health. Getting There & Away gives a brief starting point for researching travel to and from the destination. Getting Around gives an overview of the transport options when you arrive.

The peculiar demands of each destination determine how subsequent chapters are broken up, but some things remain constant. We always start with background, then proceed to sights, places to stay, places to eat, entertainment, getting there and away, and getting around information – in that order.

Heading Hierarchy Lonely Planet headings are used in a strict hierarchical structure that can be visualised as a set of Russian dolls. Each heading (and its following text) is encompassed by any preceding heading that is higher on the hierarchical ladder.

Entry Points We do not assume guidebooks will be read from beginning to end, but that people will dip into them. The traditional entry points are the list of contents and the index. In addition, however, some books have a complete list of maps and an index map illustrating map coverage.

The colour map of each destination shows highlights. These highlights are dealt with in greater detail in the text, along with planning questions and suggested itineraries. Each chapter that covers a geographical region usually begins with a locator map and another list of highlights. Once you find something of interest in a list of highlights, turn to the index.

Maps Maps play a crucial role in Lonely Planet guidebooks and include a huge amount of information. A legend is printed on the back page. We seek to have complete consistency between maps and text, and to have every important place in the text captured on a map. Map key numbers usually start in the top left corner.

Although inclusion in a guidebook usually implies a recommendation we cannot list every good place. Exclusion does not necessarily imply criticism. In fact there are a number of reasons why we might exclude a place – sometimes it is simply inappropriate to encourage an influx of travellers.

Introduction

Many people are unable to place the islands of Mauritius, the Seychelles or Réunion on a map, yet the names still evoke images of pure white sand, swaying palms and tempting azure lagoons. In fact, these beautiful islands are every bit as enticing as the islands of the Caribbean or the South Pacific, but most people are unaware of their tropical delights, at least in the English-speaking world.

Not so the French, who have long been *au fait* with these gorgeous islands, probably because France used to own Mauritius and the Seychelles, and still does own Réunion. In fact the British took over much of the region after the Napoleonic Wars, but the colonial government never really warmed to the Indian Ocean, leaving the locals to pursue their own, French-influenced way of life.

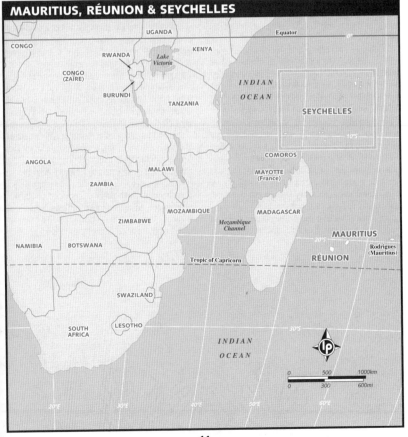

MAURITIUS, RÉUNION & SEYCHELLES

The islands' slightly enigmatic status is probably a result of this reluctant colonialism. The island of Réunion was handed back to France soon after the British took command, and is today run as a French overseas department. Mauritius and the Seychelles have both been independent for some time now, but they long languished as backwaters of the British Empire, missing out on the promotion that came the way of the Caribbean islands. From a visitor's perspective, this is all for the good, as it means these islands offer a take on the 'tropical island paradise' theme that's different from other more familiar destinations. The real beauty of these Indian Ocean islands, however, is that each has a personality of its own.

If you're searching for *the* ultimate tropical paradise, you can't beat the Seychelles, with its magical beaches and lagoons. Indeed, the Seychelles boasts some of the most striking islands on the planet and offers sensational diving and snorkelling. This paradise comes at a price, however, and only the extremely well-heeled will be able to see the best the islands have to offer.

Mauritius is much more accessible and boasts some unusual cultural attractions as well as a stunning set of tropical beaches. The island has a strongly Indian atmosphere, and many of the subcontinent's more unusual traditions live on among the Mauritian Tamil population. For the hardened beach-bunny, there are all manner of aquatic activities on offer, from windsurfing to scuba diving and even walking under the sea! Mauritius is also the cheapest of the three islands to visit; you could stay for three weeks here on a budget that wouldn't last seven days in the Seychelles or Réunion.

Réunion is the surprise package, with a live volcano and awesome alpine scenery with a luscious tropical twist. Often referred to as 'France's best kept secret', the island is virtually unexplored by all but the French. The beaches here are less impressive, but the island more than makes up for that with an incredible wilderness landscape in the interior. As a result, Réunion is a world-class destination for hikers, and there are endless opportunities for organised adventure activities such as canyoning, mountain biking and parachuting.

Apart from their natural wonders, the three islands also have a vibrant cultural mix. Each has developed differently, but all three have absorbed elements of French, British, Indian, African and Asian cultures. Each is a country of contrasts; in Mauritius, Indian culture dominates, while Réunion looks towards mainland France and the Seychelles presents a Franco-African or Creole face to the world. The result is a flamboyant potpourri of people, cuisines, languages, traditions and beliefs, and a cultural melting pot that should excite even the most experienced traveller.

Regional Facts for the Visitor

PLANNING
When to Go

For all three destinations you are advised to plan your travel well in advance, especially during the French holidays when hotels can be booked up months ahead of time. Ask your travel agent for advice on the dates of school holidays in France, which vary slightly from year to year. The Christmas to New Year period is also particularly busy. Airline reservations may be difficult to get at this time, so book well ahead to avoid disappointment. Keep in mind that many hotels hike their room rates during the peak seasons.

Sporting and leisure considerations may play a part in when you intend to visit, and weather is another important consideration. For instance, if you're planning a hiking trip to Réunion, the best time is during the dry season from around April to September.

For more information on the best times to travel to Mauritius, Réunion or the Seychelles, see Facts for the Visitor for the place you intend to visit.

What to Bring

The happiest travellers are those who pack lightly. If you plan to use buses in Mauritius or Réunion, remember that there's little space to stow luggage.

A backpack with a detachable daypack makes a good versatile combination. Travel packs are backpacks that can be converted into more civilised-looking suitcases. They are often cleverly compartmentalised, and have internal frames and special padding.

Clothing Keep clothing light. Cotton is breathable, and great in dry weather; if you're hiking, synthetics might be a good choice because they dry more quickly if you get wet. Shorts and Hawaiian shirts may be the first thing to go into the suitcase, but it's a good idea to carry a smart outfit too. Beach wear is strictly reserved for the beach in the Indian Ocean, and shorts, T-shirts and flip-flops (thongs) are banned from many night-

spots and restaurants. Smart-looking clothes will also ease your passage through customs and immigration, and will give you an air of respectability when dealing with the police or other officials if trouble should arise.

Make sure you have protection from the sun. Bring a hat, sunglasses and sunscreen. Take it easy to begin with when you go about exposing yourself to the fiery elements. It's so easy to get badly burnt, even when it's overcast, because you don't notice the damage until it's too late. Lip balm is especially good on the beach, where the sun can really pack a punch. To avoid a lobster impersonation, the golden rule is to be sun smart.

At the other extreme, a light plastic cape or mac will stop a downpour from ruining the odd day or week. It's a must during the wet season, when rain can appear out of a seemingly clear sky.

At night it cools down a bit on the coast, but not enough that you'll need woolly blankets or thick jumpers. It's a different story on the plateau around Curepipe in Mauritius and high in the cirques of Réunion. The temperature can sometimes drop to freezing, so you'll need warm clothing at night. Intending hikers should bring comfortable, strong footwear.

Equipment If you're going to be roughing it away from the resort accommodation, you may like to bring a torch (with spare batteries), a small mirror, a Swiss Army-type multipurpose knife, a first-aid kit, a sewing kit, safety pins and a small padlock (for locking rooms or luggage). That doesn't add up to much extra weight; if you're looking to save weight, bring only a thin towel.

A sheet can come in handy in budget accommodation places, especially if you're fussy about hygiene. A sarong is a good alternative, as it can be used on the beach and also as a sheet or emergency towel. It's not a bad idea to pack insect repellent, especially for staying in cheap accommodation, where the mozzies can be tenacious.

VISAS & DOCUMENTS
Passport
You must have a passport with you wherever you go; it's the most basic travel document. Make sure that your passport will be valid for the entire period you intend to remain overseas. If your passport is lost or stolen, immediately contact your country's embassy or consulate.

Visas
There are no visa requirements for Mauritius or for the Seychelles, but citizens of some countries must have a visa for Réunion. It will be much easier to get one before you leave home (for more information, see Visas & Documents in the Réunion Facts for the Visitor chapter).

Travel Insurance
A travel insurance policy to cover theft, loss and medical problems is a good idea. The policies handled by STA Travel and other student travel organisations are usually good value. Some policies offer lower and higher medical-expense options; the higher ones are chiefly for countries that have extremely high medical costs. Mauritius follows the old British national health system and has good-quality, affordable care. In Réunion, medical care is extremely good, but very expensive (and all the adventurous activities on offer mean you're more likely to need it). In the Seychelles, health care is expensive and the standards are terrible. There is a wide variety of policies available, so check the small print.

Some policies specifically exclude 'dangerous activities', which can include scuba diving, motorcycling, even hiking. A locally acquired motorcycle licence is not valid under some policies.

You may prefer a policy that pays doctors or hospitals directly rather than requiring you to pay on the spot and claim later. If you have to claim later make sure you keep all documentation. Some policies require you to contact (reverse charges) a centre in your home country, where staff immediately assess your problem.

Check that the policy covers ambulance services or an emergency flight home.

Copies
All important documents (passport data page and visa page, credit cards, travel insurance policy, air/bus/train tickets, driving licence etc) should be photocopied before you leave home. Leave one copy with someone at home and keep another with you, separate from the originals.

It's also a good idea to store details of your vital travel documents in Lonely Planet's free online Travel Vault in case you lose the photocopies or can't be bothered with them. Create your password-protected Travel Vault at www.ekno.lonelyplanet.com, then you can access it from anywhere in the world.

EMBASSIES & CONSULATES
For embassies' contact information, see the destination-specific Facts for the Visitor chapters.

Your Own Embassy
It's important to realise what your own embassy – the embassy of the country of which you are a citizen – can and can't do to help you if you get into trouble. Generally speaking, it won't be much help in emergencies if the trouble you're in is remotely your own fault. Remember that you are bound by the laws of the country you are in. Your embassy will not be sympathetic if you end up in jail after committing a crime locally, even if such actions are legal in your own country.

In genuine emergencies you might get some assistance, but only if other channels have been exhausted. For example, if you need to get home urgently, a free ticket home is exceedingly unlikely – the embassy would expect you to have insurance. If you have all your money and documents stolen, it might assist with getting a new passport, but a loan for onward travel is out of the question.

Some embassies used to keep letters for travellers or have a small reading room with home newspapers, but these days the mail holding service has usually been stopped and even newspapers tend to be out of date.

MONEY
Security
Various types of money belts and pouches are available. They can be worn around the waist or neck, or over the shoulder; leather or cotton are more comfortable than synthetics. They are only useful if worn *under* clothing – those worn outside clothing are easy prey and attract attention. At travel goods suppliers, you can also buy leather belts that have secret compartments in which you can hide your 'emergency stash' of cash.

Get used to keeping small change and a few banknotes in a shirt pocket so that you can pay for bus tickets and other small items without extracting large amounts of money which could quickly attract attention.

Don't keep all your valuables together: distribute them about your person and baggage to avoid the risk of losing everything in one fell swoop.

Make sure you know the number to call if you lose your credit card, and be quick to cancel it if it's lost or stolen. It's a good idea to make a habit of checking each day that your credit card is with you.

New-style credit card coupons do not have carbon paper inserts and offer more protection against misuse. If you sign an old-style coupon (these are still quite common in the region), be sure to ask for the carbon inserts and destroy them after use. Similarly, destroy any coupons that have been filled out incorrectly. These are worthwhile precautions against unwanted duplication of your credit card.

For more information, see Dangers & Annoyances later in this chapter.

Stolen Travellers Cheques If you're unlucky enough to have things stolen, some precautions can ease the pain. All travellers cheques are replaceable, although this does you little immediate good if you have to go home and apply to your bank. What you want is instant replacement. If you don't have the receipt you were given when you bought the cheques, rapid replacement may be more difficult. It's wise to keep an emergency stash of cash totally separate from the rest of your money. In that same place you should keep a record of cheque serial numbers, your proof of purchase slips and your passport details. The receipt should always be kept separate from the cheques, and a photocopy in yet another location is a good idea. Chances are you'll be able to get a limited amount of funds on the spot, and the rest of the funds will be available when the bank has verified your initial purchase of the travellers cheques.

Costs
The Indian Ocean is one of the world's most sought-after tropical destinations, but paradise comes at a premium and you'll need plenty of cash if you want to make even a mild splash on the scene here. The Seychelles is the most expensive country in the area, with very few options for the budget traveller. Réunion is also on the pricey side, though you can save money by self-catering and by camping or staying in mountain huts or *chambres d'hôte* (family-run B&Bs). Mauritius offers easily the best opportunities for budget travellers – US$25 per day is a realistic budget. For more information about costs, see Facts for the Visitor for the place you intend to visit.

Exchanging Money
Travellers cheques in any of the major currencies may be changed without ado in Mauritius, Réunion and the Seychelles, although French francs are probably the best bet, especially for Réunion.

Credit cards are widely accepted in Mauritius, Réunion and the Seychelles. Throughout the region there are ATMs that give cash advances in the local currency.

INTERNET RESOURCES
The World Wide Web is a rich resource for travellers. You can research your trip, hunt down bargain air fares, book hotels, check on weather conditions or chat with locals and other travellers about the best places to visit (or avoid!).

There's no better place to start your Web explorations than the Lonely Planet Web site (www.lonelyplanet.com). Here you'll find succinct summaries on travelling to most places on earth, postcards from other travellers and the Thorn Tree bulletin board, where you can ask questions before you go or dispense advice when you get back. You can also find travel news and updates to many of our most popular guidebooks, while the subWWWay section links you to the most useful travel resources elsewhere on the Web.

BOOKS

The book you are holding is the only title to cover the entire region. For a rundown on suggestions for further reading, see the Facts for the Visitor chapter for the place you intend to visit.

Note that most books are published in different editions by different publishers in different countries. As a result, a book might be a hardcover rarity in one country while it's readily available in paperback in another.

Bookshops and libraries search by title or by author, so your local bookshop or library is best placed to advise you on the availability of the recommendations given in this book.

Lonely Planet

French is the official language of Réunion and is also widely spoken in Mauritius and the Seychelles. For a comprehensive guide to French words and phrases, get a copy of Lonely Planet's *French Phrasebook*.

General

If you intend to do a lot of reading, bring paperbacks from home and hope you can swap with other travellers. There is a fairly good range of mainstream paperbacks on sale in Mauritius and the Seychelles. In Réunion, you'll find that English-language books are rare, but magazines such as *Time* and *Newsweek* are normally available in *librairies* (bookshops).

VIDEO SYSTEMS

Mauritius and Réunion use the SECAM video system, while the Seychelles uses the PAL system.

PHOTOGRAPHY & VIDEO

The Indian Ocean islands are the very image of paradise, and many photographers strive to capture that image on film. For the most comprehensive guide to travel photography, get a copy of Lonely Planet's *Travel Photography: A Guide to Taking Better Pictures* by internationally renowned travel photographer Richard I'Anson. It's in full colour throughout and designed to be taken on the road.

For terrific tips on underwater photography, see the special section 'Underwater Worlds' later in this book.

Film & Equipment

Photography Film manufacturers warn that once exposed, film should be developed as quickly as possible. If you're going to be carrying exposed film for a long time, consult a specialist photography handbook about ways of enhancing preservation. Pack everything in plastic bags before you leave home. Try to keep your film cool, and protect it in waterproof, airtight containers. Silica-gel packs distributed around your gear will assist in absorbing moisture. Always try to keep your camera and film in the shade. Black camera bags tend to absorb heat faster than white or other light-coloured surfaces.

A UV filter permanently fitted to your lens will not only cut down ultraviolet light, but will protect your lens. Other useful accessories include a small flash, a cable release, a lens-cleaning kit and a tripod. Remember to take spare batteries for cameras and flash units, and make sure your equipment is insured.

Video Make sure you keep the batteries charged, and have the necessary charger, plugs and transformer for the country you are visiting.

Blank video tapes are available in most of the tourist centres in Mauritius and Réunion, but make sure you buy the right format. In the Seychelles, there are a few stores in Victoria with video supplies. It is usually worth buying at least a few tapes duty-free to start off your trip.

Technical Tips

Take into consideration the heat, humidity, very fine sand, tropical sunlight and equatorial shadows. If you're shooting on beaches, it's important to adjust for glare from water or sand, and to keep sand and salt water well away from your equipment.

Photography The best times to take photographs on sunny days are the first two hours after sunrise and the last two before sunset. This brings out the best colours. At other times, the harsh sunlight and glare washes everything out, though you can use filters to counter the glare.

Video Properly used, a video camera can give a fascinating record of your holiday. As well as videoing the obvious things – sunsets, spectacular views – remember to record some of the ordinary details of everyday life in the place you are visiting. Often the most interesting things occur when you're actually intent on filming something else. Remember too that video 'flows', so you can shoot scenes of countryside rolling past the bus window, for example, to capture an overall impression that isn't possible with ordinary photos.

Video cameras have amazingly sensitive microphones, and you might be surprised how much sound will be picked up. This can also be a problem if there is a lot of ambient noise – filming by the side of a busy road might seem OK when you do it, but you might hear only a deafening cacophony of traffic noise when you view it back home.

One good rule for beginners is to try to film in long takes, and don't move the camera around too much. Otherwise, your video could well make your viewers seasick! Remember, you're on holiday – don't let the video take over your life and turn your trip into an extravagant Cecil B de Mille production.

Restrictions

Don't photograph or film airports or anything that looks like police or military equipment or property. In many temples and mosques, including the Hindu temple and the Grande Mosquée in St-Denis, photography is not allowed – usually there will be a sign warning against photography. If you're at all unsure, don't be afraid to ask somebody.

It may be insensitive to take photos at certain religious ceremonies, so again, it's best to ask first.

Photographing People

When taking photographs of people, it's best to ask their permission first. Different people react differently to a camera – some are happy to be photographed, while others are not. If in doubt, it's best to ask.

A zoom is a relatively unobtrusive means of taking portraits – even if you have obtained permission to take a portrait, pushing a lens in your subject's face can be disconcerting for them. A reasonable distance between you and your subject may help to reduce your subject's discomfort, and should result in more natural shots.

A video camera shoved in someone's face is probably even more annoying and offensive than a still camera. Always ask permission first.

Airport Security

If you are worried about X-ray security machines at airports ruining your film, despite assurances that they won't, simply remove your camera and film stock from your luggage and take them through separately for inspection.

TIME

Mauritius, Réunion and the Seychelles are all four hours ahead of Greenwich Mean Time (GMT) and Universal Time Coordinated (UTC). When it's noon in the Indian Ocean, it's midnight in San Francisco, 3 am in New York, 8 am in London, 6 pm in Sydney, and 8 pm in New Zealand.

WEIGHTS & MEASURES

Mauritius, Réunion and the Seychelles all use the metric system, but you may see the occasional signpost in miles. For a metric conversion chart, see the inside back cover of this book.

HEALTH

Travel health depends on your predeparture preparations, your daily health care while travelling and how you handle any medical problem that does develop. While the potential dangers can seem quite frightening, in reality few travellers to Mauritius, Réunion and the Seychelles experience anything more than perhaps an upset stomach. Health care in Mauritius and Réunion is generally of a high standard, while the Seychelles has been singled out for its poor health services. Travellers should discuss with their physician the most up-to-date methods used to prevent and treat the threats to health which may be encountered.

Predeparture Planning

Immunisations No vaccinations are officially required for travel to Mauritius, Réunion or the Seychelles. However, many doctors recommend that travellers get hepatitis A and B jabs just to be on the safe side. A yellow fever vaccination and related documentation are only necessary if you arrive from an infected area.

Plan ahead for getting your vaccinations: some of them require more than one injection, while some should not be given together. It is recommended that you seek medical advice at least six weeks before travel. Be aware that there is often a greater risk of disease with children and during pregnancy.

Record all vaccinations on an international health certificate, available from your doctor or government health department.

Discuss with your doctor the vaccinations you will need for your trip, as he or she will have the most up-to-date information. Vaccinations you should discuss further with your doctor for a trip to Mauritius, Réunion or the Seychelles include the following.

Hepatitis A Hepatitis A vaccine (eg Avaxim, Havrix 1440 or VAQTA) provides long-term immunity (possibly more than 10 years) after an initial injection and a booster at six to 12 months.

Alternatively, an injection of gamma globulin can provide short-term protection against hepatitis A (two to six months, depending on the dose). It is not a vaccine, but a ready-made antibody collected from blood donations. It is reasonably effective and, unlike the vaccine, it is protective immediately. Because it is a blood product, there are some concerns about its long-term safety.

Hepatitis A vaccine is also available in a combined form, Twinrix, with hepatitis B vaccine. Three injections over a six-month period are required, the first two providing substantial protection against hepatitis A.

Typhoid This vaccine is available as either an injection or oral capsules.

Diphtheria & Tetanus Vaccinations for these two diseases are usually combined and are recommended for everyone. After an initial course of three injections (usually given in childhood), boosters are necessary every 10 years.

Meninogococcal Meningitis Healthy people carry this disease; it is transmitted like a cold and you can die from it within a few hours. There are many carriers, and vaccination is recommended for travellers to certain parts of Asia, India, Africa and South America. It is not officially required for travellers to Mauritius, Réunion and the Seychelles, but it may be worth discussing this further with your doctor, particularly if you intend travelling to certain parts of Africa as well. A single injection will give good protection for three years. The vaccine is not recommended for children under two years of age, because they do not develop satisfactory immunity from it.

Hepatitis B This disease is spread by blood or by sexual activity. Travellers who should consider a hepatitis B vaccination include those visiting countries where there are known to be many carriers, where blood transfusions may not be adequately screened or where sexual contact is a possibility. It involves three injections, the quickest course being over three weeks with a booster at 12 months.

Polio Everyone should keep up to date with this vaccination. A booster every 10 years maintains immunity.

Yellow Fever Yellow fever is now the only vaccine that is a legal requirement for entry into many countries; the requirement is usually only enforced if you are coming from an infected area. Protection lasts 10 years and is recommended where the disease is endemic, eg Africa and South America. For travellers to Mauritius, Réunion and the Seychelles, a yellow fever vaccination and related documentation are only necessary if you arrive from an infected area. You usually have to go to a special yellow fever vaccination centre.

Cholera The current injectable vaccine against cholera is poorly protective and has many side effects, so it is not generally recommended for travellers. Very occasionally travellers are asked by immigration officials to present a certificate, even though the World Health Organisation (WHO) and all countries, including Mauritius, Réunion and the Seychelles, have dropped cholera immunisation as an entry requirement.

Health Insurance Before you travel, make sure that you have adequate health insurance. For detailed information, see Travel Insurance under Visas & Documents earlier in this chapter.

Travel Health Guides Lonely Planet's *Healthy Travel Africa* is a handy pocket-size guide which is packed with useful information. It covers pretrip planning, emergency first aid, immunisation, disease and what to do if you get sick on the road. *Travel with Children*, also from Lonely Planet, includes advice on travel health for children.

There are also a number of excellent travel health sites on the Internet. From the Lonely Planet home page there are links (www.lonelyplanet.com/weblinks/wlheal .htm) to the World Health Organization and the US Centers for Disease Control & Prevention.

Medical Kit Check List

Following is a list of items you should consider including in your medical kit – consult your pharmacist for brands available in your country.

☐ **Aspirin or paracetamol (acetaminophen in the USA)** – for pain or fever

☐ **Antihistamine** – for allergies such as hay fever; to ease the itch from insect bites or stings; and to prevent motion sickness

☐ **Cold and flu tablets, throat lozenges and nasal decongestant**

☐ **Multivitamins** – consider for long trips, when dietary vitamin intake may be inadequate

☐ **Antibiotics** – consider including these if you're travelling well off the beaten track; see your doctor, as they must be prescribed, and carry the prescription with you

☐ **Loperamide or diphenoxylate** –'blockers' for diarrhoea

☐ **Prochlorperazine or metaclopramide** – for nausea and vomiting

☐ **Rehydration mixture** – to prevent dehydration, which may occur, for example, during bouts of diarrhoea. This is particularly important when travelling with children.

☐ **Insect repellent, sunscreen, lip balm and eye drops**

☐ **Calamine lotion, sting relief spray or aloe vera** – to ease irritation from sunburn and insect bites or stings

☐ **Antifungal cream or powder** – for fungal skin infections and thrush

☐ **Antiseptic (such as povidone-iodine)** – for cuts and grazes

☐ **Bandages, Band-Aids (plasters) and other wound dressings**

☐ **Water purification tablets or iodine**

☐ **Scissors, tweezers and a thermometer** – note that mercury thermometers are prohibited by airlines

Everyday Health

Normal body temperature is up to 37°C (98.6°F); more than 2°C (4°F) higher indicates a high fever. The normal adult pulse rate is 60 to 100 per minute (children 80 to 100, babies 100 to 140). As a general rule the pulse increases about 20 beats per minute for each 1°C (2°F) rise in fever.

Respiration (breathing) rate is also an indicator of illness. Count the number of breaths per minute: between 12 and 20 is normal for adults and older children (up to 30 for younger children, 40 for babies). People with a high fever or serious respiratory illness breathe more quickly than normal. More than 40 shallow breaths a minute may indicate pneumonia.

Other Preparations Make sure you're healthy before you start travelling. If you are going on a long trip make sure your teeth are OK. If you wear glasses take a spare pair and your prescription.

If you require a particular medication take an adequate supply, as it may not be available locally. Take part of the packaging showing the generic name, rather than the brand, which will make getting replacements easier. It's a good idea to have a legible prescription or letter from your doctor to show that you legally use the medication, to avoid any problems.

Basic Rules

Food There is an old colonial adage which says: 'If you can cook it, boil it or peel it you can eat it – otherwise forget it'. Vegetables and fruit should be washed with purified water or peeled where possible. Beware of ice cream which is sold in the street or anywhere it might have been melted and refrozen; if there's any doubt (eg, from a power cut in the last day or two) steer well clear. Shellfish such as mussels, oysters and clams should be avoided, as should undercooked meat, particularly in the form of mince. Steaming does not make shellfish safe for eating.

If a place looks clean and well run and the vendor also looks clean and healthy, then the food is probably safe. In general, places that are packed with travellers or locals will be fine, while empty restaurants are questionable. The food in busy restaurants is cooked and eaten quite quickly with little standing around and is probably not reheated.

Water The number-one rule is *be careful of the water* and especially ice. If you don't know for certain that the tap water is safe, assume the worst. Reputable brands of bottled water or soft drinks are generally fine, although in some places the bottles may be refilled with tap water. Only use water from containers with a serrated seal – not tops or corks. As a general rule, tap water in Mauritius, Réunion and the Seychelles is safe to drink, but care should be taken immediately following a cyclone or bad cyclonic storm. Take care with fruit juice, particularly if water may have been added. Milk should be treated with suspicion as it is often unpasteurised, though boiled milk is fine if it is kept hygienically. Tea or coffee should also be OK, since the water should have been boiled.

Water Purification The simplest way of purifying water is to boil it thoroughly. Vigorous boiling should be satisfactory; however, at high altitude water boils at a lower temperature, so germs are less likely to be killed. Boil your water for longer in these environments.

Consider purchasing a water filter for a long trip. There are two main kinds of filter. Total filters take out all parasites, bacteria and viruses, and make water safe to drink. They are often expensive, but they can be more cost effective than buying bottled water. Simple filters (which can even be a nylon mesh bag) take out dirt and larger foreign bodies from the water so that chemical solutions work much more effectively; if water is dirty, chemical solutions may not work at all. It's very important when buying a filter to read the specifications, so that you know exactly what it removes from the water and what it doesn't. Simple filtering will not remove all dangerous organisms, so if you cannot boil water it should be treated chemically. Chlorine tablets (Puritabs, Steritabs or other brand names) will kill many pathogens, but not some parasites such as giardia and amoebic cysts. Iodine is more effective in purifying water and is available in tablet form (such as Potable Aqua). Follow the directions carefully and remember that too much iodine can be harmful.

Medical Problems & Treatment

Self-diagnosis and treatment can be risky, so you should always seek medical help. Although we do give drug dosages in this section, they are for emergency use only. Correct diagnosis is vital. An embassy, consulate or five-star hotel can usually recommend a good place to go for advice.

Antibiotics should ideally be administered only under medical supervision. Take only the recommended dose at the prescribed intervals and use the whole course, even if the illness seems to be cured earlier. Stop immediately if there are any serious reactions and don't use the antibiotic at all if you are unsure that you have the correct one. Some people are allergic to commonly prescribed antibiotics such as penicillin or sulpha drugs; carry this information when travelling – on a bracelet, for example.

Environmental Hazards

Altitude Sickness Altitude sickness is only likely to affect hikers who tackle the higher mountain peaks on Réunion. At altitudes over 2500m, less oxygen reaches the muscles and the brain, requiring the heart and lungs to compensate by working harder, which can trigger a variety of secondary symptoms. Mild symptoms of Acute Mountain Sickness (AMS) include headache, lethargy, dizziness, difficulty sleeping and loss of appetite. AMS may become more severe without warning and can be fatal. Severe symptoms include breathlessness, a dry, irritative cough (which may progress to the production of pink, frothy sputum), severe headache, lack of coordination and balance, confusion, irrational behaviour, vomiting, drowsiness and unconsciousness. There is no hard-and-fast rule as to what is too high: AMS has been fatal at 3000m,

although it usually occurs in the range of 3500m to 4500m. Symptoms usually develop during the first 24 hours at altitude but may be delayed up to three weeks.

Treat mild symptoms by resting at the same altitude until recovery, usually a day or two. Paracetamol or aspirin can be taken for headaches. If symptoms persist or become worse, however, *immediate descent is necessary*; even 500m can help. Campers should aim to set up their camp at a lower altitude than their highest point of ascent.

The drugs acetazolamide (Diamox) and dexamethasone are recommended by some doctors for the prevention of AMS; however, their use is controversial. They can reduce the symptoms, but they may also mask warning signs; severe and fatal AMS has occurred in people taking these drugs. In general we do not recommend them for travellers. Drug treatments should never be used to avoid descent or to enable further ascent.

To prevent Acute Mountain Sickness:

- Ascend slowly – have frequent rest days, spending two to three nights at each rise of 1000m. If you reach a high altitude by hiking, acclimatisation takes place gradually and you are less likely to be affected than if you fly directly to high altitude.
- It is always wise to sleep at a lower altitude than the greatest height reached during the day if possible. Also, once above 3000m, care should be taken not to increase the sleeping altitude by more than 300m per day.
- Drink extra fluids. The mountain air is dry and cold and moisture is lost as you breathe. Excessive evaporation of sweat may occur and result in dehydration.
- Eat light, high-carbohydrate meals for more energy.
- Avoid alcohol as it may increase the risk of dehydration.
- Avoid sedatives.

Fungal Infections Fungal infections occur more commonly in hot weather and are usually found on the scalp, between the toes or fingers, in the groin and on the body (ringworm). You get ringworm (which is a fungal infection, not a worm) from infected animals or other people. Moisture tends to encourage these infections.

To prevent fungal infections wear loose, comfortable clothes, avoid artificial fibres, wash frequently and dry carefully. If you do get an infection, wash the infected area at least daily with a disinfectant or medicated soap and water, and rinse and dry well. Apply an antifungal cream or powder like tolnifate (Tinaderm). Try to expose the infected area to air or sunlight as much as possible and wash all towels and underwear in hot water, change them often and let them dry in the sun.

Heat Exhaustion Dehydration and salt deficiency can cause heat exhaustion. Take time to acclimatise to high temperatures, drink sufficient liquids and do not do anything too physically demanding.

Salt deficiency is characterised by fatigue, lethargy, headaches, giddiness and muscle cramps; salt tablets may help, but adding extra salt to your food is better.

Anhydrotic heat exhaustion, caused by an inability to sweat, is quite rare. It is likely to strike people who have been in a hot climate for some time, rather than newcomers.

Heat Stroke This serious, occasionally fatal, condition can occur if the body's heat-regulating mechanism breaks down and the body temperature rises to dangerous levels. Long, continuous periods of exposure to high temperatures and insufficient fluids can leave you vulnerable to heat stroke.

The symptoms are feeling unwell, not sweating very much (or at all) and a high body temperature (39°C to 41°C or 102°F to 106°F). Where sweating has ceased the skin becomes flushed and red. Severe, throbbing headaches and lack of coordination will also occur, and the sufferer may be confused or aggressive. Eventually the victim will become delirious or convulse. Hospitalisation is essential, but in the interim get victims out of the sun, remove their clothing, cover them with a wet sheet or towel and then fan continually. Give fluids if they are conscious.

Hypothermia Too much cold can be just as dangerous as too much heat. If you are hiking at high altitudes (such as in Réunion) or simply taking a long bus trip over mountains, particularly at night, be prepared.

Hypothermia occurs when the body loses heat faster than it can produce it and the core temperature of the body falls. It is surprisingly easy to progress from very cold to dangerously cold with a combination of wind, wet clothing, fatigue and hunger, even if the air temperature is above freezing. It is best to dress in layers; silk, wool and some of the new artificial fibres are all good insulating materials. A hat is very important, as a lot of heat is lost through the head. A strong, waterproof outer layer (and a 'space' blanket for emergencies) are essential. Carry basic supplies, including food containing simple sugars to generate heat quickly and fluid to drink.

Symptoms of hypothermia are exhaustion, numb skin (particularly toes and fingers), shivering, slurred speech, irrational or violent behaviour, lethargy, stumbling, dizzy spells, muscle cramps and violent bursts of energy. Irrationality may take the form of sufferers claiming they are warm and trying to take off their clothes.

To treat mild hypothermia, first get victims out of the wind and rain, remove their clothing if it's wet and replace it with dry, warm clothing. Give them hot liquids – not alcohol – and some high-kilojoule, easily digestible food. Do not rub victims; instead allow them to slowly warm themselves. This should be enough to treat the early stages of hypothermia. The early recognition and treatment of mild hypothermia is the only way to prevent severe hypothermia, which is a critical condition.

Jet Lag Jet lag is experienced when a person travels by air across more than three time zones (each time zone usually represents a one-hour time difference). It occurs because many of the functions of the human body (such as temperature, pulse rate and emptying of the bladder and bowels) are regulated by internal 24-hour cycles. When we travel long distances rapidly, our bodies take time to adjust to the 'new time' of our destination, and we may experience fatigue, disorientation, insomnia, anxiety, impaired concentration and loss of appetite. These effects will usually be gone within three days of arrival, but to minimise the impact of jet lag:

- Rest for a couple of days before departure.
- Try to select flight schedules that minimise sleep deprivation; arriving late in the day means you can go to sleep soon after you arrive. For very long flights, try to organise a stopover.
- Avoid excessive eating (which bloats the stomach) and alcohol (which causes dehydration) during the flight. Instead, drink plenty of non-carbonated, nonalcoholic drinks such as fruit juice or water.
- Avoid smoking.
- Make yourself comfortable by wearing loose-fitting clothes and perhaps bringing an eye mask and ear plugs to help you sleep.
- Try to sleep at the appropriate time for the time zone you are travelling to.

Motion Sickness Eating lightly before and during a trip will reduce the chances of motion sickness. If you are prone to motion sickness try to find a place that minimises movement – near the wing on aircraft, close to midships on boats, near the centre on buses. Fresh air usually helps; reading and cigarette smoke don't. Commercial motion-sickness preparations, which can cause drowsiness, have to be taken before the trip commences. Ginger (available in capsule form) and peppermint (including mint-flavoured sweets) are natural preventatives.

Prickly Heat Prickly heat is an itchy rash caused by excessive perspiration trapped under the skin. It usually strikes people who have just arrived in a hot climate. Keeping cool, bathing often, drying the skin and using a mild talcum or prickly heat powder or resorting to air-conditioning may help.

Sunburn Mauritius, Réunion and the Seychelles lie close to the equator within the humid tropics, where the sun's rays are more direct and concentrated than in temperate zones. Even in the cooler highland areas, everyone will be susceptible to these hazardous UV rays.

In the tropics you can get sunburnt surprisingly quickly, even through cloud. Use a sunscreen, a hat, and barrier cream for your nose and lips. Calamine lotion, aloe vera cream or Stingose are good for mild sunburn. Protect your eyes with good-quality sunglasses, particularly if you will be near water or sand.

Diving Health
If you intend taking a dive course in Mauritius, Réunion or the Seychelles, you should have a full diving medical checkup before you leave home. In practice, most dive schools will let you dive or do a course if you're under 50 years old and complete a medical questionnaire, but the checkup is still a good idea. This is especially so if you have any problem at all with your breathing, ears or sinuses. If you are an asthmatic, or you have any other chronic breathing difficulties, or any serious inner-ear problems, you will not pass the test and should not do any scuba diving.

(For more detailed information on diving safely, see the special section 'Underwater Worlds'.)

Decompression Sickness Decompression sickness is a very serious condition usually, though not always, associated with diver error. The most common symptoms are unusual fatigue or weakness; skin itch; pain in the arms, torso or legs (joints or mid-limb); dizziness and vertigo; local numbness, tingling or paralysis; and shortness of breath. Signs may also include a blotchy skin rash, a tendency to favour an arm or a leg, staggering, coughing spasms, collapse or unconsciousness. These symptoms and signs can occur individually, or a number of them can appear at one time.

The most common causes of decompression sickness (or 'the bends' as it is commonly known) are diving too deep, staying at depth for too long, or ascending too quickly. This results in nitrogen coming out of solution in the blood and forming bubbles, most commonly in the bones and particularly in the joints or in weak spots such as healed fracture sites.

Other factors that have been shown to have a causal effect in decompression sickness include excess body fat; heavy exertion before, during or after diving; injuries and illness; dehydration; alcohol; cold water, hot showers or hot baths after diving; carbon dioxide increase (through smoking, for example); and age.

Avoid flying after diving, as this causes nitrogen to come out of the blood even faster than it would at sea level. It's not a good idea to dive in the 24-hour period before a flight, and certainly not within 12 hours. A low-altitude flight, such as a helicopter or seaplane transfer to the airport, may also be dangerous, because the aircraft are not pressurised, though the flights are usually short. Opinions vary as to the risks of flying and the time required to minimise the risks – a lot depends on the frequency, depth and duration of dives several days before the flight. Seek the advice of an instructor when planning dives during the final few days of your stay, and try to finish up with shallow dives.

Even if you take all the necessary precautions, there is no guarantee that you will not be hit by the bends. All divers have a responsibility to be aware of anything unusual about their own condition, and that of their diving buddy, after a dive.

The only treatment for decompression sickness is to put the patient into a recompression chamber. The Seychelles' two-person recompression chamber is located in the hospital in Victoria, and the interisland airplanes or helicopter will assist in a medical emergency.

In Mauritius, treatment is provided by the recompression chamber located at the headquarters of the paramilitary Special Mobile Force at Vacoas.

A chamber provides an artificial means of putting a person back under pressure similar to, or often greater than, that of the depth at which they were diving so the nitrogen bubbles can be reabsorbed. The time required in the chamber is usually three to eight hours. The treatment is usually effective, with the main problem being caused by delay in getting the patient to the chamber. If you think that you, or anyone you are diving with, are suffering from the bends, it is extremely important to get to a recompression chamber immediately.

Ear Problems Many divers experience pain in the ears after diving; this is commonly caused by failure of the ears to compensate properly for changes in pressure. The problem will usually fix itself, but injuries are often caused when people try to treat themselves by poking cotton buds or other objects into the ear.

Infectious Diseases
Diarrhoea Simple things like a change of water, food or climate can all cause a mild bout of diarrhoea, but a few rushed toilet trips with no other symptoms is not indicative of a major problem.

Dehydration is the main danger with any diarrhoea, particularly in children or the elderly, for whom it can occur quite quickly. Under all circumstances *fluid replacement* is the most important thing to remember. Soda water, weak black tea with a little sugar, or soft drinks allowed to go flat and diluted 50% with clean water are all good. With severe diarrhoea, a rehydrating solution is preferable to replace minerals and salts lost. Commercially available oral rehydration salts (ORS) are very useful; add them to boiled or bottled water. In an emergency you can make up a solution of six teaspoons of sugar and a half teaspoon of salt to a litre of boiled or bottled water. You need to drink at least the same volume of fluid that you are losing in bowel movements and vomiting. Urine is the best guide to the adequacy of replacement – if you have small amounts of concentrated urine, you need to drink more. Keep drinking small amounts often. Stick to a bland diet as you recover.

Lomotil or Imodium can be used to bring relief from the symptoms, although they do not actually cure the problem. Only use these drugs if you do not have access to toilets, eg, if you *must* travel. For children under 12 years Lomotil and Imodium are not recommended. Do not use these drugs if the person has a high fever or is severely dehydrated.

In certain situations antibiotics may be required: if you have diarrhoea with blood or mucus (dysentery), any fever, watery diarrhoea with fever and lethargy, persistent diarrhoea not improving after 48 hours, or severe diarrhoea. In these situations gut-paralysing drugs like Imodium or Lomotil should be avoided.

A stool test is necessary to diagnose which kind of dysentery you have, so you should seek medical help urgently. Where this is not possible the recommended drugs for dysentery are norfloxacin 400mg twice daily for three days or ciprofloxacin 500mg twice daily for five days. These are not recommended for children or pregnant women. The drug of choice for children would be co-trimoxazole (Bactrim, Septrin, Resprim) with dosage dependent on weight. A five-day course is given. Ampicillin or amoxycillin may be given in pregnancy, but medical care is necessary.

Amoebic dysentery is more gradual in the onset of symptoms, with cramping abdominal pain and vomiting less likely; fever may not be present. It will persist until treated and can recur and cause other health problems.

Giardiasis is another type of diarrhoea. The parasite causing this intestinal disorder is present in contaminated water. The symptoms are stomach cramps, nausea, a bloated stomach, watery, foul-smelling diarrhoea and frequent gas. Giardiasis can appear several weeks after you have been exposed to the parasite. The symptoms may disappear for a few days and then return; this can go on for several weeks. Tinidazole, known as Fasigyn, or metronidazole (Flagyl) are the recommended drugs. Treatment is a 2g single dose of Fasigyn or 250mg of Flagyl three times daily for five to 10 days.

HIV & AIDS Infection with the human immunodeficiency virus (HIV) may lead to acquired immune deficiency syndrome (AIDS), which is a fatal disease. With its links to mainland Africa, the Indian Ocean is facing a sharp upturn in cases of HIV. The small prostitution industry in Port Louis in Mauritius, St-Denis in Réunion and Victoria in the Seychelles should be regarded as extremely high risk. Any exposure to blood, blood products or body fluids may put the individual at risk.

As well as through sexual contact, the disease is often transmitted through dirty needles – vaccinations, acupuncture, tattooing and body piercing can be potentially as dangerous as intravenous drug use. HIV/AIDS can also be spread through infected blood transfusions; some developing countries cannot afford to screen blood used for transfusions.

If you do need an injection, ask to see the syringe unwrapped in front of you, or take a needle and syringe pack with you. Fear of HIV infection should never preclude treatment for serious medical conditions.

Intestinal Worms These parasites are most common in rural, tropical areas. The different worms have different ways of infecting people. Some may be ingested on food including undercooked meat and some enter through your skin. Infestations may not show up for some time, and although they are generally not serious, if left untreated some can cause severe health problems later. Consider having a stool test when you return home to check for these and determine the appropriate treatment.

Typhoid Typhoid fever is a dangerous gut infection caused by contaminated water and food. Medical help must be sought.

In its early stages sufferers may feel they have a bad cold or flu on the way, as early symptoms are a headache, body aches and a fever which rises a little each day until it is around 40°C (104°F) or more. The victim's pulse is often slow relative to the degree of fever present – unlike a normal fever where the pulse increases. There may also be vomiting, abdominal pain, diarrhoea or constipation.

In the second week the high fever and slow pulse continue and a few pink spots may appear on the body; trembling, delirium, weakness, weight loss and dehydration may occur. Complications such as pneumonia, perforated bowel or meningitis may occur.

The fever should be treated by keeping victims cool and giving them fluids as dehydration should also be watched for. Ciprofloxacin 750mg twice a day for 10 days is good for adults.

Chloramphenicol is recommended in many countries. The adult dosage is two 250mg capsules, four times a day. Children aged between eight and 12 years should have half the adult dose, and younger children one-third the adult dose.

Hepatitis Hepatitis is a general term for inflammation of the liver. It is a common disease worldwide. The symptoms are fever, chills, headache, fatigue, feelings of weakness and aches and pains, followed by loss of appetite, nausea, vomiting, abdominal pain, dark urine, light-coloured faeces, jaundiced (yellow) skin and yellowing of the whites of the eyes.

Hepatitis A Hepatitis A is transmitted by contaminated food and drinking water. The disease poses a real threat to the Western traveller. You should seek medical advice, but there is not much you can do apart from resting, drinking lots of fluids, eating lightly and avoiding fatty foods. People who have had hepatitis should avoid alcohol for some time after the illness, as the liver needs time to recover.

Hepatitis B There are almost 300 million chronic carriers of hepatitis B in the world. It is spread through contact with infected blood, blood products or body fluids, eg, through sexual contact, unsterilised needles, blood transfusions, or contact with blood via small breaks in the skin.

Other risk situations include having a shave or tattoo, or having your body pierced with contaminated equipment. The symptoms of type B may be more severe and may lead to long-term problems.

Hepatitis C Hepatitis C can lead to chronic liver disease. The virus is spread by contact with blood, usually via contaminated transfusions or shared needles. Avoiding these is the only means of prevention.

Hepatitis D is spread in the same way as hepatitis B, but the risk is mainly in shared needles.

Hepatitis E Hepatitis E is transmitted in the same way as hepatitis A, and can be very serious in pregnant women.

Sexually Transmitted Diseases

HIV/AIDS and hepatitis B can be transmitted through sexual contact – see the relevant sections earlier for more details. Other STDs include gonorrhoea, herpes and syphilis. Sores, blisters or rashes around the genitals, discharges, or pain when urinating are common symptoms. In some STDs, such as wart virus or chlamydia, symptoms may be less marked or not observed at all, especially in women. Syphilis symptoms eventually disappear completely, but the disease continues and can cause severe problems in later years. While abstinence from sexual contact is the only 100% effective prevention, using condoms is also effective. The treatment of gonorrhoea and syphilis is with specific antibiotics. There is no cure for herpes or AIDS.

Insect-Borne Diseases

Malaria The risk of malaria in Mauritius, Réunion and the Seychelles is extremely low. Almost all recorded cases involve travellers who contracted the disease elsewhere. Some doctors may still recommend malaria prophylaxis just to be safe. For your own peace of mind (as well as personal comfort!) it's wise to take the usual precautions against mosquito bites. The main messages are:

- Wear light-coloured clothing.
- Wear long pants and long-sleeved shirts.
- Use mosquito repellents containing the compound DEET on exposed areas (prolonged overuse of DEET may be harmful, especially to children, but its use is considered preferable to being bitten by disease-transmitting mosquitoes).
- Avoid highly scented perfumes or aftershave.
- Use a mosquito net impregnated with mosquito repellent (permethrin) – it may be worth taking your own.
- Impregnate clothes with permethrin, which effectively deters mosquitoes and other insects.

Cuts, Bites & Stings

Bedbugs & Lice Bedbugs live in various places, but particularly in dirty mattresses and bedding, evidenced by spots of blood on bedclothes or on the wall. Bedbugs leave itchy bites in neat rows. Calamine lotion or Stingose spray may help.

All lice cause itching and discomfort. They make themselves at home in your hair (head lice), your clothing (body lice) or in your pubic hair (crabs). You catch lice through direct contact with infected people or by sharing combs, clothing and the like. Powder or shampoo treatment will kill the lice and infected clothing should be washed in very hot, soapy water and left in the sun to dry.

As Indian Ocean families are usually large, unmarried couples have nowhere to go to get better acquainted, so some pensions, or boarding houses, rent out rooms to couples for a 'little rest'. The bed linen in such hotels can be a breeding ground for pubic lice.

Insect Bites & Stings Bee and wasp stings are usually painful rather than dangerous. However, in people who are allergic to them severe breathing difficulties may occur and require urgent medical care. Calamine lotion or Stingose spray will give relief and ice packs will reduce the pain and swelling.

Marine Dangers The Indian Ocean has its fair share of marine nasties. For more information, see the special section 'Underwater Worlds'.

Cuts & Scratches Wash any cut well, and treat with an antiseptic such as povidone-iodine. Where possible avoid bandages and Band-Aids, which can keep wounds wet. Coral cuts are notoriously slow to heal, and if they are not adequately cleaned small pieces of coral can become embedded in the wound. Avoid coral cuts by wearing shoes when walking on reefs, and clean any cut thoroughly with an antiseptic. Severe pain, throbbing, redness, fever or generally feeling unwell suggest infection and the prompt need for antibiotics, as coral cuts may result in serious infections.

Leeches & Ticks Leeches may be present in damp rainforest conditions; they attach themselves to your skin to suck your blood. Hikers often get them on their legs or in their boots. Salt or a lighted cigarette end will make them fall off. Do not pull them off, as the bite is then more likely to become infected. Clean and apply pressure if the point of attachment is bleeding. An insect repellent may keep them away.

You should always check all over your body if you have been walking through a potentially tick-infested area as ticks can cause skin infections and other more serious diseases. If a tick is found attached, press down around the tick's head with tweezers, grab the head and gently pull upwards. Avoid pulling the rear of the body as this may squeeze the tick's gut contents through the attached mouth parts into the skin, increasing the risk of infection and disease. Smearing chemicals on the tick will not make it let go and is not recommended.

Women's Health

Gynaecological Problems Antibiotic use, synthetic underwear, sweating and contraceptive pills can lead to fungal vaginal infections, especially when travelling in hot climates. Fungal infections are characterised by a rash, itch and discharge and can be treated with a vinegar or lemon-juice douche, or with yoghurt. Nystatin, miconazole or clotrimazole pessaries or vaginal cream are the usual treatment. Maintaining good personal hygiene and wearing loose-fitting clothes and cotton underwear may help prevent these infections.

Sexually transmitted diseases are a major cause of vaginal problems. Symptoms include a smelly discharge, painful intercourse and sometimes a burning sensation when urinating. Medical attention should be sought and male sexual partners must also be treated. For more information, see the Sexually Transmitted Diseases section earlier. Besides abstinence, the best thing is to practise safer sex using condoms.

Pregnancy It is not advisable to travel to some places while pregnant as some vaccinations normally used to prevent serious diseases, eg, yellow fever, are not advisable in pregnancy. In addition, some diseases are much more serious for pregnant women (and may increase the risk of a stillborn child), eg, malaria.

Most miscarriages occur during the first three months of pregnancy. Miscarriage is not uncommon, and can occasionally lead to severe bleeding. The last three months should also be spent within reasonable distance of good medical care. A baby born as early as 24 weeks stands a chance of survival, but only in a good modern hospital. Pregnant women should avoid all unnecessary medication, although vaccinations and malarial prophylactics should still be taken where needed. Additional care should be taken to prevent illness and particular attention should be paid to diet and nutrition. Alcohol and nicotine, for example, should be avoided.

Less Common Diseases
The following diseases pose a small risk to travellers, and so are only mentioned in passing. Seek medical advice if you think you may have any of these diseases.

Cholera This is the worst of the watery diarrhoeas, and medical help should be sought. Outbreaks of cholera are generally widely reported, so you can avoid such problem areas. *Fluid replacement is the most vital treatment* – the risk of dehydration is severe as you may lose up to 20L a day. If there is a delay in getting to hospital then begin taking tetracycline. The adult dose is 250mg four times daily. It is not recommended for children under nine years or pregnant women. Tetracycline may help shorten the illness, but adequate fluids are required to save lives.

Rabies Rabies is a fatal viral infection found in many countries. Many animals can be infected (such as dogs, cats, bats and monkeys) and it is their saliva which is infectious. Any bite, scratch or even lick from a warm-blooded, furry animal should be cleaned immediately and thoroughly. Scrub with soap and running water, and then apply alcohol or iodine solution. Medical help should be sought promptly for a course of injections to prevent the onset of symptoms and death.

Tetanus Tetanus occurs when a wound becomes infected by a germ which lives in soil and in the faeces of horses and other animals. It enters the body via breaks in the skin. All wounds should be cleaned promptly and adequately and an antiseptic cream or solution applied. Use antibiotics if the wound becomes hot or throbs, or if pus is seen. The first symptom may be discomfort in swallowing, or stiffening of the jaw and neck; this is followed by painful convulsions of the jaw and whole body. The disease can be fatal.

Tuberculosis (TB) TB is a bacterial infection usually transmitted from person to person by coughing, but it may be transmitted through consumption of unpasteurised milk. Milk that has been boiled is safe to drink, and the souring of milk to make yoghurt or cheese also kills the bacilli. Travellers are usually not at great risk as close household contact with the infected person is usually required before the disease is passed on.

Typhus Typhus is spread by ticks, mites or lice. It begins with fever, chills, headache and muscle pains followed a few days later by a body rash. There is often a large painful sore at the site of the bite, and nearby lymph nodes are swollen and painful. Typhus can be treated under medical supervision. Seek local advice on areas where ticks pose a danger and always check your skin (including hair) carefully for ticks after walking in a danger area such as a tropical forest. A strong insect repellent can help, and serious walkers in tick areas should consider having their boots and trousers impregnated with benzyl benzoate and dibutylphthalate.

Yellow Fever This viral disease is endemic in many African countries but is not present in Mauritius, Réunion or the Seychelles. It is transmitted by mosquitoes. The initial symptoms are fever, headache, abdominal pain and vomiting. Seek medical care urgently.

WOMEN TRAVELLERS

In general, women can expect courteous treatment in all three destinations. These are fairly traditional societies, so revealing attire is best reserved for the beach. Mauritius follows Indian traditions and women tend to swim fully clothed; bikinis are fine on private hotel beaches, but may attract stares elsewhere. You should cover your shoulders and wear trousers or a knee-length skirt if you plan to enter any temples or religious places. (Men should also dress modestly in these places; for more information, see Society & Conduct later in this chapter.)

As most visitors to these islands are couples, a woman travelling alone can expect plenty of questions on the whereabouts of her husband. If you don't want to have to answer a lot of questions about why you choose to travel alone, one possibility is to invent a mythical husband who can't get away from his work.

While the older generation will generally be respectful to women, some younger local males may regard sole female travellers as candidates for 'romantic' attention (as elsewhere, much of the blame lies with imported films that depict Western women as having 'loose morals'). Things are unlikely to go beyond long stares (dark glasses can help here), catcalls, or an inquisitive (or suggestive) *bonjour*, but most would-be suitors will back down if you firmly state that you are not interested. Some travellers to Réunion have reported verbal harassment and even threats of physical violence from local youths when going out at night. Women are advised to go out in groups if partying in the evening and never to hitch or walk alone after dark.

GAY & LESBIAN TRAVELLERS

Réunion is the most liberal of the three destinations when it comes to homosexuality, and follows French law whereby the age of consent for both homosexuals and heterosexuals is 15 years. The gay male scene is more developed than the lesbian one, but don't expect the same liberal attitudes you might find in mainland France. Overt displays of affection between members of the same sex may still be viewed with disdain, particularly away from the capital.

In Mauritius and the Seychelles, homosexuality is still illegal, although one of Mauritius' most popular politicians, Sir Gaetan Duval, was openly bisexual for much of his tenure. The Seychelles probably offers more secluded situations where you don't have to feel inhibited, but Mauritius is probably the more liberal society. Open affection in public is likely to attract stares and even jeers in both countries.

DISABLED TRAVELLERS

Réunion and Mauritius are probably the most wheelchair-friendly of the islands, with modern shopping centres that conform to international standards for disabled access. In all three destinations, most top-end hotels have wheelchair access, lifts and special bathrooms.

However, kerb ramps are few and far between, and older buildings and budget hotels often lack lifts and wheelchair access. There are only a few public toilets that accommodate wheelchairs.

SENIOR TRAVELLERS

Mauritius, Réunion and the Seychelles are all popular with senior travellers. The more upmarket hotels cater well for those who don't want to 'rough it', and offer comfortable rooms with air-conditioning (a lifesaver for those unaccustomed to the heat) and a wide array of facilities literally on the doorstep. They can arrange tours and other excursions, saving you the trouble.

While many people just opt to unwind on the beach, all three destinations offer water activities such as fishing trips, snorkelling, diving and glass-bottomed boat tours, which are open to all ages. For those who don't fancy getting wet, Mauritius and the Seychelles have a number of interesting museums and stately homes, while wildlife aficionados can take tours of the numerous nature reserves in the region.

In Réunion the emphasis is on hiking, and there are plenty of easy walks if you don't feel up to tackling the more challenging multi-day routes.

It may be helpful to discuss your proposed trip with your local doctor before setting off, especially if you plan on hiking, diving or any other energetic activities.

TRAVEL WITH CHILDREN

Children can enhance your encounters with local people, as they often possess little of the self-consciousness and sense of cultural difference that can inhibit interaction between adults. Admittedly, travelling with children can be challenging at times, and ideally the burden needs to be shared between two adults.

The upmarket hotels usually have baby-sitting services and can organise supervised water and land activities for the little ones. It's worthwhile asking about the extent of facilities offered when you make your hotel reservation.

Remember to bring along plenty of sun protection for your kids, and take extra care to prevent sunburn. Keep in mind that children are more likely to be affected by unaccustomed heat, and need time to acclimatise. Be prepared also for the minor effects often brought on by a change of diet or water, disrupted sleep patterns, or even just being in a strange place. Avoid giving your children street food, as it can sometimes bring on tummy upsets.

Nappies, lotions and baby foods are available, but the choice is somewhat limited, especially in Mauritius and the Seychelles. If there is a particular brand you swear by, it's a good idea to bring it along with you.

On the financial side, quite a few hotels and tour operators offer discounts for children – usually around 50% of the adult rate for children under 12 years of age; those below two years of age are often not charged at all.

For practical advice and information on how to make travel as stress-free as possible, for children and parents alike, get hold of Lonely Planet's *Travel with Children* by Maureen Wheeler.

SOCIETY & CONDUCT

Particular care should be taken if you attend a religious place (shrine, temple, mosque) or event. Dress and behave appropriately – don't wear singlet tops, shorts or miniskirts, and refrain from holding hands or smoking. Most holy places, including temples and mosques, require that you remove your shoes before entering – there's often a sign indicating where to leave your shoes. Don't touch a carving or statue of a deity. At some Hindu temples (such as the one in St-Denis), you also need to remove leather items such as belts. At mosques, you usually have to cover your head in certain areas, so remember to take along a scarf. If at anytime you're unsure about protocol, ask somebody. (For information on photographic etiquette, see Photography & Video earlier in this chapter.)

DANGERS & ANNOYANCES
Theft

Don't leave vital documents, money or valuables in your room. If you consider your hotel to be reliable, place your valuables in its safe and get a receipt. Make sure you package your valuables in a small, double-zippered bag that can be padlocked, or use a large envelope with a signed seal which will easily show any tampering. Count money and travellers cheques before and after retrieving them from the safe – this should quickly identify any attempts to extract single bills or cheques which might otherwise go unnoticed.

Don't take any valuables to the beach – and never tempt a passing thief by leaving your belongings unattended. Just take the minimum: swimsuit, towel, hat, T-shirt, sunscreen and enough money for a meal and drinks.

When travelling on public transport, keep your gear near you. Be extra careful in crowded places (such as the market in Port Louis), and avoid walking around with your valuables casually slung over your shoulder.

If you do have something stolen, you should report it to the police. The chances of them recovering any stolen property are remote, but you'll need a statement proving you have reported the crime if you want to claim on insurance.

For more information, see Money earlier in this chapter.

Marine Dangers
The Indian Ocean is a warm tropical ocean, so there are several aquatic nasties to watch out for, though few travellers encounter anything more serious than the odd coral cut. For detailed information, see the special section 'Underwater Worlds'.

Coconut Palms
Lying under a coconut palm may seem like a tropical idyll, but there have been some tragic accidents with plummeting coconuts. Take care when walking under coconut trees and don't lie beneath them.

LEGAL MATTERS
If you find yourself in a sticky legal predicament, contact your embassy. You should carry your passport with you at all times and keep a photocopy of the first page of your passport (with your personal details and photograph), as well as a copy of the page with your visa (if applicable).

ACTIVITIES
Water activities are the focus in Mauritius and the Seychelles, while hiking is Réunion's forte. For detailed coverage of the activities available, see the destination-specific Facts for the Visitor chapters.

Water Activities
Windsurfing, water-skiing, kayaking and pedalos are just some of the water activities offered by the main beach hotels and often made available to nonresidents for a price. Undersea walks (walks along the seabed using a diving helmet supplied with air from the surface) are extremely popular, as are tours in glass-bottomed boats. For full coverage of diving and snorkelling, see the special section 'Underwater Worlds'.

Deep-Sea Fishing Deep-sea fishing is a popular activity for travellers to all three destinations, but there is growing concern about its environmental impact. The Indian Ocean supports huge fisheries, and deep-sea angling has far less impact than commercial fishing, but the sport takes the healthiest individuals from the population, and little is known about the breeding cycles of the large predators that are the traditional targets of the sport. The tag-and-release option is growing in popularity in the region, and allows anglers to take home the trophy photograph as well as the knowledge that the fish are still going to be out there to be caught another day.

Land Activities
The options on land include mountain-bike riding, golf, horse riding, tennis, abseiling and rock climbing. In Mauritius, the Black River Gorges National Park is a popular destination for hikers, while Réunion offers many sensational hiking opportunities (see the special section 'Hiking in Réunion').

ACCOMMODATION
Although this is an expensive region to visit, it's also a great chance to play jet-setter! At the lofty top end of the market, there are some world-class luxury hotels and resorts, especially in Mauritius and the Seychelles. Indeed Mauritius and the Seychelles have traditionally been playgrounds of the rich and famous, who come here to live in style and indulge in the tempting range of water activities. But if the jet-setter scene is not for you, there are also cheaper accommodation alternatives.

The cheaper accommodation in the Seychelles can seem rather poor value for money, but Mauritius and Réunion both offer some excellent budget options, although the standard of facilities and services varies. Mauritius is probably the best destination for those seeking the tropics on a budget, with a number of extremely cheap guesthouses and self-catering apartments and bungalows, as well as some of the swankiest hotels in the Indian Ocean.

Réunion neatly covers the middle ground with a good selection of mid-range hotels as well as numerous cheaper options including camp sites, youth hostels, private gîtes, *gîtes de montagne* (mountain lodges), chambres d'hôte and *pensions de famille* (boarding houses). The Seychelles is really only for those who can afford to spend that little bit more. The top end of the range is fairly poorly represented in Réunion, with little to compare to the palatial resorts in Mauritius and the Seychelles.

Many of the mid-range and top-end hotels in all three places charge different room tariffs according to the season. Be warned that it can be difficult finding accommodation in the high season – book well ahead to avoid disappointment. If you intend staying in upmarket hotels, take advantage of package rates by booking from overseas. B&B rates include bed and breakfast. Full-board rates include all three meals, while half-board rates include breakfast and one other meal.

UNDERWATER WORLDS

The Indo-Pacific region is known to be the world's richest realm of marine flora and fauna. Mauritius, the Seychelles and the west coast of Réunion are fringed by coral reefs: fragile environments of calcareous deposits secreted by tiny marine animals known as coral polyps. Dead coral, along with shells and marine algae, forms the glorious white sand beaches of these islands; without the reefs, the beaches would erode and disappear. The reefs also provide shelter and habitat for numerous fish, shells, crustaceans, sea urchins and other marine life, which in turn provide a food source for larger fish as well as humans, both directly and indirectly. Boat trips, snorkelling and, best of all, scuba diving, will all help to open the door to this magical world below the surface.

Marine Life
Coral

Corals comes in many different shapes and sizes. When you dive or snorkel, what you are actually seeing of the coral reef is only the outer layers, a thin crust of living organisms building over the ancient skeletons of past coral reefs. The reef is constantly changing in shape and structure as the environment changes around it. Almost all the polyp skeletons are white – it's the living polyps that give coral its colourful appearance. During the day, most polyps retract to the protection of their hard skeleton, so it's only at night that the full beauty of the hard corals can be seen.

Throughout much of the Indian Ocean, coral is being decimated by a plague of the crown-of-thorns starfish, and the blame has been placed on the decimation of the starfish's primary natural enemy, the lovely – and popular – triton's trumpet shell.

The coral reefs have also been affected by superheated water from the natural phenomenon called El Nino. This has resulted in 'bleaching' of much of the hard coral in shallow-water areas. Coral bleaching occurs when the water temperature gets too high, causing the coral polyps to expel the symbiotic algae that gives corals their true colour. If the water temperature does not drop, then eventually the coral will die from the loss of the protective algae.

Inset: Descent into the underwater world (Photo: Michael Aw)

Right: Coral detail (Photo: Lawson Wood)

The near-shore reefs of the Seychelles' Beau Vallon Bay, such as Corsair Reef, were virtually wiped out by El Niño. The hard corals are still struggling, but the soft corals are in good shape. You can take great delight in discovering small pockets of growth, and the colours tend to be quite striking.

Symbiosis

The Indian Ocean is home to several thousand species of fish. This remarkable variety includes everything from tiny diamond fish, the smallest backboned animals, to huge whale sharks. Some fish are seen in the day, while others shelter in crevices and caverns in the coral and only emerge at night. Some are grazers, others are hunters. Some huddle together in groups for protection while others move around by themselves. Territorial species guard their own patch of reef fiercely, while others range freely.

A number of fish and other reef species engage in interesting symbiotic relationships, where two unrelated species get together in some activity for their mutual good.

The best recorded and, to the casual onlooker, most visible of these relationships is probably that of the anemone fish and the anemone. There are at least three recorded species of anemone fish in the Seychelles, including one that is indigenous to the area, the Seychelles anemone fish (Amphiprion fuscocaudatus), which is quite similar to the Clark's anemone fish (Amphiprion clarkii). The other species, the most common of all of the anemone fish, is the skunk anemone fish (Amphiprion akallopisos), which is a creamy brown in colour with a horizontal white line from the tip of the nose to the tip of the tail.

The brightly coloured anemone fish are a type of damselfish that have become acclimatised to living among the stinging tentacles of anemones. A typical group of anemone fish consists of several males and one larger female fish. They spend their entire life around the anemone, emerging briefly to feed then diving back into the protective tentacles at the first sign of danger. Anemone fish are not naturally immune to the anemone's sting – it is thought that they gradually gain immunity by repeatedly brushing themselves against the tentacles. Possibly the fish coat themselves with a layer of the anemone's mucus and so the anemone does not sting them, just as the anemone's tentacles avoid stinging one another.

The relationship between anemone fish and anemones is probably somewhat one-sided. The anemone fish may attract other fish within the anemone's grasp, but an anemone can live without the anemone fish, whereas the anemone fish are never seen without a protective anemone nearby.

Cleaner fish have another interesting reef relationship. The small cleaner wrasse (Labroides dimidiatus) perform a service on larger fish. They set themselves up at 'cleaner stations' and wait for customers.

The cleaners perform a small 'dance' to indicate that they're ready for action and then zip around the larger fish, nibbling off their fungal growth, dead scales, parasites and the like. They will even swim directly into the mouths of much larger fish to clean their teeth! This must be a tempting opportunity for the larger fish to get a quick free meal, but cleaner fish do not feel threatened while they're at work.

The cleaner stations are an important part of reef life; some fish regularly travel considerable distances for a clean-up and brush-up. Experimental removal of the cleaner fish from a section of reef has resulted in an increase in diseased and unhealthy fish and a fall in the general fish population.

Certain varieties of shrimps, including most of the shrimp species found in the Seychelles, also act as fish cleaners. The largest are the peppermint shrimp *(Lysmata amboinensis)* and the banded coral shrimp *(Stenopus hispidus)*. They tend to live in and around a variety of sponges and coral caves on the granite blocks or reef wall and will signal to the waiting fish with a wave of their antennae that they are open for business.

Doing a similar job on some of the larger groupers and moray eels are the hingeback cleaner shrimps *(Rhynchocinetes rugulosa)*. They are known to climb into the mouths of these fish and clean debris from the teeth.

The Pacific clown anemone shrimp *(Periclimenes brevicarpalis)* lives in association with a number of anemones, and is fairly common. This species is totally unafraid and if you extend your hand slowly, it will approach you and attempt to clean you too! This species has been known to clean human wounds and infections successfully.

The reef also has 'false cleaners'. These are tiny fish that masquerade as cleaners and then quickly take a bite out of the deceived larger fish. They've even been known to take a nip at swimmers.

It is common to see predators and prey lining up at cleaning stations, all enmity forgotten. This social truce is integral to the survival of the fish populations on the reef. These fish are not just individuals struggling to survive, they are part of an incredibly complex integrated structure which works to a firm set of guidelines that all follow. Our short journeys into their world allow us to see a small part of this ecosystem at work and to marvel at its complexity.

Top: Anenome fish (Photo: Michael Aw)

Rays

The most common species of ray found regularly in waters around the Seychelles is the manta ray *(Manta birostris)*. Look closely at the manta as it swims past you, because it may have a couple of remora or sucker-fish attached to its flanks. The remora *(Echeneis naucrates)* hitches a ride on mantas, sharks and turtles, and eats any scraps left behind by its host.

The spotted eagle ray *(Aetobatus narinari)* is a large ray with a snout somewhat like a pig's, which it uses to dig and forage beneath the sand for crustaceans and molluscs.

The electric or torpedo ray *(Torpedo pantheri)* is much smaller, and grows to a length of around 50cm. Its rounded body has two electrical organs with which it stuns its prey. It should be treated with respect – the electrical charge is between 14V and 37V.

The blue-spotted stingray *(Taeniura lymma)* is quite common in the sandy areas between the granite boulders of the Seychelles, and grows to a maximum of 50cm. It is circular in shape, covered in bright blue spots, and has a strong tail and a venomous spine.

The largest of the stingray species, and often encountered out at Shark Bank off Mahé, is the black-spotted ribbon-tail ray *(Taeniura melanospilos)*.

Sharks

Sharks are uncommon, but one of the most frequently sighted in waters around the Seychelles is the nurse shark *(Nebrius ferruginous)*, distinguishable by the two barbels on the top of its lip and small mouth. It is a fairly docile creature unless disturbed.

The white-tipped reef shark *(Triaenodon obesus)* is sometimes sighted in Mauritius and the Seychelles.

If you are extremely lucky, during winter in the Seychelles, you may get the chance to dive with the largest fish in the sea, the whale shark *(Rhincodon typus)*.

Top: Manta ray
(Photo: Michael Aw)

Eels

Moray eels are very common around all of the Seychelles islands. The giant moray *(Gymnothorax javanicus)* is the largest of all the eels found in the Seychelles.

The peppered moray *(Siderea grisea)*, at only 38cm long, is perhaps the most common around all of the Seychelles islands. It hides during the day in recesses in the reef and is an active predator by night. It is quite easily approached and has a habit of opening and closing its mouth, which looks threatening, but is actually an aid to respiration.

The undulate moray *(Gymnothorax undulatus)* is aggressive and common. Its head often protrudes from the reef.

The much rarer snowflake moray *(Echidna nebulosa)* is slightly smaller with a large dark brown to black body with irregular yellow bars and spots, yellow eyes and a cream nose and mouth.

Snake eels have a fin along the length of their back, and they live under the sand during the day. They are active foragers at night. The most common species recorded in the Seychelles during night dives is the spotted snake eel *(Myrichthys maculosus)*. Garden eels *(Heteroconger hassi)* live in vertical burrows in the softer sand areas; quite often, large numbers of them can be seen swaying gently in the current, picking off plankton as they drift past. They are extremely shy and withdraw into their burrows long before you reach them for a closer look.

Echinoderms

The widely varied group of creatures known as echinoderms includes sea urchins, starfish or sea stars, brittle stars, feather stars and sea cucumbers. It appears to be a curiously diverse group but they all share some basic structural similarities.

Starfish are highly visible since they have few natural enemies and do not hide away during daytime. Sea cucumbers, also known as bêche-de-mer, are easy to see as well.

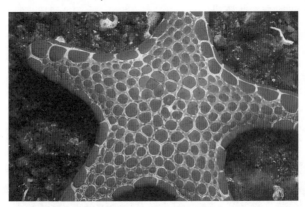

Right: Starfish
(Photo: David Bryant)

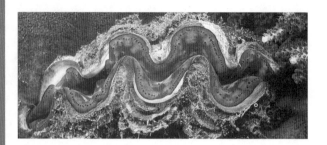

Molluscs

Like echinoderms, molluscs include members that seem to have scarcely any relationship to one another. Molluscs include a variety of shelled creatures or gastropods, the oysters, scallops and clams known as bivalves, and also the cephalopods, a group that includes octopus and squid.

The mollusc family includes the many clams that appear to be embedded in the coral. Their fleshy mantles are seen in a spectacular array of colours.

Nudibranchs, or sea slugs, are snails that have abandoned their shells and put on their party clothes. They're some of the most graceful and colourful reef creatures you can see.

Although some of the shells found in the Indian Ocean are incredibly beautiful, there are some varieties, such as the cone shell, that can fire out a deadly poisonous barb.

Dangerous Marine Life

A number of species found around Mauritius, Réunion and the Seychelles are poisonous or may sting or bite. Wild animals, including fish, must be approached carefully and sympathetically. Any creature that does not move when you approach it will have some other means of defence, so be careful.

Watch out for sea urchins, for the gaudy and easily recognisable lionfish with their poisonous spined fins, and for the cleverly camouflaged – and exceptionally poisonous – stonefish. Fire coral (*Millepora alcicornis*) should be avoided at all cost. Not a true coral, fire coral is actually a member of the jellyfish family and packs a powerful sting if touched. (For information on treating cuts, scratches and stings, see Health in the Regional Facts for the Visitor chapter.)

Make sure you wear full-shoe fins when diving, and fins or canvas shoes when snorkelling.

Although shark attacks are extremely few and far between, do be cautious, especially outside the lagoons. There have been some fatal shark attacks, particularly in Réunion (for more information, see the boxed text 'Shark Alert' in the Réunion Facts for the Visitor chapter). It's probably safest to make a habit of seeking 'shark advice' from locals before plunging into the sea.

Top: Clam
(Photo: David Bryant)

Marine Conservation

Marine turtles still occur throughout the Indian Ocean, albeit in dwindling numbers. Species include the loggerhead turtle *(Caretta caretta)*, the green turtle *(Chelonia mydas)*, the leatherback turtle *(Dermochelys coriacea)* and the hawksbill turtle *(Eretmochelys imbricata)*.

The downfall of many of these marine turtle species has been their edible flesh and eggs, highly prized by local fishermen, and their carapace (shell), which humans turn into fashionable ornaments. According to the Convention on International Trade in Endangered Species (CITES), turtles are among the most endangered species, threatened by pollution and human exploitation.

You can play a role in ensuring that turtles have a future. Please do not eat turtle meat or soup; do not buy any souvenirs made from turtles, such as hawksbill shell jewellery (commonly known as 'tortoiseshell' jewellery). Take care not to disturb turtles or hatchlings, and avoid using white light on the beach (for example, car headlights or torches), which can frighten nesting females and attract hatchlings away from the safety of the sea. Never throw plastic litter into the sea or waterways because some turtles eat plastic bags (mistaking them for jellyfish) and suffer fatal intestinal problems as a result.

In order to protect the marine environment we strongly urge you not to buy seashells or collect them from the beach, and not to buy any seashell products (such as seashell jewellery). Stocks of many of the most beautiful seashells have been cleared in many areas and some are actually endangered.

Right: Green turtle
(Photo: Simon Foale)

Seychelles

The Seychelles has four marine national parks, and several other protected marine areas, although not all the protected areas are actively managed.

Around Praslin, the Curieuse Marine National Park covers all of the area around the headlands that flank Curieuse Bay, including the waters around Curieuse Island.

Around Mahé, the Ste Anne Marine National Park was designated in 1973, and it is an extremely popular area, visited daily by glass-bottomed boats. Baie Ternay Marine National Park and Port Launay Marine National Park are both natural extensions of the Morne Seychellois National Park.

The Seychelles Marine Conservation Expedition is actively monitoring and promoting marine habitats and biodiversity. For information on its work, visit its Web site (www.dialspace.dial.pipex.com/town/avenue/aba60), which includes links to other conservation organisations that are active in the Indian Ocean.

The Nature Protection Trust of Seychelles works to protect the biodiversity of the Seychelles. Its conservation projects have included the Giant Tortoise Conservation Project on Silhouette Island. For more information, visit the trust's Web site (http://members.aol.com/jstgerlach/npts.htm).

Mauritius

In Mauritius, conservation, environmental education and preservation of marine heritage are undertaken by the Mauritius Marine Conservation Society or MMCS (☎ 696 5368). The society promotes the prohibition of spear fishing and shell and coral collecting; it also promotes the installation of artificial reefs to enhance diving opportunities and to maintain the wellbeing of the marine environment. The group is also active in reef surveys and in the monitoring of dolphins and whales in the region.

Supported by some members of the Mauritius Scuba Diving Association, environmental protection is serious business among a few dive operators. Divers can go beyond the no-gloves policy by giving their business to operators who make extra efforts in preserving the quality of the environment. At the same time, if you come upon an operator polluting or destroying the reef, make the effort to report them to the Secretary, Mauritius Marine Conservation Society, c/o MUG, Railway Road, Phoenix, Mauritius.

Left: Hermit crab
(Photo: Michael Aw)

LAWSON WOOD

LAWSON WOOD

MICHAEL AW

LAWSON WOOD

LAWSON WOOD

Underwater worlds: Coral reefs have been called the rainforests of the sea because they harbour incredible biodiversity.

MICHAEL AW

LAWSON WOOD

MICHAEL AW

LAWSON WOOD

Top: You're sure to see the coral grouper if you go diving in the Seychelles.
Middle Left: The Koran angelfish tends to be shy and solitary.
Middle Right: The squirrelfish is both edible and carnivorous.
Bottom: The hawkfish takes its name from its method of hunting.

MICHAEL AW

MICHAEL AW

MICHAEL AW

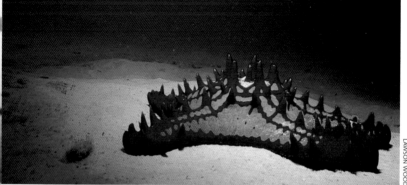

LAWSON WOOD

Top: The blue-striped snapper is commonly seen in schools around the Seychelles' *Ennerdale* wreck.
Middle Left: Your first encounter with a parrotfish is just as likely to be in a restaurant as underwater.
Middle Right: The green turtle is named for the greenish colour of its fat. It can weigh up to 375kg.
Bottom: The starfish *Protoreaster nodosus* often lives with a symbiotic shrimp.

LAWSON WOOD

MICHAEL AW

MICHAEL AW

The big, the bigeyed and the ugly: the harmless whale shark (top) is the world's biggest fish; Bloch's bigeye (middle) is commonly seen on night dives; the giant moray eel (bottom) can reach 3m in length.

Responsible Diving

The popularity of diving is placing immense pressure on many sites. Please consider the following tips when diving and help preserve the ecology and beauty of reefs:

- Do not use anchors on the reef, and take care not to ground dive boats on coral. Encourage dive operators and regulatory bodies to establish permanent moorings at popular dive sites.

- Avoid touching living marine organisms with your body or dragging equipment across the reef. Polyps can be damaged by even the gentlest contact. Never stand on corals, even if they look solid and robust. If you must hold on to the reef, only touch exposed rock or dead coral.

- Be conscious of your fins. Even without contact, the surge from heavy fin strokes near the reef can damage delicate organisms. When treading water in shallow reef areas, take care not to kick up clouds of sand. Settling sand can easily smother the delicate organisms of the reef.

- Practise and maintain proper buoyancy control. Major damage can be done by divers descending too fast and colliding with the reef. Make sure you are correctly weighted and that your weight belt is positioned so that you stay horizontal. If you have not dived for a while, have a practice dive in a pool before taking to the reef. Be aware that buoyancy can change over the period of an extended trip: Initially you may breathe harder and need more weight; a few days later you may breathe more easily and need less weight.

- Take great care in underwater caves. Spend as little time within them as possible as your air bubbles may be caught within the roof and thereby leave previously submerged organisms high and dry. Taking turns to inspect the interior of a small cave will lessen the chances of damaging contact.

- Resist the temptation to collect or buy items from marine archaeological sites (mainly shipwrecks). Respect their integrity; some sites are even protected from looting by law.

- Ensure that you take home all your rubbish and any litter you may find as well. Plastics in particular are a serious threat to marine life.

- Resist the temptation to feed fish. You may disturb their normal eating habits, encourage aggressive behaviour or feed them food that is detrimental to their health.

- Minimise your disturbance of marine animals. In particular, do not ride on the backs of turtles as this causes them great anxiety.

Diving
Safety

Qualified divers must provide proof of certification with a certification card from PADI, SSI, NAUI, FAUI or CMAS. For advanced diving, some operators may ask to check your logbook. Most instructors are members of the US-based PADI and provide high-standard safety and tuition.

A dive operator should check your ability, health and qualifications before selling you a course or taking you out on an introductory dive. All beginners must be able to swim at least 200m before proceeding. Certain medical conditions, such as asthma or having a cold, do not mix well with diving. Remember that you should allow at least 24 hours between diving and taking a flight.

Don't let having a certificate lull you into thinking that you know everything – experience is vitally important. Every diver has a logbook in which they should record every dive they make. If a proposed dive is deep or difficult, a good dive operator should check your logbook to ensure your experience is sufficient. A high proportion of diving accidents happen to inexperienced divers getting out of their depth.

Considering the ratio of accidents to the number of divers who dive in the Indian Ocean, it is clear that in most cases, training is of a very high standard. Accidents do happen, however, and emergency treatment should be sought immediately.

In the Seychelles, diving operators are all equipped to handle most medical emergencies and have ship-to-shore radio to facilitate extra help, if needed. The Seychelles' two-person recompression chamber is located in the hospital in Victoria, and the interisland airplanes or helicopter will assist in a medical emergency.

In Mauritius, treatment is provided by the recompression chamber located at the headquarters of the paramilitary Special Mobile Force at Vacoas. (For more information on diving health, see Health in the Regional Facts for the Visitor chapter.)

We strongly recommend that you sign up for insurance coverage with Divers Alert Network (DAN), a US-based dive safety organisation. For detailed information, write to Divers Alert Network, Peter B Bennett Center, 6 West Colony Place, Durham, NC 27705, USA or visit the DAN Web site (www.diversalertnetwork.org).

Seychelles

With over 900 species of fish, 100 types of shells and 50 varieties of coral, the Seychelles are a diver's paradise and an underwater photographer's dream. The five main groups of islands – namely Providence, Farquhar, Desroches, Cosmoledo and Aldabra (a Unesco World Heritage Site) – have some of the largest coral atolls in the world. In contrast to these magnificent coral atolls, the Mahé and Praslin groups in the north are granite formations with a surrounding and fringing coral reef.

Most diving takes place either very close to the shore or on the offshore granite boulders that are synonymous with diving in the

Diving Safely

Before embarking on a scuba diving, skin diving or snorkelling trip, carefully consider the following points to ensure a safe and enjoyable experience:

- Ensure you have a current diving certification card from a recognised scuba diving instructional agency (if scuba diving).
- Be sure you are healthy and feel comfortable diving.
- Obtain reliable information about physical and environmental conditions at the dive site (eg, from a reputable local dive operation).
- Be aware of local laws, regulations and etiquette about marine life and the environment.
- Dive only at sites within your realm of experience; engage the services of a competent, professionally trained dive instructor or dive master.
- Be aware that underwater conditions vary significantly from one region, or even site, to another. Seasonal changes can significantly alter any site and dive conditions. These differences influence the way divers dress for a dive and what diving techniques they use.
- Ask about the environmental characteristics that can affect your diving and how local trained divers deal with these considerations.

Seychelles, mostly from dive boats. There is shore diving in a number of locations and you can snorkel just about everywhere.

The annual Sub Indian Ocean Seychelles (SUBIOS) underwater festival is held in October. The festival combines diving activities with an underwater photography competition and film presentations. For current program information, check out the festival's Web site (www.seychelles .net/diving/subios). The Seychelles Underwater Centre's Web site (www. diveseychelles.com.sc/subios.htm) also has useful festival information.

For more information about diving, Lonely Planet's Pisces guide, *Diving & Snorkeling the Seychelles*, by Lawson Wood, includes detailed descriptions of 35 dive sites.

Conditions The best visibility and calmest seas are from March to May and September to November. Visibility can drop dramatically during November with the rise in the plankton which sweeps across the Indian Ocean, bringing with it manta rays and whale sharks. During the monsoon season, the Seychelles' rivers become swollen and the subsequent rainwater runoff can also affect visibility.

Operators choose dive sites according to the prevailing winds to allow for the best conditions. Therefore, every season offers something sensational for divers, whether it's beautiful clear waters with very occasional sightings of big fish, or poor visibility with an excellent chance of being able to dive with the largest fish in the sea, the whale shark.

Top Three Dive Sites of the Seychelles

Shark Bank This massive granite pillar off the west coast of Mahé rises from 30m deep, with several massive granite boulders on top. As the name suggests, sharks are quite often seen in the area, and large stingrays are common around the boulder outcrops. The walls are covered with bright orange sponges and white gorgonians, and the area teems with fish life not normally associated with the mainland. There is nearly always a strong current at this site, so it's best to try and reach the seabed as quickly as possible, and stay near the mooring line for additional safety. Access is by boat from Beau Vallon.

Îlot Îlot is a granite outcrop off Mahé's North Point, consisting of several large boulders topped by a couple of palm trees. Between the small island and the mainland, the current can be quite strong, but the small cluster of boulders in the centre yields one of the highest densities of life in the Seychelles. Golden cup coral festoons the canyons and gullies, and gorgonians and other soft corals abound. You're sure to see yellow-spotted burr fish, anemones and clownfish. Small peppered moray eels live in harmony with thousands of hingeback shrimps; watch out for Spanish dancer nudibranchs with symbiotic shrimps. Access is by boat only.

Ennerdale Wreck The _Ennerdale_, a former Royal Navy fleet auxiliary motor tanker, served for only three years before she sank on a sandbank after striking an uncharted rock about 11km from Victoria on 1 June 1970. The ship now lies in sections in 30m of water. Dives tend to be around the stern section where the ship is mostly intact with the wheelhouse and propeller readily accessible. The rest of the ship is largely broken up. The tangled superstructure is quite open and so allows for relatively safe exploration. The main part is slowly undergoing colonisation by small growths of soft and hard corals, with fire coral abundant on some of the upper sections. The crumpled bows tend to have a congregation of stingrays and small white-tip reef sharks, but these soon head off into the blue as you approach them. Access is by boat from Beau Vallon.

The outer islands are more susceptible than the main islands to offshore winds and the might of the Indian Ocean swell, which can travel a long way fuelled by some distant cyclone. Tidal variations and currents can be punishing.

Operators All of the dive centres on Mahé, Praslin and La Digue offer equipment and services of the highest standards. Most are dedicated five-star PADI centres with a multilingual staff, and offer the full range of certification courses in English, German, French, Italian and other languages.

Most operators in the Seychelles charge around Rs200/250 per dive (with/without your own gear). PADI beginner courses range from Rs350 to Rs500; advanced courses cost upwards of Rs1500. For live-aboard multi-day excursions, the SV *Sea Shell* (☎ 324026, fax 322978) offers three- to six-day cruises with diving for around Rs750 per person per day. The *Indian Ocean Explorer* (☎/fax 344223, e info@ioexplorer.com) runs regular 14-day dive packages to Aldabra and other islands starting at US$275 per person per day. Other Seychelles dive operators include:

Big Blue Divers (☎ 261106) Vacoa Village, Beau Vallon, Mahé
Island Ventures (☎ 247141 ext 8133, fax 515993) Berjaya Beau Vallon Bay Beach Resort, Mahé
La Digue Island Lodge (☎ 234232, fax 234100) La Digue
Le Diable des Mers (☎/fax 247104) Beau Vallon Beach, Mahé
Octopus Diving Centre (☎ 232350, fax 512350) Anse Volbert, Praslin
Pye-Koko (☎ 361361, fax 361333) Plantation Club, Pointe Lazare, Mahé
Tropi-Dive (☎ 232222) Baie Ste Anne, Praslin
Underwater Centre (☎ 247357, fax 344223) Coral Strand Hotel, Beau Vallon, Mahé

Mauritius

As a diving destination, Mauritius has been largely overshadowed by the popularity of the Red Sea, the Maldives and the Seychelles. However, the dive industry here is well developed, and caters for both beginners and advanced divers.

The fish diversity of Mauritius is documented to be similar to that of the Maldives, but astute naturalists and scientists are progressively discovering new species.

Mauritius is almost entirely surrounded by a barrier reef. Within the barrier lie turquoise lagoons providing great possibilities for snorkellers, swimmers and novice divers. Dynamic fish action and prolific coral density are only found on reefs close to the barrier and beyond. Here lie some of the best dive sites in the Indian Ocean. For more information, get a copy of *The Dive Sites of Mauritius* by Alan Mountain, which is comprehensive and well presented.

Conditions Underwater visibility varies from region to region, and from site to site, but horizontal visibility averages about 20m, and at some locations beyond 50m. Water temperature ranges from 20°C to 22°C in winter and from 26°C to 30°C in summer.

Right: White-tipped reef shark
(Photo: Michael Aw)

Top Three Dive Sites of Mauritius

Merville Aquarium Located about 1.5km offshore from Grand Baie's Merville Beach Hotel, this site in the north has the best to offer in terms of predictability of fish life. Angelfish, moray eels, scorpionfish, lionfish, damsels and butterflyfish are found in amazing numbers. The blue-striped snapper (Lutjanus kasmira) swarms the reefs in large shoals. Friendly giant morays, blue ribbon eels and stonefish are common denizens. For the macro photographer, the critters range from porcelain crabs and squat lobsters to harlequin shrimps living with sea anemones. Don't forget to look through the nooks and crannies for the octopus, which is also found in abundance. Access is by boat only, from any of the dive centres operating in the north, and the average depth of the dive is about 12m.

Colorado (Grand Canyon) This site, about 600m beyond the barrier reef at Chante au Vent (near Blue Bay) in the south, is named after the USA's Colorado River. This is the Grand Canyon beneath the sea; the sight is as breathtaking as the one in Arizona, but the adventure is 10 times more exhilarating, especially when dived in the early morning or late evening.

Sightings of black-tip sharks, kingfish, tuna and sea turtles are pretty regular, and schooling hammerheads are known to pass by in deeper water. The canyon-like structure is over 400m long. A typical route through the canyon includes a swim through a crayfish-filled tunnel, and an exit through a chimney into a large amphitheatre, decked by a large arch overhead. Ascend through the arch and swim along a narrow gorge towards a forest of gorgonian fans.

If by this stage you are not breathless absorbing the grandeur around you, you may be well and truly into decompression time. This is a deep dive, averaging 30m, but the seascape is addictive. Unfortunately, Colorado is weather dependent and often inaccessible because of rough offshore conditions. Under optimum conditions, the dive is magical and unforgettable.

Rembrant l'Herbe This is the signature site of the west region, located outside the barrier reef, offshore from Flic en Flac on the west coast. The average depth for optimum observation is about 45m. This rock pinnacle can easily be circumnavigated, and teems with an array of reef fish.

The attraction here is regular sightings of stubby grey reef sharks (Carcharhinus amblyrhynchos). Tuna, barracuda, spotted eagle rays and jacks (Caranx sexfasciatus) often swim around the pinnacle in respectable numbers. Sightings of great hammerhead have been reported by a lucky few. Fan-tailed or marbled rays (Taeniura melanospilos) are often seen foraging on this pinnacle in the afternoon. During rush hour – early morning or late evening – this site is electrifying, with feeding and spawning melees. Access is easy with a 10-minute boat trip from Flic en Flac.

Operators The majority of the dive centres in Mauritius are hotel-based, and focus on hotel guests, but they do welcome walk-in patrons. Most operate only in the region they are based in. Blue Water, Villas Caroline and Sindbad Divers are among the few independent operators that offer some form of safari to various sites around the country.

Most operators cater for two dives per day, one in the morning at about 9.30 am and another just after lunch at 1.30 pm. Beginner open-water courses, advanced course and specialist courses are widely available. Dive operators in Mauritius include:

Atlantis Dive (☎ 422 7126, fax 263 7859) Trou aux Biches
Blue Water (☎ 261 6267) Trou aux Biches
Caisson Multiplace (☎ 686 1011) Vacoas
Diving World Mauritius (☎ 421 4629, fax 263 7888) Le Mauricia Hotel, Grand Baie
Dolphin Diving (☎ 423 2693) Peréybère
Explorer (☎ 415 1544, fax 263 7859) Hotel Ambre, Belle Mare
Hibiscus Village Vacances (☎ 263 6225, fax 263 8553) Peréybère
Islandive (☎ 263 8016) Veranda Bungalow Village, Grand Baie
Karl Heinz Diving School (☎ 413 2515) Belle Mare Hotel, Poste de Flacq
La Pirogue (☎ 453 8441, fax 453 8449, e infolap@sunresort.com) Flic en Flac
Le Canonnier (☎ 263 7995) Pointe aux Cannoniers
Maritim (☎ 261 5600) Balaclava
Merville (☎ 263 8621, fax 263 8146) Merville Beach Hotel, Grand Baie
Nautilus (☎/fax 265 5495) Trou aux Biches Village Hotel, Trou aux Biches
Neptune (☎ 415 1083, fax 415 1993) Belle Mare Plage Hotel, Belle Mare
Sindbad Divers (☎ 415 1518, fax 262 7407) Cap Malheureux
Villas Caroline (☎ 453 8450, fax 453 8144, e caroline@intnet.mu) Flic en Flac

Top: Porcelain crab (Photo: Bob Halstead)

Réunion

The diving on offer in Réunion is firmly aimed at the amateur diver, with shallow dives inside the lagoon. If you're seeking something more challenging, you should contact one of the operators below to arrange a custom package (there are good opportunities to dive with sharks outside the lagoon). For general dive inquiries, call the Comité Régional de Sports Sous-Marins (☎ 33 00 95).

Most dive centres are concentrated around St-Gilles-les-Bains. Rates start at about FF210/180 per dive (without/with your own gear). All the centres also offer escorted dives for first-time divers (FF200). Dive operators in Réunion include:

Abyss Plonge (☎ 34 79 79) 7 Rue Bonnier, St-Leu
Atlantis (☎/fax 34 77 47) Zone Artisanal Pointe des Châteaux, St-Leu
Bleu Marine (☎ 24 22 00, fax 24 30 04) Port de Plaisance, St-Gilles-les-Bains
Bourbon Marine (☎ 24 45 05) Port de Plaisance, St-Gilles-les-Bains
Centre International de Plongée (☎ 24 34 11) Port de Plaisance, St-Gilles-les-Bains
Cereps Plongée (☎ 24 40 12) Port de Plaisance, St-Gilles-les-Bains
Club de Plongée et Exploration GEO (☎ 24 56 03, fax 24 33 50) Enceinte Portuaire de St-Gilles, St-Gilles-les-Bains
Corail Plongée (☎ 24 37 25, fax 24 46 38) Port de Plaisance, St-Gilles-les-Bains
Excelsus Plongée (☎ 34 73 65) Zone Artisanal Pointe des Châteaux, St-Leu
Mascareignes Plongée (☎/fax 44 27 74) Port de Plaisance, St-Gilles-les-Bains
Ô sea Bleu (☎/fax 33 16 15) Port de Plaisance, St-Gilles-les-Bains
Plongée Sous-Marine (☎ /fax 44 27 74) 121 Chemin de la Piscine, St-Paul
Réunion Plongée (☎ 34 77 77) Zone Artisanal Pointe des Châteaux, St-Leu

Left: Shallow waters are good for snorkellers or amateur divers.
(Photo: Astrid Witte & Casey Mahaney)

Snorkelling

Snorkelling is a great way to explore the underwater world with minimal equipment and without the costs associated with diving. Even the shallowest reefs are home to many colourful critters.

Before you set out, clean your mask by wetting it, then spitting into it and spreading the saliva with your fingers. Then rinse it out – this process should prevent the mask from fogging. Make sure your hair is not trapped under the seal of the mask. If water enters the snorkel, blow sharply through the tube to expel the water. If water enters the mask, breathe in through the snorkel and out through your nose while holding the top of the mask firmly to your forehead – this should clear it. For safety, always snorkel with a partner.

Watch out for sunburn, especially on your back. Wear a light T-shirt and slop on water-resistant sunscreen, and make sure your kids are equally well protected from the sun. Flippers or canvas shoes will protect your feet.

In the Seychelles, much of the coastline lies within the protection of a fringing reef, and this sheltered lagoon environment is a safe haven for swimming and snorkelling. The Ste Anne Marine National Park is a firm favourite with snorkellers – the shallow reefs and sandbars with little or no current are perfect for exploring. Small offshore granite boulders are also ideal, as they offer a varied assortment of soft and hard corals, as well as the different range of fish associated with that habitat.

Other great snorkelling spots around Mahé include Port Launay National Marine Park; Anse Soleil and Petite Anse in the south-west; and Île Souris, just south of Pointe au Sel. Off Praslin, try around Chauve Souris Island, within wading distance of Anse Volbert beach.

Most hotels and dive schools in the Seychelles sell or rent snorkelling gear (daily rates are generally between Rs30 and Rs50 for a mask, snorkel and fins).

In Mauritius, top spots include Grand Baie in the north and Blue Bay in the south. Companies running trips on glass-bottomed boats will often include snorkelling in the deal. Rental gear is widely available from dive centres in Mauritius, or you can buy your own snorkel, mask and flipper set for around Rs600.

Top: Surface-dwelling fish make friendly subjects for snorkelling photographers. (Photo: Astrid Witte & Casey Mahaney)

Underwater Photography

Underwater photography opens up whole new fields of interest to divers, and the results can be startling – at depth, flash photography reveals colours that simply aren't there for the naked eye. It used to require complex and expensive equipment, whereas now there is a variety of reasonably priced and easy-to-use underwater cameras available. It's possible to rent cameras, including underwater video cameras, from some dive operators. Disposable underwater cameras are widely available.

As with basic cameras above surface level, the best photos taken with the simplest underwater cameras are likely to be straightforward snapshots. You are not going to get superb photos of fish and marine life with a small, cheap camera, but photos of your fellow divers or snorkellers can be terrific.

More than with other types of photography, the results achieved underwater can improve dramatically with equipment expenditure, particularly on artificial lighting. As you descend, natural colours are quickly absorbed, starting with the red end of the spectrum. You can see the same result with a picture or poster that has been left in bright sunlight for too long: soon the colours fade until everything looks blue. It's the same underwater – the deeper you go, the more blue things look. Red has virtually disappeared by the time you're 10m down.

To put the colour back in you need a flash, and to work effectively underwater it has to be a much more powerful and complicated flash than above water. Thus newcomers to serious underwater photography soon find that having bought a Nikonos camera, they have to lay out as much money again for flash equipment to match. Generally the Nikonos cameras work best with 28mm or 35mm lenses. Longer lenses do not work so well underwater. Although objects appear closer underwater, with these short focal lengths you have to get close to achieve good results. Patience and practice will enable you to move in close to otherwise wary fish. With the right experience and equipment, the results can be superb.

Top: Specialised equipment is needed for the best photos at greater depths. (Photo: Michael Aw)

Getting There & Away

This chapter provides some general information on how to reach the Indian Ocean area. For much more detailed information on getting to Mauritius, Réunion and the Seychelles, see the relevant Getting There & Away chapters.

AIR
Buying Tickets

The plane ticket will probably be the single most expensive item in your budget, and buying it can be an intimidating business. There is likely to be a multitude of airlines and travel agents hoping to separate you from your money, and it is always worth putting aside a few hours to research the current state of the market. Start early – some of the cheapest tickets have to be bought months in advance, and some popular flights sell out early. Talk to other travellers – they may be able to stop you making some of the same old mistakes. Look at the ads in newspapers and magazines, consult some reference books and watch for special offers. Then phone travel agents for bargains. (Airlines can supply information on routes and timetables, but except during an interairline war they do not supply the cheapest tickets.) Find out the fare, the route, the duration of the journey and any restrictions on the ticket (see the boxed text 'Air Travel Glossary'). Then sit back and decide what is the best option for you.

You may discover that those impossibly cheap flights are 'fully booked, but we have another one that costs a bit more...' Or the flight is on an airline notorious for its poor safety standards and leaves you mid-journey in the world's least favourite airport for 14 hours. Or they claim only to have the last two seats available for that destination for the whole of July, which they will hold for you for a maximum of two hours. Don't panic – keep ringing around.

An alternative (if you trust the technology) is to book your airfare on the Internet, which can save you the hard sell. The disadvantage

of buying online is that you don't know for certain that you've got what you paid for until it arrives in the mail. Also, if budget travel agents with high street offices appear and disappear overnight, think how much easier it would be online! For Europe, one of the most reliable and trusted sites is www.ebookers.com, which is run by the British travel agent Flightbookers. This Web site provides links to regional sites for travellers in France, Germany, the Netherlands, the UK and other points of departure in Europe. You can book online through a secure connection and the booking process is transparent and relatively foolproof. Another trusted site is www.travelocity.com, which provides a similar service for travellers from the USA, or www.travelocity.co.uk for travellers in the UK (there are also numerous other sites). The fare search is based on one of the systems used by travel agents. Some travellers prefer to use these Web sites to research the cheapest fare, and then book by telephone with a trusted travel agent.

Use the fares quoted in this book as a guide only. They are approximate and based on the rates advertised by travel agents at the time of writing. Quoted airfares do not necessarily constitute a recommendation for the carrier. If you are travelling from the UK or the USA, you will probably find that the cheapest flights are being advertised by obscure bucket shops (see the boxed text 'Air Travel Glossary' for definition) whose names haven't yet reached the telephone directory. Many such firms are honest and solvent, but there are a few rogues who will take your money and disappear, only to reopen elsewhere a month or two later under a new name. If you feel suspicious about a firm, don't give them all the money at once – leave a deposit of 20% or so and pay the balance when you get the ticket. If they insist on cash in advance, go somewhere else. And once you have the ticket, ring the airline to confirm that you are actually booked onto the flight.

You may decide to pay more than the rock-bottom fare by opting for the safety of a better-known travel agent. Firms such as STA Travel, who have offices worldwide, Council Travel in the USA or Travel CUTS in Canada are not going to disappear overnight, leaving you clutching a receipt for a nonexistent ticket, and they do offer good prices to most destinations.

Once you have your ticket, write its number down, together with the flight number and other details, and keep the information somewhere separate. If the ticket is lost or stolen, this will help you get a replacement. It's sensible to buy travel insurance as early as possible. If you buy it the week before you fly, you may find, for example, that you're not covered for delays to your flight caused by industrial action.

Round the World Tickets
Round the world (RTW) tickets have become very popular in the last few years. The airline RTW tickets are often real bargains, and can work out no more expensive or even cheaper than an ordinary return ticket. Prices start at about US$1300.

The official airline RTW tickets are usually put together by a combination of two airlines, and permit you to fly anywhere you want on their route systems so long as you do not backtrack. Other restrictions are (usually) that you must book the first sector in advance and cancellation penalties then apply. There may be restrictions on how many stops you are permitted, and usually the tickets are valid for 90 days up to a year. An alternative type of RTW ticket is one put together by a travel agent using discounted tickets in combination.

Travellers with Special Needs
If you have special needs of any sort – you've broken a leg, you're vegetarian, travelling in a wheelchair, taking the baby, terrified of flying – you should let the airline know as soon as possible so that they can make arrangements accordingly. You should remind them when you reconfirm your booking (at least 72 hours before departure) and again when you check in at the airport. It may also be worth ringing round the airlines before you make your booking to find out how they can handle your own particular needs.

Airports and airlines can be surprisingly helpful, but they do need advance warning. Most international airports will provide an escort from check-in desk to plane where needed, and there should be ramps, lifts, and accessible toilets and phones. Aircraft toilets, on the other hand, are likely to present a problem; travellers should discuss this with the airline at an early stage and, if necessary, with their doctor.

Guide dogs for the blind will often have to travel in a specially pressurised baggage compartment with other animals, away from their owner, though smaller guide dogs may be admitted to the cabin. All guide dogs will be subject to the same quarantine laws (six months in isolation etc) as any other animal when entering or returning to countries currently free of rabies such as the UK or Australia.

Deaf travellers can ask for airport and inflight announcements to be written down for them.

Air Travel Glossary

Apex Apex (advance purchase excursion) is a discounted ticket that must be paid for in advance. There are penalties if you wish to change the dates.

Baggage Allowance This will be written on your ticket; the standard baggage allowance is usually one 30kg hold bag and one piece of carry-on luggage. On smaller aircraft the allowance can be less than 15kg. Excess baggage charges are steep in the Indian Ocean.

Bucket Shop Normally an unbonded travel agent specialising in discounted airline tickets.

Cancellation Penalties If you have to cancel or change an Apex ticket, there are often heavy penalties involved; insurance can sometimes be taken out against these penalties. Some airlines impose penalties on regular tickets as well, particularly against 'no-show' passengers.

Full Fares Airlines traditionally offer 1st class (coded F), business class (coded J) and economy class (coded Y) tickets. These days there are so many promotional and discounted fares available that few passengers pay full economy fare.

Lost Tickets If you lose your airline ticket an airline will usually treat it like a travellers cheque and, after inquiries, issue you with another one. Legally, however, an airline is entitled to treat it like cash and if you lose it then it's gone forever. Take good care of your tickets.

No-Shows Some airlines impose heavy penalties on passengers who fail to turn up for their flight. If you are travelling on a full fare, chances are that you will be entitled to travel on the next available flight. Those travelling on cheaper tickets may be subject to additional charges, or even lose their flight.

Onward Tickets An entry requirement for many countries is that you have a ticket out of the country. If you're unsure of your next move, the easiest solution is to buy the cheapest onward ticket to a neighbouring country or a ticket from a reliable airline which can later be refunded if you do not use it.

Open-Jaw Tickets These are return tickets where you fly out to one place but return from another. If available, this can save you backtracking to your arrival point.

Overbooking Since every flight has some passengers who fail to show up, airlines often book more passengers than they have seats. Usually excess passengers make up for the no-shows, but occasionally somebody gets 'bumped' onto the next available flight. Guess who it is most likely to be? The passengers who check in late.

Promotional Fares These are officially discounted fares, available from travel agencies or direct from the airline.

Reconfirmation If you don't reconfirm your flight at least 72 hours prior to departure, the airline may delete your name from the passenger list. Ring to find out if your airline requires reconfirmation.

Restrictions Discounted tickets often have various restrictions on them – such as needing to be paid for in advance and incurring a penalty to be altered. Others are restrictions on the minimum and maximum period you must be away.

Transferred Tickets Airline tickets cannot be transferred from one person to another. Sometimes travellers try to sell the return half of their ticket, but officials can ask you to prove that you are the person named on the ticket. On an international flight tickets are compared with passports.

Travel Periods Ticket prices vary with the time of year. There is a low (off-peak) season and a high (peak) season, and often a low-shoulder season and a high-shoulder season as well. Usually the fare depends on your outward flight – if you depart in the high season and return in the low season, you pay the high-season fare.

Children under two years of age travel for 10% of the standard fare (or free on some airlines), as long as they don't occupy a seat. They don't get a baggage allowance either. 'Skycots' should be provided by the airline if requested in advance; these will take a child weighing up to about 10kg. Children between two and 12 years of age can usually occupy a seat for half to two-thirds of the full fare, and do get a baggage allowance. Push chairs can often be taken as hand luggage.

The USA

All flights to the Indian Ocean from the USA connect through London or Paris. If you're heading to Réunion, your best option may be to fly to Paris and pick up a cheap connecting flight there. The *New York Times*, the *LA Times*, the *Chicago Tribune* and the *San Francisco Examiner* all produce weekly travel sections in which you'll find any number of travel agents' ads. Council Travel and STA Travel have offices in major cities nationwide. The magazine *Travel Unlimited* (PO Box 1058, Allston, Mass 02134) publishes details of the cheapest airfares and courier possibilities for destinations all over the world from the USA.

Canada

As for the USA, you'll have to connect through Paris or London to reach the Indian Ocean. Travel CUTS has offices in all major cities. The Toronto *Globe & Mail* and the Vancouver *Sun* carry travel agents' ads. The magazine *Great Expeditions* (PO Box 8000-411, Abbotsford BC V2S 6H1) is full of useful information.

Australia

STA Travel and Flight Centres International are major dealers in cheap airfares. Check the travel agents' ads in the Yellow Pages and telephone around. There are convenient direct Air Mauritius flights between Melbourne/Perth and Mauritius, but many travellers find it easier to fly via Singapore with Singapore Airlines. There are of course other alternatives – discuss these with your travel agent.

New Zealand

STA Travel and Flight Centres Internationa are popular travel agents. Also look through newspapers for special deals being offered Again, Singapore Airlines offers convenien connections.

The UK

Air Mauritius and British Airways operate direct flights between London and Mauritius (British Airways also flies via Kenya) British Airways and Air Seychelles cove the London to Seychelles route. Flights for Réunion generally connect through Paris; i may be cheaper to pick up a cheap flight t Paris and buy your connection there.

There are some excellent budget trave agents in London. Trailfinders in Sout Kensington produces a lavishly illustrate brochure that includes airfare details. Als in the west end of London, Flightbookers i a well-established bucket shop offering cheap fares worldwide. STA Travel also ha branches in the UK. Look in the listing magazine *Time Out* plus the Sunday paper and *Exchange & Mart* for ads. Also look ou for the free commuter magazines widel available in London – you'll often fin them outside the main railway stations.

Most British travel agents are registere with ABTA (Association of British Trave Agents). If you have paid for your flight a an ABTA-registered agent that then goe out of business, ABTA will guarantee a re fund or an alternative. Unregistered bucke shops are riskier but also sometime cheaper.

The Globetrotters Club (BCM Roving London WC1N 3XX) publishes a newslette called *Globe* which covers obscure destina tions and can help people find travelling companions.

Continental Europe

Air Mauritius and Air France offer frequen flights between Mauritius and Paris, whil Air Seychelles and Air France cover th Paris-Seychelles route. Almost all flight from Europe to Réunion go via *la métropol* (mainland France). Air France operates nin to 12 flights every week between Paris an

Réunion and the trip takes about 10 hours. The operators Air Liberté, Air Outre Mer (AOM) and Corsair (the airline of French travel agent Nouvelle Frontières) provide flights between Réunion and Paris, Lyon, Marseilles and Toulouse.

The German airline Lufthansa Condor provides connections between Mauritius and Frankfurt, Munich and Cologne, and also operates services from Frankfurt to the Seychelles. Air Mauritius flies to many European destinations including Paris, Zürich, Geneva, Rome, Munich, Frankfurt, Brussels and Vienna (the number of flights usually varies according to the season). Air Seychelles flies to Rome, Milan, Frankfurt, Zürich and Paris.

There are lots of bucket shops in Paris, Amsterdam, Brussels, Frankfurt and a few other places. However, don't take the advertised fares as gospel truth. Because of the French colonial connection, fares to the Indian Ocean are often cheaper from Paris than from other European cities.

The newsletter *Farang* (La Rue 8a, 4261, Braives, Belgium) deals with exotic destinations, as does the magazine *Globe-Trotters*, published by Aventure au Bout du Monde ☎ 01 43 35 08 95, ABM, 7 Rue Gassendi, 75014, Paris, France).

Africa

You can fly to Mauritius direct from Johannesburg, Cape Town or Durban (South Africa), Harare (Zimbabwe), Antananarivo (Madagascar), Moroni (Comoros), Nairobi (Kenya) or the Seychelles. Airlines that connect Mauritius to Africa include Air Mauritius, Air Madagascar, South African Airways (SAA) and Air Zimbabwe. You can fly directly from the Seychelles to Johannesburg and Nairobi. Air Seychelles and Kenya Air serve the routes. For fares and packages, contact the airlines or a travel agent.

Asia

Air Mauritius and Singapore Airlines operate flights between Mauritius and Mumbai (Bombay), Delhi, Kuala Lumpur, Singapore and Hong Kong. To get to anywhere in Asia

from Réunion, your cheapest option is to take the flight or boat to Mauritius and pick up a connection there. An alternative would be to fly to Madagascar and pick up the Air Madagascar flight to Singapore. There are also connections from the Seychelles to Singapore.

Hong Kong is the discount ticket capital of the region. Its bucket shops are at least as unreliable as those of other cities. Ask the advice of other travellers before buying a ticket.

Other Indian Ocean Countries

Once you get into the region, the island-hopping, if that's not too light a term in this case, becomes easier and cheaper. The best way of covering all three islands is with a round-trip air ticket using several airlines. The only condition is that you must continue your route in a circle (ie, you can't double back). This means you can also take in Madagascar, Comoros and Kenya. These round-trip air tickets are good bargains if you have the time.

Make all inquiries and bookings through a major tour operator or travel agent such as Rogers & Co Aviation in Port Louis (Mauritius) or Bourbon Voyages in St-Denis (Réunion), but not directly through the airlines. You'll have a better shot at a good deal. The same applies in your own country.

SEA

Opportunities for sea travel to Mauritius, Réunion and the Seychelles are limited to passing cruise liners, yachts and the very occasional cargo-passenger ship. The cost is high, unless you can work your way as crew. Cruise liners usually only stop for a day or two. Sea travel between the Seychelles and Mauritius is out of the question unless you have your own yacht or enough money and time to charter one. There are two passenger services between Mauritius and Réunion; see the Getting There & Away chapters for Mauritius and Réunion for details.

If you want to try crewing on a yacht, it is possible, but your chances are slim.

Remember that even if you do strike it lucky and find someone who is looking for crew, they'll be very fussy about whom they'll take. Yacht skippers normally look for someone with a bit of cash as well as sailing experience. There is no such thing as a free ride, unless you come across a rich playboy or playgirl who likes the cut of your jib. You must also have the right temperament, as conditions are difficult aboard a yacht. There's no privacy, nowhere to escape to if tension breaks and no buts about it – the skipper is boss.

Cruising time between Mauritius, Réunion and the Seychelles varies depending on the weather conditions and the direction you're heading. About 160km in 24 hours is a rough rule of thumb. There is generally no long-distance sailing between or around Mauritius and Réunion during the cyclone season. The Seychelles is situated outside the cyclone zone.

Mauritius

OLIVIER CIRENDINI

MAURITIUS

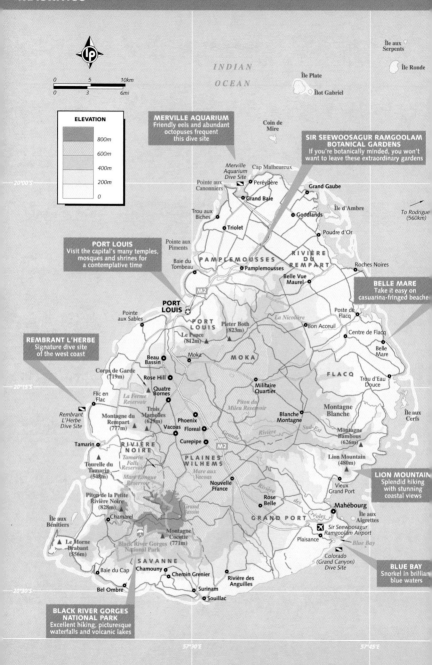

INDIAN OCEAN

Île aux Serpents

Île Ronde

Coin de Mire

Île Plate

Îlot Gabriel

ELEVATION

800m
600m
400m
200m
0

MERVILLE AQUARIUM
Friendly eels and abundant octopuses frequent this dive site

SIR SEEWOOSAGUR RAMGOOLAM BOTANICAL GARDENS
If you're botanically minded, you won't want to leave these extraordinary gardens

Merville Aquarium Dive Site

Cap Malheureux

Pointe aux Canonniers

Pereybère

Grand Gaube

Grand Baie

Île d'Ambre

Trou aux Biches

Goodlands

Poudre d'Or

Triolet

Pointe aux Piments

To Rodrigue (560km)

PORT LOUIS
Visit the capital's many temples, mosques and shrines for a contemplative time

Baie du Tombeau

PAMPLEMOUSSES

Pamplemousses

RIVIÈRE DU REMPART

Belle Vue Maurel

Roches Noires

M2

BELLE MARE
Take it easy on casuarina-fringed beaches

PORT LOUIS

Pointe aux Sables

PORT LOUIS

Pieter Both (823m)

La Nicolière

Poste de Flacq

REMBRANT L'HERBE
Signature dive site of the west coast

Le Pouce (812m)

Bon Acceuil

Centre de Flacq

Moka

MOKA

Belle Mare

Beau Bassin

Corps de Garde (719m)

La Ferme Reservoir

Rose Hill

Quatre Bornes

Militaire Quartier

FLACQ

Trou d'Eau Douce

Flic en Flac

Trois Mamelles (629m)

Phoenix

Piton du Milieu Reservoir

Blanche Montagne

Montagne Blanche

Île aux Cerfs

Rembrant L'Herbe Dive Site

Montagne du Rempart (777m)

Vacoas

Floreal

Sud-Est

Montagne Bambous (626m)

Tamarin

RIVIÈRE NOIRE

Curepipe

Grande

Rivière

M2

Lion Mountain (480m)

LION MOUNTAIN
Splendid hiking with stunning coastal views

Tourelle du Tamarin (548m)

Tamarin Falls Reservoir

PLAINES WILHEMS

Mare aux Vacoas

Piton de la Petite Rivière Noire (828m)

Mare Longue Reservoir

Nouvelle France

Rivière

Vieux Grand Port

Île aux Bénitiers

Chamarel

Grand Bassin

Rose Belle

des

Créoles

Mahébourg

Île aux Aigrettes

Le Morne Brabant (556m)

Montagne Cocotte (771m)

GRAND PORT

Sir Seewoosagur Ramgoolam Airport

Black River Gorges National Park

Plaisance

Blue Bay

SAVANNE

Chamouny

Colorado (Grand Canyon) Dive Site

BLUE BAY
Snorkel in brilliant blue waters

Baie du Cap

Chemin Grenier

Rivière des Anguilles

BLACK RIVER GORGES NATIONAL PARK
Excellent hiking, picturesque waterfalls and volcanic lakes

Bel Ombre

Surinam

Souillac

20°00'S

20°15'S

20°30'S

57°30'E

57°45'E

0   5   10km
0   3   6mi

Facts about Mauritius

In 1896, the author Mark Twain wrote of Mauritius, 'You gather the idea that Mauritius was made first and then heaven, and that heaven was copied after Mauritius.' That may be selling it a little strong these days, but Mauritius is still a delightful tropical destination, where you can laze away the days on sun-kissed beaches, indulge in wild and wonderful water activities and treat yourself to a delicious range of culinary creations.

The island, some 800km east of Madagascar, boasts endless sugar cane plantations, dramatic mountains, a vibrant cultural mix and some of the finest beaches and aquamarine lagoons in the Indian Ocean. While the Seychelles has cornered the beach market and Réunion the outdoors field, Mauritius has the most relaxed atmosphere of the three countries, and it's considerably cheaper to stay, eat and get around here than in Réunion or the Seychelles.

Many visitors tend to stay in the deluxe beach hotels and only venture out on occasional sightseeing or shopping trips, but there are plenty of far cheaper guesthouses and apartments scattered around the island. Similarly, for eating out there are places to suit all pockets, from simple sidewalk cafes to swanky seaside restaurants. The diversity of cuisine – from French to Creole – reflects the rich cultural blend of the island.

With more than half the population Hindu, the island has a distinct Indian flavour. Indians first came to Mauritius as indentured labourers, brought to work on the sugar cane fields. Moka's Mahatma Gandhi Institute was established to preserve and promote Mauritian Indian history and heritage. The island's Indian presence is perhaps most vividly highlighted during the many festivals celebrated throughout the year.

The remainder of Mauritius' population is predominantly made up of African, Chinese, French and British elements. Each group plays a part in the economy, society and administration of the country, which is structured on the British model.

MAURITIUS AT A GLANCE

Official Name: Republic of Mauritius
Area: 1865 sq km
Population: 1.18 million
Population Growth Rate: 1.18%
Capital: Port Louis
Head of State: President Cassam Uteem
Official Languages: English, French
Main Religion: Hinduism
Currency: Mauritian rupee
Exchange Rate: Rs26 = US$1
Per Capita GNP: US$3200
Inflation: 6.8%
Time: UTC +4

RODRIGUES MAPS:
Rodrigues p161
Port Mathurin p163

North Mauritius p106

Cap Malheureux
& Grand Gaube p119

INDIAN
OCEAN

Péréybère p117
Grand Baie p112

East Mauritius p140

Trou aux Biches
& Around p108
Sir S. Ramgoolam
Botanical Gardens
p121

West Mauritius p144

Port Louis
p98

Flic en Flac
p145

Curepipe
p125

Black River Gorges
National Park p132

Mahébourg
p154

Central Mauritius p124

South Mauritius p152

HISTORY

Arab traders knew of Mauritius as early as the 10th century. They called the uninhabited island Dinarobin, but did not settle it.

Mauritius has a colonial history. It has experienced four changes of 'ownership' and name between the arrival of the first inhabitants, in 1598, and independence, in 1968.

The Portuguese & the Dutch

Portuguese naval explorers did not settle Mauritius when they discovered it in the wake of Vasco da Gama's famous 1498 trip around the Cape of Good Hope, though they are credited with the first European landing. Instead, they continued on to the east coast of Africa, India and Indonesia to establish colonies.

Domingo Fernandez dropped anchor in Mauritius in 1511. He named the island Ilha do Cerne (Swan Island), perhaps after the name of his ship, or he might have been referring to the native dodo, which he perhaps took to be a sort of swan.

Rodrigues Island, 560km to the north-east, takes its name from another navigator, Don Diego Rodrigues, who called by in 1528. Rodrigues and Réunion together were named the Mascarenes, after Portuguese admiral Don Pedro Mascarenhas. Apart from introducing pesky monkeys, rats and other animals, the Portuguese did little to Mauritius. That was left to the next wave of maritime supremos, the Dutch.

In 1598, Vice Admiral Wybrandt van Warwyck landed on the south-east coast of the island, claimed it for the Netherlands and named it Mauritius, after his ruler, Maurice, Prince of Orange and Count of Nassau. It was another 40 years before the Dutch decided to try settling the country, preferring to use it as a supply base for Batavia (Java). When they did settle in Mauritius, it was around their original landing spot. Settlement ruins can be seen opposite the church at Vieux Grand Port, near Mahébourg.

The colony never really flourished and the Dutch departed for good in 1710, leaving their mark behind. They are held to blame for the extinction of the dodo and for the introduction of slaves from Africa, deer from Java, wild boar, tobacco and, above all, sugar cane. In 1642 they sent Abel Tasman off from Mauritius to explore Tasmania, Fiji and New Zealand.

The French

In 1715, Captain Guillaume Dufresne d'Arsal sailed across from Réunion, then called Île Bourbon, and claimed the island for France. Mauritius was renamed Île de France and given over to the Compagnie des Indes Orientales (French East India Company) to run as a trading base.

The French decided they would stay for good, and settlement began in 1721. Not until 1735 did things start moving under the governorship of Bertrand François Mahé de La Bourdonnais, Mauritius' first hero. Under his leadership, port facilities were expanded, the first sugar mill and hospital were built and a road network was established.

Mauritius' best known historic event – the *St Géran* tragedy – occurred during La Bourdonnais' administration. In 1744, the *St Géran* was wrecked during a storm off Île d'Ambre, near the north-east coast, while waiting to enter Port Louis to unload machinery for the new sugar mill. The event inspired Bernardin de St Pierre's romantic novel *Paul et Virginie*, an early bestseller (see the boxed text 'Paul & Virginie' in the North Mauritius chapter for more details on the tragedy).

A few years later, La Bourdonnais went off to help fight the British in India and ended up in the Bastille, imprisoned on charges of corruption in 1748. He was tried in 1751 and acquitted.

As the English gained the upper hand in the Indian Ocean during the second half of the 18th century, the Compagnie des Indes Orientales collapsed and the sugar industry strengthened. Port Louis became a free-trading base and a haven for corsairs – mercenary marines paid by a country to prey on enemy ships. The most famous Franco-Mauritian corsair was Robert Surcouf. Freebooting English, American and French pirates, who had been operating so successfully out of Madagascar towards the end of the 17th century and at the beginning of the 18th century, gave way to these licensed and semirespectable pirates.

In 1789, the French colonialists in Mauritius recognised the revolution in France and got rid of their governor. But they refused to free their slaves when the abolition of slavery was decreed in Paris in 1794.

The British

In 1810, during the Napoleonic Wars, the British moved in on the corsairs and on Mauritius. At first, they were defeated at the Battle of Vieux Grand Port, the only French naval victory inscribed on the Arc de Triomphe in Paris. Later, they landed at Cap Malheureux on the north coast and took over the island.

The Treaty of Paris in 1814 gave Île de France, along with Rodrigues and the Seychelles, to the British. They changed its name back to Mauritius, but allowed the Franco-Mauritians to retain their language, religion, Napoleonic Code legal system and sugar cane plantations. In 1835, the slaves were freed and replaced or supplemented by imported labour from India and China.

The British opened up an international market for Mauritian sugar and it became the island's *raison d'être* for the next 150 years. Indian workers continued to be indentured in their thousands. The Franco-Mauritian families produced wealthy sugar barons, and indeed continue to do so today. Through strength of numbers, the Indian workforce gradually achieved a greater say in the running of the country. The Indian political and spiritual leader Mahatma Gandhi visited Mauritius in 1901 to push for civil rights.

The island remained relatively unscathed during WWI and WWII. The greatest upheavals to the country and its one-crop economy were caused by cyclones, malaria epidemics (one in 1867 killed half the population of Port Louis), slumps and booms in the world sugar market, and the decline of the country as a maritime trade centre.

The Labour Party was founded in 1936 to fight for the labourers, and did so on the streets the following year. After the war, when a new constitution gave the vote to anyone over 21 who could write their name, the Labour Party gained support.

Under the leadership of Dr Seewoosagur Ramgoolam, who was later knighted, the Labour Party grew in strength during the 1950s. Direct opposition came from the Parti Mauricien Social Démocrate (PMSD), which represented the white and Creole populations.

Independence

Mauritius was granted independence from Britain on 12 March 1968. Sir Seewoosagur Ramgoolam was elected prime minister and remained in office for the next 13 years, eventually in coalition with the PMSD. Sir Seewoosagur continued to command reverence as a grand leader until his death in 1986, at the age of 86. His name has now been added to a host of public buildings and places.

In 1982, a coalition of the leftist Mouvement Militant Mauricien (MMM), led by Franco-Mauritian Paul Bérenger, and the Parti Socialiste Mauricien, led by Anerood Jugnauth, gained power. Jugnauth became prime minister. Bérenger became finance minister and, perhaps surprisingly, adopted a strictly monetarist policy which led to the abandonment of promised welfare measures. He also promoted South African investment in Mauritian hotels, which was opposed by Jugnauth.

The resulting tensions, and the personality clash between Jugnauth and Bérenger, led to the resignation of Bérenger and a split in the party. Jugnauth broke from Bérenger's MMM, but remained prime minister by teaming up with the Labour Party, the PMSD (under the flamboyant former mayor of Curepipe and Port Louis, Sir Gaetan Duval) and two other parties.

In August 1983, another election gave the five-party coalition victory and the chance to try to please everybody, including South Africa, with less radical policies. Jugnauth continued as prime minister and Bérenger was out in the cold.

All seemed to be going well until 1986, when three Mauritian MPs were caught at Amsterdam airport with heroin in their suitcases. The resulting inquiry opened a can of worms, implicating other politicians in drug money. Sir Gaetan became deputy prime minister and went on to compound his image as a playboy by declaring that he was bisexual.

Bérenger's MMM forced Jugnauth to go to the polls in 1987, but Jugnauth won. In the general election of 1991, a renewed alliance of Bérenger, leading the MMM, and

Jugnauth, heading the Mouvement Socialiste Mauricien (MSM), won a landslide victory. Mauritius officially became a republic in 1992. Jugnauth and Bérenger governed the country until 1995, when Jugnauth lost his seat to Navin Ramgoolam, the son of former prime minister Sir Seewoosagur Ramgoolam, leading a Labour Party–MMM coalition.

This coalition currently controls about 65% of the national assembly, with Cassam Uteem as the elected president, and day-to-day running of the country in the hands of his appointed prime minister, Navin Ramgoolam. The coalition of the MSM and Renouveau Militant Mauricien (Mauritian Militant Renewal) holds another 19% of the national assembly.

The biggest event of recent years was the riot in Port Louis in February 1999, which forced the closure of the airport and brought the country to a standstill for four days. The unrest was triggered by the death in police custody of popular seggae singer Kaya, an ardent campaigner for the rights of the disadvantaged Creole population. President Cassam Uteem was forced to mobilise the Mauritian Special Defence Force to restore law and order, and make political concessions to appease the Creole people. (For more information, see the boxed text 'Kaya' on this page.)

GEOGRAPHY

Mauritius is a volcanic island, 58km from north to south and 47km from east to west. It lies roughly 220km from Réunion; 800km from Madagascar to the west; and 5854km from Perth (Australia) to the east. It is on the same latitude as Rio de Janeiro (Brazil), Harare (Zimbabwe) and Rockhampton (Australia).

The country includes the inhabited island of Rodrigues, 560km to the north-east, and other scattered coral atolls such as Cargados Carajos and Agalega.

GEOLOGY

Mauritius is thought to be the peak of an enormous sunken volcanic chain which stretches from the Seychelles to Réunion. The island rises steeply in the south to a central plateau which then slopes gently down to the northern coast, broken by the

Kaya

It was a black day for Mauritius, and a blacker one still for the Creole community. On 21 February 1999, the singer Joseph Topize (aka Kaya) was found dead in his police cell, seemingly a victim of police brutality, after being arrested for smoking cannabis at a prolegalisation rally.

MARTIN HARRIS

As the pioneer of seggae, a unique combination of reggae and traditional *séga* beats, Kaya provided a voice for disadvantaged Creoles across the island. His death in the custody of Indian police split Mauritian society along racial lines, triggering four days of violent riots that left several people dead and brought the country to a standstill.

An autopsy cleared the police of wrongdoing, but the events have forced the Indian-dominated government to acknowledge *la malaise Créole*, Creoles' anger at their impoverished status in a country that has been dominated by Indians since independence. There is now a special government department assigned to consider the needs of Creoles.

In contrast to the violent scenes, Kaya's music is full of positive energy. The classic album *Seggae Experience*, which is available all over the island, is a tribute to the singer's unique vision.

chain of oddly shaped mountains behind Port Louis. The mountains are noted more for their curious forms than for their height. The Piton de la Petite Rivière Noire is the highest peak at 828m.

Unlike Réunion, Mauritius has no active volcanoes, although remnants of volcanic activity abound. Extinct craters and volcanic lakes, such as the Trou aux Cerfs crater in Curepipe and the Grand Bassin holy lake, are good examples. Over the aeons, the volcanoes generated millions of lava boulders, much to the chagrin of the indentured farm labourers, who had to gather up all these rocks to clear the land for sugar cane. Pyramids of these boulders dot the sugar cane fields all over the island. Some are being milled down to make grit for road building; others that have been piled up into tidy pyramids are listed monuments!

Mauritius is surrounded by a coral reef which provides several long stretches of white coral sand beaches. The reef is broken in many places. Between Souillac and Le Bouchon, on the southern coast, the sea crashes through the largest break in the reef and against the black cliffs, creating a rugged, wild coastline. There is a similar, though not so spectacular, break in the reef above Flic en Flac on the west coast.

CLIMATE

The Mauritian climate is a mixed affair. Different regions of Mauritius are affected in different ways. Up on the plateau around Curepipe, temperatures average 5°C cooler than on the coast. It can be raining up there while it's clear around the coast, and vice versa. Similarly, east coast weather differs from that of the west coast. The east coast is much drier than other areas during January and February, when the prevailing winds drive in from the east, hit the mountains, and dump rain on central and western Mauritius.

The hottest months are from January to April, when temperatures range from 25°C to 35°C. It's nice to get away from the northern hemisphere winter, but it can prove too hot and humid for some. This is also the cyclone season, and although a direct hit only

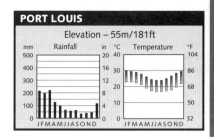

PORT LOUIS
Elevation – 55m/181ft

happens about once every 15 years, the island still suffers days of squally depression from the several cyclones that occur in the region each year. During these times, there are usually several days of heavy rain, which force most holiday-makers to stay cooped up in their hotel rooms.

There are no distinct monsoons. It can rain any day of the year. When it's not blowing from the north, the breeze comes from the south-east, courtesy of the regular trade winds.

The depths of a Mauritian 'winter' occur from July to September when temperatures average a chastening 24°C during the day and 16°C at night. This can be more pleasant. There is less rain and humidity, and less chance of frying yourself in the sun.

ECOLOGY & ENVIRONMENT

Tourism has become one of the pillars of Mauritius' economy. The expansion of tourist facilities, however, has strained the island's infrastructure and has caused all sorts of problems, including environmental degradation and excessive demand on services such as electricity, water, telephone and transport.

Conservationists are campaigning to protect the fragile marine environment, which has suffered widespread damage over the past few decades. Some of the causes include disturbance from motor boats, fishermen and divers, as well as a proliferating level of pollution. Collection of shells and coral for commercial purposes has also been damaging. We strongly urge you not to buy anything made out of turtle shell, and not to buy or take any shells from the beach.

Travellers who illegally possess or transport these items should be aware that the items are liable to confiscation on leaving Mauritius, and to fines and confiscation by customs officials in countries that have signed agreements on endangered species, including most Western countries.

(For more information on marine conservation, see the special section 'Underwater Worlds'.)

FLORA & FAUNA

Together with the Seychelles and Madagascar, Mauritius is a haven for the botanist, the biologist, the zoologist, the ornithologist and other 'ologists'.

To experience most of what the island has to offer in the way of flora and fauna, the visitor must go to the Sir Seewoosagur Ramgoolam and the Curepipe Botanical Gardens, Casela Bird Park near Flic en Flac, Domaine du Chasseur and Le Val Nature Park near Mahébourg, Île aux Aigrettes, Black River Gorges National Park, La Vanille Crocodile Park near Souillac and, for stuffed replicas, to the Mauritius Institute in Port Louis. On Rodrigues, a project involving replanting of mangroves should benefit the flora and fauna of the island. It is hoped that their restoration will mean improvement in the stocks of fish that many islanders depend on for food. (For more information, see Flora & Fauna in the Rodrigues chapter.)

The best source of information on Mauritian wildlife is the Mauritius Wildlife Appeal Fund or MWAF (☎ 211 2228), which was founded in 1984 as a charity to protect and manage the rare birds, plants, reptiles and mammals of Mauritius. The MWAF vigorously supports the creation of national parks, projects to restore the populations of endangered bird species, programs to restore and conserve endemic vegetation (including Île Ronde and Île aux Aigrettes), and the monitoring of whales, dolphins and turtles around Mauritius.

For more information, you can write to the Public Relations Officer, Mauritius Wildlife Appeal Fund, Edith Cavell St, Port Louis.

(For detailed information on the marine life of Mauritius, see the special section 'Underwater Worlds'.)

Flora

Almost one-third of the 900 plant species of Mauritius occur only on this island. Many of these endemic plants have fared poorly in competition with introduced plants, especially guava and privet, and have been depleted by introduced animals, such as deer, pigs and monkeys. General forest clearance and the establishment of crop monocultures have exacerbated the problem, so that less than 1% of Mauritius' original forest is intact. One of the best places to see the island's endemic flora is the Sir Seewoosagur Ramgoolam Botanical Gardens at Pamplemousses.

For the research and conservation of native species, the government Forestry Service together with the MWAF and the Royal Society of Arts and Sciences has set aside special vegetation plots which are protected from animal depredation and carefully weeded to remove the much faster-growing introduced species. Rare species are propagated in government nurseries and then planted in these plots where they have a better chance of survival and regeneration. It is hoped that these areas will also attract and support rare Mauritian bird species, such as the echo parakeet, the pink pigeon and the Mauritian cuckoo-shrike. Similar work is being done on Rodrigues, Île aux Aigrettes and Île Ronde.

For a tropical island, Mauritius is not big on coconut palms. Instead, casuarinas fringe most of the best beaches. These tall, slim trees look like limp-wristed pines, but although they cast needles galore, they are not members of the pine family at all. The casuarinas, which are also known as *filaos* from the Portuguese, act as useful windbreaks and grow well in sandy soil. They may not be as visually appealing as palms, but they are more aurally pleasing when you listen to the wind whistling through the branches. Along with casuarinas, eucalyptus trees have been widely planted to make up for the destruction of the original forests.

Mauritius' forests originally included the tambalacoque tree, which is also known as the dodo tree and is not far from extinction itself. You'll find it, with the services of a guide, only in the forests south of Curepipe and Mare aux Vacoas. It's a tall tree with a silver trunk and a large, strange-looking, brown seed that is half smooth and half rough. Scientists are sceptical about the rumour that the dodo acted as a germinator, feeding on the tough seed which germinated easily after being passed through the bird's stomach.

Other impressive trees, which you don't have to go off the beaten track to see, are the giant Indian banyan and the brilliant red flowering flamboyant, or royal poinciana.

Staying with shades of red, one flower you will see in abundance is anthurium, with its single, glossy petal and protruding yellow spadix. The plant originated in South America and was introduced to Mauritius at the end of the 19th century. The flower, which at first sight you'd swear was synthetic, can last up to three weeks after being cut and is therefore a popular display plant. Now grown in commercial quantities for export, it is used to spruce up hotel and business rooms and public meeting places.

Fauna

The first animal any visitor to Mauritius is likely to meet is the domestic dog, although there's nothing domesticated about it! Every second family seems to have a dog for 'security' purposes. *Chien méchant* (vicious dog) is a common notice on house gates. Although the dogs' bark is generally worse than their bite, walking along some streets in the dark can be a nightmare.

From the roadside you may also catch glimpses of the mongoose, crossing from cane field to cane field, and the Java deer, which was first imported by the Dutch for fresh meat.

You must venture further into the wild, particularly around the Rivière Noire (Black River) gorges, to come in contact with wild pigs and bands of macaque monkeys. You'll see little else and there are no dangerous animals.

Bird Life The best known representative of Mauritian bird life was the dodo, the dove that found its docility rewarded with extinction (see the boxed text 'Dead as a Dodo'). Although the dodo has become a symbol of extinction, few people realise that Mauritius still possesses several incredibly rare bird species which are as doomed as the dodo if present efforts at conservation cannot be sustained. The situation for these rare species is slowly improving, but incredibly slowly – populations of some have shrunk to fewer than ten individuals.

The Mauritius kestrel suffered a huge population decline due to pesticide poisoning, habitat destruction and hunting. The Mauritius Kestrel Conservation Program, started in 1973, has used captive breeding followed by release and management of the birds in the wild to produce an amazing recovery.

The echo parakeet is the world's rarest parakeet. Since 1985, the MWAF has been running a project to protect wild parakeets and boost their numbers through captive breeding.

The pink pigeon, the largest of all the pigeons and doves found in Mauritius, is a highly endangered species. Impediments to conservation include poor nesting results due to predation from rats and monkeys, and what one might term a public relations problem – released birds ending up in local casseroles.

The native songbirds of Mauritius, such as the Mauritius cuckoo-shrike, the Mauritius black bulbul, the Mascarene paradise flycatcher, the Mauritius fody and the Mauritius olive white-eye, are also threatened. Many of these species are already down to a couple of hundred birds.

Bird species that have already disappeared from Mauritius include the black, flightless parrot and the rail, a small wading bird.

The predominant species now include many introduced songbirds, such as the little red Madagascar fody, the Indian mynah (its yellow beak and feet make it look like it's just stepped out of a cartoon), the village weaver, and the most common bird of all on Mauritius – the red-whiskered bulbul.

Dead as a Dodo

Illustrations from the logbooks of the first ships to reach Mauritius show hundreds of plump flightless birds running down to the beach to investigate arriving sailors. Lacking natural predators, these giant flightless pigeons were easy prey for hungry sailors, who named the bird *dodo* meaning 'stupid'. It took just 30 years for passing sailors and their pets or pests – dogs, monkeys, pigs and rats – to drive the dodo to extinction; the last specimen was seen sometime in the late 1680s.

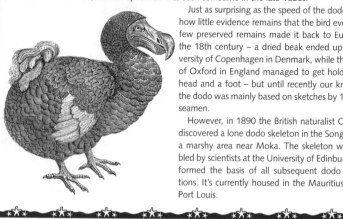

Just as surprising as the speed of the dodo's demise is how little evidence remains that the bird ever existed. A few preserved remains made it back to Europe during the 18th century – a dried beak ended up at the University of Copenhagen in Denmark, while the University of Oxford in England managed to get hold of a whole head and a foot – but until recently our knowledge of the dodo was mainly based on sketches by 17th-century seamen.

However, in 1890 the British naturalist Charles Clark discovered a lone dodo skeleton in the Songes au Mare, a marshy area near Moka. The skeleton was reassembled by scientists at the University of Edinburgh, and has formed the basis of all subsequent dodo reconstructions. It's currently housed in the Mauritius Institute in Port Louis.

National Parks

Since 1988, several international organisations have been working with the government to set up national parks in Mauritius.

The largest reserve is the Black River Gorges National Park, in the south-west of the island. It covers some 3600 hectares and preserves a wide variety of forest environments, from pine forest to tropical scrub.

Other nature reserves in Mauritius are Le Pouce, Île Ronde, Île aux Serpents, Île aux Aigrettes and Bois Sec (near Grand Bassin).

Île Cocos and Île aux Sables (small islands off Rodrigues) are both nature reserves, and are home to a large bird population.

There are many small-scale conservation areas that appear on many maps of Mauritius, although few are open to the public. Most of these are dedicated to preserving unique plant and animal species which are down to the last few individuals and are highly vulnerable to disturbance. Contact the Mauritius Wildlife Appeal Fund for information on areas you may be allowed to visit.

GOVERNMENT & POLITICS

Mauritius became a republic in March 1992 and the role of the former governor general was replaced by that of the president. The National Assembly consists of the speaker and elected and additional members. The cabinet has about 25 ministers, including the prime minister. General elections are usually held every five years (for more information, see the History section earlier in this chapter).

Mauritius has nine local government areas: Port Louis, Pamplemousses, Rivière du Rempart, Flacq, Grand Port, Savanne, Rivière Noire, Plaines Wilhems and Moka.

ECONOMY

Despite its isolation, population problems and colourful politics, Mauritius enjoys a surprisingly buoyant economy. This is largely due to the rise of industries such as textiles and tourism, which were heavily promoted during the 1980s and 1990s to relieve the pressure on the flagging sugar industry.

Today, unemployment is minimal and the rate of inflation has been reduced from a shocking 42% in 1980 to around 6.8% at the time of writing.

The sugar trade now exists in a healthy equilibrium with other industries, and exports have been steadily increasing since the 1990s. There are now approximately 600 export-oriented companies, with more than 100,000 employees.

Sugar

Until recently, the Mauritian economy could be summed up in one word – sugar. It represented more than 90% of exports, covered most of the fertile land in the country and employed most of the people. The state of the nation used to depend solely on the sugar harvest and sales. Every so often, a bad cyclone would devastate the cane crop, or a world drop in sugar prices would have bitter consequences.

A big sugar plantation ranges from 250 hectares to 1000 hectares; a small one starts at 10 hectares. A cane field is productive for between five and 10 years before it must be cleared and replanted. The cane work is mostly seasonal. The harvest is between June and September; all the cane-cutting is done by hand.

The future for these unskilled cane workers is far from secure. To compete on the world sugar stage, Mauritius is having to look towards mechanising the sugar industry, and the threat of job losses is looming large. The Sugar Industry Labour Welfare Fund (SILWF) operates centres around the country which provide free health care, a family planning institute and other social services for cane workers, but there are no welfare payouts.

Other Crops

Tea, although cultivated since first settlement, has become the second crop to sugar. It is grown mostly around Curepipe on the central plateau and is used in blending. Corn, potatoes, tomatoes, fruit and tobacco are also being encouraged as alternative crops. The export of fruit and vegetables is still very modest, although there is a growing market for Mauritius' small, sweet pineapples. The anthurium, the curious single-petalled red flower you may have seen in floral displays, is also proving to be a very popular export.

Industries

Although Mauritius is surrounded by thousands of square kilometres of ocean, its fishing industry has never been developed on a large scale. It remains primarily the domain of Creoles, and there is room for expansion. A fair amount of fish is imported from the Seychelles to satisfy local demand.

The real industry successes since the early 1970s have been the development of knitwear, textiles and footwear manufacturing, as well as tourism. Pierre Cardin, Lacoste, Calvin Klein, Marks & Spencer and other famous brands are manufactured in Mauritius. There are also lots of cheap imitations of noted designer labels.

Today, clothing is one of Mauritius' major exports. The amount of foreign investment in the industry has been remarkable. Hong Kong has supplied almost all the foreign investment in textiles. Mauritius now ranks as one of the largest exporters of woollen knitwear in the world. However, the rise of this industry has given the island some major pollution problems. The most visible signs of this pollution are the huge garbage dumps of fabric scraps that can be seen around the central plateau. Even more insidious is the discharge of chemical dyes and bleaches into the ocean.

Tourism

In 1999, some 823,000 tourists visited Mauritius, with most visitors coming from France and nearby Réunion. South Africans and Germans are the next most frequent visitors, followed by Italians, Britons and Malagasy. Australia and Japan are growing markets. Most tourists stay on the island for an average of two weeks.

Tourism is a major revenue earner, and this accounts for the ever-expanding range of hotels, apartments, guesthouses, restaurants and water activities.

POPULATION & PEOPLE

Mauritius has an estimated population of 1.18 million. With around 600 people per square kilometre, it has one of the greatest population densities in the world.

Well over half the people are Hindus (both Tamil and non-Tamil), and approximately another 180,000 are Muslims; both these segments of the population are descended from the labourers who were brought to the island to work the cane fields. Only a small percentage of the 30,000 Chinese or Sino-Mauritians came to the country as indentured labourers; most arrived as self-employed entrepreneurs. The remaining population are mainly Creoles, descendants of African slaves, and Franco-Mauritians.

Mauritius is often cited as an example of racial and religious harmony, and compared with most other countries it is. On the surface, there are few signs of conflict. However, racial divisions are still apparent, more so than in the Seychelles or Réunion. There is little intermarriage or social mixing between the racial communities.

Because Hindus are a majority and Mauritius is a democracy, Indians always win control at the elections.

Franco-Mauritians, who make up about 2% of the population, have their hands on Mauritius' purse strings and tend to screen themselves off from their former labourers in palatial private residences in the hills around Curepipe. Most of the sugar mills and other big businesses are still owned by these descendants of the *grands blancs* (rich whites), many of whom now live in South Africa and France. Unsurprisingly, almost all the luxurious holiday homes along the coast belong to Franco-Mauritians.

The Chinese are involved mostly in commerce. Most villages have one or two Chinese stores and there is a large Chinese quarter in Port Louis.

Another small group you might come across are the Chagos islanders, the Ilois as they are called in Mauritius. As inhabitants of the Chagos islands of the British Indian Ocean Territory, they were evicted from their homes when Diego Garcia was leased to the Americans as a military base. They were resettled in Mauritius by the UK between 1965 and 1973. The British paid UK£1.25 million in compensation directly to the Ilois in 1979, and moved them into housing estates in the northern districts of Port Louis.

The Mauritian government has waged a long-running campaign for the removal of US forces and the repatriation of the Chagos islanders, though this is largely motivated by the potential value of the islands as a tourist destination. In recent years, the problems of Creoles have taken centre stage and the plight of the Chagos islanders has fallen somewhat by the wayside.

EDUCATION

The government provides free education at both primary and secondary level. Further training is provided at special schools, technical institutes, handicraft training centres and teacher training centres. Several thousand students are enrolled at the University of Mauritius at Le Réduit.

The Mahatma Gandhi Institute in Moka was established in 1970 to preserve and promote Indian heritage. It offers secondary and tertiary education, as well as courses for younger children.

ARTS
Music

Western pop music is very popular, with Creoles favouring black rap artists and Indians leaning towards more mainstream dance music. The murdered US rap artist Tupac Shakur was half Indian and is something of an icon for Mauritian youths from both cultures.

There are a number of good Creole groups and singers, such as Roger Clency and Jean Claude-Monique. Ti-Frère, the most popular séga singer in the country, died in 1992. He is credited with reviving séga during the early 1950s, and his song 'Anita' has become a classic. In 1991, Radio France Internationale recorded a special Ti-Frère CD – highly recommended for séga fans. Hardcore fans may like to pick up the interactive CD-ROM *Île Maurice Séga* (about Rs750 in shops).

Séga!

The national dance of Mauritius was originally conceived by African slaves as a diversion from the injustice of their daily existence. It was through this dance that they would let down their hair at the end of a hard day in the cane fields. Couples danced the séga around campfires on the beach to the accompaniment of drums.

Because of the sand there could be no fancy footwork. So today, when dancing the séga, the feet never leave the ground and must shuffle back and forth. The rest of the body makes up for it and the result, when the fire is hot, can be extremely erotic. In the rhythm and beat of séga, you can see or hear connections with the Latin American salsa, the Caribbean calypso, and the African origins of the people. It's a personal, visceral dance where the dancers let the music take over and abandon themselves to the beat.

The dance is traditionally accompanied by the beat of the *ravanne*, a primitive goatskin drum. The beat starts slowly and builds into a pulsating rhythm which normally carries away performers and onlookers alike. Most of the big hotels offer séga soirees where diners are invited to join in the dance, but you may be lucky enough to see the dance being performed spontaneously at beach parties or family barbecues. There is about one a week at most hotels, and you can usually slip in to watch if you are not a resident.

Smaller hotels also endeavour to put on 'cultural shows'. But the séga groups tend to be amateurs just going through the motions for a bit of extra money. There's nothing worse than a lifeless séga – especially when the participants feel obliged to ask you to join in.

Séga variations danced to Creole pop music are reasonably popular in the discos, and they are sometimes more authentic than the hotel displays.

A new Mauritian musical form was invented by Creole musician Kaya (aka Joseph Topize) in 'seggae', which blends elements of séga and reggae. With his band Racinetatane, Kaya gave a voice to dissatisfied Creoles around the island. Tragically, the singer died in police custody in February 1999 (see the boxed text 'Kaya' earlier in this chapter). Kaya's classic album *Seggae Experience* is still widely available.

Ras Natty Baby is another popular seggae artist to look out for.

Literature

Mauritius' most famous contribution to world literature – one that has become entangled in the island's history – is the romantic novel *Paul et Virginie* by Bernardin de St Pierre, which was first published in 1788 (see the boxed text 'Paul & Virginie' in the North Mauritius chapter). A paperback English translation of the novel is available in St Louis bookshops.

Those who want to read a 20th-century Mauritian novel should read something by the well-known Mauritian author Malcolm de Chazal, whose most famous work is probably *Petrusmok* (1951). His other works include *Sens Plastique* (1948), *Sens Magique* (1956), *Poèmes* (1959) and *Sens Unique* (1974). Malcolm de Chazal was known as quite a character. The Swedish author Bengt Sjögren described him as an eccentric recluse who sat writing all day at the Hotel National in Port Louis, except when he walked by the seaside every morning to cogitate and watch the mighty ocean. However, according to the locals, de Chazal did not contemplate the sea, it was the sea that contemplated him.

Other writers well known in Mauritius are Robert Edward Hart, Edouard Maunick, the Masson brothers (Loys and André) and Léoville L'Homme. Mauritian humourist Yvan Lagesse has written a wry assessment of Mauritian life in *Comment vivre à l'île Maurice en 25 leçons* (How to live in Mauritius in 25 lessons). Peter Benson depicts the forced move of the Ilois (Islanders) from the Chagos Archipelago to Mauritius in his novel *A Lesser Dependency*.

Since the 1970s, literature has been published in Creole. Some examples are *Quand Montagne Prend Difé* by René Asgarally; *La Mare Mo Mémoire* (poems) by Ramesh Ramdoyal; and *La Fimé da Lizié* by Dev Virahsawmy.

Mark Twain, Joseph Conrad and Charles Baudelaire all visited the island. Joseph Conrad set a short story, *A Smile of Fortune*, in Mauritius, if you care to look for it in a collection of his works. His novel *Twixt Land and Sea* is based on a love story in Port Louis. Baudelaire's first poem, *À une Dame Créole*, was written in Pamplemousses.

Another adventure based on naval history is Patrick O'Brian's *The Mauritius Command*, about a Napoleonic swashbuckler.

(For information on nonfiction books about Mauritius, see Books in the Mauritius Facts for the Visitor chapter.)

Painting & Sculpture

The works of Mauritian artists are not widely displayed or available, which is a shame considering some of the beautiful landscapes you'd like to see captured on canvas. There are plenty of 18th- and 19th-century prints of such scenes, but the originals must have gone back to France and Britain years ago.

For contemporary paintings and sculpture, try the Port Louis Art Gallery on Mallefille St or the Max Boullé Art Gallery in Rose Hill. Galerie Hélène de Senneville (☎ 211 7317), in the Caudan Waterfront in Port Louis, sells prints and original works by local artists, including the author and painter Malcolm de Chazal. There's another branch on Route Royale near Pointe aux Canonniers at Grand Baie (☎ 263 7426).

The Naval Museum in Mahébourg has a selection of lithographs depicting local views and scenes from Bernardin de St Pierre's novel *Paul et Virginie*. The statue of the famous couple in the small park outside Curepipe town hall and one of King Edward VII in the Champ de Mars, Port Louis, were both created by Mauritius' best known sculptor, Prosper d'Epinay.

SOCIETY & CONDUCT

The island's Indian community maintains many aspects of its culture. The Mahatma Gandhi Institute in Moka was established in 1970 to actively preserve and promote Indian heritage.

Dos & Don'ts

Although beachwear is fine for the beaches, you may cause offence or invite pestering if you dress skimpily elsewhere. One traveller commented that his Mauritian friends did not consider someone stripped to the waist or wearing shorts should be taken seriously; in fact, they applied the 'foo-soo-koor' rule. According to this rule, such a person appearing in public must be either *fou* (mad), *saoul* (drunk) or *dans son cour* (inside a personal garden or backyard). Nude bathing is forbidden in Mauritius.

Mauritius has many mosques and temples – if you wish to visit, do so with respect (see Society & Conduct in the Regional Facts for the Visitor chapter).

RELIGION

Hinduism is the main religion in Mauritius. Hinduism is one of the oldest extant religions, with roots extending earlier than 1000 BC. Today, there are more than 150 temples in Mauritius. After Hindus, the greater part of the population is made up of Catholics, and then Muslims. Protestants constitute only a small proportion of the population. Mosques, churches and Hindu temples can be found within a stone's throw of each other in many parts of Mauritius.

Sino-Mauritians are less conspicuous in their worship. Many have turned to Roman Catholicism, but there are a few pagodas and Buddhist temples in Port Louis.

Catholicism is still the religion of choice for most Creoles, though it has picked up a few voodoo overtones over the years.

Many Christians pray at the shrine of Père Laval, in the Port Louis suburb of Ste-Croix. Père Jacques Laval (1803–64), a French missionary, is said to have converted more than 67,000 people to Christianity during his 23 years in Mauritius. His shrine is described in the Port Louis chapter.

LANGUAGE

It's said that when Mauritians have a community meeting, the people speak Creole, take minutes in English and discuss the outcome with government officials in French.

The official languages are English and French. English is used mainly in government and business literature. French is the spoken language in educated and cultural circles, and is used in newspapers and magazines. You'll probably find that most people will first speak to you in French and only switch to English once they realise you don't understand a word they are saying.

Creole, the common bond, derives from French and has similarities with Creole spoken elsewhere. Ironically, the Mauritian and Seychelles Creoles are more comprehensible to French people than the patois of Réunion, even though Réunion itself is thoroughly French. Most Indo-Mauritians speak Bhojpuri, derived from a Bihari dialect of Hindi.

French

French is widely spoken and understood in Mauritius and in most parts of the Indian Ocean. Most people also speak English, so non-French speakers will not be left incommunicado. However, it's not a bad idea to pick up Lonely Planet's *French phrasebook*, particularly if you intend to visit Réunion as well as Mauritius.

For a list of useful French words and phrases, see the Language chapter at the back of this book.

Creole

There are major differences between the pronunciation and usage of Creole and standard French, but if you don't speak French in the first place, you're doubly disadvantaged. (For information on Creole publications including dictionaries, see Books in the Mauritius Facts for the Visitor chapter.)

Creole is a vibrant, direct language. For starters, you might want to try the following Creole phrases:

How are you?	*Ki manière?*
Fine, thanks.	*Mon byen, mersi.*
I don't understand.	*Mo pas comprend.*
OK.	*Correc.*
Not OK.	*Pas correc.*
he, she, it	*li*
Do you have ...?	*Ou éna ...?*
I'd like ...	*Mo oulé ...*
I'm thirsty.	*Mo soif.*
Phoenix beer	*la bière zarnier* (literally 'spider beer' – the label looks like one)
Cheers!	*Tapeta!*
Great!	*Formidabe!*

Facts for the Visitor

PLANNING
When to Go

Apart from the Christmas and New Year period, Mauritius doesn't really have high and low seasons. The situation varies throughout the year and is more dependent on outside factors, such as the French holiday period, than on the weather. Consequently, factors other than the climate could determine the best time to visit.

Sporting and leisure considerations may play a part in when you choose to go. From December to March is best for diving, as the water is said to be clearer; June to August is best for surfing along the south coast; and October to March is the best time for big-game fishing, when the large predators feed closer to shore.

Maps

The map of Mauritius published by the French mapping agency, Institut Géographique Nationale (IGN), is one of the most detailed maps on the market and costs around Rs250. Also very good is the Globetrotter travel map for Rs175. It is a user-friendly map of the island and also has a number of excellent little insets of various regions, including Port Louis, Curepipe, the east, north and west coasts, Rodrigues and the Sir Seewoosagur Ramgoolam Botanical Gardens at Pamplemousses. The Macmillan map of Mauritius includes small insets for Rodrigues and Port Louis, and it is adequate for orientation, but less detailed than the IGN map. It costs Rs100.

Multimedia Ocean Indien (π 211 5242) publishes a useful free booklet called *Map of Mauritius*, which also includes street maps of Port Louis, Rose Hill, Quatre Bornes, Curepipe, Vacoas, Grand Baie and Rodrigues. You can pick up a copy at the Mauritius Tourism Promotion Authority office (π 201 1703, fax 212 5142) near the Caudan Waterfront in Port Louis.

Hikers requiring detailed information on Rodrigues should contact the Ministry for Rodrigues (π 208 8472, fax 212 6329) at the Fon Sing building, 5th floor, Edith Cavell St, Port Louis, or visit the Ministry's office (π 831 1590) in Port Mathurin, Rodrigues.

TOURIST OFFICES
Local Tourist Offices

Independent travellers in Mauritius are uncommon, which may account for the limited tourist information services on the island. You'll find most shopkeepers, bus drivers, police officers, bar staff etc very helpful without making a fuss.

The Mauritius Tourism Promotion Authority (π 208 6397, fax 212 5142) runs a friendly but somewhat uninformed tourist office at the Caudan Waterfront in Port Louis (see Information in the Port Louis chapter for details). It publishes the *Mauritius and Rodrigues Information Guide*, with extensive listings of places to eat and stay, and its Web site (www.mauritius.net) is also useful.

The Association des Hôteliers et Restaurateurs de l'Île Maurice (AHRIM) runs an accommodation booking service at the airport (π 637 3782).

Air Mauritius also seeks to promote tourism, but has only limited information at local and overseas offices. You'll probably find that the staff are too busy to devote much time to tourists – unless it's got something to do with an airline booking, of course.

Tourist Offices Abroad

Information about the island is much easier to obtain outside Mauritius. Mauritius Tourism offices around the world include:

France (π 01 44 01 46 00, fax 01 47 63 49 56) Office du Tourism de l'Ile Maurice, 24 rue Eugène Flachat, 75017 Paris
Germany (π 06171-981440, fax 980467) Mauritius Informationsbüro, Am Muhlberg 32, 61273 Wehrheim/Taunus
Italy (π 02 86 59 84) Ufficio del Turismo delle Isole Mauritius, BMK SAS Publiche Relazioni, Foro Buonaparte 46, 20121 Milano

Japan (☎ 03-5250 0175, fax 5250 0176)
Mauritius Tourist Information Bureau, Ginza
Stork building 5F, 1-22-1 Ginza, Chuo-Ku,
Tokyo 104

South Africa (☎ 31-562 1320) Mauritius
Tourism Information Service, PO Box 118,
Suite 2A, Glenashley Views, 36 Newport Ave,
Durban 4001

Switzerland (☎ 01-383 8788, fax 383 5124)
Mauritius Tourist Information Service,
Kirchenweg 5, CH-8032 Zurich

UK (☎ 020-7584 3666, fax 7225 1135) 32–33
Elvaston Place, London SW7 5NW

VISAS & DOCUMENTS

You don't need a visa to enter Mauritius if
you are a citizen of the UK, Ireland, the
USA, Australia, Canada, Japan, New
Zealand, the European Union (EU) or a
number of other countries. Initial entry is
granted for a maximum of three months. If
you change your departure plans, make sure
you don't exceed your permitted stay.

Visa Extensions

Extensions for a further three months as a
tourist are available. To apply for a visa
extension, you must go to the Passport &
Immigration Office (☎ 208 1212, fax 212
2398), Line Barracks, Port Louis (near the
Victoria Square bus station).

Applications must be submitted with one
form, two passport-size photos, your passport, an onward ticket and proof of finances.
Two letters may also be necessary – one
from you explaining why you want to stay
longer, and one by a local 'sponsor' (it can
be someone providing accommodation).
Some travellers claim they were able to extend their visa without a sponsor's letter.

Providing you can satisfy these demands
there should be no further problems, but since
the police are responsible for passport control, and quite a few visitors overstay their
entry permits, there are 'get tough' periods.

Visas for Onward Travel

It's best to apply for any visa in your own
country, as the process is usually quicker
and sometimes cheaper. Most visa applications require at least two passport photos, so
have some handy. For embassies' contact

details, see Embassies & Consulates in
Mauritius following.

India The embassy's visa section is open Monday
to Friday from 9.30 am to noon. A one-month
visa costs Rs760 and takes around five days to
process.

Madagascar The embassy is open Monday to
Friday from 9 am to 5 pm. Three-month visas
take around 48 hours to process and cost
Rs470.

Réunion The visa process takes up to a week and
costs Rs703 (cash payment in rupees required).
Apply at the visa section of the French embassy,
which is open Monday, Wednesday and Friday
from 8.15 to 11 am.

Onward Tickets

You must have an air ticket out of the country, and you'll be asked to show it at customs, so have it handy. If you do not have
an onward ticket, you could be invited to
buy one, on the spot, from Air Mauritius.

Immigration authorities will probably
also ask you to supply the name of your intended accommodation in Mauritius – if
you have not booked anything, just have a
name in your head and hope it hasn't closed
down! You could even be asked to show
proof of sufficient finances on arrival.

EMBASSIES & CONSULATES
Mauritian Embassies & Consulates

Mauritius has diplomatic representation in
the following countries:

Australia (☎ 06-281 1203, fax 282 3235) 43
Hampton Circuit, Yarralumla, ACT 2600

Belgium (☎ 02-733 9988, fax 734 4021) 68 Rue
des Bollandistes, Etterbrek, 1040 Brussels

Egypt (☎ 02-347 0929, fax 345 2425) No 5,
26th of July St, Lebanon Square,
Mohandessine, Cairo

France (☎ 01 42 27 30 19, fax 01 40 53 02 91)
127 Rue de Tocqueville, 75017 Paris

India (☎ 011-301 1112/3, fax 301 9925)
5 Kautilya Marg, Chanakyapuri, New Delhi
110021

Italy (☎ 63 449 75 86) Via Alfredeo Serranti 14,
00136 Roma

Madagascar (☎ 02-32157, fax 21939)
Route Circulaire, Anjanahary BP 6040,
Antananarivo 101

MALAYSIA

Malaysia (☎ 603-241 1870, fax 241 5115) Suite ABC, 14th floor, Bangunan Angkasa Raya, Jalan Ampangh, 50450 Kuala Lumpur
Pakistan (☎ 051-210145, fax 210076) House No 27, Street No 26, Sector F-6/2, Islamabad
South Africa (☎ 012-342 1283, fax 342 1286) 1163 Pretorius St, Hatfield, Pretoria
UK (☎ 020-7581 0294/5, fax 7823 8437) 32–33 Elvaston Place, London SW7 5NW
USA (☎ 202-244 1491, fax 244 1492) Suite 441, 4301 Connecticut Ave NW, Washington DC 20008

Embassies & Consulates in Mauritius

Countries with diplomatic representation in Mauritius include:

Australia (☎ 208 1700) Rogers House, 5 President John Kennedy St, Port Louis
Austria (☎ 208 6801) Rogers House, 5 President John Kennedy St, Port Louis (also represents Finland and Norway)
Canada (☎ 208 0821) 18 Jules Koenig St, Port Louis
Finland See Austria
France (☎ 208 4103) 14 St Georges St, Port Louis
Germany (☎ 211 4100) 32 St Georges St, Port Louis
India (☎ 208 3775) LIC building, 6th floor, Port Louis
Madagascar (☎ 697 3476) Queen Mary Ave, Floreal
Norway See Austria
UK (☎ 211 1361) Les Cascades Building, Edith Cavell St, Port Louis
USA (☎ 208 2347) Rogers House, 5 President John Kennedy St, Port Louis

CUSTOMS

Airline passengers aged 16 years and over may import duty-free goods: 200 cigarettes or 250g of tobacco; 1L of spirits; 2L of wine, ale or beer; 250ml of eau de toilette; up to 10cL of perfume.

Visitors may import a maximum of Rs700 in Mauritian currency, and take out Rs350. Duty-free items must be bought with foreign currency.

To bring in plants or plant material, you must obtain a plant permit from the Ministry of Agriculture (☎ 212 7931, 637 3194). An import permit (from the same ministry) and a sanitary certificate are required for all imported animals and animal material.

The Customs and Excise Department (☎ 240 9702, fax 240 0434) is in the IKS building, Farquhar St, Port Louis.

MONEY
Currency

The Mauritian unit of currency is the rupee (Rs), which is divided into 100 cents. There are coins of 5, 10, 20, 25 and 50 cents, and Rs1 and Rs2. The banknote denominations are Rs10, Rs50, Rs100, Rs200, Rs500 and Rs1000. There is no problem tendering old and battered notes.

Exchange Rates

country	unit		rupee
Australia	A$1	=	Rs14.90
Canada	C$1	=	Rs17.20
euro	€1	=	Rs22.90
France	FF10	=	Rs34.90
Germany	DM1	=	Rs17.20
India	Rs1	=	Rs5.60
Japan	¥100	=	Rs23.40
New Zealand	NZ$1	=	Rs11.40
Seychelles	Rs1	=	Rs4.46
Singapore	S$1	=	Rs15.00
UK	UK£	=	Rs37.80
USA	US$1	=	Rs26.00

Exchanging Money

All rates of exchange are set by the government and there is no difference from bank to bank. Banks charge a transaction fee of Rs50 for one to 10 travellers cheques and Rs5 for each additional cheque. Don't forget to take along your passport when changing money. And make sure you hang on to the encashment form, which will have to be presented if you want to change Mauritian rupees back into foreign currency. There is no black market in Mauritius.

Travellers cheques bring a better rate than cash, and there are no problems cashing the major currencies. Personal cheques on the Eurocheque system can also be cashed, but there is a hefty commission. Avoid changing money at hotels, as many charge an additional service commission.

There are increasing numbers of foreign-exchange counters around the island, and the banks at SSR airport are open for the arrival and departure of international flights.

Banking hours are from 9.15 am to 3.15 pm on weekdays, and from 9.15 to 11.15 am on Saturdays.

No restrictions apply on the amount of foreign currency you can bring in and out of the country, providing you declare it and the amount you take out does not exceed the amount you brought in.

Credit Cards Most major credit cards (such as Visa, MasterCard and American Express or AmEx) are widely accepted. Cash advances on credit cards are available from most of the major banks, including the Mauritius Commercial Bank, Barclays, the State Commercial Bank and the Shanghai Banking Corporation.

Costs

Along with Madagascar, Mauritius is among the Indian Ocean's cheapest places for visitors. However, the introduction of value-added tax (VAT) and the growth of the top end of the market have pushed prices up in recent years. In general, budget travellers should be able to get by comfortably on around US$30 per day, but this will go up markedly if you want to indulge in any water sports. At the top end of the market, the sky is the limit: A night at one of the luxury resorts can cost anything from $50 to $2000!

Unlike the Seychelles and Réunion, Mauritius does not have a heavily regulated tourism industry. Private enterprise is given a free hand. While this means that prices are competitive, it can also mean that service is variable. Just make sure you know exactly what you are getting for your money before paying. Independent tourism operators that cater for individual travellers and day or weekend visitors are concentrated at Grand Baie, Peréybère and Flic en Flac.

Costs in the lower range of the market have remained reasonably low for several years. The beauty is, the longer you stay in one place, the cheaper the rate should be for the room or apartment – and it is possible to

see all of Mauritius by basing yourself in one place. You can save on transport costs by travelling by bus, as taxis can gobble up your precious rupees.

There are no private beaches in Mauritius, so you are free to share the good hotel beaches and, at a reasonable cost in some cases, water sports facilities.

Please note that prices given in this book for accommodation, restaurants and some other services may have risen by about 5% to 10% since the time of writing.

Tipping & Bargaining

Tipping is not obligatory. In any case, most of the upmarket hotels and restaurants will include a charge on the bill for government tax and service. In budget hotels and restaurants it's not necessary to tip, although there's nothing to stop you giving something if the service has been particularly good. In major tourist areas, such as Grand Baie, there's an annoying tendency for some waiters to try to automatically extract tips – by not returning change, for example. If you use the services of an airport porter, you might want to give a small tip (around Rs20).

Bargaining is very much part of life in Mauritius. Daily accommodation rates at most places should drop by around 20% to 30% if you stay for more than a week, and further discounts are usual for off-season or long-stay occupancy.

For detailed information on tipping taxi drivers and on negotiating discounts on vehicle rental, see the Mauritius Getting Around chapter.

Taxes

In 1998, Mauritius introduced a 10% VAT on most items apart from unprepared food. At the bottom end of the market, this tax is usually included in the prices quoted for meals and rooms. In mid-range and top-end places, the tax usually isn't included.

There is also officially a 2% government tax on hotel rooms and restaurant meals, but only some places collect this charge.

At most of the cheaper *pensions* and local cafes, there are no service charges or taxes on top of your bill. Restaurants and hotels in the mid-range and at the top end of the market add 15% government tax to the bill. Be aware that many advertised tariffs do not include the tax, leaving you to find out about it only when it comes to paying the bill. To avoid confusion, it's best to ask if the room rate includes tax when you make your reservation.

POST & COMMUNICATIONS
Post
The postal service is widespread, efficient and reliable. Even the tiniest village has its own post office. Because of the rare Mauritian Blue stamp, the island is well known within world philatelic circles.

Most post offices are open from 8.15 to 11.15 am and noon to 4 pm on weekdays, and 8.15 to 11.45 am on Saturday. The last 45 minutes before closing are for stamp sales only.

The small post office in the departure section of the airport has different opening hours for almost every day of the week: Monday from 2.30 to 6 pm; Tuesday, Thursday and Friday from 2 to 6 pm; Wednesday from 2 to 4 pm; Saturday from 3.30 to 6 pm; and Sunday from 4.30 to 6.30 pm.

Sending airmail letters costs about Rs6 to Africa and Europe and Rs7 to the USA or Australia. Small/large postcards to most countries cost Rs5/12.

Most post offices have a free, reliable poste restante service. Letters are held for a maximum of around three months (if you want to extend this, speak to the postmaster). You must show some identification when collecting mail.

Telephone
The telephone service has been modernised so that most subscribers now have seven-digit numbers and international direct dialling (IDD) facilities. There are still a few hitches and glitches, and you might get dumped into the ether or misrouted.

All calls within Mauritius, from Port Louis to Grand Baie for example, cost Rs1.

There are very few public phones and even fewer that work. The local Mauritius Telecom office will usually have a card-phone and a coin-operated phone. *Télécartes* (phonecards) come in denominations of Rs30, Rs50, Rs100, Rs200 and Rs400; they are available from shops.

Alternatively, you may be able to use a phone at local shops or the post office, for a fee.

International calls can be made from private or public phones using IDD, or you can make operator-assisted calls from the Mauritius Telecom offices. The rate for a call to Australia or Europe is around Rs30 per minute. A call to the USA is about Rs35 per minute. These rates are reduced by around 25% from noon on Saturday until midnight on Sunday.

There are no area codes in Mauritius. Useful telephone numbers and prefixes include the following:

General inquiries	☎ 208 1036
Directory inquiries	☎ 90
International directory assistance	☎ 10090
International operator assistance	☎ 10091
International dialling code for Mauritius	☎ 230

Cellphone If you have a GSM phone, the coverage on the island is generally excellent. Alternatively, you can rent a cellphone from Emtel (☎ 454 5400), at 1 Boundary Rd in the centre of Rose Hill. Local calls cost Rs5 per minute off-peak and there's a charge of Rs125 per day for the handset (with a Rs5000 refundable deposit). Emtel will deliver and pick up your phone for an extra Rs500.

Fax
Hotels have fax machines for guests' use, and charge a small increment on the phone rates.

Email & Internet Access
The Internet revolution is yet to hit Mauritius. Almost the only Internet access on the island is provided by Cyberyder, which has Internet cafes in Port Louis and Curepipe. There are also a few small cafes in Quatre Bornes and Rose Hill. The usual charge is about Rs90 per hour.

INTERNET RESOURCES

The Mauritius Tourism Promotion Authority has an excellent Web site (www.mauritius .net) where you can download brochures about the island. Another excellent site is www.mauritius-info.com, which is very user-friendly and offers many useful business and tourism links.

BOOKS

For coverage of Mauritian fiction and some details of recommended authors, see Literature in the Facts about Mauritius chapter.

History & Politics

Without a doubt, *the* historian of Mauritius and the Indian Ocean was Dr Auguste Toussaint, who wrote books on pirates in general, the Surcouf brothers in particular, and the history of Port Louis – *Port Louis: A Tropical City*. He is best known for *The History of the Indian Ocean*. He died at his Forest Side home in February 1987.

For comparison, there is *A New History of Mauritius* by John Addison and K Hazareesingh, *The Truth about Mauritius* by Basdeo Bissoondoyal, and the *Historical Dictionary of Mauritius* by Lindsay Rivière. For a study of the British presence, you might like to dip into *British Mauritius 1810–1948* by Dayachand Napal.

In *Prisoners in Paradise*, Sheila Ward recounts the lives of five personalities who were imprisoned in Mauritius before independence. The characters cover an interesting historical and political span, and include the British explorer Matthew Flinders, the Malagasy prince Ratsitatane, the Kandyan chief Ehelepola from Sri Lanka, Iranian Shah Reza Khan Pahlavi, and Dr Stoyanovitch, a former prime minister of Yugoslavia.

For a more detailed account of Matthew Flinders' time in Mauritius, pick up a copy of *In the Grips of the Eagle: Matthew Flinders at Île de France* by Huguette Ly-Tio-Fane Pineo.

Another interesting roundup of visitors to the island is *They Came to Mauritius* by Derek Hollingworth.

Select Documents on Indian Immigration by Saloni Deerpalsingh & Marina Carter contains detailed information about Indian immigration to Mauritius. *Convicts in the Indian Ocean* by Clare Anderson provides more on the history of the Indian influx.

Hardcore history buffs may want to invest in the epic *A Concise History of Mauritius* by PJ Moree.

Those interested in politics should try *Untold Stories*, a collection of socio-political essays by Sir Satcam Boolell QC, or *Parliament in Mauritius* by Hansraj Mathur.

Rodrigues

The Island of Rodrigues by Alfred North-Coombes is out of print, but check second-hand bookstores and libraries. If you read French, a very useful publication is *À La Découverte de Rodrigues* by Chantal Moreau.

Flora & Fauna

For advanced reading on tropical fish, refer to either *A Field Guide to the Coral Reef Fish of the Indian & West Pacific Oceans* by RH Carcasson, or *A Guide To Common Reef Fish of the Western Indian Ocean* by KR Bock. For a look at Mauritian bird life, you could try *Birds of Mauritius* by Claude Michel. For more reading about plants and animals, there's *Fauna of Mauritius and Associated Flora* by France Staub.

You can read about Mauritian wildlife in naturalist Gerald Durrell's *Golden Bats & Pink Pigeons*. It's a funny and informative book. Durrell spent lots of time on Île Ronde off the north coast of Mauritius, where the country's only snakes (boas) live. Also recommended is *Last Chance to See* by Douglas Adams & Mark Carwardine. The authors manage to maintain a fine sense of humour while wandering around the globe in search of species that face extinction. The chapter entitled 'Rare or Medium Rare' deals with Mauritius.

Creole

Ledikasyon pu Travayer has reprinted Charles Baissac's 1888 Creole folk tale collection *Sirandann Sanpek: Zistwar an Créole*, which includes English translations, and has compiled a *Diksyoner Kreol-Anglé (Prototype Mauritian Créole-English Dictionary)*.

Editions de L'Océan Indien (EOI) is a publishing company with several outlets on the island (see Bookshops in the following section). It distributes several Creole titles, including Charles Baissac's *Le Patois Créole*, Goswami Sewtohul's *Petit Dictionnaire Français Créole*, and the popular *Parlez Créole* by James Burty David, Lilette David & Clarel Seenyen.

Cookbooks
An enduring title is *A Taste of Mauritius* by Paul Jones & Barry Andrews, which portrays island cooking at its best in mouthwatering colour. *The Best of Mauritian Cooking* by Barry Andrews, Paul Jones & Gerald Gay, and *Genuine Cuisine of Mauritius* by Guy Félix are also well worth a look.

Bookshops
The best bookshop in Mauritius is the eclectic Le Cygne Bookshop on Royal Rd in Rose Hill, with a wide selection of novels, reference books and titles on Mauritius in both English and French. Book Court at the Caudan Waterfront complex in Port Louis comes a close second, with a good range of novels and books about the island.

Editions de L'Océan Indien or EOI (☎ 464 6761) in Rose Hill publishes books about Mauritius in various languages; it also has an outlet in Curepipe (☎ 674 9065). The UK agent for EOI is Nautilus Publishing Company (☎/fax 020-8947 1912), PO Box 4100, London SW20 OXN. In France, the EOI agent is L'Harmattan (☎ 01 40 46 79 11), 16 Rue des Écoles, 75005 Paris. EOI titles are available by mail order.

Libraries
The National Library (☎ 210 9891) is on the second floor of the Fon Sing Building on Edith Cavell St in Port Louis. The collection can only be used for reference but photocopies are available. The library is open from 9.15 am to 3.30 pm on weekdays, and 9.15 to 11.30 am on Saturday.

More useful is the amenable Carnegie Library next to the Hôtel de Ville in Curepipe. It's open from 9.30 am to 6 pm on weekdays, and 9 am to 3 pm on Saturday.

You could also try the cultural centres; those that have libraries include:

Alliance Française (☎ 212 2949, fax 212 2812) 1 Rue Victor Hugo, Bell Village, Port Louis
British Council (☎ 454 9500, fax 454 9553) St Jean Rd, Rose Hill
Charles Baudelaire Centre (☎ 454 7929, fax 464 8144) 15/17 Rue Gordon, Rose Hill
China Cultural Centre (☎ 208 8547) Rue Victor Hugo, Bell Village, Port Louis

NEWSPAPERS & MAGAZINES
The main daily papers are *L'Express* and *Le Mauricien*, both in French, with the occasional article in English. Each costs Rs7. Other newspapers include *Le Quotidien*, *Mauritian Times*, *News on Sunday* and *Le Socialiste*. Weekly magazines include *Cinq Plus*, *Cinq Plus Dimanche* and *Weekend Scope*, all concentrating on cinematic and political glitterati.

British Sunday papers and French daily newspapers are also widely available. The *Mail on Sunday* and *Sunday Mirror* are available for around Rs170; broadsheets like the *Sunday Times* cost up to Rs350. *Le Figaro* and *Le Monde* both go for Rs55.

La Gazette des Îles is a good monthly magazine that's worth picking up if your knowledge of French is good enough. It contains articles on aspects of the history of Mauritius and other islands in the Indian Ocean. It is a touch heavy for the average visitor, but a boon to students of the relevant subjects.

There are two useful UK publications that have news reports and advertisements. *Mauritius News* is published monthly and can be obtained by contacting Mauritius News (☎ 020-7703 1071), PO Box 26, London SE17 1EG. *Mauritian International* is published quarterly and is available from Nautilus Publishing Company (☎/fax 020-8947 1912), PO Box 4100, London SW20 OXN.

RADIO & TV
There are three channels on Mauritian TV. The Mauritius Broadcasting Corporation (MBC) comes on from 7 am until late evening and covers important daily events.

Most of the transmission is in French, with some English and Hindi segments. See newspapers for program schedules.

The alternative is the Réseau France Ôutre-mer (RFO) station beamed across from Réunion. The presentation is slicker and it's all in French. There are also several pay-TV stations.

MBC operates a radio service which broadcasts in French, Creole, Hindi, Chinese and English. You can also tune in to the BBC World Service.

PHOTOGRAPHY

There is a plentiful supply of film at reasonable prices around the island. The best processing outlets are in Port Louis.

The main photographic shops in the centre of Port Louis are Mimosa (Agfa), which also does passport pictures and photocopying; Prophoto (Kodak) on La Chaussée, opposite the Company Gardens; and Goupile Colour Processing (Fuji) on Edith Cavell St.

Colour developing and printing can be done in one hour at many places and costs around Rs25 for processing plus Rs4.50 per print. Fuji print film costs Rs83/118 for 24/36 exposures (100 ASA). For slide film, prices start at Rs235 for Fuji Sensia for 36 exposures (100 ASA). Faster film usually costs a little more. APS film is widely available and costs around Rs120/170 for 25/40 exposures (200 ASA).

ELECTRICITY

The power supply throughout the country is 220V. British-style three-pin plugs are most common, though older establishments may also have continental two-pin sockets. It's wise to carry a travel plug that allows you to use both types of socket.

Many parts of the island experience the occasional blackout. Most hotels and guesthouses have torches or candles, and if you're staying in an apartment it's not a bad idea to buy a candle or two.

LAUNDRY

Laundry services are available at most guesthouses, bungalows and hotels. The upmarket hotels naturally charge more than the more modest places. Quite a few hotels, guesthouses and apartments provide an iron for their guests' use (free of charge). In the larger towns such as Port Louis and Curepipe there are a number of public self-service laundries that provide washing machines and dryers for a reasonable charge.

HEALTH

Should you get ill, the public health service is free to residents and visitors alike, but there may be a long wait for a consultation. The main hospitals are the Jeetoo Hospital (☎ 212 3201), Volcy Pougnet St, Port Louis; the Princess Margaret Orthopaedic Hospital (☎ 425 3031) in Candos; the Sir Seewoosagur Ramgoolam National Hospital (☎ 243 3661) at Pamplemousses; and the Jawaharlal Nehru Hospital (☎ 627 1840) at Rose Belle. The Moka Eye Hospital (☎ 433 4015) is in Moka.

A better, but more expensive, alternative is a private clinic. Among those that have been recommended are the Clinique Darné (☎ 686 1477) in Floreal; the Clinique Mauricienne (☎ 454 3063), between the university and the governor's residence in Le Réduit; and Med Point Clinic (☎ 426 7777), on Sayed Hossen Rd in Phoenix.

For general travel health information, see the Regional Facts for the Visitor chapter.

DANGERS & ANNOYANCES
Guard Dogs

Almost every Mauritian household employs some kind of dangerous-looking *chien méchant* (guard dog) to keep away undesirables. At night these beasts are allowed to run wild on the streets, causing some danger to traffic and pedestrians. In fact most of these animals will back off if confronted, but there's always the chance that they might not. It's probably best just to give them a wide berth.

Drugs

Soft drugs are available and are popular with Creole youths, but they are illegal and there are stiff penalties for offenders. It isn't worth the risk.

MAURITIUS

Exclusion from Beaches
Several travellers have complained about hotel security guards discouraging nonresidents from entering hotel beach areas. The law is quite clear: the area of beach between the high and low tide lines is public property. Most of the officious guards will back down if you calmly state that you are legally entitled to use the beach.

Shower Devices
In some budget accommodation, showers are electrically heated by a frightening looking contraption wired to the shower head. As you might expect, running water and bare electrical wires can be a 'shocking' combination. To activate the device you have to flip the electrocutioner-style switch on the wall while the water is running (yes, really), so it's best to leave your shoes or flip-flops on and not get wet until this is done. The machine can only heat a gentle flow of water, so if you want a shower with any pressure, you're best off forsaking this device and enduring the cold.

EMERGENCIES
For police or ambulance, call ☎ 999. Call ☎ 995 for fire services.

BUSINESS HOURS
Government office hours are between 9 am and 4 pm Monday to Friday. Private businesses are usually open from 8.30 am to 4.30 pm on weekdays and 8.30 am to noon on Saturday. Most shops and cafes open at 9 am and close between 3 and 6 pm. On Saturdays many close at noon. In Curepipe and Rose Hill, the shops are open an hour longer during the week, but close on Thursday and Saturday afternoons. Some restaurants are only open for lunch, or take last orders by a certain time.

PUBLIC HOLIDAYS & SPECIAL EVENTS
The following public holidays are observed in Mauritius:

New Year	1 & 2 January
Thaipoosam Cavadee	January/February
Chinese Spring Festival	January/February
Maha Shivaratree	February/March
Independence Day	12 March
Labour Day	1 May
All Saints' Day	1 November
Christmas Day	25 December
Eid al-Fitr	November/December

Apart from these holidays, there are also a handful of holidays during religious festivals; the dates vary each year. With such a range of beliefs and customs, hardly a week goes by without some celebration. You can usually find out about the latest *cavadee*, *teemeedee* or other ceremonies from the Mauritius Tourism Promotion Authority in Port Louis.

Hindu Festivals
Cavadee One of the more unusual Mauritian festivals, the Thaipoosam Cavadee takes place in January or February each year at most Hindu temples, and features acts of self-mutilation by devotees. Honouring a vow to Subramanya, the second son of Lord Shiva, pilgrims pierce their tongues and cheeks with skewers and march from their chosen temple to the banks of a river carrying the *cavadee* (a wooden arch decorated with flowers and palm leaves, with pots of milk suspended from each end of the base) on their shoulders.

The Thaipoosam Cavadee is a public holiday, but other small cavadees occur during the rest of the year at selected temples.

Teemeedee This is a Hindu and Tamil fire-walking ceremony in honour of various gods. The ceremonies occur throughout the year, but mostly in December and January. After fasting and bathing, the participants walk over red-hot embers scattered along the ground. The Hindu temples in Quatre Bornes, Camp Diable (near Savannah) and The Vale (near Goodlands) are noted for this event. A feat along similar lines is sword climbing, seen mostly between April and June. The best demonstrations occur at Mont Choisy and the villages of Triolet and Solitude (between Port Louis and Trou aux Biches).

Islamic Holidays

Muslims celebrate Eid al-Fitr to mark the end of the fasting month of Ramadan, which is the ninth month of the lunar year. Eid al-Fitr is always a public holiday.

Hijra Year	New Year	Prophet's Birthday	Ramadan begins	Eid al-Fitr	Eid al-Adha
1421	06.04.00	14.06.00	27.11.00	27.12.00	06.03.01
1422	26.03.01	04.06.01	17.11.01	16.12.01	23.02.02
1423	16.03.02	25.05.02	06.11.02	06.12.02	12.02.03
1424	05.03.03	14.05.03	27.10.03	25.11.03	01.02.04

Other Hindu Festivals Each year, most of the island's Hindus make a pilgrimage to Grand Bassin, the crater lake a few kilometres east of Le Pétrin, for the festival Maha Shivaratri. (For information about the celebration, see the boxed text 'Grand Bassin' in the Central Mauritius chapter).

Hindus celebrate the victory of Rama over the evil deity Ravana during Diwali, which falls in late October or early November. To mark this joyous event, countless candles and lamps are lit, to show Rama (the seventh incarnation of Vishnu) the way home from his period of exile.

Holi, the festival of colours, is known for the exuberant throwing of coloured powder and water, and tourists are not exempt from the odd dousing. The festival symbolises the victory of divine power over demonic strength. On the night before Holi, bonfires are built to symbolise the destruction of the evil demon Holika. This festival is held in February or March.

Other major public festivals include Ougadi (March), Pongal (January or February) and Ganesh Chaturti (September), the birthday of Ganesh, the elephant-headed god of wisdom and prosperity.

Chinese Spring Festival

The Chinese New Year is celebrated in the Chinese Spring Festival, which is a public holiday and falls around the end of January or the beginning of February. On the evening of the Chinese New Year, homes are spring-cleaned and decked in red, the colour of happiness, and firecrackers are let off to ward off evil spirits. On the following day, cakes made of rice flour and honey are given to family and friends. No scissors or knives may be used in case someone is hurt and begins the new year with bad luck.

Père Laval Feast Day

Père Laval Feast Day, in September, is the anniversary of the priest's death. Pilgrims from around the world come to his shrine at Ste-Croîx to pray for miracle cures (see the Port Louis chapter for more information).

ACTIVITIES
Water Activities

Most watery activities can be booked through your hotel or through any of the big tour operators on the island. Most of the major hotels provide items such as windsurfers and kayaks for guests' use, and some make them available to nonresidents (for a charge). Grand Baie, Trou aux Biches and Blue Bay are particularly good locations if you're interested in resort-based water activities. For detailed information on diving and snorkelling in Mauritius, see the special section 'Underwater Worlds'.

Undersea Walks This novel activity is becoming increasingly popular in Mauritius and allows nondivers the chance to experience life below the waves. Participants don lead boots and diving helmets and stroll along the seabed feeding the fish in a sort of Jules Verne journey beneath the sea. Oxygen is piped in from the surface and divers are on hand in case there are any problems. Many travellers rate the experience as a highlight of their trip.

Operators around the island include Undersea Walks (☎ 263 7820) and Angelo Club Nautique (☎ 263 3227) in Grand Baie; Aquaventure (☎ 422 7953) at Palmar Beach; and Coral Garden (☎ 631 1651) in Blue Bay.

Semisubmersibles & Glass-Bottomed Boats Several semisubmersible vessels offer undersea coral-viewing tours from Grand Baie. Operators include Croisières Australes (☎ 674 3695, fax 676 5530), which runs the yellow submarine Nessee from Grand Baie, and Blue Safari (☎ 263 3333), a proper submarine based in Mont Choisy (see the Grand Baie section in the North Mauritius chapter for more information).

Almost all the tour operators and hotels on the island can arrange trips out to the reef in glass-bottomed boats for around Rs150 per hour. Try any of the large tour operators in Grand Baie; there are also trips from Blue Bay and Trou aux Biches.

Surfing A small scene led by Aussie and South African surfers built up in the 1970s around Tamarin on the west coast (the surf movie *The Forgotten Island of Santosha* was made here), but the wave crashed and wiped out interest in surfing during the 1980s.

These days, the scene around Tamarin is fairly low key, with a small community of resident Mauritian and Réunionnais surfers. You can rent surfboards from the hotel *Chez Jacques* in Tamarin (see the West Mauritius chapter).

The surf at Tamarin itself is fairly tame; better breaks in the area include Le Morne and One Eye's (named after the one-eyed owner of Le Morne estate), both at the northern end of Le Morne Peninsula. There are also good surfing locations near the Baie du Cap. 'Lefts and Rights' is further south by Îlot Sancho, and there's a tricky break opposite the public gardens in Souillac.

The surfing season is from around June to August.

Deep-Sea Fishing The fisheries around Mauritius support healthy populations of large predators such as marlin, sailfish,

barracuda, wahoo, tuna and sharks, luring big-game fishermen from around the world.

November to March is the prime time to catch blue and black marlin, which grow to record size in these waters. The largest marlin ever caught was hooked in the area around Grande Rivière Noire. Between Grande Rivière Noire and Le Morne Peninsula the bottom plunges to a depth of 700m, and the currents attract millions of small fish pursued by huge predators. An annual fishing competition is held around Grande Rivière Noire in January or February.

Most of the big hotels run boats, and there are several Mauritian boat clubs. You can also hire cheaper local fishing boats if you're not too fussy about where you sling your hooks. You'll usually get to take home a trophy such as the nose spikes of any marlin you catch, but most operators lay claim to the rest of the fish, which they then sell to be smoked or served up at local restaurants. Tag-and-release is an option for anglers who want the thrill without depriving the ocean of these magnificent predators.

Some outfits have a minimum hire time of around six hours, and each boat can normally take five to six anglers. Expect to pay around Rs9000 per boat (for a full day) when hiring from an upmarket fishing centre or hotel. Local operators may drop to half this price or less if approached directly.

Ask your hotel or local tour operator to recommend a reputable fishing organisation, or contact one of the following:

Beachcomber Fishing Club (☎ 450 5050, fax 450 5140) Le Morne
Black River Sport Fishing Organisation (☎ 683 6547) Grande Rivière Noire
Centre de Pêche de l'Île Maurice (☎ 683 6522, fax 683 6318) Grande Rivière Noire
Organisation de Pêche du Nord (☎ 265 5209, fax 265 6267) Trou aux Biches
La Pirogue Big Game Fishing (☎ 453 8441, fax 453 8449) Flic en Flac
Professional Big Game Fishing Charter Association (☎ 683 6579, fax 683 6162) La Preneuse
Sofitel Imperial Big Game Fishing (☎ 453 8700, fax 453 8320) Wolmar
Sport Fisher (☎ 263 8358, fax 263 6309) Grand Baie

Yacht Cruises Grand Baie is the main centre for cruises, though most of the big hotels around the island offer flashy cruise packages to their guests. The travel agent Mauritours, which has offices in Port Louis (☎ 208 4739, fax 211 7617), Grand Baie (☎ 263 6056) and Rose Hill (☎ 465 7454, fax 454 1682), offers a wide range of cruises, and will ferry travellers down to the point of embarkation (usually at one of the large hotels). Cruise options from Grand Baie include day trips to Port Louis, Îlot Gabriel and Île Plate. Alternatively, you can cruise up the east coast to Île aux Cerfs. Day packages including lunch go for around Rs1300.

Perhaps the most interesting cruise on the island is a trip on the *Isla Mauritia* run by Yacht Charters Ltd in Grand Baie. Alternatively, Croisières Australes, also based in Grand Baie, has an elegant fleet of catamarans and offers a variety of day cruises. Cruise packages start at around Rs1300, including lunch and snorkelling. (For more information, see Grand Baie in the North Mauritius chapter).

Land Activities

Hiking For those interested in more than the usual beach activities, the island does offer some attractive hikes. Most hikes are in the central plateau area around the Black River Gorges National Park. The areas around Pic du Lion (north of Mahébourg) and Le Pouce (south of Port Louis) also offer some walks affording great views.

As a general rule when hiking, you should probably pay attention to 'Entrée Interdit' (Entry Prohibited) signs – they often mean you're entering a hunting reserve. 'Chemin Privée' (Private Road) signs are generally there for the benefit of motorists; most landowners won't object to the odd pedestrian. It's best to ask if you're unsure about where you should and shouldn't walk. (See Hiking the Central Plateau & Black River Gorges in the Central Mauritius chapter for details about walks in the area).

Golf There are golf courses at some of the major hotels, and some of the plusher places even offer their own golfing academies. The

Top Tips for Hikers

Special conditions apply to hiking in tropical conditions. The majority of the walks in Mauritius cross the central plateau, which is prone to tropical downpours at any time of year, especially from October to March. Rainfall is most likely in the afternoon, so you are best off starting in the morning and heading down to the (drier!) coastal plain. Trails can become treacherously slippery after rain, so good footwear is essential.

Hiking in the tropical humidity is thirsty work, so make sure you drink plenty of liquids while hiking (remember to bring your empty bottles back out with you). The damp conditions also provide a fertile breeding ground for mosquitos; apply a strong repellent if you're hiking through forested areas.

There are few serious dangers to hikers in Mauritius. If you do any bushbashing, you should watch out for spiny acacias, aloé cactuses and *framboise* bushes (thorny local shrubs). As in other mountainous areas, you should also beware of sudden drop-offs, which may be hidden by undergrowth. It's generally unwise to try and forge your own path without knowing the terrain.

Paradis hotel at Le Morne and the Belle Mare Plage Hotel at Pointe de Flacq both have 18-hole courses. Unfortunately most courses, including these two, are only open to hotel residents.

An exception to this rule is the Trou aux Biches Hotel in the north, which charges Rs550 for nine holes; equipment hire costs Rs275 (for more information, see Trou aux Biches in the North Mauritius chapter).

Tennis Tennis courts at some of the luxury hotels are open to nonresidents (for a charge of course). However, during peak tourist season, when hotels are booked out, the tennis courts may not be available to nonresidents.

Horse Riding There are opportunities for horse and pony riding at Domaine Les Pailles (☎ 212 4225, fax 212 4226), an estate run as a tourist attraction (see the Central Mauritius chapter for details). Some hotels, particularly the upmarket ones, may also be able to arrange horse riding.

WORK

It is not easy getting a work visa unless you are sponsored by a company. For more information, write to the Permanent Secretary, Ministry of Employment, Port Louis, Mauritius. Alternatively, contact your own country's Mauritian embassy.

ACCOMMODATION

Mauritius offers the full range of accommodation, from budget rooms to super-luxury suites. The main options are camping, *pensions de famille* (boarding houses), small family-run hotels, bungalows, apartments, guesthouses and luxury beach hotels.

At the budget end of the market, the most important thing to remember is that the more of you there are and the longer you stay, the cheaper the rate per person. It is possible to base yourself in one place and see all of Mauritius, especially if you hire a car. It's not a bad idea to take your own inner-sheet sleeping bag if you intend staying in pensions or cheap hotels.

December, January, July and August are usually the busiest months, and some of the top hotels implement a hefty hike in rates at these times. When it is quiet, most places will offer cheaper rates – you may even be able to slash these discounted rates. Half board is commonly available and includes breakfast and dinner.

If you don't feel like turning up unannounced, the Association des Hôteliers et Restaurateurs de l'Île Maurice (AHRIM) runs an accommodation booking service at the airport (☎ 637 3782).

The Mauritius Tourism Promotion Authority (☎ 201 1703, fax 212 5142) in Port Louis issues a list of accommodation tariffs. The tariffs are also included in the authority's *Mauritius and Rodrigues Information Guide*.

For information on accommodation taxes in Mauritius, see Taxes earlier in this chapter.

Camping

There is little assistance offered to campers. By the same token, there are few hassles. There are no official camping grounds and no restrictions, within reason, about where you can camp on public land. Few shoestring travellers or outdoor enthusiasts bring a tent, but the opportunity to use one exists. Probably the best camp sites are the public beaches, such as Blue Bay near Mahébourg, Flic en Flac, Pointe des Puits near Belle Mare, Mont Choisy, and the ones on Le Morne Peninsula. Casuarina trees provide shade and shelter. There are public toilets on some beaches, but many are in a dismal state.

The main drawback to camping, apart from the lack of facilities, is the lack of security. A good idea is to camp as close to a police station as possible, and ask the police to keep an eye on your tent. The police on the island are generally very helpful. Alternatively there are some surprisingly quiet beaches tucked away between the luxury hotels around Belle Mare and Palmar on the east coast.

Guesthouses

Guesthouses provide intimate surroundings and are a popular budget choice. Most are near the beach and offer rooms in a family home. Guesthouses are a good alternative to hotels, as you can learn a lot about local life through the owners – the atmosphere tends to be more down-to-earth. To satisfy tourist demand, there are more and more guesthouses springing up in Mauritius, particularly around the popular northern part of the island.

Pensions de Famille

Pensions de famille (boarding houses) are a budget option. They are concentrated in Mahébourg and Curepipe, with one or two at Peréybère, Quatre Bornes and Rose Hill. A few are small family affairs and offer meals. Others are loosely run by a young caretaker and rent out rooms on an hourly basis for the love trysts of frustrated local couples. Some are clean, some are grubby, but none are the absolute pits. Many have communal toilets and showers. For the sort of prices they charge, you can't afford to be fussy.

Bungalows & Apartments

There are bungalows and apartments around the coast, including seemingly hundreds in Grand Baie. In other places you may have to go looking, as they are not listed with any organisation or agency. Most will have a sign at the gate or nailed to a tree by the roadside saying *Bungalow à louer* or *Campement à louer* (Bungalow for rent), often with a telephone number. The Friday edition of *L'Express* has a page or two of *petites annonces* (classified advertisements) where you can usually find bungalows and apartments in the columns entitled *à louer* (rental).

Units range from complete bungalows, with up to four bedrooms, to small one- and two-bedroom studios with a kitchenette and bathroom. They are usually fully furnished and equipped with fridges. The more expensive ones will have a TV, a washing machine and sometimes air-con, and a more appealing interior.

If you're staying more than a few days, the bungalows are usually the best bargains. The proprietor should reduce the daily rate if you stay a week or more – ask for a discount if it is not offered. Many of the places rely on return visits by guests. Some may ask for a deposit when you make your booking. A maid or cook is sometimes included in the price or can be arranged for an additional charge – inquire when making your booking.

If possible, try to see the apartment or bungalow before you book. Some places are poorly maintained, noisy and provide limited cooking facilities. And a word of advice: make sure you check out the bed – some mattresses are positively lumpy and bumpy, leaving you grumpy in the morning after a dreadful night's sleep! Finally, if you quiver at the thought of sharing the place with creepy crawlies, come armed with a can of insect spray – huge cockroaches and spiders are not unusual, especially in the cheaper places.

Hotels

Mauritius has a wide variety of hotels, from no-frills budget places to virtual palaces on the beach.

Cheap Hotels Most of the cheap hotels are in Port Louis, with a couple in Curepipe, but most are fairly dismal. They generally cater to visiting tradesmen and business-people on tight budgets.

Urban Hotels There are several urban hotels in Port Louis, Curepipe and Quatre Bornes which are comfortable and well equipped but mainly cater to business travellers, so they lack that holiday atmosphere. They're certainly worth looking at if you find the coast a bit too hot and sticky.

Beach Hotels Mauritius is primarily a beach destination, so most travellers are looking for that perfect combination of sun, surf and sand. The beach hotels in Mauritius are certainly world-class, and offer every luxury from water sports and tennis clubs to swish restaurants, casinos and evening dinner shows. These are the places to look at for the honeymoon trip or the once-in-a-lifetime splurge. Tariffs are usually fixed at daily rates and the price drops if you book a fortnightly package. Rates are high, but still comparative with those of other luxury resorts around the world. Given the large number of beach hotels competing for customers, you should have no qualms about shopping around for the best deal and requesting discounts if you stay longer than a week.

The South African chain Sun International (☎ 401 1000, fax 401 1111, ⓔ suncro@sun resort.com) gives all its guests a Suncard on registration, which entitles the holder to various perks including discounted water sports and the opportunity to interchange accommodation with other hotels in the group. The huge Beachcomber chain (☎ 601 3232, fax 675 3240, ⓔ bcomber@bow.intnet.mu) offers its guests similar privileges.

For those with less extravagant budgets, there are numerous smaller, more homely beach resorts, though the facilities at these places are far less impressive. The best of the sand has been snapped up by the big hotel chains so these cheaper resorts tend to be relegated to the less impressive stretches of beach.

FOOD

Mauritian or Creole food is a blend of Indian, Chinese and European influences, with the emphasis on seafood. Most pensions and guesthouses offer tasty home-cooked Mauritian cuisine, though you may have to order from the manager in advance so that sufficient supplies can be obtained. Despite the dominant Indian flavour of Mauritius, there are only a handful of purely Indian restaurants. The Chinese are the main caterers and are good at blurring the lines between the various cooking traditions. For more information on Creole cooking, see the boxed text 'Delicious Mauritius', later in this chapter.

Vegetarian

Mauritians are big on seafood and meat, and even salads frequently have a sprinkling of seafood in them. If you don't mind fish you'll have no problems, but purists may struggle to find much in the way of entirely vegetarian food. Most Chinese and Mauritian menus offer a few vegetarian options, such as vegetable soup and stir-fried vegetables, but as a day-in, day-out diet this leaves something to be desired.

Probably the best choice is offered by the Indian restaurants. Many Mauritian Tamils are vegetarian, and you can find local restaurants serving vegetable *briani* (curried rice) and other potato-based curries in most towns. At the very least, you'll find dhal on almost all Indian menus.

Self-Catering

The biggest and best markets for fruit and vegetables are in Port Louis, Curepipe and the bigger towns such as Mahébourg and Centre de Flacq. Fruits and vegetables are seasonal, and prices vary accordingly. Mauritius has pretty much the same variety as the other Indian Ocean islands, but seems to get more excited over lychees and longans. To make sure you pay a fair price for your market produce, watch a local person buying the same, or compare the rates of several sellers.

The areas with a lot of self-catering accommodation, such as Flic en Flac and Grand Baie, are served by well-stocked supermarkets. Tinned and packaged food (much of it imported from South Africa) is widely available, and prices for most goods are similar to those in Europe or the USA.

To buy fish, go to the fish-landing station in each coastal village and deal directly with the fishermen. In Grand Baie, bonito costs about Rs100 per kilogram.

DRINKS

The price of all drinks purchased in bottles, whether cola, beer, rum or wine, usually includes a deposit for the bottle. Remember to take along the empties when replenishing supplies.

Nonalcoholic Drinks

Tea and coffee are hit-or-miss affairs. They're never purely Mauritian, as the local crop is used for blending. The tea is likely to be white and sweetened by condensed milk, unless you specify otherwise. Indian style *chai* and Mauritian vanilla-tea are also widely available. Instant coffee costs about the same as in the UK or Australia, but sugar and powdered milk are cheaper. Little of the French love of coffee has rubbed off on Mauritius, so you'll have to head to one of the upmarket hotels or restaurants for a decent espresso.

Soft drinks are numerous and are consumed copiously by Mauritians. Pepsi Cola, affectionately referred to as the national drink of Mauritius, is by far the most popular soft drink. The islanders are also fond of locally and commercially made yogurt drinks, many of which are available from street vendors.

The local water supply is fine to drink, but if you prefer something really cold, a 1L bottle of mineral water costs around Rs8 at the shops, or more in hotels.

Alcoholic Drinks

Beer and rum are potent, plentiful, and cheap, but not nasty. Locally brewed Guinness is popular, at Rs13 a bottle. Phoenix pilsner beer, which takes its name from the town where it's brewed, costs Rs12.50/22 for a small/large bottle. Other local brews include Blue Marlin and Strong 8.

There is a variety of brands of cane-sugar rum. The best known brand is Green Island, but Power's No 1 and Anytime are among the most popular with Mauritians. Green Island tastes better and is worth the Rs170 for a 750ml bottle.

French wine is expensive and most Mauritians drink South African wines, which cost between Rs110 and Rs230 a bottle in shops. The cheapest wines are Mauritian-bottled whites and reds for around Rs25 over the counter. The origin could be a tanker load of table wine surplus from France, or imported crystals watered down. It's just about palatable, though.

Tapeta! is Creole for 'Cheers!'

ENTERTAINMENT

Mauritians love to dance, and there are numerous nightclubs and discos, but most places cater to a younger local crowd so visitors may feel a little out of place. Probably the best place for tourist-friendly nightspots is Grand Baie.

Cinemas

Mauritians are big film buffs, but video-rental is cutting into the support base of local cinemas. Most major towns have at least one cinema, usually screening a mixture of Indian and international releases. Almost all international films are irreverently dubbed into French. Many towns also offer seedy movie houses showing ageing skin flicks.

Perhaps your only chance of catching an English-language film is at the Caudan Waterfront in Port Louis, which has the best cinema complex on the island (for more information, see Entertainment in the Port Louis chapter).

Séga Dances

The Mauritius Tourism Promotion Authority publishes information on coming events every two months or so, including a program of dancing and séga nights at most hotels and discos. Most major hotels lay on at least one séga night per week. Tickets to these events usually cost between Rs300 and Rs600 and include a buffet dinner. (For detailed information on the séga, see the Facts about Mauritius chapter.)

Casinos

Roulette, blackjack, baccarat and slot machines are some of the after-dinner diversions available for tourists at the casinos in the big beach hotels and at the plush casino at the Caudan Waterfront in Port Louis. If you intend going to a casino, tidy dress is expected (no thongs or T-shirts).

Theatres

There are two main theatres in Mauritius. One is next to Government House in Port Louis and the other is in Rose Hill. They are used mostly for local amateur productions, but host the occasional troupe from overseas. See Entertainment in the Port Louis chapter for more information.

SPECTATOR SPORTS

Soccer is the national sport, and the King George V Stadium in Curepipe is the main venue. Every town and village seems to have a soccer club, most taking their names from British teams such as Manchester United and Arsenal.

Mauritius has a busy horse-racing program from around May to the end of November at the Champ de Mars racecourse in Port Louis (for more information, see the Port Louis chapter).

SHOPPING

Some prime buys for souvenirs are model ships, clothing, Indian fabrics, basketry and embroidery. The best places to shop for them are Curepipe, Rose Hill, Quatre Bornes and Port Louis.

Given the wide choice of other things to buy in Mauritius, there is no reason to purchase items made from endangered species. For information about shells, coral and turtle products, which should not be purchased, see the special section 'Underwater Worlds'.

Model Ships

Whether or not you could conceive of having one in your home, it is difficult not to be impressed by the skill that goes into producing Mauritius' famous model ships. Small-scale shipbuilding has become a huge business and you'll see intricate replicas of famous vessels for sale all over the island; it's hard to believe that the industry dates back to only 1968, when an unknown Mauritian carved a model ship for fun and set off a whirlwind of interest.

Magnificently intricate miniature replicas of the *Bounty, Victory, Endeavour, Cutty Sark, Golden Hind* and even the *Titanic* can be bought off the shelf or made to order from a range of small factories.

For a more authentic souvenir you could buy a model of a ship that actually visited Mauritius; probably the most popular is the *Confiance*, a 1792 privateer of 26 guns, which was captained by the corsair Robert Surcouf and used in numerous raids against British merchant ships in the early 19th century.

The models are made out of teak or cheaper camphor wood, and larger ships take up to 400 hours to complete. The sails and rigging are dipped in tea to give them a weathered look.

Shop around to compare prices, which range from Rs2400 for a small model of a 19th-century cutter all the way up to

Model ships are made exactly to scale, based on the same plans used to build the originals.

Rs26,000 for a 160cm-long model of the 18th-century French vessel *Superbe*.

Some airlines discourage carrying the models as hand luggage, so sturdy specially made boxes are usually supplied by the manufacturer. Excess baggage fees in the Indian Ocean are fairly steep, so you may be better off air-freighting your purchase home. Make sure you supervise the packing to ensure that you get the right model.

One of the best places to buy a model ship is Voiliers de L'Océan (☎/fax 676 6986) on Sir Winston Churchill St in Curepipe. It employs about 35 people; the men work on the structure and the women do the rigging and sails. The staff here will be happy to show you around the small factory without any pressure to buy. The shop is open every day from 7.30 am to 6.30 pm. Comajora (☎ 676 5345, fax 675 1644) on La Brasserie St in Forest Side, a suburb of Curepipe, is also worth a look.

The biggest factory is Historic Marine (☎ 283 9404), St Antoine Industrial Estate, Goodlands, in the north of the island. It is open Monday to Friday from 8.30 am to 5 pm, and Saturday from 9 am to noon.

Several art and souvenir shops have models for sale, sometimes at reasonable prices. However, the choice is usually limited.

Clothing

After sugar and tourism, the textile industry is perhaps Mauritius' biggest earner. Many of the brand-name clothes on sale in Europe, Australia and America are produced in the factories around Curepipe, Floreal and Vacoas. Shoppers can save by buying at the source, and many of the bigger suppliers have outlet stores where you can buy items at a fraction of their usual retail price.

The Caudan Waterfront complex in Port Louis has a collection of designer-clothes shops with more conventional prices; Curepipe and Quatre Bornes also have their share of boutiques. The Sunset Boulevard complex at Grand Baie has some fancy clothing shops with fancy prices to match. Cheaper 'seconds' with minor flaws are widely available in the markets in Quatre Bornes and Rose Hill.

Alternatively, you could have a suit made to order. The turnaround time from measuring to finished product can be as little as 48 hours. Ghanty Tissus (☎ 670 0476), in the Galerie Jan Palach mall in Curepipe, charges around Rs2000 for material and Rs2500 for labour.

Local Brands As well as producing clothes for export, Mauritian companies make some stylish clothes for the local market. Fast-Forward and Habit are two local brands which will stand out among the Levis and Ralph Lauren back home. Fast-Forward has a branch in the Caudan Waterfront in Port Louis and another on Edith Cavell St, plus a branch in the Sunset Boulevard complex in Grand Baie. Habit has branches in the Caudan Waterfront, Sunset Boulevard and the Curimjee Arcade in Curepipe.

Knitwear Floreal Knitwear (☎ 698 8016) in the Floreal Square mall in Floreal is renowned for its stylish sweaters and other knitted garments. The company supplies Gap, Next and other international outfitters, but you can buy the same items before the branded labels have been added for a fraction of the final cost. Floreal Knitwear also has branches in the Salaffa Arcade in Curepipe and on Old Council St in Port Louis.

Indian Fabrics The government-authorised Handloom House at the Bank of Baroda building in Sir William Newton St, Port Louis, has a good range of Indian garments such as saris (colourful wraps for women) and churidars (long, tight-fitting trousers). There are also good Indian outfitters in Rose Hill. Cotton and silk saris start at Rs500, while churidars cost from Rs600. Silk costs around Rs450 per metre.

Stamps
Mauritius, like many island nations, prides itself on its colourful stamps and postal history. You are unlikely to find any of the truly valuable Mauritian stamps for sale (see the boxed text 'Stamp of Approval' in

---

Famous Fakes

Clothing prices in Mauritius are refreshingly low by world standards, but those who really want to save can opt for convincing copies of well-known designer brands. Well, at least some of them are convincing! At the top of the range, clothes bear the correct name, but always not the quality that should go with it; look out for minor flaws and dodgy stitching.

At the bottom end of the market, not even the names are the same as the originals, though you may have to look twice to pick the difference. Popular local makes include Kevin Kline (Calvin Klein's brother?) and Garterbillar (whose rugged clothes are similar to Caterpillar's), while fans of Adidas sportswear can choose from Adadis, Adidds, Adid As or Adiddas!

Vendors tend to congregate on President John Kennedy St in Port Louis, and in the Rose Hill and Quatre Bornes markets.

---

the Port Louis chapter), but the selection available at the Mauritius Postal Museum and the main post office in Port Louis will enhance any stamp collection.

Handicrafts & Souvenirs
For those not going to Madagascar, there are a number of shops specialising in Malagasy handicrafts, including leather belts and bags, semiprecious-stone solitaire sets, hats and baskets. Le Craft Market in the Caudan Waterfront complex and Port Louis Market both have dozens of vendors. Objects featuring the coloured earths of Chamarel are also popular. The famous sands will separate back out into differently coloured bands after they are mixed together.

The Société des Petites Entreprises Spe-cialisées (SPES) showroom on Labourdon-nais Ave, Quatre Bornes, sells chunky African-style metal jewellery, papier-mache animals, embroidery, pottery, paintings, baskets and carpets. The goods are made by a nonprofit organisation which employs disabled people.

MAURITIUS

Delicious Mauritius

MARK DAFFEY

A proud fusion of Indian, Chinese and European influences, Creole cooking is one of the highlights of the Indian Ocean region, and nowhere more so than in Mauritius. Here the Indian influence means a broad range of spices and flavours, and you can break into a *langouste* (lobster) with Creole sauce without breaking the bank.

The cornerstone of Mauritian Creole cooking is the *carri* (the Indian origins of the word are obvious), a rich, spicy onion sauce that owes a lot to Indian cooking, but includes local additions such as the aromatic leaves of the *carri poule* bush. This is one dish that is best sampled in the home, or in the kitchen of a small guesthouse, where every cook creates their own personal blend of herbs and spices. These are freshly ground on a *roche carri* (a mortar and pestle made of coarse volcanic stone). Once you've tasted a home-cooked *carri poisson* (fish curry), other meals will seem bland!

The Indian influence is also evident in the Mauritian *vindaye*, a light sauce flavoured with saffron, vinegar, onion and coriander, normally served with white fish. You'll find excellent vindaye at roadside eateries in the smaller villages.

After serving up the native wildlife as *carri dodo* and giant tortoise *daube* (stew), the early settlers of Mauritius imported game animals such as Java deer and wild boar to fill the gap. The best places to try boar or venison are the private game reserves where the animals are raised. In the south of Mauritius near Vieux Grand Port, the Domaine du Chausseur is a private hunting lodge that offers gourmet treats including roast boar with yams, and pan-fried deer brain (it's actually delicious!). Also look out for venison in *chausseur* sauce (a rich gravy made from the fresh blood of the deer).

Lobsters are plentiful off the coast of Mauritius and many restaurants will try to steer you towards the langouste when you order. It's usually served with a rougaille-like Creole sauce, a spicy tomato-based sauce with hints of ginger, thyme, garlic and chilli. It's also delicious cooked the Chinese way with garlic and butter, or with ginger. You can expect to pay Rs400 to Rs600 for fresh lobster in Mauritius. When you order, make sure that you are actually getting lobster rather than crayfish or langoustines (see the boxed text 'But I Ordered the Lobster!' in the North Mauritius chapter).

Fresh fish forms the backbone of many Mauritian dishes, and the variety of fish on offer is exceptional. Topping the list is the local *marlin fume* (smoked marlin), made from the monster marlins caught off the south-west coast. As few people can eat a whole marlin in one sitting, the fish are smoked as a means of preservation. Other fish to look out for include dorade, *sacréchien*, *vieille rouge* (grouper), *capitaine* (triggerfish) and *bourgeois* (red snapper).

Snack food is a national obsession in Mauritius, with street vendors offering inexpensive local treats at every bus station and town square. Delights you may care to sample include *roti* (lentil-flour pancakes) spread with curry sauce and hot chilli, *gateaux piments* (literally 'chilli cakes', deep-fried balls of lentils and chilli), *chana puri* (spicy dough balls), and onion *bhajees* (fried balls of onion and dough).

You can wash these titbits down with a cool glass of *lait caille*, also known as *dahi* (milk soured with vinegar), or, for sweet tooths, a glass of *alouda*, a syrupy brew of *agar* (a jelly-like substance made from seaweed, also known as china grass), milk and fruit syrup.

For dessert, try the *gateau la cire*, a sweet pastry made from cane sugar and rice starch. Finally, you can cleanse your palate with sweet local pineapples, wild guavas, or *jamblons*, tiny purple fruit with a tart grape-like flavour.

SUSAN STORM

The original fisherman's basket

SUSAN STORM

SUSAN STORM

SUSAN STORM

OLIVIER CIRENDINI

SUSAN STORM

Some like it hot: All the spice, colour and diversity of Mauritius is reflected in its cuisine.

The *séga* was first conceived by African slaves; now the dancers are slaves only to the rhythm.

Getting There & Away

AIR

Apart from the handful of people who sail in by yacht and those who arrive on the ferry from Réunion, most visitors to Mauritius fly in. You must have a return or onward ticket before arriving in Mauritius, which you should reconfirm a week prior to departure.

Expensive flights have always been the biggest deterrent to travellers. As with the Seychelles and the Maldives, the only way to cut the cost of flights is to take a package deal with hotel accommodation, or to include Mauritius in a round the world (RTW) or other circular fare. Mauritius, following the lead of the Seychelles, is now beginning to offer better deals to Europe and the UK. Most airlines offer cheaper low-season fares (the period differs from airline to airline).

Airlines

In Port Louis, Air Mauritius (☎ 208 7700, fax 208 8331) is at the Air Mauritius Centre on President John Kennedy St. Air France, Air Austral (Réunion), Air Seychelles and South African Airlines are in Rogers House at 5 President John Kennedy St. In the same building, there's an Air Mauritius office and a travel agent, Rogers & Co Aviation (☎ 208 6801). British Airways and Air Madagascar are in the Caudan Waterfront complex, while Singapore Airlines (☎ 208 7695) is at 5 Duke of Edinburgh Ave.

Departure Tax

There is a Rs300 airport tax on international departures, but this is included in the price of your ticket.

The USA

All flights from New York or Los Angeles to Mauritius go via London or Paris. A return ticket from New York to London costs around US$300 in the low season and from New York to Paris costs around US$360. From Los Angeles, you'll pay upwards of US$400 to London and US$520 to Paris (see the UK section earlier in this chapter

for the price of connections from London to Mauritius).

Australia

Air Mauritius operates flights between Melbourne/Perth and Mauritius, but this flight is notoriously overbooked. A better option is to fly Singapore Airlines via Singapore. The cost is around A$2100/2530 in the low/high season from Melbourne and A$1735/2135 from Perth.

The UK

Mauritius News and *Mauritian International* are two useful publications produced in the UK. Both have news reports and plenty of ads from travel agencies specialising in Mauritius. *Mauritius News* is published monthly and can be obtained by contacting Mauritius News (☎ 020-7703 1071), PO Box 26, London SE17 1EG. *Mauritian International* is published quarterly and is available from Nautilus Publishing Company (☎/fax 020-8947 1912), PO Box 4100, London SW20 OXN.

Several airlines fly between London and Mauritius, including Air Mauritius and British Airways. Air Mauritius flies to London twice weekly for UK£660/855 return in the low/high season and British Airways has three flights weekly for UK£790/850. A cheaper option is to fly Air France via Paris, which costs UK£594/784.

Continental Europe

Air Mauritius operates weekly flights to many European destinations including Paris, Zürich, Geneva, Rome, Munich, Frankfurt, Brussels, Vienna and London (the number of flights usually varies according to the season). Air Mauritius (☎ 01 44 51 15 55), 11 bis Rue Scribe, 75009, Paris, charges around FF5200/6625 in the low/high season for a return ticket from Paris to Mauritius; it operates about five direct flights per week.

Air France has four flights weekly between Mauritius and Paris, also for FF5200/

6625. The German airline Lufthansa Condor flies from Mauritius to Frankfurt, Munich and Cologne; the fare from Frankfurt to Mauritius is DM2161/2281. It's considerably cheaper to fly from Frankfurt to Mauritius via Paris on Air France (DM1200/1390).

Another alternative is to look for special offers between Paris and Réunion with Air France or Nouvelles Frontières (☎ 01 41 41 58 58, fax 01 40 65 99 36), 87 Blvd de Grenelle, 75015 Paris. You could then take a cheap return flight to Mauritius from Réunion.

Asia

Air Mauritius flies between Mauritius and Mumbai (Bombay) three times a week for Rs14,200, and also has a weekly flight to New Delhi for Rs14,800. Air Singapore and Air Mauritius both fly between Mauritius and Singapore twice weekly for between Rs12,789 and Rs13,860 return. Air Mauritius also flies to Hong Kong and Kuala Lumpur.

Africa

You can fly direct to Mauritius from Johannesburg, Cape Town or Durban (South Africa) with Air Mauritius and South African Airways (SAA). Prices start at around Rs10450 return (Rs11090 to Cape Town). Air Mauritius and Air Zimbabwe both have a weekly flight to Harare (Zimbabwe).

There are two flights weekly from Mauritius to Antananarivo (Madagascar) with Air Madagascar, and three with Air Mauritius (prices start at Rs7621). Air Mauritius also flies to Nairobi (Kenya) twice weekly for Rs12,475 return, and to Moroni (Comoros).

Réunion & the Seychelles

Both Air Mauritius and Austral Air have frequent flights between Mauritius and Réunion daily. A return fare (valid for one month) between Mauritius and Réunion costs Rs3650 (Rs2100 one way). The flight takes around 40 minutes and is popular with visitors from Réunion in search of a cheap holiday. This might explain why the same fare bought in Réunion costs about 50% more.

Both Air Mauritius and Air Seychelles offer connections between the Seychelles and Mauritius. Fares start at Rs6070.

SEA

On average, it takes a day to sail to Réunion and two days to return; five days to Madagascar and seven back; and 10 days to the Seychelles and two weeks back. Rodrigues, 560km to the north-east, is a seven-day sail.

Réunion

The easiest way to get to Réunion by sea is the MV *Ahinora*, a fast catamaran that takes five hours to complete the crossing. The ship is operated by MR Ocean Lines (☎ 210 7003), in the Orchard Building on Sir William Newton St in Port Louis, and leaves from in front of the Astrolabe building in the Caudan Waterfront complex. The ship sails to Le Port in Réunion on Monday, Wednesday and Friday at 8 am. Heading back the other way, it leaves Le Port (Réunion) at 8 am on Tuesday, Thursday and Sunday. A return ticket valid for one month costs Rs1945.

The MV *Mauritius Pride* operates several times monthly between Mauritius and Réunion. For information, contact Mauritius Shipping Corporation Ltd (☎ 241 2550, fax 242 5245), Nova building, 1 Military Rd, Port Louis. In Réunion, call the shipping agent Scoam (☎ 42 19 45, fax 43 25 47) at Le Port. The return fare between Mauritius and Réunion is Rs2405/3505 for a seat/cabin. Children below 12 years of age are charged half price. The one-way trip takes about 11 hours.

Several yachts call at Mauritius during the noncyclone season between June and November. They berth at Grand Baie or in Port Louis. It is possible to hitch a ride on one of these if you are willing to pay expenses and if you can crew, but the opportunities are rare. Check the noticeboard at Grand Baie Yacht Club. Alternatively, there is the remote chance of a charter, but it will be very expensive.

The Seychelles

Realistically there are no opportunities to sail from Mauritius to the Seychelles. The only way would be on a private yacht, but you would still have to face absurd immigration problems in two countries that effectively require an onward ticket for admission.

Getting Around

AIR

Domestic Air Services

There are daily flights to Rodrigues by Air Mauritius. The trip takes 1½ hours and costs Rs3150 return or Rs2800 one way. (See the Rodrigues chapter for more information.)

Air Mauritius also offers helicopter tours and charters from Sir Seewoosagur Ramgoolam (SSR) airport and a number of major hotels. If you want to arrive at your hotel in style, you can hire a helicopter for a 'Helitour' (maximum of four passengers). It costs Rs8800 for a half hour, or Rs14700 for one hour. The tour will take you over craters, waterfalls and mountains in the region of your hotel. This service is popular with honeymooners. For information and reservations, contact the Air Mauritius helicopter section (☎ 637 3552, fax 637 3424).

BUS

Bus services are frequent and can take you just about anywhere. It's best to stick to express buses whenever possible, as standard buses seem to stop every few metres and can take up to three times as long to reach the same destination. The fare is the same whether you travel standard or express.

The buses are single deck Ashok Leylands, Bedfords or Tatas, in varying states of disrepair. There are five large bus companies: National Transport Corporation, Rose Hill Transport, United Bus Service, Triolet Bus Service and Mauritius Bus Transport, along with scores of individual operators.

To offset the bombed-out appearance of many of their vehicles, the private operators give the buses dynamic, jet-set names such as 'New Lines of Power', 'Paris-Dhaka' and 'The Street Ruler'. Buses are often painted up in the livery of well-known international airlines such as British Airways and Air France.

There is no country-wide bus service. Instead there are distinct regional routes. Buses departing from Port Louis are divided into 'northern' services, which leave from Immigration Square just north of the centre, and 'southern' services, which leave from the Victoria Square bus station just south of the centre.

Southern destinations include Mahébourg, Curepipe, Flic en Flac, Rose Hill and Vacoas. Northbound buses run through the resorts of Trou aux Biches, Blue Bay, Peréybère and up to Cap Malheureux, or across the island to Flacq.

Buses also run south from Flic en Flac to Tamarin and on to Baie du Cap, while another bus connects Baie du Cap and Souillac. From Mahébourg there are connecting buses to Souillac and also up the east coast to Flacq via Grand Rivière Sud-East.

The tourist office can supply a booklet entitled *Mauritius – Information Guide*, which has a neat listing of bus operators, destinations, route numbers and departure points.

Long-distance buses only run from 6.30 am to 6.30 pm, so you'll have to rely on taxis if you want to travel earlier or later than these times (there is a late service between Port Louis and Curepipe until 8.30 pm). Local services between central Port Louis and the suburbs may run slightly later; check with the bus driver. Generally there are buses every fifteen minutes or so on the major routes, with less frequent buses on the express services.

Most divers tend to harbour Formula One racing fantasies, but the frequent stops can slow things down considerably. Try to avoid buses that go 'via' anywhere, as that can add hours to your journey time. Using a standard service, it takes approximately an hour from Mahébourg to Curepipe, an hour from Curepipe to Port Louis and an hour from Port Louis to Grand Baie. The express services take around half the time.

Fares range from Rs9 for a short trip to Rs16 for the run from Port Louis to Mahébourg. The bus conductor is often indistinguishable from the passengers, until he asks you for money. Keep some small change handy and retain your tickets, as inspectors often board to check them.

The buses are almost always packed, especially on the main routes, but turnover is quick at all the stops. If you start the trip standing, you're likely to end up sitting. You'll be told off by the conductor if you don't let disembarking passengers get off before you try to board.

Be warned that some travellers have faced problems with taking large bags or backpacks on a bus. If it takes up a seat, you will probably have to pay for that extra seat. A few travellers have even been refused entry to a full bus if they have a large bag.

For bus-related information, contact the National Transport Authority (☎ 212 1448).

CAR & MOTORCYCLE

Mauritian roads range from an excellent motorway to heavily potholed highways and minor roads. The motorway system runs from SSR airport to Port Louis and continues north.

A marvellous stretch of newly paved minor road may suddenly give way to a heavily patched and potholed major road. However, the danger comes from the drivers, not the roads. The number of buses on the roads is a hazard too, especially when they pick up speed and pass one another. Fortunately the frequency of townships and stops prevents the bus drivers from getting completely carried away. Night driving should be avoided unless you enjoy an assault course of ill-lit oncoming vehicles, unfathomable potholes and weaving pedestrians.

Mauritian drivers tend to have little consideration for each other, let alone for motorbikes. Buses are notorious for overtaking and then pulling in immediately ahead of other vehicles to pick up or drop off passengers; show extra caution. Riders should also be prepared for the elements, as sudden rain showers can come out of clear skies.

Road Rules

The speed limit is supposed to be 50km/h in the built-up areas or 80km/h on the open road. Not many people stick to these limits and the island has its fair share of accidents.

Motorists seem to think they'll save electricity by not switching on their headlights and the police are better at people control than traffic control. Driving is on the left.

Traffic congestion is heavy in Port Louis. There are many pedestrian zebra crossings but cross with care. Don't expect courtesy and don't expect drivers to be worried about insurance – you'll get knocked over.

Rental

You should ask for a discount on car, motorcycle or bicycle rental if you hire for more than a couple of days.

Car Prices for car hire aren't as low as they could be, considering the numbers of visitors who rent vehicles. Generally, drivers must be more than 23 years of age (some companies require a minimum age of 18 or 21), must have held a driving licence for at least one year and payment must be made in advance. All foreigners are technically required to have an international driver's licence if they wish to drive, but few rental agencies enforce this. It's safest to carry one, however, as the police can demand to see it.

Car rental prices differ from company to company. Rates for a small Suzuki hatchback start at around Rs700 a day with one of the independent operators (unlimited mileage). International chains such as Hertz and Avis charge from Rs1400 a day. On top of that you may be required to pay a deposit of up to Rs12,000, refundable on the safe return of the vehicle. Most policies specify that drivers are liable for the first Rs10,000 of damage in the event of an accident. This can normally be reduced by half for an additional Rs50 per day.

Avis (☎ 637 3100) and Europcar (☎ 63 3240) both have representatives at SSR airport.

Motorcycle There are only a few places where you can rent motorbikes or mopeds, which is a shame as this is a great way to explore the quiet coastal roads.

Most places charge from Rs450 a day whether you hire a moped or small motorbike (125cc). Towns offering motorcycle ire include Trou aux Biches, Grand Baie, 'lic en Flac, Mahébourg and Belle Mare see the Getting There & Around sections in he relevant chapters for more details). You hould be aware that most motorcycle hire s 'unofficial' so you may not be covered in ase of a collision.

Most of the bikes are fairly well worn, but arts are widely available should anything ail. Beware of 'imitation' parts, which are opies of genuine manufacturer spares, cast n inferior metal.

BICYCLE

Cycling isn't really a practical means of ong-distance transport in Mauritius – there s simply too much traffic – but bikes are ine for short hops along the coast. Most of he coastal plain is surprisingly flat and it's mazing how much ground you can cover n a day without killing yourself or getting addle-sore. The roads around the coast are lso quieter than the roads in the interior, so ou can relax and take in the landscape.

You really only understand the scale of he island when you cycle out of one town nd then find yourself in the next before you ealise you've left the last one.

Even if the roads seem quiet, you should e cautious when cycling on any road, es-ecially the busy main ones. Avoid cycling t night, as most roads are poorly lit and raffic can be erratic.

Rental

The cheapest rental deals start at around Rs25/100 for the hour/day. Rental models re usually mountain bikes. All should have lock. Check the state of the bike before iding off into the sunset, as some are nighty uncomfortable and look like they re about to keel over and die. To find out where you can hire a bike, ask at your hotel or contact a travel agent.

HITCHING

Hitching is never entirely safe in any country n the world, and we don't recommend it. Travellers who decide to hitch should under-tand that they are taking a small but poten-ially serious risk. If you do choose to hitch,

you will be safer if you travel in pairs and let someone know where you are planning to go. Nevertheless, you are advised not to hitch at night, and women shouldn't hitch alone – even several women together should never accept lifts from cars with only male passen-gers; make sure that there are women and/or children in the vehicle before climbing in.

Getting a lift in Mauritius is subject to pretty much the same quirks of luck and fate that you experience hitching anywhere.

BOAT

There aren't really any scheduled passenger services around the main island of Mauri-tius. Various private operators offer cruises to offshore islands, or snorkelling and fish-ing and excursions. See the listings under individual towns for more information.

Passenger Ships

The only passenger service is the MV *Mau-ritius Pride*, which runs several times each month to Rodrigues. For details see Getting There & Away in the Rodrigues chapter.

LOCAL TRANSPORT
Taxi

Taxis are the quickest and most convenient method of getting around the country, but you'll need to be savvy if you don't want to end up paying over the odds. Mauritian taxis have meters, but few drivers are will-ing to use them. You *must* agree on the price before getting into the taxi, and make sure there is no doubt about it. During the jour-ney most cabbies will also tout for future business; if you aren't careful you may find that you've agreed to be picked up first thing the next morning for an all-day island tour. If you aren't interested, make this very clear, as many drivers won't take no for an answer. Ignore sudden requests for extra petrol money en route.

Many guesthouse managers/owners have attempted to mitigate their guests' constant frustration with rip-offs by arranging prices with local taxi drivers. The quotes given under such arrangements, particularly those from small guesthouses, are often accept-able. Once you've got a feel for the rates, you can venture into independent bargaining. If you arrange a daily rate and itinerary, it helps to get the details down in writing.

The fleet of venerable British Morris Minors and Morris Oxfords has been replaced by Japanese vehicles carrying the usual taxi sign on the roof. Taxis generally have a fixed zone of operation, which is written on the side of the vehicle. If you hire a taxi from Grand Baie to the airport, for example, the driver will often include an additional fee for his journey back to base. Drivers can also charge a surcharge of Rs15 for every item of luggage over one metre in width or length.

Taxis generally charge more at night. If you want the comfort of air-con, expect to pay an extra Rs100/200 per hour/day. It's also worth remembering that some taxis charge around Rs1.30 per minute waiting time. It seems minimal, but it adds up if you want to stop for lunch or do some sightseeing on foot. Your best bet is to negotiate a fare with the driver that includes waiting time. As a rough bargaining guide, here are some of the fares you can expect to pay for one-way trips (at the time of research there were unconfirmed plans to hike up taxi rates by around 25%, so keep this in mind).

from	to	cost
SSR airport	Mahébourg	Rs300
SSR airport	Curepipe	Rs400
SSR airport	Tamarin or Port Louis	Rs650
SSR airport	Grand Baie	Rs700
Trou aux Biches	Grand Baie	Rs150
Trou aux Biches	Port Louis	Rs300
Trou aux Biches	Curepipe	Rs400
Centre de Flacq	Port Louis	Rs600

For between Rs1500 and Rs2000, you can hire a taxi for a full-day tour of sights around the island (the fare often varies with how much ground you intend to cover). This allows you to tailor your tour to suit your interests. You can cut costs by forming a group – the price should *not* be calculated per person. If you want to squeeze a tour of the whole island into one day, keep in mind that this won't leave much time for sightseeing. You're better off splitting the island tour into two days.

Although most drivers can speak both French and English, just double check before setting off to ensure you won't face a day-long communication barrier.

Share Taxi When individual fares are hard to come by, some cabs will cruise around their area supplementing the bus service.

For quick, short-haul trips they pick up passengers waiting at the bus stops and charge just a little more than the bus. Their services are called 'share taxis' or 'taxi trains'. Mind you, if you flag down a share taxi, you'll only be swapping a big sardine can for a small one, and if you flag down an empty cab, you may have to pay the full fare.

ORGANISED TOURS

The island's main tour operators take most of their bookings from overseas travel agencies or through the hotels before the visitors' arrival. If you are pushed for time but not money, the following tour operators may be worth contacting:

Le Mauricia Hotel
(☎ 263 7800, fax 263 7888) Grand Baie
Mauritius Travel & Tourist Bureau
(☎ 208 4734/39) Corner Royal & Sir William Newton Sts, Port Louis
Mauritours
Grand Baie: (☎ 263 6056) Sunset Boulevard
Port Louis: (☎ 208 5241) 10 Sir William Newton St
Rose Hill: (☎ 454 1666, 464 3078) 5 Venkatasananda St
Mautourco (☎ 674 3695, fax 674 3720) Gustave Colin St, Curepipe
White Sand Tours (☎ 212 6092) La Chaussée, Port Louis

There are also scores of smaller travel agencies, which largely cater for Mauritians going overseas.

Sandonna Villa (see Places to Stay in the North Mauritius chapter) offers a variety of trips, including a motorboat trip to Île aux Cerfs for Rs200 per person; a tour of the south-west including Curepipe, Grand Bassin, Black River Gorges National Park and Chamarel for Rs250; a tour of the south west including La Vanille Crocodile Park Souillac, Rochester Falls and Casela Bird ark for Rs250; and a tour of the south-east ncluding Domaine du Chasseur, Domaine e l'Ylang Ylang, the Mahébourg Naval Museum and Le Val Nature Park for Rs250.

The well-run Grand Baie Travel & Tours r GBTT (☎ 263 8771, fax 263 8274), close ɔ La Jonque restaurant, offers a good range f day tours. There's a 'Wild Mauritius' ɔur, which includes La Vanille Crocodile ark, the Mahébourg Naval Museum and a top for lunch at Domaine du Chasseur Rs990 per person including lunch). Other ptions include a tour of Port Louis and amplemousses (Rs385/635 without/with ɹnch); a trip to Île aux Cerfs (Rs275, lunch

not included); a tour of the south including Curepipe, Trou aux Cerfs, Grand Bassin, Black River Gorges and Chamarel (Rs550/770 without/with lunch); a visit to Domaine Les Pailles (Rs1485 including lunch); and an 'Inside Mauritius' tour, which includes Casela Bird Park, Rose Hill and Moka (Rs660/880 without/with lunch). Children are charged around half price for all tours.

Several smaller operators offer similar tour packages. Ebrahim Travel & Tours (☎ 263 7845, fax 263 8564) on Route Royale in Grand Baie offers a variety of tours including trips to the south for Rs150 per person and to Île aux Cerfs for Rs150 per person.

Port Louis

MAURITIUS

Port Louis (pronounced as either por-lwee or port loo-is) forms the administrative and business hub of Mauritius. Travellers have traditionally bypassed the Mauritian capital and headed straight for the beaches to the north and west, which is a shame because Port Louis can be a surprisingly attractive and vibrant place.

Port Louis has been bombarded by a remarkable array of natural disasters over the years, including cyclones, devastating fires and plagues (see the boxed text 'Trials of Port Louis'), but a large number of attractive Creole buildings remain. The old Creole mansions and shops are slowly being replaced by towering modern blocks and concrete developments, but for now, the city strikes a healthy balance between old and new.

During the day, Port Louis bustles as a commercial centre, with a busy market and a modern business district complete with skyscrapers and hundreds of white-collar workers. Traffic snarls are not uncommon. At night, most of the workforce returns home to Curepipe and the city can seem deathly quiet. The lively Chinese neighbourhood in the vicinity of the Jummah mosque is an exception to the rule.

The city was first settled by the Dutch, who called it Noordt Wester Haven, but it was the French governor Bertrand François Mahé de La Bourdonnais who took the initiative and developed Port Louis into a busy capital and port. La Bourdonnais is commemorated by a much-photographed statue at the seaward end of the Place d'Armes. Today, the city has a resident population of around 150,000, but most residents live in the burgeoning suburbs surrounding the old town.

Port Louis is the most multicultural town in Mauritius, with distinct Islamic, Hindu, Christian, Chinese and Creole neighbourhoods. Within the town centre are mosques, Hindu temples, Chinese pagodas and Christian churches and shrines.

HIGHLIGHTS

- Strolling through the lively and historic streets around the Port Louis market
- Shopping and dining in the plush Caudan Waterfront complex by the harbour
- Visiting the Natural History Museum & Mauritius Institute to see the dodo
- Touring Port Louis' temples, mosques and shrines

Orientation

The centre of Port Louis, where you'll find most of the businesses and sites of interest, is easily covered on foot. The only disorienting thing can be the street names. Road signs mix English and French at random; terms such as 'rue' and 'street', or 'route' and 'road', are used interchangeably. Pedestrians should also beware of names that sound similar. For example, there are three E Laurent Sts (Eugène Laurent St, Edouard Laurent St and Edgar Laurent St) within a few blocks of each other in the town centre.

The centre of Port Louis is marked by the Place d'Armes, a picturesque palm-lined avenue which runs from the Caudan Waterfront complex on the harbour to Government House. Sir William Newton St, where many of the banks have their offices, and Royal St, which runs through Chinatown, are also of interest to travellers. Chaussée St and Edith Cavell St are the main thoroughfares in the central business district.

Information

Tourist Office The Mauritius Tourism Promotion Authority (☎ 208 6397, fax 21 5142) has an office on the waterfront, close to the Caudan Waterfront complex, but only provides very mainstream information. The office is open Monday to Friday from 9 am to 4 pm, and on Saturday until noon.

Trials of Port Louis

Few cities have bounced back from as many natural disasters as Port Louis. Between 1773 and 1896 a series of fires, plagues and tropical storms all tried, and failed, to level the Mauritian capital.

First came the cyclone of 1773, which flattened 300 houses and wrecked 32 ships in the harbour. This was followed by the fire of 1816, which destroyed a fifth of the buildings in town.

There were further savage cyclones in 1818 and 1819, before cholera arrived from Manila on the frigate *Topaz*, killing an estimated 700 Port Louis residents in 1819. Then things quietened down until 1866, when malaria suddenly appeared on the scene, causing a further 3700 fatalities.

Around this time people started heading for the cooler (and safer) central plateau, so the town's population was mercifully small when the 1892 cyclone whipped through, destroying 3000 homes. The city recovered in terms of prosperity, but not in terms of population; most of the workers in Port Louis these days commute from the central plateau.

Money Port Louis is the financial capital of Mauritius and all the major banks have main offices in the vicinity of the Place d'Armes.

The State Bank of Mauritius (☎ 202 1111) is responsible for the skyscraper at the seaward end of Queen Elizabeth Ave, while the Hongkong & Shanghai Banking Corporation or HSBC (☎ 208 3161) is at the other end of the road, close to Government House. On Sir William Newton St, you'll find Barclays (☎ 212 1816) and the Mauritius Commercial Bank (☎ 202 5000). The Banque Nationale de Paris Intercontinentale or BNPI (☎ 208 4147) is opposite the main post office.

The American Express (AmEx) representative is the Mauritius Travel & Tourist Bureau or MTTB (☎ 208 2041, fax 208 8607), close to the corner of Sir William Newton and Royal Sts.

Post & Communications The main post office (☎ 208 2851) is near the harbour, at the end of Sir William Newton St. It's open Monday to Friday from 8.15 to 11.15 am and from noon to 4 pm, and on Saturday from 8 to 11.45 am. The last 45 minutes before closing are for stamp sales only. There is a free poste restante service at counter one.

Operator-assisted international calls can be made through the Overseas Telecommunications Service (OTS) office in the Telecom Tower on Edith Cavell St (call ☎ 203 7000 for inquiries). You can also receive and send faxes here. Otherwise, there are numerous payphones in the Caudan Waterfront.

Also in the Telecom Tower is the popular Cyberyder Internet cafe (☎ 203 7277), which charges Rs1.5 a minute for Internet access. It's open from 9 am to 10 pm daily (to 4 pm on Sunday). From about 3 pm on weekdays, every student in town descends on the cafe and it can be hard to get a console.

United Parcel Service (☎ 210 0345) on the corner of Dr Ferrière and President Kennedy Sts can organise air freight around the world. The office is open Monday to Friday from 8.30 am until 4.30 pm, and on Saturday from 9 am to 12.30 pm.

Travel Agencies Useful travel agencies in Port Louis include:

Mauritius Travel & Tourist Bureau (☎ 208 4739, fax 211 7617) Sir William Newton St Web site: www.mttb.com
Mauritours (☎ 212 1260, fax 212 4465) Sir William Newton St

Bookshops Port Louis has one of the best bookshops on the island – Book Court (☎ 211 9262, fax 211 9263) at the Caudan Waterfront. It has a well-displayed range of books in English and French covering a plethora of topics from cooking to economics. It also has a variety of leading newspapers and magazines from the UK and France.

There are several smaller bookshops in Port Louis, including Librairie Bourbon and Librairie Nalanda, within a few metres of each other on Bourbon St; and Librairie du Trèfle on Royal St. The range of books at these places is not as broad as at Book Court.

MAURITIUS

PORT LOUIS

PLACES TO STAY
- 6 Hotel Le Grand Carnot
- 7 Bourbon Tourist Hotel
- 33 Labourdonnais Waterfront Hotel
- 37 Tandoori Tourist Hotel
- 54 Metropole Hotel
- 58 Ambassador City Hotel
- 68 Le Saint Georges Hotel

PLACES TO EAT
- 3 Chinatown Deli
- 4 Canton
- 5 Lai Min
- 8 First Restaurant
- 13 Tandoori Express; Astrolabe Building
- 18 Cari Poulé; Singapore Airlines
- 25 La Bonne Marmite (Rocking Boat Pub); MR Ocean Lines
- 45 KFC
- 46 La Palmerie
- 50 La Floré Mauricienne
- 52 Underground Restaurant
- 53 Briani House

- 59 Co-op Cafeteria
- 61 Café du Vieux Conseil

OTHER
- 1 Police Station
- 2 Customs & Excise Department
- 9 Jummah Mosque
- 10 Merchant Navy Club
- 11 Immigration Square Bus Station
- 12 Ahinora Boat to Réunion
- 14 Main Post Office; Mauritius Postal Museum
- 15 Mauritius Tourism Promotion Authority Office
- 16 Banque Nationale de Paris Intercontinentale; Citirama Tours
- 17 Mahé de La Bourdonnais Statue
- 19 Barclays Bank
- 20 Mauritours
- 21 Mauritius Travel & Tourist Bureau; American Express
- 22 Mauritius Commercial Bank
- 23 Librairie du Trèfle

- 24 Bank of Baroda; Handloom House
- 26 Government House
- 27 Hongkong & Shanghai Banking Corporation
- 28 State Bank of Mauritius
- 29 United Parcel Service
- 30 Air Mauritius Centre
- 31 Rogers House; US Embassy; Australian High Commission; Rogers & Co Aviation; Air France; Air Austral; Air Seychelles; SAA; Air India
- 32 Caudan Waterfront Complex British Airways; Air Madagascar; Book Court; Cinemas; Harbour Cruise
- 34 Indian Embassy
- 36 Buses to Flic en Flac
- 36 Taxi Stand
- 38 Victoria Square Bus Station
- 39 Express Bus Stand
- 40 Buses to Mahébourg
- 41 Police Barracks
- 42 Passport & Immigration Office
- 43 National Library; Ministry for Rodrigues

- 44 Mauritius Telecom Tower; OTS; Cyberyder Internet Café
- 47 Company Gardens
- 48 Natural History Museum & Mauritius Institute
- 49 Port Louis Art Gallery
- 51 Photography Museum
- 55 Librairie Bourbon
- 56 Librairie Nalanda
- 57 Municipal Theatre
- 60 Floreal Knitwear
- 62 Town Hall
- 63 St Louis Cathedral
- 64 Police Station
- 65 Supreme Court
- 66 Canadian Embassy
- 67 British High Commission
- 69 French Embassy
- 70 Chapel & Shrine of Marie Reine de la Paix
- 71 Jeetoo (Civil) Hospital
- 72 German Embassy
- 73 St James Cathedral
- 74 King Edward VII Statue
- 75 Malartic Tomb

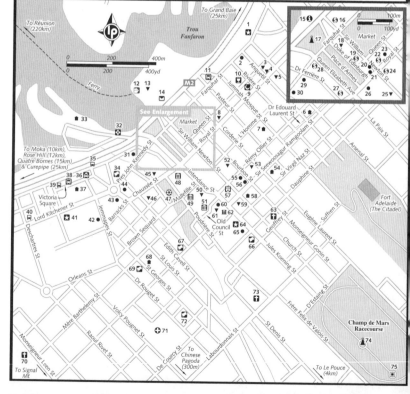

Dangers & Annoyances Pickpockets, usually operating by expertly slitting bags or pockets, are known to hang out at the Caudan Waterfront and the Port Louis market despite the police presence. A money-belt worn under clothing is a wise idea. You should stick to the well-lit main streets if you wander around Port Louis at night, as there have been reports of muggings late in the evening.

Port Louis Market

The much-touted Port Louis market isn't as authentic as the tour agents would have you believe, but it's still worth a visit to experience the hustle and bustle. The area between Farquhar and Queen Sts is where you'll find the colourful fruit and vegetable market and the less interesting T-shirt and souvenir stalls. On the seaward side of Farquhar is a somewhat pungent meat and fish market.

If you're looking for souvenirs, a wide variety of Malagasy handicrafts are available, along with 'Souvenir of Mauritius' T-shirts of varying quality. The level of hustling here can be tiresome, probably because of the number of well-heeled travellers who pass through the market. You'll have to bargain hard to pay reasonable prices; start by slashing the price you are quoted by about 30%.

For herbal cures and aphrodisiacs, you should head for the herbalists' stalls in the fruit and vegetable section. There are several vendors here selling traditional herbal medicines, which the vendors claim cure everything from obesity to stuttering. The cures are based on traditional Indian *ayurvedic* (herbal) medicine, and most take the form of leaves which you brew up into a tea. The stall run by CG Naiken has a particularly good reputation; a one-month course of 'slimming herbs' costs Rs100.

The market is open Monday to Friday from around 6 am to 5.30 pm, and on Saturday from 6 am to noon.

Natural History Museum & Mauritius Institute

Most travellers visit this museum on Chaussée St to see the famous reconstruc-

tion of a dodo. The curious looking bird was assembled by the Royal Museum of Scotland in Edinburgh in 1989, using the only complete dodo skeleton in existence (see the boxed text 'Dead as a Dodo' in the Facts about Mauritius chapter).

As well as featuring Mauritius' most famous absentee, the museum has a hall of shame of other extinct species, including stuffed examples of the Seychelles Dutch pigeon, the Bourbon crested starling, the broad-billed parrot, the Mascarene parrot and the solitaire. The museum also houses an extensive, if slightly desiccated, collection of marine animals, many of which have been repainted using their original colours.

The museum is open weekdays except Wednesday from 9 am to 4 pm, and on weekends from 9 am to noon. Admission is free.

Mauritius Postal Museum

This eclectic little museum, next door to the main post office, houses an impressive collection of Mauritian stamps and other postal paraphernalia, as well as a mock-up of the old Port Louis telegraph office. There are also replicas of the famous 'Post Office' stamps of 1847, which rank among the most valuable stamps in the world (see the boxed text 'Stamp of Approval' following). The museum is open Monday to Friday from 9 am to 4 pm, and on Saturday from 9 to 11.30 am. Admission is free (phone ☎ 208 2851 for information). The museum shop sells replica first-day covers of the famous stamps, which make nice souvenirs.

Photography Museum

This small museum and gallery (☎ 454 5242), on Old Council St near the Municipality of Port Louis buildings, is the labour of love of local photographer Tristan Bréville. On display are hundreds of old cameras and prints, and you can leaf through the vast archive of historical photos of Mauritius. The museum is open weekdays from 10 am to noon and 1 to 3 pm (Rs50 entry).

Stamp of Approval

Philatelists (stamp collectors to the rest of us) go weak at the knees at the mention of the Mauritian 'Post Office' one-penny and two-penny stamps. Issued in 1847, these stamps bore the title 'Post Office' rather than 'Post Paid'. They were recalled upon discovery of the error, but not before the wife of the British governor had mailed out a few dozen on invitations to one of her famous balls!

These stamps now rank among the most valuable in the world. The Bordeaux cover, a letter bearing both stamps, which was mailed to France in 1847, was last sold for a staggering US$3.8 million. Individual one- and two-penny stamps have been auctioned for more than US$850,000. The originals all lie in secure bank vaults, but you can see reproductions of these historic stamps at the Mauritius Postal Museum in Port Louis.

Jummah Mosque

The Jummah mosque, Mauritius' most important mosque, was built in the 1850s, and is a delightful blend of Indian, Creole and Islamic architecture; it would look equally at home in Istanbul, Delhi or New Orleans! Guests are welcome in the peaceful inner courtyard at most times, except during sermons, which take place on Thursday and Friday between 10 am and noon. (For more information on etiquette, see under Society & Conduct in the Regional Facts for the Visitor chapter.)

Père Laval's Shrine

The grave of the Catholic French priest and missionary Père Jacques Laval is something of a Lourdes of the Indian Ocean, with many miracles attributed to visits to the priest's mausoleum. The padre died in 1864 and was beatified in 1979 during a visit by Pope John Paul II. He is personally credited with thousands of conversions to Christianity.

Despite his efforts at conversion, today Père Laval is a popular figure for Mauritians of all religions. Pilgrims come here from as far afield as South Africa, the UK and France. The coloured plaster effigy of Père Laval that lies on top of the tomb has been rubbed smooth in places by pilgrims touching it in the hope of miracle cures.

The shrine is open from 8.30 am to noon and 1 to 4.45 pm on weekdays, and from 10 am to noon and 1 to 4.15 pm on Sunday. In the same complex is an attractive modern church and a shop with a permanent exhibition of Père Laval's robe, mitre, letters and photographs.

To get to the shrine, take the Cité la Cure bus or the Père Laval bus from Immigration Square, which runs out to Ste-Croix via Sir Seewoosagur Ramgoolam St and Abercrombie (Rs7).

Other Places of Worship

Other notable places of worship are the St Louis Cathedral (1932) at the south-east end of Sir William Newton St, and the St James Cathedral (1828) at the south-east end of Poudrière St. At the south-west end of Mère Barthelemy St, the chapel and shrine of Marie Reine de la Paix is a popular spot for prayers, and the attractive ornamental gardens offer great views over the city.

Place d'Armes

This major thoroughfare is lined with royal palms and leads up to Government House, a beautiful French colonial structure which dates from 1738, though the second floor was added in 1809. The statue of Mahé de La Bourdonnais at the quayside end of the avenue is to Port Louis as the Little Mermaid is to Copenhagen.

Company Gardens

Next to the Mauritius Institute on Chaussée St, this small park was once the vegetable patch of the French East India Company. Today the park is home to some truly enormous banyan trees, providing a shady retreat for lovers, strollers and statues, including that of the French poet Léoville L'Homme. The park is best avoided at night as it forms the centre of Port Louis's limited red-light district.

Fort Adelaide

Fort Adelaide is also called the citadel because it resembles a Moorish fortress. Built by the British, the fort sits high on the crown of the hill, offering splendid views over the city and beyond. The British built three other forts in Port Louis, but all are in ruins or inaccessible. There is rumoured to be a tunnel linking Fort Adelaide with Fort George, at the northern entrance to Port Louis harbour.

Signal Mount

A short walk or drive up to the radar station on top of Signal Mount will give you a stunning view of Port Louis and the surrounding coastline. The road begins at the southern end of Monseigneur Leen St.

Champ de Mars Racecourse

Also known as the Hippodrome, the 'Field of Mars' was a military training ground until the Mauritius Turf Club was founded in 1812. The police and army still use it for the odd manoeuvre in the off-season. Within the racecourse stands a statue of King Edward VII by the sculptor Prosper d'Epinay, and the Malartic Tomb, an obelisk to a French governor.

The racing season is from around May to late November, and the main race day is Saturday. The biggest race of all is the Derby, held at the end of August.

Entry into the stands costs Rs100, but admission to the central area is usually free, and you get the chance to mix with thousands of betting-crazy locals. For more information, contact the Mauritius Turf Club (☎ 208 6047) or check the local press.

Chinatown

The Chinese have traditionally occupied a quietly industrious position in the life of Port Louis. The region between the two friendship gates on Royal Road forms the centre of Port Louis' Chinatown, and this is where you'll find some of the best Chinese restaurants in town. The most interesting Chinese monument in Port Louis is the Poo Chee See Pagoda, towards the south-eastern end of Volcy Pougnet St.

Organised Tours

Citirama (☎ 212 2484, fax 212 1222) offers a half-day tour of Port Louis which takes in all the main sites around town. A ticket, which is valid for 24 hours, also entitles you to free entry to Domaine Les Pailles (described in the Central Mauritius chapter), with transfers provided by Citirama. The tour costs Rs350/200 per adult/child, and leaves at 10 am and 1 pm daily except Sunday. You can book at the Citirama kiosk by the BNPI bank.

Several companies offer boat tours around the harbour leaving from the Caudan Waterfront. Harbour Cruise (☎ 211 6560) has trips departing regularly between 10 am and 6.30 pm on weekdays, and between 11 am and 6.30 pm on weekends (Rs50/25 for adults/children). Book at the information desk in the Caudan Waterfront complex.

Places to Stay

With most travellers heading north to the beach-resort area, Port Louis isn't particularly well equipped with places to stay, but there are several budget options, as well as one very plush hotel.

Places to Stay – Budget

The best budget option is the *Tandoori Tourist Hotel* (☎ 212 2131) on Jemmapes St near the Victoria Square bus station. Security is good here, and clean singles/doubles with fan and bathroom cost Rs281/398. Some rooms tend to cop a bit of noise from the bus station.

Hotel Le Grand Carnot (☎ 240 3054, 17 Dr Edouard Laurent St) is another OK budget option, with fan-cooled rooms for Rs250/350, including breakfast. Guests don't get a key for the front door, so if you're out later than about 9.30 pm you'll have to wake the owners to get inside.

Bourbon Tourist Hotel (☎ 240 4407, 36 Jummah Mosque St) is OK, but has something of an institutional feel to it. Air-con rooms with attached bathroom go for Rs550/660, including breakfast.

The *Ambassador City Hotel* (☎ 212 0466, fax 208 5340) on Sir Seewoosagur Ramgoolam St has an OK location, but it doesn't rate well among travellers. Worn and weary air-con rooms cost Rs500/600, including breakfast. You can pay an extra Rs50 for a TV.

Nearby, the **Metropole Hotel** (☎ *212 5628*), on the corner of Sir Seewoosagur Ramgoolam and Corderie Sts, is a basic place upstairs above some shops. Fan-cooled rooms cost Rs450 for a single or double.

Places to Stay – Mid-Range

Le Saint Georges Hotel (☎ *211 2581, fax 211 0885, 19 St George St*) is a comfortable place just on the edge of the business district, aimed at businesspeople. Well-furnished air-con singles/doubles with attached bathroom cost Rs1000/1250, including breakfast. More luxurious rooms cost Rs1600/1850. It's a popular place so book well ahead.

Places to Stay – Top End

The *Labourdonnais Waterfront Hotel* (☎ *202 4000, fax 202 4040,* e *lwh@intnet .mu*), overlooking the harbour, is by far the most exclusive place to stay in Port Louis. Facilities in this grand hotel include two restaurants (see Places to Eat), a relaxing bar, a swimming pool, a health centre and a business centre. The cheapest singles/doubles will set you back Rs4565/ 6480, including breakfast. The luxurious presidential suite costs around Rs18,480. Lots of businesspeople stay here so an advance reservation is wise.

Places to Eat

Port Louis is spiced with small, cheap eating establishments ranging from cosy cafes to ramshackle roadside stalls. There's also a handful of more expensive restaurants serving Indian, Chinese, Creole or European fare. The only drawback is that most places close in the evening; those in the Caudan Waterfront complex are usually open more reasonable hours. Remember that most restaurants whack government tax onto the bill and there are few places open on Sunday.

Chinese On Royal St, *Lai Min* (☎ *242 0042*) has a good reputation for Chinese cuisine, but prices are a little elevated. Individual dishes cost between Rs70 and Rs350, or there are set menus for two or

more people starting at Rs180. It's open daily from 11.30 am to 2.30 pm and 8.30 to 9.30 pm.

On Anquetil St, the **Chinatown Deli** (☎ *240 0568*) is open later than most places and offers Europeanised Chinese food in the Rs65 to Rs150 range. It's open daily from 11 am to 10 pm.

Better Chinese food can be had at the homely *Canton* (☎ *241 4911, 15 Anquetil St*). Main dishes cost around Rs63. The restaurant is open from 10 am to 8 pm daily.

First Restaurant (☎ *212 0685*), on the corner of Royal and Corderie Sts, is at the top of a narrow stairwell. It has sweet and sour pork and other Chinese standards from Rs90 to Rs125 (Rs150 upwards for shrimp). It's open daily from 11.30 am to 2 pm and 6 to 9.30 pm.

Happy Valley (☎ *210 1228*) at the Caudan Waterfront is a friendly place on the second floor with better-than-average Chinese fare. Mains such as beef with black-bean sauce cost from Rs150. It's open daily from noon to 2 pm and 6.30 to 10 pm.

For a delicious lunch, *Charlie Snack* on Corderie St offers Chinese staples such as *bol renverse* (literally 'bowl turned over'), *riz frit* (fried rice) and wonton soup for Rs40 to Rs60. It's open from 9 am to 3 pm on weekdays only.

Indian The pleasant *Cari Poulé* (☎ *212 1295*) on Duke of Edinburgh Ave is arguably the best Indian restaurant in town. Vegetable curries start at Rs110, while meat eaters pay from Rs150 for dishes such as *rogan josh* (tomato-based curry) with lamb. It's open from 10 am to 4 pm daily. Between 7 and 11 pm on Friday and Saturday, it offers an Indian buffet for Rs300 per person.

More down-to-earth, *Tandoori Express* (☎ *210 9898*) in the Astrolabe building on the waterfront offers authentic Indian food and has tables overlooking the water. A meal of Goan fish curry, rice and naan will set you back around Rs150.

The super-cheap *Co-op Cafeteria*, in the Emmanuel Anquetil building, is only open at lunch time on weekdays; quick lunches such as curried rice cost from Rs50.

Another good Indian option is the air-conditioned *Briani House* (☎ 212 6324) on Corderie St. Briani and Creole curries cost from Rs60. It's open from 10 am to 3 pm daily except Sunday, and 6 to 8 pm from Monday to Thursday only.

Creole Housed in an appealing Creole building on Sir William Newton St, *La Bonne Marmite* (☎ 212 4406), also known as Rocking Boat Pub, offers a variety of set menus of Indian and Creole cuisine. There are four choices daily, and each meal costs Rs95. The restaurant is open from 11.30 am to 2 pm on weekdays.

La Flore Mauricienne (☎ 212 2200) on Intendance St, near Government House, is a popular place for lunch for diplomats and businesspeople. It specialises in French and Creole cuisine. It's open daily from 8.30 am to 4 pm (till 2 pm on Saturday). Main dishes cost upwards of Rs150.

The *Underground Restaurant* (☎ 212 0064), on Bourbon St between L'Homme and Rémy Ollier Sts, serves a variety of dishes including prawn curry, or chicken and chips, for around Rs60. It's open on weekdays from 11.30 am to 2.30 pm.

On Old Council St near the government buildings, the *Café du Vieux Conseil* (☎ 211 0393) offers set Creole lunch menus for Rs150 on weekdays.

La Palmerie (☎ 212 2597, 7 Sir Antelne St) is only open for lunches on weekdays. Expect to pay upwards of Rs250 for Creole and French main courses.

International The *KFC* fast-food restaurant on Chaussée St is almost the only place that stays open during a cyclone. It's open from 9.30 am to 9 pm daily (from 10 am on weekends).

Carnivores should head for *Black Steer* (☎ 211 9147) in the Caudan Waterfront complex. This popular steakhouse overlooks the harbour and offers great steaks for Rs150 to Rs200. It's open from 11 am to 11 pm daily.

L'Escale (☎ 202 4000) at the Labourdonnais Waterfront Hotel (see Places to Stay) is recommended for a dose of pampering. Main dishes range from Rs60 to

Rs350. The broad menu includes Japanese, Italian and Indian dishes. L'Escale is open from 6.30 to 11 pm daily.

The Labourdonnais Waterfront hotel also has a more upmarket seafood restaurant, *La Rose des Vents*, with goodies such as grilled lobster in a sauce of spring onion and butter (Rs150 per 100g), and other fishy mains from Rs260. Non-residents should book ahead.

Entertainment

Most of Port Louis' nightlife centres on the swish *Caudan Waterfront* complex (☎ 211 6560) overlooking the harbour. It has numerous restaurants and bars, two cinemas and a casino. The complex is very much the place to be seen in Port Louis, and at weekends, most places are packed to capacity with well-heeled Mauritian families, tourists, boisterous local youths and visiting sailors.

Bars Popular watering holes at the Caudan Waterfront include the *Keg & Marlin* (a passable copy of an English pub with live music at weekends), the French-style *Sunset Café* and the less salubrious *Shaolin* noodle-house and bar. All offer food as well as drinks and have outdoor seating overlooking the water. Most of the bars are open from noon till about 11 pm.

More down-to-earth is the *Merchant Navy Club*, at the bottom end of Rivière St, which caters mainly to visiting boat crews. The atmosphere here is suitably nautical. The bar is open from 9 am to 10.30 pm for drinks and cheap snacks such as toasted sandwiches.

Nightclub On top of the Keg and Marlin pub at the Caudan Waterfront, *Secrets* (☎ 211 9438) is a popular nightclub with varied music. It's open Friday to Sunday; call to see what's on.

Cinemas Star Cinemas (☎ 211 5361) at the Caudan Waterfront offers three screens of mainstream international releases dubbed into French, as well as the occasional English-language film. There are usually three performances a day and tickets cost Rs90.

Also in the Caudan Waterfront, Cinemaxx (☎ 210 7416) usually screens one

Hindi or Tamil film and one international release daily.

Casino If you're feeling lucky, head for the glitzy casino at the Caudan Waterfront. The slot machines are open daily except Monday from 10 am to 2 am; for blackjack and American roulette, the games room is open from 8 pm to 4 am.

Municipal Theatre This appealing theatre on Sir William Newton St has changed little since it was built in 1822, making it the oldest theatre in the Indian Ocean. Decorated in the style of the classic London theatres, it seats about 600 on three levels, and has an exquisitely painted dome ceiling with chandeliers.

There are quite frequent performances of Creole plays as well as jazz and classical music recitals. Prices vary according to what's playing, but tickets for most events cost around Rs100. Call the tourist office (☎ 208 6397) for more information.

Between 7 am and 3 pm from Monday to Saturday, you may be able to persuade the caretaker at the back entrance to put on the house and stage lights and take you backstage.

Shopping

The Port Louis market has a fair selection of T-shirts, basketry and other souvenirs, but the hard sell can get a little tiresome (for more information, see Port Louis Market earlier in this chapter). You can buy the same items without the hassle at the self-styled Craft Market in the Caudan Waterfront complex, though prices are usually higher. The Caudan Waterfront is also the place to go for designer clothes and other trendy knick-knacks (for more information, see Shopping in the Mauritius Facts for the Visitor chapter).

Most shops are open from 10 am to 6 pm Monday to Saturday, and from 10 am to noon on Sunday.

It's recommended that you don't purchase shells, coral, turtle shell or other items; purchasing them contributes to the destruction of the marine environment.

Getting There & Away

There are two major bus stations in Port Louis. Buses for northern and eastern destinations, such as Trou aux Biches, Cap Malheureux and Centre de Flacq, leave from Immigration Square, immediately north of the Port Louis market.

Buses for southern and western destinations, such as Curepipe and Quatre Bornes, use the Victoria Square terminus just south of the centre. Southbound express buses leave from a separate stand at the back of Victoria Square. National Transport Corporation (NTC) buses run to Vacoas and Quatre Bornes, while United Bus Service (UBS) buses serve Curepipe.

A few services deviate from this rule. Buses for Mahébourg leave from Deschartres St, just east of the police barracks on Lord Kitchener St. Direct buses to Flic en Flac (marked 'Luna') leave from the expressway behind the Victoria Square bus station. The first departure on most routes is at about 6 am; the last leaves at around 6 pm.

Getting Around

To/From the Airport There are no direct airport buses, but all buses between Port Louis and Mahébourg pass the airport (Rs17). You may be better off taking an express bus to Curepipe and changing to a Mahébourg-bound bus there. Allow at least two hours for the journey whichever route you take. Make sure the conductor knows where you're headed, as drivers occasionally skip the detour down to the airport terminal.

Expect to pay around Rs650 for a taxi ride from Port Louis to the airport.

Taxi In Port Louis the cabs have a printed list of tariffs that they are obliged to show you, but they might not honour them. (See the Mauritius Getting Around chapter for more information on the trials and tribulations of dealing with taxi drivers.) Ask an impartial local or your hotel staff for a rough idea of the going rate before taking a taxi. Expect to pay around Rs50 for a short hop across town. Keep in mind that taxi fares may have increased by between 5% and 10% since this book was written.

North Mauritius

The northern part of the island is divided into two districts: Pamplemousses in the west and Rivière du Rempart in the east.

The north-west coastline is practically all tourist development, with good beaches and numerous activities laid on for visitors. In contrast, there is scant development on the north-east coast, probably because there are few beaches. A plain of sugar cane fields, pockmarked with piles of volcanic boulders, stretches in between, sloping gently down to the sea.

Grand Baie is the main holiday centre, with a vast concentration of hotels, guesthouses, apartments, restaurants, shops and a small but busy beach. Peréybère, a few kilometres north-east, is similar, but considerably smaller and quieter, and somewhat cheaper.

Moving west around Pointe aux Canonniers, you'll find a 12km stretch of terrific beach where several luxury hotels have sprung up. There are still some good, clean public beaches; the biggest beach is Mont Choisy.

In the interior, the main attraction is the Sir Seewoosagur Ramgoolam Botanical Gardens at Pamplemousses. There is little else of specific fascination, but the area is certainly worth travelling around for its beauty.

BALACLAVA, BAIE DE L'ARSENAL & BAIE DU TOMBEAU

Balaclava is named after the black lava rocks in the area, rather than the Crimean battlefield. It is an attractive wild area overlooking the secluded Baie de l'Arsenal (also known as Baie aux Tortues). Here you'll find the ruins of a French arsenal, a flour mill and a lime kiln, surrounded by streams and waterfalls. The area is being developed by the big hotels, but fortunately the ruins are situated within the grounds of the Maritim Hotel, one of the more sympathetic resorts (see Places to Stay & Eat). Nonresidents can obtain permission to visit the ruins at the security hut

HIGHLIGHTS

- Indulging in a tantalising array of water activities at the cosmopolitan resort of Grand Baie
- Strolling around the fascinating Sir Seewoosagur Ramgoolam Botanical Gardens in Pamplemousses
- Enjoying the golden beaches and snorkelling at Mont Choisy, Peréybère and Trou aux Biches
- Taking a day cruise to Coin de Mire, Îlot Gabriel or Île Plate

by the entrance to the hotel grounds; the track to Balaclava begins about 30m beyond the hut to the right.

Baie du Tombeau (Tomb Bay) was so named because the area has become a tomb for so many ships. There's not much to see here apart from a dirty and polluted beach. The Dutch governor Pieter Both went down with his ship here in 1615. His name was given to a curious mountain with a balancing boulder at the summit, which is visible behind Port Louis. It was (mistakenly) predicted that the round boulder would topple off the summit when British rule ended in Mauritius.

Places to Stay & Eat

The *Maritim Hotel* (☎ 261 5600, fax 261 5670, e marbc@intnet.mu) overlooking Baie de l'Arsenal is an upmarket hotel with a great swimming beach. There are huge gardens and an assortment of facilities including *restaurants*, a golf course and a pool. Singles/doubles cost Rs4200/6400 including breakfast. Sumptuous suites start at Rs12,000/14,500.

On the bay's north side, *La Plantation* (☎ 204 3000, fax 261 5907) is a recent arrival, with good sports facilities and a nice strip of sand. Rooms cost from Rs3240/4480 on a half-board basis.

NORTH MAURITIUS

In the same area, *Le Victoria* (☎ 261 8222, fax 261 8224, e victoria@intnet.mu) is another plush modern resort belonging to the Beachcomber group, with all the usual luxury trimmings. Rates start at Rs5600/8400 on half board. The hotel offers a good range of free water sports.

The *Radisson Plaza Beach Resort* (☎ 204 3333, fax 204 3344, e radplaz@intnet.mu) nearby is luxurious but slightly soulless, despite having a great beach. Facilities include an impressive pool, water sports, a health club and several *restaurants*. Rates start at Rs6104/8140 on half board.

Getting There & Away

Baie de l'Arsenal can be reached via the A41 road, which branches off the Port Louis–Grand Baie road at Moulin à Poudre. A taxi from Port Louis to Balaclava costs around Rs300.

TROU AUX BICHES

About 20km north of Port Louis, Trou aux Biches (Hole of the Does) is an expanding resort with a pleasant – though not amazing – beach and good coral offshore. Like Flic en Flac on the west coast, Trou aux Biches is experiencing a construction explosion as more and more apartment buildings are thrown up to cater to the tourist influx.

For now, the resort retains some of its relaxed atmosphere and is quieter and cheaper than Grand Baie to the north, although it can get busy here on weekends. High-flyers can take advantage of the well-equipped resorts strung out along the coastal highway. There are also some good budget restaurants and guesthouses in Trou aux Biches, as well as one of the only public-access golf courses on the island.

Money
There's a branch of the Mauritius Commercial Bank opposite the Coralia Mont Choisy resort near Mont Choisy. The bureau de change is open from 9 am to 5 pm Monday to Saturday and 9 am to noon on Sunday.

Beaches
The beach at Trou aux Biches is nothing spectacular, although there is excellent snorkelling immediately offshore. The best beach in the area is the long strip of white sand at Mont Choisy, to the north of Trou aux Biches. The beach is shaded by casuarina trees and is usually pleasantly uncrowded during the week, although hundreds of picnicking Mauritians descend on the region at the weekend.

The beaches to the south of Trou aux Biches were reclaimed from the mangroves, an exercise that was only partly successful. Most are muddy and bordered by piles of boulders which were dredged up from the sea bottom.

Activities
There are dive schools at the Trou aux Biches Hotel, Hotel Le Cannonier and Coralia Mont Choisy (see Places to Stay for contact details). For cheap diving, try Atlantis Dive (☎ 422 7126, fax 263 7859) near La Sirène restaurant (dives start at Rs600).

Deep-sea anglers should head for the Corsaire Club (☎ 265 5209), also known as the Organisation de Pêche du Nord, near the Pescatore restaurant. Half-day fishing trips cost around Rs8000 for the whole boat.

Souvenir Snack (see Places to Eat) offers full-day trips for Rs8000 per boat.

Golfers can use the course at the Trou aux Biches Hotel for a Rs550 green fee (nine holes); club hire is Rs275.

Places to Stay
Almost every building in Trou aux Biches is available for rent in some shape or form. Most of the accommodation here is made up of apartments, villas and bungalows, usually with bathrooms, kitchens, and terraces or balconies for viewing the sunset.

Book well in advance at any hotel or guesthouse in Trou aux Biches; they can fill up in a flash – especially during the high season. On the plus side, most places should slash prices during the low season or for long bookings.

Most hotels and guesthouses can arrange excursions and car hire.

Places to Stay – Budget
Rocksheen Villa (*161 Morcellement Jhuboo, ☎/fax 265 5043*) on the road behind the police station is a friendly guesthouse run by a delightful Scottish-Mauritian couple. This place is well run and receives consistently good reports from travellers. Spotlessly clean singles/doubles with private bathroom cost Rs450/550 with breakfast. Self-catering studios are Rs550 for one or two people or Rs650 for three. It's a popular place so it's a good idea to book well ahead.

Not far from Morcellement Jhuboo is *Le Pavillon Soleil* (*☎/fax 265 8984*), a set of modern apartments surrounding a nice pool. One-bedroom apartments cost Rs800, while two-bedroom apartments which sleep up to four cost Rs1000.

Sandonna Villa (*☎ 265 5523, fax 283 7313*) on the main road is a smart guesthouse with doubles/triples (all with private bathroom) for Rs450/550. Breakfast is an extra Rs50 per person and there's a small restaurant. The owners rent out bicycles and mopeds and can arrange a good variety of tours.

If you're watching the pennies, *Auberge Chelloise* (*☎/fax 265 7196*) behind Flambeau Ltd Car Hire on Dextra Lane is good.

MAURITIUS

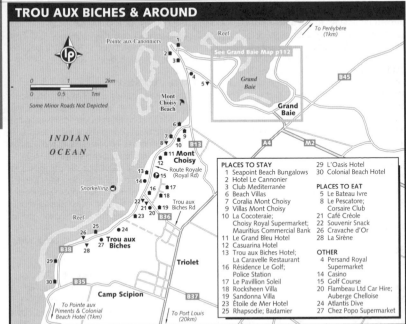

TROU AUX BICHES & AROUND

Pointe aux Canonniers

Reef

To Peréybère
(1km)

See Grand Baie Map p112

Grand
Baie

B45

Mont
Choisy
Beach

Grand
Baie

A4 M2

0   1   2km
0   0.5   1mi
Some Minor Roads Not Depicted

INDIAN
OCEAN

Route Royale
(Royal Rd)

Snorkelling

Trou aux
Biches Rd

B36

Reef

Trou aux
Biches

Triolet

B38

B35

Camp Scipion

B37

To Pointe aux
Piments & Colonial
Beach Hotel (1km)

To Port Louis
(20km)

PLACES TO STAY
1 Seapoint Beach Bungalows
2 Hotel Le Cannonier
3 Club Mediterranée
6 Beach Villas
7 Coralia Mont Choisy
9 Villas Mont Choisy
10 La Cocoteraie;
    Choisy Royal Supermarket;
    Mauritius Commercial Bank
11 Le Grand Bleu Hotel
12 Casuarina Hotel
13 Trou aux Biches Hotel;
    La Caravelle Restaurant
16 Résidence Le Golf;
    Police Station
17 Le Pavillion Soleil
18 Rocksheen Villa
19 Sandonna Villa
23 Étoile de Mer Hotel
25 Rhapsodie; Badamier

29 L'Oasis Hotel
30 Colonial Beach Hotel

PLACES TO EAT
5 Le Bateau Ivre
8 Le Pescatore;
    Corsaire Club
21 Café Créole
22 Souvenir Snack
26 Cravache d'Or
28 La Sirène

OTHER
4 Persand Royal
    Supermarket
14 Casino
15 Golf Course
20 Flambeau Ltd Car Hire;
    Auberge Chelloise
24 Atlantis Dive
27 Chez Popo Supermarket

There are just a few rooms with shared bathroom for Rs250 per person. Guests have use of a small kitchen and lounge with TV.

Résidence Le Golf (☎ 676 6525, fax 674 8775) is next to the police station and offers comfortable apartments with one/two/three bedrooms with kitchen, bathroom and TV for Rs700/900/1100. There's a small pool.

The beaches deteriorate as you head south towards Pointe aux Piments. The small **L'Oasis Hotel** (☎ 265 5808, fax 265 5207) has one of the few decent stretches of sand. Singles/doubles start at Rs725/900 and apartments (maximum of four people) cost from Rs1300 per night. There's also a restaurant and a swimming pool.

Places to Stay – Mid-Range
Travel agent Grand Baie Travel and Tours (☎ 263 8771, fax 263 8274), based in Grand Baie, offers a range of well-maintained apartments at Trou aux Biches. Good options include **Badamier** with three-bedroom

bungalows on the beach from Rs3080; **Rhapsodie** with two-bedroom bungalows on the beach from Rs1995; **Villas Mont Choisy** with studios from Rs1210 and two-bedroom bungalows from Rs1940; and **Beach Villas** with studios from Rs1630 and bungalows from Rs2420.

The **Étoile de Mer Hotel** (☎ 265 6178) is close to the beach, but it's a little run-down for the money. Singles/doubles are Rs850/1340; studios are Rs1100/1630; suites cost Rs1550/2075. Facilities include a pool and a restaurant.

On Route Royale, the **Casuarina Hotel** (☎ 265 6552, fax 265 6111) is a nicely laid out mid-range hotel with a vaguely Moorish theme. Facilities include a good pool, tennis courts and free water sports for guests. On a half-board basis, standard aircon rooms are Rs2100/Rs3200 in the low season and Rs2550/3700 in the high season. Superior rooms are Rs2250/3500 in the low season and Rs2800/4200 in the high season.

Further in the direction of Mont Choisy, *Le Grand Bleu Hotel* (☎ 265 5812, fax 265 5813, e lgbtab@intnet.mu) is an OK mid-range place with two pools and a good restaurant. Singles/doubles with air-con and bathroom cost Rs1100/1350 with breakfast or Rs1300/1700 on half board.

Nearby, *La Cocoteraie* (☎ 265 5694) offers good self-catering apartments arranged around a pool for Rs800/1000/1200 a single/double/triple. All apartments have air-con and balconies. There's a good restaurant.

Seapoint Beach Bungalows (☎ 696 4804, fax 686 7380), at Pointe aux Canonniers, is a secluded complex of self-catering bungalows on the beach. Double studios cost Rs1200, two-bedroom apartments cost Rs1400 and a duplex which sleeps six costs Rs1600.

At Pointe aux Piments, the colourful *Colonial Beach Hotel* (☎ 261 5187, fax 261 5247) is a complex of chalets with a swimming pool, a games room, snorkelling facilities and a restaurant. Singles/doubles with private bath cost from Rs1575/2160 on half board.

Places to Stay – Top End

The top dog at Trou aux Biches is the *Trou aux Biches Hotel* (☎ 265 6562, fax 265 6611, e tabhotel@intnet.mu), which dominates the nicest stretch of beach. This upmarket Beachcomber resort is set in sprawling grounds (you'll even get a map when you check in!) and offers accommodation in comfortable bungalows: standard singles are between Rs6300 and Rs8100, and doubles are between Rs9200 and Rs11800 (tariffs vary according to the time of year). All rates are on a half-board basis. The resort includes several restaurants, shops, a pool, tennis courts, baby-sitting facilities, water activities, a casino and a golf course, yet still manages to retain its human angle. This is a popular wedding venue.

The *Coralia Mont Choisy* (☎ 265 6070, fax 265 6749), further north, is another swanky hotel with well-appointed singles/doubles/triples starting at Rs3200/4200/5600 on half board. Guests can make use of good water sports facilities and a pool.

The sporty *Club Mediterranée* (☎ 209 1000, fax 263 8617), at Pointe aux Canonniers, has bungalows that vary in price from Rs2900 to Rs4270 per person including all meals and activities. Day-trippers can make use of the sports facilities for the whole day (Rs950 including breakfast and lunch), or for just the afternoon (Rs750 including lunch). The evening soirees are also open to nonresidents for Rs450, or Rs750 with dinner. Thursday and Saturday are séga nights.

Hotel Le Cannonier (☎ 263 7000, fax 263 7864), just beyond the Club Mediterranée, is a five-star Beachcomber hotel with plenty of land and water activities to indulge in. Prices for singles/doubles start at Rs4800/7000. There are two restaurants, a swimming pool and tennis courts.

Places to Eat

There is a fairly good selection of restaurants catering for most tastes, but you can always head on to Grand Baie if nothing here takes your fancy. Self-caterers can choose from the *Choisy Royal* supermarket near the Coralia Mont Choisy resort and *Chez Popo* near La Sirène restaurant.

Souvenir Snack (☎ 265 7047) near the police station is one of the best eating joints for a cheap and cheerful feed. This unpretentious little place attracts a constant stream of hungry travellers from the beach in search of sustenance. Snack lunches such as *mien frit* (fried noodles) or grilled fish start at around Rs35. It's open Monday to Saturday from 7 am to 7 pm and Sunday 7 am to noon.

Café Créole (☎ 265 6228) near Souvenir Snack has plenty of Creole dishes including *carri poisson* (fish curry) and pizzas for around Rs150. It's open daily except Monday from 9am to 2.30 pm and 6 pm to midnight and also does takeaway.

La Sirène towards Pointe aux Piments concentrates on seafood and Indian dishes. Fish-based main courses start at around Rs130 and shrimp dishes are upwards of Rs250. The restaurant is open daily from 10.30 am to 3 pm and 7 pm to 10 pm.

Nearby, the plush *Cravache d'Or* (☎ 265 7021) on Route Royale offers expensive seafood such as grilled red snapper for

MAURITIUS

around Rs350. The restaurant is open daily from noon to 1.30 pm and 7.30 to 10 pm.

La Cocoteraie (see Places to Stay) has a good restaurant with Creole dishes such as octopus curry for around Rs230. It's open daily from noon to 3 pm and 7 to 10 pm.

Le Pescatore (☎ 261 6337) is a stylish seafood restaurant overlooking the sea. Expect to pay at least Rs500 for a main course such as prawns with citronella and passion fruit. It's open daily from noon to 2.30 pm and 7 to 9.30 pm.

Le Bateau Ivre (☎ 263 8766), which translates as the Drunken Boat, is at Pointe aux Canonniers; it is a pricey but nicely presented seafood place. Unusual main courses such as grilled prawns with sea urchin butter cost from Rs350 to Rs550. Lobster is a steep Rs730. The restaurant is open daily from noon to 2 pm and 7.30 to 10 pm.

La Caravelle (☎ 265 6562) at the Trou aux Biches Hotel (see Places to Stay) offers a special Mauritian buffet dinner on Tuesday for Rs550 per person (for residents this is included in the room tariff). Nonresidents should book at least one day in advance.

Entertainment

There's a casino at the Trou aux Biches Hotel (see Places to Stay), which is open to nonresidents. The slot machines are open daily from around 10 am to 1 am, while the games room (American roulette, blackjack etc) is open from 9 pm until 4 am. Tidy dress is expected; entry is free for foreigners.

Getting There & Around

Bus There are bus stops about every 500m along the highway from Triolet to Cap Malheureux. The Triolet Bus Service runs buses to Cap Malheureux and Pointe aux Piments from the Immigration Square bus station in Port Louis; the 30-minute journey to Trou aux Biches costs Rs13.

Taxi A taxi to Grand Baie costs Rs100; to Port Louis around Rs300; to the airport Rs600; and to Curepipe about Rs400.

Car & Motorcycle In Trou aux Biches, Flambeau Ltd Car Hire (☎ 265 7894, fax

Wedding Bells

If you have ever fantasised about walking out of your wedding reception onto a tropical beach, Mauritius could be the wedding venue you've been searching for. There are dozens of splendidly equipped luxury hotels on the island offering special wedding and honeymoon packages, with perks including tropical flowers, champagne and special romantic meals for newlyweds. For that added tropical flavour, the local civil status officer can even perform the ceremony on the hotel beach.

Under Mauritian law, civil weddings can be celebrated by nonresidents upon production of a certificate of nonresidency, which can be obtained from the Registrar of Civil Status (☎ 201 1727), Emmanuel Anquetil Building, Port Louis. The application process usually takes around ten days, and requires birth certificates and passports of both parties. Alternatively, you can let someone else do the work and book a complete wedding package from abroad. The Sun International and Beachcomber chains both specialise in wedding packages (see Accommodation in the Mauritius Facts for the Visitor chapter).

261 6361) has hire cars starting from Rs900 per day with unlimited kilometres (based on three to six days). Most hotels should also be able to arrange car hire.

Flambeau Ltd also rents out mopeds for Rs500 per day and bicycles for Rs100 per day. Sandonna Villa (see Places to Stay) charges Rs400 per day for mopeds and Rs100 per day for bicycles. The Persand Royal supermarket (☎ 263 6660) out at Pointe aux Canonniers rents out 125cc motorcycles for Rs500 per day.

GRAND BAIE

This is the main holiday destination for Mauritians and visitors alike. Grand Baie used to be a tiny fishing village, but these days it resembles a mini San Tropez, with expensive boutiques, dozens of restaurants and practically everything in town catering to tourists. People either love or loathe the commercialism and the crowds.

Grand Baie was called De Bogt Zonder Eynt (Bay, or Bend, Without End) by the Dutch in the 17th century. The bay is remarkably blue and tropical-looking, but unfortunately the beach here is poor and the bay is congested with yachts. To make up for it, a huge range of water activities are on offer, including glass-bottomed boats, diving, cruising and undersea walks.

There are few other attractions in the area; most people come here to eat, drink and unwind in the company of other visitors. Grand Baie offers a wide choice of accommodation from cheap apartments to top-notch luxury resorts.

Orientation

Orientation in Grand Baie is easy, as everything is strung out along the coastal highway. The centre point of the town is the junction of the coastal highway and the road inland to Goodlands, which is also the departure point for express buses to Port Louis. The supermarkets sell maps at cheaper prices than most other shops.

Information

Tourist Offices There is no tourist office in town, but everyone in Grand Baie is keen to steer you towards this cruise package or that dive trip. The travel agents in town can provide slightly biased information on things to do in the area. Most also offer a range of tours and other services such as apartment rental and airport transfers.

Money The Mauritius Commercial Bank (MCB) is near the Grand Baie Store. The foreign exchange counter is open Monday to Saturday from 9 am to 5 pm and on Sunday from 9 am to noon. At the other end of town, Barclays has an exchange counter that is open the same hours as MCB. Other banks include the State Bank and Banque Nationale de Paris Intercontinentale (BNPI).

Post & Communications The post office is west of the centre on the main road; opening hours are from 8.15 to 4 pm Monday to Friday and from 8.15 to 11.45 am on Saturday. There's a poste restante facility here – letters are held for a maximum of three months (no charge).

You can make local and international calls from the public telephones on the main street. If they aren't working, the post office has a phone for local calls only. Making international calls from hotels is usually more expensive.

Bookshop Papyrus (☎ 263 7070), not far from the post office, is a reasonably well-stocked bookshop which sells a range of local and foreign magazines, newspapers, books and postcards, including up-to-date French and British newspapers. The shop is open every day except Sunday from 9 am to 6 pm.

Dangers & Annoyances The boom in tourism in the Grand Baie area has attracted petty thieves and burglars. The crimes are generally small-scale stuff, but you should never leave valuables unattended.

Temples

The **Surya Oudaya Sangam** is a vividly colourful Tamil temple at the west end of town; **Shiv Kalyan Vath Mandir** is an older Tamil temple towards Peréybère. Both are dedicated to Lord Shiva. Visitors are welcome but should behave with respect (see Society & Conduct in the Regional Facts for the Visitor chapter).

Coin de Mire, Île Plate & Îlot Gabriel

The two islands closest to the northern tip of Mauritius, Coin de Mire and Île Plate, make good day trips from Grand Baie.

Coin de Mire (Gunner's Quoin), 4km off the coast, was so named because it resembles the quoin or wedge used to steady the aim of a cannon. Landing here can be tricky, so most visitors tend to head for nearby Île Plate. Île Plate offers easier landing and good snorkelling, and has a lighthouse with nice views.

Îlot Gabriel is a pretty island just east of Île Plate; it's a popular lunch stop for day cruises.

MAURITIUS

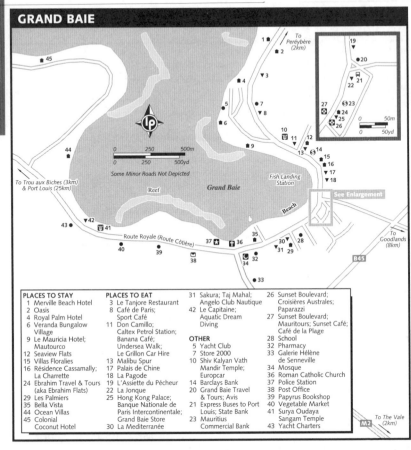

GRAND BAIE

PLACES TO STAY
1 Merville Beach Hotel
2 Oasis
4 Royal Palm Hotel
6 Veranda Bungalow
   Village
9 Le Mauricia Hotel;
   Mautourco
12 Seaview Flats
15 Villas Floralies
16 Résidence Cassamally;
   La Charrette
24 Ebrahim Travel & Tours
   (aka Ebrahim Flats)
29 Les Palmiers
35 Bella Vista
44 Ocean Villas
45 Colonial
   Coconut Hotel

PLACES TO EAT
3 Le Tanjore Restaurant
8 Café de Paris;
   Sport Café
11 Don Camillo;
   Caltex Petrol Station;
   Banana Café;
   Undersea Walk;
   Le Grillon Car Hire
13 Malibu Spur
17 Palais de Chine
18 La Pagode
19 L'Assiette du Pécheur
22 La Jonque
25 Hong Kong Palace;
   Banque Nationale de
   Paris Intercontinentale;
   Grand Baie Store
30 La Mediterranée

31 Sakura; Taj Mahal;
   Angelo Club Nautique
42 Le Capitaine;
   Aquatic Dream
   Diving

OTHER
5 Yacht Club
7 Store 2000
10 Shiv Kalyan Vath
   Mandir Temple;
   Europcar
14 Barclays Bank
20 Grand Baie Travel
   & Tours; Avis
21 Express Buses to Port
   Louis; State Bank
23 Mauritius
   Commercial Bank

26 Sunset Boulevard;
   Croisières Australes;
   Paparazzi
27 Sunset Boulevard;
   Mauritours; Sunset Café;
   Café de la Plage
28 School
32 Pharmacy
33 Galerie Hélène
   de Senneville
34 Mosque
36 Roman Catholic Church
37 Police Station
38 Post Office
39 Papyrus Bookshop
40 Vegetable Market
41 Surya Oudaya
   Sangam Temple
43 Yacht Charters

Many hotels and bungalow/flat owners can arrange boat trips to Île Plate or Îlot Gabriel for around Rs1200 per person, including lunch. Some yacht charter operations may also run day trips (see Cruises following).

Île Ronde & Île aux Serpents

Île Ronde (Round Island) and Île aux Serpents (Snake Island) are two significant nature reserves about 24km from Mauritius.

Île Ronde covers 151 hectares and scientists believe it has more endangered species than anywhere else in the world. Many of the plants, such as the hurricane palm (there are only a few left on the island) and the bottle palm, are unique to the island. The naturalist Gerald Durrell gives a very graphic description of the island in his book *Golden Bats & Pink Pigeons.*

The endemic fauna includes the keel scale boa and the burrowing boa (possibly extinct); three types of skink (Bojer's skink, Bouton's skink and Telfair's skink); and three types of gecko. Among the sea birds that breed on the island are the wedge-tailed shearwater, the white-tailed tropicbird and the gadfly petrel.

Since 1984, Île Ronde has been managed as a nature reserve by the Mauritian government and the Mauritius Wildlife Appeal Fund (MWAF). In 1986, all the goats and rabbits on the island were eradicated to give the plant species here a chance of survival. Scientists and volunteers make regular trips to the island to weed out introduced species, to plant endemic species and to conduct surveys of reptiles and birds.

Ironically, Île aux Serpents is round and has no snakes; it is a renowned bird sanctuary.

Water Activities

Hotels in Grand Baie with dive schools include Le Mauricia, Royal Palm Hotel, Merville Beach Hotel, Ocean Villas and Veranda Bungalow Village (see Places to Stay for contact details).

Private operators include Angelo Club Nautique (☎ 263 3227), Aquarius Diving (☎ 423 1361), and Aquatic Dream Diving (☎ 263 9096), all on Route Royale.

For nondivers, Undersea Walk Ltd (☎ 263 8822) beside the Caltex petrol station offers walks under the bay with a diver's helmet and weight belt for Rs750 per person. There are trips every few hours from 9 am to 3 pm. Angelo Club Nautique charges similar rates.

If you don't want to get wet, there are several semisubmersible vessels offering undersea coral-viewing tours. Le Nesseé is a distinctive yellow semisubmarine run by Croisières Australes (☎ 674 3695, fax 676 5530). It sails from Grand Baie four times daily and the one-hour trip costs Rs500 per person or Rs250 per child. Blue Safari (☎ 263 3333) is a proper submarine and leaves from the jetty by the Pescatore restaurant near Mont Choisy (Rs2000 for adults and Rs1050 for children).

For deep-sea fishing, Sportfisher (☎ 263 8358, fax 263 6309) has an office in the ocean-side section of the Sunset Boulevard arcade, and charges Rs8500/10,000 for a half/full day. Most travel agents can also arrange trips. Rates are per boat and most operators will let you split the cost with other anglers.

Cruises

Cruises are a popular activity in Grand Baie. Perhaps the most interesting is that offered by Yacht Charters Ltd (☎ 263 8395, 263 7814) on Route Royale. Its vessel, the schooner *Isla Mauritia*, was built in 1852 and was a working freighter until 1959, when the ship was refitted as a private yacht. Today the ship offers day cruises to the beach at Anse aux Filaos with lunch and traditional music for Rs1600. Contact the company directly or any of the travel agents in town.

Croisières Australes (☎ 674 3695, fax 676 5530) in the Sunset Boulevard complex offers a variety of day cruises on its luxuriously fitted catamarans. Destinations include Port Louis, Îlot Gabriel and the beach at Albion, just north of Flic en Flac. Cruise packages start at around Rs1300 including lunch and snorkelling.

Contact the travel agents in town for details of other operators; Mauritours (☎ 263 6056), in the Sunset Boulevard complex, offers the best selection.

Places to Stay – Budget

Most of the cheap accommodation in Grand Baie takes the form of bungalows or apartments. There are some excellent deals around, especially if you arrive at a quiet time of the year with three friends in tow. Most apartments are fully furnished and have a shower, kitchen, small gas cooker and fridge; only a few have air-con.

Ebrahim Travel & Tours (☎ *263 7845, fax 263 8564*) on Route Royale is otherwise known as Ebrahim Flats. Flats cost from Rs200 to Rs400 per night for a maximum of two people; Rs300 to Rs500 for a maximum of four people; and Rs450 to Rs650 for a maximum of six people. Management also organises tours and hires out cars, mopeds and bicycles.

Résidence Cassamally (☎ *263 7521, fax 263 3245*), also known as *La Résidence*, has one-bedroom self-catering apartments for Rs500, two-bedroom versions for Rs600 and a better, two-bedroom air-con flat for Rs700 per night. Prices include breakfast.

Villas Floralies (☎ 263 8269, fax 263 5379) is close to Barclays on Route Royale and offers pleasant self-catering apartments (four beds) for Rs770 and studios (two beds) for Rs500.

West of the centre, the popular *Les Palmiers* (☎ 263 8464, fax 242 8711) has a good, central location, but you should book ahead. There are two-bedroom flats (maximum of four people) for Rs600 per night and studios (maximum of two people) for Rs350 per night.

Places to Stay – Mid-Range
Apartments or bungalows to let in this range generally have better decor and facilities.

Out of town towards Peréybère, Grand Baie Travel & Tours (☎ 263 8771, fax 263 8274) manages the *Oasis*, a complex of modern apartments around a pool. Studios start from Rs1595 a double, while four-bed bungalows cost from Rs2585.

Veranda Bungalow Village (☎ 263 8015, fax 263 7369) is a beautifully laid-out complex near the yacht club at the east end of Grand Baie. The village consists of an assortment of self-catering studios and apartments that sleep from two to five people. Tariffs (including breakfast) range from Rs2450 for a basic studio to Rs4900 for a two-bedroom bungalow with verandah. All units have kitchenettes, phones, bathrooms and fans. There are also standard hotel rooms for Rs2600/3700 on half board. There is a bar, a restaurant and a swimming pool.

Closer to the centre, *Seaview Flats* (☎/fax 263 3813) is a modern complex of flats above a restaurant. Attractively furnished two-bedroom apartments with air-con, kitchen and bathroom cost Rs1450; three-bedroom apartments cost Rs1700.

West of the centre on Route Royale, *Bella Vista* (☎ 263 8489, fax 263 5195), offers singles/doubles with nice views for Rs1100/1400 with breakfast. Apartments (maximum of four people) go for Rs2000 per night. An extra bed costs Rs330.

On the coast road to Pointe aux Canonniers, *Ocean Villas* (☎ 263 6788, fax 263 8797) is another attractive option. It has two-storey units around a good pool and its own restaurant and dive school. Self-catering bungalows cost from Rs1774 a double (Rs2452 for up to four people), but rates vary throughout the year.

The pleasant *Colonial Coconut Hotel* (☎ 263 8720, fax 263 7116) is further towards Pointe aux Canonniers. Prices for singles/doubles on half board start at Rs1720/2400 in the low season and rise about 15% in the high season (November to January). On Wednesday evenings there's a traditional séga performance (Rs335). There's also a restaurant and a pool, and water activities can be arranged. It's a peaceful spot and is understandably popular, so book ahead.

Places to Stay – Top End
Royal Palm Hotel (☎ 209 8300, fax 209 8455), part of the Beachcomber group, is *the* place to stay if you're seeking pure luxury and have money to burn. Rated as one of the island's top hotels, the cheapest single/double will set you back a cool Rs12,700/19,000 including breakfast. If you're really in the mood to live it up, go for the senior suite – a luscious Rs50,000! As you would expect, the facilities here are top-notch, with a pool, restaurants and water sports galore.

Merville Beach Hotel (☎ 263 8621, fax 263 8146), further north, is much more affordable than the Royal Palm but obviously not as breathtaking. It offers the usual pool, restaurant and water sports options. It's one of the more accessible upmarket resorts, with standard rooms for Rs4975/7790 on half board. The best rooms cost Rs6275/11,198.

Le Mauricia Hotel (☎ 209 1100, fax 263 9283) is another Beachcomber hotel with a nice beach, a large pool, restaurants, tennis courts and the prerequisite water sports. Comfortable singles/doubles/triples cost Rs4800/7200/9500 on half board. Family rooms and suites are also available.

Places to Eat
You are spoiled with choices in Grand Baie. Chinese places dominate but there are also plenty of Indian, Creole and European options. However, standards and service can be pretty erratic, and a lot of the food is toned down to suit the European palate.

But I Ordered the Lobster!

Before you order the most expensive seafood dish on the menu, you should note that there is no strict convention for the naming of seafood. The normal translation for shrimps is *crevettes*, but prawns *(camarons)* may also be *crevettes*, except when they are *crevettes géantes* (in which case they shouldn't be confused with *camarons d'eau douce*, which are freshwater shrimps unless they're tiger prawns, which are also known as *rosenberghis*). Confused?

Other seafood to watch out for includes squid, which is also *mourgatte* or *calamar*, and octopus, which is also *poulpe*. The word *langouste* (lobster) covers everything from langoustines and crayfish to rock lobsters – get your waiter to explain what you're getting before you commit to a meal!

For self-caterers, the Grand Baie Store, next to the BNPI bank, and Store 2000, at the north end of town, are the best places in this area to buy groceries and other essentials. There's a vegetable market at the west end of town, open daily from 8 am to 8 pm.

There are three long-established Chinese restaurants within a stone's throw of each other on Route Royale, *La Pagode* (☎ 263 8733), *La Jonque* (☎ 263 8729) and *Palais de Chine* (☎ 263 7120). There's not much to distinguish between these places in terms of cuisine or prices. Menus include dishes such as beef with black bean sauce, and sweet and sour pork; prices start at around Rs75 for meat dishes and Rs100 for seafood. All these restaurants are open from about 11 am to 3 pm and 6 to 10 pm.

Hong Kong Palace (☎ 263 6308) is another Chinese place above the Grand Baie Store. Dishes such as shrimps with chillies, and fish with black bean sauce, cost around Rs200. The restaurant is open daily from noon to 3 pm and 7 to 10 pm.

La Charette (☎ 263 8976), also in the centre of town, offers Indian cuisine as well as Chinese and Creole dishes. Indian mains such as chicken *masala* (spicy chicken) cost from Rs150; other meals start at Rs125.

Opening hours are from noon to 3 pm and 7.30 to 11 pm daily.

For a break from Chinese food, *Don Camillo* (☎ 263 8540) near the Caltex petrol station is a popular pizzeria. Small/large pizzas cost from Rs140/170. It's open daily from noon to 2 pm and 7 to 11 pm; for evening meals you should book.

Paparazzi (☎ 263 8836) in the Sunset Boulevard complex is a stylish Italian restaurant serving authentic pizzas for Rs150 to Rs200, and pasta dishes from Rs210. It's open daily from noon to 3 pm and 7 to 11 pm.

Malibu Spur (☎ 263 6419) on Route Royale offers juicy steaks and Mexican dishes. The somewhat sexist menu includes 300g men's steaks for Rs290, and 200g women's steaks for Rs190. It's open from 11 am to 11 pm daily.

La Méditerranée (☎ 263 8019) does good French and Creole food. Mains such as *entrecôte* (sirloin steak) and *carri poulet* (chicken curry) cost from Rs190 to Rs290. This restaurant is open daily except Sunday from 11 am to 2.30 pm and 6.30 to 10.30 pm.

L'Assiette du Pêcheur (☎ 263 8589), also known as Phil's Pub, is another seafood place, with main dishes for around Rs180. It's open daily for lunch and dinner.

Sunset Café (☎ 263 9602) looks out over the bay from the Sunset Boulevard complex and is good for lunch. Crepes are Rs90, salads cost Rs160 and fish and chips costs Rs200. It's open daily from 8.30 am to 7 pm.

North of the centre, *Café de Paris* (☎ 263 8022) serves good French food such as steak with Roquefort sauce for around Rs240, as well as decent coffee. It's open from 8 am to 11 pm.

Next door, *Sport Café* (☎ 263 9188) is a garish modern place that offers grills, Creole food and loud music. Mains cost from Rs90. It's open from 8 am to midnight daily.

Nearby, *Le Tanjore* (☎ 263 6030) is a large restaurant serving Indian dishes such as chicken *pasanda* (a curry with almonds and sesame seeds). Prices vary from Rs140 for tandoori chicken to Rs600 for lobster or king prawns. It's open from noon to 3 pm and 7 to 10 pm daily.

West of the centre, *Taj Mahal* (☎ 263 4984) offers good north Indian cuisine and has several vegetarian options. Mains cost around Rs150. The restaurant is open from noon to 2 pm and 6.30 to 10 pm daily.

A few doors away, *Sakura* (☎ 263 5700) is a pricey but authentic Japanese restaurant, with dishes such as tempura and sushi for Rs295 to Rs395. You'll have to call ahead for *shabu-shabu* and sukiyaki. The restaurant is open daily from noon to 2.30 pm and 6.30 to 10.30 pm.

On the outskirts of town, *Le Capitaine* (☎ 263 8108) has a pleasant setting by the sea, but the food gets mixed reports from travellers. Dishes such as squid in Creole sauce cost from Rs185 to Rs400. It's open daily from 12.30 to 3 pm and 7.30 to 9.30 pm.

Entertainment

Most major hotels in Grand Baie lay on at least one séga night per week. Tickets usually cost between Rs300 and Rs600 (including a buffet dinner).

Hotels often have other forms of entertainment such as live music and theme evenings.

Apart from the hotels, the most popular venue in town is the *Banana Café* (☎ 263 8450), which serves cocktails until late. Other local nightspots include *Skanners* at the Sport Café, *Speedy* and *Dream On*. Entry to discos usually costs at least Rs100.

Shopping

As befits the nation's leading resort, Grand Baie has a host of boutiques selling somewhat expensive swimwear, designer clothes and souvenirs. Don't hold your breath for a bargain; prices are higher here than anywhere else in Mauritius. Your best bet for clothing is the chic Sunset Boulevard complex; there's a branch of Fast-Forward here. There's a branch of Habit near La Jonque restaurant.

For gifts to take home, there are numerous souvenir shops along the main road selling batiks, T-shirts and other souvenirs.

The supermarkets sell postcards at cheaper prices than most other shops. Here you can also pick up a snorkel, mask and flipper set for around Rs600.

Getting There & Away

Triolet buses en route from Immigration Square in Port Louis to Cap Malheureux will drop you in Grand Baie for Rs14 (one hour). Express buses run directly between Port Louis and Grand Baie every hour, also charging Rs14. The bus stop in Grand Baie is off the main road, opposite Grand Baie Travel & Tours.

Buses between Pamplemousses and Grand Baie cost Rs10.

For taxi rides from Grand Baie, expect to pay Rs100 to Trou aux Biches, Rs350 to Port Louis and around Rs700 to the airport. Taxis usually charge a little more after dark.

Getting Around

Car Ebrahim Travel & Tours (☎ 263 7845, fax 263 8564) is probably the cheapest option for car hire, charging Rs500 to 800 per day for a small hatchback. Le Grillon (☎ 263 6233) at the Caltex station charges between Rs600 and Rs1200 for cars and small jeeps, depending on how long you hire for. Europcar (☎ 263 7948) and Avis (☎ 263 7600) both have offices in town and charge from around Rs1400 per day.

Find out whether the management of your hotel or guesthouse has a special discount agreement with a local company.

Motorcycle Mopeds are widely available in Grand Baie; rental charges hover at around Rs450 per day, but you should negotiate a discount if you intend renting for a few days. A deposit of around Rs1000 per moped seems to be standard practice. One option is Ebrahim Travel & Tours, right in the centre on Route Royale, which charges around Rs400.

Bicycle Many hotels, guesthouses and travel agents can arrange bicycle hire. Rates vary, but expect to pay between Rs100 and Rs150 per day, or less if you hire for several days. Many of the independent tour operators have bikes in front of their offices; just walk down Route Royale and see what's on offer. Check out the condition of your bike before you set off, as you'll have trouble finding a lift back if you get a puncture.

PERÉYBÈRE

Peréybère is a rapidly expanding resort a couple of kilometres north of Grand Baie which caters to Mauritian holidaymakers as well as overseas visitors. It has a good beach, and a good range of budget eating places and accommodation.

On the main public beach, the persistence of souvenir pedlars and people trying to sell you excursions can sometimes become wearisome.

Activities

Most people come here just to unwind beside the beautiful azure lagoon, but there's also good snorkelling and windsurfing offshore. The best coral can be found directly off the public beach (watch out for glass-bottomed boats and water-skiers). You can buy snorkelling gear from the supermarkets in Grand Baie.

Places to Stay

In general, the cheaper places are set back from the sea.

L'Escala (☎ *263 7379, fax 240 0117*) is behind the arcade at the southern end of town, and charges Rs450 to Rs600 for self-catering studios and Rs800 for apartments that sleep four.

On Route Royale, *Peréybère Beach Apartments* (☎ */fax 263 8679*) has nicely furnished studios for Rs500, and apartments with two bedrooms, a bathroom and a kitchen for Rs700.

Also on Route Royale, *Côte d'Azur* (☎ *263 8165, fax 263 6353*) offers a variety of rooms and apartments. Air-con hotel rooms cost Rs300 a double, self-catering studios are Rs737, two-bedroom apartments are Rs1289 and well-equipped suites with four beds and hot spa cost Rs2578.

On the road behind Côte d'Azur, *Krissy's Apartments* (☎ *263 8859*) is a friendly place consisting of studios and two-bedroom self-catering apartments which cost Rs500 and Rs880 respectively.

Around the corner from Krissy's, *Fred's Apartments* (☎ *263 8830, fax 263 7531*) is one of the better options in Peréybère. Fred's caters particularly to German visitors, but all nationalities are welcome. Single/double studios cost Rs1022/1123 and two-bedroom bungalows (maximum of four people) cost Rs1612 per night, all including breakfast.

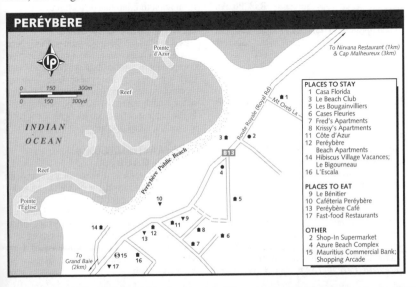

PERÉYBÈRE

INDIAN OCEAN

Reef

Reef

Pointe l'Église

Pointe d'Azur

Peréybère Public Beach

Route Royale (Royal Rd)

Mt Oreb La

B13

To Nirvana Restaurant (1km) & Cap Malheureux (3km)

To Grand Baie (2km)

0   150   300m
0   150   300yd

PLACES TO STAY
1 Casa Florida
3 Le Beach Club
5 Les Bougainvilliers
6 Cases Fleuries
7 Fred's Apartments
8 Krissy's Apartments
11 Côte d'Azur
12 Peréybère
   Beach Apartments
14 Hibiscus Village Vacances;
   Le Bigourneau
16 L'Escala

PLACES TO EAT
9 Le Bénitier
10 Caféteria Peréybère
13 Peréybère Café
17 Fast-food Restaurants

OTHER
2 Shop-In Supermarket
4 Azure Beach Complex
15 Mauritius Commercial Bank;
   Shopping Arcade

One street back from Fred's, ***Cases Fleuries*** (☎ *263 8868, fax 208 1614*) has a variety of apartments set in a lovely garden, but the atmosphere is slightly snooty. Self-catering studios cost Rs913 a double and apartments sleeping four to six range from Rs1460 to Rs1695.

Behind the new Azur Beach shopping mall, ***Les Bougainvilliers*** (☎*/fax 263 8807*) is a well-maintained complex of self-catering apartments. Studios go for Rs450 a double, two-bedroom apartments are Rs550 and three-bedroom apartments are Rs700.

Casa Florida (☎ *263 7371, fax 263 6209*) on Mt Oreb La is more upmarket. Set in a pleasant garden, self-catering single/double studios cost Rs750/880. Two-bedroom apartments with kitchen cost Rs1120 for two or Rs1340 for four people. There are also some singles/doubles for Rs550/680 or superior rooms for Rs1280/1480. All rates include breakfast. Half board costs an extra Rs150 per person. There's a swimming pool.

At the north end of the public beach, ***Le Beach Club*** (☎ *263 5104, fax 263 5202*) is a complex of nicely furnished self-catering apartments on the seafront. Studios cost from Rs1300 to Rs1450, and larger apartments with separate lounge are Rs2300. All apartments have air-con.

The upmarket ***Hibiscus Village Vacances*** (☎ 263 8554, fax 263 8553) at the southern end of the public beach offers very pleasant accommodation, plus a dive centre and restaurant. Single/double rooms are Rs1570/2070, including breakfast; on half board they're Rs1810/2550. Special séga nights are held here on Sunday.

Places to Eat

Self-caterers should head for the ***Shop-In*** supermarket in the middle of town.

For a cheap beach munch, there are several fast-food places along Route Royale serving pizza and fried chicken.

The ever popular ***Peréybère Café*** (☎ *263 8700*), across the road from the public beach, serves up Chinese dishes such as chicken with black fungus from Rs75 and more.

The cafe shouldn't be confused with ***Cafétaria Peréybère*** (☎ *263 8539*), right beside the public beach. This friendly snack place offers light meals including grilled fish, or steak and chips, for around Rs95. It's open daily from 10.30 am to 10.30 pm.

The ***restaurant*** at Fred's Apartments (see Places to Stay) serves tasty Creole meals for between Rs95 and Rs160.

Moving upmarket, ***Le Bénitier*** (☎ *263 8827*) is popular in the evenings and offers seafood standards such as fish with lemon and butter for between Rs90 and Rs180. It's open from noon to 2 pm and 7.30 to 10 pm. The bar here is open till late.

Le Bigorneau at Hibiscus Village Vacances (see Places to Stay) offers a Creole barbecue and a séga show every Sunday for Rs400. At other times, seafood dishes cost from Rs200 to Rs450. It's open from noon to 2.30 pm and 7.30 to 10 pm daily.

Arguably the best restaurant on the north coast, ***Nirvana*** (☎ *262 6068*) is 1km north of the centre and offers spectacular Indian food in a stylish dining room. Dishes from the tandoori oven include *murg makhni* (chicken with tomato-and-cream sauce) and tandoori white prawns. A main course with rice and naan bread will set you back around Rs450. The restaurant is open daily except Sunday from noon to 2 pm and 7 to 10 pm.

Getting There & Around

Buses to Cap Malheureux stop in Peréybère as well as Grand Baie. Most of the car-hire companies in Grand Baie will drop off and pick up cars in Peréybère (see Getting Around in the Grand Baie section). Find out if the management of your hotel or guesthouse has a special discount agreement with any of the local operators.

CAP MALHEUREUX & GRAND GAUBE

Cap Malheureux is a peaceful village with a picturesque church, the Nôtre Dame Auxilia Trice, and a good view of Coin de Mire island. The most northerly tip of Mauritius, it was named the 'Cape of Misfortune' after several ships were wrecked in the area.

Grand Gaube, about 6km east of Cap Malheureux, is a small fishing village with a decent beach.

MAURITIUS

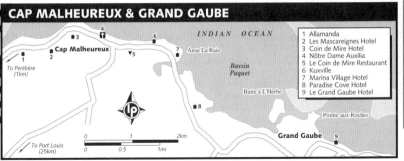

CAP MALHEUREUX & GRAND GAUBE

1 Allamanda
2 Les Mascareignes Hotel
3 Coin de Mire Hotel
4 Nôtre Dame Auxilia
5 Le Coin de Mire Restaurant
6 Kuxville
7 Marina Village Hotel
8 Paradise Cove Hotel
9 Le Grand Gaube Hotel

Places to Stay & Eat

The cheap and cheery *Allamanda* (☎ 263 8110), towards Cap Malheureux, is a complex of self-catering apartments about 2km north of Peréybère. Basic one-bedroom apartments (maximum of two people) cost Rs200 per night and two-bedroom apartments (maximum of four people) are Rs300 per night.

Coin de Mire Hotel (☎ 262 7302, fax 262 7305) is opposite Coin de Mire island and has comfortable self-catering studios (for a maximum of two people) for Rs1900. Singles/doubles/triples cost Rs1130/1325/1950 on half board (these rates apply from February to November; prices are higher in December and January). There's a pool, a restaurant, water activities, and bicycles for hire.

Kuxville (☎ 262 7913, fax 262 7407) about 1.5km east of Cap Malheureux village is a popular apartment resort with a strong German flavour. There's a small dive school here, and accommodation is in bungalows, apartments or studios, which sleep two to four people. Rates are given in euros and must be paid in foreign currency. Two-bed units cost from €60; four-bed units range from €65 to €90.

The *Marina Resort* (☎ 262 7651, fax 262 7650, e marinah@intnet.mu) is just east of Kuxville, at Anse La Raie. Spacious units with terraces or balconies start at Rs2300/ 3400 for a single/double on the ground floor, or Rs2530/3860 for a first-floor unit. Rates are on a half-board basis. Facilities include a pool, a tennis court and a restaurant.

Paradise Cove Hotel (☎ 262 7983, fax 262 7736, e pch.anse@bow.intnet.mu) at Anse La Raie is a fabulous choice if you can afford it. The standard of service at this Indian-themed hotel is very high, and luxurious singles/doubles go for Rs5450/8200, while opulent suites cost Rs6450/9200. These rates include half board. There are two restaurants, a swimming pool, tennis courts and a multitude of water activities.

The restaurant Le Coin de Mire (☎ 262 8070), opposite the church in Cap Malheureux, has a few two-bedroom and studio apartments. Prices start at Rs500 for a two-bedroom apartment without kitchen, or Rs600 with kitchen; studios start from Rs600. The restaurant itself specialises in Creole and Chinese food. It's open daily from 10.30 am to 10 pm and offers various set menus which consist of a main course and a starter or desert for Rs225 to Rs375. Individual dishes from the menu cost from Rs100 to Rs300.

Le Grand Gaube Hotel (☎ 283 9350, fax 283 9420) is an upmarket hotel with comfortable singles/doubles starting from Rs2375/3925 with breakfast (Rs2765/4705 on half board). There's a pool, a restaurant and a nice beach here, but the service can be a little variable.

Getting There & Around

There are frequent buses running between Cap Malheureux or Grand Gaube and Port Louis (which leave Port Louis from the Immigration Square bus station) for Rs15. A taxi to Port Louis will cost at least Rs500; Rs850 to the airport.

MAURITIUS

GOODLANDS

Goodlands is a fairly unremarkable regional centre. It's worth calling in to the large Historic Marine model boat-building factory at the St Antoine Industrial Estate, on the road to Poudre d'Or (see Shopping in the Mauritius Facts for the Visitor chapter). There is also an impressive Hindu temple in town.

If you're coming from Port Louis (Immigration Square bus station) there is a regular bus service to Goodlands (Rs13) and Grand Gaube via Pamplemousses (Rs15).

POUDRE D'OR

This small settlement was the setting for the events that inspired the most famous Mauritian story. The *St Géran* was wrecked in a storm and sank off the coast near here in 1744, with many lives lost. The disaster inspired the love story *Paul et Virginie*, by Bernardin de St Pierre (see the boxed text 'Paul & Virginie').

The *St Géran* was carrying machinery from France for the first sugar refinery on the island. A French dive expedition excavated the wreck in 1966 and the results on the expedition are on display at the Naval Museum in Mahébourg. A small, disappointing monument was erected on the shore near Poudre d'Or in 1944.

The village is also believed by some to be the final resting place of the treasure accrued by the infamous French pirate Olivier Levasseur, also known as La Buse (The Buzzard). About 200m north from Ste Philomène Church is a deep hole at the river's edge which is said to lead to a tunnel, perhaps connecting with another under the church or at the shore. A French team of treasure-hunting divers unofficially and unsuccessfully tried to excavate the hole, but they found only a few coins. Bel Ombre in the Seychelles has also been the subject of a long and controversial search for La Buse's treasure (see the North Mahé section in the Seychelles chapter for more information).

Buses to Poudre d'Or cost Rs13.

Paul & Virginie

Mauritius' most popular folk tale tells the story of two lovers, Paul and Virginie, who encounter tragedy when the ship that is carrying Virginie flounders on the reef. Although Paul swims out to the wreck to save her, Virginie modestly refuses to remove her clothes to swim ashore, and she drowns; Paul dies of a broken heart shortly after.

The story was written by Bernardin de St Pierre in the 18th century, but was inspired by a real-life tragedy that took place some years earlier. In 1744, the ship *St Géran* was wrecked during a storm off Île d'Ambre. Two female passengers who refused to undress to swim ashore were dragged down by the weight of their clothes. The true story is more a tragedy of social mores than one of romance!

Relics from the *St Géran* are on display in the Naval Museum in Mahébourg, while a small monument at Poudre d'Or commemorates the wreck. You'll run into Paul and Virginie everywhere in Mauritius; perhaps the most famous monument is the sculpture by Prosper d'Epinay near the town hall in Curepipe.

MARTIN HARRIS

PAMPLEMOUSSES

This small village (pronounced pamp-lay-moose, meaning 'grapefruit') was named for the citrus trees that were introduced into Mauritius from Java by the Dutch. Appropriately, it's home to the Sir Seewoosagur Ramgoolam Botanical Gardens (sometimes referred to as the Royal Botanical Gardens), which feature a stunning variety of endemic and foreign plant species.

Pamplemousses provided a testing site for new sugar cane varieties. In 1866, when a malaria epidemic hit Mauritius, the botanical gardens also acted as a nursery for the eucalyptus trees used to dry out the marshes, the breeding sites of the mosquitoes.

Sir Seewoosagur Ramgoolam Botanical Gardens

These attractive gardens are one of the most popular tourist attractions in Mauritius, but the shady avenues of palms seem to swallow the numbers. If you are not botanically minded, you probably will be after a visit. If you are so minded, you won't want to leave. The gates (all the way from Crystal Palace in London) are open each day from 8.30 am to 5.30 pm and entry is free.

SIR SEEWOOSAGUR RAMGOOLAM BOTANICAL GARDENS

1 Old Sugar Mill
2 Tortoise Pens
3 Medicinal Garden
4 Tortoise Pens
5 Sir Seewoosagur Ramgoolam Cremation Site
6 Mon Plaisir Château
7 Fernery
8 Giant Bamboo
9 Grand Bassin
10 Bernardin de St Pierre Statue
11 Lotus Pond
12 Water Lily Pond
13 Stanley Alexander de Smith Memorial
14 Liénard Monument
15 Church
16 Cemetery
17 Entrance Gate
18 Royal Palms
19 Talipot Palms
20 Post des Soupirs (Bridge of Sighs)
21 Bus Stop

The gardens are best seen with a guide, as few plants are labelled and you'll miss many of the most interesting species if you go alone. You can hire a guide by the main gates for around Rs50 per person. Make sure you negotiate a fee and the duration of your tour *before* you start. If you are happy with your guide, you may like to give a tip.

The gardens were started by Governor Mahé de La Bourdonnais in 1735, as a vegetable garden for his Mon Plaisir Château. The gardens came into their own in 1768 under the auspices of the French horticulturalist Pierre Poivre. Like Kew Gardens in England, the gardens played a significant role in the horticultural espionage of the day. Poivre imported spice plants from around the world in a bid to end France's dependence on Asian spices. The gardens were neglected between 1810 and 1849 until British horticulturalist James Duncan reinvented the gardens as an arboretum for palms and other tropical trees.

Palms, rather than flowers, constitute the most important part of the horticultural display, and they come in an astonishing variety of shapes and forms. Some of the more prominent are the stubby bottle palms, the tall royal palms lining Poivre Ave, and the talipot palms, which flower once after 40 to 60 years and then die. Other varieties include the raffia, sugar, toddy, fever, fan and even sex palms. There are many other curious tree species on display, including giant bamboo, the marmalade box tree, the fish poison tree, the chewing-gum tree and the sausage tree.

The centrepiece of the gardens is a pond filled with giant Victoria regia water lilies, native to the Amazon region. Young leaves emerge as wrinkled balls and are forced into the classic tea-tray shape by hydraulic pressure. The flowers at the centre of the huge trays open white one day and close red the next.

Another interesting attraction is the medicinal herb garden with plants that are said to cure everything from indigestion to stuttering. As you walk around, your guide will draw your attention to some of the aromatic species including ginger, cinnamon, nutmeg, camphor, eucalyptus and sandalwood.

Various international dignitaries have planted trees in the gardens, including Nelson Mandela and Indira Gandhi. The gardens also house the funerary platform where Sir Seewoosagur Ramgoolam, the first prime minister of Mauritius after independence, was cremated. His ashes were scattered on the Ganges in India. There is also an enclosure with Java deer and a pen of giant Aldabra tortoises.

The Mon Plaisir Château at the back of the gardens is now used for administration and is not open to the public. It is not the original palace; the 'old sugar mill' is also a reconstruction.

December to April is the best time to visit the gardens. It's a big place, so you'll need time and a decent map, such as the one in this book.

Getting There & Away

Pamplemousses is 11km north-east of Port Louis. To get there, take a bus to Grand Gaube, Rivière du Rempart, Roches Noires or Centre de Flacq from the Immigration Square bus station in Port Louis. There are also some direct buses from Peréybère and Grand Baie. From Trou aux Biches and Grand Baie you can also go up to Grand Gaube and change buses, or down to Port Louis and change there. Buses stop on the highway beside the gardens; it's a five-minute walk along Mapou Rd to the main gate of the gardens.

Central Mauritius

Although Mauritius is promoted primarily as a 'beach' destination, the island offers some attractive hiking opportunities for those looking for something more than sun, sea and sand. Most lowland areas have been turned over to sugar cane, but some sizeable pockets of forest remain, particularly on the steep slopes of the island's many mountain peaks, offering a variety of half-day and whole-day hikes and rambles.

The central plateau of the island is split between the Plaines Wilhems district in the south and west and the Moka district in the north and east. Plaines Wilhems is the main residential area of Mauritius, with a number of towns practically linked to each other from Port Louis down to Curepipe.

The Moka mountain range fringes the area to the north; the Black River range to the west. Quartier Militaire is at the centre of the Moka district and is, perhaps as the name suggests, the bleakest area on the island. South of Curepipe, around Mare aux Vacoas, the countryside is more appealing. The climate is cooler and less humid on the plateau and the way of life more European. The region to the south-west of Curepipe is a natural parkland and mini lake district and is pleasant for drives and walks.

The largest lake on the island is the reservoir Mare aux Vacoas. It is flanked on the west (3km away) by Mare Longue and Tamarin Falls, which are accessible from the Tamarin road.

The towns on the plateau are predominantly residential with few sites of interest, but most tourists come here for a little 'retail therapy' in the cheap clothing stores. Curepipe is traditionally the first stop, but these days Rose Hill and Quatre Bornes both offer better variety and lower prices. Phoenix and Floreal are also worth a detour for their discount clothing stores.

CUREPIPE

The area around Curepipe owes its size and prominence to the malaria epidemic of

> ### HIGHLIGHTS
>
> * Taking in the views from the rim of the Trou aux Cerfs crater in Curepipe
> * Rambling through the beautiful Black River Gorges National Park
> * Visiting Eureka, a beautifully restored Creole mansion near Moka
> * Touring the entertaining historical and cultural centre at Domaine des Pailles near Moka

1867, which caused thousands of people to flee infested Port Louis for the healthier hill country. Some claim that the name Curepipe originates from the days when soldiers from the Quartier Militaire would stop here to smoke and 'cure' (clean) their pipes, but most likely it's named after Curepipe in the south-west of France.

Curepipe is a fairly prosperous market town, but the damp weather gives most of the buildings here an ageing, mildewy quality. It can rain without warning on the plateau, so bring an umbrella. Many Franco-Mauritians live in the suburbs surrounding the town, particularly Floreal. The town is worth visiting if only to see the contrast with Port Louis. It also offers better shopping than the capital and is peaceful by comparison.

Orientation

Curepipe is bisected by Route Royale heading towards Mahébourg, which runs approximately north-south through the middle of town. Most of the banks and restaurants are on this street. The centre point of the town is the junction between Route Royale and Châteauneuf St; Châteauneuf St runs east towards the bus station.

The terminal for northbound buses (and the public market) lies on the north side of Châteauneuf St, at the junction with Victoria Ave; the terminal for southbound buses is on the south side of the street.

MAURITIUS

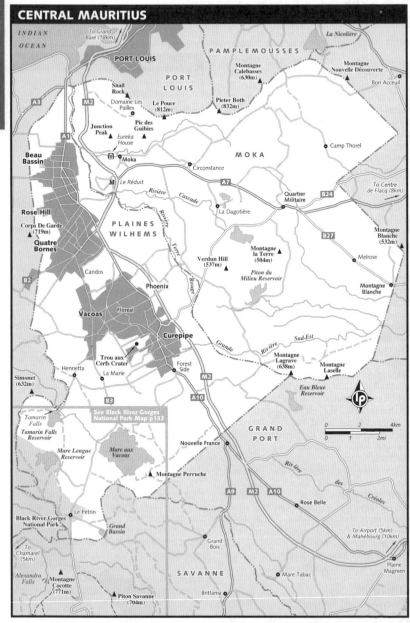

CENTRAL MAURITIUS

INDIAN
OCEAN

To Grand
Baie (18km)

La Nicolière

PORT LOUIS

PAMPLEMOUSSES

Montagne
Calebasses
(630m)

Montagne
Nouvelle Découverte

PORT
LOUIS

Bon Acceuil

Snail
Rock

A3

M2

Domaine Les
Pailles

Le Pouce
(812m)

Pieter Both
(832m)

Junction
Peak

Pic des
Guibies

A1

Eureka
House

Camp Thorel

MOKA

Moka

Circonstance

Le Réduit

Rivière

A7

Quartier
Militaire

B24

To Centre
de Flacq (8km)

Cascade

Beau
Bassin

La Dagotière

Rivière

Rose Hill

Corps De Garde
(719m)

Quatre
Bornes

B2

PLAINES
WILHEMS

Rivière

Terre

Verdun Hill
(537m)

Montagne
la Terre
(504m)

B27

Montagne
Blanche
(532m)

Melrose

Candos

Rouge

Piton du
Milieu Reservoir

Montagne
Blanche

Phoenix

Vacoas

Floreal

Curepipe

Trou aux
Cerfs Crater

Simonet
(632m)

Henrietta

La Marie

Forest
Side

M2

A10

Grande

Rivière

Sud-Est

Montagne
Lagrave
(638m)

Montagne
Laselle

Eau Bleue
Reservoir

B3

See Black River Gorges
National Park Map p132

Tamarin
Falls

Tamarin Falls
Reservoir

Mare Longue
Reservoir

Mare aux
Vacoas

Nouvelle France

GRAND
PORT

0   2   4km
0   1   2mi

Montagne Perruche

Rivière

A9

M2

A10

Rose Belle

des

Créoles

Black River Gorges
National Park

Le Pétrin

Grand
Bassin

To
Chamarel
(5km)

Grand
Bois

To Airport (5km)
& Mahébourg (10km)

Alexandra
Falls

Montagne
Cocotte
(771m)

Piton Savanne
(704m)

SAVANNE

Mare Tabac

Brittania

Plaine
Magnien

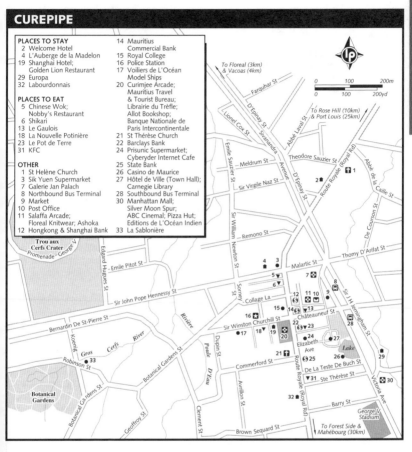

CUREPIPE

PLACES TO STAY
2 Welcome Hotel
4 L'Auberge de la Madelon
19 Shanghai Hotel;
   Golden Lion Restaurant
29 Europa
32 Labourdonnais

PLACES TO EAT
5 Chinese Wok;
   Nobby's Restaurant
6 Shikari
13 Le Gaulois
18 La Nouvelle Potinière
23 Le Pot de Terre
31 KFC

OTHER
1 St Helène Church
3 Sik Yuen Supermarket
7 Galerie Jan Palach
8 Northbound Bus Terminal
9 Market
10 Post Office
11 Salaffa Arcade;
   Floreal Knitwear; Ashoka
12 Hongkong & Shanghai Bank

14 Mauritius
   Commercial Bank
15 Royal College
16 Police Station
17 Voiliers de L'Océan
   Model Ships
20 Curimjee Arcade;
   Mauritius Travel
   & Tourist Bureau;
   Librairie du Trèfle;
   Allot Bookshop;
   Banque Nationale de
   Paris Intercontinentale
21 St Thérèse Church
22 Barclays Bank
24 Prisunic Supermarket;
   Cyberyder Internet Cafe
25 State Bank
26 Casino de Maurice
27 Hôtel de Ville (Town Hall);
   Carnegie Library
28 Southbound Bus Terminal
30 Manhattan Mall;
   Silver Moon Spur;
   ABC Cinemal; Pizza Hut;
   Editions de L'Océan Indien
33 La Sablonière

To Floreal (3km)
& Vacoas (4km)

To Rose Hill (10km)
& Port Louis (25km)

To Forest Side &
Mahébourg (30km)

Information

Tourist Office There is no tourist office in Curepipe, but the Mauritius Travel & Tourist Bureau or MTTB (☎ 676 3055, fax 675 5863) on Sir John Pope Hennessy St may be able to answer questions; it also has the usual tour services.

Money Most of the banks are on Route Royale. The two main banks, the Mauritius Commercial Bank (MCB) and Barclays, are opposite each other at the western end of Châteauneuf St. Further along the main road, towards Mahébourg, is the Banque Nationale de Paris Intercontinentale and the State Commercial Bank. Towards Port Louis is the Hongkong & Shanghai Bank.

Post & Communications The main post office (☎ 676 3085) is behind the bus station and is open from 8.15 am to 4 pm on weekdays and from 8.15 to 11.45 am on Saturdays. Poste restante is also here (free service).

The Cyberyder Internet Cafe in the Prisunic supermarket is open daily except Sunday from 10 am to 5.30 pm, charging Rs1.5 per minute.

Creole Architecture

The traditional Creole mansion is a brilliantly conceived solution to the problems associated with living in the wet tropics. Flourishes that at first appear to be ornamental – vaulted roofs and decorative pierced screens, for example – all serve a purpose, namely to keep the occupants cool and dry during the changeable tropical weather. You can see splendid examples of this vanishing architectural style in Mauritius, Réunion and the Seychelles.

The most striking feature of Creole buildings is the elaborate shingled roof, which usually rises in tiers, with ornamental turrets and rows of attic windows. These wedding-cake touches conceal a basic principle of physics. The vaulted roof-space creates a cushion of cool air over the living area that can be almost as effective as air-conditioning. This air cushion also allows for the free movement of water vapour, which eliminates the problems of dampness that plague modern concrete houses. Compare the dry and airy Creole houses of central Mauritius to the mildewed modern blocks!

The roof shingles are traditionally made from local hardwoods, the most popular being the *tamarin des hautes* (mountain tamarind), which naturally splits into flat strips. These resilient woods are able to shrink and expand with the changing temperature without splitting or becoming vulnerable to decay. The black coloration comes from a mixture of bitumen, ash from the *madrepore* tree and permanganate, applied to keep away the termites.

Another distinctive feature of Creole houses are the delicate, lace-like *lambrequins* or *dentelles* (rows of carved wooden borders) which line the roofs, windows and overhangs. These vary from simple, repetitive floral patterns to elaborate pierced *frises*; in all cases a botanical theme predominates. This fine fretwork was traditionally executed in fine-grained wood, but these days it's often just pressed from aluminium sheeting. The little decorative details over windows and doors, known as *auvents,* are also appealing.

Because of the stifling heat, Creole houses are extremely well ventilated; the old Eureka mansion near Moka boasts an incredible 109 doors and windows. However, in the heat of the summer, this was not always enough, hence the incorporation of a wide, airy *varangue* (veranda). These verandas form an integral part of the character of Creole houses. It was common for the well-heeled citizens who lived in these palatial houses to receive their guests on the veranda, sipping tea or gin and tonic and looking out over the manicured lawns of the estate.

To keep the veranda cool, most were fitted with raffia blinds, and filled with tropical plants to create a cooling humidity. Perforated screens tended to be used in place of glass because of the risk from cyclones. The roofs of the verandas were traditionally coated with *argamasse*, a traditional Indian preservative consisting of wood-lime, eggs, sugar and crushed tiles.

Many of the Creole buildings in the Indian Ocean have stood at several different locations in their lifetime. Because of their wooden construction, these remarkable dwellings could be dismantled piece by piece and reconstructed elsewhere. During the cholera and malaria epidemics of the 19th century, the Creole mansions of Mauritius moved around the countryside like chess pieces as families tried to stay one step ahead of the plagues.

This mobility has also been the downfall of many Creole buildings. Restoring Creole houses is expensive and time consuming, and many of the raw materials such as tamarind wood are in short supply. It's easier and more profitable for developers to rip down the old timber frames, and throw up brand new concrete blocks on the sturdy foundations beneath.

MAURITIUS

Creole Architecture

In the Seychelles, only a handful of old mansions have survived the push for modernisation. Most notable is the Maison de Planteur at Anse aux Courbes on Mahé, a classic Creole villa dating to 1792. As a result of the tall vaulted roof, the interior is wonderfully cool. The villa is filled with period furnishings and is open to the public. Nearby, another old Creole palace now houses the Kreol Institute. The splendid former governor's residence in Victoria is now the office of President René; you can't visit, but you may catch a glimpse of this lovely Creole building as you pass by the gates.

Mauritius has fared much better, though many of the most stunning examples of Creole architecture are privately owned and closed to the public. A visit to Eureka, a beautifully restored Creole mansion near Moka, should not be missed. Other high-profile Creole houses include the *hôtel de ville* (town hall) in Curepipe, which was moved to Curepipe from Moka in 1903; Le Réduit, near Moka, which is now used by the Mauritian military; and the Naval Museum in Mahébourg, formerly the home of the De Robillard family.

A remarkable number of old houses also survive in Port Louis. Government House and the buildings that line Place d'Armes in the centre of town are all fine examples. Possibly the most interesting Creole building on the island is the Jummah mosque on Royal St in Port Louis, which was built in the 1850s, and incorporates features of Indian, Creole and Islamic architecture.

Réunion has perhaps fared best of all the islands, probably because of the influence of the French heritage movement. The best examples of Creole town houses can be found along Rue de Paris in St-Denis (the birthplace of the poet Léon Dierx is probably the finest house here), while Hell-Bourg, high up in the Cirque de Salazie, preserves a number of more human-scaled Creole homes.

ILLUSTRATIONS BY KELLI HAMBLET

Curepipe Hôtel de Ville (Town Hall)

Bookshops Allot Bookshop and Librairie du Trèfle, both in the Curimjee Arcade, have a reasonably good selection of books and magazines in French and English. Editions de L'Océan Indien (☎ 674 9065) in the Manhattan Mall has a few title on Mauritius.

Trou aux Cerfs

Possibly the main attraction of Curepipe for tourists, apart from the shopping, is the Trou aux Cerfs crater. The volcano has been extinct for a long time and the crater floor is now heavily wooded, but the crater affords lovely views around the island. A sealed road leads gently up to and around the rim. There are benches for rest and reflection and a radar station for keeping an electronic eye on cyclone activity.

Hôtel de Ville

Located in a small park by the southbound bus station, the *hôtel de ville* (town hall) is one of the best surviving examples of traditional Creole architecture. Originally known as La Malmaison, the house was moved piecemeal from Moka in 1903.

In the gardens is an ornamental pond and a famous bronze statue of the fictitious lovers Paul and Virginie, by Mauritian sculptor Prosper d'Epinay. There are also statues of the French astronomer Abbé la Caille and the poet Paul Jean Toulet. Behind the town hall is the Carnegie Library.

Botanical Gardens

These well-kept and informal gardens are a pleasant spot for some quiet contemplation. In the middle is a stand of rare Mauritian species with several nature trails leading off from the main paths. The gardens are open daily from 6 am to 6 pm and entry is free.

La Sablonière

Near the botanical gardens on Robinson St is the house known as La Sablonière, which used to belong to the family of Mauritian poet Malcolm de Chazal. In the garden is a scale model of the Eiffel Tower dating from 1889. It's now an exclusive carpet shop, but you're welcome to look around the grounds.

Places to Stay

Accommodation is rather dreary in Curepipe, probably because most tourists opt to come here on a day trip rather than stay overnight.

Welcome Hotel (☎ 674 7292) on Route Royale is one of the best budget options, with tidy rooms with shared bathroom for Rs350/450 including breakfast.

L'Auberge de la Madelon (☎ 676 1520, fax 676 2550, 10 Sir John Pope Hennessy St) is another good choice. Comfortable rooms with private bathroom, fan, TV and phone cost Rs420/440/500 for singles/doubles/triples including breakfast.

Labourdonnais (☎ 676 1634, 270 Route Royale) is past St Thérèse Church and offers mediocre doubles with bathroom for Rs400 (Rs300 without bathroom).

Europa (☎ 676 6000, fax 676 5084) is a soulless edifice east of the lake and is often used for conferences. Characterless rooms (all doubles) cost from Rs360 per night.

The *Shanghai Hotel* (☎ 676 1965, fax 674 4267) in the town centre is the only mid-range option. Decent air-con singles/doubles cost Rs570/630 including breakfast, and rooms with fan are Rs470 (single or double).

Places to Eat

If you're self-catering, the supermarkets *Prisunic* and *Sik Yuen* have a good selection of international items.

Popular fast-food joints include *KFC* and *Pizza Hut*.

For tasty curried chicken or vegetable dishes there are several eating places in the market as well as along Châteauneuf St.

Ashoka near the post office offers good curries and other Indian staples; it's open daily except Sunday from 10.30 am to 6 pm.

Nearby, *Le Gaulois* (☎ 675 5674) offers Mauritian staples such as *carri poulet* (chicken curry) for around Rs190. It's open daily except Sunday from 9 am to 6 pm (until 1 pm on Thursday).

Le Pot de Terre (☎ 676 2204) by the Prisunic supermarket is an unpretentious snack house with grilled fish for Rs70 and *riz frit* (fried rice) for about Rs40. It's open daily except Sunday from 10.30 am to 3.30 pm.

The *Golden Lion* restaurant in the Shanghai Hotel serves tasty Chinese food.

Shikari (☎ 676 4505) on Route Royale is a pleasant Indian restaurant that serves good lamb, chicken and seafood curries; prices start at Rs90. The restaurant is open daily except Sunday from 10 am to 3.30 pm and 6.30 to 10.30 pm.

A few doors down, *Chinese Wok* (☎ 676 1548) is popular with Franco-Mauritians but serves somewhat bland Chinese food. Dishes such as beef with green peppers cost around Rs100. It's open daily except Sunday from noon to 3 pm and 6 to 9.30 pm.

Nobby's (☎ 676 1318), also on Route Royale, serves steaks, pizzas and seafood grills. Most mains cost upwards of Rs250. Nobby's is open daily except Sunday from 11.30 am to 2.30 pm and 7 to 10 pm.

For better steaks, head for *Silver Moon Spur* (☎ 674 0594) in the Manhattan Mall. Expect to pay about Rs300 for a thick-cut sirloin. It's open daily from 11 am to 11 pm.

La Nouvelle Potinière (☎ 676 2648) near the Shanghai Hotel on Sir Winston Churchill St is a popular restaurant serving mainly French cuisine. It's open from noon to 3 pm and 7 to 10 pm daily except Sunday and Wednesday. Main dishes are upwards of Rs150.

Entertainment

The Casino de Maurice offers table-based games from 8 pm until 4 am (from 2 pm on Sundays) and slot machines from 10 am to 1 am. Tidy dress is expected.

In the Manhattan Mall, the two-screen ABC Cinema shows mainstream releases daily (Rs90).

Shopping

Shops in Curepipe tend to be open from Monday to Saturday 9 am to 6 pm except Thursday when they close at around 1 pm. Most places are closed on Sunday.

There are several shopping malls in the vicinity of the northbound bus station. The Salaffa Arcade houses a number of souvenir shops as well as a branch of Floreal Knitwear and numerous cheap shoe stores. Nearby, the Galerie Jan Palach has plenty of designer stores and tailors where you can get a suit made. The Curimjee Arcade on the corner of Route Royale and Sir Winston Churchill St also has some good clothes shops including a branch of Habit.

If you're interested in model ships, Voiliers de L'Océan (☎/fax 676 6986) on Sir Winston Churchill St has one of the best selections on the island. Comajora (☎ 676 5345, fax 675 1644) on La Brasserie Rd in Forest Side also has a good selection.

For fresh fruit, vegetables and cut anthuriums, the municipal market behind the northbound bus station is open daily from early morning until 6 pm (until noon on Sunday).

Getting There & Around

Curepipe is well linked by bus to Port Louis, Mahébourg, Centre de Flacq, Moka and surrounding towns such as Rose Hill and Quatre Bornes. Most of the sights, such as the Trou aux Cerfs crater and the botanical gardens, are easy walks. Expect to pay around Rs400 for a taxi ride from Curepipe to the airport.

FLOREAL

This small suburb north-west of Curepipe has become synonymous with the high-quality knitwear produced by the Floreal Knitwear Company. Of particular interest here is the **Floreal Textile Museum** (☎ 698 8016) in the Floreal Square mall on the corner of Floreal Rd and John Kennedy Ave. Some of the workers who painstakingly put the clothes together will take you step by step through the commercial knitwear business. Although it's all to the greater glory of the Floreal Knitwear Company, it may open your eyes to how much work goes into making your favourite sweater! Entry is Rs100, and the museum is open from 9 am to 5 pm Monday to Friday, and 9 am to 4 pm on Saturday. You can buy upmarket knitwear without the brand-name labels in the shop downstairs.

Places to Stay & Eat

The *Mandarin Hotel* (☎ 696 5031, fax 686 6858) on G Guibert St offers comfortable singles/doubles with bathroom for Rs504/728

MAURITIUS

(Rs672/986 with TV) including breakfast. There's also a *restaurant*.

Kohinoor (☎ *698 6093*) on the road behind Floreal Square offers tasty Indian mains such as tandoori chicken from Rs200. It's open daily from 11.30 am to 3 pm and 6.30 to 10.30 pm.

La Clef des Champs (☎ *636 3458*) on Queen Mary Ave offers good French and Mauritian food from noon to 3 pm and 8 to 10 pm (closed Saturday evening and all day Sunday). Mains start at Rs300.

Getting There & Away

From Curepipe there are numerous buses to Port Louis, Vacoas and Flic en Flac that stop in Floreal.

PHOENIX & VACOAS

These two industrial centres don't hold much of interest for visitors. Phoenix is the home of the Phoenix Brewery, which brews Phoenix Beer and Blue Marlin. Next door to the factory, the Phoenix Glass Gallery (☎ 696 3360) sells interesting souvenirs made from glass recycled from Phoenix beer bottles. In the same area is the Phoenix Factory Shop (☎ 697 7360) which sells brand-name clothes at discounted prices.

Near Henrietta, en route from Vacoas to Mare aux Vacoas, is a stone cairn, a monument to the English navigator Matthew Flinders. Flinders arrived in Mauritius from Australia on the leaky ship *Cumberland* in 1803, on his way back to Britain and his wife. The poor bloke didn't know France and Britain were at war and he was imprisoned for more than six years. He died, aged 40, a few years after his return to England. For an interesting read on the subject, take a look at *In the Grips of the Eagle: Matthew Flinders at Île de France (1803–1810)* by Huguette Ly-Tio-Fane Pineo.

TAMARIN FALLS

These falls are awkward to reach, but it's worth the effort for a beautiful, deep, cool bathe at the bottom of the series of seven falls. There are regular buses to Henrietta from Curepipe or Quatre Bornes. From Henrietta, it's about a 2km walk to the falls.

Guavas

During the guava season, from February to June, you will see hundreds of Mauritian families scrumping the fruit from the wild trees in the Black River Gorges National Park. The small red fruits resemble tiny apples and have a tart skin but a delicious soft interior with hard seeds; they taste like fresh strawberries! In case you are worried about picking the wrong thing, you'll see vendors selling bags of the fruit throughout the season for about Rs10 a bag. Try them the Indian way, with salt and chilli.

(For details on hiking to Tamarin Falls from the south, see Hiking the Central Plateau and Black River Gorges following.)

HIKING THE CENTRAL PLATEAU & BLACK RIVER GORGES

A number of the central plateau's isolated peaks offer excellent but steep hikes with impressive views over the island. In contrast with the central plateau, the beautiful highland area south-west of Curepipe, traversed by the only mountain road in Mauritius, is like no other part of the island. Surrounded by casuarina and coniferous trees, it more resembles a North American scene than one from the tropical Indian Ocean.

The Black River Gorges National Park, formerly known as the *Réserve Forestière Macchabée* (Macchabée Forest Reserve), is the largest area of native forest on the island, and many of Mauritius's rarer plant species are found only here. The park offers a variety of forest environments including several volcanic lakes and waterfalls. Most native animal species have gone the way of the dodo, but introduced deer, wild boar and monkeys are common, and some of Mauritius's rarer birds are making a comeback.

Curepipe is a logical starting point for hikers, as there are few public transport links within the park itself. Access to most trailheads will require private transport or a taxi ride. The forestry station in Le Pétrin is the jumping-off point for several hikes in the area.

Sadly, several of the more accessible options have been turned into private hunting reserves over the years, but there are still some lovely wild spots that are open to the public.

Information

Information for hikers is fairly thin on the ground. The major tour operators may be able to recommend an experienced guide and suggest some other hiking opportunities on the island. Otherwise it's best to talk to people in the area where you plan to hike before you set out. (See the boxed text 'Top Tips for Hikers' in the Mauritius Facts for the Visitor chapter for more information on hiking conditions.)

The best reference for hikers is still *Mountains of Mauritius: A Climber's Guide* by Robert Marsh, even though some of the information is a little out of date.

All the walks described here are as popular with Mauritians as with visitors.

Maps

The IGN map (see Maps in the Mauritius Facts for the Visitor chapter) shows most of the tracks and footpaths, although a few are outdated. Roads marked in yellow on the IGN map are generally just rough vehicle tracks, sometimes passable only to 4WD vehicles, and therefore can double as walking tracks. They're all easy enough to follow, but some smaller tracks (shown on the IGN map as dashed lines) are more difficult and may be overgrown, requiring a little bushbashing.

The IGN map will be adequate for most hikers but those in search of greater detail should apply to the Ministry of Housing (☎ 212 6022), Moorgate House, Sir William Newton St, Port Louis, which produces detailed maps suitable for serious walking off the beaten track.

Central Plateau Le Pouce, near Port Louis, towers over Port Louis and Moka. It is an easy climb and makes a great introduction to walking in Mauritius, offering a splendid half-day hike with stunning views over the coast.

Corps de Garde is an impressive peak that also makes for an exhilarating half-day hike.

Le Pouce Le Pouce is a prominent thumb-shaped peak south of Port Louis. To get to the trail from central Port Louis, head for the Champ de Mars racecourse and pick up Bourguignon St on the southern side of the track. From here you should follow St Denis St and then Bathfield St as far as the school, where you turn right and head up the steps to another road which leads out into the fields.

Once you are clear of the houses, cut across the grass towards the power lines, where you'll pick up an obvious 4WD track leading up the valley. After about 1km, a narrow but discernible path branches off to the right and heads uphill. It's a slippery few kilometres up to the saddle of land below the summit, where you'll meet the wide and easy trail leading up from the Moka side.

The final ascent of the 'thumb' itself is almost vertical in places; if you don't feel up to it, just admire the views from here. The scramble to the tip of the thumb is well worth the effort though, for a panoramic view over Port Louis and the central plateau.

For a bit of variety, you can head downhill to Moka along the obvious path that winds down the hill and cuts straight across the cane fields. Once you hit the road, there are regular buses back to Port Louis. In the opposite direction, pick up a bus for Nouvelle Découverte from the Victoria Square bus station (ask the driver for Le Pouce).

Allow about three hours return from either end, or a good half day if you want to do the circuit.

Corps de Garde The wedge-shaped massif that dominates Rose Hill offers a very rewarding ascent, though it's not for anyone with vertigo.

To get to the start of the trail from central Rose Hill, follow Dr Maurice Curé St northeast from the junction with Route Royale. After about 1km, take a right turn into Surverswarnath St (you'll pass a Tamil temple on your left) and continue until you hit a staggered junction with the main road.

On the far side, follow St Anne St up to a second staggered junction near the Hart de Keating stadium and follow Cretin Ave, which leads out into the fields.

The easiest trail to follow begins just beyond the football ground and Hindu crematorium. It runs straight up to the red and white radar antenna at the top of the ridge. From here, the main track follows the ridge south, passing a huge perched boulder before reaching a tricky cliff over which you'll need to scramble. There are several more hair-raising sections to test your courage before you reach the nose, which offers amaz-ing views over the plains. Check out the Hindu temple at the bottom of the massif.

Allow about three hours for the walk if you're coming from the centre of Rose Hill; 1½ hours if you drive up to the trailhead.

Black River Gorges National Park The best time to visit the park is during the flow-ering season between September and Janu-ary. Look for the rare tambalacoque or dodo tree, the black ebony trees and the wild guavas (see the boxed text 'Guavas' earlier in this chapter). You may also run into a band of monkeys, deer or wild pigs.

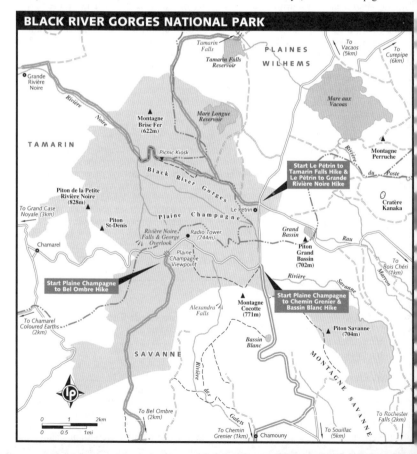

BLACK RIVER GORGES NATIONAL PARK

At Le Pétrin, one road heads east 2km to Grand Bassin while the main route climbs south, up onto Plaine Champagne. This is the rainiest part of Mauritius and the largest natural area on the island. The road's highest point (744m) is marked by a radio tower. About 3km beyond it is the Rivière Noire overlook, affording a spectacular view of waterfalls and Piton de la Petite Rivière Noire (828m), which is the highest point on Mauritius. In another 10km, the road drops to the coast at Grande Case Noyale.

Le Pétrin to Grande Rivière Noire This is a superb hike that traverses some of the finest and most scenic countryside in Mauritius. It begins at the junction of the Grand Bassin and Curepipe-Chamarel roads at Le Pétrin. The track is easy to follow through the Black River Gorges National Park, with tiny pockets of indigenous vegetation dispersed through acacia and other introduced forest.

Follow the forestry road west from Le Pétrin along the ridge through the forest and just absorb the splendid views into the Grande Rivière Noire valley. The road ends at a picnic kiosk on a fantastic viewpoint. From here the route descends precipitously along a steep and devilishly slippery track for about 1km, emerging on a 4WD track which drops down to the river.

The final stretch is an easy stroll along the river valley, though the landscape is scarred here and there by woodcutting. Eventually you come out in the cane fields; turn left at the T-junction and continue until you hit the coast road at Grande Rivière Noire.

Return to Curepipe by bus either via Souillac (you must change at Baie du Cap) or via Quatre Bornes. Buses run along these routes every half hour or so; there are no direct buses back to Curepipe. Reasonably fit walkers should allow four to five hours to do this wonderful walk.

Le Pétrin to Tamarin Falls The beginning of this hike is the same as that from Le Pétrin to Grande Rivière Noire. Follow the forestry road for just over 2km. Take the right (north) fork and continue for another 500m or so until a second fork in the road;

to reach Tamarin Falls, you must follow the left fork (the right will lead you to the road which connects the Curepipe-Chamarel road with Mare Longue reservoir).

The route is easy throughout, mostly forested with no steep or tricky bits, and often follows a scenic ridge with good views. It then descends into more open terrain near the reservoir. A detour at the end around the Seven Waterfalls of Tamarin is fun – there is a trail that drops down to the base of the falls, but you will have to explore to find it. If you have the energy, it's a fabulous finale to the walk.

Allow around three hours for this walk, more if you want to explore the falls area.

Plaine Champagne to Bel Ombre (South Coast) The trailhead for this walk is the Plaine Champagne viewpoint on the Curepipe-Chamarel road, about 2km southwest of the radio tower at the highest point on the road. The trail heads due south to Bel Ombre, passing en route a succession of wonderful views through some lovely mixed forests and plantations. The finish meanders along some rather confusing cane field tracks, but a reasonably good sense of direction will get you to the coast road without too much difficulty. From Bel Ombre, there are buses to Souillac (change there for Curepipe) and to Tamarin via Baie du Cap.

Allow about four hours for this fairly easy walk.

Plaine Champagne to Bassin Blanc & Chemin Grenier This walk begins about 3km south of Le Pétrin, where the main road makes a sharp turn to the right. A smaller sealed road continues straight ahead, descending through attractive forest and scrubland. There are excellent views over the coast, and while the walk is all on tarmac, there is rarely any traffic.

After 3km the road passes the lovely Bassin Blanc, a classic crater lake surrounded by forest. Beyond the lake the road zigzags down the valley to Chamouny and Chemin Grenier. Return from Chemin Grenier to Curepipe via Souillac, where you'll have to change buses.

MAURITIUS

Grand Bassin

According to legend, Shiva and his wife Parvati were circling the earth on a contraption made from flowers when they spied the dazzling beauty of an island and its encircling emerald sea. Shiva, who was carrying the Ganges River on his head to protect the world from floods, decided to land. After a bumpy descent, a couple of drops of water sprayed from his head and landed in a crater to form a natural lake. The Ganges expressed unhappiness about its water being left on an uninhabited island, but Shiva soothingly replied that dwellers from the banks of the Ganges would return one day to settle on the island and perform an annual pilgrimage, during which the water would be scooped out of the lake and presented as an offering.

It probably comes as no surprise that this dazzling island was Mauritius; the legendary crater lake is known as Grand Bassin (or as Ganga Talao). The majority of the island's Hindus come to the holy volcanic lake, now a renowned pilgrimage site, each year for Maha Shivaratri celebrations to pay homage to Lord Shiva.

This vast Hindu festival takes place over three days in February or March (depending on the lunar cycle) and is the largest Hindu celebration outside India. Many South African Hindus attend Maha Shivaratri in Mauritius rather than make pilgrimages to India, as for them the lake is spiritually the nearest 'branch' of the River Ganges.

In honour of Lord Shiva, the most devoted pilgrims dress in white and march from their village to the lake carrying a *kanvar*, a light wooden frame or arch decorated with paper flowers. There is no discrimination against those who can't or won't walk though; a constant stream of contract buses leaves from Bonne Terre (between Quatre Bornes and Vacoas) ferrying pilgrims to and from the sacred lake.

At the lake, pilgrims perform a *puja*, burning incense and camphor at the lake shore and offering food and flowers. By the end of the festival the lake is full of decaying offerings; this doesn't stop some pilgrims from drinking the water of the holy lake for added merit.

Visitors are welcome to attend Maha Shivaratri, but should do so with respect; dress modestly, and remove your shoes before entering temples and holy places.

Allow two hours for this easy walk, plus several hours for the bus trip back to Curepipe.

QUATRE BORNES

Though smaller than Curepipe and lacking any particular sites of interest, Quatre Bornes is easily the more pleasant of the two towns. There are some nice places to stay and eat and the atmosphere of the town is generally more upbeat. On St Jean Rd, the Orchard Centre mall and public market (Sunday and Thursday) are excellent places to pick up cheap clothes.

Orientation

St Jean Rd forms the main transect through Quatre Bornes. Most of the restaurants, hotels and banks are on this street, as well as the municipal buildings and both bus stations.

Places to Stay

Right in the centre, the **Blue Orchid Hotel** (☎ 466 3100, fax 466 2393) on St Jean Rd is a tidy modern business hotel. It has a reputable restaurant and comfortable air-con singles/doubles with bathroom and all the modcons starting from Rs1425/1650 (Rs1700/2175 on half board).

Nearby, the **Gold Crest Hotel** (☎ 454 5945, fax 454 9599) is another good upmarket option. Well-maintained air-con rooms with bathroom, TV and phone cost from Rs1075/1290 including breakfast. There's also a restaurant.

Further south on St Jean Road, the **El Monaco Hotel** (☎ 424 3915, fax 425 1072) is set back from the street in a quiet courtyard and has a nice pool and restaurant. Rooms with fan, bathroom and telephone cost from Rs560/672; these rates include breakfast.

Towards the north end of town, the *Montview Hotel* (☎ 454 7058, fax 426 6558) on Trianon Ave has a quiet location and a small pool and restaurant. Rooms with bathroom, fan, phone and TV cost Rs500/900 with breakfast (Rs575/1050 on half board).

In the same area, *La Charmeuse* (☎ 454 7254, fax 211 1789) on St Jean Rd is a friendly guesthouse, with clean rooms with fan from Rs450/600 per night.

Places to Eat
There are several restaurants on St Jean Rd. *Le Bon Choix* (☎ 465 3856) offers grills and Creole food for around Rs150. It's open daily except Sunday from noon to 2.30 pm and 6.30 to 10 pm.

Across the road, *Happy Valley* (☎ 454 6065) is a popular Chinese place and has mains such as steamed fish with ginger from Rs150. Opening hours are from noon to 2.30 pm and 6.30 to 10 pm Monday to Saturday.

Golden Spur (☎ 424 9440) in the Orchard Centre offers a variety of steaks and grills daily from 11 am to 11 pm. Mains cost around Rs300.

South of the centre on St Jean Rd, *King Dragon* (☎ 424 7888) is a stylish Chinese restaurant with the usual selection. Prices vary from Rs100 for *porc aigre-doux* (sweet and sour pork) to Rs225 for *crevettes* (prawns). It's open daily except Tuesday from 12.30 to 2 pm and 6.30 to 10.30 pm.

Getting There & Away
There are two bus stations in Quatre Bornes. Buses to Rose Hill (Rs12) stop in front of the Underground nightclub on St Jean Rd. For Flic en Flac, Curepipe, Floreal and Vacoas, you'll need to use the Railway Square terminal by the Municipality of Quatre Bornes buildings.

ROSE HILL
This pleasant hill town sits at the foot of the impressive Corps de Garde mountain. It has a more Indian atmosphere than other towns on the plateau. Rose Hill is one of the cheapest places to shop on the island and it's worth a day trip just for its relaxed non-touristy atmosphere.

Orientation
Most places of interest are strung out along St Jean Rd, which is the main thoroughfare through town. The centre point of town is the bus station at the intersection of St Jean Rd and Vandermeersch St, where you'll also find most of the shopping malls. On Route Royale you'll find branches of the major banks.

Creole Buildings
There are several impressive buildings in the centre of Rose Hill. The Municipality of Beau Bassin–Rose Hill on St Jean Rd is housed in an unusual Creole building that used to be the town railway station. Next door, **Maison Carne** is a lovely old Creole mansion that now houses the Mauritius Research Council.

Cultural Centres
Two of the most important cultural centres in Mauritius are located in Rose Hill. The British Council (☎ 454 9500, fax 454 9553) is on St Jean Rd. It has a regular program of events in English and a good library. The library is open from noon to 5 pm on Monday, 9.30 am to 5 pm Tuesday to Friday, and 9 am to 1 pm on Saturday.

On Rue Gordon, behind Maison Carne, is the Centre Charles Baudelaire (☎ 454 7929, fax 464 8144), which has an impressive schedule of plays and other events promoting French culture. The library here is open from 10 am to 5.30 pm Tuesday to Friday and 9 am to 3 pm on Saturday.

Places to Stay & Eat
Few people stop over in Rose Hill, so there are very few dining or accommodation options.

The *Riverview Hotel* (☎ 464 4957, fax 464 0630), out of town on Route Royale, has comfortable doubles for Rs400 (Rs450 with breakfast).

For a quick lunch, there are numerous basic restaurants in the vicinity of the market serving *mien frit* (fried noodles) and other Chinese staples.

Le Pekinois (☎ 465 1845) by the Esso station on Route Royale is probably your best bet for dinner. It serves Chinese food downstairs (meat dishes cost Rs80 and lobster is only Rs250) and steaks and grills upstairs (from Rs220). Opening hours are 7 to 9.30 pm daily except Monday.

Shopping

Rose Hill is a major centre for cheap locally made clothing and Indian imports such as saris and silk. The shopping malls around the bus station are a good place to start.

The colourful municipal market, which features food, flowers and household items, is just off the main road on Dr Maurice Cure St. In the surrounding streets, there is a daily street market of cheap jeans and other designer clothes. Some of the brand names are legitimate, others are subtle fakes; check the spellings carefully!

Le Cygne bookshop (☎ 464 2444) on Route Royale has probably the widest selection of books on the island.

Getting There & Away

There are regular buses from Port Louis and Curepipe to Rose Hill (Rs12). There are also buses from Rose Hill to Centre de Flacq on the east coast (Rs14).

MOKA

Bubbling brooks, waterfalls, valleys, towering mountains and some wonderful real estate make the area around the town of Moka pleasant and picturesque. Only 12km south of Port Louis, Moka is the country's centre of academia, with the University of Mauritius and the Mahatma Gandhi Institute, which promotes Indian culture.

Places to Stay

Joensu's Guest House (☎ /fax 433 4680) at Telfair roundabout is a friendly little place with singles/doubles/triples/quadruples with private bathroom for Rs300/550/650/750, including breakfast. It's a good starting point if you're walking over Le Pouce to Port Louis.

AROUND MOKA
Le Réduit

This is *the* house in Mauritius. Originally the governor's residence, Le Réduit is now used by the military.

Le Réduit, which means 'refuge', was built in 1778 by the French governor Barthélémy David, who succeeded Mahé de La Bourdonnais. It was from here in 1874 that the British governor's wife, Lady Gomm, sent out invitations to her ball with the famous Mauritian Blue stamps. They were misprinted with 'Post Office' instead of 'Post Paid' (see the boxed text 'Stamp of Approval' in the Port Louis chapter).

There is a 1km, forest-lined drive from the main gate and guard post down to the big colonial mansion. You can still walk around the gardens, although this is sometimes under armed – but polite – escort. The grounds are open Monday to Friday from 9.30 am to noon. Unfortunately, the house itself is open to the public only one day a year, on the last Sunday in August.

The countryside around Le Réduit estate is marvellous, particularly at the driveway entrance, where you look down from the roadside into the lush valley of the Rivière Cascade. Across the road is an old chapel and overgrown cemetery, where a few former governors have been laid to rest.

To get to Le Réduit, take the St Pierre bus from Port Louis, Curepipe or Rose Hill and get off at the University of Mauritius. The gate to Le Réduit is only a few hundred metres away. If you're driving or cycling, follow the Port Louis–Curepipe motorway and turn west at the roundabout to the university.

Eureka House

This renowned Creole mansion (☎ 433 4951) stands about 4km from Le Réduit, on the other side of the Port Louis–Curepipe motorway. A masterpiece of tropical construction, the house boasts 109 doors, which keep the interior deliciously cool during the hot summers. It was built in the 1830s and purchased in 1856 by Eugène Leclézio, the first Mauritian Master of the Supreme Court. Like Le Réduit, and any of the properties around this area, it has terrific views across the river valley.

The mansion has a music room, a Chinese room and a French East India Company room. It is unclear whether the rooms were always used as such or have just

JOHN HAY

A spectacular view of the Mauritian landscape

JEAN ROBERT

Botanical Gardens, Pamplemousses

SUSAN STORM

Domaine du Chasseur, South Mauritius

JOHN HAY

Champ de Mars Racecourse, Port Louis

SUSAN STORM

JEAN ROBERT

SUSAN STORM

Hinduism is the main religion in Mauritius. Most of the country's Hindus make an annual pilgrimage to Grand Bassin for the festival known as Maha Shivaratri, where they make offerings to Lord Shiva.

been created as showrooms for collections of Chinese and Indian household goods. The top floor occasionally displays paintings by local artists. On the ground floor, note the colonial shower contraption. Lining the interior walls are some fine antique maps of Asia and Africa.

The courtyard behind the house is surrounded by stone cottages which were once the staff quarters and kitchen. There is also an attractively landscaped garden.

Entry to Eureka House costs Rs165 per person. It is open from 9.30 am to 5 pm daily (it closes at 3 pm on weekends) and a guided tour around and inside the house is free and optional.

To get to Eureka, take the St Pierre bus from Victoria Square in Port Louis and get off at Moka. The turning to Eureka is about 1km north of the bus stop; walk as if you were heading back to Port Louis and the turning will be on your left just after the road to Le Pouce mountain branches off to the right.

Domaine Les Pailles

Built around the mansion of the old Pailles Sugar Estate, Domaine Les Pailles (☎ 212 4225, fax 212 4226) is an elaborate cultural and heritage centre which cost close to US$10 million to complete. The facilities here include rides in horse-drawn carriages, a miniature railway, a working replica of a traditional ox-driven sugar mill, a rum distillery producing the estate's own brew, a spice garden, a natural spring and a play area for children.

Visitors can choose to tour the site by old British army jeep, take the train or horse carriage around, or ride around the grounds on one of the estate's horses. The riding centre, Les Écuries du Domaine, offers about 42 horses for dressage and jumping and riding in the foothills. Welsh ponies are provided for children.

The centre also has a casino (open daily for all the usual games of chance) and a selection of upmarket restaurants. *La Cannelle Rouge* offers Creole fare in the Rs160 to Rs200 range. For excellent Indian food, there's *Indra,* which charges from Rs240 for most mains. *Fu Xiao* offers good Chinese food; again most mains cost from Rs240.

The cost of entry to the Domaine varies depending on which activities you want to include. For a jeep safari it's Rs490/245 for adults/children, a horse-drawn carriage ride costs Rs160/80 and a train tour is Rs140/70. More expensive packages that also include lunch and tours of the rum distillery and sugar mill are available.

To get to the Domaine, take any bus that runs between Port Louis and Curepipe and ask to be let off at Domaine Les Pailles (it's clearly signposted). From the road it takes less than half an hour on foot to the reception centre. Alternatively, take a 10-minute taxi ride from Port Louis or Moka.

East Mauritius

The east coast of Mauritius was settled by the Dutch early in the 17th century, and was one of the first parts of the country to lose its native ebony forest to the burgeoning sugar cane industry. Today, many of the cane plantations have been turned over to vegetable gardens, giving the landscape a patchy, unkempt look.

However, the beaches along the coast here are a delight. As elsewhere, many of the prime sections have been grabbed by the large hotels, but the hotel set tends to stick to its own strips of sand and surf, so the public beaches here are quieter than almost anywhere else in Mauritius. The beaches at Belle Mare and Palmar are best for seekers of sun, sand and silence. At the other end of the spectrum, the hugely popular Île aux Cerfs is one of the main tourist attractions in Mauritius, and offers several fine beaches and an alluring sandy-bottomed lagoon.

Trou d'Eau Douce, with the only budget accommodation in the area, is the jumping-off point for Île aux Cerfs. If you get tired of the beach, the Centre de Flacq is a busy market town with a strong Indian flavour.

ÎLE AUX CERFS

Day-tripping tourists long ago replaced the *cerfs* (stags) on this attractive sandy island, which belongs to the plush Le Touessrok Sun Hotel. Île aux Cerfs is joined to the smaller Île de l'Est by a picturesque sand bar. You can easily wade across the gap between the two at low tide.

The main attraction here is the casuarina-shaded beach which runs along the seaward side of both islands. But don't expect splendid isolation; this is one of the main tourist sites in Mauritius and if you stay close to the ferry jetties, it can be hard to see the sand for the sun-bronzed bodies.

Ferries dock on Île aux Cerfs, where you'll find a boathouse offering expensive water sports, souvenir stalls, several *restaurants* and a small pen with some giant Aldabran tortoises. If you're seeking solitude, you

HIGHLIGHTS

- Boating to Île aux Cerfs, popular for its water activities, sunbathing and fine cuisine
- Taking it easy on the casuarina-fringed beaches at Belle Mare and Palmar
- Touring the huge FUEL sugar mill near Centre de Flacq (June to November)

should walk around the seaward side of the island or wade across to Île de l'Est.

There are two restaurants on Île aux Cerfs. The *Paul et Virginie Restaurant* on the beach offers expensive seafood (mains start at Rs250) while *La Chaumière* on the hillside offers set Mauritian menus from Rs295. The restaurants are open daily from 12.30 to 3 pm. Alternatively, *Lors Briza* is a snack stand beside the public beach and has pizzas and other snacks for about Rs175.

Getting There & Away

Despite numerous signs to the contrary, the only official public ferry to Île aux Cerfs is that run by Le Touessrok Sun Hotel, which leaves from a jetty within the hotel grounds. The ferry runs every 15 minutes in each direction from 9 am until about 4.30 pm and the return trip costs Rs82.50 per person (Rs38.50 for children). On Île aux Cerfs, the boats dock at a jetty near the boathouse (the Le Touessrok Sun jetty is reserved for residents of the hotel).

There are also dozens of private operators offering 'public ferry' boats to Île aux Cerfs, but the return trips are usually less frequent, and some travellers have even reported being abandoned on the island by unscrupulous operators. These boats also dock at the public jetty near the boathouse.

Reliable companies include La Rochelle Boat Services (☎ 419 2902) at the Vicky Boutique on Route Royale, and Seahorse (☎ 419 5831) and Trou d'Eau Douce Co-op Ferry (☎ 419 7954), both across from the

Vicky Boutique. There isn't much difference between the companies. The return trip to Île aux Cerfs usually costs Rs80; in combination with a one-hour ride in a glass-bottomed boat it's Rs250. A tour of Île aux Cerfs and the cascades at Grande Rivière Sud-Est will cost about Rs250 without lunch, Rs600 with a chicken and fish barbecue and Rs900 with grilled lobster.

Most tours also include a trip to the waterfall near the mouth of the Grande Rivière Sud-Est. If you're driving up the coast from the south, you can take a boat from the village of Grande Rivière Sud-Est to the waterfall for around Rs200 per person; call Bateau Robert (☎ 417 6643) for details.

TROU D'EAU DOUCE
The closest accommodation to the Île aux Cerfs is found in this attractive village. The name Trou d'Eau Douce (Hole of Sweet Water) refers to a sea pool fed by a freshwater underground stream. The village has lots of character and is probably the best place to stay on the east coast if you're travelling on a budget.

Places to Stay
Right in the middle of Trou d'Eau Douce, *Auberge Etiennette* (☎ 419 3497, fax 419 7907) is a friendly little place offering several studios with fan and kitchenette for Rs400 a double. The owners can also provide meals on request.

Chez Tino (☎ 419 2769) on Route Royale has three rooms with fan, TV, balcony and kitchenette for Rs500 for one or two people. The room on the same level as the restaurant can get a little noisy.

Across the road, *Le Dodo Apartment* (☎ 419 4034) is a modern block of spacious studio apartments. The tidy rooms all come with fan, TV and balcony and cost Rs600 for one or two people.

On the coastal highway north of town, *Le Tropical Hotel* (☎ 419 2300, fax 419 2302) is a Naïade resort. It has a nice restaurant (see Places to Eat) and a free ferry to Île aux Cerfs for residents. Standard singles/doubles vary in price from Rs1960/3920 to Rs3180/4760 depending on the season.

Further north along the highway, the *Silver Beach Hotel* (☎ 419 2600, fax 419 2604) has a restaurant, a pool and a free boat to Île aux Cerfs for residents, but the place is slightly lacking in character. Singles/doubles start at Rs2800/3600 on half board.

With the Île aux Cerfs as its playground, *Le Touessrok Sun Hotel* (☎ 419 2451, fax 419 2025, **e** infotsk@sunresort.com) is easily the classiest place to stay in Trou d'Eau Douce. Situated a few kilometres south of the village proper, this intriguing hotel features a sandy islet joined to the end of a peninsula by a covered bridge. As you would expect from a Sun International hotel, the facilities here are luxurious and include a large pool, tennis courts and four restaurants, as well as the extensive water sports facilities on Île aux Cerfs. Residents have use of a free ferry service across to the island. You pay a premium for the prime location; standard rooms range from Rs7200/10,700 to Rs9850/ 14,600 depending on the season.

Places to Eat
For self-caterers, the 2000 Dumpers supermarket on Route Royale is open from 8 am to 6 pm daily.

Chez Tino (see Places to Stay) is a nice little place with reasonably priced food and a terrace overlooking the sea. Tasty Creole and Chinese seafood dishes such as shrimps in garlic butter cost around Rs150. It's open daily from 9.30 am to 2.30 pm and 7 to 9.30 pm (except Sunday evenings).

Across the road, *La Case la Paille* offers cheap snack meals such as grilled fish (Rs90) and *mien frit* (fried noodles) for Rs50. It's open from 9 am to 6 pm daily.

Restaurant Sept, south of town at Sept Croisées, specialises in Indian dishes such as prawn and fish curry. Expect to pay between Rs70 and Rs250 for a main dish. The restaurant is open daily from 11 am to 3 pm and 6 to 11 pm.

Le Tropical Hotel has a restaurant serving Creole, Chinese and European cuisine. Main dishes start from about Rs150, while gala dinners cost Rs325 and buffets are Rs375. Nonresidents should book in advance.

MAURITIUS

EAST MAURITIUS

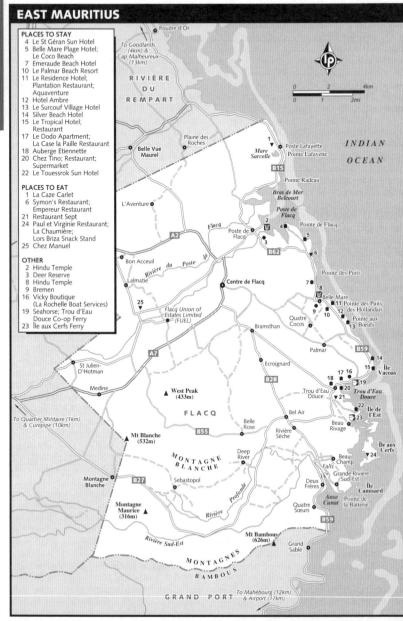

PLACES TO STAY
4 Le St Géran Sun Hotel
5 Belle Mare Plage Hotel;
  Le Coco Beach
7 Emeraude Beach Hotel
10 Le Palmar Beach Resort
11 Le Residence Hotel;
   Plantation Restaurant;
   Aquaventure
12 Hotel Ambre
13 Le Surcouf Village Hotel
14 Silver Beach Hotel
15 Le Tropical Hotel;
   Restaurant
17 Le Dodo Apartment;
   La Case la Paille Restaurant
18 Auberge Etiennette
20 Chez Tino; Restaurant;
   Supermarket
22 Le Touessrok Sun Hotel

PLACES TO EAT
1 La Caze Carlet
6 Symon's Restaurant;
  Empereur Restaurant
21 Restaurant Sept
24 Paul et Virginie Restaurant;
   La Chaumière;
   Lors Briza Snack Stand
25 Chez Manuel

OTHER
2 Hindu Temple
3 Deer Reserve
8 Hindu Temple
9 Bremen
16 Vicky Boutique
   (La Rochelle Boat Services)
19 Seahorse; Trou d'Eau
   Douce Co-op Ferry
23 Île aux Cerfs Ferry

Getting There & Around

There are no direct buses to Trou d'Eau Douce; you'll need to change at Centre de Flacq. Bus No 55 runs between Trou d'Eau Douce and Centre de Flacq every half hour from 6 am to 4 pm (Rs10). Taxis cost around Rs250 from Centre de Flacq. The Vicky Boutique (☎ 419 2902) rents bicycles (Rs100 per day) and mopeds (Rs400 per day).

PALMAR & BELLE MARE

The strip of coast north of Trou d'Eau Douce includes some of the best stretches of white sand and azure ocean in Mauritius. Belle Mare beach offers good opportunities for camping and has public toilets and a large area of casuarina trees for shade.

The water sports facilities at most of the big resorts are reserved for residents, but Aquaventure (☎ 422 7953) offers daily undersea walks for Rs750. It has a booth on the beach near the Coco Beach Hotel.

Places to Stay

At the north end of Belle Mare beach, the friendly *Emeraude Hotel* (☎ 415 1107, fax 415 1109, e htl.emeraude@intnet.mu) is across the road from the beach, but the attentive staff make up for the location. Singles/doubles are Rs1955/2800 for half board. There's a good restaurant and a pool.

Just south-east of Belle Mare village, *Le Residence* (☎ 401 8888, fax 415 5888, e residence@easynet.fr) is an upmarket place run by a French-Indonesian team and boasts an excellent Indian restaurant (see Places to Eat) as well as the usual luxury hotel facilities. High-season prices start from Rs7800 (Rs10,400 in low season) for a double overlooking the garden. The good service here would put many of the longer-established places to shame.

The more affordable *Le Palmar Beach Resort* (☎ 415 1041, fax 415 1043) shares the same strip of beach and offers a good range of water sports. Half-board rates start at Rs2650/3960 for comfortable singles/doubles. There are two restaurants and a pool.

The huge *Hotel Ambre* (☎ 415 1544, fax 415 1594, e rea.amb@intnet.mu) over-looks one of the lovely bays at Palmar and

has several restaurants, a generous pool and good water sports facilities. Its health centre offers steam baths, hydrotherapy and massage. Rates start at Rs3209/4382/5524 for a single/double/triple room on half board.

Nearby, *Le Surcouf Village Hotel* (☎ 415 1800, fax 212 1361, e sr7199@bow.intnet.mu) is an OK mid-range place with a restaurant and a pool; rooms are Rs1497/2424.

Places to Eat

The *Plantation* is a plush Indian restaurant in *Le Residence* hotel (see Places to Stay). Meals are served on a stylish terrace overlooking the ocean. The prices are similarly extravagant; mains such as tandoori chicken start at Rs390 while rock lobster is a hefty Rs1400. It's open daily from noon to 10 pm.

Emeraude Hotel (see Places to Stay) has an affordable pizzeria with pizzas (cooked in wood-fired ovens) for around Rs170. The restaurant is open daily for lunch and dinner.

Getting There & Around

There are very occasional buses from Centre de Flacq to Palmar (Rs10), but none to Belle Mare. A taxi to Belle Mare or Palmar will cost you about Rs250.

Bremen (☎ 415 1576), by the Hindu temple in Belle Mare, rents out 125cc motorcycles for Rs500 a day (it also offers tours).

POINTE DE FLACQ

The narrow spit of land at Pointe de Flacq is home to some of the most exclusive hotels in Mauritius, but there isn't much to see along the coast if you aren't staying at one of these luxurious addresses.

Hindu Temple

There is an attractive temple on a small island linked by a causeway to Poste de Flacq. It is a beautiful sight from Le St Géran Sun Hotel across the bay. The temple is open daily from sunrise to sunset. Visitors are welcome but should behave with respect.

Places to Stay

Taking up most of the peninsula at Pointe de Flacq, *Le St Géran Sun Hotel* (☎ 401 1688, fax 401 1668, **e** *infostg@sunresort.com*) is the flagship of the South African Sun International group. Among other things, the hotel has a private golf academy with a nine-hole course, a casino, a spa and three fine restaurants. For the utmost in luxury, the hotel offers the splendid self-contained Villa Royale for Rs106,650 in the low season (it's a staggering Rs200,000 over Christmas and the New Year). Standard singles/doubles cost from Rs8100/12,000.

Covering similar ground, the ***Belle Mare Plage Hotel*** (☎ *415 1515, fax 415 1993*) is a golfer's dream with a private 18-hole course and a well-respected golf academy. You can also indulge in water sports, tennis and squash or swim in the hotel's two swimming pools. In the low season (from May to September) rooms start at Rs3912/ 5738.

No-one could accuse ***Le Coco Beach*** (☎ *401 1000, fax 415 1888,* **e** *infococ@le cocobeach.com*) of subtlety; children will love the over-the-top decor and the carnival atmosphere, but adults may find it all a bit too much. Brightly decorated rooms start at Rs3150/4800 for half board. Children under 12 years can share a room with their parents for Rs730 (Rs1180 for children from 13 to 18 years). This hotel boasts an excellent program of activities for children.

Places to Eat
On Route Royale near Pointe de Flacq, ***Symon's Restaurant*** offers Creole meals such as shrimp *rougaille* (shrimp in tomato-based sauce) for around Rs200. Main dishes start at around Rs65; for a treat, try the pan-fried, Creole-style steak (Rs115). It's a clean, airy place open daily from 11 am to 2 pm and 6 to 11 pm.

Next door, the ***Empereur Restaurant*** offers good Chinese dishes such as *porc aigre-doux* (sweet and sour pork) from Rs75. It's open daily except Wednesday from 11 am to 10 pm.

Belle Mare Plage Hotel (see Places to Stay) has a Creole and European restaurant with steep prices. Main dishes start at around Rs300 and set menus are available for Rs700 per person. It's open daily from 12.30 to 3 pm and 7.30 to 9.30 pm.

North of Poste de Flacq at Poste Lafayette, ***La Caze Carlet*** (☎ *411 5622*) offers Creole food from 12.30 to 3 pm and 7 to 11.30 pm. It sometimes offers live music.

CENTRE DE FLACQ
The major settlement in east Mauritius is Centre de Flacq, a lively market town with a distinct Indian influence. There's nowhere to stay, but it's worth a visit just for the general hubbub and atmosphere. You will have to change buses here if you're heading on to Trou d'Eau Douce, Belle Mare or Palmar.

Flacq Union of Estates Limited
This sugar mill, a few kilometres west of Centre de Flacq, is the largest on the island and is even reputed to be one of the largest in the world. There are usually tours from June to late November, when cane is being harvested. These tours are held daily, except Sunday, in the afternoon. There is no admission charge but the guide will appreciate a tip.

Places to Eat
For a quick bite, there are some Indian canteens right by the public market in Centre de Flacq.

If you're self-catering, the big market in town is on Thursday and Sunday.

Close to the FUEL sugar mill, ***Chez Manuel*** (☎ *418 3599*) in the hill village of St Julien specialises in Chinese food. Main dishes range from Rs90 to Rs180. It's open daily except Sunday from 11 am to 3 pm and 6.30 to 10 pm.

Getting There & Away
The bus from Port Louis (Immigration Square bus station) to Centre de Flacq cost Rs15. Centre de Flacq is also linked by bus to Rose Hill (via the Quartier Militaire) Curepipe, Mahébourg (via the coast road) and to Grand Gaube via Rivière du Rempart and Poste Lafayette.

Taxis leave from near the market in Centre de Flacq and charge around Rs250 to go to Belle Mare. A share taxi to Port Louis will cost from Rs80 to Rs200 per person.

West Mauritius

The Rivière Noire district has many attractions. The south-west coast boasts some impressive mountains, including Le Morne Brabant, and is the centre for big-game fishing. There's a small surfing scene at Tamarin, about 6km south of Flic en Flac. Further north, most of the coastal plain is composed of cane fields, but there is a splendid strip of beach and some good diving to be had at the resort of Flic en Flac.

HIGHLIGHTS

- Swimming and diving at the beach resort of Flic en Flac
- Visiting the spectacular waterfall and curious coloured earths of Chamarel
- Surfing in laid-back Tamarin
- Deep-sea fishing at the superb Grande Rivière Noire

FLIC EN FLAC

This burgeoning resort lies off the Port Louis–Tamarin road, 3km east of the junction. The road runs through the cane fields to the coast. The name Flic en Flac is thought to come from the old Dutch name Fried Landt Flaak, meaning Free and Flat Land, which was slowly corrupted by the French into Flic en Flac.

Despite a nice beach and some pleasant places to stay and eat, Flic en Flac has become a victim of its own success, with ugly modern apartment buildings springing up all along the coast. Wolmar, 2km south of Flic en Flac, is more appealing and more exclusive. It has a number of impressive and expensive luxury resorts.

Information

There is no tourist office in Flic en Flac. Your best source of information is the Flic en Flac Tourist Agency (☎ 453 9389, fax 453 8416) on the main road, where tours and cruises can be arranged.

There's a branch of the Mauritius Commercial Bank in the Flic en Flac mall, open from 8 am to 6 pm Monday to Saturday and 9 am to noon on Sunday.

Casela Bird Park

This bird park is 1km south of the turn-off to Flic en Flac. It is well landscaped and has good views across the Rivière du Rempart valley. As well as parrots, pheasants and rare pink pigeons, there are leopards, tigers, lemurs, monkeys and deer. There are also giant tortoises, one of which is 150 years old. The park is open every day from 9 am to 5 pm; the entry fee is Rs176 on weekdays and Rs110 on weekends.

Wolmar Estate Nature Reserve

Opposite the Pirogue Sun Hotel & Casino is the private Wolmar estate (☎ 453 8463), which is open to the public as a nature reserve. Animals here include birds, deer, monkeys and boars. There are guided nature walks on Tuesday and Thursday (Rs265), 4WD jeep tours on Monday, Tuesday, Wednesday and Friday (Rs475) and cycling tours on Monday, Wednesday and Friday (Rs450, bike not included). You can book at the Flic en Flac Tourist Agency.

Diving

Some of the best dives in Mauritius are off the coast near Flic en Flac. Hotels with dive centres include the Klondike Hotel, Villas Caroline, La Pirogue Sun Hotel, the Sugar Beach Resort and the Sofitel Impérial (for contact details, see Places to Stay). For more information on diving, see the special section 'Underwater Worlds'.

Places to Stay

As a result of all the speculative apartment building, Flic en Flac is well off for accommodation, with plenty of bungalows, hotels and guesthouses. The luxury hotels are all grouped at Wolmar. They are described here roughly north to south.

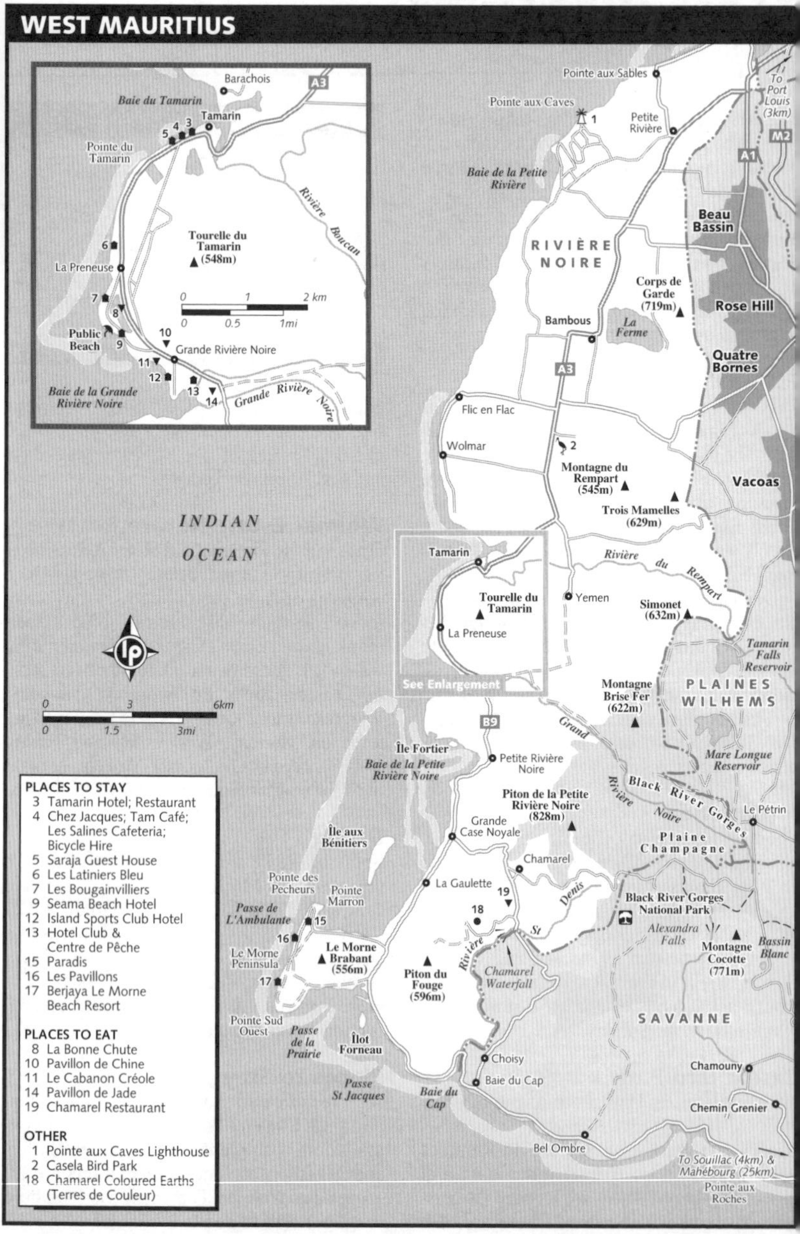

WEST MAURITIUS
Barachois
A3
Baie du Tamarin
Tamarin
Pointe du Tamarin
Rivière Boucan
Tourelle du Tamarin (548m)
La Preneuse
Public Beach
Grande Rivière Noire
Baie de la Grande Rivière Noire
Grande Rivière Noire
0 1 2 km
0 0.5 1mi
Pointe aux Sables
Pointe aux Caves
Petite Rivière
To Port Louis (3km)
M2
A1
Baie de la Petite Rivière
Beau Bassin
RIVIÈRE NOIRE
Corps de Garde (719m)
Rose Hill
Bambous
La Ferme
Quatre Bornes
A3
Flic en Flac
Wolmar
Montagne du Rempart (545m)
Vacoas
Trois Mamelles (629m)
INDIAN OCEAN
Rivière du Rempart
Tamarin
Tourelle du Tamarin
Yemen
Simonet (632m)
La Preneuse
Tamarin Falls Reservoir
See Enlargement
Montagne Brise Fer (622m)
PLAINES WILHEMS
0 3 6km
0 1.5 3mi
B9
Île Fortier
Baie de la Petite Rivière Noire
Petite Rivière Noire
Mare Longue Reservoir
Piton de la Petite Rivière Noire (828m)
Grand Rivière Noire
Black River Gorges
Le Pétrin
Île aux Bénitiers
Grande Case Noyale
Plaine Champagne
Chamarel
Pointe des Pecheurs
Pointe Marron
La Gaulette
Passe de L'Ambulante
Rivière St Denis
Black River Gorges National Park
Le Morne Peninsula
Le Morne Brabant (556m)
Alexandra Falls
Montagne Cocotte (771m)
Bassin Blanc
Piton du Fouge (596m)
Chamarel Waterfall
SAVANNE
Pointe Sud Ouest
Passe de la Prairie
Îlot Forneau
Choisy
Chamouny
Baie du Cap
Passe St Jacques
Baie du Cap
Chemin Grenier
Bel Ombre
To Souillac (4km) & Mahébourg (25km)
Pointe aux Roches
PLACES TO STAY
3 Tamarin Hotel; Restaurant
4 Chez Jacques; Tam Café; Les Salines Cafeteria; Bicycle Hire
5 Saraja Guest House
6 Les Latiniers Bleu
7 Les Bougainvilliers
9 Seama Beach Hotel
12 Island Sports Club Hotel
13 Hotel Club & Centre de Pêche
15 Paradis
16 Les Pavillons
17 Berjaya Le Morne Beach Resort
PLACES TO EAT
8 La Bonne Chute
10 Pavillon de Chine
11 Le Cabanon Créole
14 Pavillon de Jade
19 Chamarel Restaurant
OTHER
1 Pointe aux Caves Lighthouse
2 Casela Bird Park
18 Chamarel Coloured Earths (Terres de Couleur)

Klondike Hotel (☎ 453 8333, fax 453 8337) is a pleasant mid-range place offering self-catering bungalows and rooms with a sea view arranged around a stylish swimming pool, which appears to blend seamlessly with the ocean. There are also tennis courts, a dive school and a restaurant with the usual séga performances. Air-con singles/doubles are Rs1900/2800, while bungalows which sleep up to six range from Rs2000 to Rs3000; breakfast is a rather pricey Rs200.

Right on the beach, *Villas Caroline* (☎ 453 8411, fax 453 8144, e caroline@ intnet.mu) was once a budget option but both its reputation and its prices have soared over recent years. There is a great restaurant, a well-regarded dive school and also a pool. Singles range from Rs2000 to Rs3000 depending on the season; doubles cost from Rs2700 to Rs4800. Self-catering bungalows cost between Rs4800 and Rs7000 for up to four people.

Golden Reefs (☎ 453 8841, fax 453 8438) is a modern complex behind the mall on the main street. It has bungalows sleeping four to six people for Rs1000 and smaller apartments for Rs700 a double. All rooms have fridge, cooker and TV. There's a good pool.

Nearby, the friendly *Little Acorn* (☎/fax 464 8696) offers hotel-style rooms for Rs450 for one or two people as well as self-catering apartments (for a maximum of two people) for Rs550.

Easy World Apartments (☎ 453 8557, fax 464 5233) on the main road provides self-catering apartments for between Rs500 and Rs700 including breakfast. In December and January, prices increase by around Rs100.

On the street behind the Sea Breeze restaurant, *Villa Paul & Virginie* (☎ 453 8537 fax 453 8833) offers friendly and personal service. It has a great Italian restaurant and a bar. Comfortable singles/doubles with air-con are Rs880/1080. This is a popular place so you should book ahead.

Nilaya (☎/fax 453 9037), set back from the sea near the Mer de Chine restaurant, is run by an interesting Mauritian family and

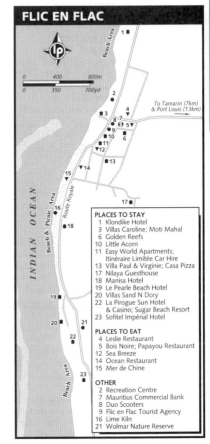

FLIC EN FLAC

To Tamarin (7km) & Port Louis (13km)

PLACES TO STAY
1 Klondike Hotel
3 Villas Caroline; Moti Mahal
6 Golden Reefs
10 Little Acorn
11 Easy World Apartments;
   Itinéraire Limitée Car Hire
13 Villa Paul & Virginie; Casa Pizza
17 Nilaya Guesthouse
18 Manisa Hotel
19 Le Pearle Beach Hotel
20 Villas Sand N Dory
22 La Pirogue Sun Hotel
   & Casino; Sugar Beach Resort
23 Sofitel Impérial Hotel

PLACES TO EAT
4 Leslie Restaurant
5 Bois Noire; Papayou Restaurant
12 Sea Breeze
14 Ocean Restaurant
15 Mer de Chine

OTHER
2 Recreation Centre
7 Mauritius Commercial Bank
8 Duo Scooters
9 Flic en Flac Tourist Agency
16 Lime Kiln
21 Wolmar Nature Reserve

is highly recommended. Spacious studio flats with private bathroom and kitchenette cost Rs800 for a single or double.

The *Manisa Hotel* (☎ 453 8558, fax 453 8562), further south, has rooms and suites, plus a swimming pool and restaurant. Single/double rooms cost Rs1600/1900 and suites cost Rs2000. All these prices are on a half-board basis. The staff can be a little indifferent here according to some travellers.

Right on the beach in Wolmar, *Le Pearle Beach Hotel* (☎ 453 8428, fax 453 8429) is a friendly mid-range place with a pleasant restaurant, a pool and the usual water sports including a dive school. Singles/doubles start at Rs2130/3320 on half board.

Next door, *Villas Sand N Dory* (☎ 453 8420, fax 453 8640) is more down-to-earth and has unremarkable rooms for Rs1300/2000. One-bedroom apartments with air-con, kitchenette, phone and TV start from Rs1400/2200, while two-bedroom apartments cost from Rs2600 for two people, Rs3000 for three and Rs3600 for four. Rates include breakfast.

La Pirogue Sun Hotel & Casino (☎ 453 8441, fax 453 8449, **e** infolap@sunresort .com) is a sprawling luxury resort belonging to the Sun group. The pyramid-shaped roof of the main building is styled after the sail of the small fishing boats or pirogues used by locals. This upmarket hotel boasts tennis courts, a pool and a casino. It also has restaurants serving Chinese meals, seafood and the usual international cuisine. Depending on the season, standard singles/doubles cost from Rs4550/6700, superior rooms cost from Rs6150/9100, and suites start at Rs12,600/18,700, all on half board. Meals can be taken in any of the restaurants at La Pirogue or the Sugar Beach resort.

The *Sugar Beach Resort* (☎ 453 9090, fax 453 9100, **e** infosbr@sunresort.com) is a very plush Sun group resort with a colonial theme. Rooms are in plantation-style houses and are surrounded by immaculately manicured lawns. There are restaurants serving Italian and international cuisine and an impressive pool, plus the usual sporting activities. Rates depend on the season. Standard rooms cost from Rs5600/8300, beachfront rooms start at Rs6650/9900 and suites start at Rs13,550/20,000; all rates are on half board. Meals can be taken in any of the restaurants at La Pirogue or the Sugar Beach resort.

Sofitel Impérial (☎ 453 8700, fax 453 8320, **e** sofitel@bow.intnet.mu) is a magnificent Japanese-style hotel with a wonderful pool and ornamental gardens. The staff here sometimes seem to have a high opinion of themselves, but the facilities at the hotel, including three restaurants, tennis courts, water sports, sauna and a golf course, are incredibly

difficult to fault. Single/double/triple rooms start at US$280/375/510 while deluxe rooms begin at US$320/430/585. For a world-class splurge, the presidential suite is available for a cool US$945 a night.

Places to Eat

Klondike Hotel (see Places to Stay) has a daily buffet dinner (accompanied by live music on Monday, Wednesday and Friday) for Rs275 per person. On Saturday there's a special barbecue buffet and séga show for Rs320 per person. Nonresidents are advised to book ahead, especially on Saturday night.

Leslie Restaurant is a little Creole place opposite the Flic en Flac mall, serving Creole meals for about Rs100. It's open daily from 11 am to 4 pm and 6 to 10 pm.

Moti Mahal at Villas Caroline (see Places to Stay) is a well-regarded Indian restaurant that is open to nonresidents. The restaurant is open daily from noon to 2.30 pm and 7.30 to 10 pm.

There are a few options in the mall, including *Papayou*, which offers light Creole meals for around Rs150. It's open daily except Friday from 9.30 am to 3.30 pm and 6 to 10 pm.

Also in the mall, *Bois Noire* is open daily except Sunday from 11 am to 3 pm and 6 to 10 pm for Chinese-influenced food. Main courses cost from Rs90.

Sea Breeze (☎ 453 8413) in the centre is very popular with locals and tourists who come for the tasty Chinese cuisine. Main dishes start at Rs95; for a splurge, try the grilled lobster (Rs350). The restaurant is open daily except Tuesday from 11.30 am to 2 pm and 6 to 10 pm.

Casa Pizza at Villa Paul & Virginie (see Places to Stay) offers great pizzas and paella for around Rs200. It's open weekday nights from 7 to 11 pm and there's live music till 1 am on Saturday and Sunday. It's very popular so book ahead.

Close to the public beach, the elegant *Ocean Restaurant* (☎ 453 8627) is another good Chinese place with mains such as chicken with cashew nuts, and beef with oyster sauce, as well as other Chinese standards from Rs90. This place is open daily from 11 am to 3 pm and 6 to 10 pm.

Mer de Chine offers snack meals such as *mien frit* (fried noodles) and grilled *poisson* (fish) for Rs70 to Rs100. It's open daily except Monday from 10 am to 3 pm and 6 to 10 pm.

Le Pearle Beach Hotel (see Places to Stay) is recommended for a special meal. There are also buffet dinners accompanied by live music for Rs375. The Mauritian buffet on Wednesday and the séga display on Saturday are recommended.

Getting There & Away

There is usually a bus from Port Louis to Flic en Flac every hour (Rs14). A taxi from Port Louis to Flic en Flac will cost you around Rs250 (one way).

Getting Around

Most of the hotels and guesthouses should be able to arrange bicycle hire – expect to pay around Rs100 to Rs150 per day.

For car hire, Easy World Apartments (see Places to Stay) offers small cars from Rs1000 per day (it's worth paying the extra Rs150 per day to reduce the excess from Rs15,000 to Rs5,000). A little further along Route Royale, Itinéraire Limitée (☎ 453 8475) also charges from Rs1000 per day (plus Rs150 for insurance).

Mopeds can be hired for Rs400 per day from Duo Scooters (☎ 243 9448) on the main road.

TAMARIN

Tamarin rode high on the wave of surfing enthusiasm that swept the island in the 1970s, but the scene has died down considerably these days. There are some good surfing spots in the bay and an OK beach (for more information, see Activities in the Mauritius Facts for the Visitor chapter). There are also a number of cheap places to stay.

The surrounding landscape is drier and harsher than elsewhere in Mauritius. Salt harvesting is a major industry in the area; Tamarin is encircled by salt evaporation ponds.

Places to Stay

There are several places to stay along the narrow roads leading down to the beach.

The *Tamarin Hotel* (☎ 483 6581, fax 483 6927) is right near the beach, but it's not the most marvellous value for money. Singles/doubles are Rs760/960 including breakfast; an extra bed is Rs180. There's a swimming pool and a restaurant.

There is something of a travellers scene at *Chez Jacques* (☎ 483 6445) on the main road down to the beach. The complex of self-catering flats can get pretty noisy, but most guests are looking for a bit of life. Apartments on the ground floor are Rs300; apartments upstairs are Rs400. There are surfboards for hire for Rs200 per day.

The basic *Saraja Guesthouse* (☎ 483 6168) on Anthurium Ave offers simple but clean rooms and self-catering apartments, both for Rs200 a double.

Places to Eat

The restaurant at the *Tamarin Hotel* (see Places to Stay) offers slightly pricey international cuisine. It's open daily for lunch and dinner.

Tam Café is a groovy coffee shop on the main street that serves snack lunches and coffee.

On the main road, *Les Salines Cafeteria* (☎ 251 0950) serves Chinese and Mauritian food such as sweet and sour fish for around Rs90. It's open daily except Tuesday from 11 am to 2 pm and 6.30 to 10 pm.

Getting There & Around

The Quatre Bornes–Baie du Cap bus service covers Tamarin and Grande Rivière Noire. You have to change at Baie du Cap for Souillac and Mahébourg, and at Quatre Bornes for Curepipe and Port Louis. The fare on any leg is around Rs12.

A taxi from the airport to Tamarin costs about Rs700; from Tamarin to Port Louis it's Rs500.

Bicycles are available for hire at Chez Jacques (see Places to Stay) for Rs100 per day. You may be able to hire a local boat for fishing, snorkelling or cruising – ask your hotel to recommend a reliable operator.

MAURITIUS

GRANDE RIVIÈRE NOIRE & LA PRENEUSE

Just offshore from the mouth of the Grande Rivière Noire estuary, the ocean bottom plunges to 700m, providing the perfect environment for jacks and other bait fish. These small fry attract big predators such as tuna, shark and marlin, which in turn attract big-game fishermen to the otherwise sleepy community of Grande Rivière Noire.

About 2km north of Grand Rivière Noire is La Preneuse. La Preneuse got its name from a French ship involved in a naval battle with the English in this area during the late 18th century. This famous battle was first recorded in *Voyages, Aventures et Combats* by Louis Garnenay; it has more recently been made into a novel, *Le Vingt Floréal Au Matin*, by Marcelle Lagesse. Martello Tower is an old lookout station here that stands with its cannons aimed at the sea.

Deep-Sea Fishing

Deep-sea fishing is the main activity here (see the boxed text 'Game for a Marlin?') and several hotels and clubs offer fully equipped boats. The Hotel Club & Centre de Pêche (see Places to Stay) charges Rs7700 for six hours of fishing, or Rs9350 for nine hours. The Island Sports Club Hotel is slightly cheaper, with half-day trips for Rs5000 and full-day trips for Rs7000. The guesthouse Les Bougainvilliers can also arrange trips for around Rs6000 a day. The Paradis and Berjaya Le Morne Beach Resort hotels on Le Morne peninsula also offer fishing trips.

The angling season runs from November to March. (For detailed information, see Activities in the Mauritius Facts for the Visitor chapter.)

Places to Stay & Eat

The accommodation and dining options are strung out between La Preneuse and Grande Rivière Noire. They are described here roughly north to south.

On the coastal road, *Les Latiniers Bleu* (☎ 483 6541, fax 483 6903) offers attractive self-catering villas in a peaceful garden setting. The villas have two to five bedrooms;

Game for a Marlin?

Surrounded on all sides by deep ocean, Mauritius is a big-game fisherman's dream. The sport was once seen as the ultimate sweetener for corporate high-flyers, but it's come downmarket in recent years and now almost anyone can take a pop at catching marlin, tuna, shark or sailfish.

Most boats employ a technique called trolling; live bait or squidlike lures are trailed along near the surface of the water where the big fish and their prey like to hang out. The emphasis is usually on satisfaction rather than challenge for the angler. Most boats trail anything from four to ten lines and have three or more crew standing by to make sure that the fisherman lands the fish.

Once the catch has been weighed and photographed, the boat owners make a second dividend by selling the fish to be smoked or served up in local hotels and restaurants. However, tag-and-release is making a slow appearance in the Indian Ocean. Game fishing has far less environmental impact than commercial fishing, but the weight and the number of fish caught has shown a marked decline since its heyday in the 1970s.

you can rent one room for Rs350 or you can rent the whole villa for Rs1300 to Rs1600. There's a swimming pool, and evening meals are available.

Les Bougainvilliers (☎ 483 6525, fax 483 6332) is on the beach at La Preneuse near the radio tower. Good double rooms cost Rs900 including breakfast (Rs700 for one person). The friendly and helpful manager can organise good deals for car hire, fishing trips and island excursions.

La Bonne Chute (☎ 483 6552) is beside the Caltex petrol station on the main road. The speciality is seafood; dishes such as steamed crab cost from Rs170 to Rs310. It's open daily except Sunday from 11 am to 3 pm and 7 to 10 pm.

The simple *Seama Beach Hotel* (☎ 483 6031, fax 483 6214) is close to the public beach at La Preneuse. Ordinary singles/

doubles cost Rs600/1100 with breakfast (Rs850/1500 on half board).

Le Cabanon Créole is a tasteful Creole cafe offering set meals such as fish in Creole sauce with rice and lentils for Rs140. It's open from 9.30 to 9.30 pm.

The *Island Sports Club Hotel* (☎ 483 5353, fax 483 6547) has rooms starting at Rs2215/3170 with breakfast (Rs2700/4140 on half board). The hotel is popular with older guests. It has a pool and a dive centre, and can organise deep-sea fishing trips and other excursions.

Right by the river mouth, the *Hotel Club & Centre de Pêche* (☎ 483 6522, fax 483 6318) is the leading angling centre in the area and (not surprisingly) has a good seafood *restaurant*. Rooms cost Rs1975/2760 on a half-board basis (it's Rs200 more from December to January). The restaurant here offers dishes such as smoked marlin salad and fish kebabs from Rs125. The restaurant is open daily from noon to 2 pm and 7.30 to 10 pm.

On the highway just north of Grande Rivière Noire, *Pavillon de Chine* is another cheap Chinese place. It's open daily from 11 am to 3 pm and 6 to 10 pm.

Pavillon de Jade, just south of Grande Rivière Noire, is a Chinese restaurant offering meals (including takeaway food) at reasonable prices. It's open daily except Monday from 11 am to 3.30 pm and 6.30 to 10 pm.

CHAMAREL

The spectacular waterfall and unusual 'coloured earths' are actually 4km south of the quiet village of Chamarel. These unusual natural phenomena feature on almost all tour itineraries, so it can be difficult to see either the sands or the waterfall for the hordes of package tourists.

Both attractions lie in the grounds of a private estate that once formed part of the estate of Charles de Chazal de Chamarel, who entertained Matthew Flinders during Flinders' captivity in Mauritius during the Napoleonic Wars. You can read more about Flinders and his time in Mauritius in Huguette Ly-Tio-Fane Pineo's book *In the Grips of the Eagle: Matthew Flinders at the Île de France, 1803–1810.*

The road to the estate begins at the gatehouse in the village of Cachette, where you must pay Rs25 per person. The road down to the coloured earths first passes a lookout point over the Chamarel waterfall. These are the highest falls in Mauritius and plunge over 100m.

A short distance further down the road is the viewing area where you can survey the coloured earths. The earths are interesting rather than amazing; the seven differently coloured layers of earth are believed to have been formed by the uneven cooling of molten rock. A large area has been cleared of vegetation so visitors can see the different colours, though in fact the earths continue over much of the surrounding countryside.

A curious quality of the coloured earth is that if it is mixed together in a tube, each colour separates again after several days. At the entrance gate you can buy various trinkets that let you put this theory to the test.

The attractions are open daily from 8.30 am to 5 pm.

Places to Eat

Just north of the falls, *Le Chamarel Restaurant* (☎ 483 1939) has great views and offers upmarket Mauritian fare including venison for upmarket prices. *Carri poulet* (chicken curry) and other mains cost from Rs230. The restaurant is open daily except Sunday from noon to 3 pm.

Getting There & Away

There are infrequent buses from Baie du Cap to Chamarel. Going in the opposite direction, you can take the Baie du Cap bus from La Preneuse, get off at Grand Case Noyale and walk uphill about 7km to the coloured earths. From Quatre Bornes there's a bus service departing daily for Chamarel (Rs15).

If you are travelling by car or taxi, you can also get here via the scenic road that crosses Plaine Champagne.

All the major tour operators run excursions to Chamarel, usually including it with Grand Bassin and Trou aux Cerfs.

MAURITIUS

LE MORNE PENINSULA

The sandy coastline stretches uninterrupted for 4km around the 'hammerhead' of the west coast, after the Paradis hotel's beach. A number of exclusive hotels have taken advantage of the spectacular setting at Le Morne, but there are some spectacular stretches of unclaimed beach here. If you don't feel intimidated by the neighbours, there's a chance to grab a secluded camping spot at the public beach beyond the Paradis hotel.

Le Morne Brabant

Reminiscent of the Rock of Gibraltar, Le Morne Brabant is very imposing. The cliffs are said to be unscaleable, but, in the early 19th century, escaped slaves managed to hide out on top. The story has it that the slaves, ignorant of the fact that slavery had been abolished, panicked when they saw a troop of soldiers making their way up the cliffs one day. Believing they were to be recaptured, the slaves flung themselves from the cliff tops. Hence the name Le Morne (The Mournful One).

Places to Stay & Eat

Dominating the peninsula, the *Paradis* (☎ *450 5050, fax 450 5140*) belongs to the Beachcomber group of hotels. Suitably luxurious singles/doubles cost from Rs11,800/13,400 on a half-board basis. Guests can enjoy the usual water sports, games and activities for free – or pay a surcharge to use the 18-hole golf course, the dive centre, the horse-riding school and the deep-sea fishing centre.

Despite having a great location, the huge *Berjaya Le Morne Beach Resort* (☎ *450 5800, fax 450 5670,* e *berjaya@intnet.mu*) is a little lacking in atmosphere. The complex includes two *restaurants*, a casino and a big pool, as well as good water sports facilities. In the low season (from April to September), rooms start at Rs5200/7800.

Dwarfed by the hotels on either side, *Les Pavillons* (☎ *450 5217, fax 450 5248*) is a small Naïade resort. This place has its own dive centre, three *restaurants* and a pool. Rates start at Rs3300 per person per night on a half-board basis.

South Mauritius

The southern region of Mauritius comprises the districts of Savanne and Grand Port, and is centred on the towns of Souillac and Mahébourg. After the commercialism of the north-west, you'll find the south coast refreshingly free from tourist developments, which greatly adds to its appeal. Much of the area is given over to sugar cane, but there are still some impressive areas of preserved forest on the slopes of the Montagnes Bambous range north-east of Mahébourg. Sun lovers can soak up the rays and indulge in the usual water sports at the peaceful resort of Blue Bay.

HIGHLIGHTS

- Visiting the Naval Museum on the outskirts of Mahébourg
- Hiking up Lion Mountain for the view over Vieux Grand Port
- Dining and rambling in the Domaine du Chasseur and Domaine de l'Ylang Ylang estates
- Exploring the rugged coastline near Souillac
- Snorkelling or just unwinding by the beach at Blue Bay

MAHÉBOURG

Mahébourg (pronounced may-burg) was named after the famous French governor Bertrand François Mahé de La Bourdonnais. Historically the town was a busy port, but these days it's something of a backwater, with a small fishing fleet and a relaxed and friendly atmosphere. All that may change if the government's plan to build a development like the Caudan Waterfront complex in Port Louis goes ahead.

As Mahébourg is the town closest to the airport, many people spend just the first or last days of their trip here, but it makes a good base from which to explore the unspoilt south coast. The bay forms a picturesque backdrop for the town, with the sea changing from one intense colour to another at great speed. The nearby Blue Bay makes a good beach stop.

Naval Museum

The Creole mansion housing the museum is set at the end of a tree-lined drive, on the outskirts of Mahébourg on the Curepipe road. It used to belong to the De Robillard family and played an important part in the island's history.

It was here in 1810 that the injured commanders of the French and English fleets were taken for treatment after the Battle of Vieux Grand Port, the only naval battle in which the French got the upper hand over their British foes. The story of the victory is displayed in the museum, along with salvaged items from the British frigate *Magicienne*, which sank in the battle. In 1933, divers on the wreck retrieved cannons, grapeshot and bottles.

Also here is the bell from the famous wreck of the *St Géran*. The ship sank on 17 August 1744, off the north-east coast of Mauritius; the bell was recovered by French divers in 1966. The disaster inspired the love story *Paul et Virginie* by Bernardin de St Pierre (see the boxed text 'Paul & Virginie' in the North Mauritius chapter).

A more recent sea disaster was the sinking of the British steamer *Trevessa*. She went down on 4 June 1923 in the Indian Ocean, 2576km from Mauritius, on her way from Fremantle in Western Australia. Sixteen men survived at sea for 25 days in an open lifeboat, which landed at Bel Ombre in south-west Mauritius. Exhibited at the museum is the men's last biscuit ration, a razor and the cigarette-tin lid used to measure out the water rations. The men's survival is commemorated each year on the anniversary of the day the lifeboat reached Mauritius (29 June) as Seafarers' Day.

Other exhibits include relics from the corsair Robert Surcouf; the furniture of Mahé de

MAURITIUS

SOUTH MAURITIUS

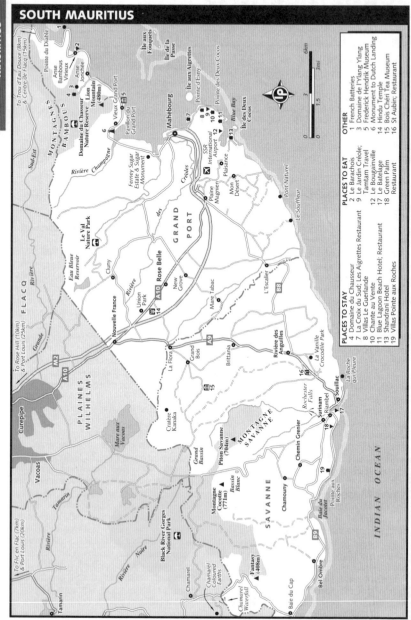

PLACES TO STAY
1   Domaine du Chausseur
7   La Croix du Sud; Les Aigrettes Restaurant
8   Villas Le Guerlande
10 Chante au Vente
11 Blue Lagoon Beach Hotel; Restaurant
13 Shandrani Hotel
19 Villas Pointe aux Roches

PLACES TO EAT
2   Le Barachois
9   Le Jardin Créole;
    Tamtam Travel
12 Le Bougainville
17 Le Batelage
18 Green Palm
    Restaurant

OTHER
1   French Batteries
3   Domaine de l'Ylang Ylang
6   Frederick Hendrik Museum
    Monument to Dutch Landing
14 Hindu Temple
15 Bois Chéri Tea Museum
16 St Aubin; Restaurant

La Bourdonnais; early Dutch and Portuguese maps of Mauritius (one based on a visit by Abel Tasman in 1642); and paintings of figures pivotal in the history of Mauritius.

The recently renovated museum (☎ 631 9329) is open daily except Tuesday and Friday from 9 am to 5 pm. Admission is free.

Nôtre Dame des Anges

Nôtre Dame des Anges church is a historic colonial church that dominates the town with its yellow spire. The original church was built in 1849, but it has been restored several times over the years, most recently in 1938. Local people visit throughout the day to make offerings at the shrines to Père Laval and other popular figures.

Places to Stay

Mahébourg caters well for independent travellers. The best of the guesthouses is the friendly *Aquarelle* (☎ 631 9479), which is set in a quiet courtyard overlooking the bay on Rue Swami Shivananda. Singles/doubles with shared bathroom start at Rs350/370 (rooms one and two have the best views), while the one-bedroom thatched bungalows in the garden cost Rs550. All prices include breakfast.

Another friendly option is the *Nice Place Guest House* (☎ 631 9419) on the corner of Rue de Labourdonnais and Rue du Hangard. It's run by a lovely Indian couple and tidy rooms cost Rs250/350. There's also an apartment with kitchen and TV for Rs400/500 (Rs600 for three people).

Less appealing is the huge *Coco Villa* (☎ 631 2192, fax 631 9646) just next to Aquarelle. This tasteless modern edifice is usually empty, but if you're still interested, singles and doubles with bathroom start at Rs550 (Rs900 with air-con).

The attractive *Hôtel Les Aigrettes* (☎/fax 631 9094) on Rue du Chaland has airy rooms with balconies, fan and TV starting at Rs450/600. There's a restaurant for residents only. Management can arrange car hire.

Pension Nôtre Dame (☎ 631 9582) is run by nuns in the convent at the Nôtre Dame des Anges church. Simple but tidy rooms with shared bathroom are Rs300/500 without breakfast, or Rs350/600 with breakfast. Ring the doorbell, and a nun will unlock the doors.

Places to Eat

For a snack meal, there are several lunch places and snack stands by the bus station.

China Delices on Rue des Cent Gaullettes is an above-average Chinese restaurant. It has excellent *riz frit* (fried rice), *mien* (noodles) and *bol renverse* (literally 'bowl turned over', a dish of rice and meat served in an upturned bowl). Prices start at Rs45. It's open from 10.30 am to 8 pm daily except Sunday.

On Rue Hollandais, *La Colombe* (☎ 631 8594) has an interesting variety of Creole and Chinese food. The *soupe aux pecheurs* (fisherman's soup) is to die for. Mains cost from Rs90. The restaurant is open from 7 am to 3 pm and 6 to 10 pm daily.

Aquarelle (see Places to Stay) has a very good restaurant that serves excellent Creole cuisine; the *carri poisson* (fish curry) here is superb. Most main dishes start at around Rs120. Nonresidents should call ahead.

By the market, *Dragon de Chine* (☎ 631 5697) offers Chinese and Mauritian seafood on an airy balcony. Dishes such as grilled fish with ginger cost around Rs200. It's open from 10 am to 10 pm daily.

Chez Patrick (☎ 631 9298) near the old Nôtre Dame des Anges church on Mahébourg Rd offers fresh seafood including squid, octopus, crab and fish in Chinese or Mauritian sauces from Rs100.

Restaurant Le Phare (☎ 631 9728) is a swish place on the seafront. It has mains such as prawns in Creole sauce from Rs425. It's open from 9.30 am to 3 pm and 6 pm until around 11 pm daily.

Entertainment

By the bus station, the modern Mahé Cinema screens Indian and international blockbusters.

An open-air amphitheatre is under construction at Pointe Canon on the seafront, and will be the venue for cultural events and plays. Call the tourist office in Port Louis (☎ 208 6397) for more information.

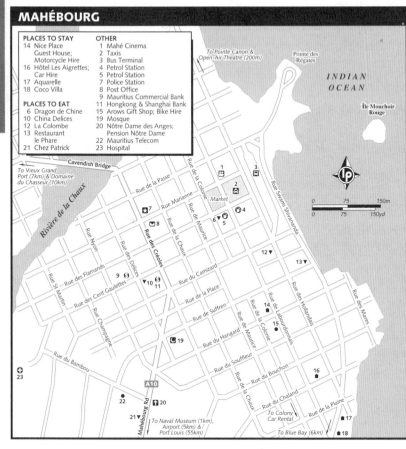

MAHÉBOURG

PLACES TO STAY	OTHER
14 Nice Place Guest House; Motorcycle Hire	1 Mahé Cinema
	2 Taxis
	3 Bus Terminal
16 Hôtel Les Aigrettes; Car Hire	4 Petrol Station
	5 Petrol Station
17 Aquarelle	7 Police Station
18 Coco Villa	8 Post Office
	9 Mauritius Commercial Bank
PLACES TO EAT	11 Hongkong & Shanghai Bank
6 Dragon de Chine	15 Arows Gift Shop; Bike Hire
10 China Delices	19 Mosque
12 La Colombe	20 Nôtre Dame des Anges;
13 Restaurant	Pension Nôtre Dame
le Phare	22 Mauritius Telecom
21 Chez Patrick	23 Hospital

Getting There & Away

There are regular buses to Curepipe (Rs14) and less frequent direct buses to Port Louis (Rs16). There are express buses to both destinations for the same prices; they leave about every hour and take half the time. The shuttle to Blue Bay runs every 30 minutes (Rs9).

On a less frequent basis, buses running north from Mahébourg go to Centre de Flacq (Rs15) via Vieux Grand Port and Grand Sable, and to Souillac (Rs14) via Rivière des Anguilles.

A taxi from SSR international airport to Mahébourg costs around Rs300.

Getting Around

Car & Motorcycle You can rent cars at the Hôtel Les Aigrettes (see Places to Stay) for around Rs900 per day. A credit card or cash deposit is required. Alternatively, Colony Car Rental (☎ 631 7062) on Rue de la Colonie charges from Rs750 per day.

The Nice Place Guest House (see Places to Stay) hires out 125cc motorcycles for Rs500 a day.

Bicycle Bicycles are available for hire from Arows Gift Shop on Rue de Labourdonnais and some local pensions and hotels for around Rs90 per day. Blue Bay makes a leisurely excursion by bicycle.

BLUE BAY

Just 6km south of Mahébourg, this attractive resort has a pleasant sandy beach and a brilliant blue lagoon with good snorkelling at the southern end. At weekends Blue Bay is a popular picnic spot for Mauritian families, but during the week it can be blissfully quiet. There are several restaurants and hotels here and visitors can indulge in the usual array of water sports.

Tamtam Travel (☎ 631 8642) on the road to Blue Bay offers trips in glass-bottomed boats and snorkelling in Blue Bay for Rs265. It also offers trips to Île aux Cerfs with lunch for Rs1210 by catamaran, Rs600 by speedboat, or Rs750 by fishing boat with freshly caught fish for lunch. Île aux Fouquets trips with snorkelling and lunch cost Rs475.

Hotel dive centres include Coral Garden (☎ 631 1651) at Chante au Vent, and Coral Dive (☎ 631 9505) at La Croix du Sud, both in Blue Bay.

Several hotels in Blue Bay offer séga nights and other extravaganzas.

Places to Stay

The plushest option is *La Croix du Sud* (☎ *631 9505, fax 631 9603*) at Pointe Jérôme on the Mahébourg–Blue Bay road. This upmarket resort offers an excellent range of facilities, including two pools, a fitness centre, tennis courts and a dive school. During the high season (October, November, January, March and April) singles/doubles/triples cost Rs2530/3180/4100 including breakfast. Rooms are Rs2050/2530/3400 at other times. Guests can take advantage of numerous water activities including windsurfing and trips to Île aux Cerfs. There is a séga night each Friday.

Villas Le Guerlande (☎ *631 9882, fax 631 9225*) is a complex of self-catering bungalows set in a pleasant garden beside the beach. A two-bedroom bungalow with kitchen, terrace and a sea view costs Rs2296 for a single or double (or Rs1736 without the view). There are also larger bungalows which cost Rs2800/3248 for

three/four people (or Rs2296/2800 without the view). All rates are for half board.

Close to the public beach, *Chante au Vent* (☎/*fax 631 9614*) is a pleasant *pension de famille* (boarding house) with its own dive centre. Doubles with bathroom start at Rs900 including breakfast (Rs1000 with kitchenette). There are also self-catering bungalows with one and two bedrooms starting at Rs1000 and Rs1200 respectively.

The *Blue Lagoon Beach Hotel* (☎ *631 9529, fax 631 9045*) is right on the excellent public beach at Blue Bay. Facilities include a small pool, a tennis court, a bar and a restaurant (see Places to Eat), and water activities are also available. During the high season (August to November and January to March) singles/doubles cost Rs1620/2600 including breakfast. At other times of year, prices drop by around 10%. Half board costs an extra Rs200 per person.

Shandrani Hotel (☎ *637 4301, fax 637 4313*) on the far side of Blue Bay is reached by a private road near the SSR airport. This hotel is set in lovely grounds and has all the facilities you would expect from a Beachcomber hotel, including a swimming pool, a tennis court and three restaurants. Rooms start at Rs11,000 on half board. Opulent suites start at a cool Rs23,000 on half board. The Shandrani has all the sport and leisure options of other luxury beach hotels, including diving, fishing and horse riding.

Places to Eat

Beside the public beach, the popular *Le Bougainville* (☎ *631 8299*) offers pizzas for Rs120 and dishes such as spaghetti with smoked marlin for Rs90 and upwards. It's open from 10 am to 3 pm and 6.30 to 10 pm daily.

At Pointe d'Esny, *Le Jardin Créole* (☎ *631 5801*) is an attractive Creole place offering mains such as chicken with chillis for Rs165 to Rs200. It's open daily except Monday from noon to midnight. There's live music here on Friday night.

Blue Lagoon Beach Hotel (see Places to Stay) has a restaurant serving a buffet dinner each night for Rs346 per person, often with a séga show. Nonresidents should book ahead.

Les Aigrettes at La Croix du Sud (see Places to Stay) offers a special séga buffet on Saturday and an Indian buffet on Tuesday, each for Rs200 per person plus tax. Nonresidents must book in advance.

Getting There & Around
The public bus to Mahébourg runs every 30 minutes for Rs9. A taxi to Mahébourg will cost Rs50.

Tamtam Travel (☎ 631 8642) at Pointe d'Esny rents bicycles for Rs75 per day.

ÎLE AUX AIGRETTES
This island nature reserve is a few kilometres off the coast. It preserves very rare remnants of the coastal forests of Mauritius. Approximately half of the island has been cleared of introduced species, and native plants are being replanted. The ecosystem is also being restored through the eradication of rats and shrews, which are imported pests that cause damage to rare plant species and prevent the reintroduction of endemic reptiles, such as the burrowing boa, the Telfair's skink and the Gunther's gecko.

The island serves as a convenient quarantine station for pink pigeons and Mauritian kestrels sent from overseas breeding schemes for eventual release into the wild. Guests at the nearby La Croix du Sud hotel on the mainland have become used to the sight of the kestrels popping over from the island for a visit.

Gerard Etienne (☎ 631 0434) offers entertaining tours to Île de la Passe on the edge of the lagoon. The ruins here belong to an old quarantine station, and are covered in graffiti dating back over four centuries. The tours are run by lively members of the Etienne family and cost Rs650, including snorkelling and a barbecue lunch by the lighthouse on nearby Île aux Fouquets (aka Île aux Phares).

VIEUX GRAND PORT
Vieux Grand Port, about 7km north of Mahébourg, was the site of the first Dutch settlement in Mauritius, Fort Frederick Hendrik. About 4km from Mahébourg, on the banks of the Rivière Champagne, is a monument commemorating the first landing by Dutch sailors, which took place on 9 September 1598 under the command of Wybrandt Van Warwyck.

The ruins of the Dutch fort can be found near the church at the northern end of Vieux Grand Port. The ruins are surrounded by a pretty park that also contains the **Frederick Hendrik Museum**. The museum traces the history of the Dutch in Mauritius. The exhibits on display include artefacts recovered from the area and records from the journals of Dutch ships. The museum is open from 9 am to 4 pm Monday to Saturday and 9 am to noon on Sunday.

Vieux Grand Port was also the site of the only French naval victory to be inscribed on the Arc de Triomphe in Paris. Relics of the 1810 battle with the English are on display at the Naval Museum in Mahébourg.

The area is devoted to sugar production; you can see the magnificent Creole mansion of the Ferney sugar estate from the coastal highway. Nearby is a monument commemorating the introduction of sugar cane by the Dutch in 1639.

AROUND VIEUX GRAND PORT
Lion Mountain
Overlooking Vieux Grand Port is Lion Mountain (Pic du Lion). This distinctive peak in the Montagnes Bambous range takes its name from its sphinx-like profile.

Lion Mountain offers a splendid half-day hike with stunning views over the coast. It's a challenging but rewarding walk that climbs up the lion's 'back', finishing at an impressive viewpoint on the 'head'. The trail begins just north of Vieux Grand Port, where the coastal highway first hits the sea.

An easy-to-find 4WD track heads inland through the sugar cane right on the point; you should turn right at the first junction and follow the trail up towards the ridge. A set of concrete steps begins on the right just after you reach the start of the forested area. The steps lead to a bunker and the trail proper begins from here, climbing through the forest to the top of the lion's back. Once here you can detour to the right for a view out over the coast before heading inland to the peak itself.

The main trail is very obvious and runs straight along the ridge and up over a rocky area to the main peak. There are a few hairy scrambles over the rocks before you reach the flat area on the lion's head. From here you can see right across the interior of the island. Return the same way you came up.

Allow around three hours for the return trip. Buses between Mahébourg and Centre de Flacq pass through Vieux Grand Port regularly, so you shouldn't have to wait long for a ride in either direction.

Anse Bambous Virieux

This small settlement is the site of a pioneering project to restore the mangroves that were destroyed by the British following the malaria epidemic of 1866 (see the boxed text 'Replanting the Mangroves' in the Rodrigues chapter).

There are nature trails through the mangroves at *Le Barachois* (☎ 634 5643), a restaurant that offers tasty seafood in small huts overlooking the water. Mains such as seafood curry with lentils cost from Rs250. It's open daily for lunch from 10 am to 4 pm.

Domaine du Chasseur

As its name suggests, Domaine du Chasseur (☎ 634 5097, fax 634 5261) or Estate of the Hunter is primarily a hunting reserve for wild boar and deer. The 900 hectares of forested mountain terrain also act as a nature reserve for monkeys and for many endemic bird species, including the Mauritian kestrel – one of the world's rarest birds of prey. You can watch the kestrels being fed white mice at around 3 pm daily.

If there are no hunters in town, visitors can hike around the estate for Rs50 (this fee is waived if you stay at the bungalows or dine at the excellent restaurant). The estate also offers guided two-hour forest walks or one-hour waterfall walks for Rs200.

Accommodation is provided on the hillside in bungalows – a great spot if you fancy a splurge away from the beach. Rates for single/double occupancy are around Rs1200/1600 with breakfast.

The estate also boasts an excellent restaurant, *Panoramour*, which is perched on the top of a hill by the helipad. The attractive thatched dining room offers lovely views over the coast and is a great place to try Creole delicacies such as venison and wild boar. Roast boar with yams costs Rs325, while venison flamed in brandy is Rs425. True gourmets may want to sample the pan-fried deer brains for Rs475. The restaurant is open daily from 8.30 am to 4.30 pm, and from 7 to 11 pm if you make a reservation.

Getting There & Away Domaine du Chasseur is 3km inland from the coastal road at Anse Jonchée, about 12km from Mahébourg. It's well signposted from the main road. If you phone ahead, it is usually possible to arrange to be picked up at the main road. Buses to Mahébourg (Rs12) and Centre de Flacq (Rs14) pass by every 30 minutes or so. A taxi from Mahébourg will cost around Rs200 one way.

Domaine de l'Ylang Ylang

This small estate (☎ 634 5668) on the road up towards the Domaine du Chasseur is the only surviving commercial perfume distillery in Mauritius. Flowers and plants grown for their essential oils include the heady ylang-ylang flower, the geranium, vetiver, lemongrass, camphor and *baie rose* (pink pepper).

The estate offers a variety of guided 4WD and walking tours. A tour of the distillery where the plant oils are extracted costs Rs75 per person; walking tours of the plantation cost Rs60, or Rs125 per person by 4WD. A tour of the plantation, distillery and forest with lunch costs Rs445 per person.

If you fall for any of the scents you smell, essential oils are available in the estate boutique. You'll pay around Rs200 for 10ml of ylang-ylang essence. Also on the estate is a good *restaurant* serving dishes such as venison in *chasseur* sauce (a rich sauce made from the fresh blood of the deer) for around Rs225.

The estate is open daily from 9am to 5 pm. To get here take the Domaine du Chasseur road and then the signposted turning on the right about 2km from the junction with the coastal highway.

LE VAL NATURE PARK

The road into Le Val starts around Union Park village, about halfway along the Mahébourg-Curepipe road. The village of Cluny, in the valley of the Rivière des Créoles, is the gateway to the park.

Many of the amazing anthurium flowers are grown at Le Val in shade houses. There are also fields full of watercress, which complements many Creole meals, and there are some attempts at prawn farming. Other facilities include a small aquarium and a deer park. Le Val is open daily from 9 am to 5 pm. Admission is Rs50 for adults and Rs25 for children.

Bus 14 runs from Curepipe to Rose Belle via Cluny (Rs13).

LE SOUFFLEUR

This impressive blowhole lies in the grounds of the Savanne sugar mill, which is just outside the village of L'Escalier on the Souillac –Plaine Magnien road. The road is signposted 'Le Souffleur' and winds for 4km through the sugar estate down to the rugged black lava cliffs. You can visit on weekdays from 7 am to 4 pm and on Saturday from 7 am to noon.

ST AUBIN

Owned by the Bois Chéri tea company, St Aubin (☎ 626 1513) is a splendid old Creole mansion which dates to 1819. Today, the traditionally furnished house offers a very good *table d'hôte* of Creole food at lunch time for Rs550. The estate no longer produces sugar, but there is an anthurium and vanilla plantation that you can walk around. St Aubin is near Grand Bois; it is open Monday to Saturday from 11 am to 3.30 pm.

BOIS CHÉRI TEA MUSEUM

This museum is also a working factory that processes the tea from the extensive estates of Bois Chéri, located about 10km south of Curepipe. Visitors are taken on a guided tour of the tea-making process. The tour finishes off with a tea tasting in the company chalet, which offers panoramic views of the coast.

Bois Chéri is on the road to Grand Bassin, which branches off the Curepipe-Souillac road at La Flora. The museum is open on weekdays from 8.30 am to 3.30 pm, and on Saturday from 8.30 to 11.30 am (closed Sunday). The 1½ hour tour costs Rs100 (call ☎ 251 1188 for more information).

BAIE DU CAP

In spite of a great variety of coastal scenery, this area has not been developed. There are some marvellous stretches of casuarina-lined beaches at La Prairie, west of the bay. There's good surf at Macondé Point, on the other side of the bay.

SOUILLAC

This town is named after the Vicomte de Souillac, the island's French governor from 1779 to 1787. Souillac itself is of little interest, but the coast here is impressively rugged and there are a few interesting places dotted around the town.

Robert Edward Hart Museum

Robert Edward Hart (1891–1954) was a renowned Mauritian poet, appreciated by the French and the English alike. He wrote in French, and translations of his poetry are hard to find. He lived out the last 13 years of his life at Le Nef, in a coral beach cottage about 500m east along the shore from the Souillac bus park.

The cottage was taken over by the Mauritius Institute and opened to the public as a museum in 1967. The bedroom and kitchen have been maintained. On display are some originals and copies of Hart's letters, plays, speeches and poetry, as well as his fiddle, spectacles and pith helmet. One of his speeches, on love and marriage, was delivered at the Curepipe hôtel de ville in 1914 for the benefit of English and French war victims. The museum (☎ 625 6101) is open from 9 am to 4 pm on weekdays and 9 am to noon at weekends. Entry is free.

Gris Gris

Continue along the road past Le Nef and the Robert Edward Hart Museum and you come to a grassy cliff top, which affords a view of the black rocky coastline where the reef is broken. There is a path here down to the rugged Gris Gris beach, where you'll see some lovely shells. The term 'gris gris' traditionally refers to 'black magic', and looking at the tortuous coastline, you can see how the area got its name. A wooden sign warns of the dangers of swimming here.

La Roche qui Pleure

La Roche qui Pleure (The Rock that Cries) is a little further east along the coast from Gris Gris and resembles a crying man. In fact it looks a lot like the profile of Robert Edward Hart. Two pictures in the Robert Edward Hart Museum show the comparison in case you can't find the actual rock.

Rochester Falls

A 5km walk north from Souillac, past the Terracine sugar mill and through the cane fields along a well-marked route, brings you to these pretty falls. The falls aren't particularly high, but they tumble over angular basalt columns created by a prehistoric volcano. The drive along the potholed tracks will test the suspension on your hire car. You may be able to persuade a taxi to take the risk for around Rs300 return from Souillac.

La Vanille Crocodile Park

Part zoo and part crocodile farm, La Vanille (☎ 626 2503) is 2km south of the hill town of Rivière des Anguilles; the turning is immediately on the right as you leave the Curepipe-Souillac road. The zoo has a successful breeding program for giant tortoises. There is also a variety of other reptiles and wildlife on display, though the commercially raised Nile crocodiles are the main attraction.

Crocodile products are on sale in the zoo shop; personally we feel that crocodiles look better without handles, but there's no strong

environmental reason not to buy. The park is open daily from 9.30 am to 5 pm. Admission costs Rs110/45 for adults/children on weekdays, and Rs90/40 on weekends.

Places to Stay

If you want to get away from it all, *Villas Pointe aux Roches* (☎ *625 6111, fax 625 6110*) is about 4km west of Souillac on the coast road. The villas are fairly unappealing white boxes, but the lovely beach and the setting among the palms are ample compensation. Singles/doubles cost Rs1344/2318 on half board. Facilities include a pool, a restaurant and minigolf.

Places to Eat

For a meal on the hop, there are some snack stands at the bus park in Souillac.

Le Batelage is a pleasant restaurant not far from Souillac which specialises in seafood. Dishes such as squid with Creole sauce cost around Rs250. The restaurant is open daily from noon to 5 pm and 7 to 9 pm.

The *Green Palm Restaurant*, on the coastal road, serves slightly humdrum Mauritian cuisine. Fish with Creole sauce and other fishy mains go for around Rs220. It's open daily from 10 am to 3 pm and 7 to 10 pm.

Getting There & Around

Souillac and Rivière des Anguilles are on the Baie du Cap–Mahébourg bus route. There are also regular buses to and from Curepipe, via Rivière des Anguilles (Rs10).

There is a bus service running direct between Curepipe, Souillac and Pointe aux Roches about three times a day. A taxi from Souillac to Villas Pointe aux Roches costs around Rs150.

Rodrigues

The rocky volcanic island of Rodrigues, 560km to the north-east of Mauritius, is often promoted as the 'other' Mauritius. The island can seem dry and rugged after the tropical lushness of Mauritius, but most people very quickly warm to the laid-back atmosphere and friendly Creole residents; everyone you meet is likely to try and strike up a conversation. As well as having some excellent deserted beaches, the island is surrounded by a pristine coral reef. There are also some attractive and rugged walks in the mountainous interior.

Although it measures only 8km by 18km, Rodrigues supports a population of about 37,000 people, almost all of African descent. Most speak Creole rather than French or English, and are strict Roman Catholics. After the abolition of slavery in Mauritius, many freed slaves chose to begin a new life here, away from their oppressors.

The economic mainstays for the islanders are fishing, subsistence agriculture, handicrafts, tourism and subsidised imports from Mauritius. The fisheries around the island are very rich, and visitors can indulge in all the usual fishing activities.

Overfarming and a succession of cyclones have stripped the island of much of its tree cover (Cyclone Bella produced wind speeds of 200km/h when it raged across the island in 1991). However, the resulting scrub is pleasant for walking, which really is the best way to see this island.

Rodrigues is receiving heavy promotion from some of the Mauritian tour operators, but for now the island still remains something of a retreat after the commercialism of Mauritius. It's not a bad idea to bring supplies of any special items you may need, such as prescription medicines or film; in Rodrigues the extra cost of transport is reflected in the price of goods imported from Mauritius.

The island is best visited in the dry season; you may struggle to fill the long rainy days from February to May.

Camping is possible just about anywhere on the island. The beaches around Pointe Coton and Grand Baie are good places to start.

History

The Portuguese had the honour of discovering Rodrigues for Europe and naming it after one of their intrepid seamen, but it was the Dutch who first set foot on the island, albeit very briefly, in 1601.

The Frenchman François Leguat and a small band of Huguenot companions sailed away from religious persecution in France and arrived here in 1691. Leguat enjoyed his paradisal existence on the island, but the lack of female company was an impediment to his complete contentment.

The island's fauna and flora was a source of wonder and of food – survival rather than conservation was the priority in those days. Leguat's journal, entitled *Voyage et Aventure de François Leguat en Deux Îles Désertes des Indes Orientales*, provides a vivid account of the group's two-year stay.

Subsequent visitors to Rodrigues set about ruthlessly removing the thousands of giant tortoises, which were a prized source of nourishment. Rodrigues also had a big flightless bird, the solitaire, which quickly went the same sorry way as the dodo.

The French returned early in the 18th century for another attempt at colonisation, but by the end of the century had abandoned

RODRIGUES

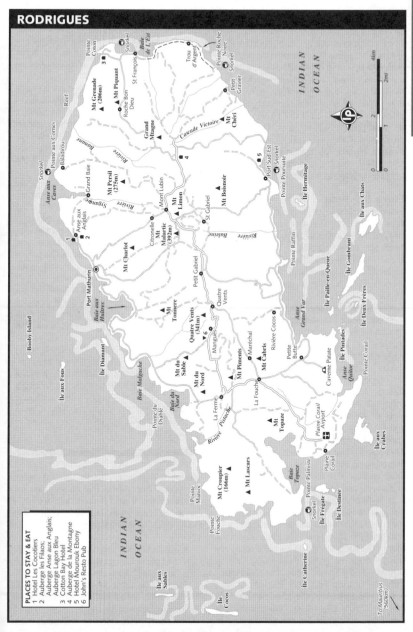

PLACES TO STAY & EAT
1 Hotel Les Cocotiers
2 Auberge les Filaos;
  Auberge Anse aux Anglais;
  Auberge Lagon Bleu
3 Cotton Bay Hotel
4 Auberge de la Montagne
5 Hotel Mourouk Ebony
6 John's Resto Pub

Rodrigues. In 1809, the British landed on the island and used it as a provisional base from which to attack and capture Mauritius.

Until it gained independence together with Mauritius in 1968, Rodrigues had an uneventful history. There is now a Ministry of Rodrigues in the Mauritian government that appoints an island secretary to look after the island's affairs. There are two political parties in Rodrigues, Organisation du Peuple Rodriguais (OPR), which is the dominant party led by Louis Serge Clair, and Mouvement Rodriguais, which is headed by Nicolas Vonmally.

Flora & Fauna

Since the island's colonisation in the 17th century, its thick forest cover has been destroyed by felling and intensive grazing; the cyclones haven't helped. The secondary growth with which the forest cover has been replaced consists mostly of introduced plant species. Of the 38 or so remaining species of plants native to Rodrigues, all but two are considered endangered, vulnerable, or rare.

Some species depend on one or two wild specimens for their continued existence; *cafe marron*, *bois pipe*, *mandrinette* and *bois pasner* are all in this precarious position.

The Mauritian government is acting to protect vegetation plots of critical importance such as Grande Montagne, Pigeon, Cascades, Mourouk, St Louis and Anse Quitor. These plots are fenced off from animal degradation and carefully weeded to remove introduced species (which grow much more quickly). Rare species are propagated in government nurseries on Rodrigues and then planted in these plots, where they have a better chance of survival and regeneration.

It is hoped that these areas will act as refuges for the island's rare endemic fauna, such as the Rodrigues warbler, the Rodrigues fody and the Rodrigues fruit bat. The warbler population has made a shaky recovery from virtual extinction in the 1960s to an estimated 65 pairs of birds. The Rodrigues fody population has also increased from very low numbers in the 1960s to approximately 200 pairs today. The extremely rare Rodrigues fruit bat spends the day in

Replanting the Mangroves

Following the 1866 malaria epidemic, in which nearly 3700 people died, the British colonial administration correctly identified the mangrove swamps around the coast of Mauritius and Rodrigues as the main breeding ground for malaria-carrying mosquitoes. As part of an organised campaign of destruction, huge tracts of mangrove were uprooted or burned and swamps were filled in with volcanic boulders. Eucalyptus trees were even brought in from Australia to dry up the marshy ground inland.

As an antimalarial strategy, the program was very successful. It was only later that scientists discovered the important role that the swamps played in the breeding cycles of many of the tropical fish that the islanders depended on for food. Further damage was done by the burgeoning beach hotels, which tried to extend the beaches by pulling up the mangroves that grew around them.

The salt tolerant trees of the *Rhizophora* genus are one of the few species that can live on the edge of the coral lagoon, and their gnarled roots provide a nursery for young fish and crustaceans.

Today the Mauritian government is taking steps to preserve the remaining mangroves, through government-sponsored replanting schemes on the north-west coast of Rodrigues and at Bambous Virieux on the south-east coast of Mauritius. Of course, what is good news for tropical fish will also be good news for mosquitoes!

communal roosts, usually in old mango trees, and becomes active at night when it searches for fruits, flowers and leaves. A common haunt for the bats is the valley about 4km south of Port Mathurin, towards Mont Lubin.

Colonies of sea birds, including the fairy tern and the noddy, nest on Île Cocos and Île aux Sables off the north-west coast.

One of the most significant projects for the environment as a whole is the replanting of the mangroves along the coast. This is particularly necessary in the north-west, where mangroves were destroyed under the British colonial administration to prevent the spread of malaria (see the boxed text 'Replanting the Mangroves' following). It is hoped that with restoration of the mangroves, the stocks of fish that many islanders depend on for food can be improved. You can see the orderly rows of mangrove saplings springing up from the mud between Baie aux Huîtres and Baie de Nord.

Dangers & Annoyances
Rodrigues' drinking water is generally neither chlorinated nor filtered. Bottled water is available from shops and most hotels; a 1L bottle costs around Rs8 but hotels and restaurants usually charge more.

PORT MATHURIN
As the administrative, commercial and industrial hub of the island, Port Mathurin is a lively little town and makes a natural base for visitors. In the evenings, the fishing jetty at the end of Rue Morrison is an attractive place to hang out and watch the sunset.

The section of town known as Camp du Roi is a burgeoning industrial development.

Information
Tourist Office There is no official tourist office on the island, but RodTours (☎ 831 2249, fax 831 2267), by the bridge near the intersection of Rue Duncan and Rue Johnston, is the local representative of Mauritours and offers fairly unbiased information about things to see and do on the island. There's another branch by the Résidences Le Tamaris apartments.

Money Barclays (☎ 831 1553), State Bank (☎ 831 1642) and Mauritius Commercial Bank (☎ 831 1833) all have offices in Port Mathurin. Opening hours are generally from 9 am to 3.15 pm Monday to Thursday and 9 am to 4 pm on Saturday. You can change money at all these banks.

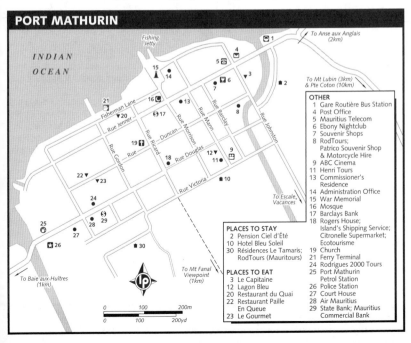

Post The main post office (☎ 831 2098) is on Rue Jenner in Port Mathurin. Opening hours are Monday to Friday from 8.15 to 4 pm and 8.15 to 11.45 am on Saturday. There are also small post offices at La Ferme and Mont Lubin.

Telephone The Mauritius Telecom office (☎ 831 1816) is on Rue Johnston and offers operator-assisted international calls and fax services. It also sells *télécartes* (phone-cards) for the cardphone located outside the office. It's open from 7.30 am to 3.30 pm Monday to Friday and from 8 am to 3.30 pm on Saturday.

Places to Stay

Pension Ciel d'Été (☎ 831 1587, fax 831 2004) on Rue Johnston in Port Mathurin is a tidy little place with singles/doubles/triples for Rs350/600/800 including breakfast or Rs500/900/1200 on half board.

Probably the best hotel in Port Mathurin is *Escale Vacances* (☎ 831 2555, fax 831 2075) a delightful small hotel with nice gardens, a lovely pool and a relaxed tropical atmosphere. Squeaky clean rooms cost Rs1265/2010 on half board (Rs1385/2250 with aircon). The restaurant here is excellent (see Places to Eat).

Résidences Le Tamaris (☎ 831 2715, fax 831 2720), owned by RodTours, is a complex of self-catering apartments with one, two and three bedrooms. Each has kitchenette, bathroom, air-con, phone and TV. Rates start at Rs875 for one bedroom, Rs1200 for two bedrooms and Rs1500 for three bedrooms. There's also a restaurant.

Hotel Beau Soleil (☎ 831 2783, fax 831 1612) on Rue Victoria is a little expensive for what you get and the service can be a tad lacklustre. Standard singles/doubles cost Rs400/750 including breakfast, or Rs500/950 on half board. Superior rooms go for Rs660/990 with breakfast, or Rs825/1320 on half board.

Places to Eat

Many people eat in their hotel or pension, but there are a handful of restaurants on the island offering traditional local cuisine.

Some items, such as lobster, are considerably cheaper in Rodrigues than in Mauritius.

Probably the nicest restaurant in Port Mathurin is the intimate little *Lagon Bleu* (☎ 831 1823) on Rue Mann. Creole dishes such as *rougaille de poisson* (fish in a tomato-based sauce) cost from Rs90 to Rs125. It's open daily from 10 am to 2 pm and 6 to 10 pm.

The little *Restaurant du Quai* (☎ 831 2840) on Fisherman Lane offers seafood and other Creole dishes for around Rs150. It's open from 10 am to 9.30 pm daily.

Le Capitaine (☎ 831 1581) on Rue Johnston serves mainly seafood dishes with a Chinese flavour. Expect to pay Rs125 for crab or squid dishes and Rs225 for lobster. The restaurant is open Monday to Saturday from 10 am to 2.30 pm and 6 to 9.30 pm.

Le Gourmet (☎ 831 1571) on Rue Duncan offers a selection of cheap Chinese and seafood dishes at lunchtime. Mains cost about Rs50. The restaurant is open Monday to Saturday from 9.30 am to 3 pm.

The *Restaurant Paille En Queue* (☎ 831 1616) is opposite Le Gourmet and has a broad menu with fare such as grilled fish with Creole sauce for around Rs60. The restaurant focuses on seafood and is open Monday to Saturday from 10 am to 3 pm and 6 to 9.30 pm.

Escale Vacances (see Places to Stay) has a pleasant restaurant and is recommended for a minor splurge. Main dishes cost between Rs90 and Rs150. It's open daily from 11.30 am to 2.30 pm and 7.30 to 9.30 pm. Nonresidents are welcome here, but advance bookings are appreciated.

Self-caterers should head straight for the *Citronelle supermarket* in Rogers House on the corner of Rue Douglas and Rue Ricard. There are also several groceries on Rue Duncan. On Wednesday and Saturday there is a *street market* on Fisherman Lane. You can also find a few vendors most days at the *gare routière* (bus station).

Entertainment

The islanders are known for their versions of old colonial ballroom and country dances such as the schottische, the waltz and the mazurka. Creoles know them as *kotis*, *laval* and *mazok*. They also have a more African version of the *séga*, known as *séga tambour*. The accordion is the main instrument played on the island. Popular local groups are Les Camarons, Racine, and Mighty Guys.

Nightlife on Rodrigues is virtually nonexistent, which is part of the island's appeal for many travellers. An exception is the Ebony Nightclub (☎ 831 1540) on Rue Jenner, which features a local band from 9 pm every Friday (Rs75 entry).

There's a tiny cinema on Rue Victoria which screens films at 7.30 pm from Wednesday to Sunday.

Shopping
Handicrafts, especially baskets and hats made from all sorts of materials, are available at shops in Port Mathurin and also at a small shop in the departure area of the airport. In the markets you can pick up all sorts of things including handicrafts, spices, local honey and dried octopus. Try the market stalls at the gare routière or the Saturday and Wednesday market by the ferry terminal.

Getting There & Away
Air Air Mauritius operates two daily flights to Rodrigues from Mauritius using ATR-42 aircraft which take 1½ hours one way. The fare is Rs3150 one way or Rs2800 return (ticket valid for a minimum stay of five days; maximum stay of one month). There is no departure tax for flights between Mauritius and Rodrigues, but you will need your passport for identification.

There is a luggage limit of 15kg per person. Each excess kilo costs Rs30, but you may get away without having to pay extra if you are just a little over. When checking in at the Mauritius airport, you may be asked how much you weigh. Don't worry, you won't have to go through the indignity of being weighed like a sack of potatoes – an approximation is fine.

The main Air Mauritius office on Rodrigues is in the ADS building in Port Mathurin (☎ 831 1558, fax 831 1959). It's open Monday to Friday from 8 am to 3.30 pm and Saturday 8 am to noon. There is also a representative at the Plaine Corail airport (☎ 831 1301); it is open for all arrivals. You should reconfirm your return ticket immediately upon arrival at the airport, and it wouldn't do any harm to call into the office in town the day before you leave just to make completely sure your name is still on the passenger list.

Boat The MV *Mauritius Pride* does the trip from Mauritius to Rodrigues twice a month. The trip takes about 27 hours one way, depending on sea conditions. Non-Mauritians pay Rs2000 return in seats or Rs3200 return in cabins, including meals. This boat is popular with locals, so try to book well ahead.

The ship leaves from Port Louis harbour in Mauritius and docks at the new passenger terminal on Fisherman Lane in Port Mathurin.

For information contact Mauritours (☎ 212 1260, fax 212 4465), Sir William Newton St, Port Louis, or try the Mauritius Shipping Corporation (☎ 241 2550, fax 242 5245) in the Nova Building, Military Rd, Port Louis. In Rodrigues, contact Island's Shipping Service (☎ 831 1555, fax 831 2089) in Rogers House on Rue Douglas in Port Mathurin.

Getting Around
To/From The Airport Flights arrive at Plaine Corail airfield at the south-west tip of the island. The 'Supercopter' bus service to Port Mathurin operates only for flight arrivals and departures and takes about 35 minutes (Rs75). The bus drops off at most hotels in Port Mathurin and Anse aux Anglais. Tour operators and most hotels and pensions can also do airport transfers (for a charge) with advance notice.

Public bus No 206 runs between Port Mathurin and Plaine Corail village every 40 minutes from 6 am to 5 pm (Rs14); it's 700m from the village to the airport terminal.

Bus & Camionette There are a number of private buses and *camionettes* (small pick-up trucks) that run from the *gare routière* (bus station) at the west end of Rue Jenner in Port Mathurin.

Car Rental Ask your hotel or pension about car hire, or contact RodTours (☎ 831 2249, fax 831 2267), which offers jeep and car hire for around Rs1350 per day. Rates drop by about Rs100 if you rent for at least three days. A cheaper option is Henri Tours (☎ 831 1823, fax 831 1726) which charges around Rs1000 per day for car rental.

Make sure you get a contact telephone number in case of a breakdown.

Motorcycle The Patrico souvenir shop (☎ 831 2044) on Rue Duncan in Port Mathurin has a few mopeds, *mobilettes* and 125cc motorcycles for hire. Daily rates are Rs300 for a moped and Rs400 for a motorbike. Some hotels and pensions may also be able to arrange moped hire.

AROUND RODRIGUES

Rodrigues is reasonably small, so most places are only a few hours' walk away – it's a great way to exercise, take in the fresh air and explore this glorious island.

The best beaches on the island are around Pointe Coton on the east coast. Probably the best is the immaculate beach at St François, though the small coves at Trou d'Argent and Petit Gravier are also magical spots.

The road system in Rodrigues is slowly being improved, though many roads are still in a poor state of repair. You'll need a motorcycle or 4WD vehicle if you want to explore beyond the limits of the sealed roads. Petrol is fairly hard to come by in Rodrigues; there are petrol stations in Port Mathurin and Mont Lubin.

Caves

At Caverne Patate, in the south-west corner of the island, there are some interesting caves with impressive stalagmite and stalactite formations. The requisite permit is issued at the Administration Office (☎ 831 1504) on Rue Morrison, Port Mathurin. The office is open from 9 am to noon Monday to Friday; a permit costs Rs200 for one to thirty people.

There are guided tours of the caves daily at 9 am, 10.30 am, 1.30 pm and 2.30 pm. You should arrive at the cave entrance on the day and time specified on your permit. Wear strong shoes and take a jacket or pullover.

To get to the caves, take the road to Petite Butte. The cave warden's hut is down a small track, close to the Centre Communal. To get here by bus, first take a bus to Rivière Cocos, then change to a bus from there to La Ferme (ask the driver to drop you off at the right spot).

Hiking

As the island is relatively small, it's perfect for simply rambling around at your own leisure. There are few signposts but the landscape is fairly open so it's pretty hard to get lost.

The high ground around Mt Limon and Mt Malartic, which are the highest points at more than 390m above sea level, offers some good hiking and nice views over the island.

Good coastal hikes include the one from Port Mathurin to Pointe Coton, and south from Pointe Coton to the gorgeous beach at Trou d'Argent. From Port Mathurin, there's an easy 1km walk from the end of Rue Ricard to a viewpoint atop Mt Fanal, which looks out over the bay.

Diving

There are several good dive locations around Rodrigues, and the marine environment around the island is remarkably well preserved. The best dives are off Pointe Coton and Pointe Roche Noire (on the east coast) and off Pointe Palmiste (on the west coast). Baladirou, at Pointe aux Cornes, is also popular.

The dive centre at the Cotton Bay Hotel (see Places to Stay) charges Rs870 per person for one dive, Rs3300 per person for five dives and Rs6300 per person for 10 dives. Nonresidents can make use of this facility – ring ahead to make an appointment.

Deep-Sea Fishing

The Auberge les Filaos (see Places to Stay) can arrange a variety of trips for deep-sea fishing. Rates vary from Rs11,500 to Rs15,000 for a full-day trip.

Organised Tours

The efficient RodTours (☎ 831 2249, fax 831 2267) on Rue Duncan in Port Mathurin, offers a variety of tours. Options include a day tour to Île Cocos for Rs600 per person including a barbecue lunch; a tour in a glass-bottomed boat to Île aux Chats for Rs600 including barbecue lunch; a snorkelling trip to Port Sud-Est for Rs350; a half-day excursion to Caverne Patate for Rs350; and a half-day tour of Port Mathurin for Rs200. The office is open weekdays from 8.30 am to 4.30 pm and Saturday 8.50 am to 12.30pm.

Henri Tours (☎ 831 1823, fax 831 1726) on Rue Mann in Port Mathurin is a down-to-earth place run by the affable and experienced Henri Meunier. A full-day island tour including the Caverne Patate costs Rs300 per person (Rs400 with lunch) while a day tour to Île aux Cocos with lunch costs Rs500 per person (Tuesday, Thursday and Saturday). Call for other options. The office is open Monday to Friday from 8 am to 4 pm and Saturday 8 am to noon.

Other operators include Ecotourisme (☎ 831 2801, fax 831 2800) in the same complex as the Citronelle supermarket, and Rodrigues 2000 Tours (☎ 831 2099, fax 831 1894) on Rue Douglas.

All these tours start in Port Mathurin, but if you book from a hotel elsewhere, pick-up will be arranged. Most of the hotels and guesthouses can also arrange tours and transport for guests.

Places to Stay & Eat

Auberge les Filaos (☎ 831 1644, fax 831 2026) at Anse aux Anglais, 2km east of Port Mathurin, is popular and well maintained. Singles/doubles with shared bathroom are Rs300/500, while rooms with private bathroom go for Rs600/800; both include breakfast. Half board costs an additional Rs150 per person. Airport transfers are available for Rs100 per person (one way); you should book in advance. Management can organise a variety of activities and fishing trips (see Fishing earlier in this chapter).

Auberge Anse aux Anglais (☎ 831 2179, fax 831 1973), right next door to the Auberge les Filaos, is also good but is more expensive. Rooms with private bathroom cost Rs600/1200 on a half-board basis only. Airport transfers cost Rs250 per person (one way). Island tours and fishing trips can be organised.

Auberge Lagon Bleu (☎ 831 1823, fax 831 1726) in the same area is owned by Henri Tours and has a few basic rooms that are good value. Singles/doubles/triples with bathroom are Rs325/600/ 800 on a half-board basis. Return airport transfers cost Rs200.

Auberge de la Montagne (☎/fax 831 4607) is a delightful *chambre d'hôte* (family-run B&B) up in the hills at Grande Montagne. Accommodation on a half-board basis costs Rs500 per person. The owner, Françoise Baptiste, prepares the absolutely delicious Creole meals.

The brand new *Hotel les Cocotiers* (☎ 831 2866, fax 831 1800, e lescocotiers@intnet .mu) is a stylish complex at Anse aux Anglais. It has a good *restaurant*, a decent-sized pool and clean, spacious air-con rooms. Rates on half board are Rs1300/ 1475 in standard rooms and Rs2075/3025 in superior rooms.

The *Hotel Mourouk Ebony* (☎ 831 3350, fax 831 3355) is in an isolated position in the Port Sud-Est area. Accommodation in comfortable bungalows (each with a shocking red roof) costs Rs2300/3580 per single/ double from November to February and during the month of August (Rs2150/3260 from March to July and from September to October); all rates are for half board. There's a small pool, a bar and a *restaurant*. Island tours and activities such as windsurfing and cycling are also available.

Cotton Bay Hotel (☎ 831 3000, fax 831 3003) at Pointe Coton is the most luxurious hotel on the island and is on an excellent beach. Standard rooms cost Rs3175/4730, superior rooms cost Rs2830/4460 and suites cost Rs4410/7420 (prices are about 5 per cent cheaper from March to July and September to October). All prices include half board. There's a good swimming pool to splash in, a games room, a tennis court and a *restaurant*. If you fancy a trot around the island, horse riding is available for Rs400 per hour. There's also a dive centre (see Diving earlier in this chapter).

One of the best seafood places on the island is ***John's Resto Pub*** (☎ *831 6306*) in the village of Mangue on the way to Plaine Corail, between Quatre Vents and La Ferme. The grilled lobster with butter is a very reasonable Rs250 while other fishy mains range from Rs60 to Rs150. This place is open daily from 8 am to 4 pm (until 2 pm on Sunday).

Getting Around

Buses running to and from Port Mathurin include Pointe Coton (Rs13), La Ferme via Mont Lubin (Rs13), Rivière Cocos (Rs13) and Baie du Nord via Baie aux Huîtres (Rs11). Buses run every 30 minutes from about 5 am to 4.30 pm Monday to Saturday on most routes, less frequently on Sunday.

OFFSHORE ISLANDS

There are many small islands dotted around Rodrigues. Commonly visited islands include Île Cocos, Île aux Sables, Île aux Chats, Île aux Crabes and Île Hermitage.

Île Cocos, barely 1km in length, and its even smaller neighbour, Île aux Sables, are both nature reserves. They are populated by several bird species, including noddies, fairy terns and frigate birds. RodTours and Henri Tours both offer guided tours of the islands with lunch (see Organised Tours earlier in this chapter). The full walk around Île Cocos takes about 45 minutes, and there are two guards who can provide directions and information about the fauna and flora.

Île Hermitage, a tiny island renowned for its beauty (and for its possible hidden treasure), is accessible by boat from Port Sud-Est (about 25 minutes) or from near Petite Butte (about 90 minutes).

Île aux Crabes, about 20 minutes by boat from Pointe Corail, is less beautiful but more peaceful. Île aux Chats is an unremarkable island, but it is surrounded by a healthy coral reef, which makes it a popular destination for tours in glass-bottomed boats and for snorkelling.

It's possible to hire local boats at Rivière Cocos for trips to Île Gombrani or Île Paille-en-Queue.

Réunion

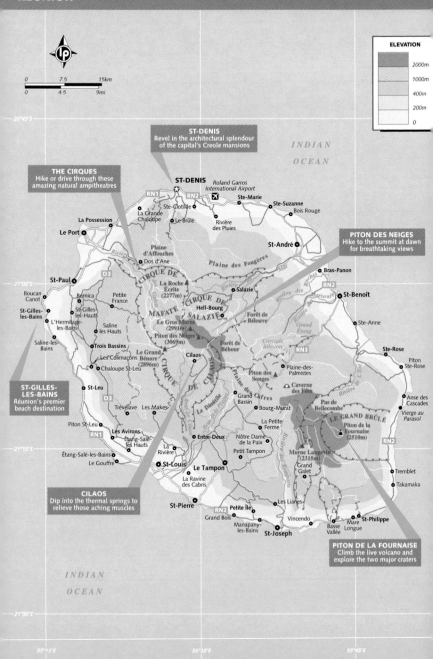

RÉUNION

ELEVATION
2000m
1000m
400m
200m
0

ST-DENIS
Revel in the architectural splendour
of the capital's Creole mansions

THE CIRQUES
Hike or drive through these
amazing natural ampitheatres

PITON DES NEIGES
Hike to the summit at dawn
for breathtaking views

**ST-GILLES-
LES-BAINS**
Réunion's premier
beach destination

CILAOS
Dip into the thermal springs to
relieve those aching muscles

PITON DE LA FOURNAISE
Climb the live volcano and
explore the two major craters

INDIAN
OCEAN

INDIAN
OCEAN

20°45'S
21°00'S
21°15'S
21°30'S

55°15'E
55°30'E
55°45'E

0   7.5   15km
0   4.5   9mi

ST-DENIS
Roland Garros
International Airport
Ste-Clotilde
Ste-Marie
Ste-Suzanne
Bois Rouge
La Grande
Chaloupe
Le Brûlé
Rivière
des Pluies
St-André
La Possession
Le Port
Plaine
d'Affouches
Dos d'Ane
Bras-Panon
St-Benoît
St-Paul
La Roche
Écrite
(2277m)
Salazie
CIRQUE DE
MAFATE
CIRQUE DE
SALAZIE
Hell-Bourg
Plaine des Fougères
Boucan
Canot
Bernica
Petite
France
Forêt de
Bélouve
Ste-Anne
St-Gilles-
les-Bains
St-Gilles-
les-Hauts
L'Hermitage-
les-Bains
Saline
les Hauts
Le Gros Morne
(2991m)
Piton des Neiges
(3069m)
Forêt de
Bébour
Cascade
Biberon
Ste-Rose
Piton
Ste-Rose
Saline-les-
Bains
Trois Bassins
Le Grand
Bénare
(2896m)
Grand
Étang
Les Colimaçons
Chaloupe St-Leu
Cilaos
Plaine-des-
Palmistes
Piton des
Songes
Anse des
Cascades
Vierge au
Parasol
St-Leu
Caverne
des Fées
Pas de
Bellecombe
LE GRAND BRÛLÉ
Trévelave
Les Makes
Grand
Bassin
Bourg-Murat
Piton de la
Fournaise
(2510m)
Piton St-Leu
Les Avirons
Étang-Salé-
les Hauts
La Petite
Ferme
Nôtre Dame
de la Paix
Étang-Salé-les-Bains
Le Gouffre
La
Rivière
Petit Tampon
Morne Langevin
(2315m)
Grand
Galet
Tremblet
Takamaka
St-Louis
Le Tampon
La Ravine
des Cabris
Entre-Deux
St-Pierre
Petite Île
Grand Bois
Les Lianes
Vincendo
Manapany-
les-Bains
St-Joseph
Basse
Vallée
Mare
Longue
St-Philippe

RN1
RN2
D3
RN2
RN3
RN2
RN1
D3
RN2

Facts about Réunion

Réunion is so sheer and lush, it looks as if it has risen dripping wet from the deep blue sea – which it effectively has, being the tip of a massive submerged prehistoric volcano. Whether you arrive by air or by sea, the island's volcanic origins are obvious, particularly if you arrive during an eruption of Piton de la Fournaise, the one remaining active cone on the island.

Predictably, many travellers draw comparisons with Hawaii – both islands have breathtaking natural landscapes, live volcanoes and a subtly tropical climate – but on arrival, you're likely to be offered a baguette and a small cup of strong black coffee rather than a palm skirt and a garland of flowers!

The island is run as an overseas department of France, making it one of the last colonial possessions in the world. French culture dominates every facet of life, from the coffee and croissant in the morning to the bottle of Evian and the carafe of red wine at the dinner table. The Réunionnais are proudly French speaking, almost to the exclusion of all other languages, and English-speakers will struggle to get by without at least a basic grasp of French.

However, the French atmosphere of the island has a firmly tropical twist, with subtle traces of Indian, African and even Chinese cultures. All of these traditions are blended in Réunion's unofficial language, Creole, and in the island's cuisine, a sort of Paris meets Bombay by way of Peking' experience. It is said that even the French have some trouble understanding the Creole of Réunion, so you shouldn't feel bad if you struggle a bit yourself.

Historically, the French have kept the secret of this beautiful island firmly to themselves – few people outside *la métropole* (mainland France, that is) know of Réunion, and even fewer know of its dramatic natural wonders. But news of Réunion's spectacular mountain countryside is starting to seep out. The hiking in the rugged interior of the island is world-class, and there is a very well

RÉUNION AT A GLANCE

Official Name: Department of Réunion
Area: 2510 sq km
Population: 717,723
Population Growth Rate: 1.75%
Capital: St-Denis
Head of State: Jacques Chirac (governed as an overseas department of France)
Official Language: French
Main Religion: Catholicism
Currency: French franc
Exchange Rate: FF7.10 = US$1
Per Capita GNP: US$8000
Inflation: 2%
Time: UTC +4

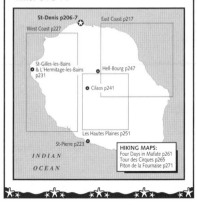

developed infrastructure of hiking trails and *gîtes de montagne* (mountain lodges) to help even the most inexperienced walkers see some of this marvellous country. If you loved Nepal or New Zealand, you'll also love Réunion.

You can also stay here in style, as Réunion enjoys most of the luxuries of mainland France. Unfortunately, this means the prices can tower nearly as high as the peaks, so a respectable budget is requisite. It would be financial suicide to arrive in Réunion on a shoestring budget, and you may risk being repatriated as *un misérable* (a pauper)!

RÉUNION

There are some good mid-range accommodation options, though you will have to compete with hordes of French tourists for the island's resources. During the French holiday season, in particular, almost every room on the island can be booked out in advance from mainland France. The solution is to plan well ahead and book your accommodation in advance, particularly if you're heading into the mountains. The excellent tourist service here can help you with itineraries and suggest alternative accommodation if your first choices are already booked up.

HISTORY

Réunion has a history similar to that of Mauritius, and was uninhabited when it was visited, but not settled, by early Malay, Arab and European mariners. The archipelago comprised of Mauritius, Rodrigues and Réunion was christened the Mascarenes by Portuguese navigator Pedro de Mascarenhas, following its European discovery in 1512. Réunion then moved through a succession of names given by the Dutch, English and French explorers who claimed to be the first to have spotted it.

1600 to 1800

In 1642, the French took the initiative of settling the island, which at the time was called Mascarin, when the French East India Company sent its ship, the *St-Louis*. No-one actually settled on Réunion until four years later, when the French governor of Fort Dauphin in southern Madagascar banished a dozen mutineers to the island. The mutineers landed at what is now St-Paul and lived in a cave for three years. In fact, this *grotte des premiers Français* (cave of the first French) still exists and is open to visitors.

On the basis of enthusiastic reports from the mutineers, the King of France officially claimed the island in 1649 and renamed it Île Bourbon.

However appealing it seemed, there was no great rush to populate and develop the island and, from around 1685, Indian Ocean pirates began using Île Bourbon as a trading base. The 260 settlers benefited from these illicit dealings until the French government and the French East India Company clamped down on them and took control at the beginning of the 18th century.

Until 1715, the French East India Company was content to provide only for its own needs and those of passing ships, but then coffee was introduced and exported, and between 1715 and 1730 it became the island's main cash crop. The island's economy changed dramatically. As coffee required intensive labour, African and Malagasy slaves were brought to the island despite French East India Company rules which forbade the use of slave labour. During this period, grains, spices and cotton were also brought in as cash crops.

Like Mauritius, Réunion came of age under the governorship of the visionary Mahé de La Bourdonnais, who served from 1735 to 1746. However, La Bourdonnais treated Île de France (Mauritius) as a favoured sibling, and Île Bourbon was left in a Cinderella role. As a result of poor management and the rivalry between France and Britain during the 18th century, as well as the collapse of the French East India Company, the government of the island passed directly to the French crown in 1764.

After the French Revolution, Île Bourbon came under the jurisdiction of the Colonial Assembly. It was at this time that the island's name was changed to La Réunion (The Joining or Meeting), for reasons known only to the Colonial Assembly. Certainly the slaves were not officially meeting with anyone. The name didn't find favour with slave owners, either, who later decided to rename the island Île Bonaparte after you-know-who.

In the late 18th century, there were a number of slave revolts, and many escaped slaves took refuge in the mountainous interior, organising themselves into villages run by democratically elected chiefs. Known as the *marrons*, these tribal chieftains were the true pioneers of the settlement of Réunion but most ultimately fell victim to bounty hunters such as François Mussard who were employed to go into the hills and hunt them down. The scars of this period of the island's history are still quite fresh in the population's psyche; there are numerous monuments around the island celebrating the achievements of French Réunionnais, but little record of the island's Creole pioneers except the names of the peaks where they were hunted down and killed.

1800 Onwards

The formerly productive coffee plantations were destroyed by cyclones very early in the 19th century, and in 1810, during the Napoleonic Wars, Bonaparte lost the island to the *habits rouges* (redcoats). On 9 July, Britain took possession of Réunion, but, five years later, under the Treaty of Paris, the spoil was returned to the French as Île Bourbon. The British, however, retained their grip on Rodrigues, Mauritius and the Seychelles.

Under British rule, sugar cane had been introduced to Réunion and quickly became the primary crop. It resulted in the dispossession of many small farmers who were forced to sell out to those with capital to invest in the new monoculture. The supplanted farmers migrated to the interior to find land and carry on with their agricultural activities. During this period, the Desbassyns brothers rose to success as the island's foremost sugar barons. The vanilla industry, introduced in 1819, also grew rapidly.

In 1848, the Second Republic was proclaimed in France, slavery was abolished, and Île Bourbon again became La Réunion. At the time, the island had a population of over 100,000 people, mostly freed slaves. Like Mauritius, Réunion immediately experienced a labour crisis, and like the British in Mauritius, the French 'solved' the problem by importing contract labourers from India, most of them Hindus, to work the sugar cane. In 1865, around 75,000 immigrants arrived on the island, and they remain largely distinct from the Muslim Indians who arrived in the early years of the 20th century.

The golden age of trade and development in Réunion lasted until 1870, with the country flourishing on the trade route between Europe, India and the Far East. However, competition from Cuba and the European sugar beet industry, combined with the opening of the Suez Canal (which short-circuited the journey around the Cape of Good Hope), resulted in an economic slump; shipping decreased, the sugar industry declined, and land and capital were further concentrated in the hands of a small French elite. Some small planters brightened their prospects by turning to geranium oil.

After WWI, in which 14,000 Réunionnais served, the sugar industry regained a bit of momentum, but it again suffered badly through the blockade of the island during WWII.

In 1936, a left-wing political group, the Comité d'Action Démocratique et Sociale, was founded on a platform of integration with France, but, after the island eventually became a Département Français d'Outre-Mer (DOM; French Overseas Department) in 1946, the group changed its mind on integration, hoping instead for self-government (with continuing infusions of capital assistance from France). The conservatives, who initially opposed integration with France for fear of losing their privileges as colonists, also did an about-face when they realised that the alternative to French integration would probably be a corrupt and chaotic independence.

Despite all the second thoughts, the island now falls under the jurisdiction of the French minister for Départements d'Outre-Mer and Territoires d'Outre-Mer (DOM-TOM). There have been feeble independence movements from time to time but, unlike those in France's Pacific territories, they have never amounted to anything. Even the Communist Party on the island seeks autonomy rather than independence, and until recently, Réunion seemed satisfied to remain totally French.

In February 1991, however, dramatic anti-government riots in St-Denis left 10 people dead, and a reactionary visit by the French prime minister Michel Rocard drew jeers from the crowds. By 1993, things appeared to have calmed down but there were still undercurrents of discontent.

As a French department, Réunion suffers from some of the ills affecting mainland France; for instance, the unemployment rate is extremely high, particularly among young

RÉUNION

Volcano Glossary

The following list of geological terms commonly used in discussions about volcanoes may be useful during a visit to Piton de la Fournaise.

basalt – a dark-coloured rock material that forms from cooled lava

bomb – a chunk of volcanic ejecta greater than 64mm in diameter that is cooled and rounded in mid-flight

caldera – the often immense depression formed by the collapse of a volcanic cone into its magma chamber

cinder slag – the mass of rough fragments of rock derived from volcanic lava

cirque – a semicircular, amphitheatre-like hollow resembling a glacial cirque (deep, steep-walled hollow)

dyke – a vertical intrusion of igneous material up through cracks in horizontal rock layers

fissure – a break or fracture in the earth's crust where vulcanism may occur

lava – flowing molten rock; the name for magma after it has been ejected from a volcano

lava cave or **lava tube** – a tunnel or cavern caused by the withdrawal of a lava stream flowing beneath an already solidified surface

magma – molten rock before it reaches the surface and becomes lava

magma chamber – a reservoir of magma from which volcanic materials are derived

obsidian – dark-coloured volcanic glass

pahoehoe – Hawaiian term for ropy, smooth-flowing lava

pillow lava – lava formed in underwater or subglacial eruptions; it solidifies immediately under water and forms pillow-like bulbs

plug – material that has solidified in a volcanic vent, revealed by erosion

pumice – solidified lava froth, so light and porous that it will float on water

scoria – porous and glassy black or red volcanic gravel formed in fountain-like eruptions

shield volcano – one with a flattish cone of oozing pahoehoe lava. Réunion's Piton de la Fournaise is a shield volcano.

sill – a finger or vein of molten material that squeezes between existing rock layers and then solidifies

people. With a French system of welfare payments for the unemployed, the island is nevertheless seen as a land of milk and honey by many Africans, and Réunion sees a continual tide of would-be immigrants.

In 1996, the minimum wage was brought to the same level as that of mainland France (the minimum welfare payment, however, remains 20% lower than that in mainland France). In 1997, the public sector went on strike in protest against a bill aimed at reducing the financial benefits of future public sector employees. The movement was supported by Paul Vergès, the Communist leader of the island, and Margie Sudre, a former minister of French-speaking communities.

Things have been fairly settled recently, though there have been growing calls in mainland France to cease social security payments to the DOM-TOMs.

GEOGRAPHY

Réunion lies about 800km east of Madagascar and 220km south-west of Mauritius. Just in case anyone was in doubt about its origins, its active volcano, Piton de la Fournaise, erupted in 1986, spewing lava into the sea and adding another few square metres to the island. In September 1992, it erupted again, but this time the lava stream stopped well short of the coast.

The island is 2510 sq km in area and has a circumference of 207km, a bit larger than Mauritius, but far less populous.

GEOLOGY

There are two major mountain zones on Réunion. The older of the two covers most of the western half of the island. The highest peak is Piton des Neiges (3069m), an alpine-class peak. Surrounding it are three immense and splendid amphitheatres: the cirques of Cilaos, Mafate and Salazie. These long, wide, deep hollows are sheer-walled canyons filled with convoluted peaks and valleys, the eroded remnants of the ancient volcanic shield that surrounded Piton des Neiges.

The smaller of the two zones lies in the south-east and is still evolving, with several extinct volcanoes and one that is still very much alive, the Piton de la Fournaise (2510m). This rumbling peak still pops its cork relatively frequently in spectacular fashion, and between eruptions quietly steams and hisses away. No-one lives in the shadow of the volcano, where lava flowing down to the shore has left a remarkable jumbled slope of cooled black volcanic rock. This volcano is undoubtedly the island's most popular and intriguing attraction.

These two mountain zones are separated by a region of high plains, while the coast is ringed by a gently sloping coastal plain which varies in width. Numerous rivers wind their way down from the Piton des Neiges range, down through the cirques, cutting deeply into the coastal plains.

CLIMATE

Réunion not only cops it from the volcano now and again, it also gets a lashing from cyclones. Cyclone Clotilde crashed into the island on Black Friday (13 February 1987), causing damage worth millions of dollars to crops, roads and buildings.

Because of the high mountains, the island's climate varies more than that of Mauritius. However, it still experiences only two distinct seasons: the hot, rainy (cyclonic) summer from October to March and the cool, dry winter from late April to September. The east coast is considerably wetter than the dry, brown west coast, but the wettest region is the heights above the east coast – the Takamaka region, the Plaine-des-Palmistes and the northern and eastern slopes of Piton de la Fournaise.

Temperatures on the coast average 21°C during winter and 28°C during summer. In the mountains, they drop to a 12°C winter

Cyclone Warning!

Réunion's cyclone warning system is based on three levels of alert.

Level one is known as a *vigilance cyclonique* (cyclone watch), and goes into effect whenever a cyclone is detected. It requires people to make sure they have enough supplies (food, batteries, candles, water etc), to cancel all hiking and boating, and to pay attention to radio communications regarding the storm's path.

The *alerte orange* (orange alert) denotes an important threat in the next 24 hours. Schools and day nurseries are closed, but businesses remain open. As a preventive measure, the population is urged to bring indoors any objects or animals that might be carried away, and to protect all doors and windows. And, of course, to listen to the radio.

The *alerte rouge* (red alert) is announced when danger is imminent. It entails a ban on driving, and the population is advised to obey the instructions broadcast by radio. Use of the telephone is also restricted.

average and an 18°C summer average. The south-east trade winds blow all year round and can make hiking around the volcano or up the Piton des Neiges uncomfortably cold in winter.

Mist and clouds surround the higher peaks and plains much of the time. They lift, drop and swirl spasmodically during the day. The best time for viewing the landscape is at first light, before the clouds begin to build and the sun starts everything steaming.

FLORA

Parts of Réunion are like a grand botanical garden. Between the coast and the alpine peaks you'll find palms, screw pines (also known as pandanus or *vacoas)*, casuarinas *(filaos)*, vanilla, spices, other tropical fruit and vegetable crops, rainforest and alpine flora. More than half the cultivable land area of Réunion is planted with sugar cane, on slopes that rise up to about 800m above sea level.

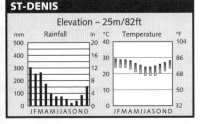

ST-DENIS

Elevation – 25m/82ft

Away from cultivated areas, especially on the east coast, the vegetation is lush and thick. Unlike the natural forests of Mauritius, which were done over by the defoliating Dutch, many of the forest species and environments of Réunion have survived to the present day. However, you won't find any of the grand rainforest trees that were once present; perhaps the best remaining example of the natural vegetation cover is found in the Forêt de Bélouve east of the Cirque de Salazie.

At the other extreme, the lava fields around the volcano exhibit a barren, moon-like face of the island. Here the various stages of vegetation growth, from a bare new lava base, are evident. The first plant to appear on lava is the one the French call *branle vert*. Its leaves contain a combustible oil. Much later in the growth cycle come tamarind and other acacia trees.

There is a large and active forestry division, the Office National des Forêts (ONF), which is more concerned with preserving than chopping the forests. Afforestation has been concentrated primarily on the Japanese cryptomerias, the tamarinds, coloured woods, casuarinas and cabbage palms.

Like any tropical island, Réunion has a wealth of flowering species, including orchids, hibiscus, bougainvillea, frangipani, jacaranda, grevillea, acacia and mimosa.

FAUNA

Since the arrival of humans, the fauna on Réunion hasn't fared as well as the flora. Réunion had dodos and giant tortoises when the island was first settled, but the early colonists and their animals made short work of them. The tortoises were boiled down for the oil in their skins; a shocking 500 individuals were needed to make one barrel of oil. Sea turtles are farmed in Réunion (see St-Leu in the Around the Coast chapter). For more information on sea turtles, see the special section 'Underwater Worlds'.

Bird Life

The crested bourbon bird is an extinct wonder; if you want to see what it looked like, you'll have to settle for the model in the Musée d'Histoire Naturelle in St-Denis.

The rarest bird on the island now is the *merle blanc* or cuckoo shrike *(Coracina newtoni)*. Creoles call it *tuit tuit*, for obvious reasons. Probably the best chance of seeing the bird is directly south of the capital, St-Denis, near the foot of La Roche Écrite. It is endemic to the island, but there is a closely related species on Mauritius.

Bulbuls, which resemble blackbirds and are locally known as *merles*, are more common.

The Mascarene paradise flycatcher is a pretty little bird with a small crest and a long, flowing red tail. It is also known as the *oiseau la vierge* because its blue head and white breast reminded early settlers of the Virgin Mary.

Other birds native to the highlands include the *tec-tec* or Réunion stonechat (the Creole name is onomatopoeic) and the *papangue* or Maillardi buzzard, a protected hawklike bird which begins life as a little brown bird and turns black and white as it grows older. It is Réunion's only surviving bird of prey. Falcons and swallows can also be seen.

Mynahs, introduced at the end of the 18th century to keep the grasshoppers under control, are common, as are the small, red cardinal-like birds known as fodies. The best-known sea bird is the white *paille-en-queue* or white-tailed tropicbird *(Phaeton lepturus)*, which sports two long tail plumes. It can often be seen soaring on the thermals created by the Piton de la Fournaise volcano. Other sea birds include visiting albatross and shearwaters. Common game birds include moorhens (which may be observed around the ponds near St-Paul and Bois Rouge) and introduced quails, francolins and partridges.

The best spots to see bird life are the Forêt de Bélouve above Hell-Bourg, and the wilderness region of Le Grand Brûlé at the southern tip of the island. Bird-watchers may want to hunt down a copy of the field guide *Oiseaux de la Réunion*. The text is in French, but there are accurate colour illustrations of all species present on the island, identified by their Latin, English, French and local names.

Insects & Spiders

The mosquitoes that plague Réunion during the rainy season can be tenacious. Oddly enough, they seem to be at their worst in St-Denis. The higher into the hills you go, the less evident the little bloodsuckers become.

The most interesting creepy crawlers are the giant millipedes – some as long as a human foot – which loll around beneath rocks in more humid areas.

Other Animals

During the rainy season, many of Réunion's roads are paved in squashed frogs! Tenrecs, which were introduced from Madagascar, don't seem to find the roads as much of a challenge as the frogs. They resemble hedgehogs, and they are few in number.

There are a few other land creatures – some lonely deer (introduced for hunters), hares (also introduced) and a few chameleons – but you'd be very lucky to spot any of them. On the bright side, there are no poisonous or toothy nasties of any description.

The rivers contain rainbow trout (introduced) and a sort of small fry that is good when cooked in a Creole curry.

GOVERNMENT & POLITICS

Since 1946, when Réunion became a Département Français d'Outre-Mer (DOM) or overseas French department, it has been party to the French economy. Other DOMs are Guadeloupe, Martinique and French Guiana. The Indian Ocean island of Mayotte has quasi-departmental status. France also has three Territoires d'Outre-Mer (TOMs) or overseas territories, which are New Caledonia, Wallis & Futuna Islands, and French Polynesia. You may see or hear the expression DOM-TOM. In 1986, France was admitted to the Indian Ocean Commission (IOC) because of its sovereignty over Réunion (and Mayotte).

Government affairs in Réunion are the responsibility of the French Minister for DOM-TOM. The department is administered by a prefect and an elected council. It is represented in the French National Assembly by five deputies, and in the French Senate by three councillors.

ECONOMY

Réunion imports about 66% of what it needs from *la métropole* (France). In turn, France imports around 71% of Réunion's exports. The island's imports are increasing at a much faster rate than its exports, and the inflation rate on the island is higher than in mainland France.

France spends an estimated 10% of its social security budget on the 1.2% of the population living in the DOM-TOMs. The official unemployment rate of Réunion is a staggering 43%.

Agriculture

The basis of the island's economy is agriculture, which, in turn, is based on the sugar cane that covers 65% of the arable land and accounts for around 80% of agricultural revenue. Molasses, rum and cane spirit are produced, but these are not widely available outside France. Several sugar factories offer tours to visitors during the cutting season around July.

Réunion is the one of the world's largest producers of geranium oil, but don't expect to see acres of beautiful flowers. The oil, used as a fixative in perfumes, is drawn from the leaves of the plants. It is still a cottage industry, concentrated mainly around Le Maïdo and Le Tampon, and most producers use a crude but effective home-made still to extract the oil.

Fragrant oil is also produced from the roots of vetiver (an Asian grass), though on a much smaller scale (around 15 tonnes annually), in the foothills near St-Pierre and St-Joseph. There were once large plantations of ylang-ylang, a bush whose yellow flowers yield an overpowering essence, but this industry down-sized considerably during the 1970s. There are still several plantations supplying the French perfume industry.

The cultivation of vanilla, which is concentrated on the east coast between Ste-Suzanne and St-Philippe, has been a limited but stable earner since the last century. Tobacco has recently made a comeback, and popular spice crops include black pepper, cloves and cinnamon. Maize, potatoes, lentils, beans, garlic and onions, and

Perfumed Isle

In keeping with the French love of perfume, Réunion has long been the garden of the great fragrance houses of Paris. The mainstays of the essential-oil business are vetiver, geranium and the evocative ylang-ylang, which you can often smell in the night air all over the island. All are cultivated in the hills, and the oils are extracted in traditional distilleries, which look like they could also be used for moonshine whisky! The cultivation of these plants is in slow decline, but certain Parisian perfumers still insist on the best oils from Réunion for their fragrances.

warm-weather fruits such as lychees, mandarins, oranges, bananas, lemons, papayas and mangoes are all produced in significant amounts.

Livestockwise, pig-breeding satisfies local consumption, while poultry farms keep the populace in eggs and in meat for the ubiquitous *carri poulet* (chicken curry).

With few good harbours, the fishing industry is small and restricted; however, Réunion oversees fish factories on the sub-Antarctic French islands of St-Paul and Amsterdam more than 3000km to the southeast.

Tourism

One of the biggest obstacles to the development of Réunion as a world-class international tourist destination (and revenue earner) is the tropical paradise image of nearby Mauritius, which is cheaper and has much better beaches. Réunion mainly attracts visitors from France and Mauritius. In 1998 there were 400,000 visitors to Réunion; 59% were visiting the island for the first time.

POPULATION & PEOPLE

Réunion has a larger land area than Mauritius, but its estimated population of 717,723 is about half that of its crowded neighbour. Réunion's population density is about 286 people per square kilometre.

Because the birth rate has been quite high for the past 25 years, the island's population is weighted in favour of youth, with 39% of the population under 20 years of age.

Réunion has the same population mix of Europeans, Indians, Chinese and Creoles as Mauritius, but in different proportions. Creoles are the largest ethnic group, comprising around 40% of the population. After the Creoles, Europeans (ie, the French) make up the largest group. Malabars (Indians) comprise about 20% of the population, the Chinese 3%, and Z'arabes (Muslims) make up about 1%.

The Europeans are involved in the island's administration and business, and are called Z'oreilles (the Ears) by the Creoles, as they may be straining to hear what's being said about them in the local patois.

ARTS

One of the greatest pleasures of visiting Réunion is experiencing Creole-flavoured French culture, or French-flavoured Creole culture. For news of cultural activities on the island, contact the Office Départemental de la Culture (☎ 41 11 41, fax 41 55 71) in St-Denis. It publishes a free monthly newsletter, *Trajectoires*, available at tourist and travel offices, which gives details of forthcoming theatre, jazz and classical music performances, exhibitions and conferences, some of which have youth and student rates.

Dance

It is interesting to see how the *séga* differs here from the versions in Mauritius, the Seychelles and Madagascar. As elsewhere, the slaves in Réunion adapted the dances of the white settlers, particularly the quadrille, to their own African rhythms, but more variations have survived in Réunion because freed slaves went on to form the majority of the island's population. The séga is now danced by everyone in Réunion in the manner of a shuffling rock step.

The more traditional slaves' dance in Réunion is the *maloya*, which has a slower, more reflective rhythm, similar to the New Orleans blues. A séga or maloya performance is often accompanied by melancholy ballads or *romances*. Séga and maloya music, as well as other Creole sounds, are available on CD for FF150 to FF200.

Instruments used to accompany the séga and the maloya range from traditional home-made percussion pieces, such as the hide-covered *houleur* drum and the maraca-like *caïambe*, to the accordion and modern band instruments.

Music

Réunion's music mixes the African rhythms of reggae, séga and maloya with the best of French, British and American rock and folk sounds. As for Creole-flavoured modern grooves, the Réunionnais leave those to their tropical cousins in Martinique and Guadeloupe, although they make popular listening in Réunion.

Compagnie Creole, a Caribbean group originally from Réunion but now based in Paris, has won greater middle-of-the-road success. Another local favourite is rastaman Michel Fock, known professionally as Ti-Fock, who adds a synthesised touch to the traditional maloya and séga rhythms.

It's all catchy stuff, and you'll hear it in bars, discos and vehicles throughout the islands of the Indian Ocean. A good selection of séga, maloya and jazz recordings is available at Megatop (☎ 41 00 41) at the corner of Rue Alexis de Villeneuve and Rue Jean Chatel in St-Denis.

In recent years, St-Denis has developed quite a lively acoustic and dance music scene. There is excellent live acoustic music several times a week at the Cyclone Cafe on Rue Jean Chatel in St-Denis; for local DJs, head to Le Rallye by Le Barachois park.

Architecture

The distinctive 18th-century Creole architecture of Réunion is evident in both the *grandes villas Creoles* (homes of wealthy planters and other *colons)* and the *tit' cases Creoles* (the homes of the common folk). The Conseil Départemental d'Architecture is actively striving to preserve the remaining examples of Creole architecture around the island. (For more information about this exotic architecture, see the boxed text 'Creole Architecture' in the Central Mauritius chapter.)

Theatre

The island has several excellent professional theatre groups, of which Théâtre Vollard (☎ 21 25 26) is the most established. Other professional troupes include Théâtre Talipot and the Théâtre Dallon.

The main venues for theatre around the island are St-Denis' Théâtre Champ Fleuri (☎ 21 16 94) on Ave André Malraux; the Théâtre du Grand Marché (☎ 20 33 99) on Rue Maréchal Leclerc, also in St-Denis; the Théâtre Luc Donat (☎ 27 24 36) on Rue de l'Église in Le Tampon; and the Théâtre de Plein Air amphitheatre (☎ 24 47 71) outside St-Gilles-les-Bains.

You can pick up theatre programs in most *syndicats d'initiative* (tourist offices). Alternatively, call the Office Départemental de la Culture (☎ 41 11 41).

Painting, Etching & Woodwork

Unlike Seychelles artists, whose artistic style is a direct response to the environment, most Réunion artists tend to ape popular European styles. French influence dominates and the imposing landscape of the island can make for interesting subject matter, but much of the work on offer is either too bright and gaudy, too ordered and dull, or too much like Gauguin! There is an argument, of course, that the Creoles have found their own artistic metier in the graffiti which covers most blank surfaces on the island.

There are at least 15 professional artists living and working in Réunion. Among them is printmaker Philippe Turpin, who etches on copper and then rolls the prints off the inky plates. But the effect, like the technique, has little to do with Creole tradition. Instead, Turpin captures the wonder of Réunion in a fantastical, almost medieval way; his renditions of the cirques resemble illustrations of fairy kingdoms. His prices are fantastic too, but the work is worth the money if you can afford it. Turpin's studio in the mountain spa village of Cilaos is open to the public.

The work of other artists can be seen at several places around the island, including Galerie Artisanale (☎ 29 56 66) at the Continent complex in St-Denis, the Boutique

RÉUNION

RÉUNION

Artisanale de L'Association Lacaze (☎ 21 55 47) at Place Sarda Garriga in St-Denis, and at Galerie Vincent (☎ 27 32 73) between Le Tampon and St-Pierre.

Woodwork, including 'East India Company' furniture and miniature replicas of Creole-style homes, is for sale at the Centre Artisanal du Bois (☎ 39 06 12) in La Rivière, St-Louis.

If you'd like to see a bit of transplanted European art, visit the Musée Léon Dierx on Rue de Paris in St-Denis.

SOCIETY & CONDUCT

Réunion has a number of mosques and temples, and visitors should dress and behave appropriately (see Society & Conduct in the Regional Facts for the Visitor chapter).

RELIGION

The Catholic faith dominates the island's religious character. It is visible in the shrines along every highway and byway, in caves and on cliff tops (many of these were constructed for family members killed in accidents on those sites), and evidenced in the many saints' days and holidays. St-Denis shuts down on Sunday, when half the city goes to *the* beach (Boucan Canot).

Hindus and Muslims follow their religions freely, and most large towns have both a temple and a mosque. Traditional Hindu rites such as *pandialé* or *teemeedee*, which features fire walking, and *cavadee*, which for pilgrims entails piercing the cheeks with skewers, often take place. (For more information on these rites, see Public Holidays & Special Events in the Mauritius Facts for the Visitor chapter.)

Interestingly, a great deal of syncretism between Hinduism, Islam and Catholicism has evolved over the years. In fact, many of the Malabar-Réunionnais participate in Catholic rites and rituals as well as those of the Indian community.

Apart from celebrating the Chinese New Year, the Sino-Réunionnais community is not very conspicuous in its religious or its traditional practices.

LANGUAGE

French is the official language of Réunion, but Creole is the most widely spoken. Few people speak English. (For some useful words and phrases in French, see the Language chapter near the back of this book.)

The Creole of Réunion is beyond the comprehension even of most French people. A word that means one thing in French can mean something completely different in Creole. And where a word does have the same meaning, Creoles usually pronounce it differently.

Creoles have quite a number of bons mots and charming idioms, which are often the result of Hindi, Arab and Malagasy influences or misinterpretations of the original French word. *Bonbon la fesse* (bum toffee) is a suppository, *conserves* (preserves) are sunglasses, the *bazaar* is the market, and *coeur d'amant* (lover's heart) is a cardamom seed. *Coco* is your head, *caze* is your house, *marmaille* is your child, *baba* is your baby, *band* means family, *le fait noir* means night, and, if the stars are out, remember that *mi aime jou* means 'I love you'.

In Creole pronunciation there are two basic rules: 'r' is generally not pronounced (when it is, it's pronounced lightly); and the soft 'j' and 'ch' sounds of French are pronounced as 'z' and 's' respectively. For example, *manzay* for *manger* (to eat), *zamais* for *jamais* (never) and *sontay* for *chanter* (to sing).

There are French-Creole dictionaries for sale in Réunion, but unfortunately there are no English-Creole dictionaries.

Facts for the Visitor

PLANNING
When to Go
Climate should be your first consideration if you want to experience Réunion at its best. Unless you have webbed feet, there's no point setting out to explore the cirques on foot if all you can expect weatherwise is swirling mist, pouring rain and mud chutes in place of walking tracks.

The only time to seriously consider hiking through Réunion's spectacular mountain country is during the dry season from April to September. For maximum spatial and climatic enjoyment, May and June are probably the best months of all (for more information, see Climate in the Facts about Réunion chapter).

The downside of climate-related trip planning is that everyone else has the same idea. You're strongly advised to book well in advance, especially during the peak tourist times. April, May and during the French school holidays from late July to early September are the busiest times to visit. In August you risk being left high and dry without accommodation unless you book in advance. The *gîtes de montagne* (mountain cabins or lodges) are packed out during this time, so if you dare brave the crowds, you may want to pack a tent. It's also worth keeping in mind that October and November can sometimes get unexpectedly busy.

The Christmas and New Year holidays also attract crowds. However, the northern winter holidays fall in the middle of Réunion's hot rainy season so there isn't much of a demand on gîtes de montagne at this time of the year.

The quietest times are during cyclone-prone February and March. The weather normally changes in April, which isn't a bad time to a visit.

Maps
Syndicats d'initiative (tourist offices) distribute several maps of the island, including the fairly good *Excursion Carte Touristique*.

You can also pick up town plans from the appropriate syndicats d'initiative.

Most island maps include at least some of the hiking trails and gîtes de montagne. For all purposes, the IGN (Institut Géographique National) 512 map of the island is currently the best and the most detailed (it costs FF58). Although it's fairly accurate, one potentially dangerous oversight is the casual placing of the gîtes. For the most part they are marked in the vicinity of where they should be rather than at the exact location. When you are trying to find a gîte at the end of a long walk, sweaty, sore and starving, and you take a wrong turn in the track, the IGN map will only be saved from the fire by its other attributes.

The best hiking maps are the TOP25 1:25,000 series produced by IGN. They cover the island in six sheets, using good relief shading and showing vegetation cover. Contour lines are at 10m intervals. The locations of the gîtes are marked accurately on these maps. For most cirque hiking, you only need to purchase two sheets (4402RT and 4405RT). Piton de la Fournaise is covered in one sheet (4406RT). The maps cost about FF70 per sheet.

TOURIST OFFICES
Local Tourist Offices
Tourist services in Réunion have the full backing of the French government, so the information and assistance available is generally excellent. While there is a definite French slant to the material on offer, most of the *syndicats d'initiative* (tourist offices) have at least one staff member who speaks English and other languages.

For information on hiking, refer to the sources described in the special section 'Hiking in Réunion' later in this book. Other queries should be taken to the main syndicat d'initiative (☎ 41 83 00, fax 21 37 76) at 53 Rue Pasteur, St-Denis, which has efficient staff members, a couple of whom speak English. There's another useful information and welcome counter at Roland Garros International Airport; the counter is open to meet international flights. The staff will offer plenty of advice and information, and can provide myriad maps, brochures and advertising.

Addresses of other syndicats d'initiative around the island are:

Bras-Panon (☎ 51 50 62, fax 51 75 47)
3 Chemin Robert, off Route Nationale, 97412 Bras-Panon
Cilaos (☎ 31 78 03, fax 31 70 30) 2 bis, Rue Mac Auliffe, 97413 Cilaos
Entre-Deux (☎ 39 69 60, fax 39 69 83) 9 Rue Fortuné Hoareau, 97414 Entre-Deux
Étang-Salé-les-Bains (☎ 26 67 32, fax 26 67 92) 74 Rue Octave Bénard, 97427 Étang-Salé-les-Bains
Hautes Plaines (☎ 59 08 92) Rue Alfred Picard, Bourg-Murat, 97418 Plaine-des-Cafres
Hell-Bourg (☎ 47 89 89) Rue Général de Gaulle, Hell-Bourg
St-André (☎ 46 91 63, fax 46 52 16) 20 Centre Commercial de St-André, 97440 St-André
Ste-Anne (☎ 51 02 57) L'Eglise de Ste-Anne, Ste-Anne
St-Gilles-les-Bains (☎ 24 57 47, fax 24 34 40) Ave Paul Julius Bénard, 97434 St-Gilles-les-Bains
St-Leu (☎ 34 63 40, fax 34 96 45) Rue du Général Lambert, St-Leu
St-Philippe (☎ 37 10 43, fax 37 10 97) Rue Leconte-Delisle, 97442 St-Philippe
St-Pierre (☎ 25 02 36) 17 Blvd Hubert-Delisle, 97410 St-Pierre
Salazie (☎ 47 50 14, fax 47 60 06) Rue Georges Pompidou, 97433 Salazie

The Comité du Tourisme de la Réunion publishes a monthly magazine called *RUN* which outlines current happenings of interest to visitors and contains articles about various aspects of the island. In addition to this, twice annually it publishes *RUN – le guide*, which is a useful directory of hotels, restaurants, discos, travel agencies and other places of interest to visitors.

These publications are available at syndicats d'initiative and at many hotels around the island. If you want to obtain a copy before you arrive in Réunion, contact the Comité du Tourisme de la Réunion (☎ 21 00 41, fax 20 25 93) at Place du 20 Décembre 1848 in St-Denis, or the office in mainland France (see the Tourist Offices Abroad section following).

Tourist Offices Abroad

For advance information on Réunion, you could contact the Comité du Tourisme de la Réunion (☎ 01 40 75 02 79, fax 01 40 75 02 73), 90 Rue de la Boétie, 75008 Paris. Yet another possibility is the Conseil Général de la Réunion (☎ 01 40 38 66 70), 78 Rue de la Chapelle, 75018 Paris, although it mainly supplies business-related information.

France's tourism representatives abroad include those in:

Australia (☎ 02-9231 5244, fax 9221 8682) 25 Bligh St, Sydney, NSW 2000
Canada (☎ 416-593 4723) 30 St Patrick St, Suite 700, Toronto, Ontario M5T 3A3
Ireland (☎ 01-703 4046) 35 Lower Abbey St, Dublin 1
South Africa (☎ 011-880 8062, fax 880 7772) 1st floor, Oxford Manor, 196 Oxford Rd (PO Box 41022, Craighall 2024), Illovo, Johannesburg
Switzerland (☎ 022-732 8610, fax 731 5873) 2 Rue de Thalberg, 1201 Geneva
UK (☎ 020-7493 5174, fax 7493 6594) 178 Piccadilly, London W1V 0AL
USA (☎ 212-838 7800, fax 838 7855) 444 Madison Ave (16th floor), New York, NY 10022

VISAS & DOCUMENTS
Visas

The visa requirements for entry to Réunion are the same as for France. There are no restrictions on nationals of the EU. Citizens of Australia, the USA, Canada, New Zealand and Israel don't need visas to visit as tourists for up to three months. Except for people from a handful of European countries, everyone else must have a visa.

Visa applications should be made to the French embassy or consulate nearest your home address.

Visa Extensions It is difficult to get a tourist visa extension except in the case of an emergency (eg, medical problems). If you have a visa extension query, contact the Service de l'États Civile et des Étrangers (☎ 40 75 80) at the Préfecture in St-Denis.

Those who don't need a visa and wish to stay for longer than three months need to apply for a *carte de séjour* (residence permit). Again, contact the Service de l'Etats Civile et des Étrangers. You could always pop across to Mauritius and then re-enter Réunion to get around this requirement.

Onward Tickets

All visitors should have an onward ticket (or they could be asked to leave money to cover the cost of one). You may also be asked to supply the name of your intended accommodation in Réunion.

Travel Insurance

EU nationals will enjoy to a certain extent the benefits of reciprocal agreements between member countries. Other nationals are advised to have medical and travel insurance. For more details, see the Regional Facts for the Visitor chapter at the beginning of this book.

EMBASSIES & CONSULATES
French Embassies & Consulates

Countries in which France has diplomatic representation include:

Australia
(☎ 02-6216 0100, fax 6216 0127) 6 Perth Ave, Yarralumla, Canberra, ACT 2600
Belgium
(☎ 02-548 8411, fax 513 6871) 65 Rue Ducale, 1000 Brussels
Canada
(☎ 13-789 1795, fax 562 3735) 42 Sussex Drive, Ottawa, Ontario K1M 2C9
Germany
(☎ 030-2063 9000, fax 2063 9010) Kochstrasse 6/7, D-10969, Berlin
Japan
(☎ 03-5420 8800, fax 5420 8847) 11-44, Chome Minami Azabu, Minato-ku, Tokyo 106
Madagascar
(☎ 20-223 9898, fax 223 9927) 3 Rue Jean-Jaurés, Ambatomena, BP 204, Tananarive
Mauritius
(☎ 230-208 4103, fax 211 0577) 14 St George St, Port Louis
New Zealand
(☎ 04-384 2555, fax 384 2577) Rural Bank Building, 34/42 Manners St (PO Box 1695), Wellington
Seychelles
(☎ 38 25 00, fax 38 25 10) Victoria House, Independence Ave, BP 478, Victoria

South Africa
April to January: (☎ 12-429 7000, fax 429 7029) 807 George Ave, Arcadia, Pretoria 0083
February to March: (☎ 12-422 1338, fax 426 1996) 78 Queen Victoria St, Cape Town 8001
UK
(☎ 020-7201 1000, fax 7201 1004) 58 Knightsbridge, London SW1X 7JT
USA
(☎ 202-944 6000, fax 944 6166) 4104 Reservoir Rd NW, Washington DC 20007

Embassies & Consulates in Réunion

Since Réunion isn't independent, only a few countries have diplomatic representation; they include:

Belgium (☎ 90 20 89 or 21 79 72, fax 90 20 88) 33 Rue Félix-Guyon, BP 785, 97476 St-Denis
Germany (☎ 21 62 96, fax 21 74 55) 9c Rue Lorraine, 97400 St-Denis
India (☎ 41 75 47, fax 21 01 70) 266 Rue Maréchal Leclerc, 97400 St-Denis
Madagascar (☎ 21 66 00, fax 21 10 08) 77 Rue Juliette Dodu, 97400 St-Denis
Seychelles (☎ 57 26 38) 67 Chemin Kerveguen, Le Tampon

CUSTOMS

Airline passengers may bring the following duty-free goods into Réunion: 200 cigarettes or 50 cigars or 250g of tobacco; 1L of spirits or 2L of wine; and 250mL of eau de toilette. If you are bringing in currency upwards of FF50,000 it must be declared at customs. For information on any customs issues, contact Réunion's customs services (☎ 90 81 00, fax 41 09 81) in St-Denis at 7 Ave de la Victoire.

The importation of plants or plant material is prohibited unless first cleared by Réunion officials. For further details, call the Réunion Plant Protection Agency (☎ 48 61 45).

The export of turtle products such as shells and decorative turtle items is banned by international wildlife trade controls, and the items may be confiscated in the country they are imported into – this applies even if the turtles were bred in captivity. At the time of writing, it was legal to produce turtle products in Réunion, although this law may change.

REUNION

MONEY
Currency

The French franc (FF) is the unit of currency and the more francs you have, the happier you'll feel about staying in Réunion. They can certainly disappear in a flash if you are not prepared for local prices!

One franc is divided into 100 centimes. French coins come in denominations of 5, 10, 20 and 50 centimes and 1, 2, 5, 10 and 20 francs. Banknotes are issued in denominations of 20, 50, 100, 200 and 500 francs.

Exchange Rates

At the time this book went to press, the exchange rates of the French franc were as follows:

country	unit		French franc
Australia	A$1	=	FF4.27
Canada	C$1	=	FF5.15
euro	€1	=	FF6.56
Germany	DM1	=	FF3.35
India	Rs100	=	FF16.77
Japan	¥100	=	FF6.48
Mauritius	Rs10	=	FF2.97
New Zealand	NZ$1	=	FF3.26
Seychelles	Rs10	=	FF13.34
Singapore	S$1	=	FF4.09
UK	£1	=	FF10.67
USA	US$1	=	FF7.10

Exchanging Money

The main banks in Réunion are Banque de la Réunion (BR), Crédit Agricole (CA), Banque Française Commerciale (BFC), BRED Banque Populaire (BRED) and Banque Nationale de Paris Intercontinentale (BNPI). There's technically no problem with changing major foreign currencies in Réunion – all of the banks offer exchange facilities – but low official exchange rates and punitive commissions on changing foreign currency travellers cheques make it sensible to carry French francs (or at least French franc travellers cheques) for your stay in Réunion.

Most banks have an ATM (known as a *guichet automatique de banque* or *GAB*), but many will only honour French credit cards. More useful to travellers are the ATMs at main post offices, which accept all the major international credit cards, regardless of where they were issued. You should have no problem using your credit card in shops, hotels or restaurants.

There were no foreign-exchange facilities at either Le Port harbour or Roland Garros International Airport at the time of writing. You should make sure you change some money into French francs before you arrive. If you do arrive without a centime, most taxis will drive you to your hotel via an ATM.

AmEx has no agent in Réunion, but AmEx cards are accepted by some ATMs, and the Crédit Agricole bank can change AmEx travellers cheques.

Travellers have reported some difficulty with Eurocheques – especially at hotels and restaurants. It's safest to have a credit card for backup, as most places seem to prefer this mode of payment.

Tipping & Bargaining

Many restaurants include service charges in their prices and surprisingly don't encourage additional tipping, but those that advertise *service non compris* (service not included) on their menus do expect something. Surprisingly, taxi drivers also don't seem to expect tips; with prices so high already, few people seem inclined to increase the agony of it all.

Few shops in Réunion are open to bargaining. However, some markets, such as the Grand Marché in St-Denis and the St-Paul market, are certainly open to some friendly haggling. Hotels have fixed tariffs, but it's definitely worthwhile asking for a discount in the low season. Similarly, if you will be staying for more than a week you may be given a better deal.

POST & COMMUNICATIONS
Post

Post offices (known as *La Poste* or *PTTs*) are open Monday to Friday from 8 am to 6 pm and on Saturday from 8 am to noon. Many close for lunch between noon and 2 pm; those that remain open through the lunch hour can get extremely crowded. There are ATMs that accept international credit cards at most post offices.

Since French post offices normally offer a vast array of services – from banking to gas bill collection – queues can be long and slow. Fortunately, there's normally a special desk or window for those poor souls who only require a couple of postcard stamps.

The main post office is in St-Denis, on the corner of Rue Maréchal Leclerc and Rue Juliette Dodu.

There's also a post office at the Roland Garros airport that is open Monday to Friday from 9.30 am to 12.30 pm and 1.30 to 4.30 pm, and Saturday 8 to 11 am.

Sending Mail
Airmail letters under 20g to anywhere within France (including DOM-TOM) and anywhere in the EU cost FF3. To the rest of the world, they're around FF4.

For packages, Surface Air-Lifted (SAL) service is significantly cheaper than regular airmail and is quite reliable.

Receiving Mail
Poste restante service is available at the main post office in St-Denis. To avoid confusion, mail should be addressed according to French tradition, with the *nom de famille* (surname or family name) first, followed by the *prénom* (first name). If you want things to run even more smoothly, tell potential correspondents to put your surname in capital letters. Poste restante costs a couple of francs tax per letter collected.

Telephone
The Réunion telephone system is efficient. There are about 500 public telephones scattered around the island and you can directly dial international numbers on them. However, very few coinphones remain in Réunion; most public telephones accept only *télécartes* (phonecards). Phonecards are available at post offices and shops; they cost FF40 for 50 units and FF80 for 120 units.

Alternatively, there are several prepaid calling cards which require you to dial a free number and enter a personal identity number before you place your call; the compensation for the inconvenience is reduced rates for international calls. Options include France Telecom, Outremer Telecom and Australes Com.

Local calls cost FF1. Calls to France are FF2.46 per minute; to Belgium or the UK FF4.93 per minute; to Australia FF7.39 per minute; to Canada or the USA FF5.91 per minute; and to India FF9.86 per minute. Charges are usually higher during peak times (ie, during business hours).

To phone Réunion from abroad, dial the international access code followed by the Réunion code (262) and the number desired.

Fax
Some shops and offices advertise that they offer fax services, and your hotel will usually let you send and receive them for a fee.

Email & Internet Access
Internet access is very thin on the ground in Réunion. About the only options are the stylish Bookc@fe at Librairie L'entrepôt on Rue Juliette Dodu in St-Denis, and Souris Net in St-Gilles-les-Bains. Both places charge around FF1 per minute.

INTERNET RESOURCES
There are several useful English-language sites covering Réunion. A hot site is www.runweb.com, which has a good selection of links with a budget emphasis. Visit www.reunion-sud.com for detailed information on the south of the island.

BOOKS
There is a fine selection of French-language books in Réunion's bookshops, predominantly in St-Denis, but if you plan to do a lot of reading in English, bring some paperbacks. The best chance of finding books in English is at the major bookshops in St-Denis (see Bookshops in the St-Denis chapter).

The Bibliothèque Departmentale (Departmental Library) is more useful than the Central Library. It's on the corner of Rue Roland Garros and Rue Jean Chatel; opening hours are from 10 am to 7 pm on Monday and 8 am to 7 pm Tuesday to Saturday.

(Remember that a bookshop is *une librairie*. The French term for a library is *une bibliothèque*.)

RÉUNION

Travel Guides

If you want the best guidebook in English (and practically the only guidebook in English), you're looking at it. The only locally available guide in English is the translation of Albert Trotet's booklet, *Tourist Guide to Réunion Island*. If you're especially interested in architecture, it's worth the investment. However, there are few English copies still available and you may have to resort to the French version, called *Guide Touristique de la Réunion*.

There are several standard French guides: the colourful *La Réunion Aujourd'hui* by Hureau & Bruyère; the detailed *Le Guide Pratique* by Serge Hoarau; the very general *À la Réunion, à l'Île Maurice, aux Seychelles*; and the oddly organised *Îles de l'Ocean Indien: Réunion, Maurice, Les Seychelles* by Jean-Pierre Jardel. In addition, there's the expanded tourist brochure-cum-book entitled *Evasions Réunion*, edited by Agostina Calderon. The photos are nice and it includes a large map.

Bonjour Réunion, which is part of the French *Bonjour* series, is a very good source of basic background material on the island and is full of fine colour photos. It purports to be a travel guide *pour voyageurs curieux* (for curious travellers), but the very limited practical information is next to useless.

Of several guides available in German, the best is *Richtig Reisen – Réunion* by Dirk & Henriette Althoff.

General

If you're looking for a French treatise on the island, the best choice is Catherine Lavaux's *La Réunion: Du Battant des Lames au Sommet des Montagnes*. In the paperback *Que Sais-Je* series, there's a general interest history book on Réunion by André Scherer.

Sous le signe de la tortue, voyages anciens à l'île Bourbon (1611–1725) is an interesting book. It contains old texts gathered by Albert Lougnon that outline the first journeys made by boat to Réunion.

Taking the emphasis off the French text, with good colour plates of the island, are the books by Folco, Salvat & Robert: *La Réunion*

has good photos from ground level, and *La Réunion – Vue du Ciel* contains magnificent aerial shots. For a cheaper, colourful alternative and an accompanying English translation of the text, there's *L'Île de la Réunion* by Claude Huc.

For pretrip reading, look out for *Blue Africa* by Australian Colin Simpson, who writes about his organised tour through Africa. It has a chapter on Réunion.

Réunion is a fascinating place for the magically minded. Creole beliefs and potions have spawned a number of books on voodoo-style sorcery. For the serious student there is a four-book set entitled *Vertus et Secrets des Plantes Médicinales des Tropiques et de la Réunion* by Dr Robert Zamore & Ary Ebroin. You will have to conjure up a couple of thousand francs for it though!

The treasure hunter extraordinaire of the island is a character called Bibique. His book *Sur la Piste des Frères de la Côte* is about the Indian Ocean pirates and their booty.

The bible of Creole cookery is *Les Délices de la Cuisine Créole*. It costs around FF3000 for the six-volume set, but it's the *crème de la crème* of cookbooks. Some of the table d'hôte restaurant owners have copies. You can also pick up some considerably cheaper (although far less impressive) cookbooks.

NEWSPAPERS & MAGAZINES

There are three daily morning papers published in St-Denis and sold around the island.

The two popular daily newspapers are the conservative *Le Journal de l'Île de la Réunion (JIR)* and the more liberal *Le Quotidien*. Each costs FF5 and carries sections on local, mainland French, Indian Ocean and world news. They're both good for features and great for up-to-date information and views on the Comoros, Madagascar and Mauritius. The *JIR* also has a large Sunday edition. Free classified advertising is available in *Le Quotidien* on Friday and in the *JIR* on Tuesday and Wednesday. Every Wednesday, *Le Quotidien* includes a page of news in English.

The communist daily, *Témoignages* (FF5), presents all these items as well, but obviously from a different perspective.

You can pick up English-language newspapers at a few places, including the airport and several of the major bookshops in St-Denis. But by far the best range of newspapers and magazines in English, French and several other languages is at Le Tabac du Rallye in St-Denis (see Bookshops in the St-Denis chapter).

There are four weekly magazines which carry the week's radio and TV programs, as well as some general-interest articles: *Télé 7*, *Télé Mag*, *Visu* and *Star Télé*.

A magazine of interest to visitors is the bimonthly *Plein Sud* which is published in Réunion but focuses on history, oddities, culture and (especially) leisure activities throughout the Indian Ocean region.

RADIO & TV

There are two Réseau France Ôutre-mer (RFO) radio stations (government stations), and scores of 'free' stations such as Radio Free-DOM, Radio Arc-en-Ciel and Radio Dominique; these cover the island and satisfy a range of creeds and tastes. Because of the mountainous landscape, radio reception can be very variable.

Television viewers have the choice of two government (RFO) channels as well as an independent station. Most of the programming on the RFOs is produced and shown in *la métropole* (mainland France) first.

PHOTOGRAPHY

There's plenty of scope for sensational photography in Réunion. The volcano may not perform on cue, but several photographers have caught it in the act and have colour shots of the eruption on display or for sale.

Stocks of film are plentiful and fresh, but rather more expensive than in Europe. A 36-exposure colour print film costs around FF58; processing is also expensive at FF4 per print and an additional FF18 per roll.

(For further information on photography in this part of the world, see Photography & Video in the Regional Facts for the Visitor chapter.)

ELECTRICITY

The electric current in Réunion is 220V AC at 50Hz. Outlets take continental two-pin plugs, so non-European visitors should use an adaptor for their electrical appliances.

LAUNDRY

All of the top-end hotels, most of the mid-range hotels and some of the budget places offer a laundry service. To cut costs, bundle together your clothes and head for a self-service laundry or dry-cleaner – these are mainly found in the larger towns.

HEALTH

Although there are definitely mosquitoes on the island, there is no malaria. However, authorities ask that visitors 'take some form of antimalarial treatment before they fall ill' if coming from Madagascar or another area where malaria is endemic (for further details see Health in the Regional Facts for the Visitor chapter).

The greatest health threat in Réunion will probably be spraining, blistering, twisting or breaking something while hiking. If the worst does happen, the best medical care is at hand. Réunion has more than 1000 doctors, 200 pharmacies and the best equipment and emergency services in the Indian Ocean.

Tap water is safe to drink everywhere on the island, but like the French in mainland France, most Réunionnais prefer bottled mineral water. Badôit, Perrier and Evian are popular imported brands; Cilaos is the local *aqua pura*.

EMERGENCIES

The emergency number for police is ☎ 17. The ambulance is on ☎ 15 and fire services are on ☎ 18.

BUSINESS HOURS

Lunches are long, relaxed affairs in Réunion; shops and businesses are generally open daily (except Sunday) from around 9 am to noon and 2.30 to 6 pm. Some shops are closed on Monday morning. On Sunday, the streets are almost eerily silent.

The main banks are open on weekdays from 8 am to 4 pm.

PUBLIC HOLIDAYS & SPECIAL EVENTS

Most of Réunion's offices, museums and shops are closed on the *jours fériés* (public holidays), which are as follows:

New Year's Day	1 January
Easter Monday	March/April
Labour Day	1 May
Victory Day 1945	8 May
Ascension Day late	May or June
Bastille Day (National Day)	14 July
Assumption Day	15 August
All Saints' Day	1 November
Armistice Day 1918	1 November
Abolition of Slavery Day	20 December
Christmas Day	25 December

Abolition of Slavery Day is taken very seriously in Réunion, particularly among the Creole population, who still occupy a disadvantaged position in society. The celebrations usually involve street parties with live reggae and *séga* music, dancing and other lively activities.

Major festivals in Réunion involve exhibitions with sales, competitions, sports events, music, dancing and various other activities. Towns and villages across the island take turns at celebrating over a week or weekend; the excuse is to honour their primary product, which can be anything from *chou chou* (a green squash-like vegetable) to sugar cane. The atmosphere is generally commercial rather than celebratory, with plenty of market stalls selling the feted produce. Beauty pageants are a popular feature, usually featuring loud rock music.

For details contact any of the syndicats d'initiative or the *mairie* (town hall) in the relevant town.

The Indian community is principally made up of Tamil Hindus and they hold some amazing rites, including *cavadees* and firewalking ceremonies. The Hindu temple in St-André is the most popular location for these events. Again, the syndicats d'initiative should have details.

Festivals in Réunion include:

Fête du Miel Vert (honey) Le Tampon, one week in mid-January

Fête du Vacoa (rope made from screw-pine fronds) St-Benoît, April
Fête du Chou Chou (chou chou) Hell-Bourg, first weekend in May
Fête de la Vanille (vanilla) Bras-Panon, 10 days in mid-May
Fête des Goyaviers (guava trees) Plaine-des-Palmistes, a weekend in June
Fête de la Canne (sugar cane) Ste-Rose, end of July
Fête de St-Paul St-Paul, two weeks in July
Foire du Bois (wood) La Rivière, St-Louis, 10 days at the beginning of August
Fête du Safran (saffron) St-Joseph, 10 days in August
Exposition des Fleurs (flower show) Le Tampon, end of September or beginning of October
Fête de la Rose (roses) St-Benoît, five days in November
Fête des Lentilles (lentils) Cilaos, a weekend in November
Fête des Mangoustans (mangosteens) St-Benoît, November
Foire de St-Pierre, St-Pierre, 10 days at the beginning of December
Fête des Letchis (lychees) St-Denis, one week in mid-December
Fête de l'Ail (garlic) Petite Île, a weekend in December

The Cross-Country for Crazies

The tortuous topography of Réunion is the setting for one of the world's most challenging cross-country races, Grand Raid, held every October or November. The route roughly follows the path of the GR R2 hiking trail which traverses the island from St-Denis to Mare Longue, near St-Philippe, taking in parts of the Mafate and Cilaos Cirques, the Plaine-des-Cafres and the lunar landscape around Piton de la Fournaise.

Covering 125km, the Grand Raid would be a challenging race over level ground, but runners also have to negotiate some 7000m of altitude change. Not for nothing is the race nicknamed the 'Cross-Country for Crazies'! The pack leaders can complete this agonising run in 16 hours, but contestants are allowed up to 60 hours to finish.

If you feel like entering, contact the organisers (☎ 20 32 00, fax 94 19 20) at BP 426, 97468 St-Denis Cedex.

ACTIVITIES

As in mainland France, the recreational emphasis in Réunion is on blood, sweat and tears, or at least it can seem that way. Most of the activities on offer involve some element of adventure, usually accompanied by strenuous effort. Whether or not anyone actually breaks new ground, however, seems to be immaterial as long as some suffering is involved! The logical conclusion of this quest for endurance is the Grand Raid, an incredible 125km race across the middle of the island (see the boxed text 'Cross Country for Crazies' earlier).

There are established clubs for just about every sort of activity you can imagine: flying, parachuting, sailboarding, hang-gliding, canyoning, equitation, mountain biking, diving, deep-sea fishing, water-skiing, sailing and numerous competitive sports. Water activities are clustered around the waterfront at St-Gilles-les-Bains, which is the holiday and leisure centre of Réunion.

Inquiries about what's on should be directed to the syndicats d'initiative or to the Office Départemental de la Culture (☎ 41 11 41, fax 41 55 71) in St-Denis. The local press should also have details on events. Another good source of information is the *RUN* magazine, available for free from the syndicats d'initiative and many hotels around the island (see Tourist Offices earlier in this chapter).

Hiking

No visitor to the island should miss the volcano and the superb rugged cirques of Cilaos, Salazie and Mafate, even if you only get as close as the villages of Cilaos or Hell-Bourg. To see the best of the cirques, of course, you'll need to hike through the peaks and valleys of the Cirque de Mafate. For the less energetic, the volcano climb makes a manageable day trip and offers some of the most unusual and impressive scenery on the island. (For more detailed information, see the special section 'Hiking in Réunion'.)

Deep-Sea Fishing

As elsewhere in the Indian Ocean region, the season for deep-sea fishing is tied to the feeding habits of bait-fish species; you stand the best chance of hooking a monster marlin from November to April. A boat with crew costs roughly FF1800/2600 per half/full day (maximum of around six people). This usually includes soft drinks and a light lunch. If you intend spending several days fishing, you should negotiate a discount. Some operators may offer individuals rates of between FF450 and FF600 per person for a half-day trip, and between FF800 and FF900 for a full day.

Contact any of the major tour operators or the fishing charters in and around St-Gilles-les-Bains:

Abaco Charter Pêche (☎ 24 34 74, fax 24 39 46)
Abalone (☎ 24 36 10)
Aloupía Pêche Sportif (☎ 68 44 06)
Alpha (☎ 24 02 02)
Blue Marlin (☎ 65 22 35)
Maevasion (☎ 85 23 46)
Marine Océan (☎ 43 98 35)
Octopus II (☎/fax 24 40 06)
Réunion Fishing Club (☎ 24 36 10, fax 24 39 46)

Les Dents du Mer

Swimmers should think twice before diving headlong into the waters around Réunion. Attacks by *les dents du mer* (the teeth of the sea) are a part of life on the island, and while the risks are statistically very low, most years see a few shark attacks on surfers, swimmers and spear fishermen.

You should avoid swimming or surfing in cloudy water, as sharks prefer an element of surprise. The mouths of rivers and streams are particularly risky spots, as the mix of fresh water and salt water turns the ocean cloudy. Swimming at night is not advisable anywhere on the island, and sharks may also be active late in the afternoon or early in the morning, particularly following rain.

The safest place for water sports is the coral lagoon along the west coast, while the exposed east coast is regarded as a high-risk zone. Surfers who paddle out beyond the reef break may be at risk anywhere along the coast. The locals know their ocean, so it's best to seek their advice before entering the water.

Surfing

There are several surfing clubs and schools, but the only surfing spots are around St-Gilles-les-Bains and St-Leu. One good location is at Ravine des Colimaçons, not far from Le Corail Turtle Farm near St-Leu. The most popular spot and surfing centre is Roches Noires beach at St-Gilles-les-Bains itself.

If you're keen to ride the waves but could do with a few pointers, contact one of the following organisations. Private lessons for beginners cost around FF135 per hour; group classes are considerably cheaper.

École de Surf Roches Noires (☎/fax 24 63 28)
    4 bis Lot des Charmilles, St-Gilles-les-Bains
Trois Bassins Surf School (☎ 66 02 45) Pointe
    de Trois Bassins, La-Saline-les-Bains
Ligue Réunionnaise de Surf (☎ 24 33 10)
    St-Gilles-les-Bains
Glissy École de Surf (☎ 33 13 13, fax 24 12 15)
    Rip Curl Proshop, Rue de la Plage,
    St-Gilles-les-Bains

Swimming

The best beaches for swimming are all on the west coast. The main tourist beaches include those at St-Gilles-les-Bains, Saline-les-Bains, Hermitage-les-Bains and Étang-Salé-les-Bains. *The* beach as far as locals are concerned is Boucan Canot.

Canyoning

For adventure seekers, there's the exhilaration of canyoning, which challenges you to abseil down rugged gorges and cliffs into water holes or lagoons below. Canyoning (with a guide) usually costs around FF250/400 per person for a half/full day. Try one of the following operators, or inquire at Maison de la Montagne (☎ 90 78 78, fax 41 84 29), 10 Place Sarda Garriga, St-Denis.

Austral Aventure (☎ 55 69 55, fax 55 83 32)
    11 Rue des Myrtilles, St-Gilles-les-Hauts
Kalanoro (☎ 51 71 10, fax 51 72 94) Bras-
    Panon
Maham (☎/fax 47 82 82) Rue Général de
    Gaulle, Hell-Bourg
Réunion Evasion (☎ 31 83 57, fax 31 80 72)
    Rue de Père Boiteau, Cilaos

Slippery Business

Tired of abseiling? Had your fill of mountain waterfalls? Why not combine the two? Canyoning is a hugely popular pastime in France and is growing in popularity around the world. It involves descending the steep walls of canyons using natural watercourses, adding the exhilaration of sliding down slippery water chutes to the already considerable thrills of abseiling. You'll need to don a wet suit though, as the water in Réunion's high mountain streams can be icy cold.

The main centres for canyoning are Hell-Bourg and Cilaos. However, the sport is very vulnerable to the vagaries of the weather. Too little rain and the watercourses will be disappointingly dry; too much and the streams transform into raging torrents which can strip canyoners from the rocks. Expect trips to be cancelled at short notice in the rainy season (from October to March).

Réunion Sensations *St-Gilles-les-Bains:* (☎ 24
    57 00, fax 24 56 57)
    Cilaos: (☎ 31 84 84, fax 31 80 85)
Ric A Ric (☎ 33 25 38, fax 86 54 85) St-
    Gilles-les-Bains

Canoeing, Kayaking, Sailboarding & Water-Skiing

Contact any of the following operators for information on these adventurous water activities.

Blue Cat (☎ 24 32 04) 2 Rue des Brisants, Port
    de Plaisance, St-Gilles-les-Bains
Location Vente (☎/fax 33 17 39) Port de
    Plaisance, St-Gilles-les-Bains
Nauti Ouest (☎ 24 43 79, fax 24 25 62) Port de
    Plaisance, St-Gilles-les-Bains
Parachute Ascensionnel Nautique (☎ 66 21 58)
    Port de Plaisance, St-Gilles-les-Bains
Ski Nautique Club de St-Paul (☎ 45 42 87)
    1 Rue de la Croix, l'Étang, St-Paul
Société Nautique de St-Paul (☎ 22 56 46)
    78 Route de la Baie, St-Paul
Société Nautique de St-Pierre (☎ 25 89 66)
    BP 123, St-Pierre
Waterworld (☎ 33 01 02, 24 32 97) Port de
    Plaisance, St-Gilles-les-Bains

Paragliding, Hang-Gliding, Abseiling & Rock Climbing

The following organisations may be helpful if you're interested in any of these activities.

Aventures Ocean Indien (☎ 24 13 42) Souris-Blanche, Trois-Bassins

Bourbon Parapente (☎ 87 58 74) Rue de Père Tabaillet, St-Leu

Centre École de Parachutisme de la Réunion (☎ 25 54 41) St-Pierre

Compagnie des Guides de la Réunion (☎ 31 71 71, fax 31 80 54) Maison de la Montagne, 2 Rue Mac Auliffe, Cilaos

Parapente Delta (Azurtech) (☎ 85 04 00, fax 33 91 36) 33 Chemin No 1, Les Avirons

Parapente Réunion (☎ 24 87 84, fax 24 87 15) 4 CD 12 des Colimaçons, St-Leu

Mountain Biking

Recently, Réunion has seen an explosion of interest in the *vélo tout terrain* (VTT) or mountain bike. (For more information, see Bicycle in the Réunion Getting Around chapter.)

Golf

There are three golf courses on the island. For nine holes, the charge is around FF160/175 on weekdays/weekends; for 18 holes you pay FF220/260. Club hire costs around FF100.

Golf Club de Bourbon (☎ 26 33 39) Étang-Salé-les-Bains

Golf Club du Bassin Bleu (☎ 55 53 58) St-Gilles-les-Hauts

Golf Club du Colorado (☎ 23 79 50) Zone de Loisirs du Colorado, La Montagne, St-Denis

Horse Riding

If the idea of exploring the countryside on horseback appeals to you, contact one of the following organisations. Most places charge between FF50 and FF140 per hour, or FF250/500 for a half/full day.

Centre Équestre Alti-Merens (☎ 59 18 84) 49 Chemin Notre Dame de la Paix, Petite Ferme

Centre Équestre du Grand-Étang (☎ 50 90 03) Route de la Plaine-des-Palmistes (RN3), St-Benoît

Centre Équestre de l'Etalon Blanc (☎ 26 55 65) Chemin Rural du Maniron, Étang-Salé-les-Hauts

Centre Équestre du Maïdo (☎ 32 49 15) Route du Maïdo, Guillaume

Centre d'Équitation du Colorado (☎ 23 62 51) 17 Chemin des Mimosas, La Montagne, St-Denis

Club Hippique de l'Hermitage (☎ 24 47 73) Chemin Ceinture, St-Gilles-les-Bains

Crinière Réunion (☎ 45 19 37) 42 Rue Henri Cornu, Cambaie, St-Paul

Eldorado La Diligence (☎ 59 10 10) RN3, Vingt-Huitième, Plaine-des-Cafres

Ranch Kikouyou, (☎ 39 60 62) Rue Cinaire BP, 19 Grand-Fond, Entre-Deux

4WD Excursions

For a guided day tour by 4WD expect to pay upwards of FF550 per person. Popular destinations include Piton de la Fournaise and Le Dimitile, or you could try creek-bashing in the Rivière des Remparts. Popular operators include:

Evasion 4x4 (☎ 59 34 12) 187 RN3, Bourg-Murat, Plaine-des-Cafres

Indi Aventure (☎ 24 23 87) 14 Rue des Lanternes, St-Gilles-les-Bains

Kréolie 4x4 (☎ 39 50 87) Grand Fond Interieur, Entre-Deux

WORK

European Union (EU) citizens have the right to live and work in Réunion for up to three months. For longer, you need an employer to apply on your behalf or to provide a guarantee of means for at least one year. This will enable you to apply at immigration for a *carte de séjour*, which will allow you to remain for five to 10 years. It's considerably harder for non-EU residents to obtain permission to work in Réunion.

If you're a native English speaker and you want to give English lessons, the going rate starts at around FF100 per hour. If you have a contact number, you can advertise your services free in *Le Quotidien* on Friday and in the *Journal de l'Île de la Réunion* on Tuesday and Wednesday.

For formal English-related employment, you could try the Chambre de Commerce et de l'Industrie. Alternatively, you may be

RÉUNION

able to find work at the Université de la Réunion as a *repetiteur* (tutor) – apply to the Faculté d'Anglais at the university. You may also be able to get work as a *maître auxiliare* (substitute teacher) – apply at the Rectorat in St-Denis. Bear in mind that you will be competing with foreign students who study French as a foreign language at the University of St-Denis.

ACCOMMODATION

Advance preparation in choosing and booking accommodation is a very good idea because of the high cost and the equally high demand. You won't be able to see, let alone appreciate, the beauty of the island if a chunk of your time is taken up in search of a place to stay. That doesn't mean there isn't a range of accommodation, but things do fill up and some places are permanently packed out.

Camping

Most of the organised camping sites have closed down in recent years. These days, camping is only really useful if you are hiking in the interior, though there's no reason why you shouldn't put up your tent at any secluded spot around the coast (there are usually 'Camping Interdit' signs if camping is forbidden).

You can *bivouac* (camp) for free in many areas in the cirques, but only for one night. Popular spots in the Cirque de Mafate include Trois Roches on GR R2 between Marla and Roche Plate; Le Grand Sable on GR R1 near Le Belier; Plaine des Tamarins on GR R1 near La Nouvelle; and the gîte de montagne at Bélouve. Setting up camp on Piton de la Fournaise is forbidden for obvious reasons.

If you're heading for the cirques in August, you may want to carry a tent and forego the urban life in the gîtes. There are also emergency shelters along some of the main hiking paths, but they provide only a roof. Remember to avoid pitching your tent under large trees, as falling branches are a danger.

Youth Hostels

Réunion has two *auberges de jeunesse* (youth hostels), at Bernica (☎ 22 89 75) and Entre-Deux (☎ 39 59 20). They are operated by the Fédération Réunionnaise des Auberges de Jeunesse (☎ 41 15 34) in St-Denis, which is an affiliate of the Ligue Française pour les Auberges de la Jeunesse (French Youth Hostels League).

Officially, the hostels are only open to Hostelling International (HI) card holders. Others may be required to become members or to purchase an international guest card for about FF100 (available at most youth hostels).

Guests over 18 years of age pay FF70 per night and an additional FF10 for breakfast. Evening meals are available for FF45 per person.

VVF Holiday Villages

The VVFs (Villages Vacances Familles), like the rural gîtes, are a French holiday institution. They are relatively quiet, low-key and nothing like a Butlins camp. In order to stay, you need to first join the VVF organisation, which costs FF50 per family per year.

There are VVFs at St-Gilles-les-Bains (☎ 24 29 39, fax 24 41 02) and in the spa town of Cilaos (☎ 31 71 39, fax 31 80 85).

Chambres d'Hôte

A *chambre d'hôte* is a small family-run bed and breakfast (B&B). Chambres d'hôte are normally tucked away in the hills and offer a window into a more traditional way of life. You may be treated like a member of the family in some places; in others you'll definitely be aware that you are a paying guest. B&B rates are from around FF150 for a double room. Hearty traditional meals cost about FF80 per person, but must be reserved in advance. You can reserve a room by telephoning the proprietor directly. Some places can also be booked through the Relais Départemental des Gîtes de France (see Gîtes Ruraux following).

Pensions de Famille

Réunion's *pensions de famille* (boarding houses) see few families; they cater mainly to Malagasy and Indian immigrants looking for work and to French students working over their summer vacation. The pensions are the cheapest places to stay in the larger towns, and many offer a kitchen for self-catering, or can provide cheap meals. St-Denis is well equipped with pensions de famille.

Rates generally range from around FF120 to FF200 per night for a double room, including breakfast. Note that standards can vary wildly from pension to pension; some places are clean and well run, others are dirty and overcrowded.

Gîtes de Montagne

Gîtes de montagne are basic mountain cabins or lodges, operated by the government through Maison de la Montagne. It is possible to organise a walking holiday using the gîtes de montagne only. Cirque de Mafate, inaccessible by road, has gîtes de montagne at Cayenne, Îlet à Bourse, Îlet à Malheur, La Nouvelle, La Plaque, Roche Plate, Grand Place and Marla. La Roche Écrite is on the route between St-Denis and the Cirque de Salazie. Bélouve and Piton des Neiges gîtes are between Salazie and Cilaos cirques. Volcan is accessible by road, on the way to the volcano at Pas de Bellecombe. There's also a gîte de montagne at Basse Vallée in the south-east of the island.

The gîtes in Réunion are generally in better condition than those in mainland France and, thanks to recently installed solar panels, they have electricity. Not all, however, get as cushy as providing warm showers. The most basic is at Piton des Neiges; it currently has no hot water or showers, but there are plans to improve facilities here.

The gîtes must be booked and paid for in advance, and charges are not refundable unless a cyclone or a cyclone alert prevents your arrival. One night's accommodation without food costs around FF83 per person. Book through Maison de la Montagne: the main office (☎ 90 78 78, fax 41 84 29) is at 10 Place Sarda Garriga, 97400 St-Denis. The Cilaos office (☎ 31 71 71, fax 31 80 54) is at 2 Rue Mac Auliffe, 97413 Cilaos. You can also book with the Pays d'Accueil de Salazie (☎ 47 89 89), Rue Général de Gaulle, in Hell-Bourg. In France, contact Maison des Gîtes de France (☎ 01 49 70 75 75, fax 01 49 70 75 76), 59 Rue St-Lazare, 75009 Paris. It's highly recommended that you book well in advance, especially during the busy tourist season.

When booking a gîte de montagne, you'll usually have to call the owner independently to book your meals (though you can pay when you arrive). Failure to do so could leave you nursing a rumbling stomach, as most gîtes just cook for the guests who have booked. Dinner costs from FF80 to FF90, and usually consists of *carri poulet* (chicken curry), *rougaille saucisse* (tomato-based sauce served with sausages) or *boucané* (smoked pork) with vegetables, plus the usual rice, *brèdes* (local spinach), *lentilles* (lentils) and *rougail* (chutney). Some owners throw in a glass of *rhum arrangé* or local wine as well. Breakfast costs around FF35 and normally consists of coffee, toast and jam.

Sleeping arrangements usually consist of bunk beds in shared rooms, so be prepared for the communal living that this entails. There are two blankets and a mattress cover per bed.

It's not a bad idea to also bring along toilet paper and a torch. It can get quite chilly at night, so warm clothing will be in order. Some places will let you cook on their wood-fired stove, but many kitchens are so grimy that you probably won't bother.

On arrival and departure you must 'book' in and out with the manager, who will collect your booking ticket. In theory, you're not meant to occupy a gîte before 3 pm or remain past 10 am. The telephone numbers of individual gîtes are listed here; for more information about the gîtes and for hiking-related information, see the special section 'Hiking in Réunion'.

Basse Vallée	☎ 37 00 75
Bélouve	☎ 41 21 23
Cayenne	☎ 43 85 42
Grand Place	☎ 43 66 76
Îlet à Bourse	☎ 43 43 93
Îlet à Malheur	☎ 43 56 96
La Nouvelle	☎ 43 61 77
Marla	☎ 43 78 31
Piton des Neiges	☎ 51 15 26
Rivière des Remparts	☎ 59 13 94
Roche Écrite	☎ 43 99 84
Roche Plate	☎ 43 60 01
Volcan	☎ 21 28 96

RÉUNION

Gîtes d'Étape

Gîtes d'étape are privately run and work in the same way as the gîtes de montagne, offering dorm beds and meals, although you can book these places directly with the owners. There are several in the Cirque de Mafate, and numerous others dotted around the island; most are in the vicinity of walking trails. The host will often offer meals or cooking facilities.

Gîtes Ruraux

Gîtes ruraux (also known as *gîtes de France*, or just 'gîtes') are private houses and lodges that families and groups can rent for self-catering holidays, normally by the week or weekend. There are over 80 gîtes ruraux in Réunion, mainly in the southern half of the island and around Plaine-des-Palmistes and Plaine-des-Cafres.

Most offer lodging for four or more people, with kitchen facilities, a fridge and hot water. You may have to bring bed sheets in some cases. Costs vary from around FF1200 to FF2700 per week and from FF500 to FF1800 for a weekend (note that not all offer bookings for just a weekend). A security bond equivalent to one week's rent is required in advance.

The handy booklet called *Île de la Réunion* contains photos and full information on each gîte. The booklet is available from the Maison de la Montagne and from tourist offices. You may book the gîtes by phoning the proprietors directly or contacting the Relais Départemental des Gîtes de France (☎ 90 78 90, fax 41 84 29), 10 Place Sarda Garriga, 97400 St-Denis. In France, contact Maison des Gîtes de France (☎ 01 49 70 75 75, fax 01 49 70 75 76), at 59 Rue Saint-Lazare, 75009 Paris.

Hotels

Réunion isn't flush with hotels, so getting a room can often be difficult. Primarily, they're found in St-Denis and around the beach resorts of the west coast, especially St-Gilles-les-Bains. Most hotels on the island are rated as one-, two- or three-star, and lots are unclassified. There is only a sprinkling of four-star hotels.

Many of the mid-range hotels attract businesspeople and can get booked out quite quickly. It's wise to make reservations well in advance so that your choices are not limited. If you will be staying for more than one week, it's worth asking for a discount when making your booking. Keep an eye open for special deals offered by hotels, particularly during the low season.

FOOD

Most restaurants are open for lunch from about noon to 3 pm and in the evening from 6.30 to 10 pm, but you may struggle to find a meal outside of these times. Many restaurants take Sunday, Monday or Tuesday as a day off. It's a good idea to ring ahead to check that the restaurant you intend dining at will be open.

Local Food

As in France proper, much time and effort is devoted to growing, preparing and enjoying food in Réunion. What's more, the Réunionnais have an array of culinary traditions to choose from – French, Indian, Chinese and Creole – and many recipes contain elements of several cuisines.

Just as in mainland France, locals begin the day with a *petit déjeuner* (breakfast) usually consisting of a bread roll or croissant with butter and jam. This is washed down with at least one cup of coffee and perhaps a glass of juice. Lunch is the main meal of the day for many people, and the restaurants fill up fast at lunchtime.

Most imaginable fruits and vegetables, as well as a few that are unknown in Europe and elsewhere, are available. Among the lesser known types, two stand out: the *tomate d'arbuste*, the sweet tree tomato that some people call tamarillo; and the pear-shaped green vegetable called *chou chou*, which was introduced from Brazil. (In Australia the chou chou is known as the choko and in Europe, the *crystophène*.)

Other common ingredients in Creole dishes are *graines*, which may be *haricots* (beans, usually red or white), *lentilles* (lentils) or *petits pois* (peas), invariably served as a creamy side dish along with *brèdes*, digestive leafy greens that resemble spinach.

Réunion is not a vegetarian's paradise. In the highlands, *poulet* (chicken), beef, goat or pork is central to practically every dish. On the coast, there is the additional choice of fish or crustaceans.

More often than not, the meat or fish available is cooked in a very mild curry (often it's little more than a tomato sauce) and served on a rice base; specialities include *carri poulpe* (octopus curry), *carri p'tit jacques* (jackfruit curry) and *carri boucané* (smoked pork curry). Vanilla or heart of palm figure in many recipes. Arabic influences are evident in the cloves, cinnamon and nutmeg in some recipes, while the Swahili contribution is coconut cream. The Chinese have contributed ginger.

If you want to spice up your meal, there is invariably a bowl of *rougail*, a spicy tomato, ginger and vegetable chutney, which is usually incendiary; just use a smidgen! The condiment evolved from the same spicy tomato stew that is served in Mauritius and the Seychelles.

Good home cooking wouldn't be the same without the cakes. They're not the fancy fruit, cream and pastry delicacies of the patisserie, but rather sweet and heavy puddings made out of sweet potatoes, chou chou, cassava or rice.

Cheap Eats

There is a dearth of budget eating houses in Réunion. Small snacks and titbits are available in shops and at street stalls all around the island. Small chicken, fish or beef samosas cost from FF2 to FF4 each. Or you can try *bon bon piments* (spicy meat fritters) and *bouchons* (Chinese-style meat dumplings) which cost around FF4 and are served with soy or pepper sauce. But unless you can subsist on snacks, you won't find much for less than FF25.

There are a few Chinese-Creole restaurants and cafes where a reasonably filling meal costs between FF30 and FF60. For a little more money, the set-menu lunches offered by most restaurants for between FF55 and FF90 are the best value.

Strange Veg

A remarkable array of curious fruits and vegetables makes it into Creole dishes alongside such staples as chicken and *boucané* (smoked pork). You may be served up *p'tit jacques* (jackfruit), *chou chou* (a green South American squash known in Australia as the choko), *margose* (a lumpy bitter melon), *combava* (a knobbly lime), *z'andouille* (a root vegetable that resembles a length of intestine) and the enigmatically named *baba figue*, the blossom of the banana tree! Heart of palm, made from the palmiste palm, is another popular ingredient.

Tables d'Hôte

Tables d'hôte dish up set meals of three or four courses accompanied by wine, punch or rum for around FF90 per person. The Creole cuisine you'll find in the tables d'hôte is rich and filling, though it rarely gets too daring; most of the time you'll wind up with carri poulet. If you like variety, you'll have to splash out on a restaurant occasionally.

There are quite a few tables d'hôte in the Cirque de Salazie, the Plaine-des-Cafres and the Plaine-des-Palmistes. Some cater for clubs and other large parties. To reserve, just telephone directly or get the local tourist office to book for you.

Most *chambres d'hôte* (B&Bs) also offer table d'hôte.

Vegetarian

Vegetarians are not particularly well catered for in Réunion. However, the French brasseries in the main towns are a refreshing exception to this rule, offering cheap and tasty salads. The French do like their meat, however, so clarify that there's no meat in your salad when you order. Creole restaurants usually offer vegetable curries and the odd vegetarian side dish, such as lentils or *achards de légumes* (pickled vegetable salad).

For versatility, your best bet is to stay in self-catering accommodation, which will allow you to whip up your favourite dishes when you get tired of the limited vegetarian options at the restaurants.

Self-Catering

When camping, hiking from gîte to gîte or renting a bungalow, the cheapest places to get provisions are the supermarkets and department stores such as Score, Champion and Super U. You'll find the same cheap and nasty prepackaged and instant food items as the ones you probably carry on outdoor trips at home. You can also get fruit and vegetables at most supermarkets, but for greater variety and better prices head for a fruit and vegetable market – such as the Petit Marché in St-Denis. All the supermarkets offer great selections of French cheese, sausage and pate.

Local cheeses are available at some supermarkets and from the smaller grocers in the highland areas. The fresh goats cheeses are very good, and baguettes are available everywhere, as are premade baguette sandwiches.

DRINKS
Nonalcoholic Drinks

Expect to pay around FF6 for a small cup of black coffee. If you want it with milk *(café au lait)*, it goes for FF8. A large coffee costs FF12/10 with/without milk. Tea, which is not as popular as coffee, is similarly priced. Many restaurants and hotels charge more.

Alcoholic Drinks

Spirits The variety of home-made rums and punches available in Réunion is astounding. The cheapest seems to be a blend of cheap *charette* rum, sugar and fruit juice. It's quite rough, and discriminating palates will want to move a bit upmarket.

A lot better is *rhum arrangé* or *punch créole*, a mixture of rum, fruit juice, cane syrup and a blend of herbs and berries. Every table d'hôte or chambre d'hôte owner will have their own tried and tested brew. Commercially produced varieties are also available in most stores, bars and restaurants. (See the boxed text 'Rhum Luck' for more information.)

Wine True to French tradition, most meals are accompanied by wine. The full French selection is available, and ranges in price from about FF20 a bottle for Vin Royal (a no-frills table wine) to several hundred

Rhum Luck

Up in the hills, almost everyone will have their own family recipe for *rhum arrangé*, a heady mixture of local rum and a secret blend of herbs and spices. In fact, not all are that secret. Popular concoctions include *rhum faham*, a blend of rum, sugar and flowers from the faham orchid; *rhum vanille*, made from rum, sugar and fresh vanilla pods; and *rhum bibasse*, made from rum, sugar and tasty *bibasse* fruit (loquats). The family rhum arrangé is a source of pride for most Creoles; if you stay in any of the rural gîtes or chambres d'hôte you can expect the proprietor to serve up their version with more than a little ceremony.

francs for a reputable label. There are also Italian and Spanish table wines for around FF30. South African wines cost from FF26 to FF250 a bottle. The spa resort of Cilaos has its own concoction, which is more like a sherry than a wine.

Beer The local brew is Bière Bourbon (it's affectionately known as Dodo); not a bad drop at all at FF8 to FF10 (ridiculously more in many restaurants and bars). A *pression* (draught) costs FF10 for a small or FF20 for a large. There is also a range of imported beers, including such surprises as Heineken Malt from the Netherlands and Tennants Stout from Scotland. A small bottle of imported beer costs between FF10 and FF15 over the counter and as much as FF40 in some bars and restaurants.

ENTERTAINMENT

There are cinemas in most population centres around the island; films are screened in Réunion shortly after their release in mainland France. Tickets cost FF45. If you're after an English-language film, don't hold your breath – they are few and far between.

For night owls, there are bars, discos and casinos dotted around the island – see the Entertainment sections under individual towns for further information. For details about theatre, see Arts in the Facts about Réunion chapter.

SPECTATOR SPORTS

The affluent European lifestyle leads to many sporting as well as cultural distractions. There is nothing particular to Réunion about the main Creole pastimes on the island: soccer, volleyball and handball are all popular, judging by the press coverage given to the local leagues. *Pétanque*, a game in which metal balls are thrown to land as near as possible to a target ball, is another favourite. Boxing, cycling, martial arts, athletics, hockey and even rugby are also popular. The surrounding Indian Ocean countries provide competition on an international basis.

For detailed information on what's on, contact the syndicat d'initiative in St-Denis.

SHOPPING

The syndicats d'initiative market a selection of local handicrafts. As with agricultural products, each town and surrounding region is known for a special craft. During WWII, when supplies were blocked, the islanders had to make their own clothes, furniture and utensils as well as grow their own food. Times were hard, but the crafts the locals took up then are now paying dividends.

The tourist and craft shops sell a variety of art prints, lithographs and poster reproductions ranging in price from FF50 to FF180.

Fruits, spices and herbs can be bought in their natural state, or in jams, compotes, pâtés, sweets, rums, punches and liqueurs. A 1L bottle of dark or white rum is about FF35, Rhum Vieux is FF60 for a 700ml bottle and Planter's Punch is around FF30 for 700ml.

Some other less localised crafts include wicker and bamboo work, hat making and stone carving. The following is a rundown of some towns and their specialities:

Cilaos The nuns in Cilaos have been doing embroidery since the beginning of the century, when Angèle Mac Auliffe, the daughter of the town's first doctor of thermal medicine, introduced the craft. There are now around 120 embroiderers and an embroidery school at Cilaos. The needlework includes everything from tablemats to huge tablecloths at prices ranging from FF60 to FF4500. For the widest selection, visit the Maison de la Broderie (☎ 31 77 48, fax 31 80 54). Cilaos also makes its own distinctive sweet wine for around FF35 per bottle.

Entre-Deux North-west of Le Tampon is Entre-Deux, which is known for slippers and scarves woven out of *chocas* fibre.

Étang-Salé-les-Hauts Artisans here make cane chairs from lilac and casuarina wood.

La Rivière, St-Louis Tamarind, olive and camphor wood is made into period furniture like that originally introduced by the French East India Company. For a good selection, visit the Centre Artisanal du Bois (☎ 39 06 12).

St-Philippe & St-André In the St-Philippe and St-André areas, the fronds of the pandanus or screw pine are made into mats, baskets and handbags of all sizes, including the traditional *tante* lunchbox (a square box). St-André also produces colourful patchwork quilts and mats known as *tapis mendiants* (beggars' mats), which cost between FF1500 and FF3300. Quilted bags are available for around FF140.

Ste-Suzanne This small seaside town is known for its bamboo work, primarily in the form of baskets and fanciful bird cages.

RÉUNION

Getting There & Away

AIR

There are flights available between Réunion and Mauritius, the Seychelles, Comoros, Mayotte, Madagascar (Antananarivo or Tamatave), South Africa (Johannesburg or Durban), Kenya (Nairobi) and mainland France. From many other international gateways, you will have to get a connecting flight from Mauritius.

Airport & Airlines

Customs and immigration procedures on arrival in Réunion are pretty much the same as in France. Roland Garros International Airport (formerly called Gillot airport) is about 11km east of St-Denis. It has no bank, so make sure you've changed some money into francs before you arrive.

There is a helpful tourist information counter (☎ 48 80 68), which is open to meet all flights. For airline arrival and departure information, call ☎ 48 81 81.

Most of the airline offices are in St-Denis and some have branches around the island. Airlines represented in Réunion include:

Air Austral (☎ 90 90 90, fax 90 90 91) 4 Rue de Nice, 97400 St-Denis
Air France
  St-Denis: (☎ 40 38 38, fax 40 38 40) 7 Ave de la Victoire, 97477
  St-Pierre: (☎ 25 06 06, fax 35 19 06) 10 Rue François de Mahy
Air Liberté (☎ 94 72 00, fax 41 68 00) 13 Rue Charles Gounod, 97400 St-Denis
Air Madagascar (☎ 21 05 21, fax 21 10 08) 2 Rue Victor Mac Auliffe, 97461 St-Denis
Air Mauritius (☎ 94 83 83, fax 94 13 23) 13 Rue Charles Gounod, 97400 St-Denis
Air Outre Mer (AOM)
  St-Denis: (☎ 94 77 77, fax 20 07 16) 7 Rue Jean Chatel, 97479
  St-Pierre: (☎ 96 17 00, fax 25 44 88) 11 Rue François de Mahy, 97410
Nouvelles Frontières (Corsair) (☎ 21 54 54, fax 20 26 37) 92 Rue Alexis de Villeneuve, 97400 St-Denis
Transports et Travaux Aériens de Madagascar (TAM) (☎ 94 38 48, fax 94 39 49) 3 Rue de Nice, 97400 St-Denis

Departure Tax

At the time of research no departure tax was charged in Réunion.

France

Fares between France and Réunion vary according to the season. It's generally more expensive to travel from July to mid-September and around Christmas time. Many airlines flying between mainland France and Réunion offer discounts for students and travellers over 60 years of age.

Air France operates at least one flight daily between Paris and Réunion (nine to 12 trips per week) and the flight takes about 10 hours. Air France splits the year into *haute* (high) season and *basse* (low) season. The high season coincides with the French holidays between December and January, and between July and September, when fares start at FF5200 return. The rest of the year is considered low season and fares are cheaper, starting from FF3890. (Prices quoted are for economy seats.) For further details, contact Air France (☎ 08 02 80 28 02), 119 Ave des Champs-Élysées, 75008 Paris.

Air France now has a great deal of competition on this route. Air Outre Mer (AOM) has up to 15 flights weekly from France. Points of departure include Paris, Lyon and Marseilles. Low season return fares begin at FF3894/4289/4300 from Paris/Marseilles/Lyon. In the high season fares cost FF5204/5599/5610. For reservations call ☎ 08 03 00 12 34 in Paris.

Air Liberté flies to Réunion from Paris, Marseilles and Toulouse (high/low season fares to Paris are FF5040/3680). For more details call the central reservations service (☎ 08 03 80 58 05) in Paris.

There are also regular flights to Paris on Corsair, which is the airline run by the French tour operator Nouvelles Frontière (☎ 01 41 41 58 58, fax 01 40 65 99 36), 8° Blvd de Grenelle, 75015 Paris. Nouvelle Frontières also has an office (☎ 21 54 54, fax 20 26 37) in Réunion at 92 Rue Alexi de Villeneuve, 97400 St-Denis. Fares are similar to the other airlines' fares.

The USA

If you're coming from the USA, your best bet is to fly to Paris first and pick up a cheap flight to Réunion from there. A return ticket from New York to Paris costs around US$360 in the low season; from Los Angeles, you'll pay upwards of US$520. (See the France section earlier in this chapter for connections to Réunion.)

Australia

If you are travelling from Australia, Singapore Airlines flies from Perth or Melbourne to Mauritius via Singapore. Fares are around A$2530/2100 in the high/low season from Melbourne and A$2135/1735 from Perth.

The UK & Continental Europe

Flights from all other destinations in Europe are usually routed via Paris. Fares from London to Réunion via Paris cost UK£784/624 in the high/low season on Air France. Special deals as low as UK£319 are often available at off-peak times. If you're coming from Germany, a ticket from Frankfurt to Réunion via Paris on an Air France flight costs DM1685/1150.

Asia

There are no direct flights to Réunion from Asia, but Mauritius is well connected to the region, with regular flights from Singapore, Kuala Lumpur and Hong Kong. Air Mauritius and Singapore Airlines service the route. From Mauritius to Réunion, there are at least 10 flights daily with Air Austral or Air Mauritius (for details, see the Mauritius & the Seychelles section following).

Africa

Air Austral provides good coverage of Africa and the Indian Ocean. Destinations and average return fares include Antananarivo in Madagascar (FF2545), Tamatave in Madagascar (FF2545), Moroni in Comoros (F4040), Mayotte (FF2653), Johannesburg in South Africa (FF3282), Harare in Zimbabwe (FF3220) and Nairobi in

Kenya (FF4040). You can also fly to Madagascar with Air Madagascar and Transports et Travaux Aériens de Madagascar (see the Airport & Airlines section earlier in this chapter).

In many respects, it's worth considering flying from A to Z with as many stopovers as you want going in one direction, rather than buying individual tickets, particularly if you'd like a stop in the Seychelles. If you choose this option, always do it through a knowledgeable travel agent and not the airlines. That way the fare may be calculated on the basis of mileage rather than the sum of your journey's parts.

Mauritius & the Seychelles

Another option for reaching Réunion is to travel via Mauritius; Air Mauritius and Air Austral both offer several flights daily between the two islands. On Air Mauritius, a return excursion fare (valid for one month) costs about FF1370 from Réunion to Mauritius (Rs2635 if you're coming the other way). The flight takes around 40 minutes.

Air Austral, Réunion's national airline, has regular flights between Réunion and the Seychelles for FF2730.

SEA

Most cruise liners give Réunion a miss in favour of the Seychelles or Mauritius. The main shipping companies are based in Le Port.

The quickest way to travel between Mauritius and Réunion by sea is the fast catamaran MV *Ahinora*, run by MR Ocean Lines, which takes five hours from Le Port in Réunion to Port Louis in Mauritius. From Réunion, there are departures at 8 am on Tuesday, Thursday and Sunday; it leaves Mauritius at 8 am on Monday, Wednesday and Friday. A return ticket valid for one month costs Rs1945 from Mauritius and FF780 from Réunion. The agent for MR Ocean Lines in Réunion is Beverly Voyages (☎ 41 41 20), 20 Rue Charles Gounod, St-Denis.

The slower MV *Mauritius Pride* sails several times each month between Port Louis and Le Port. The return fare starts at

FF940/780 in the high/low season and the trip takes around 12 hours. Note that during the summer (cyclonic) season between October and March, trips may be cancelled. For further information call the shipping agent Scoam (☎ 42 19 45, fax 43 25 47) in Le Port.

There's a chance you may be able to pick up a long-distance yacht charter in St-Gilles-les-Bains, but these boats are almost always used for deep-sea-fishing trips or cruises around the coast, and do not really offer much potential for travelling to other islands. If you do fancy this mode of transport, you may want to ask at the syndicat d'initiative in St-Gilles-les-Bains, or talk to Croisières et Découvertes (☎ 33 28 32) at Port de Plaisance, also in St-Gilles-les-Bains. You may also be able to find out about potential charters at Le Forbhan restaurant at the docks in Le Port. It's also worth asking at any tourist office, as well as having a look in the local newspapers.

Getting Around

AIR

Helicopter tours of the magnificent cirques and the volcano are understandably popular, although not with the walkers on the ground who have their peace and quiet disturbed every few minutes by the whir of the rotor blades. The tours certainly offer an exhilarating and sensational view of the landscape, and while they aren't cheap, most travellers rate such a trip as a highlight of their visit to Réunion.

Helilagon (☎ 55 55 55, fax 22 86 78) is at L'Eperon just outside St-Gilles-les-Bains. A 45-minute tour of all three cirques and Piton de la Fournaise costs FF1280 per person, or FF1080 without the volcano. To visit Salazie and Cirque de Mafate with a stop in Hell-Bourg costs FF850. For an extra FF480, you can be dropped off in Mafate at the end of the three cirques and volcano tour and be picked up again in the afternoon. Prices include transfers to the airfield from St-Gilles-les-Bains. Tours leave in the morning.

Heli Réunion (☎ 93 11 11, fax 29 51 70) offers similar tours for similar prices. For example, a tour of the three cirques and the volcano costs FF1280 (FF1080 without the volcano). A 25-minute tour over the cirques of Salazie and Mafate costs FF850. Flights leave from the heliports at Roland Garros International Airport, St-Gilles-les-Bains and Pierrefonds airport near St-Pierre. Héli-Blue (☎ 24 64 00, fax 24 16 13), also in St-Gilles-les-Bains, offers a similar range of tours at similar prices.

As well as helicopters, there are several organisations offering tours of the cirques in light aircraft. While the planes can't get you as close to the scenery, they are more affordable than the helicopter tours. Air Evasion (☎ 25 19 72, fax 25 93 34) operates tiny aircraft with large windows for viewing the landscape and charges FF880 per person for an hour's tour of the three cirque and the volcano (FF680 without the volcano). Air Intense (☎ 66 18 51) has similar tours for similar prices.

For the ultimate aerial experience, Felix ULM (☎ 43 02 59) will take you up in an ultra-light aircraft where you are exposed to all the elements. Flights for first-time fliers cost FF150; tours of the cirques start at FF350.

All flights are dependent on the prevailing weather conditions, and may be cancelled at the last minute if there is heavy cloud over the cirques.

BUS
Car Jaune

The Réunion bus service Car Jaune (Yellow Coaches), which consists of a number of formerly private lines, covers most parts of the island with several main routes. The main *gare routière* (bus station) is near Place Joffre on the St-Denis seafront. There's an information counter (☎ 41 51 10) where you can buy tickets and get *horaires* (schedules) for the different routes; it's open on weekdays from 4.30 am to 8 pm, and on weekends from 7 am to noon and 1 to 5.45 pm.

For information about buses elsewhere on the island, call the information services in St-Pierre (☎ 35 67 28), St-André (☎ 46 80 00), St-Paul (☎ 22 54 38), St-Benoît (☎ 50 10 69) or St-Joseph (☎ 56 03 90).

Fares work out at around FF0.50 per kilometre. Buses on most routes run between about 5 am and 7 pm, with about half the number of services on Sunday. You can pay the driver as you board. To get the bus to stop, you must yell *devant!* (ahead!) or clap your hands. Sometimes the radio is so loud that you also have to shout or whistle.

Line A: St-Denis to St-Pierre Express
This bus leaves approximately every hour in each direction, stopping on the highway in Le Port, St-Paul, Boucan Canot, St-Leu, Étang-Salé-les-Bains and St-Louis. It takes about 1½ hours to cover the route.
Line B: St-Denis to St-Pierre, via the coast
This is the bus to take for downtown stops in Le Port, St-Paul, St-Gilles-les-Bains, St-Leu, Étang-Salé-les-Bains, St-Louis and other towns

along the west coast. Buses leave about every 1½ hours from either end; they only go as far as St-Louis from 7.45 to 11.45 am.

Line C: St-Denis to St-Pierre, via the hills
This bus follows the same route as Line B as far as St-Leu then heads into the hills, passing through Piton St-Leu and Les Avirons before dropping back down to the coast at Étang-Salé-les-Bains. There are services every hour.

Line D: St-Denis to Chaloupe St-Leu
Line D runs hourly along the coast to St-Paul then heads into the hills, passing through St-Gilles-les-Hauts, Saline les Hauts and Trois Bassins before reaching Chaloupe St-Leu.

Line E: Chaloupe St-Leu to St-Pierre
This bus runs three times daily from Chaloupe St-Leu to St-Pierre, via Colimaçons, Piton St-Leu, Les Avirons, Étang-Salé-les-Bains and St-Louis. There are only two services on Sunday.

Line F: St-Denis to St-Benoît Express
This bus runs between St-Denis and St-Benoît every hour or so but it only makes a few stops at St-Marie, St-Suzanne, St-André and Bras Pranon.

Line G: St-Denis to St-Benoît
The regular service between St-Denis and St-Benoît runs approximately every half-hour, with frequent stops along the way.

Line H: St-Benoît to St-Pierre, via the plains
This bus runs across the Hautes Plaines several times a day, stopping in Plaine-des-Palmistes, Bourg-Murat (for the Maison du Volcan), Plaine-des-Cafres and Le Tampon.

Line I: St-Benoît to St-Pierre, via St-Philippe
This bus runs around the south end of the island about every two hours, passing through Ste-Anne, Ste-Rose, Piton Ste-Rose, St-Philippe, Vincendo, St-Joseph and Petite Île.

Line J: St-André to Salazie
There are buses every two hours between St-André and Salazie; you'll need to take a local bus to get to Hell-Bourg and other destinations deeper into the cirque. On Sunday there are only three services.

Line K: This route has been discontinued.

Line L: St-Pierre to Entre-Deux
There are buses to Entre-Deux every two hours or so (only two buses run on Sunday).

Regional Bus Services

Car Jaune provides regional minibus services for several towns on the island; these services are known as Ti' Car Jaune (from *petit*). Ti' Car Jaune buses run from St-Benoît, St-Leu, Entre-Deux and Petite Île. Regional bus companies fill in the gaps between the Car Jaune services, but these convoluted local routes can be fairly confusing, particularly if you don't speak French very well. Of most use to travellers are the buses from Salazie to Hell-Bourg, Grand Îlet and Le Bélier, and the buses from St-Pierre to Cilaos, Îlet à Cordes and Bras Sec (see the Interior chapter for more details).

CAR

The road system on the island is excellent and well signposted. Route Nationale 1, the main road around the island, approaches motorway standards in parts.

Heading into the mountains via the cirque roads – especially the route into Cilaos – is a magnificent experience. The superbly engineered roads snake through hairpin bends, up steep slopes and along sheer drops, surrounded all the while by glorious – and distracting – scenery.

The experience is likely to be marred somewhat by the local drivers, who insist on driving these roads at breakneck speeds. If you suddenly encounter an irate local inches away from your rear bumper, pull over and let them overtake rather than driving faster to appease them. You'll see enough cars turned over by the roadside to convince you that this is the correct course of action.

Road Rules

Like mainland France, Réunion keeps to the right side of the road. To drive in Réunion, you officially need an international driver's licence, but most of the car-hire firms will accept a valid European, North American or Australian licence.

Rental

With most attractions located in the hills, *location de voitures* (car hire) is extremely popular in Réunion, and rates are very reasonable, particularly if you stick to small hatchbacks. Most companies stipulate that the driver must be at least 21 to 23 years of age, have held a driving licence for at least a year, and have a passport or some other form of identification. If your personal auto insurance isn't valid in Réunion, you may also need to purchase collision damage waiver (CDW) insurance. Even with the insurance, you may be personally responsible for around FF5000 accidental damage to the vehicle; make sure you read the small print carefully.

Prices and regulations don't vary much between the main international companies. Rates start at FF250 to FF300 per day, and drop rapidly for longer hire periods. If you don't have a credit card, you will usually have to pay a cash deposit of anywhere between FF1000 and FF5000. The total hire cost is normally payable in advance.

Companies with offices at the airport include SGM/Avis (☎ 48 81 85), Budget (☎ 28 01 95), Hertz (☎ 28 05 93), National (☎ 48 83 77), Pop's Car or Nouvelle Frontières (☎ 48 81 78), Sixt (☎ 29 79 79) and Thrifty (☎ 48 81 88). Most of these companies also have representatives in St-Gilles-les-Bains and St-Pierre.

There are plenty of cheaper independent operators around the island. Most specialise in tiny hatchback cars such as Nissan Micras and Kia Prides, and rates can drop as low as FF99 per day. Be aware that most of these bargain cars are booked up in advance from mainland France. If all the cheap options are booked out you should still be able to find a small car for less than FF200 if you rent for several days.

Reliable independent operators include the following:

ADA (☎ 21 59 01, fax 21 59 01) 9 Blvd Doret, 97400 St-Denis
Au Bas Prix (☎ 22 69 89, fax 22 54 27) 35 Rue Suffren, 97460 St-Paul
Euro Location
  St-Denis: (☎ 20 06 11, fax 21 38 17) 91 Rue d'Après, 97400
  St-André: (☎ 46 52 81, fax 58 52 15) 555 Ave Bourbon
Europcar (☎ 93 14 15, fax 93 14 14) Gillot La Ferme, 97438 Ste-Marie
Garcia (☎ 21 20 20, fax 90 98 25) Place de Gare, Joffre Blvd, 97400 St-Denis
GIS Location
  St-Gilles-les-Bains: (☎ 24 09 73, fax 24 55 20) 180 Rue Général de Gaulle, 97434
  St-Paul: (☎ 45 24 84, fax 45 48 99) 79 Chaussée Royale, 97460

ITC Tropicar
  St-Gilles-les-Bains: (☎ 43 07 03, fax 42 15 74) 207 Rue Général de Gaulle, 97434
  La Possession: (☎ 24 01 01, fax 24 05 55) 12 Rue Mahatma Gandhi, 97419
LBS Location (☎ 20 22 54, fax 20 22 74) 50 Blvd Lancastel, 97400 St-Denis
Loca Ouest Evasion (☎ 24 02 75, fax 24 48 04) 11 Rue Général de Gaulle, 97434 St-Gilles-les-Bains
Location St-Gilles (☎ 24 08 18, fax 24 05 63) 216 Rue Général de Gaulle, 97434 St-Gilles-les-Bains

MOTORCYCLE

With its well-maintained roads and glorious scenery, Réunion should be a motorcyclist's dream. Sadly the adage 'Hell is other people' certainly holds true on Réunion's roads. Car drivers show little consideration for scooters and motorcycles and beginner riders should think carefully – and have a good insurance policy – before setting out on two wheels.

Rental

If that doesn't put you off, there are several companies that rent out showy road bikes as well as more sensible scooters and mopeds. Max Aventure (☎ 20 22 33, fax 21 25 45), at 46 Rue Mazagran, St-Denis, and Max Moto (☎ 21 15 25, fax 34 70 80), at 10 Ave Gaston Monnerville, St-Denis, both rent out Harleys and other large motorcycles for between FF400 and FF700. Mopeds cost from FF150 per day. Locascoot (☎ 85 88 30, fax 33 98 99), at 4 Rue Général de Gaulle, St-Gilles-les-Bains, offers scooters from FF130 per day or FF80 per day if you rent for a week.

BICYCLE

The traffic, the haste of most motorists and the steep and precarious nature of the mountain roads means that those considering cycling as a form of transport in Réunion should be prepared for some hair-raising and potentially dangerous situations.

The coastal roads are far too busy for casual cycling and the cirque roads are too steep, but the back roads and rugged terrain of the interior are ideally suited to mountain bikes.

RÉUNION

Rental

The landscape of Réunion lends itself naturally to *vélos tout terrain* (mountain bikes), and a number of challenging dirt trails have been established on the island by the Fédération Française de Cyclisme. The Maison de la Montagne at 10 Place Sarda Garriga in St-Denis represents the organisation in Réunion and can provide laminated cards showing the different trails. There are VTT stations (the starting points for the trails) at Cilaos, Entre-Deux, Piton de la Fournaise, Salazie, Ste-Rose, Le Maïdo, Plaine-des-Palmistes, Vacoa (St-Philippe) and in the hills above St-Denis.

For mountain-bike rentals, you could try the following:

Loca VTT (☎ 24 44 64) 129 Rue Général de Gaulle, St-Gilles-les-Bains
Location Bicyclettes (☎ 85 92 09) St-Gilles-les-Bains
Parc du Loisirs du Maïdo (☎ 22 96 00, fax 32 52 52) Route du Maïdo, La Petite France
Rando Bike (☎ 59 15 88) 100 Route du Volcan, Plaine-des-Cafres
Réunion Sensations (☎ 31 84 84) Rue de Père Boiteau, Cilaos
Réunion Evasion (☎ 31 83 57) Rue de Père Boiteau, Cilaos
VTT Découverte (☎ 24 55 56, fax 24 51 79) Place Julius-Bénard, St-Gilles-les-Bains
VTT Evasion (☎ 37 10 43) 64 Rue Leconte Delisle, St-Philippe

HITCHING

Hitching is never entirely safe in any country in the world, and we don't recommend it. Travellers who decide to hitch should understand that they are taking a small but potentially serious risk. If you do choose to hitch, you will be safer if you travel in pairs and let someone know where you plan to go.

The standard advice not to hitch at night applies in Réunion, too. Furthermore, women should never hitch alone and even several women together shouldn't accept lifts from vehicles with only male passengers; make sure that there are women and/or children in the vehicle before climbing in.

The run from St-Denis to St-Gilles-les-Bains is well established, but elsewhere drivers are often too busy putting the pedal to the metal to think of stopping to pick up passengers. You will stand a much better chance in the hills than on the more snobbish coastal strip.

BOAT

Yacht and catamaran charter companies run cruises around the island and further afield, mainly for diving and fishing expeditions. (For further information, see Sea in the Réunion Getting There & Away chapter and Activities in the Réunion Facts for the Visitor chapter.)

LOCAL TRANSPORT

Taxis operate in the towns on the normal hire-on-demand basis. In country areas, where there are no buses, they operate on a scheduled *taxi-collectif* (share taxi) timetable.

Regular taxi fares start with FF28 on the meter, and there's a surcharge of FF10 at night. To give you a rough idea of daytime prices, it costs FF250 to FF300 from St-Denis to Boucan Canot beach, FF100 from St-Denis to Roland Garros International Airport, and at least FF800 from St-Denis to Cilaos.

Taxi-collectifs are usually Peugeot station wagons with seating for up to eight people, which run from the main towns out to the surrounding villages. Timetables should be posted at the taxi stands. Alternatively, ask local shopkeepers or hotel or guesthouse owners. The taxi-collectifs generally circulate from around 7 am to 6 pm (although there's a later one between Cilaos and St-Louis) and they cost about the same as buses.

ORGANISED TOURS

Souprayenmestry (☎ 44 81 69) has a regular program of bus tours to the major sites: on Tuesday there's a tour of Piton de la Fournaise, on Wednesday there's a tour of the Cirque de Salazie, on Thursday there's a tour of the Cirque de Cilaos, on Friday there's a tour of Le Maïdo, and on Saturday there's a tour of the *sud sauvage* (wild south). All tours cost FF98/50 for adults/children. You can arrange to be picked up and dropped off at the main hotels in St-Gilles-les-Bains.

If you're short on time or fancy something less regimented, other itineraries can be arranged by the private tour agencies. Useful agencies include:

Atlas Voyages (☎ 33 02 20, fax 24 38 00) Gal Amandine Complex, 97434 St-Gilles-les-Bains
Bourbon Voyages
St-Denis: (☎ 94 76 94, fax 41 72 85) 14 Rue Rontaunay, 97463
St-Benoît: (☎ 50 88 88)
St-Pierre: (☎ 96 19 19)
St-Louis: (☎ 26 11 36)
St-Leu: (☎ 34 64 64)
St-Joseph: (☎ 56 69 69)
Le Tampon: (☎ 57 92 92)

Comète Voyages Réunion (☎ 21 31 00, fax 41 37 71) Corner of Rue Jules Auber and Rue Moulin à Vent, 97400 St-Denis
Nouvelles Frontières (☎ 21 54 54, fax 20 26 37) 92 Rue Alexis de Villeneuve, 97400 St-Denis
Objectif (☎ 33 08 33, fax 24 26 80) Chemin Summer, 97434 St-Gilles-les-Bains
Papangue Tours (☎ 41 61 92, fax 41 61 96) 5 Rue de Nice, 97400 St-Denis
Réucir Voyages (☎ 41 55 66, fax 21 02 51) 45 Rue Juliette Dodu, 97400 St-Denis
Réunion Voyages (☎ 33 13 43, fax 33 13 44) 82 Rue Général de Gaulle, 97434 St-Gilles-les-Bains
Tropic Voyages (☎ 21 03 54, fax 21 54 44) 15 Ave de la Victoire, 97400 St-Denis

RÉUNION

St-Denis

With its brasseries, bistros and cafe culture, St-Denis (pronounced san-de-**nee**) is a perfect reproduction of metropolitan France, down to the endless *banlieues* (suburbs) which surround the historic town centre. For fine dining and varied nightlife, the capital of Réunion is unparalleled in the Indian Ocean. However, this good living comes at a hefty premium, and even visitors with a healthy supply of cash may be surprised at how quickly their francs run out.

With most of Réunion's tourist attractions located elsewhere on the island, many tourists don't remain longer than it takes to book *gîtes de montagne* (mountain lodges). But there's plenty to see and do in St-Denis if you don't mind the cost of living. You can cut costs considerably by staying in *pensions de famille* (boarding houses) and by self-catering rather than eating out.

While St-Denis presents a prosperous and cosmopolitan face to the world, the capital is not without its problems. Graffiti is a major eyesore everywhere in the city centre, making parts of St-Denis seem more menacing than they actually are. Politicians place the blame on the high rate of unemployment in Réunion; one out of every three Réunionnais is out of work, and the rate is highest among young Creoles.

History

St-Denis was founded in 1668 by the governor Regnault. The town and the river that runs through it, the Rivière St-Denis, take their name from a ship that ran aground here in 1667. The original capital of Réunion was nearby St-Paul, but the governor Mahé de la Bourdonnais moved the capital to St-Denis in 1738. Numerous attempts at constructing a harbour near Le Barachois were foiled by a succession of cyclones.

Today, the population of this buzzing capital city and its suburbs totals about 130,000, of whom around 50,000 live in the centre. The numbers have been swelled over the years by a tide of immigrants from

HIGHLIGHTS

- Revelling in the architectural splendour of the capital's Creole mansions
- Strolling down Le Barachois, a seafront park lined with cannons and cafes
- Wandering through the Musée Léon Dierx art gallery
- Exploring the hill districts of La Montagne and Le Brûlé, for majestic views and terrific hikes

Madagascar and elsewhere in the Indian Ocean, lured by Réunion's high wages and the generous social security system.

Orientation

The main shopping area is strung out along the semipedestrianised Rue Maréchal Leclerc and the surrounding streets. Where Rue Maréchal Leclerc turns the corner at Rue Charles Gounod and heads eastward out of town, the shops head downmarket; here you find small shops and stalls selling relatively inexpensive clothing and other goods.

At the western end of the waterfront, Le Barachois is *the* place to be seen in the evenings. Here you'll find upmarket bars and sidewalk cafes as well as the Hôtel Le Saint-Denis, which is one of the town's ritziest places to stay.

Since Réunion is not an independent country, St-Denis lacks the usual complement of embassies and consulates befitting a capital city. Countries with diplomatic representation in Réunion are listed under Embassies & Consulates in the Réunion Facts for the Visitor chapter.

Information

Tourist Offices The St-Denis tourist office (☎ 41 83 00, fax 21 37 76) is at 53 Pasteur St, between Rue Juliette Dodu and Rue Jules Auber. It's signposted 'syndicat d'initiative' from Rue de Paris and Le Barachois. The staff speak English and can provide plenty of information, maps and brochures. There's a payphone here as well as toilets. The office is open Monday to Saturday from 8.30 am to 6 pm.

For hiking information and bookings, go to Maison de la Montagne (☎ 90 78 78, fax 41 84 29) at 10 Place Sarda Garriga (near Le Barachois). You can plan your itinerary using the large model of the island in the office. (For further information about hiking and gîtes de montagne, see the special section 'Hiking in Réunion'; see also Accommodation in the Réunion Facts for the Visitor chapter.) The office is open Monday to Thursday from 9 am to 5.30 pm (to 4.30 pm on Friday and to 4 pm on Saturday).

Money The main banks are all located in the city centre and all will change money. They're open Monday to Friday from 9 am to 4 pm.

If you arrive in Réunion without any francs and have to get a taxi from the airport to an ATM, the BRED Banque Populaire is probably your safest bet.

Post & Communications The main post office is on the corner of Rue Maréchal Leclerc and Rue Juliette Dodu. It is open Monday to Friday from 7.30 am to 6 pm and on Saturday from 8 am to noon. Poste restante service is available here.

There's also a post office at Roland Garros airport which is open Monday to Friday from 9.30 am to 12.30 pm and 1.30 to 4.30 pm, and Saturday 8 to 11 am.

There are a few coin phones in St-Denis. Télécartes (phonecards) can be purchased at post offices and at a number of shops. L'Igloo Glacerie (see Places to Eat) sells télécartes and is open late in the evening.

Internet Resources There is only one Internet cafe in St-Denis, the stylish Bookc@fe at Librairie L'entrepôt (see Bookshops following). There are only four consoles, but the connection is fast and the coffee is excellent. Internet access cost FF1 per minute; if you're just checking email, you can become a member for a flat rate of FF80 per month, which allows you half an hour of free online time per day.

Bookshops Librairie L'entrepôt (☎ 20 94 94) opposite the Ritz cinema on Rue Juliette Dodu is the best bookshop in town, if only for its friendly and helpful staff. The bookshop has a good selection of predominantly French-language books, as well as stationery and numerous newspapers and magazines in French and English. L'entrepôt is open Monday to Friday from 9 am to 6.30 pm and on Saturday from 9 am to 7 pm.

The attractive Librairie Papeterie Gerard (☎ 20 08 15) is on Rue de la Compagnie. It houses an excellent range of well-displayed titles (almost entirely in French) but few newspapers or magazines. It's open Monday to Saturday from 8.30 am to noon and 2 to 6.30 pm. Another option is the Alpha Librairie Papeterie (☎ 94 04 04) on Rue Alexis De Villeneuve.

Le Tabac du Rallye (☎ 20 34 66), a busy newsagent next to Le Rallye, has the best stock in town of newspapers and magazines in French and English. It's open daily from around 6 am to 11 pm. Apart from a plethora of French newspapers and magazines, it also has the widest selection of English publications in Réunion, including *The Daily Telegraph*, *The Mirror*, *The Independent*, *The Times*, *Financial Times*, *Time* magazine and *Newsweek*. Prices reflect the cost of import; tabloids cost around FF15 while broadsheets start at FF25.

Laundry Automatic Leclerc is a convenient self-service *laverie* (laundry) on Rue Maréchal Leclerc, opposite the Hotel Du Centre. It's open from 7 am to 9 pm daily and you can wash 7kg of clothes for FF30. It costs FF2 for five minutes of tumble drying.

Creole Mansions & Historic Buildings

There is a variety of impressive Creole mansions in St-Denis; the larger ones are mainly strung out along Rue de Paris between Rue Pasteur and Rue Roland Garros. They include the family home of former French prime minister Raymond Barre, and

RÉUNION

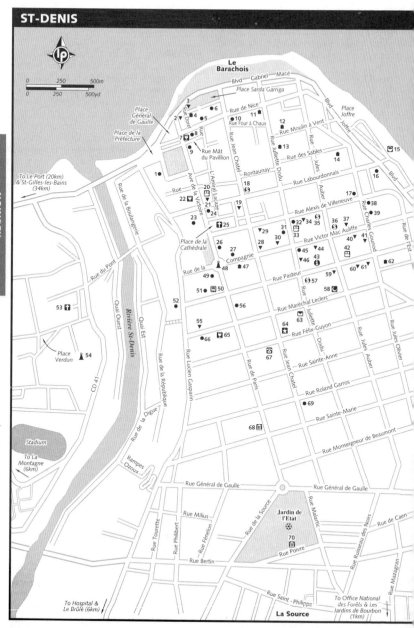

ST-DENIS

RÉUNION

Le Barachois

Blvd — Gabriel — Macé

Place Sarda Garriga

Place Général de Gaulle

Rue de Nice

Place de la Préfecture

Place Joffre

Rue Four à Chaux

Rue Moulin à Vent

Rue des Sables

Rue Mât du Pavillion

Rontaunay

To Le Port (20km) & St-Gilles-les-Bains (34km)

Rue Labourdonnais

Rue Alexis de Villeneuve

Rue Victor Mac Auliffe

Place de la Cathédrale

Compagnie

Rue Pasteur

Rue Maréchal Leclerc

Rue Félix-Guyon

Place Verdun

Rue Sainte-Anne

Rue Roland Garros

Rue Sainte-Marie

Rue Monseigneur de Beaumont

Stadium

To La Montagne (6km)

Rue Général de Gaulle

Rue Général de Gaulle

Jardin de l'Etat

Rue Milius

Rue de Caen

Rue Poivre

Rue Bertin

To Hospital & Le Brûlé (6km)

Rue Saint - Philippe

La Source

To Office National des Forêts & les Jardins de Bourbon (1km)

ST-DENIS

RÉUNION

PLACES TO STAY

4 Hôtel Le Saint-Denis;
   La Distillerie; Casino
11 Abis Hôtel
12 Hôtel Fleur de Mai
13 Le Juliette Dodu
14 Pension des Sables
47 Hôtel Central
62 Hôtel Le Mascareignes
74 Hôtel de l'Océan
77 Le Lancastel Protea
79 Pension Au Bon Refuge
81 Pension Amanda
82 Hôtel Pension les Palmiers
83 Pension du Nord
84 Hôtel du Centre
85 Pension des Îles;
   Automatic Leclerc (Laundry)
86 Select Hotel

PLACES TO EAT

2 Le Roland Garros
3 L'Oasis
19 Cyclone Café
21 Snack Soui-Mine
28 L'Igloo Glacerie
29 Le Massalé
30 Castel Bakery
34 P'tit Fleur Fané
37 Le Vieux Portail
40 Le Coquille
41 Le Touareg
44 Le Saint-Hubert
46 Les Délices d'Orient
55 Kim Son
59 Chez Piat
60 Le Mumbai
61 Les Jardins du Maroc
78 Le Pavillon d'Or

OTHER

1 Préfecture
5 Transports et Travaux
   Aux Aeriens de
   Madagascar (TAM)
6 Maison de la Montagne;
   Relais Départemental des
   Gîtes de France
7 Le Rallye; Banana's Café;
   Le Tabac du Rallye
8 Air Austral
9 Air France
10 Air Outre Mer (AOM)
15 Gare Routière (Long
   Distance Bus Terminal)
16 Garcia Car Rental
17 Beverly Voyages
18 Banque de la Réunion
20 Gaumont Cinema
22 Le First Nightclub
23 University
24 Nouvelles Frontières
25 Cathédrale de St-Denis
26 Librairie de la Réunion
27 Librairie Papeterie
   Gerard
31 Librarie L'entrepôt
32 Alpha Librarie Papeterie
33 Ritz Cinema
35 Banque Française
   Commerciale
36 Banque Populaire
   (BRED)
38 Air Mauritius
39 Air Liberté
42 Plaza Cinema
43 Syndicat d'Initiative
   (Tourist Office)

45 Air Madagascar
48 Monument aux Morts
49 Hôtel de Ville
   (Town Hall)
50 Hôtel de Ville
   Bus Terminal;
   St-Denis Bus
   Ticket Office
51 Marie (Town Hall)
52 Super U Supermarket
53 Notre Dame
   de la Délivrance
54 War Monument
56 Birthplace of Léon Dierx
57 Banque Nationale de
   Paris Intercontinentale
58 Grande Mosquée
63 La Poste (Post Office)
64 Police
65 Karoake Nightclub
66 Grand Marché & Théâtre
   du Grand Marché
67 France Telecom
   (Telephone Office)
68 Musée Léon Dierx
69 Bibliothèque
   Departmentale
   (Departmental Library)
70 Musée d'Histoire
   Naturelle
71 Super U Supermarket
72 Petit Marché
73 St-Denis Bus
   Ticket Office
75 L'Océan Bus Terminal
76 Hindu Temple
80 Église St-Jacques
87 Théâtre Champ Fleuri

INDIAN OCEAN

Rue des Limites

74
73
75
71
72
77
76

Lancastel

Blvd de l'Océan

78
Rue Maréchal Leclerc
Rue Roland Garros
Rue Sainte-Marie
Rue St-Jacques
79
85
84
83

Cemetery

Rue Voltaire

80
Place
St-Jacques
82
81

Rue de Montreuil
Rue Saint Bernard
Rue Amédée Bédier
Rue d'Après
Rue Jacob

Rue Général de Gaulle

Rue de la
d'Alsace

Lorraine

Rue de Lataniers

86

Vauban

Rue Monthyon
Rue Monthyon
Rue Bouvet

Blvd Vauban

To Roland Garros
Airport (6km) &
East Coast

Rue Jean Cocteau

87
Ave André
Malraux

Rue Bois de Nèfles

To Hôtel
Mercure Créolia;
Le Kaloupilé
(1.5km)

the birthplace of the poet Léon Dierx. Most of these palatial residences feature elaborate verandas and intricate *lambrequins* (ornamental window and door borders). The roof shingles are traditionally made from the wood of the *tamarins des hautes* (mountain tamarind) tree. (For more information, see the boxed text 'Creole Architecture' in the Central Mauritius chapter.)

Also of interest are the *hôtel de ville* (town hall), considered by many to be the city's most beautiful building; the Cathédrale de St-Denis, built between 1829 and 1832; and the Préfecture, which was begun in 1735 by Governor Dumas, and served as the headquarters of the Compagnie des Indes Orientales (French East India Company).

Musée Léon Dierx

South of the centre on Rue de Paris, the Musée Léon Dierx (☎ 20 24 82) is actually an art gallery with a large collection of paintings by artists from Réunion and mainland France. High profile *objets d'art* include a lithograph by Renoir, a bronze by Picasso and works by Chagall, Cézanne, Delacroix, Degas and Gauguin. The museum is named after the Réunionnais poet and painter Léon Dierx (1858–1912) and is housed in the old bishop's palace, which dates from 1845. It's open Tuesday to Sunday from 9 am to noon and 1 to 5 pm. Admission is free.

Jardin de l'Etat & Musée d'Histoire Naturelle

This attractive botanical garden at the southern end of Rue de Paris features numerous perfume plants, tropical oddities from around the world and lots of orchids. The original Jardin de l'Etat was established near the river in 1764 as a nursery for the experimental crops being tried out by the French East India Company, but it moved to its present location in 1773. In the gardens is a monument to agronomist Joseph Hubert from St-Benoît, who brought many useful agricultural specimens – including cloves, mangosteens, lychees and breadfruit – to Réunion. There is also a statue commemorating botanist Pierre Poivre, who performed a similar service for nearby Mauritius.

In the centre of the gardens is the Palais Législatif, dating from 1834, which houses the interesting Musée d'Histoire Naturelle (☎ 20 02 19). Very little of Réunion's natural history survived long enough to make it into the museum, but there are a few displays of extinct and nearly extinct native species including the solitaire, Réunion's equivalent of the dodo. Most of the other birds, insects and animals on display are from nearby Madagascar, though the rare coelacanth (a primitive, bony fish) was caught off the Comoros islands. The museum is open Monday to Saturday from 10 am to 5 pm. Entry costs FF10 for adults and FF5 for children.

Le Barachois

This seafront park, lined by cannons facing out to sea, is the main promenade venue in St-Denis. The park has an area set aside for *pétanque* (a game similar to bowls), cafes and a monument to the Réunion-born aviator Roland Garros. Garros was the first pilot to cross the Mediterranean and also the inventor who worked out a way of timing machinegun fire so it could be directed through a turning propeller. Nearby is Place Sarda Garriga, which has a pleasant park; it was named after the governor who abolished slavery in Réunion in 1848.

On Sundays the section of the highway that passes through Le Barachois is closed off to traffic, and the park positively heaves with promenading Creole families.

Notre Dame de la Délivrance Church

This attractive church dates from 1893 and sits on the far bank of the (usually dry) Rivière St-Denis. It's worthy of note for the shrine of St Expédit, which is permanently covered in fresh flowers, red ribbons and ceramic plaques, which are all given as thanks for answered prayers. (See the boxed text 'Mail Order Miracle' following for more information about this unusual saint.)

On the hill behind the church is a pillar commemorating the French soldiers who died defending the island from the British in the Napoleonic Wars.

Mail Order Miracle

St Expédit is one of Réunion's most popular saints, but there never actually was a person called Expédit. The origins of this 'saint who ain't' are attributed to a box of religious relics and icons that were shipped from Rome in a box bearing the Italian word *espedito* (expedited). When the box was received at a new chapel in France, the nuns mistakenly assumed that the name on the box referred to a saint and christened the chapel La Chapelle de St Expédit.

The idea was brought to Réunion in 1931 when a local woman erected a statue to the 'saint' in the Notre Dame de la Délivrance church in St Denis as a *remerciement* (thanks offering) for answering her prayer to return to Réunion.

Over the years, the saint's following has somehow twisted into a slightly sinister voodoo cult. Shrines to St Expédit, which are normally covered in brilliant red paint representing blood, are found all over the island and are used primarily for wishing ill on others. Beheaded statues are normally the result of either unanswered petitions or the fears of paranoid potential victims.

Hindu Temple

The small but wildly colourful Hindu temple stands out among the shops east of the centre along Rue Maréchal Leclerc, opposite Rue de Montreuil. If you wish to visit, do so with respect (see Society & Conduct in the Regional Facts for the Visitor chapter at the beginning of this book). Remember to remove your shoes and any leather items. Photography is not allowed.

Grande Mosquée

The Grande Mosquée (also known as the Noor-E-Islam mosque) is near the corner of Rue Maréchal Leclerc and Rue Jules Auber. The Islamic community in St-Denis is very traditional, so if you wish to visit, dress and behave with respect (see Society & Conduct in the Regional Facts for the Visitor chapter). Shoes have to be taken off and photography is not permitted.

Grand Marché

The Grand Marché on Rue Maréchal Leclerc is the main handicraft market in St-Denis. There's a mishmash of items for sale including Malagasy wooden handicrafts, fragrant spices, woven baskets, embroidery, T-shirts, furniture and a jumble of knick-knacks. The prices are rather inflated, so it's certainly worth trying to bargain them down. The market is open daily from around 8.30 am to 5.30 pm.

Organised Tours

The company Guide Péi offers tours of St-Denis that take in historic sights such as the Jardin de l'Etat and the mansions of Rue de Paris. The tours must be booked through the tourist office (☎ 41 83 00) on Rue Pasteur. A half-day tour of historic St-Denis costs FF130.

Places to Stay

There is high local demand throughout the year for accommodation (especially budget accommodation) in St-Denis, so advance booking is highly recommended. Most establishments require at least partial advance payment. Budget travellers can save money by staying in *pensions de famille*. These cheap guesthouses cater mainly to visiting French students and overseas workers so they can be a little rough and ready. The places listed below are all clean and well maintained.

Places to Stay – Budget

Many of the pensions in St-Denis went the way of the dodo during the recent government crackdown on substandard accommodation. On the plus side, this means that the remaining pensions are of a higher standard than in the past.

The best option in this bracket is *Pension des Sables* (☎ 40 91 03 or 41 78 78), superbly located on Rue des Sables. This tidy guesthouse offers shared rooms with fan for FF60 per person, or you can take a whole room for FF120/150 a single/double. There's also a snack bar and self-catering facilities. If there's no-one here, go to the tailor shop around the corner.

RÉUNION

RÉUNION

Another pleasant option is *Pension du Nord* (☎ 41 77 90) on Ruelle Pavée, just off Rue Maréchal Leclerc. Clean rooms with bathroom and fan cost FF150 for one or two people.

On Rue Maréchal Leclerc itself, *Pension des Îles* (☎ 41 65 20) is basic but clean and charges FF120/150 for simple rooms.

Nearby, the *Hôtel Pension les Palmiers* (☎/fax 41 55 55) is on a quiet alley off Rue Voltaire. Singles/doubles/triples will cost you FF150/180/220 plus FF20 for breakfast.

Pension Au Bon Refuge (☎ 20 19 86, fax 20 12 68, 13 Rue St-Jacques) is nothing very fancy but tries to cater for travellers. The cost is FF65 per person in a triple room; the whole room costs FF195. There are meals for FF50 per person. The owners can arrange tours to various places around the island.

Pension Amanda (☎ 21 57 18, 20 Rue Amédée Bédier) behind the Église St-Jacques is a comfortable option. Doubles with shared bathroom are FF130 to FF150 or there's one double with a shower for FF170. Cooking facilities are available for self-caterers.

Places to Stay – Mid-Range

The cheapest hotel in town is the *Hôtel du Centre* (☎ 41 73 02, fax 94 17 33, 272 Rue Maréchal Leclerc), which is set back from the road on a small alley. Basic but clean singles with shared bathroom cost FF120; doubles with private bathroom cost FF150.

Hôtel le Mascareignes (☎ 21 15 28, fax 21 24 19, 3 Rue Lafférière) is a good choice. Basic rooms with private bathroom start at FF180/210 plus FF30 for breakfast.

Hôtel Central (☎ 94 18 08, fax 21 64 33, 37 Rue de la Compagnie) is centrally located and provides secure parking. Single/double/triple rooms with breakfast start at FF285/355/430.

The clean *Abis Hôtel* (☎ 20 45 45, fax 20 45 46, 16 Rue Juliette Dodu) charges from FF250/280. Breakfast costs FF30 per person.

In the same area, *Hôtel Fleur de Mai* (☎ 41 51 81, fax 94 11 60) on Rue Moulin à Vent charges FF230/260 for simple rooms with air-con and bathroom.

Easily the nicest place in this price range is the lovely *Le Juliette Dodu* (☎ 20 91 20, fax 20 91 21, 31 Rue Juliette Dodu). Set in a stylish Creole building, the hotel offers singles/doubles with bathroom starting at FF415/520. Breakfast is an extra FF60.

Near Rue Maréchal Leclerc towards the ocean is *Hôtel de l'Océan* (☎ 41 43 08, fax 21 76 59, 10 Blvd de l'Océan). This hotel has 41 rooms and is rather lacking in character. Rooms cost FF250/300. Breakfast is an extra FF25 per person.

The same owners run the *Select Hôtel* (☎ 41 13 50, fax 41 67 07) west of the centre on Rue des Lataniers, off Rue Monthyon. Rooms here are also FF250/300 plus FF25 for breakfast.

Le Lancastel Protea (☎ 94 70 70, fax 20 12 05) is a vast, slightly soulless edifice near the sea on Blvd Lancastel. If you don't mind the atmosphere, rooms start at FF251/279 per night, plus FF35 for breakfast.

Les Jardins de Bourbon (☎ 40 72 40, fax 30 32 28) is a large residential-style two-star hotel above the district of Le Providence on Rue du Verger. Studios (all with a kitchenette) cost FF300 per night or FF1800 per week for one or two people.

Places to Stay – Top End

The plush *Hôtel Le Saint-Denis* (☎ 21 80 20, fax 21 97 41, 2 Rue Doret) at Le Barachois is one of Réunion's most upmarket hotels. This four-star place is centrally located and has a swimming pool, a bar and several restaurants. It is very close to the casino. Air-con rooms cost FF760/820. If you're in the mood to live it up, go for a suite, which will set you back a cool FF1100.

Overlooking St-Denis from the hillside suburb of La Providence, *Hôtel Mercure Créolia* (☎ 94 26 26, fax 94 27 27, 14 Rue du Stade) commands sensational views over the town. Although this four-star hotel is not as central as the Hôtel Le Saint-Denis, it is a touch more stately. Facilities include a large swimming pool, a sauna, a tennis court, a bar and a restaurant. Air-con doubles range from FF470 to FF850. Alternatively, the superior package entitles you to a superior room, breakfast and a hire car for FF760 per day.

Places to Eat

Thanks to the French passion for *la gastronomie*, there's a restaurant or cafe around virtually every corner in St-Denis. Lunch is something of a sacred institution for the Réunionnais and this is especially evident in St-Denis. Most restaurants and cafes fill up between noon and 2 pm and during this time getting a table can be difficult.

At lunch time, you should be able to get a reasonable *plat du jour* (special of the day) or *menu du jour* (set menu of the day) for between FF40 and FF80, but to experience *haute cuisine* (high-class cuisine) in Réunion, you'll have to bid *adieu* (goodbye) to a pile of francs.

Most cafes, bars and restaurants have a menu and price list on display, which saves embarrassing questions such as *Combien?* (How much?) Those pensions that serve meals are often a cheap option. Also reasonably cheap are the small snack bars at Le Barachois, which sell fast eats for people on the run.

Self-caterers are best off heading to the Super U supermarket on Rue Maréchal Leclerc (there's another branch on Rue de la République). For fresh fruit and vegetables, there is a wide range of cheap produce at the Petit Marché on Rue Maréchal Leclerc.

Snack Food For authentic Indian snacks and sweets, *Le Massalé* is a little snack shop near the corner of Rue Alexis de Villeneuve and Rue Jean Chatel. You'll find a mouthwatering array of samosas – fish, crab and chicken – for around FF2.50 each, as well as *catless* (cutlets in breadcrumbs) for FF12.

L'Igloo Glacerie (☎ 21 34 69, 67 Rue Jean Chatel) is *the* place to indulge in a tantalising array of wild and wonderful ice-cream creations (listed in a 20-page menu). The passion-fruit treat is to die for. Cornets or cups cost FF12 for one scoop or FF15 for two; sit-down sundaes cost from FF30. Soft-serve ice cream and snack food are sold in the annexe opposite; a *croque-monsieur* (toasted ham and cheese sandwich) is FF8.

French & Creole Near Le Barachois, *Le Roland Garros* (☎ 41 44 37) is a quiet and sophisticated place that specialises in French and Creole cuisine. Dishes such as grilled *dorade* (a type of game fish) will set you back between FF75 and FF100. At lunch time, sandwiches are FF30. There's a pleasant terrace where you can put away a few bourbons and watch the sunset. This place is open daily from 7 am to midnight.

Close by, *L'Oasis* (☎ 21 80 20), part of the Hôtel Le Saint-Denis, offers good eats in pleasant surroundings daily from 6.30 am to midnight. *Métro* (mainland French) dishes such as *confit de canard* (preserved duck) range from FF60 to FF95, while healthy salads are FF55.

The trendy **Cyclone Café** (☎ 20 00 23, 24 Rue Jean-Chatel) offers great food in chilled-out surroundings. The salad and quiche options at lunch time (FF50) are popular with office workers; the evening métro meals (FF80 to 100) pull in a younger, hipper crowd. It's open daily except Sunday for lunch and dinner. Later in the evening the restaurant transforms into a popular bar.

Le Vieux Portail (☎ 41 09 42, 43 Rue Victor Mac Auliffe) offers terrific Creole food such as chicken curry with *baba figues* (banana flower) for around FF80. It's closed on Monday and at lunch time on Saturday.

Opposite, *Le Coquille* (☎ 20 48 47) serves *moules* (mussels) in a variety of French sauces for FF65 to FF75. It's open daily for lunch and dinner except for Monday and Tuesday lunch times.

One of the best options in town is *Le Saint-Hubert* (☎ 21 95 95), a classic French brasserie on Rue Victor Mac Auliffe. Métro treats such as trout with almonds cost around FF80. It's open daily for lunch and dinner.

Chez Piat (☎ 21 45 76, 60 Rue Pasteur) is good for an intimate (if pricey) dinner. Métro mains cost about FF110. It's open daily, except Saturday lunch time, Monday evening and all day Sunday.

Le Labourdonnais (☎ 21 44 26, 14 Rue L'Amiral Lacaze) is one of the town's top French restaurants, serving métro main dishes for around FF100. It's open daily, except Saturday lunch time and Sunday.

Also serving upmarket métro cuisine is *P'tit Fleur Fané* (☎ 20 44 44, 42 Rue Alexis de Villeneuve). It's open daily except Sunday for dinner only; mains cost around FF100. It's a good idea to book ahead.

RÉUNION

Le Kaloupilé (☎ 94 26 26) at the Hôtel Mercure Créolia (see Places to Stay) offers Creole and French main courses for around FF130 and desserts for FF35. There's a poolside seafood buffet dinner every Tuesday and a barbecue buffet dinner every Thursday; each costs FF180 per person (drinks cost extra). Nonresidents are welcome, but are advised to book ahead.

Chinese, Indian & North African Out of the centre on Rue Maréchal Leclerc, *Le Pavillon d'Or* (☎ 21 49 86) offers tasty Chinese food from FF60. On Saturday night there's a dinner dance with Creole music for FF190 per person. The restaurant is open daily, except Sunday, for lunch and dinner.

Kim Son (☎ 21 75 00, 13 Rue Maréchal) is a Vietnamese restaurant at Leclerc. Dishes such as *phô* (a traditional Vietnamese soup) and *nems* (spring rolls) cost from FF60 to FF80. It's closed on Sunday.

Les Délices de L'Orient (☎ 41 44 20, 59 Rue Juliette Dodu*) is one of the better Chinese places, with dishes such as *porc à la sauce grand'mère* (pork with chillies) from FF60. It's closed on Sunday and Monday.

Le Touareg (☎ 41 22 34) on Rue Charles Gounod is an intimate Moroccan restaurant with couscous and *tajines* (stews) from FF75. It's open Tuesday to Friday for lunch, and Tuesday to Sunday for dinner.

On Rue Pasteur, *Les Jardins du Maroc* (☎ 41 06 59) is another excellent choice for Moroccan food. It's open for lunch on Saturday and Sunday and in the evening from Wednesday to Sunday. Couscous and other North African mains cost from FF85.

For good Indian concoctions, try *Le Mumbai* (☎ 94 31 57) on Rue Pasteur. It's open daily except Sunday for lunch and for dinner. Mains cost from FF80.

Entertainment

For information about cultural activities phone the Office Départemental de la Culture (☎ 41 11 41, fax 41 55 71). Another good source of information is the *RUN* magazine, available free from the tourist office and most hotels. It's also worth checking out the newspapers to see what's happening in town.

Cinemas St-Denis has three main cinemas, which generally show mainstream international blockbusters dubbed into French. The Ritz (☎ 20 09 52) on Rue Juliette Dodu and the Plaza (☎ 21 04 36) on Rue Pasteur may occasionally show English-language films. The Gaumont (☎ 41 20 00) on Rue L'Amiral Lacaze also screens less mainstream French films. Tickets cost around FF45.

Casino The casino (☎ 41 33 33) near the Hôtel Le Saint-Denis offers slot machines from 11 am to 2 am and rather more dignified games such as blackjack from 9.30 pm to around 2 am. Admission to the slot machines is free, but entry to the gaming room (for American roulette, blackjack etc) costs FF65. You'll need some form of identification and smart clothes to get past security at the door.

Discos Most of Réunion's discos are down the coast at St-Gilles-les-Bains, but there are several OK nightspots in the capital. Some of the clubs can get a little rough as the evening wears on; it's best to ask locals which clubs are currently flavour of the month.

Banana's Café (☎ 20 31 32) is a perennial favourite with the locals. By Réunion standards it's pretty chic, but hardened clubbers may find it a little chintzy. It's open every night except Monday; most people tend to roll in after 10 pm.

Other happening options include *Le First* (☎ 41 68 25, 8 Ave de la Victoire); *Le Gin-Get* (☎ 41 65 65), Rue André-Malraux; *Le 111* (☎ 21 72 36, 111 Rue Juliette Dodu*); and *Karaoke* (☎ 41 18 19, 4 Rue Maréchal Leclerc).

Theatre There are two main theatres in St-Denis. *Théâtre Champ Fleuri* (☎ 21 16 94), on Ave André Malraux at the east end of Rue Monthyon, has an excellent program of plays, music and dance. Tickets to most events cost around FF80.

Théâtre du Grand Marché (☎ 20 33 99) is, appropriately enough, beside the Grand Marché on Rue Maréchal Leclerc, and offers plays, lectures and monologues (all in French). Tickets are usually FF90.

You can pick up theatre programs at the tourist office. Alternatively, call the Office Départemental de la Culture (☎ 41 11 41).

Pubs Far and away the best pub in St-Denis is the *Cyclone Café* (see Places to Eat). After the kitchen shuts down, this atmospheric watering hole is usually buzzing, with regular live bands and the kind of friendly atmosphere you'd normally associate with your local pub. Most people opt for the draft Bière Bourbon; a small *pression* costs FF10 and for a large it's FF20.

Le Rallye (☎ 21 34 27) at the bottom of Ave de la Victoire, near Le Barachois, is a trendy bar and cafe that is a popular hangout with the university crowd. It's open every day from early morning until around midnight, with DJs on Friday and Saturday nights.

La Distillerie (☎ 21 80 20), the bar at the Hôtel Le Saint-Denis, often has live music performances – ring ahead to find out.

Getting There & Away
The *gare routière* (bus station) is near Place Joffre. For more information on buses to and from St-Denis, see the Réunion Getting Around chapter.

Getting Around
To/From the Airport Taxis between St-Denis and Roland Garros International Airport cost FF100 at any time. Cheaper and no less convenient is the regular Navette Aéroport service run by Car Jaune. The bus runs from the gare routière to the airport about once an hour between 7 am and 8.30 pm (between 7.30 am and 8 pm in the opposite direction). The fare is FF27 and the journey takes 15 minutes (longer during rush hour).

To get the regular bus into St-Denis, you need to cross the airport car park, walk under the motorway overpass and follow the road uphill. The bus stop is about 300m from the junction on the right hand side. The bus you're looking for is St-Benoît to St-Denis and it will cost around FF10 into town.

To reach the airport from St-Denis, take any St-Benoît bus from the gare routière and ask to be let off at the airport.

Bus St-Denis is relatively small and getting around the centre on foot is a breeze, but there is nevertheless a good city bus service. It goes just about everywhere in town.

Bus stops are well marked. The main bus stands are by the on Rue Pasteur near the Hôtel de Ville and on Blvd de l'Océan. The kiosks at both these stops can provide you with the free *Plan du réseau Saint-Denis Bus*, which lists bus timetables and routes. You can also pick one up from the syndicat d'initiative.

The city is divided into two zones – one zone (FF7) and all zones (FF10). You can buy tickets from the driver or at the service kiosks on Blvd de l'Océan and on Rue Pasteur. Remember to stamp the ticket in the machine by the door as you board and hang onto your ticket, as random checks are common. Weekly passes for zone one/all zones are available and cost FF56/96. Students and children pay reduced rates.

Taxi Taxis around town are generally expensive and you'll pay about FF30 for even a hop of a couple of blocks. A trip across town will set you back at least FF60.

Around St-Denis

LA MONTAGNE & LE BRÛLÉ
These hill districts behind St-Denis offer great views over the town and are starting points for hikes to Plaine d'Affouches, La Roche Écrite and even over the mountains into the Cirque de Salazie.

From Le Brûlé, there are some pleasant walks along the Route Forestière de la Roche Écrite. Another possibility is Bassin du Diable, a wild and isolated valley accessible from upper Bellepierre, the first village downhill from Le Brûlé. The track turns off to the right (headed uphill) where the bus turns around at Bassin Couderc. Allow about an hour each way.

La Roche Écrite
Like the higher Piton des Neiges, this 2277m peak is often obscured by clouds by about 10 am. Although it isn't technically *in*

the Cirque de Mafate, it does offer a spectacular view of the lower cirque and it's conveniently close to St-Denis. From the summit it's possible to drop down to Grand Îlet in the Cirque de Salazie and cross over into Mafate via the Col des Bœufs.

There are three possible routes to the peak. Option one takes you along RF1 from Le Brûlé village above St-Denis to the Gîte de Montagne de la Plaine des Chicots (three hours), then on to Caverne des Soldats, through huge slabs of lava and limestone, and up the summit (1½ hours).

Option two takes you from Le Quinzième hamlet on the La Montagne road by footpath (at least four hours) or along the GR R2 variant from the kiosk overlooking the upper Rivière St-Denis to the Plaine d'Affouches (two hours) and on to join the Le Brûlé route at the gîte de montagne (two hours). From there, it's at least 1½ hours to the summit.

Option three takes you from Dos d'Ane east along the cirque rim to the gîte de montagne (about three hours) to meet up with the previously described routes.

Places to Stay & Eat

Up in Le Brûlé, *Mme Jacqueline Lepée* (☎ *23 02 32, 17 Chemin Cimetière*) offers *chambres d'hôte* (guest rooms) for FF180/220 a single/double. There are also two self contained gîtes which cost FF1120 for the week.

Nearby, *Mme Robert* (☎ *23 00 15, 105 Route des Azelées*) is a good point of departure for walking trips to the Plaine d'Affouches and La Roche Écrite. There are two gîtes here which cost FF840 for a weekend or FF1598 for the week.

For hikers, the *Gîte de Montagne de la Plaine des Chicots* (☎ *43 99 84*) is high above St-Denis near the base of La Roche Écrite and is only accessible on foot. Dorm beds cost FF83, breakfast costs FF30 and dinner costs FF85. Bookings must be made through the Maison de la Montagne in St-Denis or Cilaos, or the Pays d'Accueil de Salazie in Hell-Bourg.

In La Montagne, *Domaine des Jamroses* (☎ *23 59 00, fax 23 93 37, 6 Chemin du Colorado*) is a charming small hotel with rooms for FF680/490 including breakfast.

Getting There & Away

Access to these areas is by taxi or bus up the steep, winding roads. To reach Le Brûlé at 800m, take bus No 2 from Rue de Paris on Blvd de l'Océan in St-Denis and change to the taxi-bus for Au Banc (FF7) at Bassin Couderc. For the trip to La Montagne, take bus No 21 or 22.

Around the Coast

There are surprising differences in atmosphere as you move around the coast of Réunion.

The east coast is Réunion's farming belt. It lacks the beaches of the west, but makes up for it with a more relaxed rural atmosphere. There are numerous *chambres d'hôte* (small, family-run B&Bs) in the area that will give you a taste of village life. The main produce of the area is sugar cane, but the region is also known for its *vanille* (vanilla).

Around the south coast of the island is the region known as *le sud sauvage* (the wild south), which sits in the shadow of Piton de la Fournaise. The tortured landscape here is the result of thousands of years of volcanic activity; there are eerie tongues of black lava slicing through the forest and even reaching the ocean at several points around the coast. Not surprisingly, very few Réunionnais tempt providence by living in the path of the lava flows!

Immediately south-west of St-Denis is Réunion's resort strip, with the best of the island's beaches and a huge variety of organised activities laid on for visitors. You could be forgiven for thinking that a piece of the south of France had been transplanted to the Indian Ocean. The main part of this sunshine coast lies between St-Gilles-les-Bains and Étang-Salé-les-Bains.

The old coastal highway between St-Denis and St-Benoît across the north-east, and the highway west from St-Denis to St-Pierre, have both been superseded by more modern expressways.

East Coast

STE-MARIE

This small village is quite rapidly being absorbed by the burgeoning *banlieues* (suburbs) of St-Denis. Just outside the village is the broad, boulder-strewn bed of the Rivière des Pluies (River of Rain),

which is dry for most of the year, but transforms into a raging torrent in the cyclone season. There's not much to see in Ste-Marie, but the shrine of La Vierge Noire (The Black Virgin) at nearby Rivière des Pluies village contains an olive-wood statue of the Virgin Mary that is believed to have miraculous powers.

Places to Stay & Eat

Le Piton Fougère (☎ *53 88 04, 272 Route des Fleurs*) uphill from Ste-Marie in Plaine des Fougères is a chambre d'hôte run by Mme Robert. Rooms cost FF220 for one or two people. Traditional Creole meals cost FF130 per person (nonguests should call ahead).

STE-SUZANNE & AROUND

The seaside village of Ste-Suzanne is one of the prettier settlements along the coast. Nearby Quartier Français was the site of the first settlement on the island; 12 mutineers exiled by Governor Provis from Fort Dauphin in Madagascar set up camp here in 1646 for three years. The area is now a major sugar-producing centre, which will become obvious as you approach from any direction.

The coastline here is fairly uninspiring and the rocky beach is unsuitable for swimming, though there is an imposing lighthouse near the western end of town.

RÉUNION

Cascade Niagara

Just beyond the church at the southern end of town is a track signposted to Cascade Niagara, a 30m waterfall on the Rivière Ste-Suzanne. After turning off the main road, go about 2km then bear right at the next two road junctions to wind up at the waterfall and attendant tropical pool. At weekends it's a popular picnic site.

Le Grand Hazier

Garden fans will especially enjoy a visit to this 18th-century sugar planter's residence. It's an official French historical monument with a two-hectare garden planted with a variety of tropical flowers and fruit trees. It's open daily for guided tours by reservation only – call ☎ 52 32 81. A tour costs FF35 per person.

Places to Stay & Eat

Mme Boucher (☎ *52 12 25, 10 Chemin Mathurine*) situated high above Ste-Suzanne in Bellevue has two gîtes that cost FF1680 for the week and chambres d'hôte for FF220 a single or double. Meals are FF100.

Towards St-André in Quartier Français, *Mme Caladama* (☎ *46 11 43, 58 Rue R Vièrgs*) has a chambre d'hôte with doubles for FF180 and *table d'hôte* meals for FF100 per person.

Dominique Aupais (☎ *52 24 82, 47 Chemin de la Renaissance*), close to Cascade Niagara, offers two self-contained gîtes set in pleasant countryside for FF1400 a week.

A very pleasant dining option is *Le Bocage* (☎ *52 21 54*) in a tranquil park by the river at the east end of Ste-Suzanne. Chinese and French mains cost around FF60. It's open daily, except Sunday evening and Monday.

ST-ANDRÉ & AROUND

This town of over 30,000 people is home to the largest Indian community in Réunion. The mainly Tamil population is descended from indentured labourers, who were imported from India to work in the sugar cane fields after slavery was abolished in 1848. The Indian atmosphere is most apparent in the Hindu temples dotted around the town. The imposing Kali Temple on Ave de l'Île de France is open to visitors (shoes must be removed before entering).

These days, St-André is a pleasant but not unusually interesting market town. The main attraction here is the Maison de la Vanille plantation. Also worth a look are Maison Valliamée, a classic Creole mansion on Rue Lagourgue, and the Grand Pharmacie Créole on Ave du Bourbon. In front of the town hall you can see examples of one of the more unusual native trees, *ficus nitida*. It is known as the *élastique* by the Creoles, because of the elastic, rubber-like gum in its bark.

Orientation

St-André is not the easiest place to find your way around. Ave de l'Île de France and Ave de la République are the main shopping streets; the tourist office and *gare routière* (bus station) are in the mall at the east end of Ave de la République, near the intersection with Rue du Lycée. The Maison de la Vanille is on the way out of town on Rue de la Gare.

Information

The Office Municipale de Tourisme de St-André (☎ 46 91 63, fax 46 52 16) is at 20 Centre Commercial de St-André, not far from the bus terminal. The office is open from 8.30 am to noon and 1.30 to 5.30 pm Tuesday to Friday, and 8.30 am to noon and 1 to 4.30 pm Saturday.

La Maison de la Vanille

Close to the centre on Rue de la Gare, this old Creole mansion and vanilla plantation is set amid lawns, gardens and vanilla plantations. It's open to the public Tuesday to Friday from 9 am to noon (last visit at 11.30 am) and 2 to 5.10 pm (last visit at 4.30 pm). Visitors can learn the elaborate process of hand pollination necessary to coax the vanilla orchid to produce those gloriously aromatic beans we know and love. Admission costs FF25 per person (entry is free for children under 13). Guided tours are available with advance notice – call ☎ 46 00 14.

Champ-Borne

This rugged coastal town is known for its ruined church, which was destroyed by a

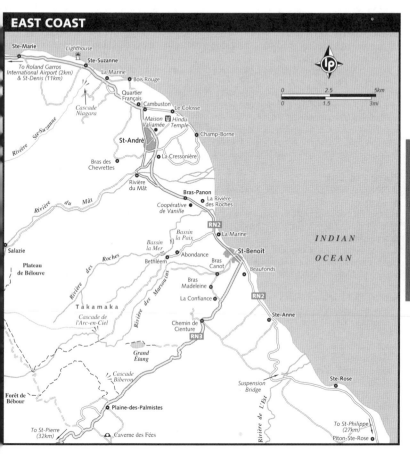

EAST COAST

tidal wave during Cyclone Jenny in 1962. There is a *restaurant* and a picnic spot near the remains. Nearby is a Hindu temple.

Sugar Refinery

The Sucerie de Bois Rouge is north of St-André on the coast. Guided tours may be arranged through the Office Municipale de Tourisme de St-André.

Special Events

Tamil fire-walking ceremonies are normally held during January. Participants enter a meditative state and then walk over red-hot embers as a sign of devotion to various deities. The Cavadee festival usually takes place in January or February. Contact the Office Municipale de Tourisme for specific dates.

Places to Stay

There's only one hotel in St-André, *Hôtel Île de France* (☎ 58 18 50, fax 50 18 55) on Rue de la Stade, where doubles cost FF230. Breakfast is an additional FF30 per person.

Around the corner is a chambre d'hôte belonging to *Mme G Cadet* (☎ 46 56 37, 92 Rue de la Stade). She charges FF130/160 for a single/double.

On the coastal road at Rivière-du-Mât-les-Bas, **Mme V Savriama** (☎ *46 69 84*) has a chambre d'hôte for FF140/170. Table d'hôte costs FF100 per head.

Above St-André in Bras des Chevrettes, **Georges de Palmas** (☎ *47 00 07, 172 Bras des Chevrettes*) offers a chambre d'hôte for FF130/170 or a gîte for FF1680 per week.

Pluies d'Or (☎ *46 18 16, 3 Allée des Sapoties*) in La Cressonnière is a delightful *pension de famille* (boarding house). Rooms cost FF140/200 including breakfast.

Places to Eat

On the way into St-André, the **Restaurant du Centre** (☎ *46 03 51*) on Rue Deschanets offers a mix of French, Chinese and Creole food from FF70. It's open for lunch daily except Sunday.

In St-André, **La Coupole** (☎ *46 94 77*) has a poor setting in the Cocoteraie mall, but good Creole and French food (mains are around FF80). It's open daily except Sunday and Tuesday nights.

South of the centre on Ave de Bourbon, **Le Restaurant Law-Shun** (☎ *46 04 08*) offers Chinese meals for around FF65. It's open for lunch and dinner daily (except Sunday).

Across from the *mairie* (town hall) in Champ Borne, **Beau Rivage** (☎ *46 08 66*) has Chinese, French and Creole dishes from FF80. It's open daily except on Sunday evenings and Monday.

Pluies d'Or (see Places to Stay earlier in this section) has a good small restaurant that specialises in home-cooked Creole cuisine.

Getting There & Away

Buses from St-Denis to St-Benoît pass through St-André (FF16.80). If you're travelling to the Cirque de Salazie from St-Denis by bus, you will have to change buses at St-André (FF10.10). There are about seven buses daily in each direction (three on Sunday). (See Getting There & Away under Salazie in the Interior chapter for onward connections to Hell-Bourg.)

BRAS-PANON

Bras-Panon, with a population of around 8500, is Réunion's vanilla capital, and most visitors come here to see (and smell!) the fragrant Coopérative de Vanille factory. The vanilla orchid was introduced into Réunion from Mexico in 1822, but early attempts at cultivation failed because of the absence of the Mexican insect that pollinates the flower and triggers the development of the vanilla pod. Fortunately for custard lovers everywhere, a method of hand-pollination was discovered in 1861 by Creole slave Edmond Albius; it's still in use today.

Information

Bras-Panon's *syndicat d'initiative* (tourist office) (☎ 51 50 62, fax 51 75 47) is next to the Coopérative de Vanille on Rue Robert, and can provide information on scenic walks and other activities in the area. The office is open weekdays from 8 am to noon and 1.15 to 5 pm.

Coopérative de Vanille

This working vanilla factory offers a hands-on display of the process of producing Réunion's famous *vanille Bourbon*. Visitors are welcome to walk around the small vanilla museum and pick up a few samples in the factory shop. It's worth a visit just for the dreamy smell. The factory is open Monday to Saturday from 8 to 11.30 am and 1.30 to 4.30 pm (from 9 am Saturday). Entry costs FF20 per person. For further information phone ☎ 51 70 12.

Places to Eat

There are no accommodation options in Bras-Panon, but there are a few restaurants.

The most convenient happens to be the **Le Vani-La** (☎ *51 56 58*) at the Coopérative de Vanille, open from 11.30 am to 5 pm daily except Sunday. Most dishes feature the local vanilla and cost around FF65.

On the main road, the friendly **Le Bec Fin** (☎ *51 52 24*) offers scrumptious Creole and Chinese dishes from FF55. It's open daily except Wednesday evening.

By the river at Rivière des Roches, **Le Beauvallon** (☎ *50 42 92*) serves local specialities such as *carri bichiques* (a curry made from tiny sprat-like fish) every lunch time for around FF80.

ST-BENOÎT & AROUND

St-Benoît is another agricultural and fishing centre. It specialises in rice, spices, lychees, coffee, maize and sugar and also in the sprat-like delicacy known as *bichiques*. These are caught at the mouth of the Rivière des Marsouins, which runs through the centre of this rather uninteresting town. The road to the Hautes Plaines turns inland here.

Domaine de la Confiance

About 6km from St-Benoît along the road towards Plaine-des-Palmistes is Domaine de la Confiance (☎ 50 90 72), a grand and gorgeous 18th-century Creole mansion. It's a protected historical monument and is attended by a garden of lush tropical vegetation and a ruined sugar mill. It's open from 8 am to noon daily except Sunday. Tours cost FF30.

Grand Étang

Around 12km from St-Benoît along the road towards Plaine-des-Palmistes, before the L'Echo lookout point, is the turning onto a 6km road/track to Grand Étang (Big Pond). This pretty picnic spot lies at the bottom of a vertical ridge separating it from the Rivière des Marsouins valley.

Places to Stay

The only option in town is the *Hôtel Le Bouvet* (☎ 50 14 96) by the ocean on Rue Amiral Bouvet. Rooms (single or double) cost FF200. Breakfast is an extra FF20 per person.

Hôtel Armony (☎ 50 86 50, fax 50 86 60) is north of St-Benoît at La Marine. It's a very plush option, with a nice swimming pool and well-appointed singles/doubles costing FF260/330. Breakfast costs FF50 per person.

Hôtel Grand Étang (☎ 50 93 24), towards Plaine-des-Palmistes by Grand Étang, has homely accommodation in the countryside. Doubles/triples cost FF250/350.

Up in the hills at Chemin de Ceinture, *Mme M Derand* (☎ 50 90 76, 20 Chemin de Ceinture) is offering a chambre d'hôte for FF165/200 a single/double. The table d'hôte costs around FF90 per person.

Places to Eat

The *Hôtel Le Bouvet* (see Places to Stay) has a restaurant that specialises in Creole and French cuisine, open daily except Sunday evening. Mains cost from FF75.

Le Dauphin Gourmand (☎ 50 42 82) on the same road serves tasty pizzas and *métro* (mainland French) grub for around FF60. It's closed on Monday night and Saturday lunch time.

L'Arum at the Hôtel Armony (see Places to Stay earlier) is open Monday to Saturday for lunch and dinner. It has French and Creole cuisine. Set meals are FF130; mains start at FF90.

Getting There & Away

From St-Benoît there's a scenic road that cuts across to St-Pierre and St-Louis in the south-west, via the Plaine-des-Palmistes and Le Tampon. Alternatively, you can continue south along the scenic coastal road through Ste-Anne, Ste-Rose, St-Philippe and St-Joseph to reach St-Pierre, passing the eerie landscape at Le Grand Brûlé, created by lava flows from Piton de la Fournaise.

There are several buses daily to St-Pierre via the high road (FF47) and about four buses via the coastal road (FF43.60). Buses to and from St-Denis leave approximately every half hour (FF20.10).

STE-ANNE

The village of Ste-Anne, about 5km south along the coast road from St-Benoît, is noted for its unusual church. The facade of the church is covered in ornamental stucco, with extravagant depictions of fruit, flowers and angels. The overall effect is flamboyant rather than tasteful, and is reminiscent of the Mestizo architecture of the Andes in South America. Credit for the construction goes to one Father Daubemberger from Alsace, who began to decorate the original church (a plain building dating from 1857) in the 1920s. He died in 1948 and was laid to rest inside the church.

In the Artisanat Réunion complex next door is the new Office de Tourisme de St-Joseph (☎ 51 02 57). It's open from 9 am to 5 pm weekdays and 9 am to noon Saturday.

RÉUNION

Between Ste-Anne and Ste-Rose is the lovely old Pont d'Anglais suspension bridge over the Rivière de l'Est, now bypassed by the main highway. It's open to pedestrians, however, and there are nice picnic spots at the southern end. It's claimed it was the longest suspension bridge in the world at the time of its construction in 1894.

STE-ROSE & AROUND
The small fishing community of Ste-Rose has its harbour at the inlet of La Marine. There's a monument here to the young English commander Corbett, who was killed when his army was defeated by the French, led by Bouvet, in 1809.

Notre Dame de la Lave
Notre Dame de la Lave is at Piton Ste-Rose, 4.5km south of town. The lava flow from a 1977 eruption went through the village, split when it came to the church and reformed again on the other side. Many people see the church's escape from the flow as a miracle of divine intervention. A wooden log 'washed up' by the lava now forms the lectern inside the church.

Anse des Cascades
This leafy picnic spot is beside the sea about 3km south of Piton Ste-Rose. The water from the hills drops dramatically into the sea near a little fishing port. There's a nice *restaurant* here.

La Vierge au Parasol
From Bois Blanc, the road continues south along the coast, then climbs and drops into the 6km-wide volcanic ravine known as Le Grand Brûlé. Just inside the ravine beside the road is the shrine La Vierge au Parasol, which features a statue of the Virgin Mary optimistically holding an umbrella as protection against the lava! A planter from Bois Blanc set it up at the turn of the century in the hope of protecting his vanilla beans from volcanic hellfire and brimstone.

Places to Stay & Eat
There are a couple of chambres d'hôte on the national highway near Ste-Rose. *Mme*

Adam de Villiers (☎ 47 21 33) at No 206 offers chambres d'hôte in a nice garden for FF200/220 a single/double. The table d'hôte here costs a steep FF120 per person.

Further south at Piton Cascade, the pleasant *Au Joyaux des Laves* (☎ 47 34 00) is a large chambre d'hôte with rooms for FF180/220. The table d'hôte starts at FF105.

By the cascades, *L'Anse des Cascades* (☎ 47 20 42) offers fresh fish dishes from FF80 every lunch time except Friday.

Across from Notre Dame de la Lave in Piton Ste-Rose, *Bel Air* (☎ 47 22 50) offers set Creole menus for FF80 every lunch time.

Just before the road drops to Le Grand Brûlé, the *Grand Brûlé* restaurant offers Creole lunches such as *boucané* (smoked pork) with heart of pandanus daily for around FF80.

Getting There & Away
The buses going from St-Benoît to St-Pierre via Ste-Rose and St-Philippe make handy stops near Notre Dame de la Lave and Anse des Cascades (FF16.80).

South Coast

ST-PHILIPPE & AROUND
This small town on the south coast is the first population centre you hit after leaving the deserted area of Grand Brûlé, the immense ravine formed by the main lava flow from the volcano. The steep slopes above known as Les Grandes Pentes, have funnelled lava down to the coast for thousands of years. Because of the lack of population, this area forms an important nature reserve for native birds.

The last flow that reached the sea down this route occurred in 1976. In March 1986 the lava took a more easterly route and crossed the main road between Pointe de Tremblet and Pointe de la Table at Takamaka and Tremblet villages. This eruption added over 30 hectares to the island's area but more than 450 people had to be evacuated and several homes were lost. The 1991 eruptions were much more low-key affairs and didn't threaten the road.

Information

At the Office de Tourisme de St-Philippe (☎ 37 10 43, fax 37 10 97), Place de la Mairie, Rue Leconte-Delisle, you can pick up information on the entire south-east coast of the island. It's open from 9 am to 5 pm daily.

Eco-Musée de St-Philippe

This quaint museum (☎ 37 16 43) is also known as Au Bon Roi Louis after the French king who encouraged the settlement of the area. It features an eclectic assortment of antiques and agricultural equipment, and visitors receive a very hands-on tour from the custodian (she'll even chop up a mountain tamarind log to show you how the roof shingles are made). It's open from 9.30 am to noon and 2 to 4.30 pm daily. Entry is FF20.

Le Jardin des Parfums et des Épices

This perfume and spice garden is located in the forest above Mare Longue and is open daily, but you must book at least one day in advance. Visits (including a guided tour) are arranged through the Office de Tourisme de St-Philippe, and cost FF40 for adults and FF20 for children.

Les Sentinelles

Near the southern end of the Grand Brûlé is a turning inland marked 'Symboise pour Volcan et Oiseaux'. About 1km along this bumpy track is a garden of bizarre sculptures known as Les Sentinelles. They were created by the local sculptor Monsieur Mayo using lava from the 1976 flow.

The *oiseaux* (birds) seen here include the imposing Maillardi buzzard.

Places to Stay

There's nowhere to stay in St-Philippe, but there are a few options near the village of Le Baril, a few kilometres to the west.

Hôtel Le Baril (☎ 37 01 04, fax 37 07 62) on the Route Nationale is a small hotel and restaurant set above the rocky shoreline. Singles/doubles are FF280/330 and the hotel has a swimming pool.

Down by the ocean in Basse Vallée, *Le Cap Méchant* (☎ 37 00 51) restaurant has a few doubles with TV and air-con for FF265. Turn down to the sea at the Basse Vallée roundabout.

Basse Vallée Gîte de Montagne (☎ 37 00 75) is about 8km above the hamlet of Basse Vallée, along the route forestière de Basse Vallée or the GR R2 variant. It charges FF83 per person per night. Breakfast is an extra FF25 and dinner is FF80. Bookings must be made in St-Denis or Cilaos through Maison de la Montagne.

Places to Eat

La Canot (☎ 37 00 36) on Rue Leconte Delisle in St-Philippe offers Creole, French and Chinese fare for around FF80. It's open daily for lunch and on Thursday, Friday and Saturday evenings.

Hôtel Le Baril (☎ 37 01 04) has a good restaurant, which offers Chinese and Creole main dishes ranging in price from FF70 to FF100. It's open daily from 11.30 am to around 10 pm.

Further south on the highway is *Chez Laurent* (☎ 37 03 07), which has tasty Chinese meals for around FF50. It's open daily except Sunday evening and Wednesday.

On the seafront in Basse Vallée, *Le Cap Méchant* (☎ 37 00 61) offers tasty Creole cuisine for lunch and dinner daily. Mains cost from FF65.

Next door, *L'Étoile de Mer* (☎ 37 04 60) offers similar fare at similar prices. It's also open daily.

Getting There & Away

St-Philippe lies on the coastal bus route between St-Benoît and St-Pierre; there are around four buses daily in either direction.

ST-JOSEPH

St-Joseph, at the mouth of the magnificent valley of the Rivière des Remparts, is a rather dull town. The area is known primarily for its production of baskets and bags from the fronds of the vacoa.

East of St-Joseph it's possible to swim at the black-sand beach of La Marine de Vincendo, the old port for the village of the same name. There's also a protected tide pool at Manapany-les-Bains.

RÉUNION

Places to Stay

M Grondin (☎ *56 51 66*) at Manapany-les-Bains on Blvd de l'Ocean has three gîtes that cost from FF1624 a week.

Overlooking the Rivière des Remparts at Grande Coude, *Jean-Pierre Chan-Shit-Sang* (☎ *56 14 44*) has several gîtes from FF1725 for the week. It also has chambres d'hôte for FF235 a double and a *gîte d'étape* (privately run lodge) that costs FF150 for one or two people. Meals are FF90.

On Chemin Sylvain Vitry, which branches off the highway towards the sea just west of the turn-off to Petite Île, *M Omarjee* (☎ *31 65 10*) has very nice singles/doubles for FF200/250. There's also a pool.

On the same road, *M Levent* (☎ *56 88 10*) rents out a gîte for FF1198 a week.

Places to Eat

Right in St-Joseph on Rue Raphaël Babet, *Pizzeria La Gondole* (☎ *56 16 12*) is great for pasta or pizza. It's open daily except Tuesday.

Also central is *La Case* (☎ *56 41 66*) on Rue Leconte Delisle. Housed in a lovely old Creole house, it serves excellent Creole mains for around FF90. It's closed Sunday, and Monday evening.

Le Tajine (☎ *37 32 51*) in Vincendo specialises in Moroccan cuisine. Couscous and other mains cost around FF70. It's open daily except Sunday and Wednesday nights.

There are a couple of cheap and cheerful Creole places on the road up to Grand Galet (Route de la Passerelle) in the Rivière Langevin valley. *La Bonne Idée* (☎ *56 70 26*) is one of the better options with Creole dishes from FF65.

Getting There & Away

St-Joseph lies on the coastal bus route between St-Pierre and St-Benoît. From St-Pierre, the fare is FF10.10.

ST-PIERRE

With a population of more than 55,000, St-Pierre is Réunion's third-largest *commune* after St-Denis and St-Paul. This moderately popular resort town is somewhat down at heel after the likes of St-Gilles-les-Bains.

Le Sitarane

Tucked away in a corner of the cemetery in St-Pierre is the grave of the African bandit and sorcerer Le Sitarane, one of the more sinister heroes of the superstitious Réunionnais. This shadowy figure was the leader of a gang of *bonhommes* (medicine men) who broke into homes in the Le Tampon area, murdered the occupants and used parts of the victims' bodies in macabre black magic rituals! Eventually, the gang was surprised while raiding a house and they were all sentenced to death by hanging in 1911.

Today, the grave of Le Sitarane is covertly used for black magic rites by Réunionnais looking to bring misfortune upon others. The grave is usually covered with offerings, from glasses of rum, candles and pieces of red cloth to neat and tidy rows of cigarettes and even the occasional beheaded rooster!

There's a mediocre beach and a string of restaurants along the seafront, but it's hard to see what all the fuss is about.

There aren't many sights in the centre of town, but if you're near the *hôtel de ville* (town hall), it doesn't take five minutes to pop inside and have a look at this 200-year-old building that was restored in 1975. The counter clerk should let you in and upstairs anytime between 9 am and 5 pm Monday to Friday.

Information

Tourist Offices The syndicat d'initiative, known as the Office de Tourisme de St-Pierre (☎ 25 02 36, fax 25 82 76), 17 Blvd Hubert-Delisle, is open from 9 am to 5.45 pm Monday to Friday and from 9 am to 3.45 pm Saturday. The staff members here are fairly uninformed.

Money The Banque de Paris Intercontinentale is on Rue des Bons Enfants, while BRED has a branch on Rue de Four à Chaux (both are open from 8 am to 4 pm weekdays). The ATM at the post office on Rue des Bons Enfants is more useful and accepts most foreign credit cards.

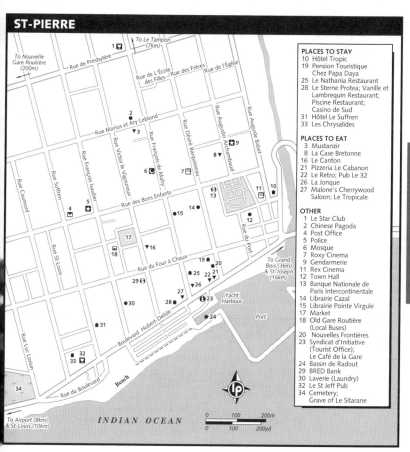

ST-PIERRE

To Nouvelle
Gare Routière
(200m)

To Le Tampon
(7km)

Rue de Presbytère

Rue de L'École
des Filles

Rue des Frères

Rue de l'Église

Rue Marius et Ary Leblond

Rue Victor de Vigoureux

Rue François de Mahy

Rue Désiré Barquissieau

Rue Augustin Archambaud

Rue Auguste Babet

Rue François Isautier

Rue Suffren

Rue Caumont

Rue des Bons Enfants

Rue St-Louis

Rue du Four à Chaux

Rue du Port

Rue Luc Lorion

Boulevard Hubert-Delisle

Rue du Boulevard

Beach

Yacht Harbour

Port

To Grand
Bois (3km)
& St-Joseph
(16km)

INDIAN OCEAN

To Airport (8km)
& St-Louis (10km)

0   100   200m
0   100   200yd

PLACES TO STAY
10 Hôtel Tropic
19 Pension Touristique
     Chez Papa Daya
25 Le Nathania Restaurant
28 Le Sterne Protea; Vanille et
     Lambrequin Restaurant;
     Piscine Restaurant;
     Casino de Sud
31 Hôtel Le Suffren
33 Les Chrysalides

PLACES TO EAT
3 Mustanzir
8 La Case Bretonne
16 Le Canton
21 Pizzeria Le Cabanon
22 Le Retro; Pub Le 32
26 La Jonque
27 Malone's Cherrywood
     Saloon; Le Tropicale

OTHER
1 Le Star Club
2 Chinese Pagoda
4 Post Office
5 Police
6 Mosque
7 Roxy Cinema
9 Gendarmerie
11 Rex Cinema
12 Town Hall
13 Banque Nationale de
     Paris Intercontinental
14 Librairie Cazal
15 Librairie Pointe Virgule
17 Market
18 Old Gare Routière
     (Local Buses)
20 Nouvelles Frontières
23 Syndicat d'Initiative
     (Tourist Office);
     Le Café de la Gare
24 Bassin de Radout
29 BRED Bank
30 Laverie (Laundry)
32 Le St Jeff Pub
34 Cemetery;
     Grave of Le Sitarane

RÉUNION

Post & Communications The main post office on Rue des Bons Enfants is open from 8 am to 5 pm weekdays and from 8 to 11 am Saturday.

Grave of Le Sitarane

St-Pierre's only real tourist attraction lies in the cemetery at the west end of Blvd Hubert-Delisle. The grave of this African sorcerer is still a popular pilgrimage spot for Réunionnais who believe in *gris gris* or black magic. (See the boxed text 'Le Sitarane'.) The grave is on the right-hand side at the west end of the cemetery.

Other features of the cemetery include some interesting Hindu graves, marked by yellow headstones in the shape of Sanskrit letters; a number of Chinese marble vaults; and some well-tended Christian graves, which are crowded with crosses and dried flowers.

Seafront

Along the main promenade, Blvd Hubert-Delisle, is the public beach, which is sandy but exposed to the wind. There is also the Bassin de Radout, a dry dock dating from the 19th century.

Market

The market, near the old gare routière, is open from 7 am to 6 pm Monday to Saturday and 7 am to noon Sunday and on holidays. Although it's primarily for fruit and vegetables, there are also some souvenir stalls here, particularly on Saturday.

Places to Stay

St-Pierre has a variety of hotels that cater for a range of budgets.

A good cheap choice is the **Pension Touristique Chez Papa Daya** (☎ 25 64 87 *during the day, 25 11 34 in the evening, 27 Rue du Four à Chaux*), not far from the beach. Singles or doubles cost FF150 with shared bathroom and FF200 with private bathroom. There's also a kitchen.

Hôtel Tropic (☎ 25 90 70, fax 35 10 32, *2 Rue Auguste Babet*) offers air-con doubles from FF170 to FF220. If you call ahead, they'll pick you up from the *nouvelle* (new) gare routière.

Right by the promenade, the charming **Le Nathania** (☎ 25 04 57, fax 35 27 05, *12 Rue François de Mahy*) is a tidy three-star place with a good restaurant. Rooms cost FF300/400 for singles/doubles, including breakfast.

Hôtel Le Suffren (☎ 35 19 10, fax 25 99 43, *14 Rue Suffren*) is also handy for the beach. It has rooms for FF360/395; prices include breakfast.

On a back street between Rue Suffren and Rue Caumont, *Les Chrysalides* (☎ 25 75 64, fax 25 22 19) is close to the sea and offers comfortable air-con rooms for FF260 a double (FF280 with TV).

Le Sterne Protea (☎ 25 70 00, fax 35 01 41) on the seafront is probably the most up-market choice in town. The least expensive rooms cost FF510/675. Breakfast is an extra FF60 per person. There's a good pool here to splash around in, and a casino.

Places to Eat

The lacklustre atmosphere in St-Pierre is somewhat made up for by the excellent restaurants in town.

For terrific ice cream, *Le Tropicale* on Blvd Hubert-Delisle offers a wide selection of *parfums* (flavours) for FF13 a scoop. It's open from noon to 7 pm daily except Monday.

Good for a beach snack is **Le Café de la Gare** (☎ 35 24 44), just behind the syndicat d'initiative. Light lunches start at FF50, while more expensive evening meals go for FF80.

For cheap eats, *La Jonque* (☎ 25 57 78) near the corner of Blvd Hubert-Delisle and Rue François de Mahy offers the usual selection of Chinese favourites from FF45. It's closed Tuesday.

Le Canton (☎ 25 08 04, 16 Rue Victor le Vigoureux) serves mainly Chinese food. It has huge lunch specials for around FF35 to FF50 and is open for lunch and dinner daily (except Sunday, and Monday and Tuesday nights).

Right on the promenade, try *Pizzeria Le Cabanon* (☎ 25 71 46) for good pizzas and métro cuisine. Expect to pay around FF90 for a meal. It's closed Monday.

Also on Blvd Hubert-Delisle, *Le Retro* (☎ 25 33 06) is a popular brasserie with French and Creole standards from FF80. It's open daily until 3 pm for lunch and until 10.30 pm for dinner.

Nearby, *Malone's Cherrywood Saloon* (☎ 25 02 22) is another lively brasserie; it offers salads from FF42 and grills from FF60. It's open every day.

On Rue Marius et Ary Leblond, check out *Le Mustanzir* (☎ 96 87 17), a good Indian restaurant. It is open daily for lunch and in the evening from Wednesday to Saturday. *Rogan josh* (curry) and other Indian treats cost about FF65.

La Case Bretonne (☎ 35 33 61) is in a lovely Creole building on Rue Archambaud and serves Bretonne cuisine. Mains cost from FF85. It's open for lunch and dinner daily except Wednesday.

Le Nathania (see Places to Stay earlier in this section) has a restaurant that serves a bit of everything – French, Creole and Chinese – with mains for around FF70. It's open daily; nonresidents should try to book ahead.

Vanille et Lambrequin at Le Sterne Protea (see Places to Stay earlier) is *the* place for a dose of pampering. The restaurant does tremendous Creole mains from FF80

France with a tropical twist: lush, green Réunion is one of the last colonial possessions in the world.

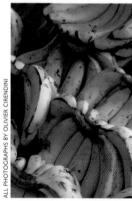

Réunion's colourful basketry is just the thing for carrying your other market purchases – such as chou chous, lychees, bananas and aubergines.

and it's open daily (bookings are recommended). Also here is the *Piscine* restaurant overlooking the pool. It's open for lunch and dinner daily and you can use the pool if you eat. The Creole buffet costs FF60.

Entertainment
Discos in St-Pierre include *Le Star Club* (☎ 35 33 62) on Rue de Presbytère; *Appolo Night* (☎ 49 58 91) on Route du Père Maître; and *Le Prestige* (☎ 49 52 60) on Route de Bois-d'Olives. All are open on Saturday and Sunday evenings.

For a drink, check out the ever popular *Malone's Cherrywood Saloon* (☎ 25 02 22) on Blvd Hubert-Delisle. Other happening places include *Aquarhum* (☎ 35 25 02) on Front de Mer, *Pub Le 32* (☎ 25 40 16) on Blvd Hubert-Delisle and also *Le St Jeff Pub* (☎ 25 76 92) on Blvd Hubert-Delisle.

At the Sterne Protea is the *Casino de Sud* (☎ 25 26 96), which offers the usual games of chance from 9.15 pm to 2 am (the slot machines are open from 10 am).

There are two cinemas in St-Pierre: *Roxy* (☎ 35 34 90), Rue Désiré Barquisseau, and *Rex* (☎ 25 01 01), Rue Auguste Babet.

Getting There & Away
Air There are just a few flights a week to Pierrefonds Airport west of St-Pierre, and no facilities for arriving visitors. Without exception, you're better off flying into Roland Garros Airport near St-Denis.

Bus Long-haul buses stop at the inconvenient new gare routière on the corner of Rues Presbytère and Luc Lorion west of town. Daily buses to/from St-Denis (FF43.60) run frequently along the western side of the island via St-Louis and St-Paul. There are also several services a day to St-Benoît via Plaine-des-Palmistes (FF47). Four buses a day go via the south-east coast road through St-Joseph and Ste-Anne (FF43.60).

Local buses use the old gare routière on Rue François Isautier.

Taxi A taxi from the new gare routière into St-Pierre costs about FF30. Call ☎ 38 54 54 if there are no taxis waiting at the bus station.

AROUND ST-PIERRE
There are a number of quiet villages in the hills around St-Pierre where you can stay and get a taste of the rural life.

There is a large concentration of gîtes and chambres d'hôte in La Ravine des Cabris in the hills north of St-Pierre.

Just outside La Ravine des Cabris on route D28, *Mme Lebon* (☎ 49 73 78, 11 Chemin Técher Maurice) offers chambres d'hôte for FF150/200 a single/double.

M Hoarau (☎ 49 55 81) is friendly and easy to find. The two gîtes cost FF2004/1120 per week/weekend. Follow the sign to 'Les Bananiers' just east of town on route D28.

Nearby on Chemin Recherchant, *Mme Lebon* (☎ 49 51 36) has three gîtes that cost from FF1680 for two people for a week and FF1904 for five people for a week.

Closer to St-Pierre in Ligne Paradis to the north, *Mme Gerbith* (☎ 49 74 83, 59 Chemin Diagonale) offers tidy chalets around a pool from FF2800 for a week and FF1300 for a weekend.

On the way into La Ravine des Cabris, *Le Vieux Domaine* (☎ 49 53 67) is a good Creole restaurant in an ornamental garden. Meals cost from FF80. It's open for lunch daily except Monday.

Further east in Grand Bois, *Demotel Résidence de Tourisme* (☎ 31 11 60, fax 31 17 51) on Allée des Lataniers is in a nice secluded location and has comfortable bungalows and rooms from FF450 (single or double). It's FF50 for breakfast, and there's a pool for guests.

West Coast

ST-LOUIS & AROUND
You have to travel to St-Louis to catch the bus to Cilaos but there's really no other reason to visit this town.

The gare routière is located on the southern side of town near a couple of snack bars and the church, which is the oldest on the island, dating from 1733.

About 1.5km west of St-Louis, at Le Camp du Gol, is the Sucrerie du Gol. You can tour this old sugar refinery daily except Sunday with prior reservation (☎ 91 05 47).

In the hills at Les Makes, 14km north of St-Louis, the Observatoire Astronomique des Makes is open daily for tours; again, you'll need to book ahead (☎ 37 86 83). Above Les Makes, the route forestière des Makes leads up to La Fenêtre, a viewpoint into the Cirque de Cilaos.

Places to Stay & Eat
There's nowhere to stay in St-Louis, but there are a few options up in the hills.

On route D3 in Bellevue, 5km north-west of St-Louis, *M Deboisvilliers* (☎ *26 73 66, 171 Rue Hubert-Delisle*) has a nice Creole house with chambres d'hôte for FF220 a double. Meals are FF100.

M Cambona (☎ *26 75 86, 175 Rue Hubert-Delisle*), a few doors down, charges FF200 a double.

M Leperlier (☎ *37 82 17, 41 Rue Paul Herman*) by the observatory in Les Makes has chambres d'hôte for FF170/220 a single/double. Meals are FF100.

Further north on the route forestière, *M Jean-Luc d'Eurveilher* (☎ *37 82 77, 55 Rue Montplaisir*) has rooms for FF130/200. Meals are FF110.

Nearby, *M Nativel* (☎ *37 85 37, 36 Rue Montplaisir*) charges FF220 a double for chambres d'hôte. Meals are FF100.

ÉTANG-SALÉ-LES-BAINS
If you're coming from the south, Étang-Salé-les-Bains is the beginning of the holiday coast, though the area remains very much an agricultural community. It's more a resort for locals than tourists, and the black-sand beach is much quieter than the coast further north around St-Gilles-les-Bains. There is some passable surf here too.

Information
The syndicat d'initiative, known as the Office de Tourisme de l'Étang-Salé (☎ 26 67 32, fax 26 67 92), is housed in the old train station on Rue Octave Bénard. It has information on the entire stretch of coast between St-Louis and St-Leu. The office is open from 8.30 am to noon and 2 to 5 pm Monday to Saturday.

Office National des Forêts (ONF) Bird Park
On the road from Étang-Salé-les-Bains to Étang-Salé-les-Hauts, just where it forks to the left to go to Les Avirons, is a two-hectare bird park operated by the Office National des Forêts. This route is beautifully crimson when all the flamboyant trees are in bloom.

Places to Stay
There aren't too many choices for accommodation in Étang-Salé-les-Bains.

Right on the roundabout in the middle of town, the *Caro Beach Village* (☎ 91 79 79, fax 91 79 80) has comfortable singles/doubles starting at FF420/520 per night. Breakfast is FF60.

Up near Étang-Salé-les-Hauts on route D110, *Mme Sanassy* (☎ 26 39 12) has three gîtes that cost from FF1904 a week and FF952 a weekend.

On route D111 in Ravine Sheunon, *Mme Savigny* (☎ 26 31 09) offers chambres d'hôte for FF150 a double.

Places to Eat
La Pirogue (☎ 26 64 28) next to the tourist office is open for lunch and dinner daily. Creole and Italian mains cost from FF70.

On the far side of the roundabout, *Le Bambou* (☎ 91 70 28) is an Italian place with pasta and pizzas from FF75. It's closed Tuesday.

L'Été Indien (☎ 26 67 33) is also on the main road, and serves fishy grills and Chinese dishes for around FF70. It's also closed Tuesday.

AROUND ÉTANG-SALÉ-LES-BAINS
For a taste of rural life, there are chambres d'hôte in several of the villages around Étang-Salé-les-Bains, including Les Avirons, about 5km north of Étang-Salé-les-Bains, and Tévelave, 11km further up the mountain.

Tévelave is the starting point for route forestière 6, which leads up into the Forêt Domaniale des Bénares. From the end of the road, you can walk to Le Grand Bénare

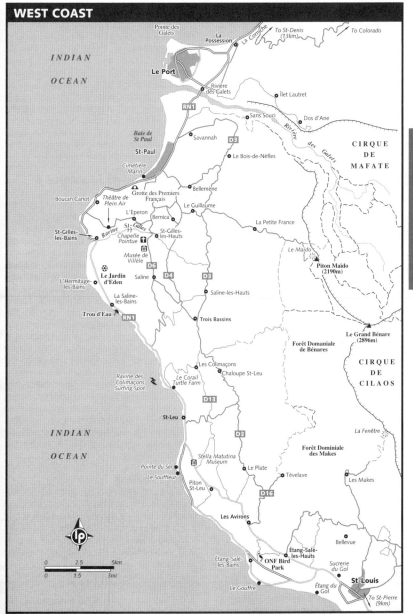

WEST COAST

INDIAN

OCEAN

Pointe des
Galets

La
Possession

To St-Denis
(13km)

To Colorado

La Corniche

Le Port

Rivière
des Galets

Îlet Lautret

RN1

Sans Souci

Dos d'Ane

Rivière des Galets

CIRQUE
DE
MAFATE

Baie de
St Paul

Savannah

D3

St-Paul

Le Bois-de-Nèfles

Cimetière
Marin

Bellemène

Boucan Canot

Théâtre de
Plein Air

Grotte des Premiers
Français

L'Eperon

Le Guillaume

La Petite France

St-Gilles
Bernica

Le Maïdo

St-Gilles-
les-Bains

Ravine

St-Gilles-
les-Hauts

Chapelle
Pointue

Piton Maïdo
(2190m)

Musée de
Villèle

D6

Le Jardin
d'Eden

D4

Saline

D3

L'Hermitage-
les-Bains

Saline-les-Hauts

La Saline-
les-Bains

Le Grand Bénare
(2896m)

Trou d'Eau

RN1

Trois Bassins

Forêt Domaniale
de Bénares

CIRQUE
DE
CILAOS

INDIAN

OCEAN

Les Colimaçons

Chaloupe St-Leu

Ravine des
Colimaçons
Surfing Spot

Le Corail
Turtle Farm

D13

La Fenêtre

St-Leu

D3

Forêt Dominale
des Makes

Stella Matutina
Museum

Pointe du Sel

Le Plate

Tévelave

Les Makes

Le Souffleur

Piton
St-Leu

D16

Les Avirons

Bellevue

Étang-Salé-
les-Hauts

Étang-Salé-
les-Bains

ONF Bird
Park

Sucrerie
du Gol

St-Louis

Le Gouffre

Étang du
Gol

To St-Pierre
(9km)

0   2.5   5km
0   1.5   3mi

LP

the nose of land that divides the Cilaos and Mafate Cirques, or even continue on to Le Maïdo and then descend into Mafate via the Sentier de Roche Plate.

Places to Stay & Eat
On route D16 on the way from Les Avirons to Tévelave, *M Idmond* (☎ 38 07 55) has a chambre d'hôte with singles/doubles for FF200/220.

Nearby, *Mme Boyer* (☎ 38 00 39, 65 Route des Vacoas) offers chambres d'hôte for FF220 a double. It's an extra FF100 for meals.

Just off route D16 on the way into Tévelave, *Mme Turpin* (☎ 38 30 67) charges FF180 a double, plus a steep FF130 for her table d'hôte.

Above Tévelave on the route forestière, *Auberge Les Fougères* (☎ 38 32 96, fax 38 30 26) is a homey rural hotel with rooms for FF220/350.

Just west of Tévelave in the village of Le Plate, *Mme Darty* (☎ 54 01 94, 419 route D3) offers chambres d'hôte for FF150/200. It's FF100 for dinner.

ST-LEU
St-Leu used to be a major centre for the sugar industry, but the town fell on hard times in 1978 when the Stella sugar refinery closed down. These days, St-Leu is best known for its surfing.

There is a break in the reef at the mouth of the Ravine des Colimaçons that generates an impressive left-handed wave regarded as one of the best in the Indian Ocean. Sharks have been known to occasionally feed in this area (see the boxed text 'Les Dents du Mer' in the Réunion Facts for the Visitor chapter), but a bigger problem is likely to be the local surfers, who have a reputation for intimidating new arrivals who want to try the wave.

Historically, St-Leu has had its share of problems, including a violent slave rebellion in 1811 and devastating cyclones in 1932 and 1989, but it was spared the cholera epidemic that devastated St-Denis and St-Louis in 1859, an event commemorated in the town's historic church.

Information
The helpful Office de Tourisme de St-Leu (☎ 34 63 40, fax 34 96 45) is just beyond the roundabout on the main road into St-Leu. This new office has brochures galore and English-speaking staff. It's open from 9 am to noon and 1.30 to 5 pm daily (closed Sunday afternoon and Monday morning).

The main road cuts straight through the middle of town. Rue de la Compagnie des Indes is where you'll find the Apolonia hotel and the post office, which has an ATM that accepts foreign credit cards.

Notre Dame de la Salette & Hôtel de Ville
Right on the main street is the recently restored chapel of Notre Dame de la Salette, built in 1859 as a plea for protection against the cholera epidemic sweeping the island. Whether by luck or by divine intervention, St-Leu was spared from the epidemic, and thousands of pilgrims come here each year on 19 September to offer thanks. Across the road is the appealing *hôtel de ville* (town hall), housed in an old store built by the French East India Company.

Surfing
Surfers should head for the mouth of the Ravine des Colimaçons, at the northern edge of town. In the right conditions, this sizable left-hander can form good tubes, but it's a tricky wave to master and amateurs are probably better off sticking to St-Gilles-les-Bains. For all board-related problems, head to Mickey Rat (☎ 34 79 00) by the tourist office.

Places to Stay
Apolonia (☎ 34 62 62, fax 34 61 61), on the corner of Rue de la Compagnie des Indes and Blvd Bonner, is a tasteful upmarket hotel. It has a pool and restaurant and a good entertainment schedule. Singles/doubles/triples will set you back FF415/600/780 including breakfast.

Inland from St-Leu on route D12, the *Iloha Village Hotel* (☎ 34 89 89, fax 34 89 90) is a very nice three-star place with great views and a decent restaurant and pool.

Singles/doubles start at FF350/390 plus FF60 for breakfast. Also on offer are a variety of self-catering bungalows from FF480 a double.

On the highway north of St-Leu, **Battants des Lames** (☎/fax 34 80 18) has comfortable bungalows around a pool. Rates start at FF330 per night for two or FF440 per night for four people.

Places to Eat

Self-caterers should visit the huge **Super-U** supermarket on the highway right in the middle of St-Leu.

Le Palais d'Asie (☎ 34 80 41, 5 Rue de l'Etang) beside the stream offers good and reasonably priced Chinese meals for around FF65. It's closed Tuesday.

By the beach just south of the centre, **La Varangue** (☎ 34 78 45, 36 Rue du Lagon) is good for a Creole feed. It's open daily for lunch.

Aux Bonnes Choises (☎ 37 76 26) opposite La Varangue serves Creole dishes for around FF75. It's closed Thursday, and Sunday evening.

Casa San Fermin (☎ 34 90 58) near Notre Dame de la Salette offers delicious Spanish dishes such as paella from FF85. It's open for lunch and dinner daily except Monday.

AROUND ST-LEU

There are several peaceful villages within 10km of St-Leu that offer accommodation in a relaxed rural setting. These include Les Colimaçons, Piton St-Leu and Chaloupe St-Leu, and can all be reached by bus (Car Jaune route 'E' from St-Pierre to Chaloupe St-Leu). Above Colimaçons, the route forestière du Piton Rouge runs east up into the Forêt Domaniale des Bénares, connecting with the trail to Le Maïdo.

Les Colimaçons is also the location of the **Conservatoire Botanique National de Mascarin** (☎ 24 92 27), an attractive garden of native plants in the grounds of the unusual Creole mansion of Chateauvieux. The gardens are open from 9 am to 5 pm daily except Monday. Entry is FF25 for adults and FF10 for children.

Le Corail Turtle Farm

Le Corail Turtle Farm (☎ 34 81 10) is 2km north of St-Leu on Route Nationale 1. This dubious attraction offers the chance to get close to commercially farmed turtles, but the thought that these magnificent creatures are being raised to make turtle-shell trinkets such as bottle openers is likely to undermine the experience. If you're still interested, the farm is open from 9 am to 6 pm daily; entry costs FF30 for adults and FF20 for children. Be aware that turtle shell may not be imported into most countries.

Stella Matutina Museum

This quirky museum (☎ 34 16 24) at the village of Stella, 4km south of St-Leu on the inland route towards Les Avirons (known as l'Allée des Flamboyants), tells the agricultural and industrial history of Réunion. It's dedicated primarily to the sugar industry, but does provide insight into the history of the island, and has exhibits on other products known and loved by the Réunionnais such as vanilla, orchids, geraniums and vetiver. It's open from 9.30 am to 5.30 pm Tuesday to Sunday. Admission is FF40 for adults and FF10 for children.

Le Souffleur

Located on the main road between St-Leu and Étang-Salé-les-Bains is Le Souffleur (The Blowhole), a rocky crevice along the seafront that spurts up a tower of water as the waves crash against it. If the sea is calm, the effect is obviously not as spectacular.

Places to Stay

Above Les Colimaçons on route D13, **Mme René** (☎ 54 80 81, No 58 bis) has chambres d'hôte for FF200 a double, and a few gîtes from FF1512 a week or FF488 a weekend.

Nearby, **M Huet** (☎ 54 76 70, 200 Chemin Potier) charges FF220 for a single or double for his chambres d'hôte. Meals are FF110.

Just off route D3 near Chaloupe St-Leu, **M Cadet** (☎ 54 85 00, 20 Chemin Payet Emmanuel) has rooms for FF150 and a gîte for FF1232 a week or FF1008 a weekend. Meals cost FF80. The road turns off near the junction with Chemin Potier.

Right in the middle of Chaloupe St-Leu, *Mme Maillot* (☎ *54 82 92, 4 Chemin des Hortensias*) offers chambres d'hôte for FF150 and table d'hôte meals for FF80. Take Chemin Boulanger, which turns off route D3 near the church.

There are numerous gîtes in Piton St-Leu. *Mme Leveneur* (☎ *34 30 81, 135 Rue A Lagourgue*) on route D11 is the easiest to find. The three gîtes here cost from FF1904 per week. The Car Jaune bus stops nearby.

Just off route D25 on a back road that runs behind the Stella Matutina Museum, *Mme Vion* (☎ *34 13 97, 22 Chemin G Thénor*) has singles or doubles for FF250. The two gîtes cost FF2240 for a week and FF952 for a weekend.

LA-SALINE-LES-BAINS

Heading north from St-Leu, the first resort you come to is La-Saline-les-Bains. It's effectively a suburb of St-Gilles-les-Bains, but the atmosphere is more mellow than in the centre of town and there's a nice strip of beach. At the southern end of town is Trou d'Eau, a popular beach for windsurfing.

Places to Stay & Eat

Right in the middle of La-Saline-les-Bains, *Hôtel Swalibo* (☎ *24 10 97, fax 24 64 29*) on Rue des Salines is a pleasant hotel with well-appointed rooms overlooking a secluded pool. Rates start at FF450/600 for a single/double room.

L'Îlot Vert (☎ *33 92 11, fax 33 92 12*) next door offers apartments sleeping two to six people from FF350 per night. There's a pool here too.

The nicest option in town is *Le Nautile* (☎ *33 88 88, fax 33 88 89*), a stylish and intimate hotel on Rue Lacaussade (turn off the highway just by the Champion supermarket). Air-con rooms with all mod-cons start at FF660/770.

Palais de L'Orient (☎ *24 68 90*) on the highway offers cheap Chinese meals daily except Tuesday. Mains cost from FF45.

By the beach on Rue des Mouettes, the *Copacabana* (☎ *24 16 31*) is open daily during daylight hours and serves Creole grills for around FF70.

At Trou d'Eau to the south, *Le Trou d'Eau* (☎ *24 17 21*) is open daily for snack lunches and Creole dinners. Meals cost from FF55 to FF95.

ST-GILLES-LES-BAINS & L'HERMITAGE-LES-BAINS

Réunion's premier beach destination comes across as either a lively party place or an overhyped tourist-trap, depending on your perspective. Certainly at the weekends, St Gilles-les-Bains can be ridiculously overcrowded, with packed restaurants, cramped beaches and all-day traffic snarls.

However, during the week, you shouldn't have to fight for a space to lay your towel and the atmosphere is much more relaxed. As well as a nice beach, St-Gilles-les-Bains boasts an excellent selection of restaurants. There are numerous water activities on offer from diving to water-skiing. The surf here isn't bad either; many amateurs hone their skills in St-Gilles-les-Bains before attempting the more challenging swells at St-Leu.

If you find the scene in St-Gilles-les-Bains a little too much, there is a pleasantly uncrowded beach with good snorkelling at L'Hermitage-les-Bains, just south of St Gilles-les-Bains.

Orientation

Almost everything of interest in downtown St-Gilles-les-Bains is on Rue Général de Gaulle, the former coastal highway. Rue de la Plage, which provides access to the main beach at Roches Noires, is just west of the main road. South of the centre at the mouth of the river is Port de Plaisance, a modern harbour complex with some expensive restaurants, centres for diving and other water sports and a good aquarium.

Information

Tourist Offices Tourist information is available from the syndicat d'initiative known as the Office de Tourisme de l'Ouest (☎ 24 57 47, fax 24 34 40) in the Galerie Amandine in the centre of St-Gilles-les-Bains. This is one of the most helpful offices on the island and it has loads of glossy brochures, booklets and souvenirs

ST-GILLES-LES-BAINS & L'HERMITAGE-LES-BAINS

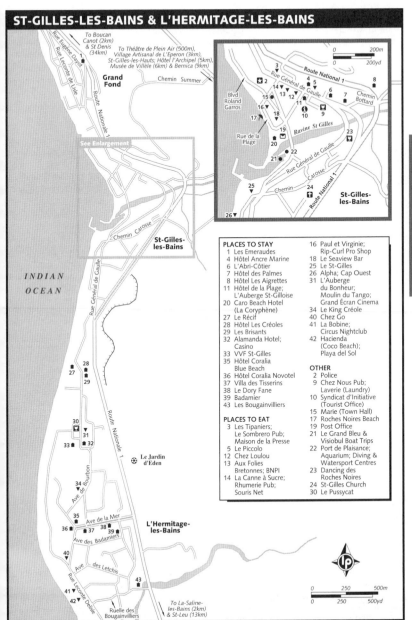

PLACES TO STAY
1 Les Emeraudes
4 Hôtel Ancre Marine
6 L'Abri-Côtier
7 Hôtel des Palmes
8 Hôtel Les Aigrettes
11 Hôtel de la Plage;
   L'Auberge St-Gilloise
20 Caro Beach Hotel
   (La Coryphène)
27 Le Récif
28 Hôtel Les Créoles
29 Les Brisants
32 Alamanda Hotel;
   Casino
33 VVF St-Gilles
35 Hôtel Coralia
   Blue Beach
36 Hôtel Coralia Novotel
37 Villa des Tisserins
38 Le Dory Fane
39 Badamier
43 Les Bougainvilliers

PLACES TO EAT
3 Les Tipaniers;
   Le Sombrero Pub;
   Maison de la Presse
5 Le Piccolo
12 Chez Loulou
13 Aux Folies
   Bretonnes; BNPI
14 La Canne à Sucre;
   Rhumerie Pub;
   Souris Net

16 Paul et Virginie;
   Rip-Curl Pro Shop
18 Le Seaview Bar
25 Le St-Gilles
26 Alpha; Cap Ouest
31 L'Auberge
   du Bonheur;
   Moulin du Tango;
   Grand Écran Cinema
34 Le King Créole
40 Chez Go
41 La Bobine;
   Circus Nightclub
42 Hacienda
   (Coco Beach);
   Playa del Sol

OTHER
2 Police
9 Chez Nous Pub;
   Laverie (Laundry)
10 Syndicat d'Initiative
   (Tourist Office)
15 Marie (Town Hall)
17 Roches Noires Beach
19 Post Office
21 Le Grand Bleu &
   Visiobul Boat Trips
22 Port de Plaisance;
   Aquarium; Diving &
   Watersport Centres
23 Dancing des
   Roches Noires
24 St-Gilles Church
30 Le Pussycat

REUNION

The office is open from 9 am to noon and 1 to 6 pm Monday; 8.30 am to 12.30 pm and 1 to 6 pm Tuesday to Friday; and from 9 am to 5 pm Saturday.

Post & Communications The main post office is near the Caro Beach Hotel; it has an ATM that accepts most credit cards. The office is open from 8 am to 4 pm weekdays and 8 to 11 am Saturday.

There are several payphones along the main street. For Internet access, Souris Net (☎ 33 26 60) in the mall by the Rhumerie Pub charges FF35 for half an hour. It's open from 9.30 am to 12.30 pm and 2 to 7 pm Monday to Saturday.

Bookshops For the latest newspapers and magazines, go to Maison de la Presse on Rue Général de Gaulle.

Aquarium
In the modern Port de Plaisance complex, the Aquarium de Réunion (☎ 33 44 00, fax 33 44 01) houses a series of extremely good underwater displays, including tanks with lobsters, barracudas, groupers and small sharks. You should probably avoid the special exhibit on shark attacks if you're planning on taking a swim! Entry is FF45 for adults and FF25 for children. Opening hours are from 10 am to 6 pm Tuesday to Sunday.

Théâtre de Plein Air
On the road between St-Gilles-les-Bains and St-Gilles-les-Hauts, the modern open-air theatre, Théâtre de Plein Air (☎ 24 47 71), is styled after Greek amphitheatres, and has the sky and ocean as a backdrop. The tourist office in town can provide a schedule of plays and other performances.

La Ravine St-Gilles
About 1km inland from the Théâtre de Plein Air, on the road to St-Gilles-les-Hauts, is a parking area and a path down to an old irrigation and water supply system. The area encompasses a stunning series of waterfalls and pools that are, from top to bottom, Bassin Malheur, Bassin des Aigrettes and Bassin du Cormoran; they're popular with swimmers.

Bassin du Cormoran, the most accessible, is reached along the lower path that cuts away from the irrigation canal about 10m from the car park. When the water level is right, the falls are excellent for swimming and provide an alternative to the beach on hot days. On weekends, the area is packed with picnickers.

Le Jardin d'Eden
The name (The Garden of Eden) may be selling it just a bit strong, but this unusual botanical garden is definitely worth a visit for anyone interested in tropical flora. Sections of the gardens are dedicated to such interesting concepts as the sacred plants of the Hindus, medicinal plants, edible tropical plants, spices and aphrodisiac plants.

Le Jardin d'Eden (☎ 33 83 16) is open from 10 am to 6 pm daily except Monday. Admission is FF30/15 for adults/children.

Water Activities
The attractive beach at Roches Noires is obviously the biggest pull at St-Gilles-les-Bains, closely followed by the surf scene. Fans of water sports should head to the Port de Plaisance complex at the mouth of the river. If beaches aren't really your thing, there are several attractions up in the hills in the direction of St-Gilles-les-Hauts.

If you fancy taking on the surf at Roches Noires, Location des Roches Noires (☎ 24 06 50) is right on the beach and rents out longboards and bodyboards for around FF40 for an hour or FF140 a day. It also offers snorkelling gear for FF20 an hour or FF80 a day. For information about local surf clubs and for other surf-related queries, go to the Rip-Curl Pro Shop on Rue de la Plage.

For more equipment-intensive water sports, head for the harbour complex. There are numerous operators here offering diving, jet-skiing, speed-boat hire, windsurfing, water-skiing and other watery activities. (See Activities in the Réunion Facts for the Visitor chapter for more information about water activities.)

Several glass-bottomed boats depart from near the aquarium. The MV *Le Grand Bleu* is a popular boat run by Croisières Découvertes

🕿 66 67 58). Cruises along the coast towards St-Leu or St-Paul take just over an hour and cost FF100 for adults and FF60 for children. Visiobul (🕿 85 23 46) offers a popular tour in an extraordinary little boat with a totally submerged glass viewing chamber. It costs FF75 for adults and FF45 for children.

Places to Stay

There's plenty of accommodation in the area, but almost everything is booked out during holiday periods and on weekends. Most of the accommodation in St-Gilles-les-Bains is actually south of the centre in L'Hermitage-les-Bains, but there are a few choices in the middle of town.

St-Gilles-les-Bains On the road down to the beach, the *Hôtel de la Plage* (🕿 24 06 37, fax 33 20 05, 20 Rue de la Plage) is a fairly hip place with nautical murals on the walls. Single rooms with fan cost FF170, air-con doubles with shared bathroom are FF180 to FF200, and air-con rooms with TV and bathroom are FF225/245 a single/double.

Above the mall in the middle of town, the *Hôtel Ancre Marine* (🕿 24 31 32, fax 24 33 85) is better than it looks from the outside. Comfortable air-con doubles are FF250, while two-bedroom apartments with kitchenette are FF350 for up to four people.

L'Abri-Côtier (🕿 24 44 64, fax 24 50 71, 129 Rue Général de Gaulle) has just a few rooms for FF180/FF200 a single/double.

The *Hôtel des Palmes* (🕿 24 47 12, fax 24 30 62) is also on Rue Général de Gaulle and offers rooms in bungalows from FF280 a double.

Right beside Roches Noires beach, the *Caro Beach Hotel* (🕿 24 42 49, fax 24 34 46), also known as La Coryphène, is a pleasant three-star place offering rooms overlooking the sea for FF610/720. Rooms without the view cost FF470/580. There's a swimming pool here.

Hôtel L'Archipel (🕿 24 05 34, fax 24 47 24) on Chemin du Théâtre is out of town on the road to St-Gilles-les-Hauts. Rooms in this attractive three-star place cost FF600/700. Breakfast is an extra FF70, and there's a nice pool and restaurant here.

The *Hôtel Les Aigrettes* (🕿 33 05 05, fax 24 30 50) is on the far side of the highway; to get here follow Chemin Bottard, which turns off Rue Général de Gaulle just before the bridge. Attractive air-con rooms cost FF280/360. It's FF60 extra for breakfast.

Les Emeraudes (🕿 24 20 20, fax 24 07 06) on Rue Eugène Dayot is on the back road between Boucan Canot and St-Gilles-les-Bains. Self-catering studios cost around FF400.

L'Hermitage-les-Bains On the main road down to L'Hermitage-les-Bains beach, *Le Dory Flane* (🕿 33 82 41, fax 33 98 52, 21 Ave de la Mer) is a popular budget option. Rooms cost FF200/250.

Nearby, *Villa Les Tisserins* (🕿 33 96 72, 25 Ave de la Mer) is a nice guesthouse with a pool. Rooms cost FF390 for two people and FF450 for four people. There is also a self-contained bungalow for FF2750 a week for two adults (children can stay for free).

In the same area, the friendly *Badamier* (🕿 33 82 79, 27 Ave des Badamiers) has simple fan-cooled units from FF180 to FF200.

Les Bougainvilliers (🕿/fax 33 82 48) on Ruelle des Bougainvilliers is a cosy guesthouse on a quiet backstreet at the other end of L'Hermitage-les-Bains. Rooms cost FF240 for one or two people and extra beds are FF60 each. There's a small pool.

A bit more upmarket, *Hôtel Les Créoles* (🕿 33 09 09, fax 33 09 19) on Ave de Bourbon is a nice three-star place with a good pool. Tidy rooms go for FF545/765.

Next door, *Les Brisants* (🕿 24 50 51, fax 24 38 85) is another holiday village, with fully equipped apartments for FF595 (maximum of four people) or FF820 (maximum of six people).

Across the road, *Le Récif* (🕿 24 50 51, fax 24 38 85) is a complex of holiday flats run by the same people as the Hôtel les Créoles. Hotel rooms are FF545/765, while self-catering flats cost FF680 for up to four people, or FF970 for up to six.

North on Ave de Bourbon, the *Alamanda Hotel* (🕿 33 10 10, fax 24 02 42) is an OK two-star place with a cheap restaurant and rooms for FF360/490/630 a single/double/triple. There's also a pool.

RÉUNION

RÉUNION

Hôtel Coralia Blue Beach (☎/*fax 24 50 25*) is a three-star place on Ave de la Mer. Comfortable slightly bland rooms are FF455/590; suites start from FF790/855. Breakfast is FF60. This hotel also has a pool and the restaurant serves French and Creole fare.

The plushest option in L'Hermitage-les-Bains is the *Hôtel Coralia Novotel* (☎ *24 44 44, fax 24 01 67*). This three-star hotel offers slightly pricey rooms from FF700/820. Breakfast is FF75 per person. Like most top-end hotels, there's a pool to splash around in, plus the usual tennis courts and restaurant.

VVF St-Gilles (☎ *24 29 39, fax 24 41 02*) is on Ave de Bourbon in L'Hermitage-les-Bains. Rooms start at FF350/540 on half board. Guests who are not members of Villages Vacances Famille must pay an annual joining fee of FF50 per family (see Accommodation in the Réunion Facts for the Visitor chapter).

Places to Eat

As the island's premier resort, St-Gilles-les-Bains is well endowed with eating places, and new restaurants are constantly coming onto the scene. Because of the continuous flow of hungry tourists, prices are higher and standards more variable than elsewhere on the island; expect to pay FF80 upwards for a meal, regardless of quality. For cheap eats, there are numerous snack-vans set up along the main street and the seafront; they serve light meals.

St-Gilles-les-Bains Right on the beach, *Le Seaview Bar* (☎ *24 43 83*) is open daily for snack meals and cocktails. Pizzas and salads cost from FF50.

Nearby, *Paul et Virginie* (☎ *33 04 53*) has fishy salads from FF40 and dishes such as *moules marinières* (mussels cooked in their own juice with onion) and steamed *bourgeois* (red snapper) ranging from FF65 to FF85.

On Rue Général de Gaulle, *Aux Folies Bretonnes* (☎ *33 02 37*) is a good Creole place with dishes such as poached prawns with vanilla for around FF90. It's open for lunch and dinner daily.

Nearby, *Chez Loulou* (☎ *24 46 36*) is a good Creole restaurant. The bakery here sells tasty samosas and sandwiches. It's closed on Sunday night, but is otherwise open for lunch and dinner.

La Canne à Sucre (☎ *24 02 56*) in the same area serves tasty Creole and French food for around FF98, and cheaper Chinese dishes from FF50. It's closed Monday.

Across the road, the atmospheric *Les Tipaniers* (☎ *24 44 87*), also known as Chez Dante, serves Creole dishes such as *civet de morue* (fish stew) from FF70.

L'Auberge Saint-Gilloise (☎ *33 17 16*) is an intimate French restaurant, open for lunch and dinner daily except Thursday. Mains go for FF90. In the evening, the owners also operate the *Pizza Sergio* van across the road; pizzas start at FF50.

Piccolo (☎ *24 51 51*) is a slightly bland-looking Italian place that offers pasta dishes from FF55. It's open for lunch and dinner daily except Thursday.

There are several expensive brasseries specialising in seafood at Port de Plaisance. *Le St-Gilles* (☎ *24 43 12*) is a favourite for swish business lunches. It has mains from FF95 and is closed Monday.

In the same area, *Cap Ouest* (☎ *33 21 56*) and *Alpha* (☎ *24 02 02*) offer similar food at similar prices. Both places are closed Monday.

L'Hermitage-les-Bains There are several excellent restaurants just off the public beach on Rue Leconte Delisle. *La Bobine* (☎ *33 94 36*) is an excellent choice, with grills and Creole dishes from FF65 to FF75. On Friday they cook up whole lambs stuffed with couscous on open fires in front of the restaurant; the delicacy costs FF80 per person.

Hacienda (☎ *33 81 43*), also known as Coco Beach, serves tasty seafood grills from FF70 to FF120. It's open every day from 6 pm until late. There is a jazz pianist on Thursday.

In the same cluster of restaurants, *Playa del Sol* (☎ *33 84 92*) serves great *gambas* (prawns) for about FF90. Couscous is served only on Friday and Saturday. The place is open for lunch and dinner daily.

Close to the beach, ***Chez Go*** (☎ *33 82 61*) is recommended for its Creole meals, which cost around FF75. It's closed Monday night and all day Tuesday.

L'Auberge du Bonheur (☎ *24 09 97*) on Ave Bourbon is a fairly uncharismatic Chinese place. Mains start at FF60 and it is closed Monday.

Nearby, ***Le King Créole*** (☎ *33 28 11*) offers pricey Creole food such as shrimps with *baie rose* (pink pepper) from FF84. It's closed Sunday and at lunch time on Thursday.

Entertainment
As one would imagine, St-Gilles-les-Bains is relatively flush with nightlife. Apart from a casino, there are discos, pubs and some music programs. For details about what's currently happening in town, ask locals or at the syndicat d'initiative.

The ***casino*** (☎ *24 47 00*) on Ave de Bourbon is open from 11 am to 2 am weekdays and from 11 am to 4 am Sunday (closed Saturday). The gambling tables (blackjack, American roulette etc) open at 10 pm and entry costs FF65.

On Ave de Bourbon is the ***Grand Écran cinema*** (☎ 24 46 66); it screens mainstream releases in French.

Three of the more well-known pubs in St-Gilles-les-Bains include ***La Rhumerie*** (☎ *24 55 99*), ***Chez Nous*** (☎ *24 08 08*) and ***Le Sombrero*** (☎ *33 03 85*).

The St-Gilles-les-Bains area has a greater density of discos than anywhere else on the island. Check the fliers posted around St-Gilles-les-Bains or ask the locals to find out which clubs are flavour of the month.

Dancing des Roches Noires (☎ *24 44 15*) on Rue Générale de Gaulle is open from 10 pm to dawn, only on Saturday.

Some of your other choices include ***Le Swing*** (☎ *24 45 98*) at Grand Fond, and ***Le Privé*** (☎ *24 07 17*) on Rue Général de Gaulle.

At L'Hermitage-les-Bains, ***Moulin du Tango*** (☎ *24 53 90*) is open from 10 pm until the wee hours of the morning every Wednesday, Friday and Saturday.

Nearby is ***Le Pussycat***, open from 11 pm Thursday, Friday and Saturday. Your other

options in L'Hermitage-les-Bains include ***Le Circus*** (☎ *33 31 46*) and ***Planet Soleil*** (☎ *33 15 00*).

Getting There & Away
Nonexpress buses between St-Denis and St-Pierre run though the centre of St-Gilles-les-Bains, stopping on Rue Général de Gaulle. The same bus also stops on the highway in L'Hermitage-les-Bains. Buses run about every half hour in either direction from 8 am to 6 pm. The trip to St-Denis takes at least an hour and costs FF22.10.

Getting Around
St-Gilles-les-Bains is a popular take-off spot for helicopter tours around the island (for details, see Air in the Réunion Getting Around chapter).

For details on car and bicycle hire in the St-Gilles-les-Bains area, see the Réunion Getting Around chapter.

BOUCAN CANOT
Just north of St-Gilles-les-Bains, Boucan Canot boasts a great beach and good surf. It's a popular spot for day-trippers so you may struggle to find a parking spot at weekends. Boucan Canot is a more exclusive address than St-Gilles-les-Bains and there are few budget places to stay or eat. All the big hotels have restaurants, or you could always pop down the road to St-Gilles-les-Bains. Camping is possible at several points on the coast just north of Boucan Canot.

Places to Stay
The intimate, family-run ***Hôtel La Villa Du Soleil*** (☎ *24 38 69, fax 24 39 09, 54 Route de Boucan Canot*) is on the back road between Boucan Canot and St-Gilles-les-Bains. This friendly hotel has a small pool and well-kept singles/doubles with air-con, TV and bathroom for FF250/290. Breakfast costs FF30 per person.

Right by the public beach, ***La Résidence les Boucaniers*** (☎ *24 23 89, fax 24 46 95*) offers a variety of well-maintained self-catering apartments. Studios are FF370/420 for two/three people; air-con apartments cost FF520/630 for four/five people. Rates go up by FF20 at the weekend. Curiously, this place is closed every Monday.

Very close to Boucan Canot beach, *Le Boucan-Canot* (☎ *24 41 20, fax 24 02 77*) used to be a good mid-range option, but it's currently being redeveloped and prices are likely to reflect the hotel's new, grander status. Call the hotel for more information.

Right on the beach, the *Hôtel Maharani* (☎ *33 06 06, fax 24 32 97*) probably comes closest to the tropical vision. This upmarket hotel has a distinctly Indian flavour, with plenty of decorative Indian fittings. Standard singles/doubles go for FF875/1080, or much swisher deluxe rooms are FF1190/1430. Facilities include a swimming pool, hot spa and a well-regarded Indian restaurant (see the following Places to Eat section).

Towards St-Gilles-les-Bains, *Le Saint-Alexis* (☎ *24 42 04, fax 24 00 13, 44 Route de Boucan Canot*) sits right on the beach, but is slightly lacking in character. Doubles start from around FF1000 (all rooms have a hot spa). Decadent touches include a swimming pool and a swish restaurant (see the following Places to Eat section).

Up on the hillside behind Les Coquillages shopping centre is *Grand Hôtel des Mascareignes* (☎ *24 36 24, fax 24 37 24*). Rooms cost FF730/790 or FF1090/1190 for rooms looking out to sea. There are all the usual extras, including a tennis court, swimming pool, snack bar and restaurant.

Places to Eat

There are only a few options in Boucan Canot; your best bet for a meal is to head for St-Gilles-les-Bains.

Beside the beach, *Le Victory* (☎ *24 47 74*) serves up seafood mains and tasty Creole favourites from FF79 to FF120. It's open for lunch and dinner daily except Thursday night.

The restaurant *Grand Hunier* at Le Saint-Alexis (see the earlier Places to Stay section) is open for lunch and dinner daily and offers a luxurious menu of Creole and métro cuisine. Most mains will cost around FF145. Nonresidents should call ahead.

At the Hôtel Maharani (see Places to Stay), Le Tandjore is an elegant Indian restaurant that looks out over the ocean. There is an Indian buffet with traditional dance on Friday, and a Creole buffet with maloya and séga dance performances on Thursday. The cost is 190FF. Nonresidents should book ahead. (For information on these dances, see Arts in the Réunion Facts for the Visitor chapter.)

ST-GILLES-LES-HAUTS & AROUND

The peaceful village of St-Gilles-les-Hauts, 6km uphill from St-Gilles-les-Bains, offers a refreshing break from the commercialism of the coast. There are some interesting attractions in the area, most notably the mountain peak of Le Maïdo, which offers stunning views and good hiking into the Cirque de Mafate. There are several options for accommodation in the small hamlets that dot the hillside above St-Gilles-les-Hauts.

Village Artisanal de L'Eperon

Housed in a picturesque old grist mill in the village of L'Eperon, the Village Artisanal de L'Eperon (☎ *22 73 01*) is now home to an informal community of artisans. Among the *objets d'art* on offer are ceramics, locally tanned leather, and lampshades made from palm fronds.

Also in the Village Artisanal is the restaurant *La Citerne* (☎ *55 52 70*), which serves Creole mains from FF70 to FF90. It's open daily except Monday.

The only public transport to L'Eperon is the infrequent short-haul bus that travels between Grand Fond and Trois Bassins, passing through L'Eperon along the way.

Musée de Villèle

South of St-Gilles-les-Hauts on route D6, the Musée de Villèle (☎ *55 64 10*) is housed in the former home of the wealthy and very powerful Mme Panon-Desbassyns (the name originated because the family's turf surrounded the *bassins* or lakes above St-Gilles-les-Bains). She was a coffee and sugar baroness who, among other things, held 300 slaves. Legend has it that she was a cruel woman and that her tormented screams can still be heard from the hellish fires whenever the volcano is erupting. She died in 1846 and her body lies in the Chapelle Pointue, which lies on the eastern side of route D6.

A bit further, on the other side of the road, is Mme Panon-Desbassyns' house and the ruins of the sugar mill. You can take a guided tour of the mansion, which was built in 1787 (the tours are narrated in French only). The caretakers conduct a lightning tour, unlocking and locking doors as you proceed. Exhibits include a clock presented to the Desbassyns by Napoleon; a set of china from Mauritius featuring *Paul et Virginie,* the love story by Bernardin de St Pierre (see the boxed text 'Paul & Virginie' in the North Mauritius chapter); a commemoration of the Réunion-born aviator Roland Garros (1888–1915); an English cannonball (a memento of British rule!); a collection of French East India Company furniture and china; and a Gobelin tapestry depicting Christ.

The well-preserved mansion is open from 9.30 am to noon and 2 to 5 pm daily except Tuesday. Admission costs FF10 per person; buy your ticket in the kiosk in the car park. You can get here on Car Jaune bus D, which runs from St-Denis to Chaloupe St-Leu.

Le Maïdo & Around

Far above St-Gilles-les-Bains on the rim of the Cirque de Mafate, Le Maïdo is one of the most impressive viewpoints in Réunion. The lookout is perched atop the mountain peak at 2204m and offers superb views over Le Gros Morne (2991m), Piton des Neiges (3069m) and Le Grand Bénare (2896m) as well as down into the cirque itself.

The name Le Maïdo comes from a Malagasy word meaning 'burnt land', and is most likely a reference to the burnt appearance of the scrub forest at this altitude. The peak is the starting point for the tough walk along the cirque rim to the summit of Le Grand Bénare, another impressive lookout (allow at least six hours for the return trip). As with other viewpoints, you should arrive early in the day if you want to see anything other than cloud.

Hikers can also descend from here into the Cirque de Mafate via the Sentier de Roche Plate, which meets the GR R2 variant that connects the villages of Roche Plate and Îlet des Orangiers (allow two to three hours to reach Roche Plate). Ambitious walkers can head in the direction of Îlet des Orangiers, following the Rivière des Galets down to the hamlet of Sans Souci near Le Port. However, there are no convenient gîtes along this route. To make a two-day trip of it without camping, you'll need to detour to Cayenne on the other side of the gorge.

The sealed route forestière du Maïdo winds all the way up to the viewpoint from Le Guillaume in the hills above St-Gilles-les-Bains, offering a long but scenic drive. It's not recommended that you leave your car here overnight.

Places to Stay & Eat

Mme Maillot (☎ 55 69 83) offers a chambre d'hôte at the far end of the Village Artisanal compound in L'Eperon. Singles/doubles cost FF180/210 including breakfast. Meals cost a steep FF110 per person.

Also in the Village Artisanal is the restaurant *La Citerne* (☎ 55 52 70), which serves Creole mains from FF70 to FF90. It's open daily except Monday.

Mme Ramassamy (☎ 55 55 06) on Chemin des Roses in Villèle has a chambre d'hôte with rooms for FF150/200. The table d'hôte costs FF100 per person. Take the road opposite the Chapelle Pointue.

Above St-Gilles-les-Hauts in Bernica, *Mme Grondin* (☎ 22 74 15) offers homely chambres d'hôte for FF175/200 including breakfast. The house is just off route D4.

Also in Bernica is *Mme Ramincoupin* (☎ 55 69 13), who has a chambre d'hôte on Chemin Bosse. She charges FF250 for singles or doubles, and offers a table d'hôte for FF100 per person.

Above Bernica in La Petite France, *Mme R Magdeleine* (☎ 32 53 50) on Chemin l'Ecole offers chambres d'hôte for FF150/200, a gîte for FF1904 a week (FF1120 per weekend) and a table d'hôte for FF80 per head. To get here, take route D7 to Guillaume and follow the Route du Maïdo.

RÉUNION

Outside La Petite France on the Route du Maïdo, *M Lougnon* (☎ 32 44 26) has chambres d'hôte for FF250 a double, two gîtes for FF2250 a week (FF1200 a weekend) and another gîte for FF1500 (FF800 a weekend).

In Bernica, there's an *Auberge de Jeunesse* (☎ 22 89 75) on Rue de l'Auberge. The cost for Hostelling International (HI) members in dorm beds is FF75. Breakfast is FF10 and dinner is available from FF50. Membership costs FF100 or FF70 if you are under 26 years of age.

Up in the hills on Route du Maïdo, *Parc Hôtel du Maïdo* (☎ 32 52 52, fax 32 52 00) offers accommodation in cosy bungalows for FF245/360. The hotel's restaurant, *Les Tamarins*, has a panoramic view of the coast and offers good Creole dishes for around FF85. There's an afternoon buffet on Sunday for FF130.

ST-PAUL

St-Paul is Réunion's second largest settlement, but it's more a place for locals than for tourists. The town was once the capital of Réunion, but these days it seems to have been left behind by the other towns along the coast. Most people come here to visit the Cimetière Marin, which lies on the highway at the south end of town, but only a few venture into the town itself.

Across the highway is the *grotte des premiers Français* (cave of the first French), a cave said to have sheltered the mutineers who arrived in Réunion in 1646, the first Frenchmen to settle on the island.

The shopping streets in the centre of St-Paul are fairly unremarkable, but there are a few relics from the town's past on the seafront promenade.

The market is held on Friday evening and Saturday morning and features stalls selling the usual Malagasy handicrafts. The market in St-Denis has a better selection.

Cimetière Marin

The only real attraction in St-Paul is the bright and well-kept cemetery at the southern end of town, which contains the remains of various famous Réunionnais, including the poet Leconte de Lisle (1818–94). The graves are clearly marked and signposted, making them easy to find.

The cemetery's star guest, however, is the pirate Olivier 'La Buse' Levasseur (The Buzzard), who was the scourge of the Indian Ocean from about 1720 to 1730, when he was captured, taken to St-Paul and hanged. His biggest catch was the Portuguese treasure ship *La Vierge du Cap;* people are still searching for the location of La Buse's treasure in Mauritius, Réunion and the Seychelles. The grave is marked by the pirates' trademark skull and crossbones, and it is usually covered with *remerciement* (thank you) plaques, cigarettes and glasses of rum, deposited by superstitious Réunionnais as part of black magic rituals.

Another interesting grave is that of Eraste Feuillet (1801–30), who died because he took a sense of remorse too far. The young sea captain accidentally struck a passer-by with an empty toilet-water bottle that he threw from his hotel room window (perhaps forgetting he was on dry land). The irate passer-by challenged Feuillet to a duel, but fortunately, his pistol jammed. Less fortunately, Feuillet had a sense of honour and offered his own weapon as a replacement – and the bugger accepted it! Feuillet's epitaph reads very simply 'Victime de sa générosité' ('Victim of his generosity').

Places to Stay & Eat

St-Paul doesn't really cater to overnight visitors. If you're killing time waiting for a bus, there are some cheap cafes around the bus station.

The restaurant *La Forgerie de la Baie* (☎ 45 57 17, fax 45 60 71) on Blvd du Front de Mer (the seafront) has a few single/double rooms for FF260/350. The Creole meals here cost around FF70. The restaurant is open daily for lunch, and from Tuesday to Saturday for dinner.

La Baie des Pirates (☎ 45 23 23) on the highway is a funky theme restaurant offering excellent seafood grills which cost around FF80. It is open Tuesday to Saturday for lunch, and Monday to Saturday for dinner.

Getting There & Away

St-Paul lies on the St-Denis to St-Pierre bus route and there are departures more or less half hourly from the gare routière in either town (FF16.80). If you just want to go to the cemetery, there's a bus stop immediately in front of the cemetery entrance, two stops on from the gare routière in St-Paul.

LE PORT & LA POSSESSION

The motorway known as La Corniche hugs the cliffs from St-Denis to La Possession, before cutting across the coastal plain to St-Paul. Most tourists zip by La Possession without even knowing it's there. They aren't missing much, as this industrial area is effectively an extension of Réunion's main port, which is appropriately known as Le Port. You may have to travel to Le Port if you are catching the boat from Réunion to Mauritius.

Getting There & Away

The terminal for passenger ferries to Mauritius is at Port Est in Le Port, but there are no bus services directly to the terminal. Nonexpress buses between St-Denis and St-Pierre (FF10.10) stop at the Port Est roundabout (ask the driver to let you off here, from where it's a 1km walk to the terminal building). Unless you're really watching the pennies, you're better off investing in a taxi (FF100 from St-Denis).

There is a small tourist information desk at the terminal, open only for arriving ferries, and a few vending-machines with soft drinks and snacks, but there are no other facilities for tourists. There is no bank here so make sure you change some money into francs before you leave. Taxis sometimes come to meet the ferries, but they will not hang around if the boat is delayed. The local firm Taxi Esther (☎ 86 35 10) operates taxis 24 hours a day.

DOS D'ANE

The isolated village of Dos d'Ane, in the hills above La Possession, is another excellent base for walks in the interior. From here you can walk to the Plaine d'Affouches and La Roche Écrite, as well as into the Cirque de Mafate via the Rivière des Galets route. An easy day's walk from Dos d'Ane will get you to the gîte de montagne at Grand Place, while a magnificent but more challenging route will take you up the beautiful Bras des Merles to Aurère.

Places to Stay & Eat

Le Galet Rond (☎/fax 32 01 56) on Rue Germain Elisabeth is a small hotel with double rooms for FF240 with a bathroom (or FF220 without a bathroom). There's a large, somewhat characterless *restaurant*; the Creole set menu is FF90 per person.

Auberge de Marie-Claire (☎ 32 00 04, 2 Allée Vivien) is another informal guesthouse; the going rate for singles/doubles is FF180/220.

M Nativel (☎ 32 01 47) on Rue Germain Elisabeth offers chambres d'hôte for FF230 a double, or beds in the gîte d'étape for FF75. Meals cost FF85. This place is a good cheap option for hikers hoping to walk from Dos d'Ane.

Getting There & Away

Unfortunately, there's no public transport to Dos d'Ane, so those without a vehicle will have to take a taxi from the small town of Rivière des Galets, which lies along the St-Denis to St-Pierre bus route.

The Interior

The interior of the island was first settled by runaway slaves, and their descendants still inhabit some of the wild remote villages in the inaccessible regions of the cirques. If the coast seems a little too close to mainland France, the interior is where you'll find the real identity of Réunion.

This rugged region is a tremendous tramping ground, with breathtaking mountain scenery and the opportunity to indulge in whatever kind of adventure sport takes your fancy. It's up to you how far you take the thrills and spills of course; if abseiling down a waterfall seems too much like hard work, there are dozens of easy walks where you can just soak up the awe-inspiring environment around you. (For detailed information on hiking in the interior, see the special section 'Hiking in Réunion'. For information on the other adventure activities on offer in the interior, see also Activities in the Réunion Facts for the Visitor chapter.)

The Cirques

Like the leaves of a three-leaf clover, the cirques of Cilaos, Salazie and Mafate dominate the heart of the island. Although they superficially resemble volcanic craters, they are actually the product of the same erosional forces that sharpened the peak of the Matterhorn in Switzerland.

The whole island was once the dome of a vast prehistoric shield volcano, centred on Piton des Neiges, but the collapse of subterranean lava chambers formed the starting point for the creation of the cirques. Millions of years of rainfall and erosion did the rest, scouring out the amphitheatres that are visible today.

Even if you don't fancy hiking through the cirques, it's worth taking a road trip through these amazing amphitheatres just for the views. Whether you come by bus or private car, you will have to negotiate a hair-raising series of corkscrew turns, nar-

HIGHLIGHTS

- Exploring the intriguing cirques of Cilaos, Salazie and Mafate
- Dipping into the *sources thermales* (thermal springs) in Cilaos to relieve those aching muscles
- Splashing under the towering Cascade du Voile de la Mariée falls near Hell-Bourg

row tunnels, hairpin bends and precarious viaducts. The locals treat these roads like mountain motorways, so be prepared to pull over and let others whiz past.

The landscape here is other-worldly and surreal, sometimes revealed in all its breathtaking splendour and other times hidden by swirling banks of cloud. If you see a photo opportunity, snap it up immediately; the chances are it will be enveloped in cloud if you wait even a few minutes.

The cirques were first settled by escaped slaves or *marrons* (see the boxed text 'Marrons' following), who were later followed by families from Normandy and Brittany. The atmosphere in these communities is quite different from the cosmopolitan vibe on the coast.

CIRQUE DE CILAOS
Cilaos

The biggest settlement in any of the cirques is Cilaos, high in the cirque of the same name, which developed as a spa resort at the end of the 19th century. The thermal baths fell out of favour some time ago, but the bottled mineral water industry and the growing interest in hiking have revived the town's fortunes.

The name, pronounced see-**la**-oos, is thought to be derived from the Malagasy term *tsy laosana* (place from which one never returns). These days, most people come to Cilaos to leave the town, on foot, for the cirques of Cilaos, Mafate and Salazie. (For detailed information on short walks and

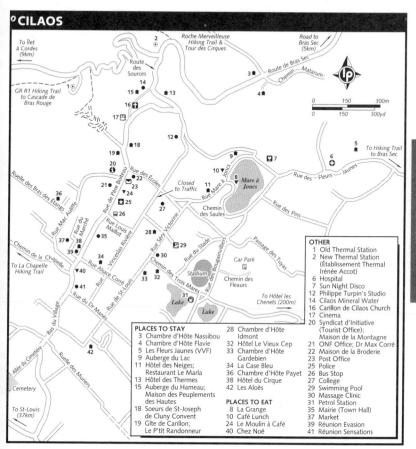

°CILAOS

To Îlet à Cordes (9km)

GR R1 Hiking Trail to Cascade de Bras Rouge

Roche Merveilleuse Hiking Trail & Tour des Cirques

Road to Bras Sec (5km)

Route des Sources

Route de Bras Sec

Chemin – Matarum

To Hiking Trail to Bras Sec

Ruelle des Bras des Étangs

Rue de Père Boiteau

Rue des Écoles

Closed to Traffic

Rue Mare à Joncs

Mare à Joncs

Rue des – Fleurs Jaunes

Rue des Pins

Chemin des Saules

Passage des Tuyas

Rue Mac Auliffe

Chemin de la Chapelle

To La Chapelle Hiking Trail

Rue du Marché

Rue Louis Maillot

Rue Séry Victorine

Vincendas Rivière

Rue des Bougainvilliers

Rue du Stade

Chemin des Trois Mares

Rue Alsace Corré

Rue de St-Louis

Stadium

Car Park

Chemin des Fleaurs

To Hôtel les Chenets (200m)

Lake

Lake

Bas du Village

Rue du Dr Manès

Allée du Cimetière

Ruelle des Muriers

Cemetery

To St-Louis (37km)

0   150   300m
0   150   300yd

PLACES TO STAY
3 Chambre d'Hôte Nassibou
4 Chambre d'Hôte Flavie
5 Les Fleurs Jaunes (VVF)
9 Auberge du Lac
11 Hôtel des Neiges; Restaurant Le Marla
13 Hôtel des Thermes
15 Auberge du Hameau; Maison des Peuplements des Hautes
18 Soeurs de St-Joseph de Cluny Convent
19 Gîte de Carillon; Le P'tit Randonneur

28 Chambre d'Hôte Idmont
32 Hôtel Le Vieux Cep
33 Chambre d'Hôte Gardebien
34 La Case Bleu
36 Chambre d'Hôte Payet
38 Hôtel du Cirque
42 Les Aloès

PLACES TO EAT
8 La Grange
10 Café Lunch
24 Le Moulin à Café
40 Chez Noë

OTHER
1 Old Thermal Station
2 New Thermal Station (Établissement Thermal Irénée Accot)
6 Hospital
7 Sun Night Disco
12 Philippe Turpin's Studio
14 Cilaos Mineral Water
16 Carillon de Cilaos Church
17 Cinema
20 Syndicat d'Initiative (Tourist Office); Maison de la Montagne
21 ONF Office; Dr Max Corré
22 Maison de la Broderie
23 Post Office
25 Police
26 Bus Stop
27 College
29 Swimming Pool
30 Massage Clinic
31 Petrol Station
35 Mairie (Town Hall)
37 Market
39 Réunion Evasion
41 Réunion Sensations

RÉUNION

---

longer hikes around Cilaos and the cirques, see the special section 'Hiking in Réunion').

The area is known for the production of lentils, local embroidery and sweet red and white wines reminiscent of sherry and tawny port. The population here is mostly descended from settlers from Brittany and Normandy, so the French atmosphere can be quite pronounced.

Orientation Rue de Père Boiteau, which runs to the tourist office, is the main shopping street, with a supermarket, a pharmacy, a post office and several restaurants.

The Carillon de Cilaos church is the main landmark; on foggy days the illuminated blue cross on the spire forms a beacon for hikers. There is a big clump of places to stay and eat near the Mare à Joncs, Cilaos' biggest lake.

The various hiking routes all begin north of town, where Route des Sources meets the Îlet à Cordes and Bras Sec roads.

Information Cilaos' *syndicat d'initiative* (tourist office), known as the Office de Tourisme de Cilaos (☎ 31 78 03, fax 31 70 30), is at the corner of Rue Mac Auliffe and Rue de Père Boiteau. This office is particularly

Marrons

Perhaps from a sense of shame, there is little mention made in Réunion of the earliest settlers of the rugged interior of the island. During the 18th century, a number of resourceful Malagasy and African slaves escaped from their owners and forged the first inroads into this unforgiving environment. Some of them established private utopias in inaccessible parts of the cirques, while others grouped together and formed organised communities with democratically elected leaders.

Sadly this sense of liberty was to be short lived. Most of the renegades or *marrons* were hunted down and captured or killed by bounty hunters such as François Mussard, lending their names to the locations where they made their last stands, such as Mafate and Enchaing.

The Maison du Peuplement des Hauts in Cilaos does something to redress the balance, celebrating the achievements of these unsung heroes of the cirques.

helpful, with numerous brochures, and the staff can speak English and other foreign languages. It's open Monday to Saturday from 8.30 am to 12.20 pm and 1.30 to 5.30 pm, and Sunday from 9 am to 1 pm. This is also the Cilaos headquarters for Maison de la Montagne (☎ 31 71 71, fax 31 80 54), which will book *gîtes de montagne* (mountain lodges) and provide hiking information.

There aren't any banks in Cilaos, but fortunately there's an ATM at the post office if you run out of francs while stocking up for your hike.

There are several doctors in town if you pull something while hiking. One option is Dr Max Corré (☎ 31 71 72) on Rue Mac Auliffe. Masseurs Gary Swaenpoël and Christine Navarro (☎ 31 72 07) run a private clinic at 1 Chemin des Trois Mares on weekdays from 2.30 to 5 pm.

Sources Thermales The *sources thermales* (thermal springs) of Cilaos were first brought to the attention of the outside world in 1815 by a goat hunter from St-Louis, M Paulin

Técher. A track into the cirque was constructed in 1842, paving the way for the development of Cilaos as a colonial health spa. The spring is heated by volcanic chambers far below the surface, and the water contains bicarbonate of soda with traces of magnesium, iron, calcium, sulphur and a weak radioactivity. It's said to cure rheumatism, among other bone and muscular ailments.

The first thermal station was opened in 1896, but the source was ruined in a cyclone in 1948 and the spa closed down. The project was revived in 1971, only to close in 1987 because of damage to the buildings from the chemicals in the spa water. The latest incarnation of the Cilaos spa is the Établissement Thermal Irénée Accot (☎ 31 72 27, fax 31 76 57) at the north end of town, which is open Monday to Saturday from 8 am to noon and 2 to 6 pm (closed Wednesday afternoon) and on Sunday from 9 am to 5 pm.

All manner of health treatments are offered, from *aérobains* (spas) and hydromassage (with jets of spring water) to traditional hands-on shiatsu. A 15-minute shiatsu massage costs FF70, a hydromassage is FF110, or you can pay FF530 for the full monty, with massages, water therapy and a sauna. Perfect for relaxing after your hike!

Maison de la Broderie The originator of Cilaos' embroidery tradition was Angèle Mac Auliffe, the daughter of the town's first doctor of thermal medicine. Looking for a pastime to fill the long, damp days in the cirque, Angèle established the first embroidery workshop with 20 women producing what later evolved into a distinctive Cilaos style of embroidery.

The present school and workshop was set up by the Sisters of Nôtre-Dame-des-Neiges convent in 1953. The nearby Maison de la Broderie or Embroidery House (☎ 31 77 48, fax 31 80 54), on Rue des Écoles, provides a venue for both teachers and students. Here, they embroider and sell children's clothes, serviettes, place settings and tablecloths. The centre is open Monday to Saturday from 9.30 am to noon and 2 to 5 pm, and on Sunday from 9.30 am to noon. Admission (including a guided tour) costs FF5 per person.

Maison du Peuplement des Hauts

Close to the town's church, downstairs from the Auberge du Hameau, this enigmatic 'eco museum' (☎/fax 31 88 01) is dedicated to the marrons who first settled the unforgiving landscape of the cirques. The displays are interesting and informative and provide a much needed monument to the unsung Creole heroes of Réunion (see the boxed text 'Marrons' earlier in this chapter). It's open daily except Tuesday from 10 am to 12.30 pm and 2.30 to 6 pm; entry costs FF30.

Philippe Turpin's Studio
Philippe Turpin is a printmaker whose studio (☎ 31 73 64) is open to the public. (For more information about his work, see Arts in the Facts about Réunion chapter.)

Places to Stay
Cilaos is well endowed with accommodation options, but it can become crowded during the tourist season – for peace of mind, you're advised to book ahead.

Hostels If you're really watching the pennies, the convent run by the *Soeurs de St-Joseph de Cluny* (☎ 31 71 22, 80 Rue du Père Boiteau) offers dorm beds for FF50 per person. You'll need to bring your own sleeping bag.

The rather ageing *Auberge du Hameau* (☎ 31 70 94, 5 Chemin Séminaire) is above the Maison du Peuplement des Hauts and offers single/double rooms on full board only for FF230/338.

The *Auberge du Lac* (☎ 31 76 30, 13 Rue Mare à Joncs) is right beside the Mare à Joncs and offers just a few rooms for FF200 a double, plus FF30 per person for breakfast.

Villages Vacances Familles (VVF) You'll need to join the VVF to stay at *Les Fleurs Jaunes* (☎ 31 71 39, fax 31 80 85), on Rue des Fleurs Jaunes behind the hospital. Rooms cost from FF350/540 per single/double on half board. The VVF annual membership fee is FF50 per family; non-members may join on the spot.

Chambres d'Hôte & Gîtes Close to the centre, *M Idmont* (☎ 31 72 47, 9 Rue Séry Victorine*) offers comfortable chambres d'hôte for FF220 a double; the table d'hôte meal service is an extra FF100.

Nearby, *Mme Gardebien* (☎ 31 72 15, 50 Rue St-Louis*) offers a business-like chambre d'hôte with single/double rooms for FF150/200; meals are FF90.

Close to the church, the *Gîte de Carillon* (☎ 31 82 88) is a private *gîte d'étape* (privately run mountain lodge) with clean dorm beds for FF75 and meals for FF65.

La Case Bleu (☎ 31 77 88, 15 Rue Alsace Corré*) is a youth-oriented gîte d'étape run by the hiking store Réunion Evasion. Beds cost FF80 per person.

M Payet (☎ 31 77 99) near the tourist office offers OK chambres d'hôte for FF225/250. The table d'hôte is FF100.

Mme Nassibou (☎ 31 71 77) offers accommodation right by the junction of Route de Bras Sec and Chemin Matarum. Chambres d'hôte cost FF150 for a single or double, or there are beds in the gîte d'étape for FF60 per person. Meals costs FF75.

Just downhill in an alley off Chemin Matarum, *Mme Flavie* (☎ 31 72 23) offers chambres d'hôte for FF120/160. Meals are FF100.

Hotels The *Hôtel des Neiges* (☎ 31 72 33, fax 31 72 98) on Rue Mare à Joncs is a very pleasant budget hotel. Appealing wooden rooms with bathroom cost from FF160 for a single or a double (FF185 with breakfast). Swisher rooms in the new block cost from FF210 (FF270 with breakfast).

The friendly *Les Aloès* (☎ 31 81 00, fax 31 87 86) on Rue de St-Louis offers cosy heated doubles with TV and bathroom for FF380.

Hôtel du Cirque (☎ 31 70 68, fax 31 80 46) is right on the main drag, Rue de Père Boiteau. Slightly ordinary rooms cost FF340/370 including breakfast.

Much better is the very upmarket *Hôtel Le Vieux Cep* (☎ 31 71 89, fax 31 77 68, 2 Chemin des Trois Mares*), which has a nice pool and offers comfortable rooms from FF470/500 including breakfast.

At the far end of Chemin des Trois Mares, the colourful *Hôtel les Chenets*

RÉUNION

(☎ *31 85 85, fax 31 87 17*) is an upmarket place with a pool and restaurant. Rooms start at FF500/630 including breakfast. Dinner is FF150 extra.

Built in 1936, the historic ***Hôtel des Thermes*** (☎ *31 89 00, fax 31 74 73, 8 Route des Sources*) is the oldest hotel in Cilaos. The cheapest rooms are FF310/360, or you can pay FF540/600 for the best rooms in the house.

Places to Eat Cilaos is noted for its lentils and home-made sweet wine. You'll get lentils with most meals, particularly at the chambres and tables d'hôte, and probably a sip of the wine too. Bottles of *vin de Cilaos* are also available from the tourist office or streetside vendors for about FF30.

A popular cheapie is the restaurant at the ***Auberge du Hameau*** (see Places to Stay), which offers Creole meals from FF50. It's open from 12.15 to 1.30 pm for lunch and 7 to 8 pm for dinner.

Le Petit Randonneur (☎ *31 79 55*) offers lunches only from FF50. It's open every day except Wednesday.

Beside the Mare à Joncs, ***Auberge du Lac*** (see Places to Stay) offers tasty *plats du jour* (daily specials) from FF60. This popular place is open daily for lunch and dinner except Sunday evening and Monday.

Nearby, ***Café Lunch*** offers very cheap Creole lunches for FF40 to FF60. It's closed on Wednesday.

Just down the road, ***Le Marla*** at the Hôtel des Neiges (see Places to Stay) offers homey Creole meals such as *rougaille saucisse* (tomato-based sauce with sausages) and *achards des legumes* (pickled vegetable salad) for around FF70. It's open daily for lunch and dinner.

Run by the same owners, ***La Grange*** occupies a picturesque location by the Mare à Joncs. It's open every evening except Wednesday for upmarket Creole food. Mains start at FF80.

On Rue de Père Boiteau, ***Le Moulin a Café*** (☎ *31 80 80*) is a pleasant little Creole and *métro* (mainland French) style place open daily except Friday for lunch and dinner. Mains cost from FF65.

Further along Rue de Père Boiteau, ***Chez Noë*** (☎ *31 79 93*) offers Creole favourites such as *carri poulet* (chicken curry) for around FF60. The atmosphere is better than the food. It's open daily except Monday for lunch and dinner.

The ***Hôtel du Cirque*** (see Places to Stay) has a broad menu with Creole, Chinese and French mains from FF75. It's open every day for lunch and dinner.

The plush restaurant at the ***Hôtel des Thermes*** (see Places to Stay) is a nice place to treat yourself after a few days of hiking in the cirques. Métro dishes start at FF100 (the set lunch is cheaper at FF98). This place is open every lunch time and evening.

The ***Hôtel Le Vieux Cep*** (see Places to Stay) has the nicest restaurant in town, with excellent Creole dishes from FF90. It's open daily for lunch and dinner.

Entertainment If you want to catch a movie, there's a small ***cinema*** (☎ *31 73 25*) opposite the church, which is only open on Saturday night (entry FF15). Beside the lake, the ***Sun Night*** disco (☎ *31 87 98*) is open from Friday to Sunday till late (entry FF60).

Shopping There are two excellent outdoor suppliers in town who can provide everything you need for a hike. Réunion Sensations (☎ *31 84 84*) on Rue de Père Boiteau is well stocked and also offers an excellent program of canyoning trips (prices start at FF230/430 for a half/full day).

Réunion Evasion (☎ *31 83 57*) across the road has an impressive supply of outdoor gear including climbing equipment and spares for *vélos tout terrain* (mountain bikes, also known as VTTs). It also rents out sleeping bags for FF40 per day.

Getting There & Away Cilaos is 112km from St-Denis by road and 37km from the nearest coastal town, St-Louis. The road through the cirque is magnificent, but hair raising in sections, particularly when you see the way the locals drive it! Before the road was built, visitors to the cirque had to walk from Le Pavillon, where the road crosses the Bras de Cilaos (wealthier visitors were carried up the valley by palanquin!).

Buses from St-Pierre to Cilaos run via St-Louis, so you can save time if you're coming from St-Denis by changing here. There are about six buses daily between St-Pierre and Cilaos (FF16), with half the number of services on Sunday. The last service to Cilaos leaves St-Pierre at 5.15 pm; going in the reverse direction, the last bus leaves Cilaos at 4 pm.

Buses leave Cilaos for Bras Sec about once an hour (only four buses on Sunday) from 7.30 am to 7.30 pm (FF6.50). The last bus back to Cilaos leaves at 4 pm, but it's only an hour's walk back to Cilaos if you miss it.

For Îlet à Cordes there are buses every two hours (only three buses on Sunday) from 7.20 am to 7.05 pm (FF6.50). Don't miss the last bus back at 4 pm. Another option for Îlet à Cordes is the transfer service offered by the Société Cilaosienne de Transport (☎ 31 85 87), which costs FF40 for two people.

Getting Around Outdoor suppliers Réunion Sensations (☎ 31 84 84) and Réunion Evasion (☎ 31 83 57), both on Rue de Père Boiteau, rent out mountain bikes for about FF80/110 for a half/full day.

Mr Grondin, meet Mr Grondin

The first French settlers in the cirques were a handful of families from Normandy and Brittany, who brought many of their local traditions, as well as their surnames, with them. This tiny group went on to populate the entire area, a fact that becomes obvious when you look at the tiny range of surnames in the cirques; in some villages, almost every resident is called Payet, Grondin, Houroau or Bégue. People on the coast may spread uncharitable rumours to explain the closed nature of these communities; in fact, most of the cirque-dwellers like their peace and quiet, and have no interest in coming down to the hectic seaside strip!

Around Cilaos

Staying in the middle of Cilaos is handy for the restaurants and activities in town, but for hikers who want to get a head start, Îlet à Cordes or Bras Sec make good bases.

Bras Sec Near the river in Bras Sec, *Mme Boyer* (☎ 25 77 61) runs a friendly little chambre d'hôte, with rooms for FF170 a double (FF190 with breakfast). Other meals cost a very reasonable FF60.

Just beyond the church on the main road, *M Jean-Paul Dijoux* (☎ 31 72 73, 29 Chemin Saül) has a gîte d'étape for FF90 per person including breakfast; meals are an extra FF100.

A bit further south, *M Christian Dijoux* (☎ 25 56 64, 40 Chemin Saül) offers chambres d'hôte for FF220 for a single or double; meals are FF100.

Îlet à Cordes Chambres d'hôte are available from *Mme Payet* (☎ 35 18 13, 13 Chemin Terre Fine) in Îlet à Cordes for FF200/220, and the table d'hôte is FF100 per person.

Nearby is a chambre d'hôte run by *M Grondin* (☎ 25 38 57), who charges FF220 a double, and who also has dorm beds in a gîte d'étape for FF100.

CIRQUE DE SALAZIE

The Cirque de Salazie, the wettest of the three cirques, is busier and more varied than the Cirque de Cilaos. It's a bit 'flatter' (although 'flat' is not the first word that will spring to mind when you see it!), but the scenery as you approach is nearly as awesome. The name is thought to derive from the Malagasy word *salazane*, which means 'sentry stakes'.

(For detailed information on the Tour des Cirques, a hiking route that takes in the Cirque de Salazie, see the special section 'Hiking in Réunion'.)

Salazie

The village from which the Cirque de Salazie takes its name lies at the eastern entrance to the cirque. You'll have to change buses here if you're heading up to Hell-Bourg, but otherwise there's not much to see, and there are no places to stay. The post office here has an ATM which accepts major international credit cards.

Tourist Office The Syndicat d'Initiative de Salazie (☎ 47 50 14, fax 47 60 06) occupies a small office opposite the *mairie* (town hall) in Salazie. It is open Monday to Saturday from 9 am to 3 pm, and Sunday from 9 to 11 am. It has the usual stock of glossy brochures and leaflets.

Places to Eat On the main road in Salazie, *Restaurant Le P'tit Bambou* (☎ 47 51 51) serves good Creole and Chinese lunches only for around FF65. Desserts cost from FF18. It's closed on Wednesday.

Le Viole de la Mariée (☎ 47 53 54), by the waterfall of the same name, offers very good Creole lunches from FF80. It's closed Monday.

Getting There & Away The road alongside the gorge of the Rivière du Mât from St-André to Salazie winds past superb waterfall displays. In places, swinging bridges cross the chasm to small farms clinging to the slopes. The road to Grand Îlet and Le Bélier turns off the Hell-Bourg road just south of Salazie.

There are buses from Salazie to Hell-Bourg about every two hours from 6.45 am to 6.20 pm (FF10). In the reverse direction, there are services from 6.10 am to 4 pm. There is no Sunday service.

There are about seven buses daily from Salazie to St-André between 5.30 am and 4.40 pm (in the reverse direction, buses run from 6.10 am to 5.45 pm). On Sunday buses leave Salazie at 8 am, 12.40 pm and 2.40 pm (8.30 am, 1.30 pm and 5.45 pm from St-André). The fare is FF10.10.

Grand Îlet & Le Bélier

These two villages lie about 12km east of Salazie, at the base of the ridge that separates the Cirque de Salazie and the Cirque de Mafate. Above Le Bélier are the mountain passes of Col de Fourche and Col des Bœufs, which form the main pedestrian routes between the two cirques.

Many people drive up here to hike into Mafate over the Col des Bœufs; the road to Grand Îlet and Le Bélier branches off the Salazie–Hell-Bourg road near the Cascade du Voile de la Mariée. Car thieves are known to operate in the public car park at the Le Bélier trailhead. Secure parking is available from Chez Titine (☎ 47 71 84) on the road to Camp Pierrot for FF50 per night. Transfers to/from Col des Bœufs cost FF100 one way.

Committed hikers can walk from Grand Îlet all the way to St-Denis via La Roche Écrite (the gîte de montagne at the Plaine des Chicots is the only place to break the hike). There are several chambres d'hôte in Grand Îlet and Le Bélier which make good starting points for walks.

Places to Stay & Eat In Grand Îlet, the main road makes a right-angle turn to Le Bélier at the start of Rue de l'Église, where you'll find the appealing old Creole church and many of the chambres d'hôte.

Right in the middle of Grand Îlet, *Mme Jeanine Grondin* (☎ 47 70 66) has a few chambres d'hôte near the church on Rue de l'Église for FF100/150 a single/double. The table d'hôte here costs FF90.

Mme Jeanne Marie Grondin (☎ 47 70 51) has a chambre d'hôte nearby on Rue du Père Jouanno, and charges FF120/150 (FF180/200 with private bathroom).

The chambre d'hôte run by *Mme Christine Boyer* (☎ 47 70 87) costs FF180/200, with table d'hôte meals for FF100. To get here, follow the road signposted to La Nouvelle uphill from the church, and turn left along the track at the top of the hill.

Further into the hills on the Route du Bélier, *Mme Campton* (☎ 47 73 59) offers attractive chambres d'hôte for FF180/200.

In Le Bélier itself, *M Boyer* (☎ 41 71 62) on Chemin Camp Pierrot charges FF180/200 for chambres d'hôte. To get here, turn left by the turn up to the Col des Bœufs car park.

On the Plaine des Chicots, above Grand Îlet on the way to La Roche Écrite, is *Plaine des Chicots Gîte de Montagne* (☎ 43 99 84); book through the Maison de la Montagne in St-Denis or Cilaos, or the Pays d'Accueil de Salazie in Hell-Bourg. Beds cost FF83, breakfast is FF30 and dinner is FF85.

Getting There & Away Buses from Salazie to Grand Îlet and Le Bélier leave at 8 am and 1, 3 and 6 pm (FF12). Heading back to Salazie there are services at 7 am, noon, 2 and 4 pm. There is no Sunday service.

Hell-Bourg

Hell-Bourg is the main community in the Cirque de Salazie, with numerous Creole houses in a beautiful setting in the centre of the natural amphitheatre. A sign outside the village proclaims that Hell-Bourg is *l'un des plus beau villages de France* (one of France's most beautiful villages). The town takes its curious name from former governor Admiral de Hell; the town itself is anything but!

Hell-Bourg served as a thermal resort until its springs dried up. Visitors can still see the Hôtel des Salazes, which once accommodated the thermal crowd but is now a private residence, and the ruins of the old baths. While Cilaos is known for its lentils, Hell-Bourg is locally synonymous with *chou chou*, a green, pear-shaped vegetable

imported from Brazil in 1834. There's also a trout farm just outside town.

Popular day hikes from Hell-Bourg include Les Sources Pétrifiantes and Piton d'Enchaing. The town makes a pleasant alternative to Cilaos if you're planning to hike up to Piton des Neiges or the Cirque de Mafate. Hikers doing the Tour des Cirques route will have to pass through Hell-Bourg as they cross the Cirque de Salazie. (For detailed information on all of these hiking possibilities, see the special section 'Hiking in Réunion'.)

Information The helpful Pays d'Accueil de Salazie (☎ 47 89 89) on the main road in Hell-Bourg is the local tourist information centre and can also arrange bookings at the gîtes de montagne. It's open weekdays from 8 am to 4 pm, and weekends from 9.30 am to noon and 2 to 3.30 pm.

Creole Buildings There are numerous appealing Creole buildings in Hell-Bourg, which date back as far as the 1860s. Several of the shops in Hell-Bourg sell *Les Cases de Hell-Bourg*, a glossy guide which lists the most impressive structures (FF20).

RÉUNION

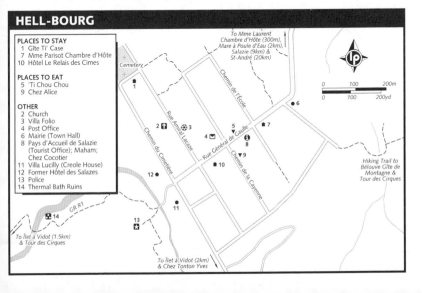

HELL-BOURG

PLACES TO STAY
1 Gîte Ti' Case
7 Mme Parisot Chambre d'Hôte
10 Hôtel Le Relais des Cimes

PLACES TO EAT
5 'Ti Chou Chou
9 Chez Alice

OTHER
2 Church
3 Villa Folio
4 Post Office
6 Mairie (Town Hall)
8 Pays d'Accueil de Salazie
    (Tourist Office); Maham;
    Chez Cocotier
11 Villa Lucilly (Creole House)
12 Former Hôtel des Salazes
13 Police
14 Thermal Bath Ruins

To Mme Laurent
Chambre d'Hôte (300m),
Mare à Poule d'Eau (2km),
Salazie (9km) &
St-André (20km)

Cemetery

Chemin de l'École

Rue Amiral Lacaze

Chemin du Cimetière

Rue Général de Gaulle

Chemin de la Cayenne

0   100   200m
0   100   200yd

Hiking Trail to
Bélouve Gîte de
Montagne &
Tour des Cirques

GR R1

To Îlet à Vidot (1.5km)
& Tour des Cirques

To Îlet à Vidot (2km)
& Chez Tonton Yves

Thermal Bath Ruins The old spa at Hell-Bourg is found in the ravine near the western end of town, and it's a nice short walk from the centre. Head downhill from the Hôtel Le Relais des Cimes along the main street. Where the street begins climbing to the *gendarmerie* (police station), bear right and follow the track down to the river, where you'll see the blue-tiled ruins of the old baths. There's not much left now, but it's a quiet and leafy spot. Cross the clunky steel bridge and climb the hill and you'll connect with the Îlet à Vidot road.

Villa Folio This late-19th-century flower and palm garden at 5 Rue Amiral Lacaze is planted densely around a series of walls, walkways, kiosks, terraces and fountains. You'll find a variety of tropical flowering plants including camellias, orchids, anthuriums, asters and nasturtiums. You can visit between 9 and 11.30 am and between 2 and 5 pm daily except Wednesday (FF25 per person). Call ahead to let the staff know you're coming (☎ 47 80 98).

Activities Maham (☎ 47 82 82), on the main road, can organise canyoning and rock-climbing trips in the area. It also rents out VTTs (mountain bikes) for FF80/100 per half/full day.

Places to Stay On Ave Général de Gaulle, *Mme Parisot* (☎ 47 83 48, fax 47 83 40) runs a lovely gîte d'étape spread over several old Creole houses. The cost per person is FF80, breakfast is FF20, and you can get dinner for FF90.

Gîte Ti' Case (☎/fax 47 87 80) on Rue Amiral Lacaze is more like an informal guesthouse. Singles/doubles cost FF100/250 per night. Meals cost FF80.

Mme Madeleine Laurent (☎ 47 80 60) has a pretty gîte d'étape just downhill from Hell-Bourg towards Mare à Poule d'Eau. She charges FF100 per person including breakfast.

West of Hell-Bourg in Îlet à Vidot, *Chez Tonton Yves* (☎ 47 84 22) offers chambres d'hôte for FF220 (for one or two people). Table d'hôte meals cost FF110 per person.

The only hotel in town is the *Hôtel Le Relais des Cimes* (☎ 47 81 58, fax 47 82 11) on Rue Général de Gaulle, which has comfortable rooms for FF320/400, including breakfast. Some people say the service here can be a little indifferent.

Places to Eat On Rue Général de Gaulle *'Ti Chou Chou* (☎ 47 80 93) serves up the local vegetable in a variety of combinations; try the cod with chou chou for FF65. It's open every day.

The excellent *Chez Alice* (☎ 47 86 24) on Chemin de la Cayenne serves up hearty regional dishes such as *truites aux poivreux* (trout with pepper) for around FF70. It's open daily except Monday for lunch and dinner (get here early for lunch if you want a seat).

Chez Cocotier (☎ 47 84 01) on Rue Général de Gaulle offers a Creole *menu du jour* (set menu of the day) for FF80. It's closed Wednesday evening and all day Thursday.

The *Hôtel Le Relais des Cimes* (see Places to Stay) has a restaurant which serves treats such as the local Hell-Bourg *truites* (trout) with vanilla for around FF150. It's open every day for lunch and dinner.

Getting There & Away There are buses from Hell-Bourg to Salazie about every two hours from 6.10 am to 4 pm (except Sunday). In the reverse direction, there are services from 6.45 am to 6.20 pm. The fare is FF10.

Around Hell-Bourg

On the road from Salazie to Hell-Bourg, at the top of the hair-rasing corkscrew section, is the village of Mare à Poule d'Eau with its superb viewpoint, known as Le Point du Jour. From here you have a stunning view over the peaks of Salazie, or, alternatively, a view of dense cloud, depending on the weather.

Just north of Mare à Poule d'Eau, below the turn-off to Grand Îlet, is the Cascade du Voile de la Mariée (Bridal Veil Falls). These towering falls drop in several stages from the often cloud-obscured heights into the ravine at the roadside.

CIRQUE DE MAFATE

Despite its remoteness, the Cirque de Mafate is populated and there are several villages large enough to support shops and other minor enterprises. Not much happens in these sleepy little places but they provide a few trappings of civilisation if you're walking through the cirque. There are no roads into the cirque (though the surfaced *route forestière* or forestry road runs right up to the pass at Col des Bœufs), so the villages of La Nouvelle, Roche Plate, Marla, Îlet à Bourse, Îlet à Malheur, Grand Place and Aurère are accessible only on foot.

For information on hiking in the area, and on the settlements of Marla, La Nouvelle and Roche Plate, see the special section 'Hiking in Réunion', which details 'Four Days in the Cirque de Mafate'. The map in that section shows the settlements of Îlet à Bourse, Aurère, Grand Place and Cayenne.

Îlet à Bourse

This pleasant village has an awesome view down the cirque and makes a convenient first night stop if you're coming over Bord à Martin from Le Bélier.

Îlet à Bourse Gîte de Montagne (☎ 43 43 93) offers beds for FF83 per person, while breakfast/dinner is an extra FF25/75.

Aurère

Undoubtedly the grottiest of the Mafate communities, Aurère is nevertheless beautifully positioned, perched Machu-Picchu-like above the precipitous canyon of the Bras Bémale and beneath the Piton Cabris.

M Georget Boyer (☎ 55 02 33) has a private gîte with beds for FF65. Evening meals are FF70 per person.

Grand Place & Cayenne

These two tiny communities lie above the rushing Rivière des Galets near the cirque's main outlet.

The *Gîte de Montagne – Le Pavillon* (☎ 43 66 76) is atop the hill in Grand Place, while the *Grand Place Gîte de Montagne – La Cayenne* (☎ 43 85 42) is down in the valley at Cayenne. Beds in both gîtes cost FF83 (breakfast/dinner is an extra FF25/75).

Les Hautes Plaines

Réunion's only cross-island road passes through the Plaine-des-Palmistes and the Plaine-des-Cafres, collectively known as les Hautes Plaines (the High Plains). These relatively large open areas actually form the saddle that separates the massif, comprised of the three cirques, from the volcano, Piton de la Fournaise. Because there's a road from here that approaches within a few kilometres of the summit, nearly all visitors to the volcano approach from this side. If you're feeling particularly energetic you can also hike from here into the Cirque de Salazie and the Cirque de Cilaos. (For detailed information on hiking in the volcano area and the cirques, see the special section 'Hiking in Réunion'.)

PLAINE-DES-PALMISTES

There were once large numbers of palm trees on the Plaine-des-Palmistes (hence the name), but thanks to heavy consumption of heart-of-palm salad, now there are almost none (see the boxed text 'Have a Heart'). The village actually consists of three communities: Le Premier and Le Deuxième on the highway, and La Petite Plaine to the south-west.

> ### Have a Heart
>
> The Plaine-des-Palmistes was once covered in palmiste palms, but early settlers developed a taste for salads made from the apical bud of the tree, known as the 'heart of palm'. The palm dies once the bud is removed, earning this wasteful salad delicacy the title 'millionaire's salad'. The Plaine-des-Palmistes was stripped bare in a few generations, but the tree is protected these days, and the heart of palm on offer in restaurants is commercially grown.
>
> Other curious ingredients that are popular in Creole salads include the leaves of the blue *choka* (the 'Vera Cruz' agave species), and the tasty interior of the pandanus tree, or screw pine.

Information

The Pays d'Accueil des Hautes-Plaines is housed inside the Domaine des Tourelles (☎ 51 39 92), a lovely old Creole building just north of the centre. It's open from 8.30 am to 5 pm on weekdays, and 10 am to 5 pm on weekends.

Cascade Biberon

The Cascade Biberon is an easy detour from Le Premier. It's signposted from the highway near the Les Alazées hotel. The falls are about 2km along an obvious track (when you cross the Ravine Sèche, just follow the electricity wires to find the next stretch).

Piton des Songes

On the summit of Piton des Songes or Peak of Dreams (1270m) are a cross, a shrine and a small reservoir pond. From the peak, it's possible to see across the plain and down to St-Benoît and the sea. You can park here and walk up in a few minutes.

Places to Stay

Just north of Le Premier, *Mme Grondin* (☎ *51 33 79, 17 Rue Doreau*) offers chambres d'hôte for FF150/180 a single/double. Meals are FF100. The turning is on the left if you're coming from St-Benoît.

Mme Rivière (☎ *51 33 45*) runs a gîte d'étape at Rue Eugène Rochetaing in Le Deuxième. It costs FF80 per person (including breakfast); dinner is FF90.

In La Petite Plaine, *M Jista* (☎ *51 37 33*) has a gîte d'étape on Rue Henri Pignolet (near the turn-off to the Forêt de Bébour), with beds for FF80 per person.

Hôtel des Plaines (☎ *51 35 67, fax 51 44 24*) in Le Deuxième is a rather ordinary three-star hotel with standard rooms for FF285/340 (plus FF35 for breakfast).

Les Azalées (☎ *51 34 24, fax 51 39 89*) is a friendly small hotel on the highway in Le Premier. Neat rooms cost FF245 for a single or a double; breakfast is FF35 per person.

Ferme Auberge le Pommeau (☎ *51 40 70*) is on Rue de Peindray d'Ambelle in Le Premier. Lovely rooms with bathroom cost from FF260/305.

Places to Eat

Les Platanes (☎ *51 31 69*) on the main road has Creole lunches daily except Tuesday, and is also open Friday and Saturday evenings. Meals cost about FF65.

Hôtel des Plaines (see Places to Stay) has a French and Creole restaurant which is open daily for lunch and dinner, but the meals on offer are somewhat expensive at FF75 to FF200.

The restaurant at the *Ferme Auberge le Pommeau* (see Places to Stay) serves superb Creole cuisine for around FF95. It's open daily for lunch and dinner.

Getting There & Away

Plaine-des-Palmistes lies on the cross-island highway between St-Benoît and St-Pierre. The bus fare from St-Pierre to the Domaine des Tourelles in Plaine-des-Palmistes is FF30.10. From St-Benoît to Plaine-des-Palmistes, it's FF20.10.

PLAINE-DES-CAFRES

The Plaine-des-Cafres, once a refuge for runaway slaves from the coast, offers a gently sloping, almost European landscape, hemmed in between the cirques and Piton de la Fournaise.

The Plaine-des-Cafres formally begins at Col de Bellevue, at the top of the winding road from Plaine-des-Palmistes, and ends at the rather humdrum regional centre of Le Tampon (the name is derived from the Malagasy word *tampony*, which refers to a small hill). North of Le Tampon on Route Nationale 3 or the RN3 (the cross-island road) are numerous small settlements which are named for their distance from the sea – Le Quatorzième (14th), for example, is 14km from the ocean. There are numerous places to stay on or close to the cross-island road.

The most interesting place on the Plaine-des-Cafres from a visitor's perspective is Bourg-Murat, where the Route Forestière du Volcan turns off to Piton de la Fournaise. Bourg-Murat presents several accommodation and dining choices, and it's also the location of the informative Maison du Volcan museum.

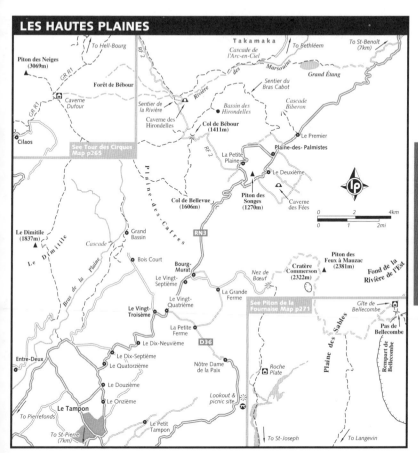

LES HAUTES PLAINES

RÉUNION

Information

The Hautes Plaines tourist office (☎ 59 08 92) is just behind the Maison du Volcan on Rue Alfred Picard in Bourg-Murat. The office is open weekdays from 9 am to 5 pm and on Saturday from 9 am to 4 pm.

Grand Bassin

This picturesque basin, known as *la vallée perdue* (the lost valley), is formed by the confluence of three rivers: the Bras Sec, the Bras de Suzanne and the Bras des Roches Noires. It's a quiet community with a lovely waterfall and a handful of gîtes. To get here,

follow the road to the end of Bois Court from Vingt-Troisième village. The 2km track down to Grand Bassin begins on Rue Roland Hoareau.

La Maison du Volcan

If you wish to know more about the behaviour of volcanoes in general and Piton de la Fournaise in particular, visit La Maison du Volcan or Volcano House (☎ 59 00 26) in the village of Bourg-Murat on the cross-island road. Here, a team of scientists keep a close watch on the volcano's moods, and are poised to issue a formal warning if things look to be gathering steam inside the crater. This place is open Tuesday to Sunday from 9.30 am to 5.30 pm (last entry at 4.45 pm) and admission is FF40/10 for adults/children.

Places to Stay

There are numerous gîte and chambre d'hôte options, but many are close to the highway, and only a few are really convenient for hikers. The villages of La Grande Ferme, La Petite Ferme and Nôtre Dame de la Paix are all convenient for trips to the volcano. Places to stay are listed here roughly north to south.

Bourg-Murat to Le Tampon There are several pleasant hotel options in and around Bourg-Murat.

La Diligence (☎ *59 10 10, fax 59 11 81*) is a horse ranch and hotel, just off the highway north of Bourg-Murat in Vingt-Huitième. Accommodation in the old but passable bungalows costs FF250/295/350 a single/double/triple; breakfast is FF32 per person. There's a nice restaurant here with a hearty open fire. Also at the hotel, the cheaper *Gîte de Bellevue* (☎ *59 15 02*) is a gîte d'étape with beds for FF70 per person.

The cosy *Auberge du Volcan* (☎ *27 50 91, fax 59 17 21*) is right in Bourg-Murat and guests can unwind in front of the log fire. Single or double rooms cost FF180 and breakfast is FF20 per person.

The same owners run the *Hôtel le Volcan* across the road. The building is newer but not as cosy. Rooms cost FF180/240.

Hotel Ecrin (☎ *59 02 02, fax 59 36 10*) is just downhill from the turn-off to the volcano. Tidy rooms start at FF160/220, or FF280/340 in the new annexe. There are also a few self-catering apartments for FF500 a double.

There are a few convenient gîtes and chambres d'hôte right on Route National 3 (RN3) which aren't too far from the turn-off to the volcano.

On RN3 in Le Vingt-Cinquième, *Mme Combelles* (☎ *59 29 79*) charges FF215/240 for her chambres d'hôte. Good Creole meals are FF100.

In Le Vingt-Quatrième, *Les Géraniums* (☎ *59 11 06, fax 59 21 83*) is a hotel with a good reputation but, according to some travellers, it doesn't always live up to it. Rooms cost FF310/350; breakfast is an additional FF50.

Mme Alicalapa-Tenon (☎ *59 10 41, 62 RN3*), nearby the police station in Le Vingt-Quatrième, has chambres d'hôte from FF160 a double, with table d'hôte meals for FF80.

On the highway in Le Vingt-Deuxième, *M Lacouture* (☎ *59 04 91*) offers chambres d'hôte for FF150/180, and gîtes from FF1680 for the week (FF985 for the weekend).

Also on RN3 in Le Vingt-Deuxième, *Mme Rivière* (☎ *27 59 78*) has a chambre d'hôte with rooms for FF150/180; meals are FF100.

On the highway at Le Vingtième, 5km from Le Tampon, *Chez Céline* (☎ *59 02 32, 192 RN3*) is a chambre d'hôte with rooms for FF240 a double and table d'hôte meals for FF100.

La Grande Ferme, La Petite Ferme & Nôtre Dame de la Paix Right on Route Forestière du Volcan in La Grande Ferme, *M Techer* (☎ *50 03 10*) offers a gîte at FF1860 for the entire week and FF890 just for the weekend.

On Chemin Grande Ferme in La Grande Ferme, *M Dalleau* (☎ *59 28 07*) offers chambres d'hôte at FF230 for a single or a double.

Nearby, *Mme Guesdon* (☎ *27 59 25*) has a popular chambre d'hôte by the playing field in La Grande Ferme. Rooms cost FF200/220 and meals are FF80 per person.

In La Petite Ferme near the turn-off to Grande Ferme, *Mme Robert* (☎ *59 20 59*) has chambres d'hôte for FF250 a double and two gîtes at FF2246 for the week (FF1232 for the weekend).

South of La Petite Ferme on Chemin Nôtre Dame de la Paix (the D36), *Mme Mussard* (☎ *27 57 59*) offers chambres d'hôte for FF180 a double. Meals are FF85.

Grand Bassin & Bois Court In Grand Bassin, rooms at the gîte d'étape of *Mme Jeanne-Marie Nativel* (☎ *27 51 91*) cost FF150 including breakfast. Other meals are FF80.

Other options in Grand Bassin include **Mme Sery-Picard** (☎ *27 51 02*), with dorm beds for FF50 per person, including breakfast, and **Mme Josie Rivière** (☎ *59 03 66*), with dorm beds for FF70. Both gîtes offer table d'hôte meals for FF80.

Places to Eat

If you're staying in a gîte or a chambre d'hôte, most places will also offer home-cooked Creole food. For those passing through, there are restaurants at several of the hotels.

Right by the tourist office in Bourg-Murat, **Relais du Commerson** (☎ *27 52 87*) serves Creole and Chinese food. It's open from 7 am to 8 pm daily.

Auberge du Volcan in Bourg-Murat (see Places to Stay) is recommended for its Creole dishes, which cost around FF75. The restaurant is open daily except Sunday evening.

La Diligence (see Places to Stay) offers Creole and French dishes from FF80 in its cosy restaurant. It's open daily for lunch and dinner.

The restaurant at **Les Géraniums** (see Places to Stay) also specialises in Creole and French fare. It's open daily from 11.30 am to 10.30 pm. Nonresidents should book ahead.

On Rue de Père Favron, just before the police station in Le Vingt-Quatorzième, **Auberge du 24eme** (☎ *59 08 60*) offers excellent home-cooked Creole dishes ranging in price from FF95 to FF150. It's open daily for lunch and dinner.

Chez Cocotier (☎ *59 08 30*), at La Ravine Blanche near Le Vingt-Troisième, is open every day, except Sunday night and Monday. Creole and French main courses cost from FF70.

Entertainment

The Théâtre Luc Donat (☎ *27 24 36*), on Rue de l'Église in Le Tampon, stages many of the musical and theatrical productions that play in St-Denis. Le Tampon also has a cinema on Rue Hubert Delisle, showing mainly French-language films.

Getting There & Away

There are about three buses daily each way between St-Benoît and St-Pierre via Le Tampon, Plaine-des-Cafres and Plaine-des-Palmistes. From St-Pierre to Bourg-Murat, the fare is FF16.80. Coming from St-Benoît, it's FF20.10 to Plaine-des-Palmistes and FF33.50 to Bourg-Murat.

ENTRE-DEUX

This community got its strange name, which means 'between two', because it is situated between two rivers – the Bras de Cilaos and the Bras de la Plaine, which together form the Rivière St-Étienne. It's a friendly enough village in itself, but most visitors come here for the tough hike up the slopes of Le Dimitile to a super view over the Cirque de Cilaos. If you leave at dawn, the ascent and descent of Le Dimitile (1837m) can be done in a single day; plan on at least 16 hours. If you want to hike up but you're not superhuman or you don't want to cut things too closely for a single day, there are several gîtes d'étape at Le Dimitile.

Information

The Entre-Deux tourist office (☎ 39 69 80, fax 39 57 70) is at 9 Rue Fortune Hoareau, near the arboretum. It's open Tuesday to Friday from 8 am to 3 pm, and on the weekend from 8 to 11 am.

Places to Stay & Eat

The **Auberge de Jeunesse** (☎ 39 59 20) is north of the centre in Ravine de Citron (on the way to Le Dimitile). It charges the standard FF75 per person (for Hostelling International members). Evening meals cost FF50 and breakfast is FF10 per person.

Mme Jacqueline Corré (☎ *39 53 43, 7 Impasse des Jasmines*) has chambres d'hôte at Grand Fond Intérieur, north of the main settlement. Rooms cost FF75 per person, including breakfast. Dinner is FF80.

In Grand Fond Extérieur, a little further north, **M Lavocat** (☎ *30 60 62, 20 Rue Cinaire*) charges FF200/220 for singles/doubles for his chambres d'hôte. There's also an equestrian centre here.

RÉUNION

In Ravine de Citron, north-east of town, *Mme Vienne* (☎ *39 64 03, 35 Rue Defaud*) charges FF175/250. Meals are FF90.

Nearby, *Mme Clain* (☎ *39 65 43, 1 Chemin de la Source Raisin*) charges FF250/350, with table d'hôte meals from FF100.

Le Grillardin on Rue Herbert Delisle has Creole meals for around FF75. This place is open daily.

Up on Le Dimitile, *M Beldan* (☎ *39 50 46*) charges FF70 per person for a bed and FF90 for a meal. *M Payet* (☎ *39 66 42*) offers a room, breakfast and meal for FF170 per person. *M Bardil* (☎ *39 60 84*) charges FF80 for a bed, and FF90 for a meal.

Getting There & Away
Minor bus lines operate between Entre-Deux and the *gares routières* (bus stations) in St-Pierre and St-Louis. Buses run every two hours or so from St-Pierre (there are only two buses on Sunday).

HIKING IN RÉUNION

Instead of showing serene lagoons, postcards from Réunion usually depict a more tortured landscape of sharp mountain crests, forested valleys, tumbling waterfalls and surreal volcanic tuff. The natural environment is remarkably intact, with a huge variety of flora, from tropical rainforest to gnarled thickets of giant heather. There is a slightly eerie lack of fauna, as few of the tropical species that colonised the island have been able to adapt to the exposed and chilly conditions of the interior. Formed from one mighty dead volcano (Piton des Neiges) and one very alive volcano (Piton de la Fournaise), the island is a paradise for hikers, adventure-sports enthusiasts or indeed anyone who is receptive to the untamed beauty of a wilderness environment.

For many visitors, hiking is the *raison d'être* of a trip to Réunion. Thanks to the Office National des Forêts (ONF), the island boasts nearly a thousand kilometres of hiking trails. The Grande Randonnée (GR) offers two superbly maintained trails with numerous offshoots. GR R1 does a tour of Piton des Neiges, passing through Cilaos, the Fôret de Bélouve, Hell-Bourg and the Cirque de Mafate. GR R2 makes an epic traverse across the island all the way from St-Denis to St-Philippe via the three cirques, the Hautes Plaines and Piton de la Fournaise.

The trails are well maintained, but the tropical rainfall can eat through footpaths and wash away steps and handrails. Even experienced hikers should be prepared for tortuous ascents, slippery mud chutes, and narrow paths beside sheer precipices. The days can be humid and hot, the nights damp and surprisingly chilly.

The trails described in this section are popular hikes, though there are countless variations, and they should be well within the capabilities of any reasonably fit adult; children should be able to do the walks with a little extra time. The hiking times given are for an average hiker carrying a light day-pack and taking only brief breaks.

(For more information on the towns and villages that you may pass through, such as Cilaos and Hell-Bourg, see the Interior chapter.)

Planning
Information
Information on the mountains is provided by the Maison de la Montagne. The staff here are extremely well informed, and can provide guides and arrange tours for *randonneurs* (walkers). They also organise bookings for the invaluable *gîtes de montagne* (mountain lodges) that are strategically located around the cirques. Many people book the gîtes de montagne from mainland France, so don't make the mistake of leaving your booking to the last minute.

The main branch of the Maison de la Montagne is in St-Denis near Le Barachois at 10 Place Sarda Garriga (☎ 90 78 78, fax 41 84 29). The office is open Monday to Thursday from 9 am to 5.30 pm, on Friday from 9 am to 4.30 pm, and on Saturday from 9 am to 4 pm.

Maison de la Montagne also has an office in Cilaos (☎ 31 71 71, fax 31 80 54) at 2 Rue Mac Auliffe. This office is open Monday to Saturday from 8.30 am to 12.20 pm and from 1.30 to 5.30 pm. It is also open on Sunday from 9 am to 1 pm, and on some holidays.

In Hell-Bourg, you can get hiking information at the Pays d'Accueil de Salazie (☎ 47 89 89) on the main road. It's open weekdays from 8 am to 4 pm and weekends from 9.30 am to noon and 2 to 3.30 pm.

What to Bring

Good shoes are essential for hiking the trails of Réunion, which are of gravel and stone and which are often very steep, muddy or slippery. Hiking shoes with good ankle support are better than sneakers.

Be sure to carry water (at least 2L for a day's hiking), a raincoat, a warm top, sunscreen, insect repellent and a torch. If you intend sleeping out at altitude, you'll need a decent sleeping bag, as temperatures in the cirques can fall rapidly at night. The gîtes provide sheets and blankets.

You will be able to buy most last-minute supplies at a sporting-goods store. Cilaos has several excellent outdoor suppliers (for more information, see Cilaos in the Interior chapter).

Maps

Réunion is covered by the six 1:25,000 scale maps published by the Institut Géographique National. Map number 4402 RT is one of the most useful for hikers, since it covers Cirque de Mafate and Cirque de Salazie as well as the northern part of the Cirque de Cilaos. It also covers the whole of GR R1. These maps show trails and gîtes. They are sold all over the island, including at the Maisons de la Montagne in St-Denis and Cilaos.

Money

There are ATMs at the post offices in Salazie and Cilaos. Carry plenty of francs, as meals and beds in private gîtes must be paid for in cash.

Books

Several excellent route guides in French are available at the Maison de la Montagne, but there are none in English. However, the French guides are still useful for their maps.

The definitive guide to walks along GR R1 and GR R2 is the Topoguide *L'île de la Réunion*, published by the Fédération Française de la Randonnée Pédestre. It uses 1:25,000 scale IGN maps, and includes eight one-day hikes of varying degrees of difficulty.

Cirque de Mafate, Découverte et Randonnée, published by the ONF, details 26 hikes in the Cirque de Mafate. This small, high-quality guide also describes the fauna, flora and population of Mafate's *îlets* (villages) and includes a 1:25,000 scale map.

Sentiers Marmailles is designed with children in mind, and describes 46 outings that can be covered in less than two hours.

A broader range of walks is covered by *50 Itinéraires de Promenades Pédestres à la Réunion*, from simple strolls lasting a couple of hours to more athletic hikes.

OLIVIER CIRENDINI

DEANNA SWANEY

OLIVIER CIRENDINI

DEANNA SWANEY

agged peaks, swirling mists and tumbling waterfalls: hikers in Réunion's dramatic cirques have it all,
even a solar-powered hot shower at the end of the day.

ADRIAN VADROT

Day two of the Tour des Cirques offers superb views of the Cirque de Salazie.

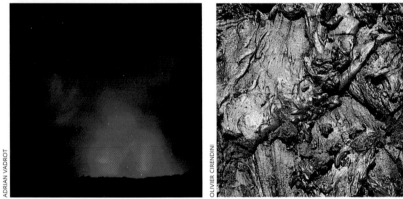

ADRIAN VADROT

Piton de la Fournaise goes off!

OLIVIER CIRENDINI

Volcanic rock

ADRIAN VADROT

Camping Interdit: Camping around the volcano is forbidden for obvious reasons.

Accommodation & Food

Most of the accommodation for hikers consists of *gîtes de montagne* (mountain lodges, mostly found in isolated locations on the trails themselves) or of small, family-run B&Bs known as *chambres d'hôte* (mostly found in the villages at the ends of the hiking trails). Some of the gîtes on the walking trails are more accurately described as *gîtes d'étape*, which are privately run and offer dorm beds and meals. There's often little to separate the different types of gîtes in terms of comfort or facilities. Showers are often solar-heated and are rarely piping hot; some places can be downright cold at night. Your choice of where to stay will most likely be based on where you can find a room. There are also a few hotels in Hell-Bourg and Cilaos for that last night of luxury (and central heating) before you set out.

The gîtes de montagne are managed by the Maison de la Montagne; to book, you must pay up front at the Maison de la Montagne in Cilaos or St-Denis or the Pays d'Accueil de Salazie (see Information earlier in this section). When you pay, you will receive a ticket to be given to the gîte's manager. You must call the owner to book your meals. Private gîtes can usually be booked directly with the owners.

If all this organisation doesn't fit in with your idea of adventure, camping is permitted in most areas, but only for one night at a time. Some spots (the Trois Roches waterfall near Roche Plate in Mafate, for example) are extraordinarily popular, and you may have to fight for a decent space to set up your tent. Camping is not permitted around Piton de la Fournaise.

Most gîtes offer Creole meals, which are normally hearty, but may be a little rustic for some palates. Most places serve up *carri poulet* (chicken curry), *boucané* (smoked pork) or the local *rougaille saucisse*, often with local wine or *rhum arrangé* (rum punch) thrown in. Breakfast is usually just a cup of coffee with toast and jam.

If you plan to self-cater, you'll need to bring plenty of carbohydrate-rich food. Instant noodles are light and filling, while chocolate and other sugary snacks can provide the energy necessary to make that last mountain ridge. There are cooking facilities at a few gîtes, but you are best off bringing a camping stove. Some villages in the cirques have shops where you can purchase a very limited variety of food (few places stock anything more wholesome than biscuits and canned beans).

Safety

In Réunion, as elsewhere, safety is basically a matter of common sense and being prepared. Leave early enough in the morning to reach your planned destination before dark; see that you have enough water; equip yourself with good hiking footwear; and check the weather report before setting out. There are plenty of hikers in the cirques, but you are taking an appreciable risk if you hike alone.

Minor muscle injuries and sprains can be enough to put you out of action. If you do pull something, an elastic bandage and muscle balm may be enough to get you to your immediate destination, but rest is essential for the muscles to repair. Also be prepared for blisters, particularly in wet conditions.

In a real emergency, lifting both arms to form a 'V' is a signal to one of the many helicopter pilots who fly over the island daily that you need help. The gîtes are equipped with radiotelephones with which you can contact emergency services.

Climate

The best time to hike is during the dry season, from around April to September; May and June are probably the best months of all. The weather is extremely changeable from one part of this small island to the other. For example, you can leave Col des Bœufs shrouded in mist and arrive at the village of La Nouvelle under a blazing sun.

The weather in Réunion has a tendency to become worse as the day goes on. As the hours pass, the island's uplands seem to delight in 'capturing' any cloud that happens to come their way. An early start is therefore one of the best defences against the vagaries of the elements.

Considerations for Responsible Hiking

The popularity of hiking is placing great pressure on the natural environment. Please consider the following tips when hiking, and help preserve the ecology and beauty of Réunion.

Rubbish

• Carry out all your rubbish. If you've carried it in, you can carry it out. Empty packaging weighs very little anyway and should be stored in a dedicated rubbish bag. Make an effort to carry out rubbish left by others.

• Never bury your rubbish: Digging disturbs soil and ground cover and encourages erosion. Buried rubbish may also take years to decompose, especially at high altitudes.

• Minimise the waste you must carry out by taking minimal packaging and taking no more food than you will need. If you can't buy in bulk, unpack small-portion packages and combine their contents in one container before your trip. Take reusable containers.

• Don't rely on bought water in plastic bottles. Disposal of these bottles is creating a major problem. Use iodine drops or purification tablets instead.

• Sanitary napkins, tampons and condoms should be carried out despite the inconvenience.

Human Waste Disposal

• Contamination of water sources by human faeces can lead to the transmission of hepatitis, typhoid and intestinal parasites such as giardia amoebas and roundworms. It can cause severe health risks not only to members of your party, but also to local residents and wildlife.

• Where there is a toilet, please use it. Where there is none, bury your waste. Dig a small hole 15cm deep and at least 100m from any watercourse. Consider carrying a lightweight trowel for this purpose. Cover the waste with soil and a rock. Use toilet paper sparingly and bury it with the waste.

You can get information on weather conditions in specific parts of the island over a 24-hour period by telephoning the Méteo France voice service (☎ 08 36 68 02 02). Broader forecasts, updated twice a day, are also available (☎ 08 36 68 00 00). Storm-watch bulletins are available on ☎ 08 36 65 10 10. All these services are in French.

Organised Tours

The hiking trails are well established and well mapped, but you may get more information about the environment you are walking through if you go with a local guide. The Maison de la Montagne publishes *Objectif Pleine Nature*, a guide to organised adventure trips on the island. Simple guided walks start at FF900 for two days, while a seven-day tramp costs upwards of FF3800, including meals and accommodation. More expensive itineraries that include adventure activities such as mountain biking and canyoning are also available. For more information, contact the Maison de la Montagne in Cilaos or St-Denis, or the Pays d'Accueil de Salazie in Hell-Bourg (see Information earlier in this section for contact details).

Considerations for Responsible Hiking

Washing
- Don't use detergents or toothpaste in or near watercourses, even if they are biodegradable.

- For personal washing, use biodegradable soap and a water container (or even a light-weight, portable basin) at least 50m away from the watercourse. Disperse the waste water widely to allow the soil to filter it fully before it finally makes it back to the watercourse.

- Wash cooking utensils 50m from watercourses using a scourer instead of detergent.

Erosion
- Hillsides and mountain slopes are prone to erosion. It is important to stick to existing tracks and avoid short cuts. If you blaze a new trail straight down a slope, it will turn into a water-course with the next heavy rainfall and eventually cause soil loss and deep scarring.

- If a well-used track passes through a mud patch, walk through the mud: walking around the edge will increase the size of the patch.

Fires & Low-Impact Cooking
- Don't depend on open fires for cooking. The cutting of wood for fires in popular hiking areas can cause rapid deforestation. Cook on a light-weight kerosene, alcohol or Shellite (white gas) stove and avoid those powered by disposable butane gas canisters.

- If you patronise local accommodation, select those places that do not use wood fires.

- Fires may be acceptable below the tree line in areas that get very few visitors. If you light a fire, use an existing fireplace rather than creating a new one. Don't surround fires with rocks as this creates a visual scar. Use only dead, fallen wood. Remember the adage 'the bigger the fool, the bigger the fire'. Use minimal wood, just what you need for cooking. In huts, leave wood for the next person.

- Ensure you fully extinguish a fire after use. Spread the embers and douse them with water.

Four Days in the Cirque de Mafate

Surrounded by ramparts, crisscrossed with gullies, and studded with narrow ridges, Mafate is the wildest and most remote of Réunion's cirques. There are no roads into the cirque (though the surfaced *route forestière* or forestry road runs right up to the pass at Col des Bœufs), so the villages of La Nouvelle, Roche Plate, Marla, Îlet à Bourse, Îlet à Malheur, Grand Place and Aurère are accessible only on foot.

The cirque was named after a runaway slave, the chieftain and sorcerer Mafate, who took refuge in the ramparts of the cirque. He was hunted down and killed in 1751 by François Mussard, a hunter of runaway slaves whose name is now remembered only because it has been given to a dank, dark cave near Piton des Neiges.

Mafate is accessible by four paths: from Cilaos via the Col du Taïbit (2082m); along the banks of the Rivière des Galets from Dos d'Ane or Sans Souci; from Hell-Bourg via the Col des Bœufs or Col de Fourche (1942m); or via Piton Maïdo, which involves a precipitous descent into Roche Plate. Most people take the easy option and hop over the ridge via the Col des Bœufs.

In the Cirque de Mafate, there are gîtes de montagne at Îlet à Bourse, Grand Place, Cayenne, Roche Plate, La Nouvelle and Marla (remember to book through the Maison de la Montagne). In addition, there are some gîtes d'étape in La Nouvelle which may be of use to hikers. Most routes are well signposted, but of course you should always carry a good map.

The following itinerary takes you through some of the most interesting and scenic parts of Mafate, but numerous other options exist (talk to the staff at the Maison de la Montagne). This hike can also be combined with the Tour des Cirques, which is described later in this section.

The car park at Le Bélier is a popular prowling ground for thieves – secure parking is available from Chez Titine (☎ 47 71 84) downhill from Le Bélier on the road to Camp Pierrot. The cost is FF50 per night. Transfers to/from the car park at Col des Bœufs cost FF100 for one person or FF150 for two or more people.

Day One: Petit Col Car Park to La Nouvelle

(Walking time: about two hours)

The trail, a GR R1 variant, begins in Le Bélier, but the first hour follows the Haut Mafate forestry road up to the Petit Col car park, so most people choose to begin the walk from the car park.

From the car park, it only takes 15 minutes to reach the Col des Bœufs, from where you'll get your first glimpse of the Cirque de Mafate. Ahead, GR R1 plunges steeply down to the forested Plaine des Tamarins. The *tamarin des hautes* (mountain tamarind) trees are cloaked in a yellowish lichen called *barbes de capucin* (monk's beard), and the low cloud often creates a slightly spooky atmosphere, like something from Tolkien's *Lord of the Rings*.

FOUR DAYS IN THE CIRQUE DE MAFATE

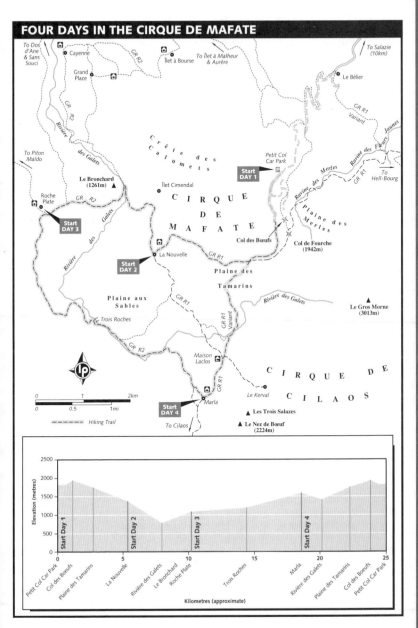

Follow the path signposted to La Nouvelle (the other branch heads south to Marla), which meanders through the forest in a fairly leisurely fashion, before dropping rapidly to the village of La Nouvelle. There are some absolutely stunning views of Le Grand Bénare on the cirque rim as you descend.

La Nouvelle used to be a cattle-raising centre, but tourism has very much taken over as the village's main source of income. There are only about 130 inhabitants, but the numbers are swelled daily by the jet-setters who drop out of the sky by helicopter for lunch. The village has several shops, a school, an interesting shingle-roofed chapel and, unique in the cirque, a payphone (you'll need a phonecard to use it).

Places to Stay & Eat As you enter La Nouvelle, the gîte belonging to *J Cuvelier* (☎ *43 49 63*) is signposted down a narrow trail on your right. To stay here costs FF70 per person, plus FF30/80 for breakfast/dinner.

La Nouvelle Gîte de Montagne (☎ *43 61 77*) offers beds for FF85 per person plus FF35/100 for breakfast/dinner. In the attractive Creole building behind this complex is the private gîte of *Andre Bègue* (☎ *43 61 77*), which costs FF80 per person, or FF180 for a double room.

The trail north from La Nouvelle passes in front of the chapel and the wooden-framed *Épicerie Bègue Alain*, which is the best-stocked grocery in the village.

The blue building behind the chapel is the private gîte of *Sylvio Bègue* (☎ *43 43 10*), a tidy place with beds for FF100 (dinner is FF70).

Just beyond is the gîte of *S P Bègue* (☎ *43 51 74*), where beds cost FF60 per person and meals cost FF75.

Day Two: La Nouvelle to Roche Plate via Le Bronchard
(Walking time: about four hours)

The trail to Grand Place, Cayenne and Roche Plate via Le Bronchard turns downhill just after the La Nouvelle chapel and heads into the maize fields, before plummeting into the valley of the Rivière des Galets. This steep and often treacherous descent is not for the faint-hearted, though reassuring handrails are provided for some of the steeper sections.

To make up for the risk, the views are to die for (figuratively speak-ing!) and an exhilarating hour or so will get you to the bottom of the cirque, where you can take a well-deserved splash in the river. The trail along the valley floor continues to Grand Place and Cayenne, but you should ford the river and start the arduous ascent up the far side of the valley.

When you reach the white metal cross at Le Bronchard (1261m) the worst is over. The final stretch descends not into the ravine as it first appears, but slowly down to the village of Roche Plate. Ignore the turn-off to the right marked 'Îlet à Cordes', and the trail to 'Marla, Trois Roches and La Nouvelle' which branches off to the left as you enter the village. The village of Roche Plate sits at the foot of the majestic Piton Maïdo (2182m).

Places to Stay & Eat The nice tidy *Roche Plate Gîte de Montagne* (☎ 43 60 01) is uphill from the school and ONF office, and has hot water, a kitchen and a fine view over the cirque. It charges FF83 for beds and FF25/75 for breakfast/dinner.

Further along this path is the village *grocery* and the private *Auberge de Bronchard* (☎ 43 83 66), which has double rooms for FF220 including breakfast and dinner.

Day Three: Roche Plate to Marla via Trois Roches
(Walking time: about four to five hours)

The trail on to Marla via Trois Roches begins where the trail from La Nouvelle enters Roche Plate. The first section rises steadily through a dry landscape studded with *chokas* (an agave species). Towering overhead are the peaks of Le Grand Bénare, Col du Taïbit, Le Gros Morne and Col de Fourche. Apart from one significant drop, the path stays fairly level before descending in earnest to the waterfall at Trois Roches (about 2½ hours from Roche Plate).

This curious waterfall drops through a narrow crack in a bed of grey granite that has been perfectly polished into ripple patterns by aeons of erosion, and is a popular camping spot. The falls are named for the huge boulders (there are actually seven, not three) that were deposited here by prehistoric torrents.

Marla is about 1½ hours beyond the falls. The trail crosses the river and then follows the left bank, passing through a rather arid landscape of eroded volcanic cinders from Piton des Neiges. After about 20 minutes, the trail crosses the river, just downstream from a pile of vast alluvial boulders, and climbs the far bank to Marla in about 40 minutes (take the left fork when the path divides or you'll miss the village altogether).

At an altitude of 1620m, Marla is the highest îlet in Mafate. Its name is said to be derived from a Malagasy term meaning 'many people', but these days, the town consists of only a few houses.

After you reach Marla, you can elect to end your hike by crossing the Col du Taïbit to Cilaos (for more information, see day four of the Tour des Cirques section following).

Places to Stay & Eat The trail into Marla passes between the red-roofed *Marla Gîte de Montagne* (☎ 43 78 31) and the private *gîte* run by the same owner. The gîte de montagne has beds for FF83 per person. The private gîte costs FF55 per person. Breakfast/dinner costs FF25/75 extra at both places.

The well-stocked village shop and another private gîte are run by *M Giroday* (☎ 43 83 13), who offers beds for FF55, plus breakfast/dinner for FF30/75.

Day Four: Marla to Col des Bœufs
(Walking time: about three hours)

This easy last day picks up GR R1 at the north end of the village. The trail is signposted to La Nouvelle, Col de Fourche and Col des Bœufs, and should get you to Maison Laclos within about 30 minutes. This ancient dwelling was abandoned in the aftermath of Hurricane Hyacinthe, which came through in 1980, and can be used as a shelter or as a camping site. From there, you should pick up the left-hand (northward) trail to La Nouvelle (the trail on the right ascends to the Plateau du Kerval, at 1768m).

A very short distance on, you'll reach a second junction. The main GR R1 trail returns to La Nouvelle, but you can cut out some distance by taking the right-hand fork, a GR R1 variant, which cuts straight back up (northward) to the Plaine des Tamarins (allow about 1½ hours). This trail connects with the main GR R1 trail into the cirque, from where it's an easy hour back to the car park at Col des Bœufs.

Tour des Cirques

This four-day walk roughly follows the path of GR R1 and is best started in Cilaos, which has excellent facilities for walkers and the added advantage of a health spa where you can unwind after your hike. The hike overlaps with days one and four of the 'Four Days in the Cirque de Mafate' hike, so you can easily extend the walk by combining the two routes.

Day One: Cilaos to Caverne Dufour
(Walking time: about four hours)

The trail starts just north of Cilaos, where Route des Sources hits the roads to Îlet à Cordes and Bras Sec, and rises through the casuarina forest to the Plateau des Chênes. Take the right fork towards La Roche Merveilleuse (The Marvellous Rock); the left fork leads along the ridge to Col du Taïbit. The trail crosses the forestry road several times before it reaches La Roche Merveilleuse, and then descends to meet the Bras Sec road. Try not to end up on the Sentier de Découverte, a circular nature trail around La Roche Merveilleuse.

From here, the trail follows the Bras Sec road for about 500m, branching off to the left through a forest of cryptomerias (a species of a cedar-like tree native to Réunion) at Le Bloc. If you like, you can cut out this first section of the walk and get a lift straight to the picnic area at Le Bloc by car or bus.

From Le Bloc, the path climbs steadily through the cryptomerias to the Plateau du Petit Matarum, where the forest changes to stunted giant heather bushes (known as *branles* or *brandes*), cloaked in wisps of lichen. It's uphill all the way from here to the gîte. Once you gain the saddle, there's a turning on the right to Plaine-des-Cafres, and a short distance further on, you'll come to the slightly ramshackle-looking **Gîte de la Caverne Dufour, Piton des Neiges** (☎ *51 15 26*) at

HIKING IN REUNION

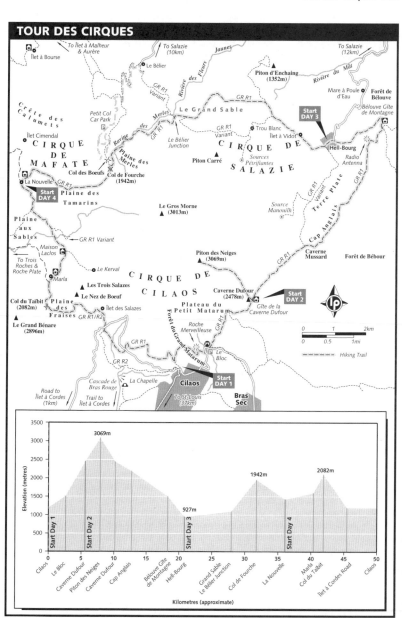

TOUR DES CIRQUES

To Îlet à Malheur & Aurère
Îlet à Bourse
To Salazie (10km)
Jaunes
To Salazie (12km)
Le Bélier
Rivière des Fleurs
Piton d'Enchaing (1352m)
Rivière du Mât
Mare à Poule d'Eau
Forêt de Bélouve
GR R1 Variant
GR R1
Bélouve Gîte de Montagne
Crête des Calumets
Petit Col Car Park
Le Grand Sable
Start DAY 3
Îlet Cimendal
Ravine des Merles
GR R1 Variant
Trou Blanc
Hell-Bourg
CIRQUE DE MAFATE
Plaine des Merles
Le Bélier Junction
CIRQUE DE SALAZIE
Radio Antenna
Piton Carré
Sources Pétrifiantes
Îlet à Vidot
Col des Boeufs
Col de Fourche (1942m)
La Nouvelle
Start DAY 4
GR R1 Variant
Terre Plate
Plaine des Tamarins
Le Gros Morne (3013m)
Source Manouilh
Cap Anglais
Plaine aux Sables
GR R1 Variant
Piton des Neiges (3069m)
GR R1
Caverne Mussard
Forêt de Bébour
Maison Laclos
To Trois Roches & Roche Plate
Le Kerval
CIRQUE DE CILAOS
Caverne Dufour (2478m)
Start DAY 2
Marla
Les Trois Salazes
Le Nez de Boeuf
Gîte de la Caverne Dufour
Col du Taïbit (2082m)
Plaine des Fraises
Îlet des Salazes
Plateau du Petit Matarum
GR R1/R2
Roche Merveilleuse
Le Grand Bénare (2896m)
GR R1
Forêt du Grand Matarum
GR R2
Le Bloc
Road to Îlet à Cordes (1km)
Cascade de Bras Rouge
La Chapelle
Cilaos
Start DAY 1
Trail to Îlet à Cordes
To St-Louis (37km)
Bras Sec

0 — 1 — 2km
0 — 0.5 — 1mi

- - - - - Hiking Trail

Elevation profile:

3500
3000 — 3069m
2500
2000 — 1942m — 2082m
1500
1000 — 927m
500
0

Start Day 1 | Start Day 2 | Start Day 3 | Start Day 4

Elevation (metres)

Cilaos | Le Bloc | Caverne Dufour | Piton des Neiges | Caverne Dufour | Cap Anglais | Bélouve Gîte de Montagne | Hell-Bourg | Grand Sable | Le Bélier Junction | Col de Fourche | La Nouvelle | Marla | Col du Taïbit | Îlet à Cordes Road | Cilaos

0 5 10 15 20 25 30 35 40 45 50

Kilometres (approximate)

2500m. The gîte is more comfortable than it looks, but there are no showers or hot water. Beds cost FF83 per person. Dinner is an extra FF90, and breakfast costs FF30 (both should be booked in advance).

Day Two: Caverne Dufour to Hell-Bourg via Piton des Neiges

(Walking time: three hours return to Piton des Neiges, plus three hours to Hell-Bourg)

Because the summit of Piton des Neiges is usually cloaked in cloud by midmorning, most people choose to stay overnight at the gîte, starting out for the peak the following morning. For your best chance of a decent view, you should leave the gîte at or before dawn. The path begins directly opposite the gîte; making it to the summit takes about 1½ hours. Markers are easily recognisable in white on the rock face, making the trail easy to follow in the dark, but you should bring a torch if you start out before dawn.

The landscape becomes increasingly rocky the higher you climb, and the final section rises steeply over shifting cinders that make for slippery footing. At the summit, there are few traces of vegetation, and the red, black and ochre rock leaves little doubt about the mountain's volcanic origins.

The active life of this vast volcano, which can be considered the true progenitor of the island of Réunion, took place more than 450,000 years ago, when floods of thick lava poured from the peak. With its collapse, the crater created the starting point for the cirques of Salazie, Mafate and Cilaos. Unlike Piton de la Fournaise, which is still active, the volcano here last hotted up around 30,000 years ago.

On a clear day, the whole island is spread out beneath you. If you didn't beat the cloud to the summit, you may just be confronted by an enveloping cloak of white.

The trail on to Hell-Bourg runs north across the saddle and skirts the rim of the Cirque de Salazie, passing through giant heather forest. It's a bit of a mud chute so watch your footing. After 1½ hours, you'll reach a white painted cross at Caverne Mussard, with excellent views over the Cirque de Salazie. If you just want some creature comforts, you can take the GR R1 variant straight downhill from here to the southern end of Hell-Bourg (two hours), emerging near the stadium and the trout farm.

More interesting is the walk along the cirque rim through the lush Fôret de Bélouve. Just beyond the turn-off, the trail begins a series of slippery ascents and descents through a marshy area of heather forest. Anchored metal ladders and wooden boardwalks are provided to help you over the boggiest sections. Once you start to see ferns among the trees, the worst is over.

From here, the trail enters an enchanted tropical forest, with primordial ferns and huge trees draped in sheets of moss. The woods suddenly seem to come alive with the sound of birdsong. Walking is easier through this lush area, and plaques describe some of the wildlife you are seeing and hearing. After an hour you'll reach a radio antenna on the lip of the cirque. This point offers spectacular views over Hell-Bourg and plenty of photo opportunities.

Following the gravel forestry road for another kilometre, you'll come to the appealing *Bélouve Gîte de Montagne* (☎ 41 21 23), which is a breath of fresh air after the simple gîte at Caverne Dufour. Beds cost FF83 per person (plus FF25/90 for breakfast/dinner). Campers can set up for free (one night only) by the lookout in front of the gîte.

The gîte is located at the head of an old logging cableway that was used to transport felled *tamarin des hautes* (mountain tamarind) trees down to Hell-Bourg to be used in the construction of Creole houses. The cableway terminal now houses a small logging-industry museum.

The final descent to Hell-Bourg follows the cableway into the valley. Cut through the garden of the gîte and bear left at the lookout. After an hour or so, you'll hit the first few farms and, a short distance beyond, the start of the town proper. The trail emerges by the park on Rue Général de Gaulle. Treat yourself to a meal and a hot shower when you arrive! (For more information on accommodation options, see Hell-Bourg in the Interior chapter.)

Day Three: Hell-Bourg to La Nouvelle
(Walking time: about seven hours)
Start this day's walk by taking the track at the end of Rue Général de Gaulle in Hell-Bourg to the thermal bath ruins; this track connects with the Îlet à Vidot road, which will take you to the car park in Îlet à Vidot.

From the car park, a dirt road descends into the valley, reaching a turning on the left to Le Grand Sable, Trou Blanc and Les Sources Pétrifiantes after about 500m. You should ignore the turn-off and continue straight ahead, passing a turning on the right to Piton d'Enchaing. The track ascends rather uneventfully for the next 1½ hours, crossing several ravines, before skirting along the edge of a large plantation of casuarina trees at Le Grand Sable (the trail from Trou Blancs emerges from the forest about 500m further on). The trail then drops down to cross one of the tributaries of the Rivière des Fleurs Jaunes. There's an excellent bivouac on the far bank where the trail to Le Bélier turns off through the woods. Allow about three hours from Hell-Bourg to reach this point.

From here, you should take the left fork, which follows the river upstream before climbing through the forest to meet the walking trail from Le Bélier near Col de Fourche after about 1½ hours. From here it's about 45 minutes to the saddle, where you'll catch your first glimpse of Mafate.

The walk into Mafate makes for a long and tiring day, but the last stretch from the Col de Fourche to La Nouvelle is all downhill. On the

Tour des Cirques – Day Three Side Trips

If you have energy to spare on day three, you could incorporate one of the following side trips along the way. They also make good day trips from Hell-Bourg.

Les Sources Pétrifiantes

These iron-rich hot springs are popular with day hikers from Hell-Bourg. Take the GR R1 from Îlet à Vidot, then turn left along the GR R1 variant to Trou Blanc where the track divides. After 2km on this track, the route to the falls branches off to the left. Allow about four hours for the return trip.

Piton d'Enchaing

This enticing 1352m peak is a popular but challenging day hike from Hell-Bourg. The peak was named after an escaped slave who used this lofty vantage point to spy on the movements of bounty-hunters in the Cirque de Salazie (see the boxed text 'Marrons' in the Interior chapter).

To get to the peak, start out as for the walk to Les Sources Pétrifiantes, but follow the right fork when the trail divides. A short distance further on, the trail to Piton d'Enchaing branches off to the right. Allow about 2½ hours each way from Hell-Bourg.

far side, the path descends on ageing wooden steps to meet the better track from the Petit Col car park.

The final section, from Col des Bœfs to La Nouvelle, is the same as the first day of the 'Four Days in the Cirque de Mafate' walk, crossing the atmospheric Plaine des Tamarins and descending on the far side to the village of La Nouvelle in about 1½ hours. (For more information on this part of the route, including a rundown of accommodation options in La Nouvelle, see day one of Four Days in the Cirque de Mafate earlier in this section.)

Day Four: La Nouvelle to Cilaos

(Walking time: about six hours)

This final day will take you back to the modern comforts of Cilaos, passing through some stunning countryside on the way.

The first section takes you down to the village of Marla via Maison Laclos, beginning with a steep descent into the Ravine Gérien. It's a fairly easy 1½ hour walk to Marla, passing some nice views of the cirque, but be sure to ignore the branches off to 'Marla par passerelle' and Plaine aux Sables.

Marla consists only of a few houses, but the village shop sells snacks and drinks. At the southern end of town you'll meet the trail to Trois Roches and Roche Plate, where you turn left (south) towards the reservoir. The trail ascends steadily towards the obvious low point on the ridge, reaching Col du Taïbit in about 1½ hours. If you reach this viewpoint early in the morning, there are magnificent views over the Cirque de Mafate, and down the Cirque de Cilaos to St-Louis and the coast.

The trail (GR R1/R2) descends slowly to the plateau at Îlet des Salazes, before dropping steeply through drier country to cross the Îlet à Cordes road after about two hours. You could always pick up a lift to Cilaos here, but die-hards should continue behind the concrete wall on the far side of the road (watch out for traffic) and descend into the valley. The trail divides just beyond. GR R2 turns right and follows the far bank of the Bras des Étangs, while GR R1 stays on the same side of the valley as the Îlet à Cordes road and so offers the better views.

The latter trail (GR R1) descends to the valley bottom and crosses the river, rising steeply on the far side to cross the Îlet à Cordes road a second time. The final ascent takes you through mixed forest to the top of the ridge. From here Cilaos seems an unattainable distance away, but you should persevere! The final stretch slopes gently down to Cilaos, meeting the turn-off down to Route des Sources after about an hour.

Depending on how you feel, you could stop off at the spa in Cilaos for a massage, or hit one of the restaurants in town for a well-earned Bourbon beer!

Short Walks from Cilaos

There are some excellent short walks and day walks from Cilaos. The following walks are shown on the Tour des Cirques map in this special section (for more detailed mapping of the trailheads, see the Cilaos map in the Interior chapter).

Cascade de Bras Rouge

This pretty waterfall is a popular picnic stop and lies 1½ hours (walking time) from Cilaos on the GR R2 route to the Col du Taïbit and Mafate. You can pick up the trail from the Îlet à Cordes road just outside Cilaos, or take a shortcut via the old thermal station in Cilaos (take the road opposite the Soeurs de St-Joseph de Cluny convent).

Bras Sec & Palmiste Rouge

You can hike across to these two pretty villages near Cilaos for a taste of rural life in the cirques. From Cilaos, the hiking trail to Bras Sec descends to cross the Ravine du Bras de Bejoin near the hospital on Rue des Fleurs Jaunes. It takes about an hour to reach Bras Sec. You can take the bus back to Cilaos.

From the southern end of Bras Sec, you can pick up the Sentier des Calumets trail which runs to the village of Palmiste Rouge via the Bonnet de Prêtre (Priest's Bonnet), the obvious peak south-east of Bras Sec. Allow about 2½ hours each way.

Roche Merveilleuse

This appealing viewpoint lies on the GR R1 route from Cilaos to Hell-Bourg, which starts up near the Hôtel des Thermes in Cilaos. Take the right fork at the Plateau des Chênes. Allow an hour each way.

La Chapelle & Îlet à Cordes

An interesting cave, La Chapelle is just down river from the Cascade de Bras Rouge, but you have to go the long way round to get here. The trail begins on Rue de la Chapelle at the south-west end of Cilaos. After about 1.5km, the trail to the cave branches off to the right. Allow four hours for the return trip.

You can also use this route to get to Îlet à Cordes; the trail continues straight ahead at the junction to La Chapelle and crosses the Ravine de Bras Rouge. Allow at least four hours one way to reach Îlet à Cordes.

Getting There & Away

From Cilaos, the Société Cilaosienne de Transport (☎ 31 85 87) offers transfers to Îlet à Cordes (FF40 for two people) and to the trailheads at Le Bloc (on the GR R1 route to Hell-Bourg) and Taïbit (on the GR R1/GR R2 route to Col du Taïbit and Mafate), saving you about an hour's walking time each way.

If you have driven up and you are worried about leaving your car, M Begoni (☎ 31 80 94) on Chemin des Fleurs in Cilaos offers secure parking for FF40 per night.

Piton de la Fournaise

Piton de la Fournaise is a bubbling, smouldering volcano that is probably Réunion's most renowned feature. The walk to the summit is extremely popular, and therefore crowded, but the fascinating tortured landscape more than makes up for the crowds.

Neither the main crater, Dolomieu (also known as Brûlant), nor the smaller crater to the north, Bory, has erupted for centuries. All the recent action has taken place in the tiny craters on the south flank of the volcano. The last eruption took place at the Piton de Partage in 1998.

While the volcano walk is popular, it still makes for a challenging day. The landscape around the volcano is harsh and arid, despite the mist which can drench hikers to the skin. The chilly wind whips away moisture, leaving walkers dehydrated and breathless. At times it can feel like you are walking on Mars, with only the dry crunch of the cinders underfoot for company.

The morning is the best time to climb the volcano, as you stand a better chance of clear views, but this time also brings the biggest crowds. The path from the ridge across the lava plain can resemble a trail of ants, with hundreds of walkers all breaking for the peak at the same time.

Most people make a circuit of the Dolomieu crater, starting from the **Gîte de Bellecombe (Gîte de Volcan)** (☎ 21 28 96). Accommodation

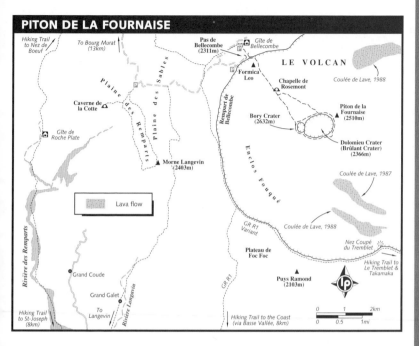

PITON DE LA FOURNAISE

Hiking Trail to Nez de Boeuf

To Bourg Murat (13km)

Pas de Bellecombe (2311m)

Gîte de Bellecombe

LE VOLCAN

Formica Leo

Chapelle de Rosemont

Coulée de Lave, 1988

Plaine des Sables

Caverne de la Cotte

Plaine des Remparts

Rempart de Bellecombe

Bory Crater (2632m)

Piton de la Fournaise (2510m)

Gîte de Roche Plate

Dolomieu Crater (Brûlant Crater) (2366m)

Morne Langevin (2403m)

Enclos Foucqué

Coulée de Lave, 1987

Lava flow

GR R1 Variant

Coulée de Lave, 1988

Nez Coupé du Tremblet

Rivière des Remparts

Plateau de Foc Foc

Hiking Trail to Le Tremblet & Takamaka

Grand Coude

GR R1

Puys Ramond (2103m)

Grand Galet

To Langevin

Rivière Langevin

Hiking Trail to St-Joseph (8km)

Hiking Trail to the Coast (via Basse Vallée, 8km)

0 1 2km

0 0.5 1mi

at the gîte costs FF83 per person, plus FF90 for dinner and FF30 for breakfast. Alternatively, you can begin the crater circuit from the Pas de Bellecombe car park 600m further on from the gîte. The return walk from the gîte to the summit and around the summit is approximately 13km and takes five hours under optimum conditions.

The trail skirts the crater rim to the left (east) of the car park before dropping abruptly to the floor of the immense U-shaped outer crater, known as Enclos Foucqué. The route across the lava plain is marked with white paint-spots. The liquid origin of the rocks is quite apparent here – it feels a little like walking on soggy ground. There are endless snags where you can turn an ankle, so take care as you pick your way across the lava formations.

On the way, you'll pass a small scoria cone, Formica Leo, and a cavern in the lava known as Chapelle de Rosemont. From here, the right-hand path climbs steeply and directly to the 2632m-high, 200m-wide Bory Crater, while the left fork takes a more gradual route up to La Soufrière, the northern wall of the gaping 900m-wide Dolomieu Crater.

Once at the top, you can decide whether to do the circuit around both craters or just traverse the track that connects the Bory and La Soufrière routes along the northern rims. While walking along the rim, beware of large fissures, holes and, most of all, overhangs. Leave the way you came – there are no safe routes across the recent lava flows to the south-east.

Hiking from Bourg-Murat
The four-hour hike to the volcano from Bourg-Murat via the Sentier Josemont is regarded as something of a walk for masochists, as it's easy to pick up a ride along the Route Forestière du Volcan instead.

Hiking from St-Joseph
A more challenging and interesting alternative to the hike from Bourg-Murat is the two-day hike up the stunning gorge of the Rivière des Remparts from St-Joseph, breaking the journey at the **Gîte de Roche Plate** (☎ *59 13 94*). Beds here cost FF83 per person, plus FF30/100 for breakfast/dinner. This trail climbs to the viewpoint at Nez de Bœuf on the road to the volcano.

Hiking from Le Tremblet
Near Tremblet, there's a GR R2 trailhead from which the extremely energetic can climb to the summit of Piton de la Fournaise. To reach the trailhead, take the coastal bus route between St-Benoît and St-Pierre, and get off the bus at the 'Kiosque' stop. It's a steep, rugged and wet walk and is considered one of Réunion's most challenging, so don't take it lightly.

Plan on two to three days to reach the gîte at Pas de Bellecombe. An alternative route follows the 1986 flows from the village of Takamaka (get off the bus at 'Roche à Jacquot') and joins the Le Tremblet route at the Abri du Tremblet bivouac gîte.

Getting There & Away
For those with a vehicle, getting to the volcano couldn't be easier because of the all-weather Route Forestière du Volcan, which climbs from Bourg-Murat all the way to Pas de Bellecombe on the crater's outer rim. This point is just a couple of hours' walking from the summit. Check out the lookout over the Rivière des Remparts at Nez de Bœuf and the sinister Cratère Commerson on the way up.

Seychelles

SEYCHELLES

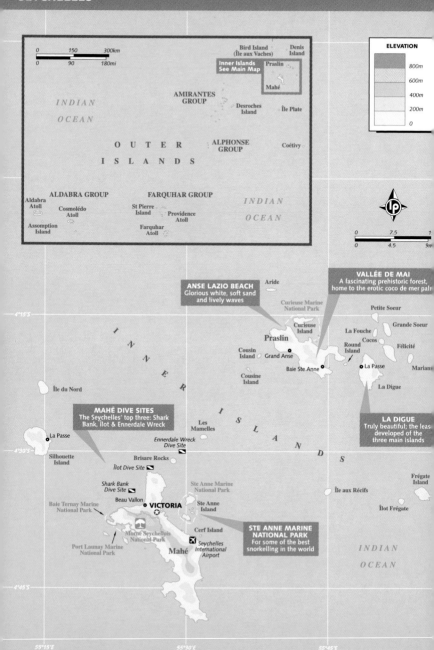

ELEVATION

800m
600m
400m
200m
0

Inset map (OUTER ISLANDS)

0   150   300km
0   90   180mi

Bird Island
(Île aux Vaches)   Denis
Island

**Inner Islands
See Main Map**

Praslin

Mahé

INDIAN

OCEAN

AMIRANTES
GROUP

Desroches
Island   Île Plate

O U T E R   ALPHONSE
GROUP   Coétivy

I S L A N D S

ALDABRA GROUP   FARQUHAR GROUP   *INDIAN*

Aldabra
Atoll   St Pierre
Island   *OCEAN*
Cosmolédo
Atoll   Providence
Atoll

Assomption
Island   Farquhar
Atoll

Main map

Aride

VALLÉE DE MAI
A fascinating prehistoric forest,
home to the erotic coco de mer palm

ANSE LAZIO BEACH
Glorious white, soft sand
and lively waves

Curieuse Marine
National Park

Petite Soeur

Grande Soeur

4°15'S

Curieuse
Island

La Fouche
Cocos   Félicité

Praslin   Round
Island

I N N E R   Cousin
Island   Grand Anse   La Passe   Marian

Baie Ste Anne   La Digue

Cousine
Island

Île du Nord   La Digue

MAHÉ DIVE SITES
The Seychelles' top three: Shark
Bank, Îlot & Ennerdale Wreck

Les
Mamelles

LA DIGUE
Truly beautiful; the leas
developed of the
three main islands

Ennerdale Wreck
Dive Site

Brisare Rocks

La Passe   Îlot Dive Site   Frégate
Island

4°30'S

Silhouette
Island

Shark Bank
Dive Site   Ste Anne Marine
National Park   Île aux Récifs

Beau Vallon

Baie Ternay Marine
National Park   **VICTORIA**   Ste Anne
Island   Îlot Frégate

Morne Seychellois
National Park   Cerf Island   **STE ANNE MARINE
NATIONAL PARK**
For some of the best
snorkelling in the world

INDIAN

Port Launay Marine
National Park   Mahé   Seychelles
International
Airport   *OCEAN*

4°45'S

55°15'E   55°30'E   55°45'E

Scale bars

0   7.5   1
0   4.5   9m

Seychelles

Facts about the Seychelles

Among the estimated 115 coral islands that make up the Seychelles are some of the most beautiful island getaways in the Indian Ocean, or indeed the world. Here you can find the lush, tropical paradise you may have seen in seductive advertisements or glossy travel brochures. If the idea of sipping a cocktail on a palm-fringed tropical beach appeals, the Seychelles is probably for you.

In fact, the Seychelles can seem far more – or far less – impressive than the seductive images in the brochures suggest, depending on how much you can afford to spend on your sojourn in paradise. Many of the best islands and most glorious beaches have been nabbed by the expensive upmarket hotels and resorts, and what is left behind for travellers with shallower pockets can fall a long way short of the tropical idyll that is promoted by the Seychelles Marketing Board.

Behind the relaxed tropical image of the Seychelles lurks an intriguing and often dangerous political background. Since President France Albert René grabbed power in 1977 from the elected leader of the former British colony, the Seychelles have periodically harboured spies as well as tourists. The CIA, the KGB and MI5 flitted through the islands during the Cold War era, mixing with communist troops from North Korea and Tanzania, Russian advisers, US military personnel from a satellite tracking station, mercenaries, private detectives, exiled rebels, diplomats and the Mafia.

Most travellers to the Seychelles just spend a day or two on the main island, Mahé, then make a beeline for the more easy-going and exotic islands of Praslin or La Digue. For those who really want to play jet-setter there are a handful of smaller, more secluded island hideaways.

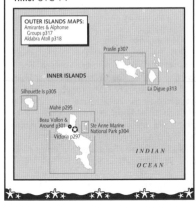

HISTORY

Until the 17th century the Seychelles were uninhabited, though there are ancient tombs on Silhouette Island which are attributed to shipwrecked Arab sailors. The islands were first spotted by Portuguese explorers, but the first recorded landing was left to a British East India Company ship in 1609.

Settlement and Colonisation

The first settlers were pirates and privateers, who used the islands as a temporary base and provisions stop during lulls in their maraudings. The famous French pirate Olivier 'La Buse' Levasseur is believed by many to have deposited his treasure somewhere in the islands, possibly around Bel Ombre on Mahé (see the boxed text 'Pieces of Eight' in the Mahé section).

In 1742, the great Mahé de La Bourdonnais, the governor of Mauritius (then known as Île de France), sent Lazare Picault to check out the islands. Picault named the main island after his governor (and the bay where he landed after himself) and laid the way for the French to claim possession of the islands 12 years later. They were named the Seychelles in honour of the finance minister to Louis XV, Jean Moreau de Sachelles.

The first batch of the French and their slaves arrived on Ste Anne Island in 1770. After a few false starts, the settlers began growing spices, cassava, sugar cane, coffee, sweet potatoes and maize, at the same time eating their way through the large colonies of giant tortoises.

During the 18th century, the British began to take an interest in the islands. Rather than risking life and limb to fend off British attacks, the French governor Queau de Quinssy lowered the French flag and surrendered to the British frigates, raising the French flag again as soon as the British ships had departed! The 'great capitulator', as de Quinssy became known, was to repeat this manoeuvre about a dozen times before the Seychelles became a British dependency of Mauritius, after the Napoleonic Wars and the Treaty of Paris in 1814.

De Quinssy was allowed to remain in charge until 1827. He changed his name to De Quincy in deference to his new masters and lived out his days in the Seychelles. His tomb is at Government House in Victoria, Mahé.

The British did little to develop the islands except increase the number of slaves. When slavery was abolished in 1835, the slaves were released. French remained the main language and French culture too was dominant.

Over the years the islands have been used as a holding pen for numerous political prisoners and exiles, many of whom actually had a great time here. The British even tossed around the idea of turning the islands into a concentration camp for Boer prisoners of war or Irish republican rebels, but this never happened. As recently as 1956, the rebellious Archbishop Makarios of Cyprus was housed in the governor's lodge at Sans Souci on Mahé. Later, the Southern Maldivian rebel Abdullah Afif Didi was also imprisoned on the island.

In 1903 the Seychelles became a crown colony administered from London. The country went into the political and economic doldrums until 1964, when political parties were formed. France Albert René, a young lawyer, founded the Seychelles People's United Party (SPUP). His colleague in law and grandson of a Chinese immigrant, James Mancham, led the new Seychelles Democratic Party (SDP).

1966 Election & Independence

In 1965, an Australian journalist wrote: 'Hardly anything happens in the Seychelles. People show virtually no interest in politics …the clocks chime twice for those who were not awake the first time'. However, the next 20 years resulted in a complete and stunning transformation of the sleepy, forgotten islands, with events that would wake up the world.

Mancham's SDP, made up of the islands' businesspeople and planters, won the elections in 1966 and 1970. René's SPUP fought on a socialist and independence ticket. In June 1975 a coalition of the two parties gave the appearance of unity in the lead up to independence from the UK, which was granted a year later. Mancham became the first president and René the prime minister.

The flamboyant Sir Jim (as James Mancham was known) – poet and playboy – placed all his eggs in one basket: tourism. He jet-setted around the world with a beautiful socialite on each arm, and he put the Seychelles on the map.

The rich and famous poured in for holidays or to stay and party, party, party. Adnan Khashoggi and other Arab millionaires bought large tracts of land on the islands. Film stars and celebrities went there to enhance their romantic, sexy images. *Goodbye Emmanuelle* was filmed on La Digue.

However, according to René and the SPUP, the wealth was not being spread evenly or fairly and the country was no more than a rich person's playground. René said that poor Creoles were little better off than slaves.

So on 5 June 1977, barely a year after independence, René and a team of Tanzanian-trained rebels carried out an almost bloodless coup while Mancham was in London attending a conference of Commonwealth leaders. As Mancham said at the time, 'It was no heroic deed to take over the Seychelles. Twenty-five people with sticks could seize control.' René brought in Tanzanian and North Korean soldiers to make sure that any opposition would need more than that to take over the country.

An attempt to do so came in November 1981, when a band of mercenaries, led by ex-Congo 'dog of war' Colonel Mike Hoare, bungled a chance to invade. The group posed as a South African rugby club on an annual binge, but a customs officer discovered weapons in one of their suitcases. Two people died in a shoot-out at the airport before the mercenaries beat a hasty retreat by hijacking an Air India plane back to South Africa. Five mercenaries, the advance guard, were rounded up, tried and sentenced to death. They were later released and deported. In 1992 the South African government paid the Seychelles government eight million rupees as compensation for the attempted coup.

In the following years, René went on to consolidate his position by deporting many of the members and supporters of the outlawed SDP. Opposed to René's one-party socialist state, these *grands blancs* (rich whites) set up 'resistance movements' in the UK, South Africa and Australia.

The country fell into disarray as the tourist trade dried to a trickle. In 1982 there was a mutiny of NCOs (non-commissioned officers) in the Seychelles army, and a coup plot by Seychelles expatriates was discovered taking place in a London hotel room. Bombings and murders on the islands continued into 1983 as part of a campaign of civil disruption by supporters of the SDP.

In December 1984, thorough intelligence gathering by the Seychelles government foiled another coup plot in the early stages of planning in South Africa. A year later, Gerard Hoareau, the immigration chief under Mancham and the leader of the Seychelles resistance movement in the UK, was machine-gunned to death outside his London home. In 1986 there was another attempted coup by majors from within the Seychelles army.

Facing growing international criticism, as well as the threat of withdrawal of foreign aid, René pulled a political about-face in the early 1990s; he abandoned one-party rule, but ensured that the conditions imposed on the new opposition parties would alienate supporters of his arch rival, Mancham.

Multiparty elections were held in July 1992, under the watchful eye of Commonwealth observers. René and his Seychelles People's Progressive Front (SPPF) won 58.4% of the votes; Mancham, who had returned to the Seychelles with a hefty Special Air Force (SAS) security team from the UK, fielded 33.7% for his SDP and contested the results as rigged and unfair.

In November 1992, a draft constitution was thrown out after a referendum failed to achieve the required 60% of votes in favour. The opposition, most notably Mancham's SDP, campaigned successfully against proposed links between presidential election results and the allocation of National Assembly seats. In 1993, a modified constitution based on a multiparty system was implemented.

Elections held in 1993 resulted in René retaining power, while the SDP's star has continued to wane. René again surged to victory in the 1998 election, and even Mancham himself abandoned the SDP in favour of the more popular Seychelles National Party in 1999. The languishing SDP is now in the hands of Father Wavel Ramkalawan. The next elections are due in 2003.

GEOGRAPHY & GEOLOGY
The Seychelles lies about 1600km off the coast of East Africa, its nearest neighbour. There are roughly 115 islands, with a combined area of only 455 sq km, situated between the equator and the 10th parallel south.

SEYCHELLES

The central islands are granite, the main three being Mahé, Praslin and La Digue. The outlying islands are coral atolls. The granite islands, which do not share the volcanic nature of Réunion and Mauritius, appear to be peaks of a huge submerged plateau that was left behind by India when the continental plates shifted about 65 million years ago. The highest point in the islands is Morne Seychellois (905m) on Mahé.

CLIMATE

The Seychelles lies outside the cyclone zone, which makes it a safer bet than Mauritius or Réunion for visits between November and April. But the islands do catch the south-east trade winds, making many beaches unsuitable for swimming between June and November.

The seasons are defined by the beginning and end of these winds, which usually blow from May to October. During the rest of the year, the islands experience the north-west monsoon winds that bring the rain, especially in January. The turnaround periods between the two winds are the calmest.

The rain generally comes in sudden, heavy bursts. Mahé, the most mountainous island, and lofty Silhouette Island get the highest rainfall. January is the wettest month by far, and July and August are the driest. The temperature is constant throughout the year, between 24°C and 30°C, as is the humidity, at around 80%.

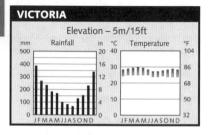

ECOLOGY & ENVIRONMENT

The Seychelles government has traditionally tried to balance tourist developments with the protection of the natural assets that attract the tourists (and therefore revenue) to the islands. However, the rising population of the islands is putting a strain on that policy. In 1998, the government authorised a vast land-reclamation project for the northeast coast of Mahé, providing valuable land for housing and development, but marring this area of the coastline indefinitely.

Much of the marine life in the Seychelles is protected, but that doesn't stop unscrupulous operators offering souvenirs made from coral and other marine species. We strongly urge you not to buy anything made out of turtle shell or to buy or collect seashells. (For detailed information on marine conservation, see the special section 'Underwater Worlds'.)

FLORA & FAUNA

The islands are a haven for wildlife, particularly birds and tropical fish. The government's conservation policies include the formation of several marine and nature reserves. Because of the islands' isolation and the comparatively late arrival of humans, there are many species unique to the Seychelles. Some are plentiful, some are rare and some are now extinct. (For more information on the marine life of the Seychelles, see the special section 'Underwater Worlds'.)

Flora

The coconut palm and the casuarina are the most common trees on the islands. There are a few banyans – a giant one shades the road at Ma Constance, about 3.5km north of Victoria. You're also likely to see screw pines, bamboo and tortoise trees (so named because the fruit looks like the tortoises that eat it). Virgin forest now exists only on the higher parts of Silhouette Island and Mahé, and in the Vallée de Mai on Praslin, which is one of only three places in the world where the giant coco de mer palm grows. The other two are Silhouette and Curieuse Islands.

Out of about 200 plant species, 80 are endemic. These include the *bois rouge*, which has broad, reddish leaves and red wood, the giant and very rare *bois de fer*, and the *capucin*, named because its seed resembles the hood of a Capuchin monk.

In the high, remote parts of Silhouette Island and Mahé, you may come across the insect-eating pitcher plant, which either clings to adjacent trees or bushes or sprawls along the ground.

On the floral front, there are plenty of orchids, bougainvilleas, hibiscuses, gardenias and frangipanis.

The Botanical Gardens in Victoria are well kept and provide a pleasant and interesting walk. The Vallée de Mai on Praslin is a must. For chance discoveries, get away from the beach for a day and head into the hills on Mahé, Silhouette or Praslin.

Fauna

Common mammals and reptiles around the islands include the fruit bat or flying fox, the gecko, the skink and the tenrec (a hedgehog-like mammal imported from Madagascar). There are also some small snakes, but they are not dangerous.

Insect life in the Seychelles is represented by more than 3000 species. Among the more interesting insects are the lumbering rhinoceros beetle, whose larvae cause considerable damage by feeding on young shoots of coconut palms; the giant tenebrionid beetle of Frégate Island; and the various kinds of wasp, which excel in creating mud pots attached to vegetation, rocks or walls. Despite an impressive appearance, the giant millipedes, palm spiders and whip scorpions are not life threatening, but you can expect a nasty reaction if you handle them.

Tortoises The French and the English wiped out the giant land tortoises from all the islands except Aldabra, where there are still a few thousand left. Several tortoises have been brought to the central islands, where they now munch their way around pens at hotels. There is a free-roaming colony on Curieuse Island. Perhaps the biggest daddy of all is in the Cousin Island bird sanctuary (although Bird Island's operators also claim that distinction for Esmeralda). Giant tortoises, central to the Seychelles coat of arms, are endemic to only two regions in the world: one is the Seychelles, the other is the Galápagos Islands, off Ecuador.

Bird Life Almost every island seems to have some rare species of bird: on Frégate and Aride are the magpie robins (known as *pie chanteuse* in Creole); on Cousin you'll find the bush warbler; La Digue has the *veuve* (paradise flycatcher); and Praslin has the black parrot. The bare-legged scops owl and the Seychelles kestrel live on Mahé, and Bird Island is home to millions of fairy terns.

In general there are plenty of herons, fodies, sunbirds, lovebirds, egrets, owls, mynahs, sparrows, shearwaters, petrels, plovers, boobies, sooty terns and gulls.

Four of the islands are bird sanctuaries – Bird, Cousin, Aride and Frégate. The Vallée de Mai on Praslin and the Veuve Reserve on La Digue are also protected reserves.

GOVERNMENT & POLITICS

The Seychelles is a republic. The current president, France Albert René, heads a cabinet of around 10 ministers with specific portfolios. In 1993 the constitution was reformed to incorporate multiparty politics and in July 1993 René won elections held under this revised constitution. He retained power in the 1998 elections; elections are due again in 2003.

ECONOMY

The Seychelles are very Westernised islands with most of the trappings of a Western economy. The minimum wage, however, is still around Rs1900 (US$340) per month.

The islands were, and still are, labelled an idyllic paradise, with plenty of fish in the sea and fruit on the trees; a place where traditional work patterns are very different from Western ones. But the René government's importation of foreign skills and workers means these patterns are slowly changing.

With the influence of the former Soviet Union on the wane, the country is moving slowly towards privatisation and a free-market economy. The most significant recent change has been abandonment of the Seychelles Marketing Board's monopoly on some foods.

Despite wages that are high in comparison with those in other Indian Ocean countries, the standard of living of most Creoles is lower than you might expect, mostly because of the disproportionately high cost of living.

Tourism

The mainstay of the islands' economy is tourism, as it was before the socialist revolution or coup of 1977. Ever since the coup, attempts have been made to promote other industries, but the tourism industry continues to account for at least half the country's gross national product, and provides employment for 20% of the workforce. There are more than 140,000 visitors to the Seychelles annually. To maintain this high level of tourist interest, the Seychelles Marketing Board (SMB) is very active in promoting the islands' tropical image around the world.

Fishing & Agriculture

The most successful alternative to tourism has been commercial fishing. Victoria is home to the huge Indian Ocean Tuna tuna-processing plant, which can process up to 200 tonnes of fish per day. However, environmentalists are becoming concerned at the outflows from the plant into the Ste Anne Marine National Park, and even sports fishermen are reporting reduced numbers of fish.

The Seychelles' 320km Exclusive Economic Zone, proclaimed in 1977, includes fisheries rich in tuna and red snapper. Although fish is the staple diet of the Seychellois, this is changing with the greater availability and choice of agricultural produce. A recent addition is the prawn farm on Coëtivy, which supplies the local market.

The Seychelles Marketing Board is responsible for all aspects of the agricultural sector, including production, processing, packaging and distribution of products. It sets and controls prices for some local produce, but no longer does this for fruit and vegetables. Copra and cinnamon have traditionally been the main agricultural exports, but the government's first concern is to become self-sufficient in food.

Other Industries

Other industries include the manufacture of paint, detergents, plastics and packaging products, and joint foreign ventures.

POPULATION & PEOPLE

The most recent population figure for the Seychelles is 79,164. Every shade and hue of skin and hair imaginable exists in the Seychelles, arising out of a mixture of European, African, Indian, Chinese and Arab genes. No creed or colour can be said to have dominated since the 1977 coup, when most of the *grands blancs* (rich whites) were dispossessed.

Most Seychellois are Catholic, but marriage is an unpopular institution (the reasons cited are that it doesn't last and it's expensive), which means high levels of illegitimacy. At one point in the 1970s, more than 50% of the population was illegitimate. Because of this, the islanders have acquired a largely undeserved reputation for promiscuity, a situation fuelled by the early promotion of the Seychelles as a tropical Garden of Eden with all the associated lust, temptation and sin.

That image has been 'cleaned up' by the socialist government and the tourist board now promotes packaged weddings and honeymoons on the islands, leaving any erotic suggestiveness to the famous coco de mer nut. The high incidence of HIV/AIDS is also a disincentive to put anyone's reputation for promiscuity to the test.

In the Seychelles the colonial backlash is still somewhat evident, although it's not nearly as strong as it was a few years back. With the sense of national pride and identity that developed after independence and the coup came a more aloof attitude to visitors. But generally, the people are friendly and helpful.

EDUCATION

The education system has developed considerably since René's takeover. Nowadays, between the ages of 3½ and 5½, children can attend a noncompulsory creche education program. Primary and secondary level schooling is compulsory up to age 15½. There are several fee-paying schools.

Until the early 1990s, school-leavers were obliged to spend a year in the National Youth Service (NYS), a communist boot-camp where youths would be separated from their families and indoctrinated in the teachings of Marx and Engels by Russian, Cuban and Angolan tutors. These days, the cadets in the NYS camps at Port Launay and Cap Ternay are there on a voluntary basis.

The Polytechnic at Mont Fleuri provides a wide range of academic, technical and vocational courses for students between the ages of 16½ and 20½.

ARTS

The Seychelles was uninhabited when it was settled, so the Creoles are the closest the country has to an indigenous population. Many aspects of their African origins survive, including the séga and moutia dances.

The government has formed the National School of Music and the National Cultural Troupe (NCT) to foster Creole cultural identity and tradition. They have produced some fine singers, dancers and writers. Creole culture is also preserved and promoted through the colourful Festival Kreol (see the boxed text 'Festival Kreol' following).

Dance

The sombre *moutia* is the traditional dance of the Seychelles, and has strong African and Malagasy rhythms. The songs are prayers that the slaves turned into work chants, similar to the early black gospel music of the USA. They are accompanied by slow, repetitive dance routines. The moutia is normally danced around an open fire and serves as the primary evening entertainment.

European influences are evident in the *contredanse*, which has its roots in the court of Louis XIV of France, as well as the *mazok*, which is reminiscent of the French waltz, and the *kosez*, which is a type of quadrille.

The Seychelles version of the *séga* differs little from that of Mauritius. Séga dance displays are held at most of the large hotels at least one night a week and you may even be lucky enough to stumble onto a more spontaneous celebration.

Music

The Indian, European, Chinese and Arabic backgrounds of the Seychellois are reflected in their music. The accordion, banjo

---

Festival Kreol

The vibrant Festival Kreol aims to preserve and promote Creole culture. Held every year around the end of October, this week-long festival is an explosion of Creole cuisine, fashion, art, music and dance. Creole artists from other countries are invited to participate, and the festival provides young artists with a platform on which to unleash their creative talent. Other events often held during the Festival Kreol include street theatre, forums to discuss Creole literature and linguistics, photographic exhibitions, puppet shows and dance competitions. There are various Creole handicrafts and knick-knacks on sale.

The Festival Kreol has a different venue each year – for more detailed information, contact the Ministry of Culture (☎ 321333) at the National Library in Victoria.

---

and violin music brought to the islands by the early European settlers has blended with that of the *makalapo*, a stringed instrument with a tin sound box; the *zez*, a monochord sitar; African skin drums; and the *bom*, a bowed instrument.

Patrick Victor is one of the best-known musicians on the islands for his Creole pop and folk music; you can buy his recordings in most souvenir and music shops. Other popular local stars are David Philoe, Jonise Juliette, Serge Camille, Jones Camille and Hudson Dorothe. The late Raymond Lebon is also popular.

On a more traditional level are the roving *camtole* bands, which feature fiddle, banjo, accordion and drums. They sometimes accompany the contredanse, a dance similar to the quadrille.

Literature

The Kreol Institute on Mahé was set up to research and promote Creole culture, specifically literature. It publishes books in Creole and sells books written by Creole authors.

Art

Over the past several decades, more and more artists and craftspeople have settled in

SEYCHELLES

the Seychelles and spawned a local industry to cater for the souvenir-hungry tourists (see Shopping in the Seychelles Facts for the Visitor chapter). The tourist office can provide a brochure that lists local artists.

Lorenzo Appiani was responsible for the sculptures on the roundabouts at each end of 5th June Ave in Victoria. The Freedom Square monument known as Twa Zwazo is said to represent the continents of Africa, Europe and Asia, each of which has played a part in the development of the Seychellois people.

Theatre

Creoles once performed impromptu street theatre known as *sokwe*, but the practice has all but disappeared. Theatre arts aren't yet popular with the Seychellois; public performances these days concentrate on music and dancing. However, the success of the Creole comedy *Bolot Feray* has encouraged greater interest in play writing and theatre performance. For more information about theatrical performances contact the Ministry of Culture (☎ 321333) at the National Library in Victoria.

SOCIETY & CONDUCT

The Seychellois are quite traditional in their attitudes, and society continues to be largely male dominated. Fortunately for women, the tourism industry is regarded as quite an equal-opportunity employer.

Because birth control is frowned on for religious reasons, many of the problems that afflict mainland Africa, such as rapid population growth and HIV/AIDS, are also beginning to affect the Seychelles.

Dos & Don'ts

Skimpy beachwear is OK for the hotel pool and beaches, but you may attract lingering gazes and pestering elsewhere. If you want to bathe topless, you're best doing so on secluded beaches, unless you don't mind being ogled. If you visit a shrine or other holy place, dress and behave with respect. (For detailed information on appropriate behaviour, see Society & Conduct in the Regional Facts for the Visitor chapter.)

RELIGION

Most Seychellois are Catholic and the majority are avid churchgoers. But there is also a widespread belief in the supernatural and in the old magic of spirits known as *gris gris*. Sorcery was outlawed in 1958, but there are quite a number of *bonhommes* and *bonnefemmes di bois* (medicine men and women) practising their cures and curses and concocting potions for love, luck and revenge. These rituals and beliefs resemble those of Caribbean voodoo, but they are practised only on a limited scale.

LANGUAGE

English and French are the official languages of the Seychelles. Most people speak both, although French Creole is the lingua franca. *Kreol seselwa* was 'rehabilitated' and made semi-official in 1981, and is increasingly used in newspapers and literature. These days, most Seychellois will use English when speaking to tourists, French when conducting business, and Creole in the home. (For a guide to French and a list of useful words and phrases, see the Language chapter at the back of this book.)

Seychelles Creole is similar to that of Mauritius and Martinique, but differs remarkably from that of Réunion. In the local patois, the soft pronunciation of certain French consonants is hardened and some syllables are dropped completely. The soft 'j' becomes 'z', for example. The following phrases may help you venture into Creole:

Good morning/ Good afternoon.	*Bonzour.*
How are you?	*Comman sava?*
Fine, thanks.	*Mon byen, mersi.*
What's your name?	*Ki mannyer ou appel?*
My name is ...	*Mon appel ...*
Where do you live?	*Koté ou resté?*
I don't understand.	*Mon pas konpran.*
I like it.	*Mon kontan.*
Where is ...?	*Ol i ...?*
How much is that?	*Kombyen sa?*
I'm thirsty.	*Mon soif.*
Can I have a beer, please?	*Mon kapa ganny en labyer silvouplé?*

Facts for the Visitor

PLANNING
When to Go
The best times to visit depend on what you like to do. Diving is best from March to May and September to November. The south-east trade winds (usually from May to October) provide good conditions for sailing or windsurfing. The rain can fall in short torrents during the wet season, yet it can be overcast for days during the cooler, drier periods.

Hotel prices shoot up and accommodation can be hard to find during the peak seasons (from December to January and from July to August). Easter can also get busy.

Maps
The tourist offices have a reasonably good map of the major islands – Mahé, Praslin and La Digue; this map also has a small inset of Victoria. Travel agents also stock basic maps for tourists. The Seychelles Survey Department in Independence House, Victoria, offers detailed maps of the individual islands. It's open from 8.30 am to noon and 1 to 4 pm on weekdays.

TOURIST OFFICES
Local Tourist Offices
The Seychelles Ministry of Tourism (☎ 224030) has its head office at Independence House, Victoria (PO Box 92). It has a tourist office full of brochures nearby on Independence Ave (see Information in the Victoria section).

Tourist Offices Abroad
There are Seychelles tourist offices in the following countries:

Belgium (☎ 02-640 2505, fax 640 4905) 30 Square du Sol, Bosch (PO Box 8), 1050 Brussels
France (☎ 01 42 89 97 77, fax 01 42 89 97 70) 32 Rue de Ponthieu, 75008 Paris
Germany (☎ 069-29 20 64, fax 29 62 30) Hoch Strasse 15, D60313 Frankfurt
India (☎ 011-331 1122, fax 335 0027) Trac Representations, F-12 Connaught Place, New Delhi 110001
Italy (☎ 05 686 90 56, fax 06 686 81 27) Via Giulia 66, 00186 Rome

Japan (☎ 03-5449 0461, fax 5449 0462) Berna Heits, 4-A3 Hiroo 5-4-11, Shibuya, Tokyo 150
South Africa (☎ 011-791 0300, fax 791 0052) 480 Cork Ave, Ferndale 2194, Johannesburg
UK (☎ 020-7224 1670, fax 7486 1352) 2nd floor, Eros House, 111 Baker St, London W1M 1FE
USA (☎ 212-687 9766, fax 922 9177) 235 East 40th St, Suite 24A, New York, NY 10016

VISAS
You don't need a visa to enter the Seychelles, just a valid passport, an onward ticket, booked accommodation and sufficient funds for your stay. Upon arrival at the airport, you will be given a visitor's visa for up to a month, depending on the departure date printed on your onward ticket.

Visa Extensions
If you wish to extend your visa, apply with proof of funds and your onward ticket at the Immigration Office (☎ 224030, fax 225035), Independence House, on the corner of Independence and 5th June Aves in Victoria. Processing takes about a week. The office is open from 8 am to noon and from 1 to 4 pm Monday to Friday.

You can extend the visa by up to three months free of charge. Thereafter the cost is Rs200 per three-month extension. You can only stay one year on a visitor's visa.

EMBASSIES
Seychelles Embassies & Consulates
Seychelles has diplomatic representation in the following countries:

Australia (☎ 08-9291 6570, fax 9291 9157) 23 Marri Cres, Les Murdie, Perth, WA 6076
France (☎ 01 42 30 57 47, fax 01 42 30 57 40) 51 Ave Mozart, 75016, Paris
Germany (☎ 069-59 82 62, fax 59 70 16) Oeder Weg 43, D-60318, Frankfurt
Mauritius (☎ 251 0013, fax 238 4526) 616 St James Court, St Denis St, Port Louis
UK (☎ 020-7224 1660, fax 7487 5756) 2nd floor, Eros House, 111 Baker St, London W1M 1FE
USA (☎ 212-972 1785, fax 972 1786) 820 Second Ave, Suite 900F, New York, NY 10017-4504

SEYCHELLES

Other countries in which the Seychelles has diplomatic representation include Austria, Canada, Denmark, Finland, Greece, Hong Kong, India, Indonesia, Israel, Italy, Japan, Jordan, Kenya, Madagascar, Malaysia, Netherlands, Norway, Pakistan, Philippines, Singapore, South Africa, Spain, Sweden, Switzerland and Thailand.

Embassies & Consulates in the Seychelles

Following are the addresses of the major foreign embassies and consulates in the Seychelles:

France (☎ 382500) Victoria House, Victoria
Germany (☎ 261222) PO Box 132, Mont Fleuri
India (☎ 224489) PO Box 488, Le Chantier
Madagascar (☎ 344030) PO Box 68, Plaisance
Netherlands (☎ 261200) PO Box 372, Glacis
UK (☎ 225225) PO Box 161, Victoria House, Victoria
USA (☎ 225256) PO Box 251, Victoria House, Victoria

Other countries represented in the Seychelles include Belgium, China, Cuba, Cyprus, Denmark, Finland, India, Monaco, Norway, Russia and Switzerland.

CUSTOMS

The international airport is 10km south-east of Victoria. You are permitted to bring in 1L of spirits or wine; up to 200 cigarettes or 250g of tobacco; 200mL of perfume or eau de toilette. Spear guns, along with other weapons and ammunition, are forbidden, as is any food or agricultural produce.

When leaving the Seychelles do not take any shells, coral, preserved fish or turtle products. Such items are liable to confiscation; purchasing goods made from endangered species directly contributes to their extinction. If you are taking home a coco de mer nut, make sure you have the requisite export certificate.

MONEY
Currency

The unit of currency is the Seychelles rupee (Rs), which is divided into 100 cents (¢). Banknotes come in denominations of Rs10, Rs25, Rs50 and Rs100; there are coins of Rs1, Rs5, 1¢, 5¢, 10¢ and 25¢.

Although the rates of exchange fluctuate daily, the rupee is generally strong and stable.

Exchange Rates

The exchange rate is set by the Central Bank of Seychelles. At the time this book went to press, exchange rates were as follows:

country	unit		rupee
Australia	A$1	=	Rs3.20
Canada	C$1	=	Rs3.86
euro	€1	=	Rs4.92
France	FF10	=	Rs7.50
Germany	DM1	=	Rs2.51
India	Rs100	=	Rs12.57
Japan	¥100	=	Rs5.16
Mauritius	Rs10	=	Rs2.23
New Zealand	NZ$1	=	Rs2.44
Singapore	S$1	=	Rs3.26
UK	UK£1	=	Rs8.49
USA	US$1	=	Rs5.65

Exchanging Money

There are some complex rules governing foreign exchange in the Seychelles. Without exception, if you want to change Seychelles rupees back into foreign currency, you must go back to the same bank with the original receipt that was given to you when you obtained the rupees. Most banks will also let you prepay your departure tax (US$40) at the same time. The tax must be paid by credit card or in foreign currency.

Hotels and guesthouses sometimes offer cheaper 'black-market' rates for foreign exchange, but you won't be able to exchange these rupees when you leave the country.

Victoria has numerous banks; the four main banks are Barclays (☎ 244101), the Seychelles Savings Bank (☎ 225251), Banque Française Commerciale (☎ 323096) and Nouvobanq (☎ 225011). Barclays and Nouvobanq also have offices at the airport that are open for all flights.

Credit Cards Major credit cards (such as Visa and MasterCard) are accepted in most hotels, restaurants and shops, and most banks give cash advances against the cards. AmEx card holders can visit Travel Services

Seychelles (TSS) (☎ 322414, fax 321366), which will issue a credit slip that can then be redeemed in any of the banks.

Costs

The Seychelles is an expensive destination by anyone's standards, so don't arrive on a shoestring budget. Accommodation is regulated by the tourist board; camping is forbidden and prices, availability and the standard of accommodation are strictly controlled by the state.

At the bottom end of the market, things can seem very poor value, but you generally get more for your money as you move up the price scale. If you're watching the pennies, you can save money by skipping the overpriced breakfasts offered by the guesthouses. Even if you keep to the less expensive places, you will struggle to get by on less than US$70 a day.

Tipping & Bargaining

Tipping is welcomed but not obligatory. A 10% service charge is added to your bill in hotels and restaurants.

In general, there's a relaxed approach to bargaining. Gentle prompting can sometimes produce discounts for car rental, but the prices marked in shops are seldom negotiable. Markets are more open to a bit of friendly haggling.

POST & COMMUNICATIONS
Post

Airmail postcards to all international destinations cost Rs3. Airmail letters weighing up to 10g cost Rs3.50 to Europe or Australia, Rs4 to the USA or Canada, and Rs3 to Indian Ocean or African destinations. Aerograms cost Rs2.50.

For heavy packages, you're probably best off talking directly to the Air Seychelles freight department at the airport (☎ 384010). If you're leaving the country, excess luggage can be sent unaccompanied for considerably less than the usual excess luggage fee.

Telephone

The telephone system, run by Cable & Wireless, is one of the world's most modern.

Telephone cards, known as Phonocards, are available for Rs30 (30 units), Rs60 (60 units) and Rs105 (120 units). Unfortunately there are few working public phones. The phone at the Cable & Wireless office (☎ 284000) on Francis Rachel St in Victoria is usually your best bet; telegram, telex and fax services are also available here.

Local Calls Local calls within and between the three main islands cost Rs0.825 for up to three minutes. Calls to the outlying islands of Desroches, Coëtivy and Farquhar cost Rs3.60 per minute.

If you wish to contact vessels at sea in the vicinity of the Seychelles, call ☎ 375733. These radiotelephone calls are charged at the rate of Rs2.50 per minute.

International Calls You can make international calls direct using international direct dialling (IDD). The rate per minute for a call to Europe, the USA, Australia or the Indian Ocean is Rs8.89. If you are tempted to phone from your hotel room, remember that hotels often add a hefty mark-up to this rate. Cheaper rates apply all weekend and from 7 pm to 7 am on weekdays. Call ☎ 151 for the international operator.

INTERNET RESOURCES

The Web site of the UK Seychelles Tourist Office (www.seychelles.uk.com) has good background information on the islands. At www.sey.net you'll find useful information on activities and hotels. The site at www.seychelles.net carries advertising from many local companies.

BOOKS
History & Politics

There are a couple of interesting books on the Seychelles worth reading before you go to the islands so you can compare 'then' and 'now'. One of the more picturesque of these is *Forgotten Eden* by Atholl Thomas. It's long out of print, but is still considered to be one of the best books on the country. More politically biased (on the side of the first president, James Mancham) is *Political Castaways* by Christopher Lee.

SEYCHELLES

A more recent account is Mancham's own story of his rise and fall in *Paradise Raped*. Mancham's locally published collection of poetry *Reflections & Echoes from Seychelles* is available from the library in Victoria.

France Albert René has his say about the history of the Seychelles United People's Party, the revolution and the necessity of a one-party state in *Seychelles: The New Era*. The government has also published the *White Book*, which gives full details of the failed mercenary coup attempt by 'Mad Mike' Hoare in 1981. Mad Mike's own version of the bungled coup, *The Seychelles Affair*, adopts a more novelistic approach to events.

In *The Treasure Seeker's Treasury* by Roy Nevill, the author expounds on the hunt for the treasure of the pirate Olivier 'La Buse' Levasseur at Bel Ombre on Mahé. In *Island Home*, Wendy Weevers-Carter writes about life on Rémire Island in the isolated Amirantes Group.

Cookbooks

Sir James Mancham may have fallen out of favour in the Seychelles, but his mum's recipes have not in Eveline Mancham's *La Cuisine Seychelloise*. Traditional Seychelles cuisine is the focus of *Dekouver Marmit*, compiled by the Ministry of Education & Culture.

Flora & Fauna

There are eight books in the *Seychelles Nature Handbooks* series, which deals with most aspects of nature on the islands – shells, reef life, natural history, birds, fish and plant life. Another title that flora and fauna buffs will find interesting is Francis Friedmann's *Flowers & Trees of Seychelles*.

The life and work of artist Marianne North, who visited the Seychelles in 1883 to paint the flora, is set out in *A Vision of Eden*. Another good book that covers the beautiful flora of the islands is *The Beautiful Plants of Seychelles* by Adrian & Judith Skerrett.

Ornithologists will be interested in *The Birds of Seychelles and the Outlying Islands*

and *Birds of the Republic of Seychelles*. Also worth a look are Adrian Skerrett's *Beautiful Birds of Seychelles*, and Adrian Skerrett & Ian Bullock's *A Birdwatchers Guide to Seychelles*.

Aldabra Alone by Tony Beamish looks at life among the giant tortoises, robber crabs and other incredible natural phenomena during an expedition to the Aldabra Group. Al Venter's *Underwater Seychelles* is fairly widely available.

NEWSPAPERS & MAGAZINES

The only daily paper is the government-controlled *Nation*, which costs Rs2 (Rs7 for a weekend edition). It contains stories in English, French and Creole, and carries cinema, TV and radio programs and advertisements.

The Antigone bookshop gets the Sunday papers from the UK (usually on Monday). *Time* (Rs35), *Newsweek* (Rs19) and other magazines are also usually available.

Other papers include *Regar* (Rs7), which is trilingual and published weekly, and the *People* (Rs3), published weekly in three languages.

RADIO & TV

The Seychelles Broadcasting Corporation (SBC) provides radio broadcasts daily from 6 am to 10 pm. It also provides TV broadcasts from 6 to 8.30 am and 1 pm to midnight Monday to Friday, and 6 am to midnight at weekends. Most programs are imported from England or France.

PHOTOGRAPHY

It's best to stock up on film from duty-free shops before you arrive, because it's cheaper than in the Seychelles. However, there's a plentiful supply here as well, and there are several decent developing studios. The main players in Victoria are Photo-Eden (☎ 322457), next to the Pirates Arms, and Fujicolor (☎ 224966) on the far side of Independence Ave. The average cost for a 36-exposure 200 film is Rs30; slide film costs from Rs40 for 36 exposures. (For useful tips, see Photography & Video in the Regional Facts for the Visitor chapter near the beginning of this book.)

ELECTRICITY

The current is 240V AC. The plugs in general use have square pins and three points. You'll probably experience at least one power cut during your stay, so be sure to keep a torch (flashlight) or a candle handy.

LAUNDRY

Laundry services are widely available at guesthouses and hotels.

HEALTH

The main outpatient clinic (☎ 388000) is at Mont Fleuri in Victoria, near the Botanical Gardens. The casualty unit at the hospital is open 24 hours. There is a hospital at Baie Ste Anne on Praslin (☎ 232333), and a smaller hospital on La Digue (☎ 234255).

Some travellers have been critical of the standard of public health care in the Seychelles. If you have any concerns, you're best off asking at your hotel for a recommendation on a reliable private doctor. You must pay for prescribed medicines or drugs at the pharmacy.

No vaccination certificates are required for entry into the Seychelles. The islands are free of malaria, yellow fever and most other nasties.

Just because the sun doesn't shine all the time, don't be fooled into thinking you won't burn. The Seychelles is close to the equator and even on overcast days you may be surprised how quickly the sun's rays do their damage. For your own comfort as well as your health, use plenty of sunscreen.

Tap water is safe to drink, although it has more of a chlorinated taste on Mahé than on Praslin.

(For more general information on travel health, see the Regional Facts for the Visitor chapter near the beginning of this book.)

DANGERS & ANNOYANCES

Petty theft is very common. Don't take valuables to the beach and *never* leave belongings unattended on the beach – even if you're just going in for a quick dip. Nothing of any value should be left in your rental car, especially if it's a Mini Moke (the lock-box at the back is a favourite target for thieves).

For detailed information on underwater dangers and nasties, see the special section 'Underwater Worlds'.

EMERGENCIES

Call ☎ 999 for emergency services.

BUSINESS HOURS

Offices and shops keep British rather than French hours, opening at 8.30 am, lunching between noon and 1 pm, and closing at 4 pm (government offices) or 5 pm (shops). On weekends, most shops are open only on Saturday mornings. Shops are generally open later in the villages.

In Victoria, the banks are open from 8.30 am to 12.30 pm and 2 to 3.30 pm Monday to Friday, and from 8.30 to 11.30 am on Saturday. At the airport, bank counters are open for incoming and departing international flights.

See the individual island sections for the details of post office hours.

PUBLIC HOLIDAYS & SPECIAL EVENTS

Public holidays in the Seychelles are observed as follows:

New Year	1 & 2 January
Good Friday	March/April
Labour Day	1 May
Liberation Day	5 June
Corpus Christi	10 June
National Day	18 June
Independence Day	29 June
Assumption	15 August
La Digue Festival	15 August
All Saints' Day	1 November
Immaculate Conception	8 December
Christmas Day	25 December

For information about the Festival Kreol, which is held in late October, see the boxed text 'Festival Kreol' in the Facts about the Seychelles section earlier.

ACTIVITIES

For visitors the main leisure pursuits are water activities – water-skiing, paragliding, snorkelling, diving and the like. There are plenty of water sports experts around to teach holiday-makers, at a pretty price of course. These activities are thrown in for free if you're staying at a big hotel. If not, the water sports centre at the Berjaya Beau Vallon Bay Beach Resort (☎ 247141) on Mahé is open to nonresidents. As an indicator, windsurfing usually costs about Rs100 per hour, while water-skiing is around Rs600 per hour.

(For detailed information on diving and snorkelling in the Seychelles, see the special section 'Underwater Worlds'.)

Deep-Sea Fishing

The Seychelles supports extremely rich fisheries for big game fish such as sharks, tuna and marlin. Numerous operators have jumped on the boat, so to speak, offering all-inclusive trips where they do everything for you but put the fish on the hook. Many of these can be booked through the Marine Charter Association (☎ 322126, fax 224679) beside the Yacht Club in Victoria. Alternatively, you can book trips through Mason's Travel (☎ 322642, fax 225273) or Créole Holidays (☎ 224900, fax 225111) in Victoria for around Rs2000/3000 for a half/full day. For something a bit cheaper, the Boathouse restaurant (☎ 247868) in Beau Vallon offers fun fishing trips around Silhouette Island for Rs550 per person.

Lone Wolf Charters (☎ 234127) on La Digue offers trips for Rs1800/3000 per half/full day.

Hiking

Because the islands are relatively small and the roads little travelled (away from North Mahé), walking is a pleasurable activity just about anywhere in the Seychelles. There are still lots of wild, hilly and mountainous areas where you can escape the crowds, appreciate the islands' natural scenery and enjoy some of the many alternatives to beach-oriented activities.

The Tourism Division of the Ministry of Tourism & Transport has produced a good set of 10 hiking brochures which describe individual hiking routes, the natural history of the islands and points of interest along the way. It also has informative material on fauna and flora. The brochures are avail-

able for Rs5 each from the tourist office in Victoria.

None of the routes is more than a few kilometres long, but you should still carry energy-rich snacks and more water than you expect to need; you'll sweat buckets climbing in this humidity. Make sure you take sunscreen and a hat as protection from the equatorial sun. If you have a camera or other valuables, place them in a waterproof container to protect them from the frequent tropical downpours that occur throughout the year. Footwear with good treads is also essential since the almost perpetually muddy mountain tracks turn to ski slopes after rain.

From the environmental point of view, keep to the trail as much as possible; carry out all your rubbish; don't pick or damage plants; and don't try to capture or worry wild creatures, although it's difficult to avoid the immense palm spiders that boobytrap everything in the forest (see the boxed text 'Palm Spiders' following).

If you prefer to try a guided walk, get in touch with local mountain guide Basil Beaudoin (☎/fax 241790), who leads hiking and bird-watching trips of varying difficulty into the Mahé back country. Basil knows his stuff and charges Rs300 for an informative day walk with lunch. Popular options include Morne Seychellois and the steep Trois Fréres peak.

Palm Spiders

Arachnophobes may have a difficult time in the Seychelles. Every tree branch and telephone wire is draped in sheets of tough sticky silk belonging to the huge palm spider. Despite its size – the female has a leg span of up to 10cm – this obtrusive arachnid is harmless to humans. Like other members of the genus *Nephila*, its web silk is extremely strong, something you will no doubt discover if you try to walk off the beaten track anywhere in the Seychelles. If you look closely at the webs, you may see the tiny male who spends his whole life staying out of the way of the female, only approaching to mate when she is distracted by a meal.

Golf

The Reef Hotel & Golf Club (☎ 376251, fax 376296), at Anse aux Pins on Mahé, has a golf course which is open to nonresidents for Rs60/100 for nine/18 holes; club hire costs Rs80. Residents of the hotel are charged half price.

ACCOMMODATION

About 75% of accommodation is on Mahé and is registered and regulated by the Seychelles Ministry of Tourism. This does ensure a certain standard of service and facilities, but you might feel that you don't get a lot for your money, particularly at the bottom end of the market. Options include resorts, hotels, self-catering apartments and guesthouses. Camping is forbidden everywhere on the islands.

Virtually all the luxury hotels and a couple of the guesthouses charge higher rates for the three peak periods: Christmas–New Year, Easter, and July and August. The majority of the hotels will impose what they call a 'Christmas supplement' from late December to early January. Make sure you verify the tariff when making your reservation, as many hotels charge very different rates at different times of the year.

Accommodation is limited on Praslin and La Digue and you are strongly advised to book well ahead.

Prices given in this chapter for hotels and guesthouses are expected to rise by around 5% each year.

FOOD

Creole cuisine in the Seychelles is centred on fish, which is usually cooked in a tasty tomato-based sauce and served with rice and incendiary chilli relish. You'll probably be able to try job fish, tuna, shark, barracuda, octopus, squid, *bourgeois* (red snapper), cordonnier, parrotfish and *vielle* (grouper) cooked in several different ways.

The most popular cooking styles are *daube*, a sweet sauce or stew, and *rougaille*, a tomato-based sauce served with fish or sausages. Other popular dishes are *carri coco*, a mild meat or fish curry with coconut cream; fish marinated in lemon; and *brèdes*,

a local variety of spinach or Chinese cabbage. Also popular is 'millionaire's salad', made from the apical bud of the palmiste palm. The palm dies when the 'heart of palm' has been removed.

The Creoles are big on soups. The *tec-tec* soup, which contains small shells, is delicious. On the meat side, pork is becoming more popular. Sweet potatoes, cassava and breadfruit also form a big part of the daily Creole diet.

The wide choice of tropical fruits includes passion fruit, star fruit and custard apples, which grow all over the island. A fair bit of imagination goes into making desserts; try the *nouga*, a sweet and sticky coconut pudding.

Eating Out

There are about four price levels from which to choose. The cheapest places to eat are the takeaway counters in Victoria where you can fill up for around Rs25. Then there are a few economical restaurants around the islands where you can eat for between Rs40 and Rs80.

Some of the guesthouses do good set-menu meals for between Rs80 and Rs100. At hotels and higher-class restaurants expect to pay at least Rs100 for a modest meal.

Self-Catering

At the Seychelles Marketing Board (SMB) supermarket on Albert St in the centre of Victoria you can buy most imported foodstuffs, household items, wines and spirits. You'll pay about Rs5 for long-life milk, Rs8 for a packet of pasta, Rs8 for a kilo of rice and Rs7 for a box of six eggs. You can get very cheap fish at the market in Victoria or directly from the fishermen.

DRINKS

For those who don't trust the water, there is bottled mineral water (Rs6/8 a small/large bottle). Soft drinks such as Coke and ginger ale cost Rs3. The cost of all bottled drinks includes a deposit of Rs1. Cartons of Liquifruit brand fruit juices cost Rs3.

The local lagers, Seybrew and EKU, are excellent and cost around Rs8.50 in shops, but double or more in hotels and restaurants. The Seychellois are also fond of their Guinness, for Rs10 per bottle.

There are a few expensive wines available from the SMB supermarket in Victoria. Expect to pay upwards of Rs65 for a bottle of fairly ordinary South African or Greek wine; French wine costs at least twice that. The local rum is just about palatable and comes in plastic bottles at a cost of around Rs60 a litre.

ENTERTAINMENT

The only cinema on the islands is the Deepam Cinema in Victoria (see Victoria later in this chapter for details). There are few nightspots in the Seychelles, but most hotels fill the gap with séga shows and private discos for residents. Your hotel will usually provide a list of activities.

The Berjaya Beau Vallon Bay Beach Resort (North Mahé) and the Plantation Club (South Mahé) each have a casino open to nonresidents. On Praslin there's the grandiose Casino Des Îles.

SHOPPING
Paintings & Sculpture

There are many talented painters and other artists in the Seychelles. The best-known artist is the painter Michael Adams, whose home and studio (☎ 361006, fax 361200) are at Anse aux Poules Bleues in the south-west of Mahé. Adams' work is easily the most distinctive on the islands, and features on local calendars and promotional material. His work is highly collectable so bring plenty of rupees if you're thinking of buying.

Other artists worth checking out are Gerard Devoud (☎ 361313), who exhibits at the Valmer Resort in Baie Lazare (South Mahé) and George Camille (☎ 224667), who exhibits at the Kaz Zanana gallery in Victoria (Mahé). If you're on La Digue, pop in and have a look at Barbara Jenson's studio (☎ 234406, fax 376356). Sunstroke (☎ 242767) on Market St in Victoria sells work by many Seychelles artists.

Italian-born sculptor Antonio Filippin specialises in wood sculpture; there's an impressive range of his work on display at the Plantation Club resort in Baie Lazare. You will pay upwards of Rs5000 per piece.

Batik

Ron Gerlach's batik studio (☎ 247875), on the beach at Beau Vallon, has nice dresses (Rs230), shirts (Rs150), sarongs (Rs125) and other garments in silk or cotton. There are also some T-shirts and cards for sale. The studio is open from 10 am to 5 pm Monday to Friday.

Model Ships

There is only one workshop in the Seychelles, compared with the scores in Mauritius, so the prices for a model Victory or Bounty are a lot dearer here. The factory La Marine (☎ 371441) is at La Plaine St André, just south of Anse aux Pins on Mahé. It's open from 7.30 am to 5 pm Monday to Friday and 8 am to 3.30 pm on Saturday. The models range in price from Rs3000 to Rs30,000. Make sure they are well packed and check up on all possible freight and duty fees at the other end.

Coco de Mer

You can read more about this famous nut of nuts in the Praslin section. If you want to own one of these famously erotic seeds, be prepared to part with upwards of Rs1500 (US$265)! Only some nuts take the erotic shape most buyers are after. Make sure that you are given an export permit and receipt when you buy – otherwise your purchase may be confiscated at the airport. Genuine nuts come in their natural husky state and will need to be polished. Beware of prepolished souvenir nuts, which often aren't coco de mer at all.

Souvenirs

There is a cluster of souvenir stalls opposite the post office in the centre of Victoria, and countless shops are dotted around the three main islands. It's a shame to deny the Creole traders a living, but read the information on marine conservation in the special section 'Underwater Worlds' before you contemplate going back home with a set of shark dentures or a sprig or two of coral.

Getting There & Away

AIR

Seychelles International Airport sits on an area of reclaimed land about 10km south-east of Victoria. Apart from the occasional luxury yacht, all arrivals to the Seychelles are by air.

Air Seychelles, the national carrier, has a tiny fleet, but it serves an impressive range of destinations around the world. Air France, British Airways and Lufthansa Condor provide the main connections to Europe. Air Kenya flies twice a week to Nairobi; this flight forms the last leg of the code-share KLM Royal Dutch Airlines flight from Amsterdam. If you're flying from Europe, the cheapest option may be to fly first to Holland and then pick up this code-share flight to the Seychelles.

The Russian airline Aeroflot used to fly regularly between the Seychelles and Moscow, but its services have been suspended; they may have been reinstated by the time you read this. In addition, there are chartered flights from Europe during the high season, mainly from Italy.

Airlines

The Air Seychelles office (☎ 381300, fax 225933) is in Victoria House, near the clock tower in Victoria. British Airways (☎ 224910, fax 225596), Air Mauritius (☎ 322414, fax 321366) and Air France (☎ 322414, fax 225048) are all at Kingsgate House on Independence Ave in Victoria. Aeroflot (☎ 225005, fax 224170) and Air Austral (☎ 323262, fax 323223) have offices in the same building as the Pirates Arms restaurant on Independence Ave, Victoria. Kenya Airways (☎ 322989, fax 324162) is at Cooperative House, Manglier St, Victoria.

Departure Tax

There is a US$40 departure tax on all international flights. This can be paid at the airport or prepaid at the major banks. It must be paid in foreign currency or by credit card. You can change Seychelles rupees back into foreign currency at the airport, but only if you previously brought them from Barclays or Nouvobanq. In either case you will need the original encashment form (issued when you change foreign currency into Seychelles rupees).

The USA

As is the case with Mauritius and Réunion, visitors from the USA will need to connect via Paris or London to reach the Seychelles. A return ticket from New York to London costs around US$300 in the low season; from New York to Paris costs around US$360. From Los Angeles you'll pay upwards of US$400 to London and US$520 to Paris. (See The UK earlier in this section for the price of connections to the Seychelles.)

Australia

Return flights to the Seychelles from Melbourne via Singapore cost around A$1880 on Air Seychelles (higher rates apply over the Christmas period). Another option is to fly to Europe (see Continental Europe earlier in this chapter) or Africa (see Africa later in this chapter) and catch a flight from there to the Seychelles. You could also fly direct to Mauritius (with Air Mauritius) and get a flight from there to the Seychelles.

The UK

A return ticket from London to the Seychelles on British Airways costs around UK£700/860 in the low/high season. On Air Seychelles, a return fare from London is around UK£800/545 in the high/low season. The cheapest route from London to the Seychelles is to fly via Amsterdam with KLM Royal Dutch Airlines and Kenya Airways, which costs UK£350/570.

Continental Europe

Most visitors from Europe arrive on hotel-flight package holidays. Air France flies from Paris to the Seychelles four times a week, charging FF4850/6730 for a return ticket in the high/low season. The other main European connection is on the German airline Lufthansa Condor, which has a single weekly flight between the Seychelles and Frankfurt for DM1926. You'd be better off flying via Paris on Air France (DM1630/1300 in the high/low season) or via Amsterdam on KLM Royal Dutch Airlines/Kenya Airways (DM1350/1150). Keep your eyes peeled for special discounts and promotions, which pop up from time to time.

Africa

The Seychelles is not particularly well connected with Africa. The only direct flights are the twice-weekly flights to and from Nairobi with Kenya Airways (Rs1960), and the twice-weekly flight to and from Johannesburg with Air Seychelles (Rs4072). You can easily pick up connections to other African destinations from Nairobi or Johannesburg.

Mauritius & Réunion

There are no bargain return flight deals from the Seychelles to Réunion or Mauritius and vice versa. You would be better off taking the Seychelles as a stopover en route from Europe to Mauritius or other countries. A ticket between the Seychelles and Mauritius with Air Seychelles or Air Mauritius costs around Rs1660 (this fare is valid for a stay of one month).

SEA

Cruise liners regularly call into Victoria, but there are no passenger services directly to the Seychelles. Plenty of yachts visit during the cruising season from April to October.

If you do arrive by yacht, you must wait offshore near the Victoria lighthouse, switch to VHF channel 16 and wait for a customs and health clearance to proceed to the inner harbour. You will be given a two-week visa. The authorities will permit pets only if they are kept on board. Any firearms or spear guns must be handed over for safekeeping, to be collected when you leave. Don't make the mistake of trying to bribe the officials.

If you want to leave the Seychelles by yacht, there are a few each year looking for crew members. Check the notice board at the Yacht Club in Victoria.

Getting Around

AIR
Domestic Air Services

Air Seychelles (☎ 381300, fax 225933) takes care of all interisland flights operating out of Seychelles international airport. The only regular scheduled flights are between Mahé and Praslin, with around 20 flights per day. The fare for the 15-minute hop is Rs343 return.

The airline offers transfers to the resort islands of Frégate, Desroches, Bird and Denis only as part of accommodation packages at the resorts. You should check the schedule with the hotel when you book (fares are given under the individual resorts).

Check-in time is 30 minutes before departure and the luggage limit is only 10kg (Rs3 per kilo for excess luggage) – you may be able to stretch the rules if you are connecting with an international flight, but don't bet on it. Fortunately there is a luggage storage facility at the international airport (no charge). Alternatively, if you are returning to a hotel on Mahé, the hotel may be able to store your luggage for you.

Bookings can be made through travel agents or though Air Seychelles. The planes are 20-seat Twin Otters, nine-seat Britten-Norman Islanders and 17-seat Trislander aircraft.

Helicopter

Helicopter Seychelles (☎ 373900, fax 373 055) operates scenic helicopter flights as well as some interisland transfers. A 30-minute buzz over Mahé, La Digue or Praslin costs Rs2200 for up to four people. The company also offers transfers from Mahé to La Digue (Rs640 one way), and from Mahé to the exclusive Silhouette Island Lodge (Rs902 return for guests only; see the Silhouette Island section later in this chapter).

BUS

An extensive bus service operates throughout Mahé. A limited service operates on Praslin. The fleet mainly consists of ageing Indian Tata buses, accompanied by a few small Italian Iveco vans, which fill up quickly at the terminus in Victoria and are often difficult to board at other stops in town. Standing passengers are not always allowed, so it's best to board at the bus station if you can.

Destinations and routes are usually marked on the signboard at the front of the bus. There is a flat rate of Rs3 wherever you want to go on the island; pay the driver as you board. On Mahé and Praslin the bus stops have signs and shelters and there are also markings on the road. When you want to get off you should shout *'Devant'*. Let passengers disembark before you try to board or you'll get a dressing down from the driver!

There are 37 bus routes on Mahé. The principal destinations from Victoria are Beau Vallon (for Beau Vallon beach), Anse aux Pins (for the airport and lagoon), Port Launay (for the Morne Seychellois National Park and the Port Launay and Baie Ternay Marine National Parks) and Baie Lazare. Check the signboards for routes. There's a bus each hour on most routes from early morning until around 7 pm. Timetables and maps of each route are posted at the central bus park in Victoria.

Services from Victoria run later than services heading into town. On most routes the last bus going towards Victoria leaves at around 6 pm; in the reverse direction services may run as late as 8.30 pm. If you're depending on the buses, check the time of the last bus or you may face a long walk home.

On Praslin, the basic route is from Anse Boudin to Anse Kerlan (via Anse Volbert, Baie Ste Anne and Grand Anse). Buses run in each direction every hour from 6 am to 6.30 pm. Some go via Anse Consolation and others via the Vallée de Mai. As on Mahé, fares are fixed at Rs3.

CAR

Most of the road network on Mahé is sealed and in good shape. The worry is not the road surface so much as the bends and the speed at which some drivers take them. On Praslin most of the major roads are surfaced, but on La Digue and the other islands none of them are.

Locations of petrol stations on Mahé include Francis Rachel St in Victoria; opposite the airport in Pointe Larue; opposite the Kaz Kreol restaurant in Anse Royale; by the Plantation Club in Baie Lazare; by the Berjaya Mahé resort in Port Glaud; and on the road from Victoria to Beau Vallon.

On Praslin the only petrol stations are at Baie Ste Anne and Grand Anse.

Petrol costs around Rs6.5 a litre. As a rough guide, you can expect to use about 8L of petrol per day in a Mini Moke doing 140km a day.

Road Rules

Drive on the left, and beware of drivers with fast cars and drowsy brains – especially late on Friday and Saturday nights. The speed limit is supposed to be 40km in Victoria and the villages and 65km on the open road, but few people stick to it. If you run over something that explodes like a pistol shot while driving at night, you've probably hit a giant African snail. These huge molluscs were imported as a delicacy by the French and have overrun the islands.

Rental

Mini Mokes are *the* hire cars in the Seychelles. 'Moking is not a wealth hazard' is the motto of one car-hire firm. But at around Rs400 a day, unfortunately, it is.

Many of these underpowered vehicles have some sort of mechanical defect. Make sure that basic essentials such as brakes, steering, gears, lights and seatbelts actually work – and don't be shy about asking for something to be fixed or to have the car replaced with another one that might at least have more acceptable foibles! Make certain you have the hire company's telephone number for out of office hours in case of a breakdown.

The plastic covers that purport to keep out the rain are mainly cosmetic; anything more than a light shower and you'll be as wet inside the vehicle as you would be outside.

You should never leave any valuables unattended in your vehicle. If you have to use the flimsy trunk security box, you should use your own padlock, and be prepared for the worst when you return to your vehicle. In general the Seychellois are honest folk, but petty theft is becoming a popular leisure activity among bored teenagers.

The standard daily hire rate for a Moke is set at a steep Rs400, including insurance. There is no per kilometre rate. You may be able to get the rate down to Rs300 per day if you rent for three days or more; most companies will make offers if you approach them individually. After the Moke, Suzuki open jeeps are the most popular vehicles at around Rs425. Sedan cars are available for Rs450, or Rs475 with air-con.

There are more than 30 car-hire companies to choose from, and as the government limits each firm to a certain number of vehicles and sets the hire rates, there's little difference between them. Possible options include:

Austral Car Rental (☎ 232015) Côte d'Or, Praslin
Avis (☎ 224511) Victoria House, Victoria, Mahé
Europcar/Tropicar (☎ 373336) Providence Industrial Estate, Mahé
Explorer Cars (☎ 233311) Grand Anse, Praslin
Hertz (☎ 322447) Revolution Ave, Victoria, Mahé
Prestige Car Hire (☎ 233226) Grand Anse, Praslin
RAM Car Hire (☎ 266333) St Louis, Mahé
Victoria Car Hire (☎ 376314) Anse aux Pins, Mahé

BICYCLE

Bicycles are the principle form of transport on La Digue. On Praslin and Mahé the pressure is on visitors to rent mokes, so this inexpensive form of transport is hard to find. Côte d'Or Bicycle Hire (☎ 232071) at Anse Volbert on Praslin has bikes for Rs50 per day.

The Seychelles isn't really substantial enough to justify bringing your own bike. One poor traveller had his bike impounded by customs for most of his stay while he waited to get a licence and a bell!

HITCHING

Hitching is never entirely safe in any country in the world, and we don't recommend it. Travellers who decide to hitch should understand that they are taking a small but potentially serious risk. If you do choose to hitch, you will be safer if you travel in pairs and let someone know where you are planning to go. Nevertheless, you are advised not to hitch at night, and women shouldn't hitch alone – even several women together shouldn't accept lifts from cars with only male passengers; make sure that there are women or children in the vehicle before climbing in.

BOAT
Interisland Ferries

There are regular ferry services between Mahé, Praslin and La Digue. Services leave from the interisland quay in Victoria (at the end of Flamboyant Ave), from Baie Ste Anne jetty on Praslin and from La Passe jetty on La Digue. For all other islands you have to charter a boat, take a tour or hitch a ride on a government vessel or fishing boat.

Mahé to Praslin In a move that seems solely designed to sting visitors, the appealing schooner services from Mahé to Praslin have been replaced by the expensive Cat Cocos ferry (☎ 324843). There are two services daily in each direction from Monday to Thursday, three services each way on Friday and Sunday, and no ferries on Saturday. The fare for this one-hour trip is a steep Rs280 (Rs340 in the air-con lounge). Considering the cost, it's probably worth paying the extra Rs3 and flying to Praslin!

Mahé to La Digue The schooners *La Belle Edma* (☎ 234013) and *Clarté* (☎ 234254) still operate from Monday to Friday between Mahé and La Digue, taking three hours for the crossing. If you don't get seasick it's quite a romantic way to travel. *La Belle Edma* and *Clarté* leave Mahé at 10 and 11 am respectively, both returning from La Digue at 5 pm. The one-way fare is quite reasonable at Rs50. You can use this as a cheap route to Praslin, connecting with one of the regular schooners from La Digue to Praslin.

Praslin to La Digue Two schooners, the *Silhouette* and *Lady Mary II*, run daily for the 30-minute trip between Praslin and La Digue. The one-way ticket costs Rs35 per person; luggage costs Rs5 per piece. It's a good idea to book ahead – most hotels will do this for you. For details about both schooners, call ☎ 232329.

There are departures from Praslin daily at 7, 9.30 and 10.30 am, and 2.30 and 5 pm. From La Digue, there are departures at 7.30, 10 and 11.30 am, and 3.30 and 5.30 pm. The trip can be a rocky one, sometimes spraying unsuspecting passengers with water – make sure your camera or video camera is well protected. See if you can spot flying fish skimming over the waves.

Charters

Most tours to islands should include landing fees – make sure you ask before paying.

The Marine Charter Association or MCA (☎ 322126, fax 224679), beside the Yacht Club in Victoria, has about 30 members who offer a variety of boats for hire at a variety of purposes and at a variety of high prices. There are schooners, yachts, launches and motor cruisers for cruising, ferrying, fishing, diving and just about any other water activity you can think of.

The best months for cruising are April and October; the worst months are January, July and August. Most boat owners charge around Rs3500 per day for the vessel on overnight trips, or around Rs400 per person for a day trip with a minimum of six people. They usually drop the rates during quiet periods.

Several independent boat-owners offer charter services that are a bit more intimate than the organised tours. On La Digue, Michelin (☎ 234043) conducts a variety of boat excursions, including a trip in a glass-bottomed boat with snorkelling stops for Rs200/400 for a half/full day.

Makaira Boat Charter (☎ 233445) at Grand Anse offers day cruises to Anse Lazio for Rs300, as well as Cousin and Curieuse Islands and St Pierre Islet trips for Rs450 with a barbecue lunch and big-game fishing trips for Rs1800/2500 for a half/full day.

The Maison des Palmes hotel (☎ 233411) at Grand Anse offers transfers to Anse Lazio for Rs75. Your other options include a three-island trip for Rs445 with lunch, and half-day trips to Cousin Island only for Rs215.

VPM Yacht Charter (☎/fax 225676) at the interisland quay in Victoria on Mahé offers yacht tours in style. It's best to contact the company directly for a rundown of itineraries and costs.

The delightful SV *Sea Shell* and SV *Silhouette* are a pair of old Dutch schooners that offer live-aboard cruises around the inner islands with activities such as deep-sea fishing, scuba diving and kayaking thrown in. Rates start at Rs750 per person per day on full board, as part of a cruise for two, three, five or six days.

Sunsail (☎ 023-9222 2229, fax 9221 5125) is a reputable UK yacht-charter company that offers various yachting possibilities in the Seychelles. To find out more, contact. The Port House, Port Solent, Portsmouth, Hampshire, PO6 4TH, UK.

Outer Island Services

If you simply must see Aldabra at any cost, the *Indian Ocean Explorer* (☎/fax 344223) offers regular cruises to Aldabra and other outer islands, which are for a minimum of eight days. For the Aldabra trip, you'll need to fly down to meet the boat on Assomption Island. Rates start at US$275 per day including all meals. Scuba diving is extra. Call for a schedule of sailings.

There is a very remote chance you may be able to get a berth as a paying or non-paying crew member on one of the schooners to the outer islands, but few of the islands cater for independent travellers. Try your luck with the skippers at the ferry piers at Victoria, Praslin and La Digue.

The Seychelles Island Foundation (☎ 321755) at New Port, Victoria, runs a ship to the Aldabra Group for government workers and scientists. If you are feeling confident, you may be able to wrangle permission to visit Aldabra from the Ministry of National Development at Independence House, Victoria.

LOCAL TRANSPORT
To/From the Airport

A taxi to Victoria from the airport costs about Rs75. From Beau Vallon to the airport, expect to pay Rs85. Large pieces of luggage incur an extra charge of Rs5. If you arrive during the day and have no mobility problems with your luggage there is a bus stand about 20m away, directly opposite the airport gates near the petrol station. Buses run about every hour between 6 am and 7.30 pm. The fare to Victoria is Rs3.

Taxi

Taxi fares on Mahé and Praslin are set by the government. On Mahé you pay Rs15 for the first kilometre and Rs5 for each additional kilometre regardless of the number of passengers. There is also a charge of about Rs11 for each 15 minutes of waiting time, and drivers can charge Rs5 for each major piece of luggage and for the outward journey to a pick-up point.

Some examples of fares are as follows: Victoria to the airport is Rs75; from Victoria to Beau Vallon is Rs35; Victoria to Baie Lazare is Rs150; and the airport to Grande Anse is Rs95.

Alternatively, you can hire a taxi for a set period and arrange a fee with the driver. If you want to query any fare, get a receipt from the driver and contact the head of the Taxi Owner Drivers Association (☎ 323895) at Olivier Maradam St, Victoria.

On Praslin, taxis cost Rs18 for the first kilometre, and Rs6 for each additional kilometre. Luggage and waiting charges are the same as on Mahé. From the Baie Ste Anne jetty to the Paradise Sun Hotel at Anse Volbert is Rs51; from the airport to Vallée de Mai is Rs50; and from Baie Ste Anne jetty to Baie Ste Anne village is Rs25.

There are only a couple of taxis on La Digue, where the prices are about the same as on Praslin.

ORGANISED TOURS

The main tour operators and travel agents in the Seychelles have their head office in Victoria, usually with sub-offices on Praslin and La Digue (see those sections for details). Travel Services Seychelles (TSS), Créole Holidays and Mason's Travel are the largest operators; independent travellers use them mainly to arrange trips to the smaller islands and snorkelling tours of Ste Anne

Marine National Park. Otherwise, these operators are busy with hotel package tourists.

Most tours include a guide, lunch, entrance fees and transfer to and from your hotel. Some hotels, especially the upmarket ones, run their own tours. Most of the tour operators offer a discount for children.

The cheapest and perhaps most popular tours are the glass-bottomed-boat trips around the Ste Anne Marine National Park off Victoria, which run most days of the week to a different island each day. A full-day excursion with lunch on Cerf or Round Islands includes a chance to go snorkelling and costs about Rs410/250 per adult/child.

If you contact Patrick at the Marine Charter Association (☎ 322126, fax 224679) you can arrange to charter a small boat for almost half the normal price, with the added advantage of a small group (minimum two people) instead of the usual 40 or so. A half-day trip costs about Rs150 per person and a full-day trip costs Rs200 per person, including snorkelling equipment (but not lunch).

Mahé

HIGHLIGHTS

- Snorkelling, swimming or diving in the crystal clear water around the island
- Sunning it up, then feasting on seafood on beautiful Beau Vallon beach
- Walking through the stunning granite landscape
- Touring Ste Anne Marine National Park in a glass-bottomed boat

Mahé was named by the French in honour of the 18th-century governor of Mauritius, Mahé de La Bourdonnais, and is by far the largest and most developed of the Seychelles islands. It is home to the country's capital, Victoria (no prizes for guessing who that was named after), and to about 88% of the country's 73,000 people.

MAHÉ

PLACES TO STAY
1 Sunset Beach Hotel
2 Le Northolme Hotel
3 Le Pti Payot
4 Vacoa Village
5 Auberge Louis XVII
7 Berjaya Mahé Beach Resort
8 Le Meridien Barbarons
9 Carefree
10 La Retraite
12 Reef Hotel & Golf Club
13 Lalla Panzi
18 Auberge de Bougainville
22 Valmer Resort
23 Plantation Club
24 Lazare Picault Hotel
25 Chez Batista & Restaurant

PLACES TO EAT
15 Ty-Foo
17 Kaz Kreol
20 Anchor Café & Pizza
21 Splash Cafe

OTHER
6 Tea Factory
11 Golf Course
14 Craft Village;
   Restaurant Vye Marmit;
   Kreol Institute
16 Maison de Planteur;
   La Marine Model Ships
19 Le Jardin du Roi

SEYCHELLES

Mahé is only about 27km long and between 3km and 8km wide. A range of granite peaks runs from north to south along the length of the island, including the island's highest point, Morne Seychellois (905m), which overlooks Victoria. Most of the settlements and roads in Mahé stick to the narrow coastal strip, while the densely forested interior, with its towering granite boulders, has been left relatively undisturbed.

As Mahé is the most populous of the Seychelles islands, much of the coast is given over to housing, so there are only a few spots that fit the picture-postcard ideal. The mountainous interior and the rugged beaches to the south-west are probably your best bet for a bit of seclusion. On the north-west coast, Beau Vallon beach falls nicely between the two extremes, with a quiet and attractive white sand beach as well as some excellent restaurants and places to stay.

Elsewhere, large areas of the island have been devoted to industrial developments. To ease the island's housing crisis, the north-east coast from Anse Étoile to the airport has been given over to a huge land reclamation project that is likely to alter the appearance of the island forever. Although nearly 85% of the country's tourist accommodation and restaurants are on Mahé, most visitors now head for the less developed and more beautiful islands of Praslin and La Digue.

Orientation

The coastal highway hugs the beach for most of the coast, breaking only at the rugged southern tip of the island and the Morne Seychellois National Park in the north-west corner. A number of smaller roads cross the interior, linking the east and west coasts. The airport is on the coast at Pointe Larue, about 10 km from Victoria.

VICTORIA

With a population of only about 27,000 people, Victoria is one of the smallest capital cities in the world. Officially it's the only 'town' in the Seychelles (all the other settlements on the islands are 'villages'), but it doesn't feel like much more than a village itself. The town centre consists of only a few blocks, so it's easy to find your way around.

Aside from a few notable old buildings, the centre of Victoria is too clean and modern looking to have a great deal of atmosphere. The focal point of downtown is *l'horloge* (the clock tower), a replica of the clock tower on London's Vauxhall Bridge, which was brought to Victoria in 1903 when the Seychelles became a crown colony.

The old courthouse beside the clock tower will appeal to fans of Creole architecture, and there are also a few attractive old houses and shops along Francis Rachel St (named after the lone 'martyr' of the 1977 coup) and Albert St.

Information

Tourist Office The friendly tourist office (☎ 225313, fax 224035) on Independence Ave has a selection of brochures and general tourist information for visitors. If you're interested in hiking, this is the place to stock up on the guides for individual routes (Rs5 per guide). The office has a good map of Mahé, Praslin and La Digue (free of charge). You can also pick up a copy of *Visitor's Seychelles*, a free booklet with extensive tourist information. The office is open weekdays from 8 am to 5 pm and Saturday from 9 am to noon.

Money Victoria is uniquely well endowed with banks. The major players are Barclays, Nouvobanq and Banque Française Commerciale, all with branches close to the clock tower. As well as offering bureau de change facilities and ATMs, the banks will let you pay your airport departure tax (US$40) in advance.

The banks are open Monday to Friday from 8.30 am to 12.30 pm and 2 to 3.30 pm, and Saturday from 8.30 to 11.30 am. If you want to change back local currency before you leave, you'll need to return to the same bank, with your original exchange receipt or ATM advice slip.

Post The main post office (☎ 225222), on the corner of Independence Ave and Albert St, is open Monday to Friday from 8 am to 4 pm, and Saturday from 8 am to noon.

VICTORIA

PLACES TO STAY
16 Hilltop Guest House
35 Hotel Bel Air
51 Sunrise Small Hotel

PLACES TO EAT
13 Barrel Bar
17 Marie Antoinette
19 Sandy's Takeaway
29 Vanilla 2000
30 Pirates Arms; Aeroflot; Alliance Française
40 Sure Good Chinese Takeaway; Digitech Internet

OTHER
1 Cathedral of the Immaculate Conception
2 Bus Terminal
3 Cat Cocos Ferry to Praslin; Schooner Ferries to La Digue
4 Barclays Bank
5 Deepam Cinema
6 Kenya Airways
7 SMB Supermarket
8 Taxi Stand
9 Lovenut
10 Sunstroke Souvenirs; Zimas Kreol Gallery
11 Sir Selwyn Selwyn-Clarke Market
12 Mason's Travel
14 Tamil Temple; Foodnest Takeaway
15 Kaz Zanana
18 Hertz
20 Police Station
21 Travel Services Seychelles (TSS)
22 Clock Tower
23 Main Post Office
24 Natural History Museum
25 Kingsgate House; British Airways; Air France; Air Mauritius; Créole Holidays
26 Seychelles Savings Bank
27 Independence House; Immigration Office; Seychelles Ministry of Tourism;
28 Tourist Office
31 Barclays Bank
32 Crafts Market
33 Victoria House; Air Seychelles; Nouvobang; Antigone; American Consulate; UK & French Embassies
34 National Museum of History
36 State House
37 Atlas Internet; Sam's Pizzeria
38 SPUP Museum
39 Petrol Station
41 Mosque
42 Cable & Wireless
43 Independence Monument
44 Marine Charter Association (MCA)
45 Yacht Club
46 Jardin des Enfants
47 National Library & Archives
48 Indian High Commission
49 Botanical Gardens
50 Hospital

Telephone The Cable & Wireless office (☎ 322221) is on Francis Rachel St and is open daily from 7 am to 9 pm for cable, fax, telex and phone services. The service on Sundays can seem a little relaxed.

Email & Internet Access Atlas Internet (☎ 304060) is the only Internet service provider in the Seychelles. You can go on-line at its Internet Bureau on the second floor of the Maison Suleman building on Francis Rachel St. It's open from 9 am to 8 pm daily except Sunday, and charges Rs10 for 15 minutes.

Travel Agencies The main three travel agents in the Seychelles are Mason's Travel (☎ 322642, fax 225273), on Revolution Ave; Créole Holidays (☎ 224900, fax 225111), in Kingsgate House on Independence Ave; and Travel Services Seychelles or TSS (☎ 322414, fax 321366) on Albert St. Their offices are open from 8 am to 4 pm on weekdays and 8 am to noon on Saturday. (See Organised Tours later in this section for some of the tours on offer.)

Bookshops The only bookshop of any note in Victoria is Antigone (☎ 225443, fax 224668) in the Victoria House arcade. It is open weekdays from 9 am to 4.30 pm and on Saturday from 9.15 am to noon. It stocks a fairly wide collection of novels in English, German and French, and some good books on the Seychelles. British and French newspapers and magazines are also available, but prices reflect the cost of import.

Libraries The National Library (☎ 321333), also the Ministry of Culture, is housed in a large building on Francis Rachel St. It is open from 8.30 am to 5 pm weekdays. You can borrow a book by leaving a deposit of Rs50, and can take out two books at a time.

Medical Services Victoria has a large hospital (south of the town centre) and a number of good private clinics. See the Health section earlier in the Seychelles chapter for information on medical services on Mahé.

Natural History Museum
The Natural History Museum (☎ 321333) is next to the main post office, right in the heart of town. The museum is devoted to the curious natural history of the Seychelles, including two of its most interesting inhabitants, the crocodile of the Seychelles and the giant tortoise of the Seychelles. Both of these, sadly, have vanished from the main islands. Other exhibits include giant coconut or robber crabs, a good collection of local shells, insects and spiders and some rather grotesque dried-out fish.

The museum is open Monday to Friday from 8.30 am to 4.30 pm and Saturday from 8.30 am to 12.30 pm. Admission is Rs10.

National Museum of History
Not to be confused with the Natural History Museum, the National Museum of History (☎ 225253), on State House Ave, has a well-displayed collection of historical artefacts of the Seychelles. In pride of place is the Stone of Possession, which was laid in 1756 by Corneille Nicolas Morphey to commemorate French possession of the islands. The other exhibits relate to the settlement of the island.

The National Museum is open Monday, Tuesday, Thursday and Friday from 8.30 am to 4 pm and Saturday from 8.30 am to noon. Entry is Rs10.

Sir Selwyn Selwyn-Clarke Market
When it first opened, the revamped covered market on Market St was something of a tourist gimmick, but over the years it's evolved into quite a lively, bustling place. Early morning is the best time to come, when the fish traders display an astonishing variety of fish, from parrot fish to barracudas. The market is open from 7 am till 4 pm on weekdays and 6 am to noon on Saturday.

Botanical Gardens
These pleasant gardens (☎ 224644) are near the hospital, just past Le Chantier roundabout and the Sans Souci road exit, at the south end of town. Only a few of the trees have been labelled, but the coco de mer

palms from Praslin need no introduction. Many of the specimens here were planted by British dignitaries during the last century. Within the gardens is a cafeteria, a pen of giant tortoises, an orchid garden and a souvenir shop. The gardens are open daily from 6 am to 6 pm; entry is free.

Organised Tours

The three main tour operators are pretty much interchangeable in terms of prices and the tours they offer. For example, Mason's Travel offers a full-day bus tour of Mahé including lunch for Rs220/120 per adult/child (a half-day tour is Rs140/74). Tours in glass-bottomed boats to Ste Anne Marine National Park cost Rs410/245. Day tours of the attractions on Praslin and La Digue are Rs630/325 by boat and Rs830/600 by plane. Deep-sea fishing trips are also on offer from Rs2500/3600 for a half/full day.

Créole Holidays and TSS both offer very similar packages at the same prices. All agents also offer car hire and yacht charters, and can arrange walking tours on nature trails around the islands. (See Travel Agencies earlier in this section for contact details.)

Places to Stay

There are several guesthouses dotted around the suburbs of Victoria, but no hotels.

Closest to the centre, the *Hilltop Guest House* (☎ 266555) is behind the Marie Antoinette restaurant on Serret Rd, off the road to Beau Vallon. The prices are about as reasonable as you'll find in the Seychelles; a single/double costs Rs175/350 including breakfast.

Hotel Bel Air (☎ 224416, fax 224923), on the road to Bel Air and Sans Souci, is a pleasant old colonial house on a rise overlooking Victoria. Including breakfast, singles/doubles/triples cost Rs450/540/680, or Rs520/680/890 on half board.

Quite close to the Botanical Gardens, the *Sunrise Small Hotel* (☎ 224560, fax 225290) is a friendly Chinese-run guesthouse that charges Rs325/400 per room. Home-cooked meals cost Rs75.

Nearby, *Auberge Louis XVII* (☎ 344411, fax 344428) is grander and more expensive.

This serene hilltop retreat has sea views, a little pool and a restaurant. Rooms cost Rs500/650 including breakfast or Rs590/820 on half board.

Places to Eat

Relatively speaking, Victoria isn't a bad place for cheap eats. There is a profusion of takeaway places offering Creole staples such as *poisson rougaille* (grilled fish in tomato sauce) and chicken curry.

On Independence Ave, *Pirates Arms* (☎ 225001) is a popular open-fronted cafe and restaurant, though it has a slightly institutional atmosphere. Mains such as fried job-fish cost around Rs45. It's open Monday to Saturday from 9 am to midnight and Sunday from 4 to 11 pm.

Sandy's (☎ 322099), on Revolution Ave, is a bargain takeaway place that is open daily except Sunday from 11 am to 2.30 pm and 6 to 9 pm. Fish or beef rougaille costs around Rs20.

For Chinese food, *Sure Good Chinese Takeaway* (☎ 241238) offers a good range of dishes for around Rs60 (Rs22 to take away). It's open Monday to Saturday from 11 am to 11 pm, and Sunday from noon to 2 pm and 6 to 11 pm.

On the road from Victoria to Beau Vallon, *Marie Antoinette* (☎ 266222) is an atmospheric and popular Creole restaurant in a beautiful old Creole house. The restaurant is open daily except Sunday from 12.30 to 3 pm and 7.30 and 10 pm. The set menu costs Rs110.

On Francis Rachel St, *Sam's Pizzeria* (☎ 322499) offers good pizza and pasta options from 7 am to 11pm daily. Expect to pay Rs50 for a meal.

Entertainment

The *Deepam Cinema* (☎ 322585) on Albert St screens American films every evening. Tickets cost Rs15 on the balcony or Rs12 in the broken seats downstairs.

Getting There & Away

For information on transport to other islands from Victoria see the Seychelles Getting Around section earlier in this chapter.

SEYCHELLES

NORTH MAHÉ

The most developed and populous area of Mahé lies to the north of an imaginary east-west line from the airport to Grande Anse. While there are still some lovely spots along the coast here, the whole east coast from the airport to Anse Étoile has recently been marred by a huge and ugly land reclamation project designed to ease the island's housing shortage. Considering the cost of holidaying in the Seychelles, it's best to demand some paradise for your money and stick to the north and west coasts of North Mahé.

Beau Vallon Beach

The lovely white-sand beach at Beau Vallon used to be the most popular beach in the Seychelles, but with most tourists moving directly on to the islands of Praslin and La Digue, Beau Vallon can be surprisingly quiet these days. The sand is fine (there's plenty of it) and numerous palms and taka-maka trees provide shelter for sunbathers. It's also one of the few beaches where the water is deep enough for swimming (watch out for large swells between June and November).

In Beau Vallon village, where the road from Victoria forks to Bel Ombre (west) and Glacis (north-east), there is a petrol station, a Barclays (☎ 247391) ATM, some small supermarkets, a few souvenir shops and the police station.

Buses leave regularly from Victoria for Beau Vallon, either the long way around via Glacis, or straight over the hill via St Louis. The last bus to Victoria leaves by 7.30 pm, but it's an easy 40-minute walk over the ridge if you miss the last bus.

Tea Factory

This working tea factory (☎ 378221) and restaurant is on the Sans Souci road about 3km from Port Glaud. There are free tours of the tea-making process on weekdays from 8.30 am to noon.

Walks

The tourist office produces a series of guides entitled *Nature Trails and Walks in Seychelles,* which describe a number of casual rambles and more serious hikes in the interior of Mahé.

Danzilles to Anse Major The walk to this lovely and secluded beach passes through the unspoilt Morne Seychellois National Park, fringed by some impressive glacis rock formations. The walk starts beyond the village of Danzilles; follow the road that turns along the coast just beyond La Scala restaurant. The beach is blissfully quiet (except on Wednesday when the tour groups arrive), and is good for swimming, though there can be strong currents. Return by the same route.

Trois Frères Peak Trois Frères peak, which forms the mountain backdrop for Victoria, lies in Morne Seychellois National Park. The steep (somewhat challenging) walk to its 699m summit begins at Sans Souci Forest Station on the Forêt Noire route, about 5km from Victoria. The trailhead is well signposted from the road.

Sans Souci to Morne Blanc The rather imposing white bulk of Morne Blanc and its almost sheer 500m face make a great hiking destination. Although the track is only 600m long, it is quite steep, climbing 250m from start to finish. Unless you're very fit, plan on about an hour for the trip up.

The beginning of the route is signposted 250m up the road from the tea factory, along the Forêt Noire cross-island road, and the trail is marked by intermittent yellow splotches of paint on trees. The return is via the same route.

Places to Stay

Beau Vallon *The* place to stay at Beau Vallon is the ***Coral Strand Hotel*** (☎ *247036, fax 247517*), right on the beach where the old coast road meets the ocean. Single/double rooms cost Rs680/750 including breakfast or Rs780/1000 on half board. There's a dive school, water sports and a restaurant.

The other top-end option is the ***Berjaya Beau Vallon Bay Beach Resort*** (☎ *247141, fax 247943*), further west off the Bel Ombre road, but this place mainly caters to the package-tour groups. Singles/doubles/triples

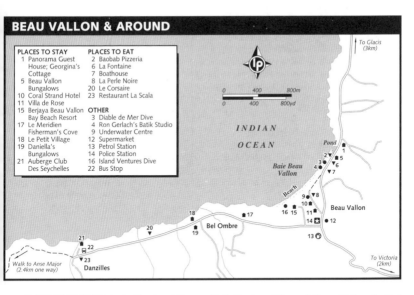

BEAU VALLON & AROUND

PLACES TO STAY	PLACES TO EAT
1 Panorama Guest House; Georgina's Cottage	2 Baobab Pizzeria
	6 La Fontaine
5 Beau Vallon Bungalows	7 Boathouse
	8 La Perle Noire
10 Coral Strand Hotel	20 Le Corsaire
11 Villa de Rose	23 Restaurant La Scala
15 Berjaya Beau Vallon Bay Beach Resort	**OTHER**
	3 Diable de Mer Dive
17 Le Meridien Fisherman's Cove	4 Ron Gerlach's Batik Studio
18 Le Petit Village	9 Underwater Centre
19 Daniella's Bungalows	12 Supermarket
	13 Petrol Station
21 Auberge Club Des Seychelles	14 Police Station
	16 Island Ventures Dive
	22 Bus Stop

cost Rs1356/1446/1672 including breakfast and Rs1565/1859/2153 on half board. Also here is a good dive and water sports centre and a casino.

Villa de Rose (☎ 247455), in the same area, is a well-run guesthouse with air-con rooms for Rs350/500 including breakfast. Self-catering apartments cost Rs680 for up to four people.

In Mare Anglaise, at the north end of Beau Vallon beach, *Le Pti Payot* (☎ 261447, fax 261094) is highly recommended. Attractive chalets with views of the beach cost Rs500 for up to four people. Air-con costs an extra Rs30.

A little further south, *Vacoa Village* (☎ 261130, fax 261146) is a complex of apartments in a lovely garden full of glacis boulders. Studios go for Rs500 a double including breakfast, while two-bedroom apartments cost Rs650 for up to four people.

For travellers with shallower pockets, *Georgina's Cottage* (☎ 247016, fax 247945) is an excellent homey guesthouse just a few minutes' walk from the Beau Vallon restaurants. There's a communal kitchen and a washing machine. Rooms cost Rs250/350 including breakfast.

Bel Ombre West of Beau Vallon in Bel Ombre, the *Meridien Fisherman's Cove* (☎ 247247, fax 247742) is a splendid choice if you can afford it. Facilities are top-notch and include a dive centre, three restaurants, a golf course and a pool. During the low season, rates begin at Rs1470/2060 including breakfast or Rs1690/2500 for half board. Rates increase by Rs100 per person in the high season.

Auberge Club Des Seychelles (☎ 247550, fax 247703) is at Danzilles, 1.5km from Bel Ombre, and offers thatched huts scattered about the headland. The rates for single/double/triple rooms are Rs640/810/1000 including breakfast or Rs765/1060/1375 on half board. The management organises a weekly walk to Anse Major with a 'Robinson Crusoe Picnic' and return transport by boat.

Daniella's Bungalows (☎ 247212, fax 247784) offers accommodation in well-kept bungalows. Rooms cost Rs400/500; rates include breakfast.

Just across the road, *Le Petit Village* (☎ 247474, fax 247771) offers charming log cabins overlooking the ocean. Air-con studios cost Rs810 a double; for four people in a two-bedroom apartment, it costs Rs1400.

Glacis The *Sunset Beach Hotel* (☎ 261111, fax 261221) near Glacis is an exclusive holiday village on a peaceful bay, and has a pool and a restaurant. Rates start at Rs1315/1525/2265 for singles/doubles/triples including breakfast. Half board costs an extra Rs180 per person.

The long-established *Le Northolme Hotel* (☎ 261222, fax 261223) is set on a pleasantly rugged stretch of coast just to the south. Rooms start at Rs1080/1260 including breakfast or Rs1260/1650 on half board.

Port Glaud Just south of Port Glaud is the *Berjaya Mahé Beach Resort* (☎ 378451, fax 378517). This rather unsightly multistorey edifice broke the tradition that all hotels on the islands should be no taller than the height of a palm tree. Facilities are OK, with a pool, tennis courts and water sports. Standard rooms cost Rs920/990 including breakfast (Rs1085/1320 in the high season).

Grande Anse On the other side of Grande Anse, *Le Meridien Barbarons* (☎ 378253, fax 378484) is a popular resort set around an impressive pool. Well-appointed rooms go for about Rs925/1060 including breakfast and Rs1055/1320 on half board. Prices vary throughout the year, so ask when you book.

Places to Eat

Beau Vallon Right on the beach, the *Baobab Pizzeria* (☎ 247167) is something of a local legend, offering tasty and reasonably priced pizzas and pasta dishes for about Rs35. The sand-floored restaurant is open daily except Tuesday, from 11.30 am to 3.30 pm and 6 to 10 pm.

Just across the road, the *Boathouse* (☎ 247868) offers a magnificent fresh fish barbecue every evening except Monday from 7.30 pm. You can eat all you want to (including scrummy deserts) for Rs85.

Next door, *La Fontaine* (☎ 247841) cooks up Creole seafood dishes for around Rs85. It's open daily from 11.30 am to 10 pm.

La Perle Noire (☎ 247046), by the Coral Strand Hotel, is open daily for dinner from 7 pm. It offers delicious Italian and Creole dishes for around Rs85.

Pieces of Eight

Bel Ombre is one of several possible locations of the fortune in treasure stolen by the legendary pirate Olivier Levasseur, known as 'La Buse' ('The Buzzard'). When La Buse was finally caught and hanged in Réunion in July 1730, he is said to have tossed a piece of paper into the crowd and shouted 'Find my treasure, he who can'.

A cryptogram that belonged to an old Norwegian whaling skipper, and strange markings on the shore rocks at Bel Ombre, have led several treasure seekers to dig up this particular stretch of coast. A retired Englishman, Reginald Cruise-Wilkins, devoted the last years of his life to the search in the 1940s, but found nothing more than a few tantalising coins and pieces of weaponry.

However, he may have been looking in the wrong place. Poudre d'Or in north Mauritius is just one of several other contenders for the title of final resting place of La Buse's fortune.

Bel Ombre Right near the water in Bel Ombre village, *Le Corsaire* (☎ 247171) offers Creole dishes such as fish with ginger sauce from Rs75. This restaurant is open for dinner only from 7.30 pm. It's closed on Monday.

Restaurant La Scala (☎ 247535) is at the end of the coast road, and specialises in Italian food. Interesting mains such as pasta with smoked sailfish cost around Rs85. It opens for dinner at 7 pm from Monday to Saturday; it's closed on Sunday and all through the month of June.

SOUTH MAHÉ

The southern half of Mahé is less mountainous and less populated than the north. There are some pleasant beaches around the southern tip of the island, but most of these are more suitable for sunbathing and just playing in the sand than for swimming as the lagoon rarely gets more than waist-deep. The best strips of sand are at Anse Bougainville, Anse Parnel, Anse Forbans and Anse Marie-Louise.

Around the headland, the beaches are too exposed and wild for swimming, but are great places to just watch the surf. Anse Intendance and Police Bay, right at the tip, are both splendid spots. You can walk there from the village of Quatre Bornes, which is accessible by public bus.

Craft Village

The rather contrived craft village (☎ 376100) at Anse aux Pins is a collection of craft shops grouped around the *Vye Marmit Restaurant* (☎ 376155). The craft shops sell a variety of local products such as straw hats and prints of tropical fish. The shops are open daily from 10 am to 6 pm. The restaurant is open daily from 11 am to 2 pm and 6 to 11 pm; Creole mains cost from Rs55.

Maison de Planteur

This beautifully restored Creole house is just south of the craft village at Anse aux Corbes. It's full of period furnishings, and looks much like it must have when it was built in 1792. You can visit on weekdays from 10 am to 5 pm (Rs10).

Le Jardin du Roi

Located in the hills of Anse Royale, Le Jardin du Roi (☎ 371313, fax 371366) is a sprawling and lush garden that owes its existence to Pierre Poivre, the French spice entrepreneur. There is a self-guided walk in the spice gardens, and you can help yourself to star fruit and other tropical delights as you wander around.

The gardens are open daily from 10 am to 5.30 pm. Admission costs Rs20 (it's free for children under 12 years of age).

Places to Stay

East Coast It's close to the airport, but *Carefree* (☎ 375237, fax 375654) is nothing to write home about. Singles/doubles/triples are Rs330/385/495 including breakfast, and Rs420/565/765 for half board. There's also a restaurant here.

Further south, *La Retraite* (☎ 375816) is a cheap and cheerful guesthouse in Anse aux Pins village. Simple rooms cost Rs200/270 including breakfast.

Nearby, the quiet *Lalla Panzi* (☎ 376411, fax 375633) is good value, with rooms for Rs220/280 including breakfast (air-con is Rs25 extra).

The *Reef Hotel & Golf Club* (☎ 376251, fax 376296) is a popular place. Adding to its appeal, it has budget package tours, a pool, tennis courts and a golf course. Rates start from Rs640/700 including breakfast, or Rs760/940 for half board.

In an isolated spot on the east coast, *Auberge de Bougainville* (☎ 371788, fax 371808) is a lovely old plantation house surrounded by a wooden veranda. Rooms cost Rs320/390 including breakfast, or Rs380/535 on half board. There is also a restaurant here; the set menu costs Rs90.

West Coast The *Lazare Picault Hotel* (☎ 361111, fax 361177), on the hillside overlooking the Baie Lazare, has comfortable rooms with great views for Rs415/525.

Chez Batista (☎ 366300, fax 366509) further south has a very cute seafront restaurant (see Places to Eat) and offers comfortable chalets for Rs385/660/865 for a single/double/triple including breakfast, and a few cheaper single/double rooms for Rs360/575.

The swish *Plantation Club* (☎ 361361, fax 361333) is a vast resort at Pointe Lazare, and has some towering glacis boulders in the garden. This popular hotel offers rooms with ocean views for Rs1250 a double plus an obligatory Rs80 for breakfast. There's a pool, a dive centre, tennis courts and a gallery featuring sculptures by local artist Antonio Filippin.

Across the road, the *Valmer Resort* (☎ 361313, fax 361159) offers spanking new self-catering villas with all mod-cons. One-bedroom villas cost Rs448/616; two-bedroom villas cost Rs952/1288. Painter Gerard Devoud has a gallery here.

Places to Eat

East Coast Near Pointe au Sel, *Ty-Foo* (☎ 371485) offers cheap and cheerful Chinese meals daily from 11 am to 2.30 pm and 6 to 10 pm. Most of the main courses cost around Rs55.

SEYCHELLES

Kaz Kreol (☎ *371680*) is close to Anse Royale village, and offers pizzas and seafood for about Rs90. It's open daily except Monday from noon to 4 pm (until 9 pm Friday to Sunday).

West Coast At Anse à la Mouche, *Anchor Café & Pizza* (☎ *371289*) serves cheap eats such as pizzas and grills for around Rs35. It's open daily from around 10 am to 11 pm.

The cosy **Splash Café** (☎ *361500*) at Baie Lazare is run by the sister of American actor Tom Hanks, but a better reason to visit is the tasty snack food. Burgers and other light meals cost from Rs35. It's open from 8.30 am to 4.30 pm daily except Monday.

Chez Batista at Anse Takamaka (see Places to Stay) is an easy-going eatery with a sand floor. It offers grilled fish, good pizzas and *gambas* (prawns) in the Rs75 to Rs100 range. It's open every day from 9 am to 10 pm.

STE ANNE MARINE NATIONAL PARK

This park is just off the coast near Victoria and consists of six islands. Long Island houses a prison, Ste Anne Island has a National Youth Service camp, and Cachée Island is reserved for the birds, but visitors are permitted to land on Cerf, Round and Moyenne Islands. The snorkelling in the park is impressive and highly recommended, though the effect of the land-reclamation project in the bay remains to be seen.

The islands are primarily visited on glass-bottomed-boat tours run by Mason's Travel, Créole Holidays and TSS (see Organised Tours earlier in this section), but you may be able to arrange a cheaper deal at the Marine Charter Association (☎ 322126, fax 224679) in Victoria.

Moyenne Island

Moyenne is probably the best marine park island to visit, as the fauna and flora have been carefully regenerated. Among the species you might see here are coco de mer palms and giant Aldabran tortoises. Day tours in a glass-bottomed boat are organised through Mason's Travel and cost Rs410/255

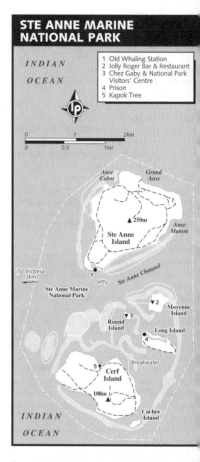

STE ANNE MARINE NATIONAL PARK

1 Old Whaling Station
2 Jolly Roger Bar & Restaurant
3 Chez Gaby & National Park Visitors' Centre
4 Prison
5 Kapok Tree

for adults/children, including lunch at the *Jolly Roger Bar & Restaurant* when you get to the island.

Round Island

This island, like Curieuse Island near Praslin, was once home to a leper colony but these days it's better known for the offshore snorkelling and its restaurant *Chez Gaby*, which serves good Creole creations.

TSS and Créole Holidays both offer glass-bottomed-boat tours priced at around Rs410/250 per adult/child, which include snorkelling stops and lunch at Chez Gaby.

SARINA SINGH

JOHN HAY

JOHN HAY

JOHN HAY

Indulge your Robinson Crusoe fantasies on the islands of the Seychelles.

Fishy business: Canned tuna and frozen fish are among the Seychelles' biggest export earners, although the environmental effects of the commercial fishing industry are controversial.

Cerf Island

About 40 people live on Cerf Island, including Wilbur Smith, the South African novelist. As with Moyenne and Round Islands, there is good snorkelling and a restaurant, *Kapok Tree*, which offers Creole seafood dishes.

TSS and Créole Holidays both charge around Rs410/250 for a glass-bottomed-boat tour including lunch at the Kapok Tree, or you may be able to hire a boat from the Marine Charter Association.

SILHOUETTE ISLAND

This imposing island is 20km from Mahé. It is named not for its moody profile at sunset, but for a French minister – though the atmosphere is certainly romantic enough once you arrive on shore. With steep forested mountain peaks rising from the ocean above stunning palm-shaded beaches, Silhouette Island is a truly magnificent island hideaway.

Sadly, the romance is reserved for guests of the exclusive Silhouette Island Lodge. You may be able to stop off at one of the beaches if you charter a boat for some deep-sea fishing from Mahé, but otherwise you'll either have to make the investment, or gaze over at the island from Beau Vallon beach and wonder.

Pirate Jean François Hodoul made the island his base, and there's 'gold in them thar hills', or so the tourist brochures would have you believe. If you want to search for it, there are caves to explore. If nothing else, they contain stalagmites and stalactities.

The island probably offers more things to do than any of the other exclusive island resorts. As well as some lovely beaches, there are numerous walking trails through the forest, including to the mist-shrouded peak of Mont Pot à Eau (621m), the island's highest point, which should confirm the feeling of having a paradise island all to yourself.

Places to Stay

The plush *Silhouette Island Lodge* (☎ *224003, fax 224897*) offers excursion packages only, which require a minimum stay of three days. The attractive bungalows are all very close to the ocean and cost Rs900/1190/1772 per single/double/triple, and an extra Rs902 per person for helicopter transfers from Mahé.

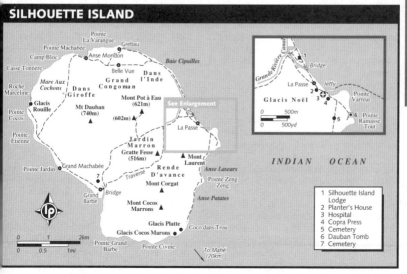

SILHOUETTE ISLAND

Map legend:
1 Silhouette Island Lodge
2 Planter's House
3 Hospital
4 Copra Press
5 Cemetery
6 Dauban Tomb
7 Cemetery

Praslin

HIGHLIGHTS

- Relaxing on the glorious Anse Lazio beach
- Encountering the fauna of the nearby islands, especially Cousin Island
- Meandering through Vallée de Mai, a fascinating prehistoric forest

Praslin is the second-largest island in the Seychelles, and has perhaps the friendliest atmosphere of the three main islands. In terms of development and tourism, it falls somewhere between Mahé and La Digue. The landscape is lush and tropical and the mood slow and easy, as befits such a tropical island paradise.

Like Mahé, Praslin is a granite island, with a ridge of mountains running east-west along the centre. The island measures 12km long and 5km across at its widest point, and lies about 45km north-east of Mahé. It's named after the Duc de Praslin, a French minister of state who was guillotined in the French Revolution.

The main attraction here, apart from some lovely beaches, is the Vallée de Mai. This forest reserve is one of the few places where the unusual coco de mer palm will grow (see the boxed text 'Lovely Bunch of Coconuts' following). The forest sits in the shadow of Praslin Island Peak (367m), the island's highest point.

The 5000 inhabitants of Praslin are scattered around the coast in a series of small settlements. The most important settlements from a visitor's perspective are the resorts of Anse Volbert (also known as the Côte d'Or) and Grand Anse. At the south-west tip of the island is Baie Ste Anne, Praslin's main port.

Information

Tourist Office There's a small tourist office (☎ 233346) at the Praslin airport terminal. It provides basic information about the island and can also help with accommodation bookings. The office is open from 8 am to 2 pm and 3.15 to 4 pm weekdays, and on Saturday from 8 am to noon.

Money There are several banks on the island. Grand Anse has branches of Barclays (☎ 233344), Banque Française Commerciale or BFC (☎ 233940) and Seychelles Savings Bank (☎ 233810). There's another BFC at Anse Volbert and a Barclays in Baie Ste Anne. All of these banks are open from 9 am to 2.30 pm on weekdays and 9 to 11 am on Saturday.

Post The main post office (☎ 233212) on Praslin is next to the police station at Grand Anse. Opening hours are from 8 am to noon and 1 to 4 pm weekdays.

Travel Agencies The travel agencies Créole Holidays (☎ 233223), Travel Services Seychelles or TSS (☎ 233441) and Mason's Travel (☎ 233211) all have offices at Grand Anse, and all offer an array of excursions to various islands. The offices are open from 8 am to 4 pm on weekdays and 8 am to noon on Saturday.

Vallée de Mai

Praslin's World Heritage-listed Vallée de Mai has the greatest concentration of coco de mer palms in the Seychelles – an estimated 4000. Other palms here include the palmiste palm, the latanier palm, the splayed traveller's palm and Chinese fans. Their collective fronds are an artist's dream; the way the sunlight filters through the forest ceiling and hits the various greens and oranges of the leaves is really something. Also look out for the black parrot of the Seychelles, which exists only on Praslin.

The Vallée de Mai is open every day from 8 am to 5.30 pm. Entry costs Rs40. In the interests of conservation, visitors are asked not to touch the trees or remove things from the forest. Smoking is also forbidden.

Beaches

The best beach on Praslin (indeed one of the best in the Seychelles) is Anse Lazio, 8km from Anse Volbert, on the north-west side of the island. The sand here is spectacular

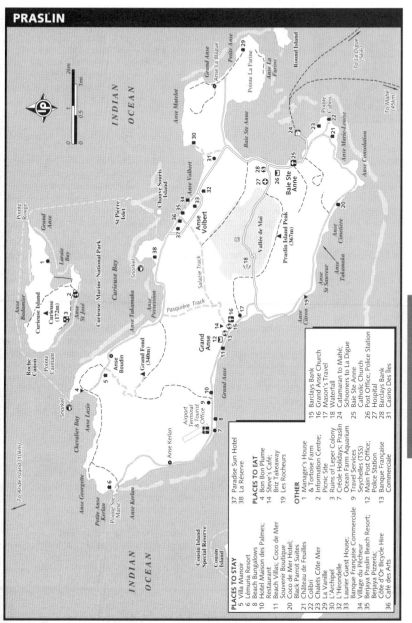

PRASLIN

PLACES TO STAY
5 Villa Manoir
6 Lémuria Resort
8 Beach Bungalows
10 Hotel Maison des Palmes;
   Restaurant
11 Beach Villas; Coco de Mer
   Souvenir Boutique
20 Coco de Mer Hotel;
   Black Parrot Suites
21 Château de Feuilles
22 Colibri
23 Chalets Côte Mer
29 La Vanille
30 L'Archipel
32 L'Hirondelle
33 Laurier Guest House;
   Banque Française Commerciale
34 Berjaya Praslin Beach Resort;
   Berjaya Pizzeria;
   Côte d'Or Bicycle Hire
36 Café des Arts

37 Paradise Sun Hotel
38 La Réserve

PLACES TO EAT
4 Bon Bon Plume
14 Steve's Café;
   Briz Takeaway
19 Les Rocheurs

OTHER
1 Manager's House
   & Tortoise Farm
2 Information Centre;
   Picnic Site
3 Ruins of Leper Colony
7 Créole Holidays; Praslin
   Ocean Farm Aquarium
9 Travel Services
   Seychelles (TSS)
12 Main Post Office;
   Police Station
13 Banque Française
   Commerciale

15 Barclays Bank
16 Grand Anse Church
17 Mason's Travel
18 Waterfall
24 Catamaran to Mahé;
   Schooners to La Digue
25 Baie Ste Anne
   Catholic Church
26 Post Office; Police Station
27 Hospital
28 Barclays Bank
31 Casino Des Îles

Lovely Bunch of Coconuts

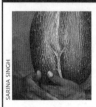

SARINA SINGH

The famously erotic nut of the coco de mer palm grows naturally only on Praslin, Silhouette and Curieuse Islands, and some of the trees in the Vallée de Mai are close to 1000 years old. This rare palm may seem a little tame by today's standards, but you can see why these strange fruit excited the 17th-century sailors who first stumbled upon them after months at sea. In fact, the occasional nut had washed up on the shores of other continents long before, sparking legends of a curious underwater tree (hence the name coco de mer, or coconut of the sea).

More recent travellers have also been inspired by the coco de mer. General Gordon of Khartoum, who visited Praslin in 1881, was so moved by the Vallée de Mai that he seriously proposed it as the location of the original Garden of Eden. The coco de mer palm, Gordon believed, was the tree of good and evil knowledge used to test Adam and Eve. Its fruit, he wrote, 'externally represents the heart, while the interior represents the thighs and belly, which I consider as the true seat of carnal desires...'

Only female trees produce the erotically shaped nuts, which can weigh up to 20kg. The male tree possesses a rather phallic flowering catkin, adding to the coco de mer's steamy reputation.

Harvesting of the nuts is strictly controlled by the Seychelles government – expect to pay around Rs1500 (US$265) for an unpolished coco de mer.

the lagoon is incredibly blue and there is good swimming and snorkelling offshore. Also here is a terrific restaurant called Bon Bon Plume (see Places to Eat).

The beaches at Grand Anse are disappointing, but there is a nice stretch of sand at Anse Volbert. Right at the southern tip of the island, Anse Consolation and Anse Marie-Louise are also pretty spots.

The waters around the tiny St Pierre Islet, off Anse Volbert, are good for snorkelling and some sloshing around.

Boat trips organised by hotels such as the Paradise Sun Hotel and private operators cost around Rs45 per person.

Aquarium

Praslin Ocean Farm Aquarium (☎ 233150) is a commercial pearl farm with over 40,000 giant clams. Visitors can learn about the pearl-culturing process and also see sharks and other fish in the small aquarium.

The aquarium is open from 8 am to 6 pm Sunday to Friday; entry costs Rs25/10 for adults/children.

Organised Tours

Mason's Travel, Créole Holidays and TSS (see Travel Agencies earlier in this chapter)

all offer similar excursions at similar prices and can organise car hire, boat charters, water activities and general travel arrangements.

A full-day bus tour of Praslin including Anse Lazio and the Vallée de Mai costs around Rs225/105 for adults/ children, including lunch. A morning tour of the Vallée de Mai alone costs Rs135/60. Other options include a day tour of the Vallée de Mai and La Digue for Rs410/200 including lunch, and a day tour of just La Digue for Rs315/200 including lunch. Call the agents for more details.

Places to Stay

Most visitors favour Praslin over Mahé so demand for accommodation is high, as are the prices. To avoid disappointment, book your accommodation well in advance; this is essential during the high season.

Places to Stay – Budget

Budget options are pretty thin on the ground in Praslin.

A 10-minute walk from the stunning beach at Anse Lazio, *Villa Manoir* (☎ 575848, fax 261115) has just two self-catering apartments for Rs200/300 a single/double with breakfast. You can also get cheap snack meals here.

Beach Villas and *Beach Bungalows* are two friendly budget places at opposite ends of Grand Anse. Comfortable rooms cost Rs285/400. For reservations call ☎ 233445 or fax 233098.

L'Hirondelle (☎/fax 232243) is one of a few cheap places at Anse Volbert. It offers doubles with shared bathroom for Rs350, doubles with private bathroom for Rs375, and self-catering apartments for Rs410/450 a single/double.

Laurier Guest House (☎ 232241, fax 232362) in the centre of Anse Volbert is a friendly guesthouse and bungalow complex with its own restaurant. Rates start at Rs280/400/450 per single/double/triple in rooms or Rs300/450/500 in the bungalows. Rates include breakfast.

At Pointe Cabris, just south of Baie Ste Anne, *Colibri* (☎/fax 232302) has a tranquil setting overlooking the bay. The attractive wooden villas cost Rs300/450 with breakfast (Rs370/600 on half board). There are lovely views but no beach.

Places to Stay – Mid-Range

At Petite Anse to the north of Baie Ste Anne, *La Vanille* (☎ 232178, fax 232284) is set on a lovely secluded beach. Standard rooms go for Rs470/680 with breakfast (Rs585/900 with all meals). Water sports are available.

The splendid *Hotel Maison des Palmes* (☎ 233411, fax 233880) is the best choice at Grand Anse. Pleasant thatched units cost from Rs807/862/941 per single/double/triple with breakfast. There are lots of water activities on offer. Prices go up by around Rs100 in the high season.

Chalets Côte Mer (☎/fax 232367) at Pointe Cabris offers clean rooms for Rs630/730 and tidy apartments for Rs580 a double (Rs700 for three people). There's a discount of 15% if you book directly with the owners.

Café des Arts (☎ 232170, fax 232155) is a very cosy British-run place with its own art gallery. Beautifully laid out rooms cost from Rs630/700/930 per single/double/triple.

Places to Stay – Top End

Top of the top-end places in Praslin is the brand new *Lémuria Resort* (☎ 281281, fax 281000) at Petite Anse Kerlan. There's a pool, a private 18-hole golf course, three restaurants and four bars. Rates start at Rs1960 per person including breakfast.

Close to Anse Lazio, *La Réserve* (☎ 232211, fax 232166) at Anse Petite Cour is an impressive place, with plantation-style mansions beside a private beach. The well-appointed rooms start at Rs1950 a double (Rs2050 in the plush air-con villas by the beach).

There are some good choices at Anse Volbert. The *Berjaya Praslin Beach Resort* (☎ 232222, fax 232244) is right on the beach and has a swimming pool, a tennis court and the usual water activities, but is missing a certain warmth. The rates for standard rooms are Rs1020/1110 with breakfast; Rs1230/1520 on half board.

The *Paradise Sun Hotel* (☎ 232255, fax 232019) at the west end of Anse Volbert beach is well laid out and has a better-than-average strip of sand. The rooms cost from Rs1600/2200 on a half-board basis. As you'd expect, there's a pool, a restaurant and a dive school.

The relaxed *Village du Pêcheur* (☎ 232224, fax 261221) at Anse Volbert offers rooms from Rs845/890 in the garden and from Rs1400/1305 right by the beach. Rates include breakfast. There's a good restaurant here (see Places to Eat).

L'Archipel (☎ 232242, fax 232072) has a lovely secluded location at the eastern end of Anse Volbert. Good rooms cost Rs1876/1988 with breakfast, or Rs2128/2492 on half board (the rates increase between late December and early January). This place is a real retreat and has a fine restaurant.

Château de Feuilles (☎ 233316, fax 233916) is a beautifully conceived tropical getaway on the Pointe Cabris estate south of Baie Ste Anne. Double rooms in the main house cost Rs1450, while thatched bungalows in the garden start at Rs1850 a double. There's a lovely restaurant.

The *Coco de Mer Hotel* and *Black Parrot Suites* (☎ 233900, fax 233919) share a pool, a restaurant and a dive school. They are located on a secluded but ordinary beach near Anse Cimetière. In the low season, rooms at

SEYCHELLES

the Coco de Mer cost from Rs1190/1320 with breakfast; suites at the Black Parrot cost from Rs1755/2025 on half board. In the high season, prices increase by about 30%.

Places to Eat
Self-caterers can choose from the small supermarket in Grand Anse and a few small stores in Grand Anse and Baie Ste Anne. You can buy fresh fish from the fishermen at Baie Ste Anne.

There are only a few takeaways on Praslin. One option is *Briz Takeaway* near the church in Grand Anse, which offers the usual dishes, such as *rougaille poisson* (fish in a tomato-based sauce) with rice for around Rs20. It's open from 11.30 am to 2.30 pm and 4.30 to 10 pm.

Nearby, *Steve's Café* (☎ 233215) is another good cheapie, with takeaway meals for Rs22 (Rs40 if you eat in). It's open from 8 am to 10.30 pm Monday to Saturday.

At the Berjaya Praslin Beach Resort (see Places to Stay) in Anse Volbert, the beachfront *Berjaya Pizzeria* offers great pizzas from Rs60. It's open daily from 11.30 am to 9.30 pm – you can eat in or take away.

Bon Bon Plume (☎ 232136) is a palm-thatched restaurant located by the gorgeous Anse Lazio beach. Because of the location, prices are a little elevated; mains such as grilled fish with Creole sauce cost from Rs100 to Rs225. It's open daily for lunch only from noon to 3 pm.

Village du Pêcheur (see Places to Stay) has a pleasant restaurant that is open daily to nonresidents. Lunch is served from 12.30 to 2.30 pm and dinner from 7.30 to 9.30 pm. Creole mains cost from Rs60.

On the south-west coast at La Pointe, *Les Rocheurs* (☎ 233034) has a slightly high opinion of itself, but has excellent Creole food. It's open from 11.30 am to 2 pm and 6 to 9 pm. Mains cost from Rs150.

Hotel Maison des Palmes at Grand Anse (see Places to Stay) has a charming restaurant that is open daily for lunch and dinner. On Wednesdays there's a grill night with music, and on Saturdays there's a Creole buffet with music. Nonresidents pay Rs150 and must book ahead.

Entertainment
Most of the large hotels have their own entertainment programs, usually on the weekend. Nightlife is pretty limited on Praslin and most people seem to like it that way.

Casino Des Îles (☎ 232500) is the major entertainment venue. The slot machines are open daily from noon to 2 am, while the games room (for blackjack, roulette, poker etc) is open from 7.30 pm to 3 am. The usual dress codes apply. If you call ahead they'll even pick you up from your hotel.

Getting There & Away
Praslin's airport terminal is 3km from Grand Anse. (For flight information, see the Seychelles Getting Around section.)

The expensive Cat Cocos catamaran provides the main boat connection to Mahé. You can save money by taking the schooner from Mahé to La Digue and then picking up one of the regular schooners between La Digue and Praslin. (See the Seychelles Getting Around section for routes, times and prices.)

Hopping around the small islands of Praslin is done by chartered boat; trips are usually organised through the hotels or the tour operators (see Travel Agencies earlier in the Praslin section).

Getting Around
Praslin has a decent bus service as well as the usual pricey taxis.

For car hire, try Explorer Cars (☎ 233311) Prestige Car Hire (☎ 233226) or Austral Car Rental (☎ 232015). There are petrol stations at Baie Ste Anne and Grand Anse. Car rental costs the same as on Mahé.

You can rent bikes for Rs50 per day from Côte d'Or Bicycle Hire (☎ 232071) at the entry road to the Berjaya Praslin Beach Resort at Anse Volbert village. Most hotels should be able to arrange bicycle hire for their guests.

(For more information on taxis, buses and car hire, see the Seychelles Getting Around section earlier in this chapter.)

CURIEUSE ISLAND
This island, just 1.5km off the north coast of Praslin, was a leper colony from 1833 until

1965. As part of a curious reciprocal arrangement, lepers from Mauritius were traded for mentally ill Seychellois. The theory was that the Seychelles had more isolated islands where the disease could be contained.

The island's information centre is housed in the old doctor's house at Anse St José. The charming Creole building is a national monument, and is open daily from 9 am to 5 pm.

The island is given over to a breeding scheme for hundreds of giant Aldabran tortoises – visitors can come as part of an organised tour and be shown round by the wardens. Look out for the curious glacis formations en route.

Getting There & Away

Most visitors to Curieuse Island arrive on a 'Three Islands' day trip (Cousin, Curieuse and St Pierre) organised by Créole Holidays, Mason's Travel or TSS (see Travel Agencies earlier in the Praslin section). This trip costs around Rs450 per person (almost half price for children) including lunch.

COUSIN ISLAND

Approximately 1km in diameter and about 3km off the south-west coast of Praslin is Cousin Island, which is run as a nature reserve by Bird Life Seychelles (☎ 225097). Numerous species breed here, including the black noddy, the *paille en queue* (white-tailed tropicbird), and the extremely rare brush warbler and magpie robin. It's an amazing experience to walk through thick forest with birds seemingly nesting on every branch.

To minimise the effect on the local bird life, Cousin can only be visited as part of a guided tour. Visitors can get close enough to the birds to photograph them, but tripods and close-up lenses are not allowed. A small booklet, sold for Rs3 on the island, will take you through the flora and fauna. Keep an eye open for George and Georgina, a pair of very elderly Aldabra tortoises who plod after visitors in the hope of having their leathery necks stroked.

Getting There & Away

Cousin is included on the 'Three Islands' tours run by Créole Holidays, Mason's Travel

and TSS (see Travel Agencies earlier in the Praslin section). For bird lovers, Créole Holidays offers full-day tours of Cousin Island for Rs315/195 per adult/child. Your hotel may also be able to organise day trips.

ARIDE ISLAND

The most northerly of the granite islands, Aride Island lies 10km to the north of Praslin. The island was purchased for the Royal Society for Nature Conservation in 1973 by Christopher Cadbury (of chocolate fame). The nature reserve supports the greatest concentration of sea birds in the area, including large colonies of lesser noddies, roseate terns and frigate birds (the frigate birds are noted for their giant wingspan). The island can be reached by boat between April and October only, as the winds and seas can make landing difficult and dangerous at other times.

Getting There & Away

Weather permitting, you can take a tour from Praslin with Mason's Travel, Créole Holidays or TSS for Rs400/195 for adults/children, including lunch (for contact details, see Travel Agencies earlier in the Praslin section). Your hotel may also be able to arrange trips.

Seychelles Sea Birds

Cousin and Aride Islands support huge colonies of black (lesser) noddies during the south-east monsoon. During the birds' elaborate courtship, the male bird offers his mate leaves until he finds one to her satisfaction (she indicates her approval by defecating on it!). This leaf then forms the keystone of the nest for the season.

Another prevalent species is the wedge-tailed shearwater, which breeds in burrows from October to March. The noise of shearwater colonies has to be heard to be believed; the bird mates for life and when its companion, who hasn't been seen for the past year, turns up all hell breaks loose. The birds have a large wingspan and their 'runways' are well defined; you may see them lined up for their predawn departure for the day's fishing.

La Digue & Other Inner Islands

HIGHLIGHTS

- Just relaxing amid the laid-back ambience and friendly folk
- Diving, snorkelling and deep-sea fishing
- Bird-watching on Denis and Bird Islands, home to millions of feathery creatures

LA DIGUE

La Digue is truly beautiful and is easily the least developed of the three main islands, though it's certainly not undiscovered. Most tourists to the Seychelles make a stop on the island, so you'll have to make that little bit more effort to find a quiet place in the sun. Fortunately, there are some lovely isolated beaches on the south-east coast where you can escape the crowds and indulge your Robinson Crusoe fantasies.

La Digue is only about 5km from Praslin, and regular schooners ferry day-trippers between the two islands. For the moment, the island is cheaper to stay on than either Mahé or Praslin, and it has a quieter, more laid-back feel. Tourist developments on this lovely island have thus far been fairly subtle affairs; the island's developers even went as far as to disguise the cellphone transmitters on La Digue as palm trees. Most of the 2000 or so inhabitants are involved in fishing, agriculture or tourism.

Information

Tourist Office The La Digue tourist office (☎/fax 234393) is right next to the pier. It can organise transport around the island and can also help with tours. It's open Monday to Friday from 8 am to noon and 1 to 4 pm, and Saturday from 9 am to noon.

Money There are several banks on La Digue. Banque Française Commerciale (☎ 234560), opposite the jetty in La Passe, and Seychelles Savings Bank (☎ 234135), opposite the hospital, are both open normal bank hours for foreign exchange. Barclays (☎ 234148), opposite La Digue Island Lodge Hotel, is open Monday, Wednesday and Friday from 10.30 am to 2 pm.

Post La Digue's post office (☎ 234036) is next to the police station, near the pier at La Passe. It is open weekdays from 8 am to noon and 1 to 4 pm. There is one mail collection per day.

Travel Agencies Travel Services Seychelles or TSS (☎ 234429) has an office in the arcade by the pier; Mason's Travel (☎ 234227, fax 234266) is close to the La Digue Island Lodge. Both are open Monday to Friday from 8 am to noon and 1 to 4 pm, and Saturday from 8 am to noon. They can arrange various activities including fishing trips, helicopter flights and inter-island trips.

Beaches

Most new arrivals head straight for the beach at Anse Source d'Argent, a classic white-sand beach backed by a gallery of naturally sculpted granite boulders that would have made Henry Moore proud. Although the scenery is superb, it can get pretty crowded here, and the lagoon is much too shallow for swimming. The path down to the Anse Source d'Argent runs through the old L'Union coconut plantation, which is run as a museum, so you will probably have to pay the Rs10 entry fee.

On the far side of the island, Grand Anse is another stunning beach, and it sees less visitors because of the effort required to get there (but you can easily walk or cycle the 4km or so from La Passe). Again, the beach is better for sunbathing than swimming, this time because of strong offshore currents. There's a snack bar here offering tasty grilled fish and other light meals, open daily from 9 am to 6 pm.

The best beaches on La Digue are north of Grand Anse at Petite Anse and Anse Cocos. The path to Petite Anse begins behind the beach at Grand Anse. Watch out for giant millipedes, huge land crabs and palm spiders as you cross over the headland (See the

LA DIGUE

PLACES TO STAY
1 Hotel L'Ocean
  & Restaurant
2 Patatran Village
10 Villa Authentique
12 Chez Marston
13 Choppy's Beach
  Bungalows
14 Fleur de Lys
17 La Digue Island Lodge
  & Pool Restaurant
19 Le Romarin
20 Calou Guest House
21 Bernique Guest House
22 Sitronnel Guest House
23 Château St Cloud
28 Paradise Fly
  Catcher's Lodge
31 L'Union Self-Catering
  Chalets
34 Villa Mon Rêve

PLACES TO EAT
4 Tarosa Cafeteria
7 Bakery; Michelin
  (Bicycle Hire)
24 Zerof
36 Snack Bar

OTHER
3 Tourist Office
5 Tati's Cycle Hire
6 Hospital
8 Post Office;
  Police Station; Payphone
9 Banque Française
  Commerciale; Helicopter
  Seychelles; Kokosye;
  Travel Services Seychelles
11 Seychelles Savings Bank
15 Cable & Wireless
16 Mason's Travel
18 Barclays Bank;
  Gregoire's Store
25 School
26 Church
27 Petrol Station
29 Barbara Jenson's Studio
30 Old Cemetery
32 Plantation House
33 L'Union Estate
  & Copra Factory
35 Abandoned Settlement

boxed text 'Palm Spiders in the Seychelles Facts for the Visitor section). The beach here is quiet, palm-fringed and idyllic, though there are strong currents here too. The idyllic Anse Cocos is reached by a rather vague track at the north end of Petite Anse.

L'Union Estate & Copra Factory

At one time, the main industry on La Digue was coconut farming, centred on L'Union Estate coconut plantation south of La Passe. These days the estate is run as an informal museum, with demonstrations of the process of extracting oil from copra (dried coconut

meat). Also in the grounds is the imposing State Guest House (which is used for presidential guests), an old colonial cemetery and an enclosure containing a number of giant tortoises which you can feed with the vegetation provided. It's open from around 7 am to 7 pm; entry costs Rs10.

Veuve Reserve

This small forest reserve is the last refuge of the black paradise flycatcher (*Terpsiphone corvina*), which the Creoles call the *veuve* (widow) because the male bird appears to be in mourning with its streaming black tail feathers. Endemic to the Seychelles, there are thought to be fewer than 50 pairs left, with just five or six nesting pairs in the reserve itself. Entry to the reserve is free. The information centre near the entrance of the reserve is open Monday to Friday from 8 am to 4 pm.

Barbara Jenson's Studio
North of L'Union Estate & Copra Factory is this studio (☎ 234406, fax 376356). Originally from England, Jenson came to the Seychelles in 1984 and her paintings reflect her love of the islands, particularly La Digue. The studio is open daily from 9 am to 6 pm.

Scenic Flights
The Helicopter Seychelles office (☎ 375400) is located in the Social Security building in La Passe. It's open daily from 9 am to noon and 2 to 5 pm. A 30-minute buzz over La Digue costs Rs2200 for up to four people.

Organised Tours
Many hotels can arrange a tour of the island or boat charters to other islands (see the Seychelles Getting Around section earlier in this chapter).

Mason's Travel offers various tours (some on request). A two-hour guided tour of the island costs Rs115 per person. For tours to other islands, see the relevant entries later in this section.

Places to Stay
Places to stay on La Digue are limited and the island is becoming increasingly popular with travellers, so don't leave bookings to the last minute.

Places to Stay – Budget
The charming *Château St Cloud* (☎/fax 234346), inland from the main settlement, is a former plantation house which offers comfortable single/double rooms for Rs250/400 including breakfast (Rs300/500 for half board). It's relaxed and informal – meals are eaten at a shared table.

Nearby, *Bernique Guest House* (☎ 234229, fax 234288) is a complex of clean bungalows; rates are Rs310/420 including breakfast (Rs400/570 on half board).

Sitronnel Guest House (☎ 234230), just south of Bernique, is an unpretentious guesthouse with rooms for Rs200/400 including breakfast; Rs300/550 for half board.

Le Romarin (☎ 234115), just north of Bernique, is a cheap option with just a few rooms for Rs150/200; breakfast is a steep Rs50 per person.

Across the road, *Calou Guest House* (☎/fax 234083) has five rooms for Rs385/525 on a half-board basis only.

Closer to the jetty, *Villa Authentique* (☎/fax 234413) is a very homy place run by a friendly Creole family. Single/doubles/triples cost Rs300/450/600 on a half-board basis.

Another good cheapie is *Chez Marston* (☎/fax 234023), not far from the hospital. Clean self-catering units cost Rs200/400.

Further south on the shore, *Choppy's Beach Bungalows* (☎ 234224, fax 234088) is a bit more upmarket. Rooms in the garden cost Rs575/650 with breakfast; better beach rooms cost Rs725/800. Half board is an extra Rs75 per person.

Beside the Veuve Reserve, *Paradise Fly Catcher's Lodge* (☎/fax 234015) offers well-appointed rooms in duplexes with a shared kitchen and living room. The charge is Rs300/400 with breakfast or Rs600/800 on half board.

Places to Stay – Top End
Patatran Village (☎ 234333, fax 234344) is an attractive complex of chalets in a tranquil location overlooking the sea at Anse Patates. Rates for a standard single/double room start from Rs530/780 for half board or Rs750/1120 for full board. There's also a good restaurant here (see Places to Eat).

Not quite so luxurious, *Hotel L'Ocean* (☎ 234180, fax 234308), near Patatran Village, offers singles/doubles/triples for Rs640/850/970 including breakfast. It also has a pleasant restaurant.

La Digue Island Lodge (☎ 234232, fax 234100), near Anse La Réunion, is a large, resort-style hotel that is certainly luxurious enough, but is a little lacking in warmth. Rooms vary in price from Rs1045/1515 in the garden to Rs1410/2095 by the beach.

All rates are on half board. There's a pool, a restaurant and a dive centre.

The same owners also manage *L'Union Self Catering Chalets* in the L'Union Estate, with self-contained chalets on the beach for Rs1825 for up to four people.

Places to Eat

For self-caterers, *Gregoire's* near La Digue Island Lodge is a fairly well-stocked supermarket, open Monday to Saturday from 8 am to 6.30 pm.

Behind Michelin bicycle hire near the pier is a small *bakery* with freshly baked bread for about Rs6.

The best option for a cheap lunch is the *Tarosa Cafeteria* (☎ 234250), near the pier, with snack meals such as salads (Rs25), omelettes (Rs35) and sandwiches (Rs25). It's open daily from 10 am to 6 pm.

Zerof (☎ 234067), opposite the Veuve Reserve, has an emphasis on Creole cuisine. The main courses cost around Rs65; takeaway dishes cost Rs25. It is open daily from noon to 9 pm.

Choppy's Beach Bungalows (see Places to Stay) has an OK restaurant open daily from noon to 3 pm and 7 to 9.30 pm. There's a tasty Creole buffet twice a week (ring to check when) which costs Rs100 per person. Nonresidents should book ahead.

The restaurant at *Hotel l'Ocean* (see Places to Stay) offers reasonably priced Creole food; mains such as *carri poulpe* (octopus curry) range from Rs75 to Rs90. It's open daily from noon to 10 pm.

At La Digue Island Lodge (see Places to Stay), the *Pool Restaurant* offers burgers and sandwiches by the hotel pool for Rs45, or main meals for around Rs90. It's open daily from noon to 5 pm.

The restaurant at *Patatran Village* (see Places to Stay) is recommended for a treat. Set seafood lunches are Rs110, while evening mains start at Rs100. Lunch is served daily from noon to 2.30 pm; dinner is served from 7 to 9.30 pm.

Getting There & Away

You can get to La Digue by boat or helicopter from either Mahé or Praslin. See Getting Around near the beginning of this chapter for details.

Getting Around

Taxi There are only about three taxis on La Digue, as most people get around on bicycle or on foot. A one-way ride from the pier to Grand Anse costs around Rs60. There is a surcharge of Rs5 per item of luggage.

Bicycle As only essential motor vehicles are allowed on La Digue, cycling has become the modus operandi. The island is relatively small, so cycling is a relaxing and easy way to get around, though in the high season the island's roads can start to resemble the Tour de France. There are loads of bikes to rent; most places charge around Rs10/25 per hour/day. Michelin (☎ 234043) and Tati's Cycle Hire (☎ 234250) are both near the pier and both charge Rs10/25 per hour/day.

Walking If you can't ride a bike, don't despair. The island is small enough to cover comfortably on foot. It's a great place to ramble around at leisure, with plenty of alluring beaches to stop at for a cool dip if you work up a sweat. Several walks and hikes are described earlier in this chapter.

Ox Cart The ox carts are mainly hired out by tour groups. Talk to the tourist office about hiring one if this easy-going mode of transport appeals to you.

Boat Your hotel may be able to recommend a reputable private boat operator. (See the main Seychelles Getting Around section near the beginning of this chapter.)

FÉLICITÉ ISLAND

This mountainous island, 3.5km north-east of La Digue, has good walking trails and excellent snorkelling sites. It is run as an extremely luxurious resort by La Digue Island Lodge, and the whole island is available for rent according to the motto 'own your island'. The minimum number of guests is two and the maximum is eight. Once a reservation has been confirmed, no other

SEYCHELLES

reservation is allowed to overlap with the confirmed stay of the guests on the island.

The minimum length of stay is three days. Rates start at around Rs7000 for two people and rise to a maximum of Rs20,325 for eight people. The price includes full board, all drinks, snorkelling gear and even use of the lodge yacht. Also included in the rates is the transfer – around 30 minutes by boat – from La Digue or Praslin. Contact La Digue Island Lodge (☎ 234232, fax 234100).

If you can't afford to stay here, you can always visit on a day trip. La Digue Island Lodge offers day trips to Félicité at Rs300 per person including lunch. Mason's Travel charges Rs310/155 for adults/children, with lunch included.

FRÉGATE ISLAND

This privately owned granite island, 56km east of Mahé and about 20km south of La Digue, was once a hang-out for pirates, who left strange markings on the rocks – today it's a stronghold for the rare magpie robin and the giant tenebrionid beetle, as well as a few giant tortoises. Guests at the hotel can indulge in bird-watching and hunting for treasure, or can just lie on the splendid golden sand at Anse Victorin, one of the best beaches in the islands.

Places to Stay

This magnificent island is reserved for guests of the exclusive *Fregate Island Resort*. Bookings can only be made through the resort's office in Germany, and rooms start at a staggering US$1070 per night. Plane transfers from Mahé cost an extra Rs3700. For information contact Astride Oberhummer, Egerlaender Str 47, Offenbach 63069, Germany (☎ 69-8383 7635).

BIRD ISLAND

True to its name, this tiny flat coral island, 96km north of Mahé, is dominated by birds, birds, birds. Sooty terns nest here between May and October, and other migratory species, including fairy terns and common noddies, descend on the island throughout the year. A visit is an awesome and immensely enjoyable experience, but it takes some travellers a while to become accustomed to the sights, smells and noises of the bird world.

The island, which measures only 1km by 2km, is covered in palms and ringed by a white coral beach. It is open only to guests of the Bird Island Lodge. Apart from being an obvious magnet for ornithologists, Bird Island is also good for snorkelling, swimming, diving, windsurfing, deep-sea fishing and simply lazing around.

Turtles breed on the island's beaches, while their land-bound relatives lumber around the interior. One of these giant tortoises, Esmeralda, is in the Guinness Book of Records as the oldest tortoise in the world. She is actually a he, and is believed to be more than 150 years old.

Places to Stay

Bird Island Lodge (☎ 323322, fax 323335) offers attractive wooden bungalows with verandas facing the sea. Singles go for Rs1155/1815/2500 for one/two/three nights, and doubles cost Rs2310/3300/4565. Rates include return airfares and all meals. Contact the Bird Island office (☎ 224925, fax 225074) on Independence Ave in Victoria for information on booking and flight schedules.

DENIS ISLAND

Ideal for the well-heeled ornithologist, the privately owned Denis Island is similar to Bird Island, but is more exclusive. The island was named after the French navigator Denis de Trobriand, who discovered it in 1773. The coral island is south-east of Bird Island and about 80km from Mahé. It belongs to the Denis Island Lodge, which offers guests scuba diving, deep-sea fishing and land-based sports.

Places to Stay

Denis Island Lodge (☎ 321143, fax 321010) has luxurious thatched and secluded chalets dotted among the coconut trees. The minimum booking is three nights – rates start at Rs2581/2967/4060 per single/double/triple on full board, plus Rs1190 per person for air transfers.

Outer Islands

HIGHLIGHTS

- Playing jet-setter at the exclusive resorts
- Living out your Robinson Crusoe fantasies in isolated splendour
- Descending into the amazing underwater world around the Aldabra Atoll

The majority of the Seychelles islands are scattered widely hundreds of kilometres to the south-west of the main Mahé group. They fall into three main groups – Amirantes, Farquhar and Aldabra. Sadly, most of the outer islands are inaccessible to travellers, and those you can visit are run as extremely exclusive resorts.

Only a few of the outer islands are inhabited, by about 500 fishermen and research and agricultural workers employed by the Seychelles Island Foundation (☎ 321755). The main industry of these islands is copra (dried coconut meat), used in the production of coconut oil. There are also fledgling attempts at aquaculture; perhaps the most successful is the prawn farm on Coëtivy. You may be able to obtain permission to visit some of the far-flung islands from the Seychelles Island Foundation.

AMIRANTES GROUP

The largest of the three groups, the Amirantes, lies about 250km south-west of Mahé. The islands were named Ilhas do Amirante (Admiral Islands) in 1501 by Vasco da Gama, the Portuguese explorer.

The main island in the group is Desroches, which is now a luxury resort, the **Desroches Island Resort** (☎ 229003, fax 229002). You can only visit on a three-day excursion package costing Rs1725/2300 per single/double plus Rs1100 per person for air transfers.

ALPHONSE GROUP

Further south, the Alphonse Group is another cluster of coral islands that are only really accessible to private yachts.

The largest island in the group, the tiny Alphonse Island, is home to the brand new **Alphonse Island Resort** (☎ 322682, fax 321322), which offers luxurious chalets for Rs2372/3040. Air transfers from Mahé cost about FF1245.

ALDABRA GROUP

This is the best known, most remote and most interesting of the outer island groups. Aldabra lies more than 1000km from Mahé – in fact the Aldabra Atoll is closer to Madagascar (400km) and Tanzania (800km) than to its own capital. The islands are only really accessible to scientists, though you may be able to swing permission to visit from the Seychelles Island Foundation (☎ 321755). The group is thought to have been discovered around the 9th century by Arab seafarers, who called it Al Khadra; through the centuries and various European pronunciations, the name has became Aldabra.

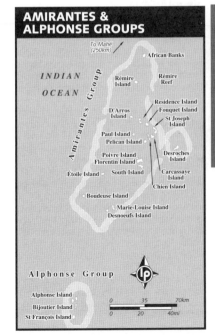

AMIRANTES & ALPHONSE GROUPS

To Mahé (250km)

INDIAN OCEAN

Amirantes Group

African Banks
Rémire Island
Rémire Reef
Residence Island
D'Arros Island
Fouquet Island
St Joseph Island
Paul Island
Pelican Island
Poivre Island
Florentin Island
Desroches Island
Étoile Island
South Island
Carcassaye Island
Chien Island
Boudeuse Island
Marie-Louise Island
Desnoeufs Island

Alphonse Group
Alphonse Island
Bijoutier Island
St François Island

0   35   70km
0   20   40mi

SEYCHELLES

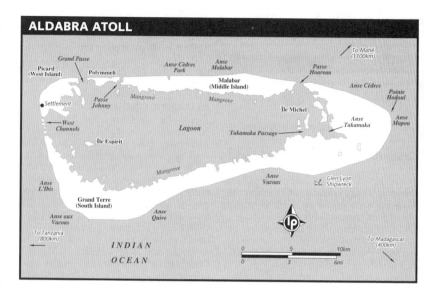

ALDABRA ATOLL

Aldabra Atoll

Aldabra Atoll is one of the world's largest coral atolls. It stretches for 22km east to west and contains four major islands – Picard (West Island), Polymnieli, Malabar (Middle Island) and Grand Terre (South Island) – which enclose a huge tidal lagoon. The underwater environment here is magnificent.

Aldabra is home to about 20,000 giant tortoises, although at the turn of the century they were almost killed off. Many ended life as food for hungry sailors, but still more were boiled up for the oil in their skins.

Turtles lay their eggs on the atoll, and flocks of migratory birds, including ibises, flamingos, herons and frigate birds, fly in and out in their thousands. Other interesting species include the white-throated rail, the sole remaining flightless bird species in the Indian Ocean, and the giant robber crab, which climbs coconut trees and cuts down the nuts with its pincers!

Aldabra was declared a nature reserve some years ago by the Seychelles government and has now been listed as a World Heritage Site by Unesco.

The atoll is inhabited only by scientists, and only for three months of the year. It has a scientific station with generator-powered electricity. The Seychelles government is keen to see more scientists make use of the station. Assomption Island, 27km south of Aldabra, has the nearest airstrip to Aldabra.

Cosmolédo Atoll

The Cosmolédo Atoll, which includes Astove Island, is a ring of 12 tiny islands 110km east of Assomption Island in the Aldabra Group. The largest of these islands is Wizard Island (Grand Île), which covers less than 2 sq km. The islands have been more or less ignored by outsiders, and still serve as nesting sites for the tern, the booby and the rare red-tailed tropicbird.

FARQUHAR GROUP

This group of islands – Farquhar Atoll, Providence and St Pierre – lies about 700km south-west of Mahé. The lagoon of Farquhar Atoll is a popular resting point for yachts and schooners. Copra production and fishing are carried out by the very few inhabitants. Île du Nord in the Farquhar Atoll has an airstrip.

Language

Creole is a blend of French and assorted African languages and is spoken in Mauritius, Réunion and the Seychelles. However, there are variations in the Creole dialect between these three countries. For instance, Seychelles Creole is fairly similar to that of Mauritius, but differs significantly from the Creole spoken in Réunion. For further details and some useful Creole words, see Language in Facts about Mauritius, Facts about Réunion and Facts about the Seychelles.

FRENCH

Along with local and Creole dialects, French is spoken in all three destinations. You'll often find that menus on the islands are mostly in French, with Creole variations in some cases.

An important distinction is made in French between *tu* and *vous*, which both mean 'you'. *Tu* is only used when addressing people you know well, children or animals. When addressing an adult who is not a personal friend, *vous* should be used unless the person invites you to use *tu*. In general, younger people are less insistent on this distinction, and they may use *tu* from the beginning of an acquaintance.

The following list of words and phrases should help you with basic communication. For a more comprehensive guide to the French language, get a copy of Lonely Planet's *French phrasebook*.

Basics

Yes.	*Oui.*
No.	*Non.*
Maybe.	*Peut-être.*
Please.	*S'il vous plaît.*
Thank you (very much).	*Merci (beaucoup).*
You're welcome.	*Je vous en prie.*
Excuse me.	*Excusez-moi.*
I'm sorry/ Forgive me.	*Pardon.*

How?	*Comment?*
Why?	*Pourquoi?*
Where?	*Où?*
When?	*Quand?*
Who?	*Qui?*
What?	*Quoi?*
Which?	*Quel* (m)/*Quelle* (f)?
with	*avec*
without	*sans*

Greetings & Civilities

Hello/Good morning.	*Bonjour.*
Good evening.	*Bonsoir.*
Goodbye.	*Au revoir.*
How are you? (polite)	*Comment allez-vous?*
How are you? (informal)	*Comment ça va?/ Ça va?*
I'm fine, thanks.	*Bien, merci.*
Madam/Mrs	*Madame*
Ms/Miss	*Mademoiselle*
Sir/Mr	*Monsieur*

Small Talk

What's your name?	*Comment vous appelez-vous?*
My name is ...	*Je m'appele ...*
What country are you from?	*De quel pays êtes-vous?*
I'm from ...	*Je viens de ...*

Language Difficulties

Do you speak English?	*Parlez-vous anglais?*
I understand.	*Je comprends.*
I don't understand.	*Je ne comprends pas.*
Could you please write it down?	*Est-ce que vous pouvez l'écrire?*

Getting Around

What time does the ... leave/arrive?	*À quelle heure part/arrive ...?*
boat	*le bateau*
bus	*le bus*
plane	*l'avion*

I want to go to ...	Je voudrais aller à ...
How long does the trip take?	Combien de temps durera le trajet?
next	prochain
first	premier
last	dernier
ticket	billet
timetable	horaire

I'd like to hire a ...	Je voudrais louer ...
bicycle	un vélo
car	une voiture
motorcycle	une moto

Directions

Where is ...?	Où est ...?
How do I get to ...?	Comment dois-je faire pour arriver à ...?
Is it near/far?	Est-ce prés/loin?
Go straight ahead.	Continuez tout droit.
Turn left/right.	Tournez gauche/droite.
at the next corner	au prochain carrefour
behind	derrière
in front of	devant
towards	vers
left	gauche
right	droite
on	sur
under	sous
between	entre
north	nord
south	sud
east	est
west	ouest

Signs

Entrée	Entrance
Sortie	Exit
Ouvert	Open
Fermé	Closed
Chambres Libres	Rooms Available
Complet	No Vacancies
Renseignements	Information
Interdit	Prohibited
Gendarmerie	Police Station
Police	Police
Toilettes, WC	Toilets
Hommes	Men
Femmes	Women

Around Town

I'm looking for ...	Je cherche ...
a bank	une banque
an exchange office	un bureau de change
the ... embassy	l'ambassade de ...
my hotel	mon hôtel
the police	la police
the post office	la poste
a public telephone	une cabine téléphonique
the tourist office	le syndicat d'initiative
the beach	la plage
a church	une église
the hospital	l'hôpital
a library	une bibliothèque
the museum	le musée
the park	le parc
a pub/bar	un bar
a travel agency	une agence de voyages

| I'd like to make a telephone call. | Je voudrais téléphoner. |

I'd like to change ...	Je voudrais changer ...
some money	de l'argent
travellers cheques	des chèques de voyage

Accommodation

I'm looking for ...	Je cherche ...
the youth hostel	l'auberge de jeunesse
the camping ground	le camping
a hotel	un hôtel

I'm going to stay ...	Je resterai ...
one night	un jour
two nights	deux jours
a week	une semaine

How much is it ...?	Quel est le prix ...?
per day	pour par jour
per week	par semaine
per month	par mois

I'd like ...	*Je voudrais ...*
a single room (air-conditioned)	*une chambre simple (climatisée)*
a double room	*une chambre double*
a bedroom	*une chambre*
a double bed	*un grand lit*
twin beds	*lits jumeaux*
an extra bed	*un lit supplémentaire*
a bathroom	*une salle de bain*
a shower	*une douche*
a washbasin	*un lavabo*
hot water	*eau chaude*
a balcony	*un balcon*
a window	*une fenêtre*
a terrace	*une terrace*
a sea view	*une vue sur la mer*
full board	*pension complète*
half board	*demi-pension*
facilities	*facilités*
dining room	*salle à manger*
kitchen	*cuisine*
television	*télévision*
swimming pool	*piscine*
towels	*serviettes*
(not) included	*(non) compris*
on request	*sur demande/ sur commande*
price/tariff	*prix/tarif*

Food

breakfast	*petit déjeuner*
lunch	*déjeuner*
dinner	*dîner*
meal	*repas*
special of the day	*le plat du jour*
the bill	*l'addition*
I'm a vegetarian.	*Je suis végétarien/ végétarienne.* (m/f)
I don't eat meat.	*Je ne mange pas de viande.*

Seafood

fish	*poisson*
mussels	*moules*
octopus	*poulpe*
seafood	*fruits de mer*
sea urchins	*ourites*
squid	*calmar*
trout	*truite*
tuna	*thon*

Meat

meat (generic)	*viande*
bacon	*lard*
beef	*bœuf*
chicken	*poulet*
duck	*canard*
goat	*chèvre*
ham	*jambon*
mutton	*mouton*
pork	*porc*
rabbit	*lapin*
hare	*lièvre*
mixed grill	*grillades*

Vegetables

avocado	*avocat*
beans	*haricots*
cabbage	*chou*
carrot	*carotte*
cassava	*manioc*
cauliflower	*chou fleur*
cucumber	*concombre*
eggplant	*aubergine*
french fries (chips)	*pommes frites*
lentils	*lentilles*
lettuce	*laitue*
onion	*oignon*
peas	*petits pois*
potato	*pomme de terre*
salad	*salade*
sweet potato	*patate douce*
tomato	*tomate*
vegetables	*légumes*

Fruit

apple	*pomme*
apricot	*abricot*
banana	*banane*
coconut	*noix de coco*
custard apple	*corossol*
fruit	*fruit*
grapefruit	*pamplemousse*
guava	*goyave*
lemon	*citron*
mango	*mangue*
orange	*orange*
passionfruit	*grenadelle*
peach	*pêche*
pear	*poivre*
pineapple	*ananas*
star fruit	*carambol*

Desserts

cake	*gâteau*
cream	*crème*
dessert	*dessert*
ice cream	*glace*
pancake; crepe	*crêpe*
pastries	*pâtisseries*

Condiments

chilli	*piment*
curry	*carri*
ginger	*gingembre*
mustard	*moutarde*
pepper	*poivre*
salad dressing	*vinaigrette*
salt	*sel*
sugar	*sucre*
sweet and sour	*aigre-doux*
vinegar	*vinaigre*

Miscellaneous

bread	*pain*
butter	*beurre*
cheese	*fromage*
cup	*tasse*
eggs	*oeufs*
fork	*fourchette*
glass	*verre*
jam	*confiture*
knife	*couteau*
napkin	*serviette*
noodles	*nouilles*
pasta	*pâtes*
plate	*assiette*
rice	*riz*
spoon	*cuiller*
thick soup	*potage*
vegetarian	*végétarien*

Drinks

beer	*bière*
brandy	*cognac*
coffee	*café*
drinks	*boissons*
fruit juice	*jus de fruit*
hot chocolate	*chocolat chaud*
lemonade	*limonade*
milk	*lait*
mineral water	*l'eau minérale*
tea	*thé*
wine	*vin*

Shopping

How much is it?	*C'est combien?*
May I look at it?	*Est-ce que je peux le/ la voir?*
Do you accept credit cards?	*Est-ce que je peux payer avec ma carte de crédit?*
It's too big/small.	*C'est trop grand/petit.*
more/less	*plus/moins*
cheap/cheaper	*bon marché/moins cher*
I'm looking for ...	*Je cherche ...*
a grocery shop	*une épicerie*
a supermarket	*un supermarché*
the market	*le marché*
a pharmacy	*une pharmacie*
a bookshop	*un librairie*
condoms	*préservatifs*
disposable nappies	*couches coulottes*
hat	*chapeau*
matches	*alumettes*
sanitary napkins	*serviettes hygiéniques*
soap	*savon*
sunscreen	*crème haute protection*
toilet paper	*papier hygiénique*
toothpaste	*dentifrice*

Health

I need a doctor.	*Il me faut un médecin.*
Where is the hospital?	*Où est l'hôpital?*
I'm ...	*Je suis ...*
diabetic	*diabétique*
epileptic	*épilectique*
asthmatic	*asthmatique*
anaemic	*anémique*
I'm allergic ...	*Je suis allergique ...*
to antibiotics	*aux antibiotiques*
to penicillin	*à la penicilline*
to bees	*aux abeilles*

Time, Dates & Numbers

What time is it?	*Quelle heure est-il?*
It's ... o'clock.	*Il est ... heures.*
today	*aujourd'hui*
tomorrow	*demain*
yesterday	*hier*

Emergencies

Help!	*Au secours!*
Call a doctor!	*Appelez un médecin!*
Call the police!	*Appelez la police!*
Leave me alone!	*Fichez-moi la paix!*
I'm lost.	*Je me suis égaré/ égarée.* (m/f)

the/this morning	*le/ce matin*
the/this afternoon	*l'/cet après-midi*

Monday	*lundi*
Tuesday	*mardi*
Wednesday	*mercredi*
Thursday	*jeudi*
Friday	*vendredi*
Saturday	*samedi*
Sunday	*dimanche*

January	*janvier*
February	*février*
March	*mars*
April	*avril*
May	*mai*
June	*juin*
July	*juillet*
August	*août*
September	*septembre*
October	*octobre*
November	*novembre*
December	*décembre*

0	*zéro*
1	*un*
2	*deux*
3	*trois*
4	*quatre*
5	*cinq*
6	*six*
7	*sept*
8	*huit*
9	*neuf*
10	*dix*
11	*onze*
12	*douze*
13	*treize*
14	*quatorze*
15	*quinze*
16	*seize*
17	*dix-sept*
18	*dix-huit*
19	*dix-neuf*
20	*vingt*
21	*vingt-et-un*
22	*vingt-deux*
30	*trente*
40	*quarante*
50	*cinquante*
60	*soixante*
70	*soixante-dix*
80	*quatre-vingts*
90	*quatre-vingt-dix*
100	*cent*
1000	*mille*

one million	*un million*

Glossary

achards de légumes – pickled vegetable salad

baba figue – the blossom of the banana tree
baie rose – pink pepper
bibliothèque – library
bichiques – sprat-like seafood delicacy
bom – stringed instrument with a bulbous gourd-shaped body
bon bon piment – spicy meat fritter
bouchon – Chinese-style meat dumpling
bourgeois – red snapper
brèdes – variety of spinach or Chinese cabbage found in the Seychelles
briani – curried rice; sometimes known as biryani

camtole – in the Seychelles, a traditional roving band featuring fiddle, banjo, drums and accordion
carri boucané – smoked pork curry
carri coco – mild meat curry with coconut cream
carri p'tit jacques – jackfruit curry
carri poulet/poulpe/poisson – chicken/octopus/fish curry
carte de séjour – residence visa
catless – cutlets in breadcrumbs
chambre d'hôte – small, family-run B&B
chou chou – squash-like vegetable, also known as *choux choux*
civet de morue – fish stew
combava – a knobbly lime
Compagnie des Indes Orientales – French East India Company

daube – sauce or stew
dorade – a type of game fish, also known as daurade, found on menus throughout the Indian Ocean region

gamba – prawn
gare routière – bus station
gendarmerie – police station
gîte d'étape – privately run mountain lodge
gîte de montagne – mountain lodge
grands blancs – rich whites

guichet automatique de banque (GAB) – automated teller machine (ATM)

hôtel de ville – town hall (see also *mairie*)

jour férié – public holiday

la métropole – mainland France as known in Réunion
le menu du jour – set menu of the day
le plat du jour – special of the day
librairie – bookshop

mairie – town hall; in Réunion, whether a town has a *mairie* or a *hôtel de ville* depends on the local-government status of the town
makalapo – stringed instrument with a tin sound-box
maloya – Réunion slave dance
margose – a lumpy bitter melon
marrons – in Réunion, slaves who escaped from their owners and settled the interior of the island; most were later hunted down and killed by bounty hunters
masala – literally 'mix'; usually refers to a mixture of different spices
métro cuisine – the cuisine of mainland France
mien frit – fried noodles
moules marinières – mussels cooked in their own juice with onions
moutia – a sombre, traditional dance of the Seychelles

nouga – sweet, sticky coconut pudding

Office National des Forêts (ONF) – Réunion's forestry division

Pays d'Accueil – the name given to one of Réunion's tourist information bodies
pension de famille – boarding house
porc à la sauce grand'mère – a dish of pork with chillies (literally, pork in grandma's sauce)
porc aigre-doux – sweet and sour pork

ravanne – primitive goatskin drum which traditionally accompanies the séga dance

rhum arrangé – a mixture of rum, fruit juice, cane syrup and a blend of herbs and berries

riz frit – fried rice

rogan josh – a tomato-based curry

rougail – a spicy chutney popular in Réunion

rougaille saucisse – tomato-based sauce with sausage

séga – dance of African origin

sokwe – impromtu street theatre

syndicat d'initiative – tourist office

tamarin des hautes – mountain tamarind

taxi collectif – in Réunion, scheduled share taxis that run between main towns out to surrounding villages

télécarte – telephone card

tomate d'arbuste – the sweet tree-tomato that is also called tamarillo

vélo tout terrain – mountain bike, also known as VTT

z'andouille – a root vegetable that resembles a length of intestine

zez – monochord sitar

LONELY PLANET

You already know that Lonely Planet produces more than this one guidebook, but you might not be aware of the other products we have on this region. Here is a selection of titles that you may want to check out as well:

Africa on a shoestring
ISBN 0 86442 663 1
US$29.99 • UK£17.99 • 199FF

French phrasebook
ISBN 0 86442 450 7
US$5.95 • UK£3.99 • 40FF

Read This First: Africa
ISBN 1 86450 066 2
US$14.95 • UK£8.99 • 99FF

Madagascar
ISBN 1 86450 215 0
US$17.99 • UK£11.99 • 139FF

Healthy Travel Africa
ISBN 1 86450 050 6
US$5.95 • UK£3.99 • 39FF

**Diving & Snorkeling
The Seychelles**
ISBN 1 55992 097 1
US$14.95 • UK£7.99 • 110FF

East Africa
ISBN 0 86442 676 3
US$24.99 • UK£14.99 • 180FF

Southern Africa
ISBN 0 86442 662 3
US$27.99 • UK£16.99 • 189FF

**Available wherever books
are sold**

Index

Abbreviations

M – Mauritius   R – Réunion   S – Seychelles

Text

A

abseiling
    Réunion 189
accommodation 31-2
    Mauritius 82-3
    Réunion 190-2, 257
    Seychelles 287
activities, *see* specific activities
agriculture
    Mauritius 65
    Réunion 175-6, 229, 249
    Seychelles 278
air travel 51-5
    jet lag 22-3
    to/from Mauritius 89-90
    to/from Réunion 196-7
    to/from the Seychelles 289-90
    within Mauritius 91
    within Réunion 199
    within the Seychelles 290
Aldabra Atoll (S) 318, **318**
Aldabra Group (S) 317-18
Alphonse Group (S) 317, **318**
Amirantes Group (S) 317, **318**
angling, *see* deep-sea fishing
animals, *see* birds, dodos,
    marine life, wildlife, tortoises
Anse Bambous Virieux (M) 157
Anse Cocos (S) 312
Anse des Cascades (R) 220
Anse Jonchée (M) 157
Anse Lazio (S) 306-8
Anse Major (S) 300
Anse Royale (S) 303
Anse Source d'Argent (S) 312
Anse Victorin (S) 316
Appiani, Lorenzo (sculptor) 280
aquariums
    Réunion 232
    Seychelles 308
architecture 126-7, *see also*
    Creole architecture, historic
    buildings

Bold indicates maps.

Aride Island (S) 311-12
art galleries
    Mauritius 68
    Réunion 177-8, 208, 236, 243
    Seychelles 314
Assomption Island (S) 318
Aurère (R) 239, 249

B

Baie de L'Arsenal (M) 105-6
Baie du Cap (M) 158
Baie du Tombeau (M) 105-6
Baie Ternay Marine National
    Park (M) 40
Balaclava (S) 105-6
Bambous Virieux (S) 162
banking hours
    Mauritius 73
    Réunion 185
    Seychelles 285
bargaining
    Mauritius 73
    Réunion 182
    Seychelles 283
basketry
    Mauritius 87
    Réunion 195, 209, 221
Basse Vallée (R) 221
Bassin Blanc (M) 133-4
Bassin Couderc (R) 213
batik
    Seychelles 288
Battle of Vieux Grand Port (M)
    59, 151
Beau Vallon (S) 300-3, **301**
beaches, *see also* specific
    beach names
    Mauritius 107, 117, 141,
        158-9
    Réunion 232, 235
    Seychelles 300, 302-3, 305,
        306-8, 312-13, 316
beaches, exclusion from in
    Mauritius 78
Bel Ombre (M) 133, 151, 302

Belle Mare (M) 141
Bellevue (R) 226
Bérenger, Paul 59
Bernica (R) 237, 238
bicycle rental
    Mauritius 93, 116, 141,
        147, 154, 156
    Réunion 202, 245, 248
    Seychelles 292, 315
bicycle travel
    Mauritius 93
    Réunion 245
    Seychelles 292, 315
Bird Island (S) 316
Bird Life Seychelles (organisa-
    tion) 311
birds, *see also* dodos
    Mauritius 63, 143, 157, 162-3
    Réunion 174, 226
    Seychelles 277, 311, 313-14,
        316, 318
Black River Gorges National
    Park (M) 130-4, **132**
Blue Bay (M) 155-6
boat travel 55-6
    to/from Mauritius 90
    to/from Réunion 197-8
    to/from the Seychelles 290
    within Mauritius 81, 93
    within Réunion 187, 197-8
    within the Seychelles 286,
        292-3
Bois Chéri tea museum (M) 158
Bois Court (R) 252-3
books 16, *see also* literature
    diving 43, 45
    hiking 131
    Mauritius 75-6
    Réunion 183-4, 256
    Seychelles 283-4
    travel health 19
bookshops
    Mauritius 76
    Réunion 205
botanical gardens, *see* gardens
    & parks

Bold indicates maps.

Boxed Text

MAP LEGEND

CITY ROUTES

Freeway .... Freeway
Highway .... Primary Road
Road .... Secondary Road
Street .... Street
Lane .... Lane
=== Unsealed Road
Pedestrian Street
Stepped Street

REGIONAL ROUTES

.... Tollway, Freeway
.... Primary Road
.... Secondary Road
.... Minor Road

BOUNDARIES

.... International
.... State
.... Cliff

HYDROGRAPHY

.... River, Creek
.... Lake
.... Dry Lake; Salt Lake
.... Waterfalls

TRANSPORT ROUTES & STATIONS

.... Ferry
.... Walking Trail
.... Path
.... Pier or Jetty

AREA FEATURES

.... Building
.... Park, Gardens
.... Market
.... Sports Ground
.... Beach
.... Cemetery
.... Campus
.... Plaza

POPULATION SYMBOLS

✪ CAPITAL .... National Capital
◉ CAPITAL .... State Capital
● CITY .... City
● Town .... Town
● Village .... Village
.... Urban Area

MAP SYMBOLS

■ .... Place to Stay
▼ .... Place to Eat
● .... Point of Interest

✈ Airport	⛳ Golf Course	🅿 Parking	🏄 Surf Beach
🏦 Bank	✚ Hospital	🌳 Picnic Area	🏊 Swimming Pool
🚌 Bus Station	🛖 Hut	🚔 Police Station	🚕 Taxi Rank
🏕 Camping Area	💻 Internet Cafe	📮 Post Office	☎ Telephone
🕳 Cave	🔭 Lookout	🍺 Pub or Bar	🛕 Temple
✝ Church	🗿 Monument	🏛 Ruins	🎭 Theatre
🎬 Cinema	☪ Mosque	🛍 Shopping Centre	⬛ Tomb
🤿 Dive Site	🏛 Museum	🤿 Snorkelling	ℹ Tourist Information
✉ Embassy	🏞 National Park	🏠 Stately Home	🚉 Transport

Note: not all symbols displayed above appear in this book

LONELY PLANET OFFICES

Australia
Locked Bag 1, Footscray, Victoria 3011
☎ 03 9689 4666 fax 03 9689 6833
email: talk2us@lonelyplanet.com.au

USA
150 Linden St, Oakland, CA 94607
☎ 510 893 8555 TOLL FREE: 800 275 8555
fax 510 893 8572
email: info@lonelyplanet.com

UK
10a Spring Place, London NW5 3BH
☎ 020 7428 4800 fax 020 7428 4828
email: go@lonelyplanet.co.uk

France
1 rue du Dahomey, 75011 Paris
☎ 01 55 25 33 00 fax 01 55 25 33 01
email: bip@lonelyplanet.fr
www.lonelyplanet.fr

World Wide Web: www.lonelyplanet.com *or* AOL keyword: lp
Lonely Planet Images: lpi@lonelyplanet.com.au